MILLER'S

collectors
cars

collectors
cars

GENERAL EDITOR
Dave Selby

FOREWORD
Paddy Hopkirk

MILLER'S COLLECTORS CARS PRICE GUIDE 2003/4

Created and designed by
Miller's Publications
The Cellars, High Street
Tenterden, Kent TN30 6BN
Telephone: 01580 766411
Fax: 01580 766100

General Editor: Dave Selby
Project Co-ordinator: Philip Hannath
Editorial Co-ordinator: Deborah Wanstall
Editorial Assistants: Joanna Hill, Maureen Horner
Designer: Kari Reeves
Advertisement Designer: Simon Cook
Jacket Design: Victoria Bevan
Advertising Executive: Jill Jackson
Advertising Administrator & Co-ordinator: Melinda Williams
Advertising Assistant: Elizabeth Ellender
Production Assistants: Caroline Bugeja, Gillian Charles, Ethne Tragett
Additional Photography: Elizabeth Bennett, Classic & Sportscar Magazine, Simon Clay,
Bob Dunsmore, Haynes Motor Museum, Don Heiny, Gordon L. Jolley,
LAT Photographic Library, Charles Leith, Robin Saker, Mark Squire, Roger Stowers,
The National Motor Museum at Beaulieu
US Advertising Representative: Katharine Buckley,
Buckley Pell Associates, 34 East 64th Street, New York, NY 10021
Tel: 212 223 4996 Fax: 212 223 4997 E-mail: buckley@moveworld.com

First published in Great Britain in 2002
by Miller's, a division of Mitchell Beazley,
imprints of Octopus Publishing Group Ltd,
2–4 Heron Quays, London E14 4JP

© 2002 Octopus Publishing Group Ltd

A CIP catalogue record for this book is
available from the British Library

ISBN 1 84000 631 5

Illustrations and film output by CK Digital, Whitstable, Kent
Printed and bound by Toppan Printing Co (HK) Ltd, China

Front cover illustration:

A Chevrolet Corvette Sting Ray,
designed by Bill Mitchell in the early 1960s.
Photograph © Octopus Publishing Group Ltd

6

Contents

Acknowledgments

The publishers would like to acknowledge the great assistance given by our consultants:

Malcolm Barber — Montpelier Street, Knightsbridge SW7 1HH
Tel: 020 7393 3900

Tom Falconer — Claremont Corvette, Snodland, Kent ME6 5NA

Simon Johnson — Military Vehicle Trust, 7 Carter Fold, Mellor, Lancs BB2 7ER

Brian Page — Classic Assessments, Stonechat House, Moorymead Close, Watton-at-Stone, Herts SG14 3HF

Mike Penn CEI, Tech Eng ITE, Mairso — Haynes Motor Museum, Sparkford, Nr Yeovil, Somerset BA22 7LH

Mike Smith — Chiltern House, Ashendon, Aylesbury, Bucks HP18 0HB

Neil Tuckett — Marstonfields, North Marston, Bucks MK18 3PG

Peter W. Card BSc — Bonhams, 65 Lots Road, Chelsea, London SW10 1HH

We would like to extend our thanks to all auction houses, their press offices, and dealers who have assisted us in the production of this book, along with the organisers and press offices of the following events:

Beaulieu September Autojumble & Automart
Goodwood Festival of Speed
Rétromobile, Paris
The War & Peace Show
London Classic Car Show

How to use this book

It is our aim to make the guide easy to use. Marques are listed alphabetically and then chronologically. Commercial Vehicles, Replica, Kit & Reproduction Cars, Restoration Projects, Racing & Rallying, Military Vehicles and Children's Cars are located after the marques, towards the end of the book. In the Automobilia section, objects are grouped alphabetically by type. If you cannot find what you are looking for, please consult the index on page 348.

ALFA ROMEO 27

1949 Alfa Romeo 6C 2500S, 2443cc double-overhead-camshaft 6-cylinder engine, 90bhp, box-section chassis, 4-wheel independent suspension.
£18,000–22,000 / $26,000–32,000 ➤ Bon
Its Portello factory devastated by wartime bombing, Alfa Romeo did not resume car production until 1946, when the pre-war 6C 2500 re-emerged clothed anew as the Freccia d'Oro (Golden Arrow). A development of the 2300 and destined to be the last of the separate-chassis Alfas, the 2500 had been introduced in 1939. Styled in-house, but strongly influenced by Touring, the Freccia d'Oro five-seat sports saloon was built alongside coupé and cabriolet versions featuring bodies by the likes of Pinin Farina, Touring and Ghia, plus a six/seven-seat *berlina* on a longer wheelbase.

1960 Alfa Romeo Guilletta Sprint Coupé, 1290cc engine, 4-speed manual gearbox, left-hand drive, total restoration, complete mechanical overhaul, new chromework, bare-metal respray in red, new red interior, exceptional condition throughout.
£8,500–10,000 / $12,500–14,500 ➤ H&H
The Guilletta Sprint was launched in 1954 at the same time as the 1900 Super Sprint. It came with the 1298cc engine and two-seat coupé body which was at first part alloy with sliding Perspex windows.

▶ **1964 Alfa Romeo 2600 Spider,** 2584cc double-overhead-camshaft 6-cylinder engine, 145bhp, 5-speed manual gearbox, 64,000 miles from new.
£16,000–18,000 / $23,000–26,000 ➤ CGC

Alfa Romeo Montreal (1970–77)
Price in 1972: £5,077/$7,362 (£800/$1,160 less than BMW 3.0CSi).
Production: 3,925.
Engine: 2593cc quad-cam V8.
Transmission: ZF five-speed manual.
Power output: 200bhp at 6,550rpm.
Brakes: Servo-assisted ventilated discs all-round.
0–60mph: 7.5 seconds.
Top speed: 137mph.

Miller's Starter Marque

Starter Alfa Romeos: 1750 & 2000 GTV; 1300 Junior Spider, 1600 Duetto Spider, 1750 & 2000 Spider Veloce; 1300 & 1600 GT Junior; Alfasud ti & Sprint
- Responsive, eager and sweet twin-cam engines, finely balanced chassis, nimble handling and delightful looks are just some of the character traits of classic Alfas from the mid-sixties onward. They are also eminently affordable. For the kind of money that gets you an MGB or TR Triumph, you could be a little more adventurous and acquire an engaging Alfa Romeo sporting saloon or convertible.
- That's the good news; the bad news is that the unfortunate reputation Alfas of the 1960s and 1970s earned for rusting was deserved. Take a magnet along. Classic Alfa owners – *Alfisti* as they prefer to call themselves – have a saying: 'You pay for the engineering and the engine, but the body comes free.' Bear in mind too that maintenance costs are likely to be pricier than those of an MG or TR Triumph.

ALFA ROMEO Model	ENGINE cc/cyl	DATES	CONDITION 1	2	3
24hp	4084/4	1910–11	£25,000	£16,000	£12,000
12hp	2413/4	1910–11	£18,000	£11,000	£8,000
40–60	6028/4	1913–15	£32,000	£24,000	£14,000
RL/RLSS	2916/6	1921–22	£40,000	£24,000	£14,000
RM	1944/4	1924–25	£28,000	£17,000	£13,000
6C 1500	1487/6	1927–28	£50,000*	£20,000+	£10,000+
6C 1750	1752/6	1923–33	£100,000+	£80,000+	–
6C 1900	1917/6	1933	£18,000	£15,000	£12,000
6C 2300	2309/6	1934	£30,000+	£18,000	£15,000
6C 2500 SS Cabriolet/Spider	2443/6	1939–45	£100,000	£50,000	£40,000
6C 2500 SS Coupé	2443/6	1939–45	£60,000	£40,000	£30,000
8C 2300 Monza/Short Chassis	2300/8	1931–34	£1,500,000+	£400,000+	–
8C 2900	2900/8	1935–39	£1,500,000+	£1,000,000	–

Value is very dependent on sporting history, body style and engine type.
*The high price of this model is dependent on whether it is 1500 supercharged/twin overhead cam, and with or without a racing history.

Price Boxes
give the value of a particular model, dependent on condition and are compiled by our team of experts, car clubs and private collectors.
Condition 1 refers to a vehicle in top class condition, but not concours d'élégance standard, either fully restored or in very good original condition.
Condition 2 refers to a good, clean roadworthy vehicle, both mechanically and bodily sound.
Condition 3 refers to a runner, but in need of attention, probably to both bodywork and mechanics. It must have a current MOT.
Restoration projects are vehicles that fail to make the Condition 3 grading.

Information Box
covers relevant information on marques, designers, racing drivers and special events.

Source Code
refers to the 'Key to Illustrations' on page 332 that lists the details of where the item was sourced. Advertisers are also indicated on this page. The ➤ icon indicates the item was sold at auction. The ⊞ icon indicates the item originated from a dealer. The 🚗 icon indicates the item belonged to a member of a car club; see Directory of Car Clubs on page 336.

Miller's Starter Marque
refers to selected marques that offer affordable, reliable and interesting classic motoring.

Caption
provides a brief description of the vehicle or item, and could include comments on its history, mileage, any restoration work carried out and current condition.

Price Guide
these are based on actual prices realised shown in £sterling with a US$ conversion. Remember that Miller's is a PRICE GUIDE not a PRICE LIST and prices are affected by many variables such as location, condition, desirability and so on. Don't forget that if you are selling, it is quite likely you will be offered less than the price range. Price ranges for items sold at auction include the buyer's premium.

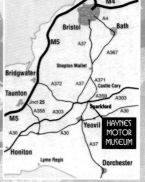

Foreword

Who would have thought many years ago that classic cars would have become so popular? The *Miller's Collectors Cars Price Guide* has an amazing array of both cars and memorabilia that devotees can own and enjoy. It is gratifying to find that the Miller's guide helps the enthusiast on a budget and offers buying suggestions – this is an invaluable guide for the car buff.

I am honoured to have been associated with so many of the cars that are represented in this book, Austin 7, the first Volkswagen Beetle, Triumph TR2, Sunbeam Alpine and Rapier, Austin Healey 3000 and Sprites, MG and of course Mini Cooper S – all of them now classic cars.

In 1964, the Mini Cooper pictured above, beat the rest of the world's car manufacturers to win the Monte Carlo Rally, and I was fortunate enough to be its driver. In July 2001 the Mini was reborn. It is a wonderful looking car with breathtaking road holding capability and is destined to become an outstanding classic car of the 21st century.

I hope you enjoy this year's edition and that it will help guide you to find your own piece of motoring history that you can own and enjoy for many years to come.

14

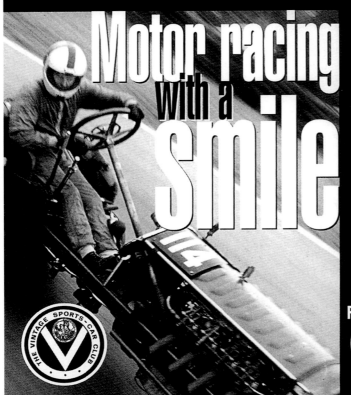

The State of the Market

The past 12 months have been dominated by the tragic events of 11 September 2001 although the worldwide effect on the economy has not been as serious as was first thought. Certainly this is true as far as the classic car market is concerned. The foot and mouth epidemic also played its part in depressing trade last year.

It has been a good year for veteran cars and true for early primitives. Christie's sold the 1894 Santler for £146,750 ($213,000) and Bonhams made £124,700 ($181,000) for the 1896 Arnold Dogcart. Two Edwardian Napiers – a 1908 Tourer and 1908 Open Drive Limousine each sold for £89,500 ($130,000) at Bonhams Hendon auction. Previously, in their December Olympia sale the unusual 1913 Thames Coach from The National Motor Museum realized £47,700 ($69,000).

Automobilia has been increasingly popular with Bonhams selling items worth over £2,000,000 ($2,900,000) – scale models doing particularly well. H & H at Buxton are now regularly including automobilia in their sales, as are Cheffins in Cambridge and Lambert & Foster in Kent.

A recent high for RTS in East Anglia was the Heritage Engineering version of the 1950's Lister Jaguar with a 4.2 litre E-type engine which sold for £22,575 ($33,000). Purely Classics in Southend continued to cater for the lower end of the classic market and automobilia. Among the provincial houses, H&H have turned in satisfactory results, with auctions consistently achieving 70 per cent of entries sold. The late Lord Riverdale's 1908 Sheffield-Simplex Toy Tonneau, sold for £68,250 ($100,000) at this sale, again emphasizing the strength in the early veteran market. H&H also sold the 1952 Connaught A- type single seater for £106,000 ($154,000). Cheffins are steadily building up a reputation for interesting and successful sales, doing particularly well with pre-war Rolls-Royce entries. The 1924 Silver Ghost made £50,500 ($73,000).

Edwardian Silver Ghost Rolls-Royces have also had a good year, with Bonhams selling a stunning 1911 Limousine at their Summer Vintage sale at Beaulieu last year for £309,500 ($449,000), while Christie's sold the oldest known Silver Ghost, dating from 1907, for £322,920 ($468,500) at Pebble Beach, USA. This continues to be their flagship sale, together with a sale at the Rockerfeller Plaza, New York, each spring.

Despite the talk of economic recession in the USA, their auction market has held up well. Bonham's Quail lodge, California sale, saw excellent results such as, £1,178,175 ($1,708,500) paid for a 1937 Bugatti Type 57S Atalanta Coupé and £96,000 ($139,000) for a 1967 Toyota 2000 GT with 15,000 recorded miles. In January the Barrett-Jackson Scottsdale sale totalled over £16,000,000 ($26,000,000). Similarly, RM Auctions realized £1,600,000 ($2,500,000) for the late Terry Cohn's Alfa Romeo Monza.

Bonhams continue to expand both at home and abroad. The auction at the Museum of Transport in Boston was added to their schedule in May with over 90 per cent of all lots sold. One of the highlights was the 1932 Bugatti type 49 Coupé which sold for £58,260 ($85,000) to a UK collector. Bonhams, at the Historic Festival at Silverstone last year, sold an exciting barn discovery – a 1932 Alfa Romeo 8C2300 Spider Corsa for £1,063,000 ($1,542,000). In terms of one marque sales the auction held by Bonhams each May, in association with Aston Martin Works Service, proves very popular and top price last year was the Aston Martin DB4 Vantage GT at £129,100 ($187,000). The following year this exclusive Aston Martin sale saw a 2000 Vantage Volante SWB special edition realize £254,500 ($369,000). The Bonhams Europe Ferrari sale at Gstaad, Switzerland in December was combined with jewellery and watches and proved as successful as ever, with a top price of £689,390 ($1,000,000) being paid for a 1961 Ferrari 250 GT SWB Competition Berlinetta and £271,848 ($394,000) for a 1958 Ferrari California Spyder LWB.

Coys continued to hold successful sales throughout the year. Their London sale in April saw the *Inspector Morse* Jaguar MK2 fetch an incredible £52,000 ($75,500). Coys were also at Techno Classica, Essen, in the spring, a first for them, achieving a 51 per cent sold rate. Bonhams were in Monaco for their annual auction during Grand Prix week successfully selling 35 cars, with a top price of £276,639 ($401,000) being paid for a first production Ferrari F50 roadster.

British Car Auctions (BCA) also continued to hold regular classic vehicle sales, mainly concentrating on the £10,000–20,000 ($14,500–30,000) classic market at Blackbushe and Bridgewater, overall selling a large percentage of the cars on offer. Lambert and Foster in Kent also returned to the auction scene after an absence of some years with sales of both cars and automobilia, again concentrating on classics under £10,000 ($14,500), and Barons, at Sandown Park now see more successful sales with their first £300,000 ($435,000) auction total.

Unrestored cars and restoration projects continue to amaze – the auction of the of the late Paul Kunkel's collection saw a 1955 Maserati A6G 2000 Berlinetta by Zagato fetch £276,500 ($401,000).

The overall picture is that the auction scene has remained stable, although selective at all levels. Bottom of the range classics are plentiful and remain extremely reasonable, particularly for the first time buyer. Jaguar was the most popular marque at auction in Europe last year followed by Mercedes-Benz, MG and Rolls-Royce. Our advice is keep a watching brief – bargains can still be had.

Malcolm Barber

Drive a Bargain

Every year, as I settle down to read *Miller's Collectors' Cars Price Guide* there's one thing I can be sure of – I'm about to discover some fascinating cars I never knew existed.

Some of them are delightfully implausible, like the bizarre and strangely appealing Crosley Crosmobile shown on page 89 of this edition. Others are one-off coach-built stunners with stellar price tags. As I pore over the thousands of pictures my wish list of 'must haves' grows ever longer. Another thing that never fails to surprise me is what tremendous bargains classic cars often are.

Since the last edition a unique set of economic forces has come into play, and the sharpest analysis you're likely to get from the experts is 'it's been a funny old year', and the future looks just as unpredictable.

To make sense of the present it helps to understand the past. In the boom years of the late 1980s classic cars made headline news as prices soared; old metal was precious metal, an 'alternative vehicle of investment' as the housing and stock markets disappointed and faltered. The Ferrari 365GTB/4 Daytona told the story of the times. If you wanted a valuation on yours, the auction houses would ask whether you required this morning's or this afternoon's value, such was the joke when Daytonas were a cinch at a quarter of a million pounds. The punch line wasn't so funny when the false market collapsed in the early '90s and the Daytona, like countless 'blue chip' investments sagged on its suspension at under £100,000/$145,000. In the last year on the UK open auction market no Daytona fixed-head, other than competition variants, topped £80,000/$116,000, while the lowest auction price was $49,900/$72,000.

At these kinds of prices if you're after a Daytona it's probably worth holding out until the vendor throws in a full tank of petrol. This is today's reality in a year that's seen the classic car market sidelined on the hard-shoulder of larger events.

In the first half of last year, the foot and mouth outbreak played havoc with classic car events, including auctions. Then, in the wake of September 11, several East Coast USA auctions were, quite rightly, cancelled as a mark of respect. In the UK the auction calendar was unaffected, but something very strange happened in the aftermath of that terrible tragedy. Virtually every auction after September 11 until the end of 2001 was overflowing, with auction catalogues often selling out and percentage sales rates well up. The domestic sale of the year was, without doubt, Bonhams' (formerly Bonhams & Brooks) Olympia sale on December 3 which took £3.75/$5.4 million in a bustling atmosphere reminiscent of the red-braced Yuppie era of the late 1980s.

But don't panic! Old timers tell me there was a mini consumer spending boom in the late 1930s. As Europe teetered on the brink of war people thought "What the hell! I might as well enjoy it while I can."

Alongside the September 11 effect, a slowdown in the stock market and uncertainty in the housing market mirror the late 1980s. This time though, interest rates are low, money's cheap and savings are unrewarding.

After a very flat first half of 2001 the classic car market picked up nicely. By the end of the year the number of cars offered at auction was almost exactly the same as the year before – just over 4,700. Likewise, the sale rate was almost exactly on a par, with 2,650 cars sold at auction in 2001.

Of course, 2000 wasn't a particularly great year to follow, but recent patterns are reassuringly healthy. In a market not driven by debt, crash-and-burn hedonism or attention-seeking displays of wealth, when Jaguar XJ220s come up at auction they often don't sell. If they do, it's generally between £115,000/$167,000 and £130,000/$188,500. They just don't impress people any more. As for Rolls-Royce Silver Shadows, the auction ball-park price range of £4,000/$5,800 to £9,000/$13,000 gives them little more than marginal appeal.

Instead, I'm seeing knowledgeable enthusiasts pursuing their next driving experience. A flaky Mk 2 Jag may sell at £3,000/$4,400 to £6,000/$8,700, but a real gem above £20,000/$29,000 will be more keenly contested. Another tell-tale sign is that pre-war iron is also selling more readily – Model T Fords, Austins and Morrises etc. – although prices aren't escalating. They're not going to return any great dividend, but are a tinkerer's delight and to me that's a healthy recreational pursuit.

I'd venture that classic cars are at their most affordable for years, with a greater choice than ever before, and for a list of the top-ten classic buys look no further than your own enthusiasm. As Robin Lawton of auctioneers BCA observes: "Not a lot's going to change over the next year or two. Buy wisely and you'll not be paying depreciation." With stocks plentiful and prices broadly stable it gives enthusiasts the assurance that they can indulge without fearing that values will plummet or soar beyond reach, as they did in the boom. With regard to the early 1990s, Simon Hope of H & H Classic Auctions notes that "those briefly inflated values encouraged many costly restorations and today, if you buy wisely, you can buy a really sound car for less than the cost of its restoration. The boom also led to many cars being restored that would otherwise have been scrapped."

Those cars have added to the classic car pool, while other wider economic factors have swelled it to a point of oversupply. Simon Hope observes, "Thousands of cars are being repatriated from right-hand-drive export markets like Australia, New Zealand and South Africa. In South Africa in particular, where the economy and classic car market has collapsed, cars that are worth next to nothing there are coming back to the UK, where at least they're worth something."

Robin Lawton reckons between 500 and 700 Mk 2 Jaguars have been repatriated from South Africa in the last two years alone. MG T-Series Midgets have also come back in their hundreds, putting further pressure on the UK market. Laurence Sayers-Gillan of Barons Auctions highlights another strain on the UK classic car market: "The downward pressure on new and used car prices has filtered through to mainstream classic cars. As far as the borderline classic car enthusiast is concerned I'm not sure how tempted they'll be by a £25,000/$36,250 E-Type Jaguar when you can buy a new BMW Z3 for less; likewise at £6,000/$8,700 for a 30-year-old MGB Roadster or the same amount for a five-year-old Mazda MX5."

In short, it's a buyer's market with plentiful stock and it's looking to stay that way for a while. Now is not the time to 'invest in an appreciating asset', but to drive a bargain – and enjoy.

Buying a classic car is not an end in itself, but merely a passport to a whole range of pleasures. I get a tremendous kick just driving my Volvo P1800S in daily use. There's a delicious appeal in driving a car that's thwarted the scrapyard and defied the cynical planned obsolescence of the manufacturer. The more hard-core enthusiasts would have you believe that old cars are viable transport, even practical and sensible, with zero road tax for cars built before 1973 and favourable insurance rates.

Then there's tremendous pleasure to be had with others on any number of classic car runs throughout the season, many taking in stunning scenery. If you want to change up a gear, your classic car can also open the door to competitive driving in stage rallies or in circuit racing. You can compete at any level from a one-day regularity rally on public roads, to a re-creation of the Monte Carlo Rally, Peking to Paris, a raid in the Andes, London to Mexico, even round the world. It's all been done in classic cars. There are shows to attend and friends to meet at club events. In winter, why not while away the time reading some of the vast fund of motoring writing stretching back over the course of a motoring century and more?

I can think of no other hobby that opens up so many roads to sheer pleasure, and I hope this latest edition of *Miller's Collectors Cars Price Guide* sets you off on an enjoyable journey down memory lane.

Dave Selby

AC

For some enthusiasts, the legend and myth of the awesome Anglo-American Cobra eclipses all ACs before or since. Certainly, the company had come a long way since 1907 when it produced its first utility vehicles under the company name Auto-Carriers. After WWI, ACs began to take on a sporting character, and in 1922 an AC became the first 1500cc car to cover 100 miles in one hour. After 1945, ACs continued to appeal to discerning and necessarily well-healed sporting drivers, but the car that really brought the company to wider notice was the lovely Ace of 1954, which American racer Carroll Shelby transformed and mutated into the fearsome Cobra. Although the first incarnation of the Cobra expired in 1968, its legend has given rise to a later series of continuation Cobras and spawned a whole kit-car cottage industry producing 'fake-snakes' as the pretenders are termed by those who are lucky enough to own the real thing.

1908 AC Auto-Carrier Tricar, restored 1986, new body.
£4,000–5,000 / $5,800–7,250 ⚒ Bon
Formed in 1904, Autocars and Accessories of Thames Ditton originally developed a three-wheeled commercial carrier with tiller steering as a competitor to the horse and cart, the driver being placed behind the load. A single-cylinder air-cooled 648cc engine drove through a two-speed epicyclic gearbox mounted on one side of the rear wheel, the brake drum being housed on the other side of the wheel. A passenger version was introduced in 1908, the passenger taking the place of the box van. The AC Sociable followed in 1910, accommodating the driver and passenger in the front, side by side. A three-seat version was also listed, the driver sitting behind the two front passengers.

1955 AC 2 Litre Saloon, triple SU carburettors, 76bhp, 4-speed Moss gearbox, partially restored, engine and gearbox rebuilt, wiring renewed, brakes overhauled, road springs repaired and reset, front and rear bumpers rechromed, new window rubbers, all instruments restored and recalibrated, wood trim and headlining refurbished, in need of finishing.
£4,000–5,000 / $5,800–7,250 ⚒ CGC
Launched in 1947, the AC 2 Litre owed a lot to pre-war design trends. Its continued use of AC's venerable overhead-camshaft six and a beam-axle front suspension design lent it a 'vintage' feel. Nevertheless, it was a spacious and well-appointed four-seat touring car offering respectable acceleration and an 84mph top speed.

1935 AC 16/56 Drophead Coupé, 1991cc 6-cylinder engine, 4-speed manual gearbox with synchromesh, 3-position drophead coupé coachwork, Rudge Whitworth-type knock-off wire wheels, finished in red, grey leathercloth hood, black interior trim, coachwork and all mechanical components in good condition.
£12,000–15,000 / $17,500–21,750 ⚒ BRIT
The origins of AC date back to 1904, with the founding of Autocars & Accessories Ltd at West Norwood in London. The company manufactured a three-wheeled light delivery van, designed by John Wellar. By 1908, a passenger car was being built, also a three-wheeler, known as the Sociable, which remained in production until the outbreak of WWI in 1914. By then the company was operating from Thames Ditton in Surrey, and following wartime munitions work, Wellar went on to design a six-cylinder, overhead-camshaft engine of 1.5 litres, this being increased to 1991cc during 1922. It became AC's staple power unit, remaining in production until 1963, by which time continuous development had increased its power output from the initial 35bhp to 103bhp. Between 1921 and 1929, under the directorship of S. F. Edge, ACs were used extensively in competition and enjoyed much success. In 1926, the Hon Victor Bruce and W. J. Brunell drove to victory in the Monte Carlo Rally, a six-cylinder AC being the first British car to win this prestigious event. However, financial difficulties arose during 1929 and production virtually ceased until the Hurlock brothers acquired the company in the following year. From then on, AC concentrated on the manufacture of high-quality sporting cars.

1957 AC Ace Bristol, 1971cc 6-cylinder engine, 120bhp, 4-speed manual gearbox with overdrive, 4-wheel independent suspension, front disc/rear drum brakes, original Bristol engine, recent 5-year chassis-up restoration, only run-in mileage since, finished in navy blue, black hide interior.
£45,000–50,000 / $65,000–72,000 ⚒ RM

AC Model	ENGINE cc/cyl	DATES	CONDITION 1	2	3
Sociable	636/1	1907–12	£14,000	£9,000	£6,000
12/24 (Anzani)	1498/4	1919–27	£14,000	£11,500	£7,500
16/40	1991/6	1920–28	£18,000	£15,000	£11,000
16/60 Drophead/Saloon	1991/6	1937–40	£24,000	£21,000	£15,500
16/70 Sports Tourer	1991/6	1937–40	£35,000	£26,000	£18,000
16/80 Competition 2-Seater	1991/6	1937–40	£55,000	£45,000	£35,000

1958 AC Ace, 2 litre overhead-camshaft 6-cylinder engine, 4-wheel independent suspension, chassis stripped and repainted 1993, mechanical overhaul, interior reupholstered, good condition throughout.
£32,000–36,000 / $46,000–52,000 ≁ **Bon**
In tuned form, the Ace enjoyed great success in production sports car racing, winning its class at Le Mans in 1959. In 1955, AC had added a hardtop version – the fastback-styled Aceca – and both models became available with the more powerful Bristol engine before production ceased in 1963.

1954 AC Aceca Bristol, 1971cc 6-cylinder engine, extensively restored, bills in excess of £30,000/$43,500, black paintwork showing signs of blistering, red interior in excellent condition, Motor Show car, ex-Donald Campbell.
£25,000–28,000 / $36,000–40,000 ≁ **H&H**
This particular car was the prototype Aceca coupé and was displayed at the Motor Show in 1954. Subsequently it was owned by Donald Campell, who had the Bristol engine fitted.

▶ **1987 AC Cobra Mk IV by Autokraft,** 5 litre Ford V8 engine, fuel injection, 5-speed manual gearbox, 4-wheel disc brakes, coil-spring suspension, finished in black, 1 of only 348 produced, fewer than 1,000 miles from new.
£34,000–38,000 / $50,000–55,000 ≁ **RM**

1959 AC Ace/Cobra, 4.7 litre Ford V8 engine, left-hand drive Ace chassis, 427 Cobra-style bodywork, imported into the UK from USA 1989, partially dismantled.
£7,000–10,000 / $10,200–14,500 ≁ **Bon**

1961 AC Greyhound, 1971cc Bristol engine with D-type-specification cams and cylinder head, overdrive gearbox, restored 1997–2000, finished in silver, red leather upholstery.
£16,000–18,000 / $23,000–26,000 ≁ **H&H**

AC Cobra (1962–68)

Production: Estimates vary from 560 to 580 for the 289 model and 316 to 510 for the 427 model.
Engine: 289cu.in (4727cc); 427cu.in (6997cc).
Power output: 289, 271–370bhp; 427, 355–425bhp.
Transmission: Four-speed manual.
Brakes: Discs all-round.
Maximum speed: 289, 136+mph; 427, 165mph.
0–60mph: 289, 5.2–5.5 seconds; 427, 4.2 seconds.
The story of the AC Cobra started in Surrey in 1954 with the launch of AC's neat, lean and agile Ace, an expensive, bespoke sports car powered by a rather vintage six-cylinder unit. In 1962, American Carroll Shelby gave it a massive steroid shot, pumping up the chassis, suspension, brakes and aluminium body to cope with a series of fire-breathing Ford V8s. The first 75 cars used 4.2 litre engines, then grew to 4.7 to create the 289 – the engine's capacity in cubic inches. Performance figures were shattering, but still Shelby wanted more and, in an attempt to realize his goal of winning Le Mans, he squeezed in a stonking 7 litre V8 and beefed up the chassis still more to create the Cobra 427. The Cobra 427 never won Le Mans, although competition Cobras won races in other categories all over the world, and on the streets the car marketed as 'the fastest production car ever sold to the public' was – and still is – just about the loudest, proudest, most raucous and primal four-wheeled projectile around.

◀ **1989 AC Cobra Mk IV by Autokraft,** 5 litre Ford V8 engine, fuel injection, 225bhp, Borg Warner 5-speed manual gearbox, Salisbury limited-slip differential, 0–100mph in 13.3 seconds, finished in red, black Everflex hood and tonneau, wind wings, Nardi woodrim steering wheel, black Connolly leather interior, 3,000 miles from new, excellent condition.
£33,000–37,000 / $48,000–53,750 ⟋ Bon

Convinced that a market existed for an inexpensive sports car combining European chassis engineering and American V8 power, Texan racing driver Carroll Shelby concocted an unlikely alliance between AC Cars and the Ford Motor Company. The former's Ace provided the simple twin-tube chassis frame – supplied with four-wheel disc brakes for the Cobra – into which was persuaded one of Ford's small-block V8s. Production ended in 1968, but resumed in 1980 under the auspices of Brooklands-based Autokraft.

1991 AC Cobra Mk IV, 5000cc Ford V8 engine, 5-speed manual gearbox, twin sidepipes, finished in metallic dark blue, black leather seats, 5,000 miles from new, 1 of a limited number of lightweights built.
£40,000–45,000 / $58,000–65,000 ⊞ BC

1967 AC 428 Convertible, coachwork by Frua, 7014cc V8 engine, 345bhp, 4-speed manual gearbox, top speed 140mph, 0–60mph in around 6 seconds, 4-wheel disc brakes, factory converted to left-hand drive, chassis tuned for firmer ride, finished in green, black interior, air conditioning, very good condition throughout.
£45,000–50,000 / $65,000–72,000 ⟋ Bon

In essence, the AC 428 was a Cobra Mk III with a longer wheelbase and a body styled by Frua. During its production life (1965–73), fewer than 80 examples were made.

◀ **1971 AC 428 Coupé,** coachwork by Frua, 7014cc V8 engine, chrome wire wheels, finished in white, original black leather interior trim, fewer than 41,000 miles from new, excellent condition throughout.
£14,000–18,000 / $20,000–26,000 ⟋ H&H

AC Model	ENGINE cc/cyl	DATES	CONDITION 1	2	3
2 Litre	1991/6	1947–55	£7,000	£4,000	£1,500
Buckland	1991/6	1949–54	£9,000	£5,500	£2,500
Ace	1991/6	1953–63	£30,000	£25,000	£20,000
Ace Bristol	1971/6	1954–63	£45,000	£30,000	£25,000
Ace 2.6	1553/6	1961–62	£38,000	£32,000	£29,000
Aceca	1991/6	1954–63	£22,000	£16,000	£11,000
Aceca Bristol	1971/6	1956–63	£28,000	£20,000	£12,000
Greyhound Bristol	1971/6	1961–63	£16,000	£12,000	£8,000
Cobra Mk II 289	4735/8	1963–64	£90,000	£80,000	£60,000
Cobra Mk III 427	6998/8	1965–67	£135,000	£100,000	£80,000
Cobra Mk IV	5340/8	1987–92	£55,000	£40,000	£28,000
428 Frua	7014/8	1967–73	£19,000	£15,000	£10,000
428 Frua Convertible	7014/8	1967–73	£30,000	£20,000	£16,000
3000ME	2994/6	1976–84	£15,000	£10,000	£8,000

Racing history for Cobra will put the price at £100,000–120,000+.

Alfa Romeo

The Milanese company started life in 1909 as ALFA (Anonima Lombardo Fabbrica Automibili), produced its first cars in 1910 and became Alfa Romeo when industrialist Nicolo Romeo took control in 1915. In the 1920s, Alfa Romeo produced some exquisite sporting machines and dominated grand prix racing for a decade before being overwhelmed by the might of the Mercedes and Auto Union teams in the mid-1930s. Post-1945 Alfas became more accessible, and many models from the 1960s onwards have sometimes been tagged 'poor man's Ferraris'. That may sound like a put-down, but it should be regarded as a compliment – albeit a little backhanded – for there are very few poor handling Alfa Romeos, and most have all the characteristics to engage keen drivers with their lithe, lean and sure-footed agility.

1928 Alfa Romeo 6C 1500 Sport Spider, coachwork by Zagato, 1487cc double-overhead-camshaft 6-cylinder engine, 54bhp, 4-speed manual gearbox, 4-wheel drum brakes, older restoration, original body, oldest known survivor of its type.
£75,000–80,000 / $109,000–116,000 ↗ RM
After joining Alfa Romeo in 1923, Vittorio Jano created the all-conquering P2. After its instant success was followed by a series of victories, Alfa Romeo steered Jano's talents to a line of passenger cars to succeed the RL and RM models. Jano took a clean sheet of paper and created a legendary 1.5 litre six that was to set new standards for lightweight high-performance motor cars, the 6C 1500. In its naturally-aspirated and supercharged variants, this car would go on to beat much larger and more powerful machinery. In the hands of both professional and gifted amateur drivers from Campari to Eyston, Alfa's 6C 1500 was a potential winner in any event, and it frequently fulfilled its potential.

▶ **1963 Alfa Romeo 2600 Spider,** double-overhead-camshaft 6-cylinder engine, triple Dellorto carburettors, 145bhp, 5-speed manual gearbox, substantial restoration 1986–90, engine rebuilt late 1990s, fewer than 5,000 miles since, uprated shock absorbers, resprayed red, black interior trim, good to excellent condition.
£8,000–11,000 / $11,500–16,000 ↗ COYS
The Alfa Romeo 2600 Spider was launched in 1962 and represented a return for the marque to the high-class, luxury six-cylinder cars that in the past had proved so successful. Its chief rivals were the Maserati 3500GT Spyder and Lancia Flaminia Convertible, both similar in appearance and performance.

1949 Alfa Romeo 6C 2500S, 2443cc double-overhead-camshaft 6-cylinder engine, 90bhp, box-section chassis, 4-wheel independent suspension.
£18,000–22,000 / $26,000–32,000 ↗ Bon
Its Portello factory devastated by wartime bombing, Alfa Romeo did not resume car production until 1946, when the pre-war 6C 2500 re-emerged clothed anew as the Freccia d'Oro (Golden Arrow). A development of the 2300 and destined to be the last of the separate-chassis Alfas, the 2500 had been introduced in 1939. Styled in-house, but strongly influenced by Touring, the Freccia d'Oro five-seat sports saloon was built alongside coupé and cabriolet versions featuring bodies by the likes of Pinin Farina, Touring and Ghia, plus a six/seven-seat *berlina* on a longer wheelbase.

ALFA ROMEO Model	ENGINE cc/cyl	DATES	CONDITION 1	2	3
24hp	4084/4	1910–11	£25,000	£16,000	£12,000
12hp	2413/4	1910–11	£18,000	£11,000	£8,000
40–60	6028/4	1913–15	£32,000	£24,000	£14,000
RL/RLSS	2916/6	1921–22	£40,000	£24,000	£14,000
RM	1944/4	1924–25	£28,000	£17,000	£13,000
6C 1500	1487/6	1927–28	£50,000*	£20,000+	£10,000+
6C 1750	1752/6	1923–33	£100,000+	£80,000+	-
6C 1900	1917/6	1933	£18,000	£15,000	£12,000
6C 2300	2309/6	1934	£30,000+	£18,000	£15,000
6C 2500 SS Cabriolet/Spider	2443/6	1939–45	£100,000	£50,000	£40,000
6C 2500 SS Coupé	2443/6	1939–45	£60,000	£40,000	£30,000
8C 2300 Monza/Short Chassis	2300/8	1931–34	£1,500,000+	£600,000+	-
8C 2900	2900/8	1935–39	£1,500,000+	£1,000,000	-

Value is very dependent on sporting history, body style and engine type.
*The high price of this model is dependent on whether it is 1500 supercharged/twin overhead cam, and with or without a racing history.

1964 Alfa Romeo 2600 Spider, 2584cc double-overhead-camshaft 6-cylinder engine, 145bhp, 5-speed manual gearbox, brakes overhauled, finished in red, reupholstered 1988, black leather upholstery in very good condition, 1 of 103 right-hand-drive cars built, 64,000 miles from new.
£16,000–18,000 / $23,000–26,000 ➤ CGC

1971 Alfa Romeo Giulia 1300 Super Berlina, left-hand drive, 2 owners from new, never restored or modified, original condition throughout.
£1,500–2,000 / $2,000–3,000 ➤ Bon
Successor to the popular Giulietta, the Giulia saloon was launched in 1963. Despite its boxy unitary-construction body, the newcomer was a paragon of aerodynamic efficiency and possessed a distinctly sporting nature, its 1.6 litre 92bhp twin-cam four-cylinder engine making it a genuine 100mph car. Under the skin, the Giulia featured a five-speed manual gearbox, independent front suspension, coil-sprung live rear axle and, early cars excepted, disc brakes all-round. The Giulia 1300, readily distinguishable by its two-headlamp front end, appeared in 1964, the Ti version with 82bhp proving almost as quick as its big brother. The Ti theme was further improved upon by the succeeding Giulia 1300 Super which, courtesy of a raised compression ratio and two twin-choke Weber carburettors, produced 89bhp, an output good enough for a top speed in excess of 100mph.

1960 Alfa Romeo Guilletta Sprint Coupé, 1290cc engine, 4-speed manual gearbox, left-hand drive, total restoration, complete mechanical overhaul, new chromework, bare-metal respray in red, new red interior, exceptional condition throughout.
£8,500–10,000 / $12,500–14,500 ➤ H&H
The Guilletta Sprint was launched in 1954 at the same time as the 1900 Super Sprint. It came with the 1298cc engine and two-seat coupé body which was at first part alloy with sliding Perspex windows.

1966 Alfa Romeo Giulia Spider, 1570cc double-overhead-camshaft engine, 92bhp, 5-speed gearbox, original right-hand-drive car, finished in red, black interior, well maintained, good overall condition.
£8,000–10,000 / $11,500–14,500 ➤ COYS

The Alfa Romeo Spider has enjoyed a cult following ever since one was driven by Dustin Hoffman to the strains of Simon and Garfunkel in the film *The Graduate*.

1965 Alfa Romeo Giulia Sprint Speciale, coachwork by Bertone, left-hand drive, finished in white, red interior in correct PVC and cloth, fewer than 37,000 miles from new, largely original and unrestored, in need of attention.
£8,000–10,000 / $11,500–14,500 ➤ Bon
Bertone created the extraordinary Sprint Speciale body in 1957, when it was hailed as futuristic and a masterpiece. The style was created for the Alfa Romeo Giulietta, but so profound was its impact that it was retained when the Giulietta was replaced by the slightly larger Giulia. Only 1,366 examples were made.

1964 Alfa Romeo Giulia Sprint GTC Cabriolet, left-hand drive, restored 1994–95, finished in red, black interior, 3 owners from new, good condition.
£11,000–14,000 / $16,000–20,500 ⚲ Bon
The coupé version of the Giulia Ti sports saloon, the Giulia Sprint GT, was launched in 1963. Clothed in four-seat coachwork by Bertone, it utilized the 1.6 litre version of Alfa's twin-cam four. Power output was 106bhp, sufficient to propel the Sprint to a top speed of around 112mph. Mechanically, the new coupé was much the same as the saloon and featured a five-speed manual gearbox, independent front suspension, coil-sprung live rear axle and disc brakes all round. The GTA competition version enjoyed considerable success, winning the European Touring Car Championship three years running from 1966 to 1968. Almost as rare as the GTA was the cabriolet-bodied GTC, the only four-seat convertible in the Giulietta/Giulia family, only 999 examples of which were produced between 1964 and 1966.

◄ **1966 Alfa Romeo Giulia Sprint GT Veloce,** restored, good condition throughout.
£3,000–4,000 /$4,400–5,800 ⚲ Bon

1975 Alfa Romeo 1600 GT Junior, 1570cc 4-cylinder engine, cylinder head overhauled, finished in yellow, original grey and black cloth interior, sound mechanical order, well maintained.
£2,000–2,500 / $3,000–3,600 ⚲ BRIT

Miller's Starter Marque

- **Starter Alfa Romeos:** *1750 & 2000 GTV; 1300 Junior Spider, 1600 Duetto Spider, 1750 & 2000 Spider Veloce; 1300 & 1600 GT Junior; Alfasud ti & Sprint.*
- Responsive, eager and sweet twin-cam engines, finely balanced chassis, nimble handling and delightful looks are just some of the character traits of classic Alfas from the mid-1960s onwards. They are also eminently affordable. For the kind of money that gets you an MGB or TR Triumph you could be a little more adventurous and acquire an engaging Alfa Romeo sporting saloon or convertible.
- That's the good news; the bad news is that the unfortunate reputation Alfas of the 1960s and 1970s earned for rusting was deserved. Even that has its up-side, because the suspicion still lingers and helps keep prices comparatively low. In fact, most of the Alfas you're looking at will by now have had major surgery at least once, so you should be able to find one with plenty of metal. Even so, take a magnet along. Classic Alfa owners – or *Alfisti* as they prefer to call themselves – have a saying: you pay for the engineering and the engine, but the body comes free. Bear in mind too that maintenance costs are likely to be pricier than an MG or Triumph TR.

Restored values

The cost of a professional restoration will have an influence on, but no direct relation to, a car's market value. A restored car can have a market value lower than the cost of its restoration.

1974 Alfa Romeo GTV Coupé, 1962cc 4-cylinder engine, finished in yellow, good condition.
£2,000–2,500 / $3,000–3,500 ⚲ H&H

1970 Alfa Romeo Montreal Coupé, coachwork by Bertone, original, 2 owners from new, very good condition throughout.
£5,000–6,000 / $7,250–8,750 ➣ Bon
Inspired by Bertone's Alfa-based styling exercise, which had been exhibited at the 1967 Montreal Expo, the two-seat Montreal coupé débuted at the Geneva Salon in 1970. Unlike the Expo prototype, which had used Alfa's 1.6 litre four-cylinder engine, the production Montreal employed a 'civilized' 2593cc version of the T33 sports car's four-cam V8. The front-mounted, dry-sumped engine produced 200bhp at 6,500rpm courtesy of electronic ignition and Spica mechanical fuel injection, and drove the rear wheels via a five-speed ZF gearbox. Sourced from the contemporary Giulia 1750 GTV, the running gear comprised independent front suspension plus disc brakes all-round. The Montreal was good for a top speed of 137mph and, despite the hefty price tag, proved very popular.

1972 Alfa Romeo Montreal, dry-sump V8 engine, 4 Weber 42DCNF carburettor conversion, left-hand drive, resprayed.
£5,500–6,500 / $8,000–9,500 ➣ CGC

Cross Reference
See Colour Review (page 65)

Alfa Romeo Montreal (1970–77)
Price in 1972: £5,077/$7,362 (£800/$1,160 less than BMW 3.0CSi).
Production: 3,925.
Engine: 2593cc quad-cam V8.
Transmission: ZF five-speed manual.
Power output: 200bhp at 6,550rpm.
Brakes: Servo–assisted ventilated discs all-round.
0–60mph: 7.5 seconds.
Top speed: 137mph.

1983 Alfa Romeo Alfetta 2000 SL Saloon, double-overhead-camshaft 4-cylinder engine, 5-speed transaxle, finished in blue and silver, grey cloth interior, limited-edition model, 38,000 miles from new, excellent condition.
£2,000–2,500 / $3,000–3,600 ➣ H&H

ALFA ROMEO Model	ENGINE cc/cyl	DATES	CONDITION 1	2	3
2000 Spider	1974/4	1958–61	£14,000	£9,000	£4,000
2600 Sprint	2584/6	1962–66	£11,000	£7,500	£4,000
2600 Spider	2584/6	1962–65	£13,000	£8,000	£5,000
Giulietta Sprint	1290/4	1955–62	£10,000	£7,000	£4,000
Giulietta Spider	1290/4	1956–62	£12,000	£6,000	£4,500
Giulia Saloon	1570/4	1962–72	£5,000	£3,000	£1,500
Giulia Sprint (rhd)	1570/4	1962–68	£10,500	£6,000	£2,000
Giulia Spider (rhd)	1570/4	1962–65	£11,000	£8,000	£4,000
Giulia SS	1570/4	1962–66	£16,000	£11,000	£5,000
GT 1300 Junior	1290/4	1966–77	£7,000	£5,500	£2,000
Giulia Sprint GT	1570/4	1962–68	£7,500	£5,000	£2,000
1600GT Junior	1570/4	1972–75	£7,000	£4,000	£2,000
1750/2000 Berlina	1779/ 1962/4	1967–77	£4,000	£2,000	£1,000
1750GTV	1779/4	1967–72	£7,000	£6,000	£2,000
2000GTV	1962/4	1971–77	£6,500	£4,000	£2,000
1600/1750 (Duetto)	1570/ 1779/4	1966–67	£10,000	£7,500	£5,000
1750/2000 Spider (Kamm)	1779/ 1962/4	1967–78	£9,000	£6,000	£3,000
Montreal	2593/8	1970–77	£9,000	£8,000	£5,000
Junior Zagato 1300	1290/4	1968–74	£7,000	£5,000	£3,000
Junior Zagato 1600	1570/4	1968–74	£8,000	£6,000	£4,000
Alfetta GT/GTV (chrome)	1962/4	1972–86	£4,000	£2,500	£1,000
Alfasud	1186/ 1490/4	1972–83	£2,000	£1,000	£500
Alfasud ti	1186/ 1490/4	1974–81	£2,500	£1,200	£900
Alfasud Sprint	1284/ 1490/4	1976–85	£3,000	£2,000	£1,000
GTV6	2492/6	1981–	£4,000	£2,500	£1,000

Watch for Zagato coachwork on early coupé models – very desirable.

Allard

Long before he became a car maker in his own right, Sydney Herbert Allard had built up a wealth of valuable experience by competing widely in various forms of motor sport. At the age of 19, in 1929, he was already racing three-wheeled Morgans and selling cars at his family's south London Ford dealership. In the 1930s, he was a major force in trials and hillclimbs, and by 1936 he had built his first Allard special,

based on a Ford V8 chassis and sparse body that even included bits of a Bugatti Type 57. These early specials developed into the big, hairy-chested sports cars that were the company's staple offerings, all of which were produced in limited numbers. Sydney Allard drove his own creations to win the 1949 British Hillclimb Championship and the 1952 Monte Carlo Rally.

1948 Allard M-Type Drophead Coupé, 3600cc sidevalve Ford V8 engine, finished in black, burgundy interior, 1 of 500 built, maintained regardless of cost, excellent condition throughout.
£15,000–18,000 / $22,000–26,000 ➶ H&H

The first post-war production models of the Allard Motor Company, founded in 1946, featured American Ford sidevalve V8s, more often than not fitted with Sidney's own alloy speed equipment, such as intake manifolds and cylinder heads. By the early 1950s, larger American overhead-valve V8s from Cadillac and Chrysler became available. In true hot rod fashion, Sidney wasted no time in shoehorning these into his J2 and J2X sports-racing models. The first Cadillac engine was immediately installed into Allard's own J2 racing car, which was entered in the 1950 Tour of Sicily and in the same year at Le Mans, where Allard finished third overall.

ALLARD Model	ENGINE cc/cyl	DATES	CONDITION 1	2	3
K/K2/L/M/M2X	3622/8	1947–54	£18,500+	£12,000	£8,000
K3	var/8	1953–54	£24,000	£15,000	£11,000
P1	3622/8	1949–52	£19,500	£13,000	£8,000
P2	3622/8	1952–54	£22,000	£18,000	£11,500
J2/J2X	var/8	1950–54	£60,000+	£50,000	£35,000
Palm Beach	1508/4, 2262/6	1952–55	£12,000	£10,000	£5,500
Palm Beach II	2252/ 3442/6	1956–60	£25,000+	£20,000	£11,000

Alldays

◀ **1914 Alldays Midget 8.9bhp Two-Seater,** 875cc vertical twin-cylinder monobloc engine, 3-speed gearbox, quarter-elliptic springs, brass oil side lamps, folding brass-framed windscreen, hood, bulb horn, side mounted spare wheel, oil rear lamp, finished in maroon with black wings, pleated black upholstery, original.
£9,000–11,000 / $13,000–16,000 ➶ Bon

One of the UK's longest-established engineering establishments, The Alldays & Onions Pneumatic Engineering Company began building cars as early as 1898, continuing in production until 1918. The first commercially viable car was the twin-cylinder 10/12hp model, introduced in 1905. The later Alldays Midget catered for the cyclecar fashion of the immediate pre-WWI years.

Alvis

Always sporting of nature, generally elegant and occasionally surprisingly innovative, Alvis trickled along from 1919 to 1966 aloof from the automotive mainstream, producing a select strain of often memorable vehicles. The Coventry company was an early proponent of front-wheel drive, which appeared in 1928 on the 12/75. In the 1930s, the handsome and fast

Speed 20 tourers were never so extrovert as to be bold, but were assuredly self-confident. Some early post-war offerings were initially a little wayward – for example, the whale-like TB14 and TB21 – but perhaps no Alvis was ever more elegant than the last-of-line TD, TE and TF21 models, which brought car making to a close when Rover took control in 1966.

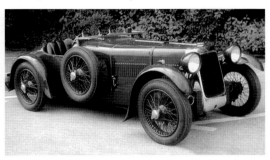

1928 Alvis 12/75, restored to original specification at a cost of over £60,000/$87,000, correct specification.
£40,000–45,000 / $58,000–65,000 ✈ COYS
The front-wheel-drive Alvis was introduced in 1928, but was never intended for the ordinary motorist. Instead it was a super sports car to be sold only to experienced drivers for road and competition use. Production began as a result of huge demand, the car initially being developed in 1925 to dominate the 200 mile Brooklands endurance race. This concept was soon proven in competition, two production blown cars finishing sixth and ninth at Le Mans and first in their class. Four cars were entered for the Tourist Trophy race of the same year where, after a glorious battle, Leon Cushman's supercharged car was just beaten into second place.

▶ **1929 Alvis Silver Eagle 2 Litre Sports Tourer,** coachwork by Cross & Ellis, 1991cc engine, twin carburettors, 100mph speedometer, Bluemels sprung steering wheel, refurbished 1989 at a cost of £25,000/$36,250, coachwork restored, recommissioned 2000, finished in British racing green with red wheels, brown leather upholstery, 1 owner 1949–2000.
£22,000–26,000 / $32,000–38,000 ✈ Bon
The Silver Eagle was one of the few British vintage motor cars capable of cruising at a steady 70mph, and it was in just such a model that E. J. P. Eugster raced the Blue Train Express from St Raphael to Calais, a distance of 746 miles, beating the speeding train by a comfortable margin of three hours.

1932 Alvis 12/50 TJ Atlantic Saloon, coachwork by Carbodies, 1645cc 4-cylinder engine, all equipment and instrumentation fully functional, finished in green with black wings, green leather upholstery, seats reupholstered, original interior wood trim, good condition throughout.
£7,000–8,000 / $10,250–11,500 ✈ BRIT
Founded immediately after WWI by T. G. John, Alvis quickly gained a reputation for high-quality sporting motor cars. The 12/50 appeared in 1923, being fitted with numerous styles of coachwork, from the outright sporting 'duck's back' two-seaters to well-appointed saloons. The model continued in production until 1932. The final TJ-series 12/50 and 12/60 models were fitted with a longer-stroke 1645cc engine.

ALVIS Model	ENGINE cc/cyl	DATES	CONDITION 1	2	3
12/50	1496/4	1923–32	£20,000	£13,000	£7,000
Silver Eagle	2148	1929–37	£16,000	£12,000	£8,000
Silver Eagle DHC	2148	1929–37	£20,000+	£13,000	£9,000
12/60	1645/4	1931–32	£15,000	£10,000	£7,000
Speed 20 (tourer)	2511/6	1932–36	£35,000+	£28,000	£18,000
Speed 20 (closed)	2511/6	1932–36	£25,000	£18,000+	£11,000
Crested Eagle	3571/6	1933–39	£10,000	£7,000	£4,000
Firefly (tourer)	1496/4	1932–34	£14,000+	£10,000	£6,000
Firefly (closed)	1496/4	1932–34	£7,000	£5,000	£4,000
Firebird (tourer)	1842/4	1934–39	£13,000	£10,000	£6,000
Firebird (closed)	1842/4	1934–39	£7,000	£5,000	£4,000
Speed 25 (tourer)	3571/6	1936–40	£38,500	£30,000	£20,000
Speed 25 (closed)	3571/6	1936–40	£23,000	£17,000	£12,000
3.5 Litre	3571/6	1935–36	£35,000	£25,000	£18,000
4.3 Litre	4387/6	1936–40	£44,000+	£30,000	£22,000
Silver Crest	2362/6	1936–40	£14,000	£10,000	£7,000
TA	3571/6	1936–39	£18,000	£12,000	£8,000
12/70	1842/4	1937–40	£10,000	£8,000	£6,000

1935 Alvis Silver Eagle Saloon, coachwork by Holbrook, 2362cc overhead-valve 6-cylinder engine, 4-speed gearbox, mechanically restored, finished in black, original interior, excellent running order.
£12,000–14,000 / $17,500–20,500 ⊞ AVON

1959 Alvis TD21 Saloon, 2993cc 6-cylinder engine, manual gearbox, wire wheels, restored mid-1990s, finished in maroon, grey hide interior trim, all mechanical components in good condition, 60,000 miles from new.
£7,500–8,500 / $10,800–12,300 ⚒ BRIT

1961 Alvis TD21 Saloon, coachwork by Park Ward, 2993cc 6-cylinder engine, manual gearbox, excellent condition.
£9,000–10,000 / $13,000–14,500 ⊞ UMC

▶ **1963 Alvis TE21 Saloon,** 2993cc 6-cylinder engine, automatic transmission, extensively restored late 1980s, recent mechanical work, finished in blue, grey leather interior trim, coachwork and structure in good condition.
£5,500–6,500 / $8,000–9,500 ⚒ BRIT

1949 Alvis TA14 Four-Door Saloon, subject of 7-year restoration, over £10,500/$15,225 spent on new parts, finished in dark green, green whipcord upholstery, coachwork and paintwork in very good condition, interior as new, engine seized.
£6,000–7,000 / $8,700–10,200 ⚒ Bon
Alvis' first post-WWII model was the TA14, developed from the pre-war 12/70. It was powered by a four-cylinder 1892cc engine fitted with a single horizontal SU carburettor. It boasted a maximum speed of 74mph with 25mpg fuel economy.

1961 Alvis TD21 Saloon, 2993cc 6-cylinder engine, 120bhp, automatic transmission, servo-assisted disc brakes, older restoration, little recent use, fair/good condition.
£4,500–5,500 / $6,500–8,000 ⚒ Bon
Originally registered to Alvis Cars, this particular TD21 is thought to have been the works demonstrator and possibly the Motor Show car.

ALVIS Model	ENGINE cc/cyl	DATES	CONDITION		
			1	2	3
TA14	1892/4	1946–50	£9,500	£8,000	£4,500
TA14 DHC	1892/4	1946–50	£14,000	£11,000	£5,000
TB14 Roadster	1892/4	1949–50	£15,000	£10,000	£8,000
TB21 Roadster	2993/6	1951	£16,000	£10,000	£7,000
TA21/TC21	2993/6	1950–55	£12,000	£9,000	£5,000
TA21/TC21 DHC	2993/6	1950–55	£17,000	£13,000	£10,000
TC21/100 Grey Lady	2993/6	1953–56	£13,000	£11,000	£5,000
TC21/100 DHC	2993/6	1954–56	£19,000	£15,000	£9,000
TD21	2993/6	1956–62	£11,000	£8,000	£4,000
TD21 DHC	2993/6	1956–62	£22,000	£16,000	£10,000
TE21	2993/6	1963–67	£15,000	£10,000	£7,000
TE21 DHC	2993/6	1963–67	£22,000	£16,000	£8,000
TF21	2993/6	1966–67	£16,000	£12,000	£8,000
TF21 DHC	2993/6	1966–67	£28,000	£17,000	£13,000

American Motors

1979 American Motors Pacer Squire Station Wagon, 258cu.in overhead-valve 6-cylinder engine, 120bhp, 3-speed automatic transmission, finished in metallic copper with *faux*-wood trim.
£2,000–2,500 / $3,000–3,500 ⚒ Bon
When released in 1975, the Pacer was offered with a choice of straight-six engines: the standard 232cu.in unit and an optional 258cu.in engine. Subsequently, the latter became the base unit and a 304cu.in V8 was added as the engine option, which required selection of power steering and brakes. The standard transmission was a column-change three-speed manual, with optional floor shift; a Torque-Command automatic was also optional.

Amilcar

◀ **1925 Amilcar CGS Two-Seater Sports,** fitted with 1000cc CCCS engine, restored 1980s, including new bodywork, finished in white, black upholstery.
£13,000–15,000
$18,750–21,750 ⚒ Bon
Of all the small French sporting cars produced after WWI, the Amilcar is one of the most famous and successful. The CGS featured a 1074cc engine, large front-wheel brakes, a robust chassis and leaf-spring suspension.

Armstrong-Siddeley

▶ **1938 Armstrong-Siddeley Sports Foursome Saloon,** 2394cc engine, restored, finished in green and black.
£11,000–12,000
$16,000–17,500 ⊞ BLE

ARMSTRONG–SIDDELEY Model	ENGINE cc/cyl	DATES	CONDITION		
			1	2	3
Hurricane	1991/6	1945–53	£10,000	£7,000	£4,000
Typhoon	1991/6	1946–50	£7,000	£3,000	£2,000
Lancaster/Whitley	1991/ 2306/6	1945–53	£8,000	£5,500	£2,500
Sapphire 234/236	2290/4 2309/6	1955–58	£7,500	£5,000	£3,000
Sapphire 346	3440/6	1953–58	£9,000	£5,000	£2,000
Star Sapphire	3990/6	1958–60	£10,000	£7,000	£4,000

◄ **1949 Armstrong-Siddeley Whitley 18hp,**
2309cc 6-cylinder engine, 4-speed synchromesh
gearbox, body-off restoration c1992, converted to
unleaded fuel, finished in pale yellow and brown,
brown leather interior trim partially replaced,
woodwork refurbished, trophy winner, good
condition throughout.
£7,000–8,000 / $10,200–11,600 ⚒ BRIT
Armstrong-Siddeley, formed in 1919, came
about as a result of the merging interests of
Armstrong-Whitworth and Siddeley-Deasey.
Throughout the company's 41 years of car
manufacture, products were always of the
highest quality. The post-war models,
introduced in 1945, had striking styling and a
specification that included torsion-bar front
suspension together with hydro-mechanical
brakes. The Whitley 18hp saloon succeeded
the Lancaster model and was available as a
four- or six-light saloon, a limousine or a coupé.

Arnold

► **1896 Arnold 1½hp Dogcart,** chassis no. 1, engine no. 1,
subject of considerable restoration work, new crankshaft and
new cam follower, new belts, new wheels, sprag brake,
period candle carriage lamps, 4 bells, finished in green and
black, 1 of only 2 surviving examples, trophy winner, complete
and continuous history, VCC dating plate, full working order.
£100,000–120,000 / $145,000–174,000 ⚒ Bon
W. Arnold & Sons, an agricultural and milling
engineering company, became a Benz importer, then
obtained a licence to build Benz-type motor cars. In
1896, the decision was taken to build a car of its
own design, but very much on the lines of the
contemporary Benz. At about this time, The Motor
Car Club announced its Tour to Brighton. The new
Arnold car could not be readied in time, so a Benz
chassis was modified to accept the prototype Arnold
engine. Henry Hewetson, a business associate of the
Arnolds, drove the car to Brighton, winning a gold
medal in the process. Following this achievement, the
car returned to the works, where Arnold transmission
gear was fitted and the car was completed to
Arnold's own design. A subsequent owner designed
and fitted his own patented electric starter.

Arnolt

◄ **1959 Arnolt Bristol,** coachwork by Bertone,
Bristol chassis, left-hand drive, restored, finished
in red, 1 of 142 built.
£28,000–31,000 / $40,500–42,000 ⚒ BJ
Arnolt Bristol cars were sold exclusively by
S. H. 'Wacky' Arnolt of Chicago.

Aston Martin

Many people equate Aston Martin's glory years with the heyday of James Bond: those classic years when Bond was Connery and 007 drove a DB Aston. But it was only a few years before silver-screen stardom that Aston Martin was also creating a name for itself in international motor racing with a vigorous works programme that culminated in a Le Mans win in 1959 for the DBR1. Those dizzy heights were a long way from the day in 1913 when Robert Bamford and Lionel Martin set up Bamford & Martin Ltd in London's South Kensington and started tuning and developing Singer 10s. In 1919, the first prototype Aston Martins were produced – the name was formed from the Aston Clinton Hillclimb and Lionel Martin's surname. Since then, production has always remained limited, and it was not until 1984 that the 10,000th Aston Martin, a V8 model, was built. For much of its life, Aston Martin's existence has been precarious. It first went bankrupt in 1925; then in 1947, industrialist David Brown took over, heralding the era of the glamorous DB – or David Brown – Astons, which came to full bloom in the 1960s. On the road, the DB4, 5 and 6 models were the stuff of dreams – literally – with a DB4 costing approximately the same as two E-Type Jaguars. Yet the company still struggled financially. In 1972, David Brown gave up the struggle – losses were reckoned at £1 million/$1.45 million a year – and after several changes of ownership, the company's future became secure when Ford took over in 1987.

1931 Aston Martin International Tourer, full chassis-up restoration 1990s, rebuilt 1.5 litre engine, including strengthened bottom end, steel connecting rods, ES pistons and Le Mans camshaft, Le Mans rear axle, 21in wire wheels, originally fitted with saloon body, since replaced with an original International 2/4-seat standard sports body, original upward-opening windscreen, previously owned by Aston Martin team driver K. S. Peacock.
£35,000–40,000 / $51,000–58,000 ✒ Bon

1951 Aston Martin DB2 Vantage, 1 of only 19 of the first DB2s fitted with Vantage engines from the outset, Alfin drum brakes, twin master cylinder, believed 1 of only 12 works prepared cars, rebuilt late 1990s, finished in original black with cream wheels, tan interior, original, excellent condition throughout.
£27,000–30,000 / $39,000–43,500 ✒ COYS

1952 Aston Martin DB2 Vantage, older restoration, history file containing invoices totalling c£36,500/$52,925, finished in red, black leather interior, very good condition.
£24,000–28,000 / $35,000–41,000 ✒ Bon
This DB2 was displayed by Aston Martin at the 1952 London Motor Show. The engine was converted to Vantage specification in 1952.

1953 Aston Martin DB2 Drophead Coupé, 2.6 litre double-overhead-camshaft 6-cylinder engine, front suspension by coil springs and trailing arms, rigid rear axle located by coil springs, parallel trailing arms and panhard rod, finished in metallic blue, blue leather interior, good original condition.
£40,000–45,000 / $58,000–65,000 ✒ COYS
The DB2 was offered between 1950 and 1953, during which time 410 were made. Of the total production, only 49 were drophead coupés.

ASTON MARTIN Model	ENGINE cc/cyl	DATES	CONDITION		
			1	2	3
Lionel Martin Cars	1486/4	1921–25	£26,000+	£18,000	£16,000
International	1486/4	1927–32	£50,000	£28,000	£16,000
Le Mans	1486/4	1932–33	£60,000	£40,000	£32,000
Mk II	1486/4	1934–36	£40,000	£30,000	£25,000
Ulster	1486/4	1934–36	£80,000+	£50,000	-
2 Litre	1950/4	1936–40	£40,000	£25,000	£18,000

Value is dependent upon racing history, originality and completeness.
Add 40% if a competition winner or works team car.

1953 Aston Martin DB2/4, 2580cc 6-cylinder engine, 125bhp, 4-wheel drum brakes, independent trailing-link/coil-spring front suspension, live rear axle on coil springs located by parallel arms and panhard rod, restored 1990s, finished in British racing green, beige interior, excellent condition throughout.
£30,000–35,000 / $44,000–51,000 ↗ COYS

Fine car though the DB2 was, its sales had been affected by the limitations of two seats and minimal luggage space. As a result, Aston Martin redesigned the rear of the car to incorporate two occasional rear seats, at the same time raising the roof line slightly to increase headroom and fitting a larger rear window in an opening lid. As such, this Aston, named DB2/4, was arguably the world's first hatchback. Other changes included a one-piece windscreen, reshaped quarterlights, repositioned headlights and a 6in (15cm) increase in overall length.

1954 Aston Martin DB2/4,
2.6 litre double-overhead-camshaft
6-cylinder Vantage engine,
rectangular-tube chassis,
trailing-arm independent front
suspension, restored 1994–2001,
finished in navy blue, light blue
leather interior, very good
condition throughout.
£26,000–30,000
$38,000–44,000 ↗ Bon

◄ **1957 Aston
Martin DB2/4
Mk II,** 2922cc
double-overhead-
camshaft 6-cylinder
engine, little use
since 1973.
£9,000–11,000
$13,000–16,000
↗ Bon

ASTON MARTIN Model	ENGINE cc/cyl	DATES	CONDITION		
			1	2	3
DB1	1970/4	1948–50	£30,000+	£20,000	£16,000
DB2	2580/6	1950–53	£30,000+	£18,000	£14,000
DB2 Conv	2580/6	1951–53	£45,000+	£28,000+	£17,000
DB2/4 Mk I/II	2580/ 2922/6	1953–57	£30,000	£18,000	£14,000
DB2/4 Mk II Conv	2580/ 2922/6	1953–57	£45,000	£30,000	£15,000
DB Mk III Conv	2922/6	1957–59	£45,000	£28,000	£18,000
DB Mk III	2922/6	1957–59	£30,000	£20,000	£15,000
DB4	3670/6	1959–63	£40,000+	£25,000+	£16,000
DB4 Conv	3670/6	1961–63	£60,000+	£35,000+	-
DB4 GT	3670/6	1961–63	£140,000+	£100,000	-
DB5	3995/6	1964–65	£48,000	£32,000	£20,000
DB5 Conv	3995/6	1964–65	£55,000+	£38,000	-
DB6	3995/6	1965–69	£30,000	£20,000	£16,000
DB6 Mk I auto	3995/6	1965–69	£28,000	£18,000	£14,000
DB6 Mk I Volante	3995/6	1965–71	£50,000+	£32,000+	£28,000
DB6 Mk II Volante	3995/6	1969–70	£60,000+	£40,000+	£30,000
DBS	3995/6	1967–72	£14,000+	£10,000	£8,000
AM Vantage	5340/8	1972–73	£15,000	£12,000	£9,000
V8 Vantage Oscar India	5340/8	1978–82	£30,000+	£20,000	£10,000
V8 Volante	5340/8	1978–82	£50,000+	£35,000	£25,000

Works/competition history is an important factor, as is Vantage and short-chassis specification.

◄ **1959 Aston Martin DB Mk III,** 2922cc engine, 4-speed manual gearbox with overdrive, over £15,000/$21,750 spent since 1997, finished in red, black interior, very good condition throughout. **£26,000–28,000 / $38,000–41,000** ↗ H&H
The final DB2/4 package came with a new 'droop snoot' and a 162bhp engine, as well as Girling front disc brakes, a hydraulically actuated clutch and optional overdrive. In all, 551 examples were produced, and although it was effectively a DB2/4 Mk III, it has always been referred to as the DB Mk III.

1959 Aston Martin DB4, restored, fitted with DB5 automatic transmission, negative-earth alternator electrics, halogen headlamps, Kenlowe electric fan, electronic fuel pump, electric windows, new Connolly hide upholstery and trim, Willans seatbelts, period Radiomobile radio, excellent condition.
£48,000–54,000 / $70,000–78,000 ↗ Bon
Launched at the 1958 London Motor Show, the Touring-styled DB4 established a look that would survive, with only minor revision, until 1970. A new design by Tadek Marek, the DB4's all-alloy, twin-cam six featured 'square' bore and stroke dimensions of 92mm, for a displacement of 3670cc, and developed 240bhp at 5,500rpm. The David Brown gearbox was a new four-speed all-synchromesh unit. A strong platform-type chassis replaced the DB2/4's multi-tubular space-frame, the latter being considered incompatible with Touring's *Superleggera* body construction, which employed its own lightweight tubular structure to support the aluminium body panels. The DB2/4's trailing-link independent front suspension gave way to unequal-length wishbones, while at the rear the DB4 sported a well-located live axle instead of its predecessor's De Dion set-up.

1960 Aston Martin DB4, 3670cc 6-cylinder engine, 4-speed manual gearbox, 140mph top speed, restored.
£36,000–42,000 / $52,000–61,000 ⊞ VIC

Although the David Brown era is considered by many to be Aston Martin's golden period, the company struggled to make a profit on its cars. A friend once asked David Brown if he could buy an Aston Martin at cost price. David Brown replied, 'I would love to sell it to you at cost, but I couldn't possibly charge you that much.'

1966 Aston Martin DB6, 3995cc engine, automatic transmission, converted to unleaded fuel, new stainless-steel exhaust, finished in silver-blue, blue interior, excellent condition.
£20,000–24,000 / $29,000–35,000 ↗ H&H

Aston Martin DB6 (1965–71)

Price in 1967: £5,084/$7,370 for Vantage saloon.
Production: 1,753.
Engine: 3995cc, straight-six, double overhead cam.
Power: 282–325bhp (325bhp was Aston's claimed output for Vantage-spec engine).
Transmission: ZF five-speed manual or Borg-Warner automatic.
Brakes: Four-wheel discs.
0–60mph: 6.1–6.7 seconds.
0–100mph: 15 seconds.
Top speed: 148+mph.
If James Bond had ever hung up his Walther PPK and settled down with wife and kids, the DB6 with its identifying uplifted Kamm tail would have been the Aston for him. With four proper seats, the option of automatic transmission and power steering, it was almost becoming practical. Of the classic DB series, which started with the DB4 in 1958, the DB6 is also the fastest, but in the eyes of some enthusiasts is, with its automatic option and power steering, a little softer and less outrightly sporting than its forbears. Consequently the DB6, although the most civilized of the classic DB Aston saloons, is the least prized and most affordable, and in today's market something of an Aston bargain.

1966 Aston Martin DB6, 3995cc 6-cylinder engine, manual gearbox, good condition.
£27,000–30,000 / $39,000–43,500 ⊞ CCW

The DB6 may ooze pure-bred Bulldog Britishness, but the styling is an evolution of the Touring of Milan designed DB4. Prince Charles owns a DB6 Volante. At top speeds the upturned tail was said to reduce aerodynamic lift by half. Six DB6 estates were built by coachbuilder Harold Radford.

1967 Aston Martin DB6, automatic transmission, finished in red, 10,000 miles in last 12 years, good condition throughout.
£16,000–18,000 / $23,000–26,000 ⚒ BARO
The DB6 was the last of the true DB models, being replaced by the William Towns designed DBS in 1969. Obvious changes from the DB5 were the subtle upswept Camm tail rear and the steeper rake of the front screen, necessary due to the extra 4in (10cm) in chassis length. Not so obvious was the change to conventional steel fabrication of the body frame, rather than the lighter and more expensive *Superleggera* construction used on its predecessor.

1969 Aston Martin DB6, 3995cc double-overhead-camshaft 6-cylinder engine, 5-speed manual gearbox, finished in burgundy, beige leather interior.
£32,000–36,000 / $46,000–52,000 ⊞ VIC

1968 Aston Martin DBS, fitted with 5343cc Jaguar V12 engine, automatic transmission, period Webasto sunroof, finished in British racing green, tan interior.
£7,500–9,000 / $10,875–13,000 ⚒ H&H

1971 Aston Martin DBS V8, subject of extensive chassis renovation early 1990s at a cost of £20,000/$29,000, finished in original metallic turquoise, re-Connollised beige leather interior.
£9,000–11,000 / $13,000–16,000 ⚒ Bon

1973 Aston Martin Vantage, automatic transmission, invoices totalling over £16,500/$24,000, finished in British racing green, light tan leather interior.
£9,000–11,000 / $13,000–16,000 ⋌ Bon
After Sir David Brown's departure, Aston Martin DBS production continued under new owners Company Developments. The car was restyled with a new two-headlamp front end, reminiscent of the DB Mk III and DB4, but mechanically remained much as before. Named Vantage, the six-cylinder model came with the 325bhp C-type Vantage engine and was good for 148mph. Only 70 Vantages had been made when production ceased in July 1973.

1974 Aston Martin V8 Vantage, subject of extensive renovation 1996, including engine rebuild to Vantage X-specification, upgraded oil and water systems, large-bore induction/exhaust systems, suspension upgraded to Vantage specification, uprated front and rear anti-roll bars, reconditioned wheels, auxiliary driving lamps, remotely-activated security system, bare-metal respray in metallic pale blue, exterior brightwork rechromed, leather-trimmed Recaro electric front seats, rear seat belts, upgraded air conditioning system, vehicle tracking and relocation system, c70,000 miles from new, excellent condition throughout.
£30,000–34,000 / $43,000–49,000 ⋌ Bon

1977 Aston Martin V8, 5340cc V8 engine, fair condition.
£9,000–11,000 / $13,000–16,000 ⊞ CCW

1977 Aston Martin V8, aluminium front air dam, sliding stereo cover, finished in silver-blue, good condition throughout.
£11,000–12,500 / $16,000–18,000 ⋌ BARO

1978 Aston Martin V8 Vantage, 5341cc double-overhead-camshaft V8 engine, 400bhp, 5-speed all-synchromesh manual gearbox, independent double-wishbone front suspension with coil springs, telescopic dampers and anti-roll bar, De Dion rear suspension with coil springs and telescopic dampers, servo-assisted 4-wheel disc brakes, electric sunroof, lockable fuel filler caps, completely restored by Aston Martin mid-1980s, engine uprated to Series 3 Vantage specification and converted to unleaded fuel, flared wheel arches and sill skirts, 1987-series alloy wheels, 1 of only 172 built in 4th series of V8s, finished in blue, magnolia interior.
£20,000–30,000 / $29,000–43,000 ⚒ C
This car was owned originally by the singer Elton John, who refers to it as 'The Beast'. In the 1980s, when he was president of Watford football club and his team was doing particularly well, it was painted in the team colours: yellow with a black and red stripe. He recalled HRH Prince Philip saying, 'Oh, it's you who owns that ghastly car, is it? We often see it when we're driving into the back of Windsor Castle. I've seen it so many times and thought, "Who owns that ghastly car?"'

1986 Aston Martin V8 Vantage Zagato Coupé, finished in metallic grey, black leather interior, 1 of 19 built, 2 owners and 11,000 miles from new.
£70,000–80,000 / $102,000–116,000 ⚒ Bon
With the introduction of the Vantage Zagato in 1986, Aston Martin renewed its association with one of Italy's most illustrious coachbuilders, Zagato having been responsible for the celebrated DB4GT. Part of Zagato's brief had been to shed some of the standard Vantage's not inconsiderable weight, which was achieved by shortening the car by over 6½in (17cm); with the redesigned superstructure, body and use of composite materials, the car tipped the scales some ten per cent lighter than the standard model. The 5.3 litre quad-cam V8 was to Vantage X specification, producing 32bhp at 6,200rpm. The manner of its installation, though, created controversy, the Zagato's low sloping bonnet, penned in the expectation of a dry-sumped engine, meant that a power bulge was required to clear the quartet of Weber carburettors.

A known continuous history can add value to and enhance the enjoyment of a car.

◄ **1987 Aston Martin V8 Volante,** 5340cc double-overhead-camshaft V8 engine, fuel injection, automatic transmission, 4-wheel disc brakes, fewer than 22,000 miles from new.
£35,000–40,000
$51,000–58,000 ⚒ Pou

1988 Aston Martin V8 Volante, 305bhp, fuel injection, automatic transmission, 140mph top speed, left-hand drive, finished in white, lined power-operated hood, burgundy hide interior, 34,000 miles from new, very good condition throughout.
£30,000–35,000 / $44,000–51,000 ↗ Bon

The Aston Martin V8 made its debut as the DBS V8 in 1969 and continued in production for a further 19 years, a record-breaking production run that saw 2,919 cars sold, making this the most successful Aston Martin ever. It had always been intended that the DBS would house the new Tadek Marek designed V8 engine, but production difficulties meant that the car appeared first with the 4 litre six of the concurrent DB5. Styled in-house by Bill Towns, the four-seat DBS employed a platform-type chassis with independent suspension all-round: wishbone and coil spring at the front, De Dion with Watts linkage at the rear. Bigger and more luxuriously appointed than the DB6, the heavyweight DBS disappointed some by virtue of its slightly reduced performance, but there were no complaints when the quad-cam 5340cc V8 arrived in 1969. With an estimated 315bhp available, the DBS V8 could reach 100mph in under 14 seconds, running on to a top speed of over 150mph, a staggering performance in those days, and one that fully justified the claim that it was the fastest production car in the world.

◄ **1980 Aston Martin Lagonda,** factory converted to unleaded fuel, resprayed, re-Connollised upholstery, excellent condition throughout.
£9,000–11,000 / $13,000–16,000 ↗ Bon

When the Lagonda name reappeared on Aston Martin's new super saloon, the car was the sensation of the 1976 London Motor Show. Clothed in striking 'razor-edged' bodywork penned by William Towns, the Lagonda boasted an interior every bit as luxurious as the exterior was futuristic. Production ceased in May 1990, by which time 645 cars had been built.

► **1986 Aston Martin Lagonda,** 5340cc V8 engine, finished in black, grey interior.
£11,000–13,000
$16,000–18,850 ↗ H&H

1989 Aston Martin Zagato Volante, automatic transmission, 5,000 miles from new, 'as new' condition.
£50,000–60,000 / $73,000–87,000 ⊞ CCW

Audi

1985 Audi Quattro UR Roadster, 250bhp engine, Treser spoiler/air-duct kit, wheel spokes shaped to direct air over the brakes, headlamp washers, central locking, electric windows, heated seats, air conditioning, cruise control, electrically operated hood, recently refurbished, finished in red, red leather upholstery, very good condition.
£8,000–10,000 / $11,500–14,500 ✗ COYS
Walter Treser played a major part in the development of the Quattro, and was in charge of Audi's rally team in 1980 and 1981. Then he left to set up his own tuning firm, which was to become one of the most well-known Audi tuning companies of the era. Aside from engine conversions up to 350bhp, Treser made all sorts of modified parts – from bespoke instrument panels to radical body modifications.

▶ **1987 Audi Quattro Turbo,** 2226cc 5-cylinder engine, finished in dark blue, dark grey leather interior trim, good condition throughout.
£6,500–7,500 / $9,500–11,000 ✗ BRIT

1985 Audi Quattro Coupé, 2226cc 5-cylinder engine, 5-speed manual gearbox, finished in red, brown interior trim, 2 owners and 41,750 miles from new, very good condition throughout.
£2,400–2,700 / $3,500–4,000 ✗ H&H

Austin

Even before the young Herbert Austin set up car manufacturing under his own name in 1905, he had already built up considerable practical knowledge and valuable experience in the fledgling motor industry. In 1894, the young engineer had seen his first horseless carriage, a three-wheeled Bollée, and a year or so later he had built his own vehicle along broadly similar lines. In 1900, after producing further prototypes, he set Wolseley on the road to car manufacture with a capable four-wheeled voiturette, but left in 1905 after a dispute with Wolseley directors. In 1906, the Austin Motor Company Ltd at Longbridge, on the outskirts of Birmingham, produced its

first car, a 25/30hp touring model. Then, for 80 years, Austin remained a major player at the core of the British motor industry, until in 1987 the Austin name was finally dropped from the renamed Rover Group. At various times in its history, Austin was the largest British car maker. As for the cars, Austin's greatest legacy must surely be the two modest machines that transformed British motoring on each side of a World War. The Austin 7 of 1922 brought motoring en masse to the middle classes, and in 1959 the new Austin Se7en, as it was originally badged, brought motoring to millions in a pocket-sized world-beater better known as the Mini.

1929 Austin 7 Chummy, older restoration, little recent use, finished in blue and black, with quantity of small spares plus hood frame, very good condition.
£3,000–3,500 / $4,500–5,000 ✗ CGC

1929 Austin 7 Wydoor Top Hat Saloon, 747cc engine, 3-speed gearbox, restored, finished in blue with black wings, grey cord upholstery.
£2,750–3,500 / $4,000–5,000 ✗ Bon

Miller's is a price GUIDE not a price LIST

AUSTIN Model	ENGINE cc/cyl	DATES	CONDITION		
			1	2	3
7 Swallow 2-Seater Sports	747/4	1927–32	£11,000	£8,500	£7,000
7 Swallow 4-Seater Saloon	747/7	1929–32	£10,000	£7,500	£6,000
Important coachbuilt versions.					

◀ **1930 Austin 7 Two-Seater Boat-Tail Sports**, 747cc, high-compression head, 4-speed gearbox, completely rebuilt, finished in green, tonneau cover, tan interior.
£4,500–5,500 / $6,500–8,000 ↗ H&H

1930 Austin 7 Tourer, completely restored 1998, fewer than 3,000 miles since, finished in green and black, black hood and side screens, black interior, very good condition.
£5,250–5,750 / $7,500–8,500 ↗ Bon
Ruggedly built, economical and easily maintained by the home mechanic, the 7 was offered initially only as the Chummy tourer. However, standard saloon, fabric saloon and coupé models, plus a roomier tourer, were on offer by 1927. With the introduction of restyled short-scuttle bodies in June 1930, the range lost its vintage look.

1930 Austin 7 Top Hat Saloon, 747cc, restored late 1970s, finished in blue and black, black interior trim, museum displayed for many years, very good condition throughout.
£2,700–3,200 / $4,000–4,700 ↗ H&H

Miller's Starter Marque

- **Starter Austins:** *Austin 7; A55/A60 Cambridge; A90/95/99/105/110 Westminster; Nash Metropolitan; A30/35/40; 1100 & 1300.*
- Although post-war Austin models were in general pretty populous, not all are in plentiful supply. The ones we've chosen above are blessed with a good survival rate, spares and club support, and generally possess those Austin virtues of sturdy and sensible dependability. From the pre-war period, the Austin 7 is eminently viable as a run-while-you-restore car, with little to baffle the DIY mechanic.
- One of the most engaging Austins of the post-war era is the Austin/Nash Metropolitan. They should really have called it the Neopolitan, for this quaint little dolly-mixture of a car came in a choice of dazzling ice-cream colours – red, yellow and turquoise over white. The hardtop versions all had white roofs and lower bodies, making them resemble a white-sliced sandwich with a variety of sickly fillings. The Metropolitan, was built initially by Austin for the American Nash company as a 'sub-compact,' or two-thirds-scale Yank tank. Available over here from 1957.

AUSTIN Model	ENGINE cc/cyl	DATES	CONDITION		
			1	2	3
25/30	4900/4	1906	£35,000	£25,000	£20,000
20/4	3600/4	1919–29	£20,000	£12,000	£6,000
12	1661/4	1922–26	£8,000	£5,000	£2,000
7/Chummy	747/4	1924–39	£7,000	£5,000	£2,500
7 Coachbuilt/Nippy/Opal etc	747/4	1924–39	£10,000	£9,000	£7,000
12/4	1861/4	1927–35	£5,500	£5,000	£2,000
16	2249/6	1928–36	£9,000	£7,000	£4,000
20/6	3400/6	1928–38	£12,500	£10,000	£8,000
12/6	1496/6	1932–37	£6,000	£4,000	£1,500
12/4	1535/4	1933–39	£5,000	£3,500	£1,500
10 and 10/4	1125/4	1932–47	£4,000	£3,000	£1,000
10 and 10/4 Conv	1125/4	1933–47	£5,000+	£3,500	£1,000
18	2510/6	1934–39	£8,000	£5,000	£3,000
14	1711/6	1937–39	£6,000	£4,000	£2,000
Big Seven	900/4	1938–39	£4,000	£2,500	£1,500
8	900/4	1939–47	£3,000	£2,000	£1,000
28	4016/6	1939	£6,000	£4,000	£2,000

Prices for early Austin models are dependent on body style: landaulette, tourer, etc (eg. Austin Heavy 12/4 Tourer will command a higher price).

1934 Austin 7 Nippy Sports, 747cc engine, completely rebuilt using all original panels, little use since, finished in red with red interior.
£7,000–8,000 / $10,200–11,500 ✗ H&H
The Nippy was introduced in the middle of 1933 and came with rounded-back two-seat coachwork, a curved front axle, under-slung rear springs and a tuned 21bhp engine.

► **1934 Austin 7 Tourer,** converted from a saloon, folding hood and side screens, finished in cream and black, brown leather interior, last used 1999.
£2,500–3,000 / $3,500–4,500 ✗ CGC

1934 Austin 7 Saloon, 747cc, 4-speed gearbox, recently restored at a cost of £9,000/$13,000, finished in burgundy and black, burgundy leather interior, excellent condition throughout.
£7,000–8,000 / $10,200–11,500 ✗ Bon

1935 Austin 7 Ruby Saloon, 747cc 4-cylinder engine, finished in maroon and black, good mechanical condition, paintwork and interior trim in need of attention.
£2,000–2,500 / $3,000–3,600 ✗ BRIT
In August 1934, the Austin 7 range underwent a major facelift, along with the rest of the Austin range. The restyling boosted sales, with the 7 remaining a bestseller. The saloon was designated Ruby, while the two-seat tourer and cabriolet bore the titles Opal and Pearl respectively.

1937 Austin 7 Ruby Saloon, restored to original condition.
£2,250–2,750 / $3,300–4,000 ⊞ UMC

1937 Austin 7 Pearl Cabriolet, 747cc 4-cylinder engine, bare-metal respray in dark red and black 1994, red Rexine hood, original red interior in need of restoration, 1 owner since 1965, various spares.
£3,200–3,800 / $4,700–5,500 ⚒ **BRIT**
The Pearl cabriolet was a versatile little car, providing the advantage of an open touring model while retaining the profile of the saloon.

1937 Austin 7 Ruby Saloon, 747cc 4-cylinder engine, recent extensive body-off refurbishment, engine, gearbox, rear axle, steering and braking system rebuilt, exhaust system replaced, wheels respoked, resprayed maroon, black leatherette interior trim to original pattern, in need of finishing, good condition.
£1,900–2,300 / $2,500–3,500 ⚒ **BRIT**

1936 Austin 10 Sherborne Saloon, 1125cc sidevalve 4-cylinder engine, engine rebuilt, 5,000 miles covered since, new springs, retrimmed in red leather.
£4,000–5,000 / $5,800–7,250 ⚒ **Bon**
By 1936, a significant part of Longbridge production was dedicated to the 10hp model. Styling changes had seen the introduction of an enamelled radiator surround, while the Sherborne model had the fashionable swept tail.

1933 Austin 10 Saloon, 1125cc sidevalve 4-cylinder engine, 4-speed synchromesh gearbox, 12-volt electrics, engine rebuilt at a cost of over £1,700/$2,500, interior retrimmed, sound condition.
£3,500–4,000 / $5,000–5,800 ⚒ **Bon**
Introduced in the spring of 1932, the Austin 10 proved an outstanding success, outselling every other Austin, including the 7.

1937 Austin 10/4 Cambridge Saloon, much chromework replated, black paintwork showing signs of age, original brown leather upholstery and grey cloth headlining, boot contains original luggage trunk, very original.
£2,000–2,500 / $3,000–3,500 ⚒ **CGC**
Powered by a three-bearing 1125cc sidevalve four-cylinder engine producing 32bhp and driving through a four-speed manual gearbox, the 10/4 of 1937–39 was capable of over 60mph. Its specification included all-round semi-elliptic leaf springs and Girling drum brakes.

◀ **1947 Austin 10 GSI Saloon,** engine completely rebuilt, fewer than 2,000 miles since, finished in black with gold coachlines, brown leather seats, wood-effect dashboard, sunshine roof, rear window blind, window rubbers replaced where necessary, chrome slightly tarnished in places, 55,000 miles from new, good overall condition.
£3,750–4,500 / \$5,500–6,500 ⟋ CGC
This GSI saloon remained with its original owner's family until 1993; so devoted was he to his Austin that when he died his widow had the car bricked up in their garage so as not to be reminded of him.

1928 Austin 12 Five-Seater Tourer, rebuilt, finished in grey and black, new hood and frame, red leather upholstery, good condition throughout.
£10,000–11,000 / \$14,500–16,000 ⟋ Bon
Introduced in 1922 alongside the 7 and 20hp models, the 12hp was powered by a conventional four-cylinder sidevalve engine and, like its big brother, reflected just a hint of American influence. This car was supplied new to Australia and carries Melbourne coachwork, very similar to the British Clifton Tourer.

1948 Austin 16 Saloon, rolling restoration project, wheels recently stove enamelled in cream, black paintwork in poor condition, brown leather interior in need of repair, otherwise sound mechanical and structural condition, spare gearbox.
£1,750–2,250 / \$2,500–3,250 ⟋ CGC
Launched in 1945 and featuring Austin's first overhead-valve engine, the 16hp was a direct development of the 12hp model introduced in 1939. The 2199cc four-cylinder engine provided relaxed, torquey performance, combining a 75mph top speed with 25mpg.

AUSTIN Model	ENGINE cc/cyl	DATES	CONDITION 1	2	3
16	2199/4	1945–49	£3,000	£2,000	£1,000
A40 Devon	1200/4	1947–52	£2,000	£1,200	£750
A40 Sports	1200/4	1950–53	£6,000	£4,000	£2,000
A40 Somerset	1200/4	1952–54	£2,000	£1,500	£750
A40 Somerset DHC	1200/4	1954	£5,000	£4,000	£2,500
A40 Dorset 2-door	1200/4	1947–48	£2,000	£1,500	£1,000
A70 Hampshire	2199/4	1948–50	£3,000	£1,500	£1,000
A70 Hereford	2199/4	1950–54	£3,000	£1,500	£1,000
A90 Atlantic DHC	2660/4	1949–52	£10,000	£6,000	£4,000
A90 Atlantic	2660/4	1949–52	£6,000	£4,000	£3,000
A40/A50 Cambridge	1200/4	1954–57	£1,200	£750	£500
A55 Mk I Cambridge	1489/4	1957–59	£1,000	£750	£500
A55 Mk II	1489/4	1959–61	£1,000	£750	£500
A60 Cambridge	1622/4	1961–69	£1,000	£750	£500
A90/95 Westminster	2639/6	1954–59	£2,000	£1,500	£750
A99 Westminster	2912/6	1959–61	£1,500	£1,000	£500
A105 Westminster	2639/6	1956–59	£3,000	£1,500	£750
A110 Mk I/II	2912/6	1961–68	£2,000	£1,500	£750
Nash Metropolitan	1489/4	1957–61	£3,500	£2,000	£750
Nash Metropolitan DHC	1489/4	1957–61	£6,000	£3,000	£1,500
A30	803/4	1952–56	£1,500	£800	-
A30 Countryman	803/4	1954–56	£1,500	£1,000	-
A35	948/4	1956–59	£1,000	£500	-
A35 Countryman	948/4	1956–62	£1,500	£1,000	-
A40 Farina Mk I	948/4	1958–62	£1,250	£750	£200
A40 Mk I Countryman	948/4	1959–62	£1,500	£1,000	£400
A40 Farina Mk II	1098/4	1962–67	£1,000	£750	-
A40 Mk II Countryman	1098/4	1962–67	£1,200	£750	£300
1100	1098/4	1963–73	£1,000	£750	-
1300 Mk I/II	1275/4	1967–74	£750	£500	-
1300GT	1275/4	1969–74	£1,800	£1,000	£750
1800/2200	1800/2200/4	1964–75	£1,500	£900	£600
3 Litre	2912/6	1968–71	£3,000	£1,500	£500

◄ **1948 Austin 16 Saloon,** 2199cc engine, extensively restored, engine and gearbox replaced, front and rear axles overhauled, brakes refurbished, new radiator and wiring loom, resprayed in original sage green, instruments restored, upholstered in caramel leather, Bakelite trim refurbished, new window rubbers, some finishing required to interior. **£3,500–4,500 / $5,000–6,500** ⚹ CGC This particular car has made frequent television appearances in dramas such as *The Camomile Lawn, A Perfect Hero, Charmer, Over Here* and *Ain't Misbehaving.*

► **1936 Austin 18/6 Norfolk Saloon,** restored, finished in black over silver, good condition. **£3,750–4,500 / $5,500–6,500** ⚹ Bon First shown in 1926, Austin's new six-cylinder model was built initially in 20hp (3400cc) and 16hp (2249cc) versions, before an 18hp (2510cc) example on the smaller chassis joined the range in 1933. The 16/18 shared its chassis with the Heavy 12/4 and was updated in similar fashion, gaining synchromesh gears for 1934 and a painted radiator surround as part of a major restyle for 1935. Built in five-seat and seven-seat saloon variants, the 18 lasted until 1937, the 16 having been dropped from the range the previous year.

◄ **1954 Austin A30 Four-Door Saloon,** recently refurbished at a cost of £1,500/$2,175, finished in cream, red Rexine interior, good overall condition. **£1,000–1,300 / $1,500–2,000** ⚹ CGC The A30 was an important car for Austin. One of the company's first proper post-war designs, it was also the first recipient of, and test-bed for, the A-series engine. A small, light and compact design, the A30 could reach over 60mph with just 800cc at its disposal. A four-speed gearbox helped keep things on the boil and make the most of the model's nimble handling. Understandably economical, it also offered greater sophistication than its pre-war predecessors.

Austin Cambridge A55/A60 & Morris Oxford V/VI (1959–71)

Production: 1,207,000.
Prices in 1960: Austin A55, £801; Morris Oxford, £815; Wolseley 15/60, £936; MG Magnette, £1,012; Riley 4/68, £1,028.
Engine: 1489 and 1622cc overhead-valve four-cylinder.
Power output: 53–68bhp.
Transmission: Four-speed manual; optional automatic on some models.
Brakes: Girling hydraulic drums all-round.
Maximum speed: 80–90mph
0–60mph: 19.5–24 seconds.
The names above are only a sample from BMC's biblical model christening book. Lump them together, mix in the Wolseley, MG and Riley four-cylinder variants with their own mystic-rune model names and/or numbers, and the only generic term anyone's ever been able to come up with is 'Big Farinas', on account of the fact that the design was penned by Italy's Pinin Farina

studio. That's what they later came to be called by banger racers, who drove droves of them to destruction, little appreciating the nuances that once had served as slight social distinctions in the pecking order of the suburban driveway.
One thing the banger boys did appreciate though was the hefty monocoque hull and the fact that, for a while, there were hoardes of them at scrap prices. In the early 1960s, these Big Farinas also earned praise for their compliant ride, and owners would also have considered their straightforward mechanics, capacious boot and spacious family accommodation of more note than outright pace or the fact that the Big Farinas persisted with drum brakes to the last.
Austins and Morrises were the plain-Jane motors with no frills. The Wolseley added wood and leather garnish, the MG offered a more peppy engine, and the Riley combined the MG performance with the Wolseley trim.

1957 Austin A35 Two-Door Saloon, 948cc 4-cylinder engine, restored, show winner.
£2,500–3,000 / $3,500–4,500 🚗 AUS

1958 Austin A35 Four-Door Saloon, 948cc 4-cylinder engine, poor condition.
£300–400 / $440–580 🚗 AUS

From the 1950s into the 1970s, many Austin models were offered with only slight variations in trim, decoration and specification as Morris, MG, Wolseley, Riley and Vanden Plas.

1962 Austin A35 Van, 1100cc 4-cylinder engine, converted to Countryman specification with side windows.
£2,250–2,750 / $3,250–4,000 🚗 AUS
During the 1950s and 1960s, commercial vehicles did not attract purchase tax like passenger vehicles, making them cheaper, and a common dodge was to convert small vans into estates by fitting side windows and extra seating.

▶ **1966 Austin A35 Van,** 848cc 4-cylinder engine, dealer converted with Countryman side windows.
£1,750–2,250 / $2,500–3,250 🚗 AUS

Austin A30/A35 (1951–59)

Body styles: Two- and four-door saloon, Countryman estate, van and pick-up (very rare, only 497 produced).
Engine: 803cc (A30) and 948cc (A35) overhead-valve four-cylinder.
Transmission: Four-speed manual.
Brakes: Hydro-mechanical drums.
Power output: 28bhp at 4,500rpm (A30); 34bhp at 5,100 rpm (A35).
0–60mph: 38 seconds (A30); 29 seconds ((A35).
Top speed: 65mph (A30); 75mph (A35).
Fuel consumption: 35–45mpg.
Price in 1951: £529.
Production: 576,672.
When the baby Austin A30 appeared in 1951, the peanut-shaped and sized four-seater was intended to rival the Morris Minor launched in 1948. But shortly after the baby Austin appeared, the two rivals merged under the BMC banner. Even though it was a moderate success, the Austin was rather overshadowed by the million-selling Minor. Nevertheless, the A30 was a pert and capable economy package. It was the first Austin to feature unitary construction and was powered initally by a peppy little 803cc overhead-valve engine, the first of the famous A-series engines, which went on to power the Mini and Metro.

In 1956, the A30 was updated to become the A35. Externally it featured a larger rear window and other detail changes, but underneath it had a 948cc engine that considerably improved performance. Saloon production ended in 1959 with the arrival of the Mini, but A35 vans continued through to 1968.
For: Four-seat starter classic that's more distinctive for not being a Morris Minor. A30/35 is based on mostly easy-to-find BMC mechanics.
Against: Depending on your point of view, the skinny tyres and narrow track make the A30/A35 either particularly entertaining – or hazardous – particularly in high crosswinds.
Pick of the bunch: The bigger-engined A35. If the conditions are right, with a following gale, you might even contemplate overtaking.
Austin asides: In 1994, a 1967 A35 van that had belonged to the lamented F1 champion James Hunt until his death in 1993 fetched a world record auction price of £3,800. When he hung up his racing overalls, Hunt still used the A35 on weekends to transport the budgerigars that he bred and exhibited. He once said, 'The car is great to drive. I've kept it on cross-ply tyres so that is slides more, which makes it tremendous fun in the wet.'

Austin A40 (1958–67)

Price in 1958: £676.7s.
Production: 340,000.
Engine: 948cc overhead-valve four-cylinder; 1098cc from October 1962.
Transmission: Four-speed manual.
Power: 34–37bhp for 948cc; 48bhp for 1098cc.
Brakes: Hydro-mechanical drums; full hydraulic drums from October 1961.
0–60mph: 29–30 seconds for 948cc; 23 seconds for 1098cc.
Maximum speed: 73–75+mph for 948cc; 83mph for 1098cc.

Now nearly forgotten and rarely seen on the roads, in its day the Austin A40 represented something of a quiet revolution. It was launched to replace the cute peanut-shaped A35 and by comparison offered crisply modern looks, thanks to its Italian Pininfarina styling. Austin ads touted the new A40 as 'the world's most advanced small car', a bold claim that didn't quite stack up at launch and certainly couldn't be justified in any way when the Mini was launched a year later. Nevertheless, the A40 was roomy for its size, pleasant to drive, predictable in handling and perky enough. These last qualities attracted the motorsport crowd, who raced and rallied them with verve, but where the A40 really

scored was as a family carry-all. One of its handiest features was the fold-flat rear seat, which made it a really versatile little load carrier with reasonably easy access from the drop-down boot lid. A year later, the Countryman version featured a split tailgate with lift-up rear window to create a first-generation small hatchback, still recognizable in modern offerings in concept and execution. For a brief period, the A40 was thoroughly modern, but the competition soon massed around it in the shape of outside rivals like the Triumph Herald and Ford Anglia, as well as in-house competition from BMC's advanced front-wheel-drive 1100 range. By 1967, the once-modern A40 looked decidedly dated and gently faded away. Today, the A40 remains largely overlooked and humbly priced, and is all the more appealing for that, because for near banger money, you could have an easy-maintenance about-town classic carry-all. Out of town, on the M40, an A40 could even lose your licence – if you're really trying and the cop who stops you has an unreasonable loathing of A40s.
For: Cheaper and more capable all-round than the obviously cute Austin A30/A35.
Against: Low survival rate; rust prone; no problem with mechanical parts, but some body parts and trim scarce.

◄ **1956 Austin A50 Cambridge Saloon,** 1489cc 4-cylinder engine, converted to unleaded fuel, stainless-steel exhaust, new shock absorbers, finished in black, original tan leather interior, good condition throughout.
£1,400–1,800 / $2,000–2,500 ➚ BRIT
Reviving a name first used on the 1936–39 10hp model, the post-war Cambridge was of unitary construction, initially with a choice of 1200 and 1500cc engines, the smaller variant being known as the A40.

1956 Austin A40 Cambridge Saloon, 1200cc 4-cylinder engine, finished in blue, blue/grey interior, 6,600 miles from new, excellent condition throughout.
£2,200–2,600 / $3,200–3,800 ➚ H&H
This car spent much of its life bricked up in a garage.

1966 Austin Princess Vanden Plas, restored, finished in dark green, 39,000 miles from new, excellent condition.
£3,000–4,000 / $4,400–5,800 ⊞ VIC

Austin-Healey

Donald Mitchell Healey had been making bespoke and relatively expensive sporting cars in limited numbers (see Healey) since 1946, but in 1952 his cars burst into the automotive mainstream when his new Healey Hundred debuted at the October Earls Court Motor Show. Donald Healey's dream was of a cheap, true 100mph sports car, and by the time of the show he had already sewn up a deal with Austin boss Leonard Lord for the use of the rugged four-cylinder engines and transmissions of the Austin A90 Atlantic in his Healey Hundred. However, such was the rapturous reception of the new Healey that, more or less overnight, Lord decided it would make sense to build the complete car rather than just supply the engines. And so the Austin-Healey 100 was born. From 1953 to 1968, the Big Healey, as it became known, grew in stature to become one of the immortals, a handy tool in rallies and on race-tracks, and beloved of spirited drivers the world over. Of course, though, one must not forget 'the little Healey', the cute Frog-eye Sprite, a sporting cherub with a winning smile and oodles of charm.

1956 Austin-Healey 100/4, 2660cc 4-cylinder overhead-valve engine, 90bhp, 4-speed synchromesh gearbox with overdrive, independent front suspension, hydraulic disc front/drum rear brakes, wire wheels, fold-down windscreen, rust-free ex-California car, subject of complete nut-and-bolt restoration, rebuilt engine, carburettors and hydraulics, stainless-steel exhaust, suspension bushes and brakes replaced, instruments rebuilt, new steering wheel, red leather interior.
£20,000–22,000 / $29,000–32,000 ✗ RM

1955 Austin-Healey 100/4, 2660cc 4-cylinder engine, 4-speed overdrive gearbox, extensively refurbished late 1980s, converted to right-hand drive, 100M-type louvred bonnet, bare-metal respray in red, new black leather interior to original spec, bodywork and structure in very good condition.
£16,000–18,000 / $23,000–26,000 ✗ BRIT

c1955 Austin-Healey 100S, 2660cc 4-cylinder overhead-valve engine, aluminium cylinder head, 4-speed synchromesh gearbox, 4-wheel Dunlop disc brakes, independent front suspension by coil springs and wishbones, rigid rear axle on semi-elliptic leaf springs, centre-lock wire wheels, restored, finished in white and blue, blue leather interior, 1 of only 55 built, very original.
£92,500–110,000 / $135,000–160,000 ✗ GO
Developed as a special competition version of the Austin-Healey 100, the 100S model benefited from a Weslake designed four-port aluminium cylinder head, strengthened chassis frame, aluminium-panelled body and Dunlop disc brakes. A distinctive smaller radiator grille was incorporated, together with a low Perspex windscreen and louvred bonnet. No hood or side screens were provided. This new sports racing car proved very successful in international competition in the hands of both private and professional drivers. This particular car's first owner was the Brazilian Formula 1 Gordini and Ferrari works driver Hermandos da Silva Ramos.

AUSTIN-HEALEY Model	ENGINE cc/cyl	DATES	CONDITION 1	2	3
100 BN 1/2	2660/4	1953–56	£20,000	£14,000	£8,000
100/6, BN4/BN6	2639/6	1956–59	£18,000	£13,500	£8,000
3000 Mk I	2912/6	1959–61	£20,000	£13,000	£8,500
3000 Mk II	2912/6	1961–62	£22,000	£15,000	£9,000
3000 Mk IIA	2912/6	1962–64	£23,000	£15,000	£11,000
3000 Mk III	2912/6	1964–68	£24,000	£17,000	£11,000
Sprite Mk I	948/4	1958–61	£10,000	£6,000	£3,000
Sprite Mk II	948/4	1961–64	£5,000	£3,000	£2,000
Sprite Mk III	1098/4	1964–66	£4,500	£3,000	£1,500
Sprite Mk IV	1275/4	1966–71	£5,000	£3,000	£1,500

Austin-Healey Sprite Mk I (1958–61)

Price in 1958: £668.17s.
Production: 38,999.
Body style: Two-seat roadster.
Construction: Unitary body/chassis.
Engine: BMC A-series 948cc, four-cylinder, overhead-valve.
Power output: 43bhp at 5,200rpm.
Transmission: Four-speed manual, synchromesh on top three ratios.
Suspension: Front: independent, coil springs and wishbones. Rear: quarter-elliptic leaf springs, rigid axle.
Brakes: Hydraulic, drums all-round.
Maximum speed: 84mph.
0–60mph: 20.5 seconds
Millers miscellany: The Frog-eye Sprite gets its nickname from the headlamp pods on the bonnet, but Donald Healey originally wanted to use retractable lamps like the later Lotus Elan. Cost ruled these out, however.

1956 Austin-Healey 100/6, tuned engine, uprated 4-wheel disc brakes, restored at a cost of c£15,000/$21,750, finished in gunmetal grey, red upholstery.
£13,000–15,000 / $19,000–22,000 ➶ COYS
In 1952, Donald Healey showed his Healey 100 at the London Motor Show, and by the time the show closed the car had attracted so much attention that arrangements had been made for production to be undertaken by Austin. In September 1956, the Austin-Healey 100/6 was introduced, using the six-cylinder, 2639cc BMC engine, which produced 102bhp at 4,600rpm, and was a great deal more flexible and smoother than the earlier four-cylinder model. The 100/6 was phenomenally successful on the road and in international rallying, being campaigned by many of the best-known drivers of the day.

1963 Austin-Healey 3000 Mk IIA, 2912cc 6-cylinder engine, left-hand drive, extensively restored 1990–95, only 500 miles covered since, finished in red and white, black vinyl hood, red interior to original specification.
£13,500–15,000 / $19,500–22,000 ➶ BRIT
By 1962, the Austin-Healey 3000 Mk IIA had been introduced. This model benefited from a fully convertible hood and the convenience of wind-up windows. Power was up to 132bhp, which equated to a top speed approaching 120mph.

Miller's Starter Marque

- **Starter Austin-Healeys:** *Sprite MkI 'Frog-eye'; Sprite II–V.*
- The Donald Healey Motor Company and Austin had already forged close links in the early 1950s with the co-operative Austin-Healey 100. In 1958, its little brother, the Sprite, was born, a spartan little sports car designed down to a price, and based on the engine and running gear of the Austin A35 saloon, with a bit of Morris Minor too. The A35 saloon was perfectly adequate, admirable even, but the sports car that borrowed so many components from it was something separate altogether. Curvaceous and captivating, nimble and peppy, it belied its stock origins. It was affordable too, yet the Frog-eye really was a sports car and had a sweet raspberry exhaust note to prove it.
- In 1961 the Frog-eye was reclothed in the more conventional skin of the MG Midget; the Sprite versions endured until 1971, while the Midget soldiered on until 1979.
- All Austin-Healey Sprites are viable restore-while-you-drive cars with readily available parts, and a strong club and specialist network.

1966 Austin-Healey 3000 Mk III, 2912cc overhead-valve 6-cylinder engine, 150bhp, 4-speed manual gearbox, front disc/rear drum brakes, recent nut-and-bolt restoration, engine, carburettor, starter, dynamo and distributor rebuilt, new clutch, braking system, wiring harness and chrome wire wheels, stainless-steel exhaust, new top, resprayed in red.
£20,000–23,000 / $29,000–33,000 ➶ RM

1967 Austin-Healey 3000 Mk III BJ8 2+2, restored, finished in red, 65,000 miles from new, excellent condition throughout.
£19,000–21,000 / $27,500–30,500 ➶ BARO

◄ **1959 Austin-Healey Sprite Mk I,** restored to original specification 2000, engine and gearbox rebuilt, suspension and brakes overhauled, wheels and running gear repainted, new floorpan, boot floor, sills and wing top strips, bare-metal respray, all chromework replated or replaced, new tonneau and hood, glassfibre hardtop, period-style boot rack, interior completely retrimmed.
£6,500–7,500 / $9,500–11,000 ✗ Bon
Intended to make sports-car motoring more affordable, the Sprite entered production in March 1958. Its unitary-construction bodyshell featured a distinctive forward-hinging bonnet/wings topped by two 'frog-eye' headlamps, ensuring instant recognition and the now familiar nickname. Despite a spartan level of equipment – even the front bumper was listed as extra – the Frog-eye sold well, which was not surprising, as there was nothing to compete with it on price or performance.

1959 Austin-Healey Sprite Mk I, 1275cc engine, restored 1999–2000, finished in Old English white, black interior, good condition throughout.
£4,000–5,000 / $5,800–7,250 ✗ Bon

1960 Austin-Healey Sprite Mk I, 948cc 4-cylinder engine, 4-speed gearbox, original all-steel car, resprayed in red, correct weather gear including side screens, Waxoyled.
£5,000–6,000 / $7,250–8,700 ✗ H&H

Ballot

1926 Ballot 2LTS Touring Sport Four-Seater, 2 litre overhead-camshaft engine, originally supplied with saloon body, subject of 15-year restoration, fitted with Lagache-Glazmann-style coachwork, brakes converted to hydraulic operation, bills totalling over £51,500/$75,000, quantity of spares.
£26,000–30,000 / $37,700–43,500 ✗ Bon
A former marine engineer, Ernest Ballot founded his company in 1910 in Paris to manufacture internal-combustion engines for cars and stationary use. By 1919, Ballot was producing complete chassis with engines featuring twin-cam multi-valve cylinder heads designed for racing. As well as competing in the French, Italian and Spanish Grands Prix, Ballots ran in the Targa Florio and the Indianapolis 500, winning several events with spectacular performances. From 1921, a 93mph 2LS road car was offered with a twin-cam, four-valves-per-cylinder engine. By 1923, the 2LT single-cam was available to the British market, about 1,500 examples being built. In more sporting form, from 1926, was the 2LTS, or Touring Sport, model. The 60bhp four-cylinder overhead-camshaft engine was smooth and docile, but could rev more freely compared to the touring model, having hemispherical combustion chambers with inclined valves, and larger inlet and exhaust manifolds. A stronger gearbox was also provided. About 500 were produced.

Bentley

After working as a railway engineer and enjoying his recreation as an enthusiastic motorcyclist, Walter Owen Bentley undertook his first commercial automotive venture in 1912, when he took over an agency selling three makes of French car just off London's Baker Street. During WWI, he worked on aero engines, and in 1919 founded Bentley Motors. The first 3 litre prototype took to the road in 1920, with production getting under way at Cricklewood in north-west London in 1922. Two years later a 3 Litre won Le Mans, and the legend was cemented with further Le Mans victories in 1927, 1928, 1929 and 1930. Yet Bentley's formidable racing reputation wasn't enough to keep the company in the black, and it fell into receivership in 1931, to be taken over by Rolls-Royce in 1933. The subsequent refined Derby built, Rolls-Royce designed Bentleys became known as 'the silent sports car' and many were graced with supremely elegant bodies. After WWII, production resumed at Crewe. The Mk VI Bentley of 1946 represented a turning point as the first Rolls-Bentley product to be offered with an off-the-shelf factory body, although special bodies were still available. By 1955, the standard-bodied Bentley S-series was little more than a Rolls-Royce with a Bentley radiator. However, in the 1980s, Bentley began to emerge from the shadow of Rolls-Royce and regain its true sporting identity. In today's market, S-series and T-series Bentleys can often be slightly cheaper than their Rolls-Royce counterparts.

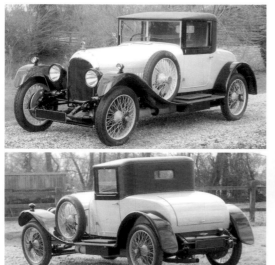

1925 Bentley 3 Litre Short-Chassis Light Tourer, original Vanden Plas coachwork, finished in dark blue, original blue hide interior, 4 owners from new, complete, never restored.
£67,000–75,000 / $98,000–109,000 ⊞ BC

◄ **1924 Bentley 3 Litre TT Replica Single Coupé,** coachwork by Park Ward, close-ratio A-type gearbox, restored over 3½ years, finished in grey and black, fawn interior, 1 of only 71 TT replicas built between 1922 and 1924.
£65,000–75,000 / $94,000–109,000 ⚒ Bon
This car was built to the special order of HRH Prince George, later The Duke of Kent.

1926 Bentley 3–4½ Litre Tourer, coachwork by Vanden Plas, 4389cc overhead-camshaft 6-cylinder engine, c100bhp, 4-speed manual gearbox, 4-wheel drum brakes, suspension by semi-elliptic leaf springs, fitted with later 4½ Litre engine, Kenlowe fan, original coachwork badge, bodywork restored, finished in green, correct period instrumentation, green leather interior, seats reupholstered, original fabric side panels.
£100,000–120,000 / $145,000–174,000 ⚒ C
Introduced in 1922, the 3 Litre model was quickly developed through active campaigning at the instigation of its designer, Walter Owen Bentley. Their successes in the Tourist Trophy and later at Le Mans were legendary. By 1926, the 3 Litre was losing its competitive edge, and the Bentley enthusiast was looking for an improved big four-cylinder car. W. O. Bentley answered their call with a new model with a 4.5 Litre engine. It matched the success of its forebear, over 650 units being built.

BENTLEY Model	ENGINE cc/cyl	DATES	CONDITION 1	2	3
3 Litre	2996/4	1920–27	£100,000	£75,000	£40,000
Speed Six	6597/6	1926–32	£300,000	£250,000	£160,000
4½ Litre	4398/4	1927–31	£175,000	£125,000	£80,000
4½ Litre Supercharged	4398/4	1929–32	£600,000+	£300,000	£200,000
8 Litre	7983/6	1930–32	£350,000	£250,000	£100,000
3½ Litre Saloon & DHC	3699/6	1934–37	£70,000	£30,000	£15,000
4¼ Litre Saloon & DHC	4257/6	1937–39	£70,000	£35,000	£20,000
Mk V	4257/6	1939–41	£45,000	£25,000	£20,000

Prices are dependent on engine type, chassis length, matching chassis and engine nos, body style and coachbuilder, and original extras like supercharger, gearbox ratio, racing history and originality. Many specials built upon the 'Derby' Bentley chassis and Mk VI.

◀ **1928 Bentley 4½ Litre Four-Seater Tourer,** 4500cc, supplied originally with Freestone & Webb coupé coachwork, since fitted with replica Vanden Plas four-seat open coachwork, same family ownership for last 40 years, excellent condition.
£120,000–130,000 / $174,000–188,000 ✗ H&H
Fitted with two-seat open coachwork, this car appeared in the film *School for Scoundrels*, starring Terry Thomas and Ian Carmichael.

From 1919 to 1931, total Bentley production was just 3,024 cars.

1934 Bentley 3½ Litre Sports Saloon, coachwork by Park Ward, paint faded, leather tired, original, in need of recommissioning.
£12,000–15,000 / $17,400–22,000 ✗ COYS
The first of the Derby Bentleys was also the first to be marketed as 'The Silent Sports Car', such was its considerable refinement. The 3½ Litre soon gained a reputation for pace and fine handling combined with the elegance of hand-built coachwork supplied by various leading coachbuilders in saloon, drophead coupé and touring guises. As such, it found favour with many owner/drivers. Its separate chassis, complete with centralized lubrication system, employed leaf-spring suspension and hydraulic shock absorbers front and rear, while the brakes were power assisted by Rolls-Royce's gearbox-driven mechanical servo. Detail modifications were introduced during the 3½ Litre's three-year production life, including adjustable shock absorbers in 1935. Production ended the following year, after 1,177 examples had been manufactured.

1935 Bentley 3½ Litre Four-Seater Drophead Special, 3669cc overhead-valve 6-cylinder engine, originally fitted with Park Ward drophead coupé body, new lightweight four-seat body commissioned 1969, finished in yellow, black leather interior, good general condition.
£15,000–18,000 / $22,000–26,000 ✗ Bon

1935 Bentley 3½ Litre Drophead Coupé, coachwork by Park Ward, original 3500cc 6-cylinder engine, restored, finished in black, red interior.
£44,000–48,000 / $64,000–70,000 ✗ H&H
This car was bought some years ago by the newspaper magnate Eddie Shah, who paid £43,000/$62,500 when it was in need of complete restoration. Then he spent over £85,000/$123,000 on it; a further £20,000/$29,000 has since been spent.

1937 Bentley 4¼ Litre Sports Saloon, coachwork by Park Ward, correct specification, new cylinder head, finished in black and silver, original grey leather interior, good mechanical condition.
£22,000–24,000 / $32,000–35,000 ⊞ RCC

1937 Bentley 4¼ Litre Four-Door Allweather Tourer, coachwork by Vanden Plas, Ace wheel discs, R100 headlamps, wind-up windows, finished in dark green, beige hood, beige leather interior, correct and complete, structurally and mechanically sound.
£60,000–65,000 / $87,000–94,000 ⊞ RCC

1939 Bentley 4¼ Litre Drophead Coupé, coachwork by Vanden Plas, wind-up windows, finished in black and cream, red leather interior, good condition throughout.
£60,000–65,000 / $87,000–94,000 ⊞ RCC

1949 Bentley Mk VI Cresta Continental, coachwork by Pinin Farina, nut-and-bolt restoration to original specification at a cost of c£120,000/$174,000, finished in dark green, beige Connolly hide upholstery, nominal mileage since restoration.
£120,000–130,000 / $174,000–188,000 ⋋ Bon
The Cresta Continental was inspired by the enthusiasm of three European businessmen: Walter Sleator, managing director of Garage Franco-Britannique (Rolls-Royce agents in Paris), Georges Daninos of Forges et Ateliers de Construction d'Eure de Loire (later Facel) and Georges Paulin, celebrated designer of the Embiricos Le Mans car. Their plan was to urge Rolls-Royce at the end of WWII to continue its development of a long-distance continental touring sports saloon. Sadly, Paulin did not survive the hostilities, but Sleator and Daninos used their influence to persuade Lord Hive of Rolls-Royce to release to them a batch of 17 modified Bentley chassis, based on the new Mk VI model. Modifications to the chassis included a lower radiator core and shell, lower steering column rake, a higher-ratio rear axle, a speedometer calibrated in both kilometres and miles per hour, and a 'Continental' chassis plate. Sleator and Daninos commissioned Pinin Farina to design and build the coachwork for the first Cresta Continental, which was exhibited at the Paris Salon in 1948 and caused a sensation. This car was the third chassis built in 1948 to carry the Cresta coachwork. However, it is Farina bodied, the coachbuilding features being markedly different from the Facel-Metallon cars. It is believed that Farina built just one car of the Cresta genre, and it is a matter of conjecture whether the coachwork on this chassis was originally fitted to the Daninos car, the very first of the line.

1951 Bentley Mk VI Four-Door Saloon, engine refurbished 1994, brakes overhauled, finished two-tone grey, red leather interior, correct specification.
£13,000–15,000 / $19,000–22,000 ⊞ RCC

1962 Bentley Special, Daimler 4.5 litre V8 engine, close-ratio gearbox, chassis shortened to improve handling, completely restored 1989–93, engine stripped and rebuilt, rewired, resprayed in British racing green, reupholstered black interior.
£18,000–20,000 / $26,000–29,000 ⋋ COYS
When Rolls-Royce was able to resume production after WWII, it broke with tradition by offering its mainstream models, whether Rolls-Royce or Bentley, as a standard package with factory supplied bodywork. Unfortunately, these bodies were susceptible to rust, although as the bodies deteriorated the chassis and mechanical components remained usable. As a result, a small industry grew up to strip these cars to their chassis and build vintage-style specials on the more modern running gear.

1950 Bentley Mk VI Fixed-head Coupé, coachwork by Park Ward, 4257cc overhead-valve 6-cylinder engine, 135bhp, 4-speed manual gearbox, 4-wheel drum brakes hydraulically operated to front, mechanical with servo to rear, independent suspension by coil springs and wishbones with lever-arm hydraulic dampers to front, rigid axle with semi-elliptic leaf springs and adjustable lever-arm hydraulic dampers to rear, left-hand drive, restored, finished in sand over sable, original tan leather interior, air conditioning, woodwork in need of repolishing.
£33,000–37,000 / $48,000–54,000 ⋋ C
The post-war Bentley Mk VI, launched in May 1946, was an entirely new departure in terms of engineering and design. In production numbers, it was almost mass-produced, with over 5,000 cars leaving the line between 1946 and 1952, compared with 2,500 units of the 3½ Litre and 4¼ Litre models produced between 1932 and 1939. The car was compact in design and very much an owner/driver vehicle, with a comprehensive interior specification that added heater and demisters, leather upholstery, radio, picnic tables, vanity mirrors and reading lights. The distinctive radiator carried a forward-sloping winged 'B' fixed to a dummy radiator cap.

1951 Bentley Mk VI Foursome Drophead Coupé, coachwork by Park Ward, 4257cc F-head engine, restored, no major modifications to original specification, finished in black and silver, grey leather upholstery, wooden fascia and door cappings.
£30,000–35,000 / $44,000–51,000 ⋋ Bon

BENTLEY Model	ENGINE cc/cyl	DATES	CONDITION 1	2	3
Abbreviations: HJM = H.J. Mulliner; PW = Park Ward; M/PW = Mulliner/Park Ward					
Mk VI Standard Steel	4257/ 4566/6	1946–52	£16,000	£10,000	£5,000
Mk VI Coachbuilt	4257/ 4566/6	1946–52	£25,000	£20,000	£12,000
Mk VI Coachbuilt DHC	4566/6	1946–52	£40,000+	£30,000	£20,000
R-Type Standard Steel	4566/6	1952–55	£12,000	£10,000	£7,000
R-Type Coachbuilt	4566/6	1952–55	£25,000	£20,000	£15,000
R-Type Coachbuilt DHC	4566/ 4887/6	1952–55	£50,000+	£35,000	£25,000
R-Type Cont (HJM)	4887/6	1952–55	£80,000+	£40,000	£29,000
S1 Standard Steel	4887/6	1955–59	£15,000	£10,000	£7,000
S1 Cont 2-door (PW)	4877/6	1955–59	£30,000	£25,000	£20,000
S1 Cont Drophead	4877/6	1955–59	£80,000+	£75,000	£50,000
S1 Cont F'back (HJM)	4877/6	1955–58	£50,000	£35,000	£25,000
S2 Standard Steel	6230/8	1959–62	£15,000	£9,000	£6,000
S2 Cont 2-door (HJM)	6230/8	1959–62	£60,000	£40,000	£30,000
S2 Flying Spur (HJM)	6230/8	1959–62	£45,000	£33,000	£22,000
S2 Conv (PW)	6230/8	1959–62	£60,000+	£50,000	£35,000
S3 Standard Steel	6230/8	1962–65	£16,000	£11,000	£9,000
S3 Cont/Flying Spur	6230/8	1962–65	£45,000	£30,000	£25,000
S3 2-door (M/PW)	6230/8	1962–65	£30,000	£25,000	£10,000
S3 Conv (modern conversion – only made one original)	6230/8	1962–65	£40,000	£28,000	£20,000
T1	6230/6, 6750/8	1965–77	£10,000	£8,000	£4,000
T1 2-door (M/PW)	6230/6, 6750/8	1965–70	£15,000	£12,000	£9,000
T1 Drophead (M/PW)	6230/6, 6750/8	1965–70	£30,000	£20,000	£12,000

1954 Bentley R-Type Saloon, 4566cc, automatic transmission, finished in metallic grey, grey interior, original specification, very good condition.
£9,000–10,000 / $13,000–14,500 ⤴ H&H

◀ **1951 Bentley Mk VI Standard Steel Saloon,** 4257cc 6-cylinder engine, manual gearbox, sliding roof, major engine overhaul 1994, brakes and dynamo overhauled, finished in silver and grey, original red leather upholstery, original specification in all major respects.
£9,500–11,000 / $14,000–17,000 ⤴ Bon

1950/1969 Bentley Mk VI Special, fitted later 4.9 litre S1 6-cylinder engine, gas flowed and ported cylinder head, Garrett AiResearch turbocharger, Powr-Lok limited-slip differential 16in wheels, finished in gold over red, bucket seats.
£19,000–21,000 / $28,000–31,000 ⤴ CGC
The most well known of the Mk VI specials built by Bentley stalwart Harry Rose, this car featured in much of his company's promotional material. A mobile showcase, its specification embodied his ideal of recycling staid, decaying Mk VI saloons into exciting, dynamic sports cars. Its donor chassis was modified by removing 12in (30.5cm) from the rear and adding the same amount behind the front suspension, thus retaining the 10ft (305cm) wheelbase. This greatly improved the weight distribution and handling characteristics of the chassis. Further improvements came from the lightweight glassfibre two-seat body tub with integral loadbearing floor. The car's racetrack potential was amply demonstrated by both Harry Rose and his daughter, former Bentley Driver's Club chairman, Ann Shoosmith.

◀ **1954 Bentley R-Type Saloon,** 4566cc 6-cylinder engine, automatic transmission, good condition.
£11,000–12,000 / $16,000–17,500 ⤴ BLE

1954 Bentley R-Type Saloon, 4566cc 6-cylinder engine, 4-speed manual gearbox, standard steel coachwork, finished in burgundy and black, original light grey leather interior.
£10,000–11,000 / $14,500–16,000 ⊞ AVON

1955 Bentley R-Type Four-Door saloon, coachwork by H. J. Mulliner, automatic transmission, finished in black, brown leather interior, coachwork and underside sound, very good mechanical condition, original and correct.
£18,000–20,000 / $26,000–29,000 ⊞ RCC

Bentley R-Type Continental (1952–55)

Production: 208.
Body style: Two-door fastback saloon.
Construction: Steel chassis, alloy body.
Engine: 4566 or 4887cc straight-six, twin SU carburettors.
Power output: Never declared, but at least 165bhp.
Transmission: Four-speed automatic or manual.
Maximum speed: 115–120mph.
0–60mph: 13.5 seconds.

By the early 1950s, the racing-green exploits of the Le Mans conquering Bentleys were a fast-fading memory. The cars that had been once, so distinguished were now little more than Rolls-Royce companion models. For those who favoured formal roadwear, there was the Rolls Silver Dawn; the Bentley equivalent was the R-Type, hardly cravat casual, but a little cheaper and a touch more sporting. But there was one exception, the beautiful Bentley R-Type Continental with an exquisite coachbuilt fastback body formed in the wind-tunnel and crafted in aluminium by H. J. Mulliner. It would have been sleeker and more slippery still, but

Rolls-Royce wouldn't allow the height of the bluff radiator to be reduced by more than 1½in (4cm). Here was a car that cocked a snook at post-war austerity with its astronomical price tag of £7,608/$11,032 (that's close on £500,000/$725,000 in today's money). Yet not only was it the most expensive production car in the world, it was, with its own twin-carburettor version of the Rolls-Royce engine, also the fastest production four-seater of its day. With its genuine and serene 100mph cruising speed, you could drive from London to Monte Carlo and arrive fresh enough to play the tables. *Autocar* magazine lamented that 'such a car is bound to be costly, and the British, who make it cannot own it; but it goes abroad as proof that a nation where the creators are constantly subjected to the debasement of their own living standards can still keep alive the idea of perfection for others to enjoy.' In fact, 100 of the 208 Mulliner fastback Continentals did go abroad, and today the wonderful R-Type Continental is the most coveted of all post-war Bentleys.

1955 Bentley R-Type Saloon, 4500cc 6-cylinder engine, automatic transmission, original metal sliding sunroof, finished in dark blue over black, grey leather interior.
£14,850–16,500 / $22,000–24,000 ⊞ BC

1955 Bentley S1 Four-door Saloon, 4.9 litre 6-cylinder engine, twin SU carburettors, 4-speed automatic transmission, coil-and-wishbone independent front suspension, restored 1996 at a cost of £21,000/$30,500, transmission overhauled, new rear wings, new inner sills and front sill box sections, bare-metal respray in two-tone blue.
£9,000–10,000 / $13,000–14,500 ⋔ Bon

◄ **1955 Bentley S1 Continental,** coachwork by H. J. Mulliner, 4887cc 6-cylinder engine, overhead inlet/side exhaust valves, twin SU carburettors, 4-speed automatic transmission, 4-wheel drum brakes, independent front suspension by coil springs and wishbones, rigid rear axle on semi-elliptic leaf springs, restored at a cost of £60,000/$87,000 early 1990s, finished in grey over black, red leather interior, bench front seat with divided adjustable squab, air conditioning, 18th of 101 built.
£65,000–75,000 / $94,000–109,000 ⋔ C

1956 Bentley S1 Sports Saloon, coachwork by James Young, 10-year nut-and-bolt restoration, full engine and mechanical rebuild, invoices totalling £100,000/$145,000, finished in silver over burgundy, burgundy interior, believed to be 1 of only 7 remaining with James Young coachwork.
£25,000–28,000 / $36,000–40,000 ➶ H&H

1956 Bentley S1 Four-Door Saloon, 4887cc 6-cylinder engine, 3-speed automatic transmission, £20,000/$29,000 spent in last 10 years, new exhaust system, complete body renovation, bare-metal respray in green, new tan upholstery, excellent condition.
£9,000–10,000 / $13,000–14,500 ➶ H&H

1957 Bentley S1 Four-Door Saloon, power steering, new chassis c1980, finished in dark blue and pale grey, blue and grey leather interior, 1 owner from new, correct, excellent condition.
£14,000–16,000 / $20,000–23,000 ⊞ RCC

1956 Bentley S1 Continental Drophead Coupé, coachwork by Park Ward, 4.9 litre 6-cylinder engine, automatic transmission, left-hand drive, recently resprayed in original metallic pale grey, original hood and original grey leather interior in need of refurbishment, interior woodwork very good, 2 owners and fewer than 43,500 miles from new, very good mechanical condition.
£125,000–140,000 / $180,000–203,000 ➶ Bon

1960 Bentley S2 Continental Flying Spur, coachwork by H. J. Mulliner, 6230cc overhead-valve V8 engine, twin SU carburettors, 4-speed automatic transmission, hydro-mechanical power-assisted drum brakes, power steering, independent front suspension by unequal-length wishbones and coil springs with anti-roll-bar, semi-elliptic leaf-spring rear suspension with single radius rod, older restoration, resprayed in dark green, interior completely refurbished, upholstered in green leather, air conditioning.
£35,000–45,000 / $51,000–65,000 ➶ C
The Bentley S2 was the high-performance version of the Rolls-Royce Silver Cloud, which had gained a brand-new 6.2 litre V8 engine in 1959. The Continental was the higher-performance version of the Bentley, which came with power steering and hydro-mechanical power-assisted brakes. The original intention was for the Continental chassis to be equipped with only two-door coachwork, and it was 1957 before the company permitted H. J. Mulliner to build a four-door body. The six-light saloon was given the name Flying Spur. The first car built on an S1 chassis wore a chrome winged mascot. The Flying Spur was continued throughout the S-series cars. This particular example was formerly owned by Elton John.

◀ **1961 Bentley S2 Continental Flying Spur Saloon,** coachwork by H. J. Mulliner, 6230cc V8 engine, 4-speed automatic transmission, 4-leading-shoe front drum brakes, power-assisted steering, finished in dark blue, power-operated steel sunroof, electric windows, Bosch hazard warning system, light cream leather upholstery, factory-fitted air conditioning, original and unrestored condition.
£50,000–60,000 / $72,000–87,000 ➶ Bon
This Bentley Continental Flying Spur was first owned by film director Mervyn Le Roy, whose screen credits include *Little Caesar*, *I Am a Fugitive from a Chain Gang* and *Random Harvest*. In total, 388 cars were built on the Continental S2 chassis. This is one of only 13 left-hand-drive examples of H. J. Mulliner's four-door Flying Spur.

1961 Bentley S2 Four-door Saloon, finished in black, green leather interior, 1 of only 57 S2 models built on the long-wheel-base chassis, very good condition.
£11,500–13,500 / $17,000–20,000 ✗ **Bon**
With development of its dependable six-cylinder engine nearing an end, and facing competition from faster rivals in the United States market, Rolls-Royce turned to V8 power as the 1960s approached. Introduced in the autumn of 1959, the Rolls-Royce Silver Cloud II and Bentley S2 appeared externally unchanged from their Silver Cloud and S-Type predecessors, although their performance was considerably enhanced by the new 6230cc aluminium engine. Power-assisted steering was standard, and there was no longer the option of a manual gearbox. The Silver Cloud II and S2 remained in production until superseded by the restyled Cloud III and S3 in 1962.

1961 Bentley S2 Standard Steel Saloon, 6230cc V8 engine, automatic transmission, restored early 1990s, transmission and brakes overhauled, new sills, new rear half-wings, resprayed in silver-grey over blue, blue upholstery and interior in good condition.
£6,000–8,000 / $8,700–11,500 ✗ **Bon**

1964 Bentley S3 Four-Door Saloon, restored 1993, extensive bodywork renovation, partial respray in original two-tone green, new headlining, door seals and windscreen, new Connolly leather interior trim, woodwork revarnished, 2 owners from new, good to very good condition.
£12,000–14,000 / $17,500–20,500 ✗ **Bon**

▶ **1964 Bentley S3 Continental Drophead Coupé,** coachwork by Mulliner Park Ward, 6230cc overhead-valve V8 engine, c220bhp, 4-speed automatic transmission, 4-wheel drum brakes, independent front suspension by coil springs, semi-elliptic rear leaf springs, older restoration, mechanics rebuilt where necessary, finished in dark metallic blue, new magnolia Everflex hood, new magnolia leather interior, electric hood mechanism in need of some attention, formerly owned by Elton John.
£45,000–55,000 / $65,000–80,000 ✗ **C**

1962 Bentley S3 Continental Flying Spur Saloon, coachwork by H. J. Mulliner, factory-fitted air conditioning, 1 of 311 cars built on the S3 Continental chassis, displayed at the 1962 Motor Show, good condition throughout.
£30,000–35,000 / $44,000–51,000 ✗ **Bon**
Launched in 1962, the Bentley S3 and its Rolls-Royce equivalent, the Silver Cloud III, retained the existing 6.2 litre V8 engine, although with larger carburettors, a new distributor and raised compression ratio. Most obvious among many changes from the S2 was the adoption of a four-headlamp lighting arrangement, the absence of sidelights from the wing tops and a slightly lower radiator shell. Inside, there was revised accommodation with separate front seats and increased room for rear passengers. Despite the popularity of the standard steel bodywork, independent coachbuilders continued to offer alternatives, perhaps the most stylish being those produced to clothe the Bentley Continental.

> A known continuous history can add value to and enhance the enjoyment of a car.

1972 Bentley T1 Saloon, finished in metallic silver mink, scarlet leather interior, chrome furnishings in very good condition, slight blemishes to paintwork, otherwise very good condition.
£8,000–9,000 / $11,500–13,000 ⋏ CGC

1983 Bentley Mulsanne Turbo Saloon, automatic transmission, new turbocharger, recent brake overhaul, finished in red, black leather interior, good overall condition.
£9,000–10,000 / $13,000–14,500 ⋏ CGC
The introduction of the Mulsanne Turbo at the 1982 Geneva Motor Show represented a change of fortune for Bentley. Before, the differences between its models and those of sister marque Rolls-Royce had been largely cosmetic, but now the Bentley cars had been given a character very much of their own. With some 300bhp courtesy of its force-fed 6.75 litre V8, the Mulsanne Turbo was capable of an easy 135mph and 0–60mph in under 7 seconds.

1975 Bentley Corniche Convertible, coachwork by Mulliner Park Ward, 6750cc overhead-valve V8 engine, 225bhp, 3-speed automatic transmission, 4-wheel power-assisted disc brakes, independent front suspension by lower wishbones and coil springs, rear suspension by trailing arms and coil springs, automatic levelling, later model wheels, Sundym glass, power hood, hood cover, finished in dark metallic blue, magnolia leather interior, c43,000 miles from new, formerly owned by Elton John, very good condition throughout.
£25,000–35,000 / $36,000–51,000 ⋏ C
The Corniche was announced in early 1971. The name and model were a new identity for the existing, coachbuilt two-door design based on the Silver Shadow, which had been available since 1967 from Mulliner Park Ward. It benefited from improved performance over the standard model, and for the first time cruise control was introduced, while the interior featured a revised dash layout.

1984 Bentley 8 Saloon, 6.7 litre V8 engine, automatic transmission.
£9,500–11,000 / $14,000–16,000 ⊞ BLE

1990 Bentley Continental Convertible, coachwork by Mulliner Park Ward, finished in dark blue, parchment upholstery, fewer than 29,500 miles from new, excellent condition.
£55,000–65,000 / $80,000–94,000 ⋏ Bon
A key factor in Rolls-Royce's marketing strategy for the 1980s was the relaunch of Bentley. To rekindle interest in the marque, a name from its past was resurrected – 'Continental' – and applied to the two-door model previously known, like its Rolls-Royce equivalent, as the Corniche. Introduced in March 1971, the Corniche was a revised version of the Mulliner Park Ward bodied two-door variant of the Rolls-Royce Silver Shadow and Bentley T-series saloons, themselves notable as the Crewe factory's first unitary-construction cars. In Corniche form, Rolls-Royce's well-tried 6.7 litre V8 produced around ten per cent more power than standard and proved capable of propelling the car to a top speed of over 120mph with sports-car-beating acceleration to match. The model proved a major success for Rolls-Royce, and although its exterior style remained recognizably Silver Shadow, the Corniche/Continental benefited from the regular updates and improvements made to the contemporary Silver Spirit range, remaining in production well into the 1990s, the last (convertible) examples being delivered in 1995.

Berkeley

◀ **1960 Berkeley T60 Roadster,** Excelsior engine, restored 1994–96, c300 miles since, modified with fore-and-aft seat adjustment, child's seat restraint and interior light, new hood and frame, finished in red, black interior, unused for last 3 years, assorted spares including new starter motor, excellent condition.
£2,500–3,000 / $3,600–4,400 ✗ Bon
Produced between 1956 and 1961, the Laurie Bond designed Berkeley was unique at the time of its introduction in featuring not only a transverse engine and front-wheel drive, but also a glassfibre monocoque bodyshell with aluminium reinforcement. The 322cc Anzani two-stroke, twin-cylinder engine was soon dropped in favour of a similar, but more reliable, Excelsior unit, while later developments included the 700cc Royal Enfield powered B95 and B105 models.

Bitter

▶ **1986 Bitter SC Coupé,** automatic transmission, sunroof, alloy wheels, 'space-saver' spare, engine converted to unleaded fuel, finished in metallic brown, tan leather interior, 1 family ownership and fewer than 50,000 miles from new.
£4,500–5,000 / $6,500–7,250 ✗ Bon
Eric Bitter began building his Opel-based cars in the early 1970s, launching the Senator/Monza-based SC in 1981. The latter's body was made in Italy and the car assembled by Bitter in Germany until Steyr Daimler Puch took over the work in 1983. Powered by Opel's 3848cc overhead-camshaft inline six, the 140mph SC was built in coupé, saloon and cabriolet forms.

BMW

Bayerische Flugzeug Werke, as the company was called originally, was founded in 1916 to make aero engines, becoming Bayerische Motoren Werke in 1922 with the beginning of motorcycle production. Car production followed in 1928 with the Dixi, an Austin 7 built under licence. The first true BMW, the four-cylinder, 800cc 3/20 appeared in 1932, followed by a range of fine touring and sports cars. The pinnacle of the company's pre-war achievements was the lithe 2 litre 328, which, fitted with a beautiful streamlined body, won the 1940 Mille Miglia. The 328 undoubtedly had a strong influence on the shape of William Lyons' post-war Jaguar

XK120. After the war, BMW survived the nationalisation of its Eisenach factory, by then in East Germany, and several financial crises. The 507 V8-engined roadster – aimed at the Yankee dollar – was beautiful, but extortionately over-priced. The Isetta microcars at first brought salvation, then threatened oblivion as sales slumped in the late 1950s. The turn-around came in 1961 with the launch of the neat Michelotti styled 1500 and 1800 models, which helped create BMW's modern reputation for superbly built prestige cars. It's amazing that strong hints of the original Michelotti designs remain even in today's accomplished BMWs.

◀ **c1938 BMW 327 Cabriolet,** single-carburettor engine, older restoration, unused for several years, in need of recommissioning, otherwise very good condition.
£12,000–15,000
$17,500–21,750 ✗ Bon
Introduced in 1938, the 327 sports tourer used the shortened 326 saloon chassis, shared by the 320, but with semi-elliptic rear springing in place of torsion bars. BMW's six-cylinder overhead-valve engine had been enlarged to 1971cc and developed around 60bhp in the 327, which could also be ordered with the 328 sports car's 80bhp unit.

BMW Model	ENGINE cc/cyl	DATES	CONDITION 1	2	3
Dixi	747/4	1927–32	£7,000	£3,000	£2,000
303	1175/6	1934–36	£11,000	£8,000	£5,000
309	843/4	1933–34	£6,000	£4,000	£2,000
315	1490/6	1935–36	£9,000	£7,000	£5,000
319	1911/6	1935–37	£10,000	£9,000	£6,000
326	1971/6	1936–37	£12,000	£10,000	£8,000
320 series	1971/6	1937–38	£12,000	£10,000	£8,000
327/328	1971/6	1937–40	£30,000+	£18,000	£10,000
328	1971/6	1937–40	£60,000+	-	-

A known continuous history can add value to and enhance the enjoyment of a car.

Miller's Starter Marque

- **Starter BMWs:** *1502, 1602, 2002, 2002 Touring.*
- There's a 'Beemer' that won't burn a hole in your wallet, and can make you beam from ear to ear as you snick through the gears and enjoy its sporting response.
- We're talking about the '02 series two-door saloons, which were launched in Germany in 1968. When they arrived in Britain in 1971, they were not particularly cheap: the 2002 model was £120 more than a Rover P6 2000, and only £170 less than a Mk II 3.4 Jaguar – yet on the BMW there was not a piece of polished wood or hide trim in sight. Instead, the '02 models rewarded sporting drivers with their spirited performance and pert handling.
- They are also easy to live with and generally robust, with good availability of quality reasonably priced spares.
- **Performance:** All except the 1502 are good for 100mph, and the fuel-injected 2002 Tii offers a sizzling 0–60mph time of 8.2 seconds and 118mph top speed. This and the twin-carb 2002 Ti are the best buys in performance terms, but many have been mistreated by a succession of boy racers whose only pretence to maintenance is applying go-faster decals. The 1602, plain 2002 and 1502 make sensible down-market alternatives.
- **Rust:** Particular points to watch include the jacking points, which can eventually fall out and leave the sills prone to rotting from the inside out. Look inside the boot too. Generally, though, rust problems are no worse than any other steel monocoque saloon.
- **Engines:** BMW engines are famed for their smooth and reliable performance and, if looked after, are good for more than 80,000 miles. On starting from cold, listen for rattling from the top end, which indicates camshaft/follower wear. The engines need an oil change around every 5,000 miles, so look for supporting documentation that confirms regular maintenance.
- All in all, this Beemer's pretty straightforward, but there are a couple of more exotic options. Cabriolets are undoubtedly desirable, but have some nasty rust-traps, particularly behind the rear seat where the hood is stowed. If you're not careful, Cabriolet restoration costs could spiral beyond your reach.
- Likewise, the rare 2002 Turbo is an enthusiast's car rather than an every-day user. For a start, only 51 were sold in the UK. If you can find one, you'll get performance – and shattering bills to match.

1957 BMW 502 Saloon, 3168cc V8 engine, finished in silver, largely in good condition, but in need of some attention and cosmetic refurbishment, spare gearbox and partially dismantled second engine.
£2,500–3,000 / $3,600–4,400 ⟋ BRIT
First seen in 1954, the BMW 502 was the first post-war German car to feature V8 power, the major engine components being constructed of aluminium. Based on the 501, BMW's first post-war offering, the 502 had a better specification, more chrome, built-in fog lamps and indicators and, from late 1955, a wraparound 'panoramic' rear screen. Initially, the engine displaced 2.6 litres, but an enlarged 3.2 litre version, the basis of that used in the 507 roadster and coupé, was offered from 1955.

1971 BMW 1602 Convertible, 4-cylinder engine, 4-speed manual gearbox, completely restored 1995, finished in white.
£3,500–4,000 /$5,000–5,800 ⟋ BARO

1972 BMW 2002, finished in red, black interior, 34,000 miles from new, excellent condition.
£3,000–3,500 / $4,400–5,000 ⟋ COYS
It was BMW's 1600 saloon of 1966, with new two-door, medium-sized bodywork, that really sealed the German manufacturer's path on the road to success. Faster derivatives soon joined the 1600 with the extremely popular 2002 launched in January 1968. In basic form, its 1998cc engine produced 100bhp, and BMW used a derivative to win the 2000cc class of the 1968 European Touring Car Championship.

BMW Model	ENGINE cc/cyl	DATES	CONDITION 1	2	3
501	2077/6	1952–56	£9,000	£7,000	£3,500
501 V8/502	2580, 3168/8	1955–63	£10,000+	£5,000	£3,000
503 FHC/DHC	3168/8	1956–59	£25,000+	£20,000	£15,000
507	3168/8	1956–59	£120,000+	£70,000	£50,000
Isetta (4 wheels)	247/1	1955–62	£7,000	£3,000	£1,200
Isetta (3 wheels)	298/1	1958–64	£8,000	£2,500	£1,500
Isetta 600	585/2	1958–59	£3,000+	£1,800	£500
1500/1800/2000	var/4	1962–68	£1,800	£800	£500
2000CS	1990/4	1966–69	£5,500	£4,000	£1,500
1500/1600/1602	1499/ 1573/4	1966–75	£3,000+	£1,500	£800
1600 Cabriolet	1573/4	1967–71	£6,000	£4,500	£2,000
2800CS	2788/6	1968–71	£5,000	£4,000	£1,500
1602	1990/4	1968–74	£3,000	£1,500	£1,000
2002	1990/4	1968–74	£3,000	£2,000	£1,000
2002 Tii	1990/4	1971–75	£4,500	£2,500	£1,200
2002 Touring	1990/4	1971–74	£3,500	£2,000	£1,000
2002 Cabriolet	1990/4	1971–75	£5,000+	£3,000	£2,500
2002 Turbo	1990/4	1973–74	£10,000	£6,000	£4,000
3.0 CSa/CSi	2986/6	1972–75	£8,000	£6,000	£4,000
3.0 CSL	3003/ 3153/6	1972–75	£16,000	£10,000	£7,500
MI	3500/6	1978–85	£50,000	£40,000	£30,000
633/635 CS/CSI	3210/3453/6	1976–85	£7,000	£3,000	£2,000
M535i	3453/6	1979–81	£4,500	£3,000	£2,500

▶ **1979 BMW M1 Coupé,** 3500cc 6-cylinder engine, air conditioning, 1 of 450 built, original condition. **£35,000–40,000 / 50,750–58,000** ✗ BJ

1972 BMW 3.0 CSL, 3 litre 6-cylinder engine, genuine BMW 'Batmobile' spoiler kit, finished in white with blue and red stripes, black cloth interior, engine rebuilt and converted from fuel injection to triple carburettors 1988–89, 6,400 miles covered since, 1 of 500 original right-hand-drive cars from a total of only 1,039, excellent mechanical condition. **£8,500–9,500 / $12,300–13,800** ✗ COYS
The aggressive styling and performance of the BMW CSL, or Coupé Sport Leichtmetal, made it a popular and successful choice for drivers in the 1970s European Touring Car Championships. Success in this event was used by BMW to promote the new road-going lightweight version of the 3.0 litre CS that was already in production. This homologation special featured an aluminium bonnet, boot and doors, which saved a total of 300lb (136kg) in weight over the standard steel-bodied CS.

1984 BMW 635 CSi, 6-cylinder engine, switchable automatic transmission, BBS-style alloy wheels, sunroof, finished in silver, navy blue leather interior, air conditioning, heated seats. **£2,200–2,800 / $3,200–4,000** ✗ COYS
Launched in the late 1970s, the 635 CSi soon became the flagship of the BMW range until it was superseded by the M6 variant in the mid-1980s.

Bristol

Nestling at the end of London's Kensington High Street, hard by the Hilton Hotel, there's a tiny showroom that proclaims in red neon 'Bristol Cars Ltd'. This is the single retail outlet of what has to be the most British car you can buy. The story of Bristol Cars started in 1947, when the Bristol Aeroplane Company branched out into car manufacture with an anglicized version of the pre-war BMW 327. Bristol's famed six-cylinder engine was derived from a pre-war BMW unit. Combining handcrafted coachwork and luxury appointments, Bristols earned the appellation 'The Businessman's Express'. In the early 1960s, Bristol Cars Ltd, as it had become, adopted Chrysler V8 power to endow its luxury sports saloons with extra urge. At their best, the V8 Bristols could offer near-Jaguar or Ferrari performance, but with most un-Ferrari-like quiet.

Miller's Compares

I. **1948 Bristol 400 Coupé,** 1971cc triple-carburettor engine, 85bhp, older restoration, finished in white, beige interior, period HMV radio, 1 owner since 1973, fewer than 4,000 miles covered since 1974, completely original.
£8,500–10,000 / $12,300–14,500 ⚲ H&H

II. **1949 Bristol 400 Coupé,** restored, fitted with front disc brakes, resprayed in Old English white, retrimmed tan interior by Bristol at a cost of over £6,300/$9,000, inertia seat belts, 24,000 miles from new.
£14,000–16,000 / $20,300–23,200 ⚲ COYS
When the Bristol Aeroplane Company began to build cars as well as aircraft in 1946, it came as no surprise that its first model, the 400, displayed a high degree of engineering integrity. With an 80bhp engine driving through a four-speed gearbox, the Bristol 400 boasted a top speed of 95mph together with surefootedness and excellent cornering. Maximum speed was assisted by the smooth aerodynamic lines of the 400's body, styled and built by Bristol in steel with an aluminium bonnet and doors, and featuring a BMW-style grille.

On the face of it, these white Bristol 400s look very similar. Both have had loving attention over the years, with devoted owners commissioning some of the restoration from Bristol Cars, which doesn't come cheap. However, it is over 25 years since car I was in top concours fettle, and these days its restoration could do with refreshing. Car II was restored much later, in the late 1980s, and has stood up better.

◀ **1958 Bristol 406 Saloon,** 2216cc engine, completely restored 1992, finished in burgundy, beige interior, 1 of 178 built, very good condition throughout.
£5,500–7,000 / $8,000–10,200 ⚲ H&H
This particular 406 was originally registered to Tony Crook, the owner of Bristol Cars, and it featured in the road tests carried out by *Autocar* and *Motor* magazines. According to the chassis records, it was the fifth chassis laid down, the first four being prototypes, and it was used as the works demonstrator until 1960. The first engine fitted was a development engine, but this was replaced in 1959 with the final production unit.

▶ **1963 Bristol 407 Sports Saloon,** 5200cc engine, completely restored at a cost of over £40,000/$58,000, finished in blue and silver, burgundy interior, air conditioning.
£15,000–18,000
$21,750–26,000 ⚲ H&H
The Bristol 407 was introduced in 1961, and during a production run of just over two years, 88 two-door saloons were produced. This was the first of the Anglo-American Bristols, being fitted with a 250bhp Chrysler engine, which was married to a three-speed automatic transmission; it was good for 125mph.

BRISTOL Model	ENGINE cc/cyl	DATES	CONDITION 1	2	3
400	1971/6	1947–50	£16,000	£14,000	£8,000
401 FHC/DHC	1971/6	1949–53	£28,000	£14,000	£8,000
402	1971/6	1949–50	£22,000	£19,000	£12,000
403	1971/6	1953–55	£20,000	£14,000	£10,000
404 Coupé	1971/6	1953–57	£22,000	£15,000	£12,000
405	1971/6	1954–58	£15,000	£12,000	£10,000
405 Drophead	1971/6	1954–56	£22,000	£19,000	£16,000
406	2216/6	1958–61	£12,000	£8,000	£6,000
407	5130/8	1962–63	£15,000	£8,000	£6,000
408	5130/8	1964–65	£14,000	£10,000	£8,000
409	5211/8	1966–67	£14,000	£11,000	£7,000
410	5211/8	1969	£14,000	£10,000	£6,000
411 Mk I–III	6277/8	1970–73	£16,000	£11,000	£8,000
411 Mk IV–V	6556/8	1974–76	£12,500	£9,500	£7,000
412	5900/ 6556/8	1975–82	£15,000	£9,000	£6,000
603	5211/ 5900/8	1976–82	£10,000	£7,000	£5,000

1972 Bristol 411 Mk II, completely restored, finished in metallic blue, tan leather interior, 1 of only 474 produced, excellent condition.
£14,000–15,000 / $20,300–21,750 ⊞ TIHO

1977 Bristol 412 Convertible, restored 1991, converted to unleaded fuel, new starter motor, finished in Jaguar ocean blue, black leather interior, 1 of only 75 aluminium-bodied 412s built, concours winner, very good condition.
£7,000–9,000 / $10,200–13,000 ↗ CGC
Introduced in 1975, the 412 was Bristol's first convertible since the 1950s. The Zagato styled body with its targa top/roll-over bar arrangement offered greater versatility and saloon-like levels of refinement. Fitted with the established 6556cc Chrysler V8 and Torqueflite automatic transmission, it was an impressive performer.

BSA

1932 BSA Three-Wheeler, 1021cc twin-cylinder engine, soft top, finished in black, brown interior, good condition throughout.
£4,500–5,500 / $6,500–8,000 ↗ H&H
BSA had begun motorcycle manufacture in 1910, and by the late 1920s the company was the largest motorcycle producer in Britain, if not the world. It was from the BSA factory at Small Heath that the new car emerged, a three-wheeler designed by F. W. Hulse. It competed with the Morgan three-wheeler and, although slower, it was more comfortable and easier to drive.

Bugatti

1935 Bugatti Type 57 Ventoux, rear wheel spats, finished in black, red leather interior, excellent condition.
£120,000–130,000 / $174,000–188,500 ✗ COYS
The Type 57, in its various forms, was the mainstay of Bugatti's production car output from 1934 onwards. Although primarily conceived as a road car, it did well in competition, and versions twice won at Le Mans. The 3.3 litre, double-overhead-camshaft, straight-eight engine was completely new, and it was offered initially in unblown form to keep the price down. Even so, it produced 140bhp, which meant that any T57 was good for 95mph, and the model revitalized the company's fortunes. A road test in *Motorsport* in 1934 revealed that the speed could be dropped to 10mph in top gear and the engine would pick up cleanly. Road-holding was typical of Bugatti: the car could take a 60-degree corner at 60mph 'without any reduction in speed. The car neither rolled, slid nor gave any indication that the manoeuvre was at all unusual.' So confident was Bugatti of the car that it did not even fit a rev-counter, because 'no harm results even if the engine speed reaches 5,500rpm.'

1937 Bugatti Type 57S Atalante Coupé, coachwork by Gangloff, only minor alterations are thought to include the addition of bumpers and modification to the lights and fuel filler cap, all carried out by Gangloff in the 1950s, finished in black, original leather upholstery, never the subject of a full restoration, maintained to a high standard, excellent running condition.
£1,000,000+ / $1,450,000+ ✗ Bon

The Type 57S made its first appearance in 1936. Although derived from the well established Type 57, the 57S was radically different. Only some 40 examples were built, and it was claimed to be the fastest production road-going sports car available at the time. The chassis was all new, and it was lowered most effectively by having the rear axle pass through the side members. The Type 57S engine had a capacity of 3257cc and featured dry-sump lubrication with a lightened crankshaft and high-compression pistons. Most customers seem to have decided that Jean Bugatti's rakish Atalante coupé design suited the 57S chassis best, and some 20 such cars were built, with coachwork executed by either the Bugatti factory or nearby coachbuilder Gangloff. A handful of later models were supercharged and designated Type 57SC.

BUGATTI Model	ENGINE cc/cyl	DATES	CONDITION 1	2	3
13/22/23	1496/4	1919–26	£40,000	£32,000	£25,000
30	1991/8	1922–36	£45,000	£35,000	£30,000
32	1992/8	1923	£45,000	£35,000	£30,000
35A	1991/8	1924–30	£110,000+	£90,000	£80,500
38 (30 update)	1991/8	1926–28	£44,500	£34,000	£28,000
39	1493/8	1926–29	£120,000	£90,000	£80,000
39A Supercharged	1496/8	1926–29	£140,000+	-	-
35T	2262/8	1926–30	£140,000+	-	-
37 GP Car	1496/4	1926–30	£110,000+	£90,000	£75,000
40	1496/4	1926–30	£50,000	£42,000	£35,000
38A	1991/8	1927–28	£48,000	£40,000	£35,000
35B Supercharged	2262/8	1927–30	£300,000+	£170,000+	-
35C	1991/8	1927–30	£170,000+	-	-
37A	1496/4	1927–30	£125,000+	-	-
44	2991/8	1927–30	£60,000+	£40,000	£35,000
45	3801/16	1927–30	£150,000+	-	-
43/43A Tourer	2262/8	1927–31	£180,000+	-	-
35A	1991/8	1928–30	£140,000	£110,000	£90,000
46	5359/8	1929–36	£140,000	£110,000	£90,000
40A	1627/4	1930	£55,000	£45,000	£35,500
49	3257/8	1930–34	£60,000+	£45,000	£35,500
57 Closed	3257/8	1934–40	£60,000+	£35,000	£30,000
57 Open	3257/8	1936–38	£90,000++	£60,000	£55,000
57S	3257/8	1936–38	£250,000+	-	-
57SC Supercharged	3257/8	1936–39	£250,000+	-	-
57G	3257/8	1937–40	£250,000+	-	-
57C	3257/8	1939–40	£140,000+	-	-

Racing history is an important factor with the GP cars, also whether supercharged and low chassis.

Buick

Buick is one of those names that has steered a steady course through the mainstream of the American auto industry, yet the man who founded the marque was actually a Scot. David Dunbar Buick moved to the USA at an early age, and by 1903 he had built and tested his own car. By 1908, Buick had left the company and the dynamic William Crapo Durant was in control, using Buick as the basis of General Motors. The millionth Buick was built in 1923, and throughout most of its life since the marque has provided stout service as a General Motors middle-market brand.

◀ **1918 Buick E-Six-45 Four-Door Tourer,** 3958cc overhead-valve 6-cylinder engine, exposed valve gear, export model, right-hand drive, right-hand gear change, detachable wheel rims, weather equipment, new silencer, spare cylinder block and head, valves with springs and cages, exhaust manifold, hood frame support clamps and headlamp glass.
£11,000–13,000 / $16,000–18,850 ⚒ Bon
David Dunbar Buick built his first automobile in Detroit, Michigan, in 1903. Just five years later, his departure from the Buick Motor Company coincided with it becoming the cornerstone of General Motors, under its new owner, William C. Durant.

BUICK Model	ENGINE cc/cyl	DATES	CONDITION 1	2	3
Veteran	various	1903–09	£18,500	£12,000	£8,000
18/20	3881/6	1918–22	£12,000	£5,000	£2,000
Series 22	2587/4	1922–24	£9,000	£5,000	£3,000
Series 24/6	3393/6	1923–30	£9,000	£5,000	£3,000
Light 8	3616/8	1931	£18,000	£14,500	£11,000
Straight 8	4467/8	1931	£22,000	£18,000	£10,000
50 Series	3857/8	1931–39	£18,500	£15,000	£8,000
60 Series	5247/8	1936–39	£19,000	£15,000	£8,000
90 Series	5648/8	1934–35	£20,000	£15,500	£9,000
40 Series	4064/8	1936–39	£19,000	£14,000	£10,000
80/90	5247/8	1936–39	£25,000	£20,000	£15,000
McLaughlin	5247/8	1937–40	£22,000	£15,000	£10,000

Various chassis lengths and bodies will affect value. Buick chassis fitted with British bodies prior to 1916 were called Bedford-Buicks. Right-hand drive can have an added premium of 25%.

◀ **1939 Buick Series 40 Straight Eight Coupé,** 5300cc 8-cylinder engine, left-hand drive, finished in black, new tan leather interior trim, 3 owners and 44,000 miles from new, paint thin in places, otherwise good original condition.
£8,000–10,000 / $11,500–14,500 ⚒ H&H

1953 Buick Skyark, 322cu.in V8 engine, Dynaflow automatic transmission, 4-wheel hydraulic drum brakes, coil-spring front suspension, Kelsey-Hayes chrome wire wheels, hydraulically-operated top, windows and seats, chassis-up restoration early 1980s, finished in white, original black and white leather seats.
£28,000–34,000 / $40,500–50,000 ⚒ Bon
When new, this particular Skylark is said to have been a college graduation present to grape juice heiress Jan Welch and was customized for her.

◀ **1955 Buick Special Riviera,** V8 engine, finished in black over grey over white, excellent condition throughout.
£6,000–8,000 / $8,700–11,600 ⚒ CGC

1960 Buick Electra Four-Door Hardtop, 401cu.in overhead-valve V8 engine, 325hp, automatic transmission, independent front suspension, finished in metallic dark green, tinted glass, original green vinyl and fabric interior, original push-button radio, never restored, excellent condition.
£4,000–6,000 / $5,800–8,700 ⚒ Bon

▶ **1970 Buick Riviera,** 455cu.in V8 engine, Turbo 400 automatic transmission, 0–60mph in 8 seconds, black vinyl interior, 55,000 miles from new, original condition.
£3,500–4,500 / $5,000–6,500 ⚒ CGC

BUICK Model	ENGINE cu. in/cyl	DATES	CONDITION 1	2	3
Special/Super 4-Door	248/ 364/8	1950–59	£6,000	£4,000	£2,000
Special/Super Riviera	263/ 332/8	1950–56	£8,000	£6,000	£3,000
Special/Super Convertible	263/ 332/8	1950–56	£8,500	£5,500	£3,000
Roadmaster 4-door	320/ 365/8	1950–58	£11,000	£8,000	£6,000
Roadmaster Riviera	320/ 364/8	1950–58	£9,000	£7,000	£5,000
Roadmaster Convertible	320/ 364/8	1950–58	£16,000	£11,000	£7,000
Special/Super Riviera	364/8	1957–59	£10,750	£7,500	£5,000
Special/Super Convertible	364/8	1957–58	£13,500	£11,000	£6,000

Colour Review

1928 Alfa Romeo 1500S Tourer, retaining all period fittings, original paint, trim faded, fewer than 50,000 miles and 2 owners from new.
£75,000–90,000 / $109,000–130,500 ⚒ COYS

One of the world's most renowned car designers, Vittorio Jano, created his best and most successful designs for Alfa Romeo. He joined the company in 1923, his first design being the successful P2 grand prix car. His second project was the 6C production series, culminating in the 1750 Gran Sport, perhaps the greatest sports-racing car of the 1930s. The 6C was so named because of its six-cylinder engine, which began life as a 1.5 litre, overhead-cam unit of monobloc construction, the crankcase and cylinder head cast in iron, and the crankshaft running in five main bearings. This was fitted to a chassis of two wheelbases: 122in (310cm) for six/seven-seat coachwork and 114in (290cm) for four-seat coachwork. Both chassis were stiffly sprung, providing excellent roadholding. Fully compensated rod-operated brakes worked on all four wheels, as did the handbrake. The 6C 1500 was first shown in 1925. This car is a rare example of the second series of 1500cc cars. The 'S' designation denotes a short chassis and uprated twin-cam engine.

1933 Alfa Romeo 6th Series 6C 1750 Gran Sport Spider, coachwork by Touring, 1752cc double-overhead-camshaft 6-cylinder engine, original-style Memini carburettor, Roots-type supercharger, recent extensive restoration, new hide upholstery, otherwise very original.
£250,000+ / $362,500+ ⚒ Bon

1930 Aston Martin International Short-Chassis Tourer, coachwork by Bertelli, original specification in all major respects, worm-drive rear axle, fold-flat windscreen, full weather equipment, new fuel pumps and lines, rebuilt magneto and dynamo, new front wheel bearings, good original condition.
£40,000–45,000 / $58,000–65,250 ⚒ Bon

1927 Alvis 12/50 SD, coachwork by Carbodies, 1496cc overhead-valve 4-cylinder engine, 50bhp, engine and gearbox rebuilt, converted to full-flow oil system, 12 volt electrics, Marchal headlamps, additional driving lamps, black canvas hood and tonneau cover, side screens, dashboard retains original ivorine facing, full complement of Smiths instruments, interior including dickey seat trimmed in brown leather.
£30,000–35,000 / $43,500–50,750 ⚒ CGC

Founded in 1920, T. G. John Ltd, or Alvis as it later became known, quickly established itself as a force to be reckoned with in car, aero and military engineering. Its front-wheel-drive, all-independently-sprung racing cars of 1928 were a world first. Pioneer in production car design as well, the company introduced independent front suspension in 1933 and the world's first all-synchromesh, four-speed gearbox a year later. The dynamic force behind these innovations was Alvis' chief engineer, G. T. Smith Clarke, a man whose achievements match those of Henry Royce, W. O. Bentley and Alec Issigonis. It was Smith Clarke who relentlessly honed the 12/50 until it became one of the finest sports cars available in the vintage period, regardless of size or cost.

1956 Aston Martin DB2/4 Drophead Coupé, 3 litre double-overhead-camshaft 6-cylinder engine, 180bhp, 4-speed manual gearbox, independent front suspension, Girling front disc brakes, Alfin rear drums, recently restored, resprayed in original colour, dark blue leather interior.
£60,000–70,000 / $87,000–101,500 ⚒ RM

◄ **1961 Aston Martin DB4 Series III Vantage,** coachwork by Touring, 3670cc double-overhead-camshaft 6-cylinder engine, 4-speed manual gearbox with overdrive, independent coil-sprung wishbone front suspension, coil-sprung live rear axle located by Watts linkage and parallel trailing arms, 4-wheel disc brakes, factory uprated to Vantage specification, £30,000/$43,500 spent on restoration late 1980s, parchment hide upholstery, excellent condition throughout.
£44,000–48,000 / $63,800–69,600 ⚒ COYS
Third-series DB4s were only built in 1961; later that year, the fourth series appeared, some of which were built to Vantage specification, producing 266bhp. The original owner of this DB4 was so envious of the higher performance that he returned the car to Newport Pagnell to have the car uprated to Vantage specification.

1965 Aston Martin DB5, £35,000/$50,750 spent on recent restoration, correct automatic transmission and power steering, cream leather upholstery.
£65,000–70,000 / $94,250–101,500 ⚒ COYS

◄ **1990 Aston Martin Virage,** 6.3 litre all-alloy V8 engine, 4 valves per cylinder, 465bhp factory conversion, suspension and brakes uprated, body improved with Vantage styling front and rear, 18in spoked alloy wheels, black leather interior, fewer than 35,000 miles from new, very good overall condition.
£35,000–45,000
$50,750–65,250 ⚒ COYS

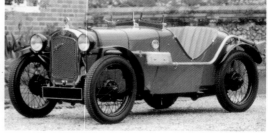

1930 Austin 7 TT Ulster-style Sports, modified running gear from 1929 model, period Luvax shock absorbers.
£9,000–11,000 / $13,000–16,000 ⚒ Bon
Encouraged by racing successes in 1929, Austin built a new team of Ulsters for 1930. The first of the big events that year was the JCC Double 12 in May, for which three works Ulsters were entered. Arthur Waite was paired with the Earl of March in a supercharged car, with Frazer Nash and Gunnar Poppe in a similar car, and the Barnes brothers in an unsupercharged version. This example has a pressurized re-created Ulster engine in the style of the Barnes brothers' car, purchased in 1963 over the telephone from a scrap dealer, just for the cylinder head. The scrap dealer was too lazy to remove the cylinder head, and when the whole engine was collected, it was found to be fitted with an Ulster sports cylinder head. Apart from the crankcase, the pressurized engine contained sports Austin parts, all for 30 shillings!

1928 Austin 7 Chummy, older restoration, new beige interior.
£5,000–6,000 / $7,250–8,700 ⚒ COYS
Considering the enormous success of the Austin 7, it is ironic that Sir Herbert Austin had to personally finance its development in the face of opposition from the Austin board. Despite a peak of £10 million/ $14.5 million turnover resulting from armaments production during WWI, the company had been forced into receivership in 1921 due to labour problems and a failed share flotation. With the 7, however, Austin became a pioneer of the light car, producing a model for the masses that was well built, reliable and inexpensive. This formula was continued throughout its long life until production ended in 1939.

1934 Austin 12/4 Berkeley Saloon, 1861cc 4-cylinder engine, 4-speed manual gearbox, brown leather upholstery, 2,000 miles recorded since restoration, very good condition throughout.
£7,000–9,000 / $10,200–13,000 ⚒ Bon

1954 Austin A30 Four-Door Saloon, 803cc 4-cylinder overhead-valve engine, 4-speed manual gearbox, good condition.
£2,000–2,500 / $3,000–3,600 🚗 AUS

1955 Austin-Healey 100/4, 2660cc 4-cylinder engine, twin SU H4 carburettors, 90bhp, 3-speed manual gearbox with overdrive on second and third gears, hydraulic disc front/drum rear brakes, completely restored.
£16,000–18,000 / $23,000–26,000 ⚒ Pou

1930 Bentley 6½ Litre Speed Six Drophead Coupé, coachwork by H. J. Mulliner, original engine, replacement chassis fitted in 1931, totally restored over 4 years at a cost of c£200,000/$290,000, concours winner, excellent condition throughout.
£300,000+ / $435,000+ ⚒ Bon
Although the 6½ Litre had been conceived as a touring car to compete with Rolls-Royce's New Phantom, in Speed Six form it proved admirably suited to competition: in 1929, Barnato/Birkin's Speed Six won the Le Mans 24-hour race ahead of a trio of 4½ Litre Bentleys, and Barnato/Kidston repeated the feat in the following year's Grand Prix d'Endurance at the Sarthe circuit, ahead of the similarly-mounted duo of Clement and Watney. The 6½ Litre was produced for four years, during which time 544 chassis were completed, 182 of them to Speed Six specification.

1937 Bentley 4¼ Litre Three-Position Drophead Coupé, coachwork by Gurney Nutting, overdrive, original coachwork, tan weather equipment and matching hide interior, engine rebuilt, 12,000 miles covered since, recent £6,000/$8,700 service.
£100,000–120,000 / $145,000–175,000 ⚒ COYS
The Bentley 4¼ Litre, introduced in 1936, was the last of the 1930s 'Rolls-Bentley' sporting cars. Although by the time it appeared W. O. Bentley had left the company to head design at Lagonda, the overall design followed the principles he had laid down. Bentley's company had been taken over by Rolls-Royce in 1931 (some say to stifle the 8 Litre Bentley, which promised to be stiff competition) and 'W.O.' was retained to supervise a new range of cars, which combined Rolls-Royce components with Bentley's sporting values. The result was advertised as 'The Silent Sports Car'. This particular car starred in the James Bond blockbuster *Never Say Never Again*, being driven by Sean Connery in several scenes.

1959 Bristol 406 Zagato, extensively refurbished, engine rebuilt, original triple Solex carburettors, interior trimmed in cream leather, 1 of only 6 built, very good overall condition.
£40,000–45,000 / $58,000–65,250 ➤ CGC
In 1947, the Bristol Aeroplane Company diversified into car production, making the most of its knowledge of aeronautical engineering and manufacturing practice. Thus, although the Bristol 400 was based on a pre-war BMW 326 chassis and 2 litre BMW 328 engine, it set new industry benchmarks for aerodynamics, stability and high-speed cruising ability – all qualities that Bristol considered to be as valid on the road as they were in the air. The 406, launched in 1958, was equipped with four-wheel disc brakes, while overdrive was standard on the manual gearbox. The straight-six engine, the last to be fitted to a Bristol, was enlarged to 2216cc and developed 105bhp. Zagato judged it the perfect platform for one of its designs, with characteristic 'double-bubble' roof. Thus, this particular car appeared on the Zagato stand at London's 1959 Motor Show.

1913 Bugatti Type 13 Two-Seat Voiturette, fully restored 1990s, virtually no use since, rebuilt engine with single Zenith carburettor, wire wheels plus set of original wooden wheels, 'Summa' brass headlamps, outside levers, single rear mounted spare wheel, lightweight competition coachwork, minimal instrumentation, wood-rimmed steering wheel, upholstered in buttoned black leather.
£40,000–50,000 / $58,000–72,500 ➤ Bon
Ettore Bugatti set up business at Molsheim in 1909, initially building light cars developed from the Type 10, which he had constructed in the cellar of his house. The 'Petit Pur Sang', Type 13, was built on a 79in (200cm) wheelbase chassis and had a four-cylinder, eight-valve engine, which had a onepiece cylinder block, mounted on an aluminium crankcase, and displaced 1327cc. Early examples had the flat-top radiator, but by 1913 the characteristic 'horseshoe' style had taken its place. At 6,000 francs for a chassis, Bugatti's jewel was expensive, but its performance justified the cost.

1936 Bugatti Type 57 Atalante Coupé, 3257cc 8-cylinder engine, completely restored to 'as new' condition.
£275,000+ / $398,750+ ➤ Bon
Launched in 1934, the Type 57 range gave Bugatti a civilized rival to the products from Alfa Romeo and Delahaye. Its success is revealed by the production figures: 680 examples of the various Type 57 models were built between 1934 and 1940, and the Type 57 chassis was the basis of the post-war Bugatti Type 101. One of the most extravagant body styles was the Atalante sports coupé. It set new design standards with its steeply raked windscreen, low roof, compact passenger cabin and long, sweeping tail. A two-seater, the Atalante was bodied either by the Bugatti factory or by the marque's preferred coachbuilder, Gangloff. This particular car features factory *toit ouvrable* coachwork, in which the fixed roof surround is equipped with a roll-back, bureau-style panel, allowing fresh-air motoring in summer and the comfort of a closed coupé in winter, while retaining the split rear window and roof profile of the standard Atalante. It is believed to have a long pre-war competition history, including appearances in the Liège-Rome-Liège Rally, the Rallye des Alpes and the Monte Carlo Rally.

◀ **1904 Cadillac Model B Surrey,** 4-seat coachwork, Surrey top, restored, many spare parts including original reconditioned radiator, purpose-built tandem-axle trailer, VCC dating certificate.
£27,000–32,000 / $39,000–46,500 ➤ Bon
Founded by Henry Leland and Robert Faulconer, the Cadillac Automobile Company of Detroit completed its first car in October 1902, the firm's superior manufacturing technology – precision gear cutting was a speciality – soon establishing it as the foremost builder of quality cars in the USA. The Cadillac's single-cylinder engine was mounted horizontally, beneath the front seat, and drove via a two-speeds-plus-reverse planetary transmission and chain drive to the rear axle. The first 1903 model curved-dash Cadillac continued for 1904 as the Model A, a more refined Model B with box-shaped 'bonnet', pressed-steel frame, I-beam front axle and transverse front spring being added at the same time.

1953 Cadillac Eldorado Convertible, 331cu.in overhead-valve V8 engine, 210bhp, 4-speed automatic transmission, unrestored, blue leather and white vinyl interior, c22,000 miles from new, original condition.
£65,000–70,000 / $94,250–101,500 ⚒ Bon

1959 Cadillac Eldorado Biarittz Convertible, 390cu.in overhead-valve V8 engine, Tri-Power induction system, 345bhp, automatic transmission, power steering and brakes, power top, windows and seats, air conditioning, c36,500 miles from new, 100 miles covered since engine rebuild.
£50,000–60,000 / $72,500–87,000 ⚒ Bon
In 1957, Chrysler's Virgil Exner had taken GM – and all of the automotive world – by surprise with the spectacular and trend-setting fins and airy greenhouse of its new cars, particularly the Fury. General Motors was accustomed to being the industry's style leader and was not happy about being out-styled by the Chrysler Corporation. As a result, bolder styling and taller fins were implemented throughout the GM ranges, but one car stood out from them all – the 1959 Cadillac Eldorado Biarittz.

1954 Chevrolet Corvette Custom Roadster, 327cu.in 1968 Corvette L79 V8 engine, Edelbrock 600S aluminium inlet manifold and dual 4-barrel carburettors, 350bhp, 4-speed manual gearbox, 1995 Corvette C4 4-wheel independent suspension and 4-wheel disc brakes, 1957-model bonnet, CenterLine aluminium wheels, custom instruments, 1957-model steering wheel, interior trimmed in red Connolly leather.
£90,000–100,000 / $130,500–145,000 ⚒ RM

The price paid for a car can vary according to the country in which it was sold. To discover where the car sold, cross reference the code at the end of each caption with the Key to Illustrations on page 332.

◄ **1911 Delage 10hp Three-Seat Voiturette,** 1592cc Ballot 4G sidevalve monobloc engine, radiator calormeter, Ducellier oil side lamps, oil rear lamp, acetylene BRC Lenticulaire Parabolique brass headlamps, double-twist bulb horn, brass rear-view mirror, 8-day clock, oil pressure gauge, alternative lightweight spyder seat for third passenger.
£11,000–13,000 / $16,000–18,750 ⚒ Bon
Production of the first Delage motor cars began in 1905, the earliest light cars being powered by a single-cylinder De Dion-type engine. These were marketed in Britain as the Baby Friswell. Early production concentrated on light cars, and Delage products enjoyed considerable success in voiturette racing. Delage used other proprietary engines from Chapuis-Dormier and Ballot before producing its own engines for all models.

1949 Delahaye 148L, coachwork by Antem, 3557cc 6-cylinder engine, triple carburettors, 130bhp, Cotal electro-mechanical 4-speed gearbox, 4-wheel cable-operated drum brakes, wire wheels.
£30,000–40,000 / $43,500–58,000 ⚒ Pou
In late 1935, Joseph Paul took delivery of a Delahaye 135 Competition, at the wheel of which he gained a respectable racing record, including a second place overall at Le Mans. In 1950, the car was fitted with a new body credited to Jean Antem, who was nicknamed 'the couturier of the sports car', and carried on racing successfully. In 1979, the car was restored to its original form, and in 1988 the Antem body was fitted to this 1949 Delahaye 148L chassis as part of a three-year restoration project.

1965 Ferrari 275 GTS Convertible, chassis no. 7799, 3286cc V12 engine, 3 Weber downdraft carburettors, 260bhp, 5-speed synchromesh gearbox, 4-wheel independent suspension, 4-wheel disc brakes, c£38,000/$55,100 spent within the last year, engine rebuilt, resprayed, brightwork excellent.
£100,000–110,000 / $145,000–159,500 ⚒ RM
Designed and built by Pininfarina, the 275 GTS shared its engine, chassis and suspension with Ferrari's contemporary berlinetta, the 275 GTB. With the latest 3.3 litre version of the alloy Colombo V12, the car also featured a five-speed transaxle mounted in unit with the rear axle for better weight distribution. The body was entirely new, having a cleaner and more muscular look, with open headlights, an 'egg-crate' grille and vents in the wings.

1987 Ferrari Testarossa, 4943cc flat-12 engine, Bosch fuel injection, 390bhp, 5-speed manual gearbox, 4-wheel independent suspension, 4-wheel ventilated disc brakes, right-hand drive, brown and tan interior, c7,500 miles and 2 owners from new, showing minor signs of age.
£35,000–45,000 / $50,750–65,250 ⚒ C
The Testarossa was the replacement for the BB series, which had run for 12 years. The 12-cylinder Boxer engine had been redesigned and retained only the displacement of its predecessor. With new four-valve heads, power and torque were increased, while fuel consumption was reduced. This particular Testarossa was given to Elton John by his record company, MCA, to celebrate his 40th birthday, at a party held at Lockwell House, in Rickmansworth. A large red ribbon and feather boa decorated the car.

1970 Fiat Abarth 595 SS, 594cc rear-mounted air-cooled twin-cylinder engine, 32bhp, 4-speed manual gearbox, 4-wheel independent suspension, drum brakes, left-hand drive, restored using a rust-free original Abarth shell, removable roof panel, correct engine, badging and main instrumentation, original black Nardi steering wheel, black interior.
£8,000–10,000 / $11,500–14,500 ⚒ C
The 595 SS was based on the Fiat 500, Abarth increasing the engine capacity to 594cc, just under the limit for the European 600cc racing saloon class. High-compression pistons were fitted together with a special camshaft, an alloy sump, and Abarth rocker covers and air filter. The engine cover was held open by a prop, while the exhaust system was a special Abarth item. This package, together with lowered suspension, flared arches and 10in rims, amounted to what was known as the Assetto Corsa SS model.

1923 Ford Model T Roadster 'Snow Machine', 2896cc 4-cylinder sidevalve engine, 20bhp, 2-speed planetary transmission, left-hand drive, fully restored, concours winner, excellent condition throughout.
£10,000–12,000 / $14,500–17,500 ✗ Bon
In addition to its ordinary road wheels, this car has the factory option of interchangeable front-axle mounted skis for use in snow.

1957 Ford Custom Wagon, 351cu.in Ford racing engine, aluminium cylinder heads, fuel injection, supercharger, 510bhp, Borg Warner 6-speed gearbox, 4-wheel air-bag suspension system, 12-point adjustable shock absorbers, 4-wheel disc brakes.
£80,000–90,000 / $116,000–130,500 ✗ BJ

1923 Hillman 11hp Speed Model Two-Seater, older restoration, CAV headlamps, Toby side lamps, one-piece folding windscreen, four-branch outside exhaust, rear-mounted spare wheel, running-board mounted tool and battery boxes, fawn duck hood, trimmed in antique black hide, museum-stored for 20 years, in need of recommissioning.
£8,000–9,000 / $11,500–13,000 ✗ Bon

1931 Ford Model A Slant-Windshield Cabriolet, 3.3 litre engine, dickey seat, completely restored early 1990s, fewer than 1,000 miles since, excellent condition throughout.
£10,000–11,000 / $14,500–16,000 ✗ Bon
Introduced in December 1927, the Model A Ford was of a more complex design than the Model T, but it featured a broadly conventional 3.3 litre, four-cylinder, 40bhp sidevalve engine, four-wheel brakes, and a new three-speed gearbox. No fewer than 4,500,000 Model As were manufactured and sold in just four years. This car is believed to be the only 'slant-windshield' example in the UK.

> The price paid for a car can vary according to the country in which it was sold. To discover where the car sold, cross reference the code at the end of each caption with the Key to Illustrations on page 332.

1966 Ford Shelby GT 350 Mustang Convertible, 289cu.in V8 engine, 306bhp, 4-speed manual gearbox, independent front suspension, concours condition.
£110,000–130,000 / $159,500–188,500 ✗ RM
Ford was quick to recognize the good that Carroll Shelby had done for its image with his Cobras. Initially, the GT 350 was conceived as a way of improving the stature of the Mustang, which was facing stiff competition as the muscle car wars began to heat up. As a result, the 1965 models were thinly disguised racing cars with stiff suspension, competition brakes and few creature comforts. Although they were successful on the track, it soon became apparent that road cars needed to be more user-friendly, so for 1966 a host of revisions softened the hard edges, creating a legendary street machine. A convertible was never offered officially, but four experimental soft-tops were built by Shelby to evaluate convertible production for the following year. All were highly optioned and included air conditioning – a feature not even available on the coupés. They were retained by Shelby and used by him and his staff before being sold as used cars. This example is one of only two equipped with four-speed manual gearboxes, and the only red convertible built.

◄ **1934 Hillman 9.8hp Aero Minx Streamline Saloon,** sliding sunshine roof, individual front seats with occasional rear seat, sunburst-pattern door panels, beige interior, restored, thought to be sole surviving unmodified example.
£10,000–12,000 / $14,500–17,500 ✗ Bon
The two-door Aero Minx Streamline Saloon adopted the 10/30hp engine of the Hillman Minx, uprated with a high-compression cylinder head and Stromberg downdraught carburettor. The chassis was much modified to accommodate the low seating position and the sleek streamlined body, being upswept at the front and downswept at the rear. The coachwork was designed to achieve optimum aerodynamics. Extra-long front and rear semi-elliptic springs and hydraulic shock absorbers gave good road-holding.

◀ **1933 Jaguar SS1 Coupé,** restored mid-1980s, very good condition.
£25,000–30,000 / $36,000–43,500 ⚡ COYS
The SS1 was Sir William Lyons' first venture into outright car manufacture, and represented a massive leap from his previous work producing bespoke coachbuilt bodies for motorcycle sidecars and production car chassis from established manufacturers. The model demonstrated Lyons' styling flair, soon to become a feature of every SS and Jaguar model until his retirement.

1955 Jaguar XK140 Roadster, completely restored mid-1990s, C-type cylinder head, twin exhausts, chrome wire wheels, twin fog lamps, tonneau cover, interior trimmed in biscuit leather.
£35,000–40,000 / $50,750–58,000 ⚡ COYS
The XK140 was introduced in 1954 as the successor to the XK120. It was easily distinguishable from its predecessor because of its more substantial front and rear bumpers, a radiator grille with fewer slats and a chrome strip that ran along the centre of the bonnet and boot. Under the bonnet, the XK140 had a superb 3.4 litre six-cylinder engine, which was basically the same as the Special Equipment XK120 unit and thus capable of producing 190bhp at 5,600rpm, compared to the 160bhp of the standard XK120. Like the XK120, however, the XK140 had independent front suspension, but it was fitted with rack-and-pinion steering, which marked a huge improvement.

1969 Jaguar E-Type Series II Coupé, 4235cc double-overhead-camshaft 6-cylinder engine, 246bhp, 4-speed manual gearbox, 4-wheel independent suspension, 4-wheel disc brakes, professionally restored, carburettors rebuilt, new radiator core and fans, suspension bushings and most rubber parts replaced, braking system rebuilt, fuel tank cleaned and sealed, bare-metal respray, chrome and brightwork replaced or replated as necessary, new interior trim and carpets.
£16,000–18,000 / $23,000–26,000 ⚡ RM

1964 Jaguar E-Type Coupé, 3781cc, complete ground-up restoration in 1991, 2,500 miles since, cylinder head converted for unleaded fuel, 47,800 miles and 3 owners from new.
£16,000–18,000 / $23,000–26,000 ⚡ H&H

1993 Jaguar XJ220, 3498cc double-overhead-camshaft V6 engine, aluminium cylinder heads and block, 4 valves per cylinder, twin turbochargers, 542bhp, 5-speed all-synchromesh gearbox, 4-wheel independent suspension by unequal-length wishbones, inboard coil springs with dampers and anti-roll bars, 4-wheel ventilated and cross-drilled outboard disc brakes with 4-pot calipers, 1 of only 80 built, owned from new by Elton John, fewer than 900 miles recorded.
£120,000–140,000 / $174,000–203,000 ⚡ C
In 1988, after four years of development, Jaguar announced that it would be using the knowledge gained in racing to launch its own supercar, a prototype of the XJ220 appearing at the Birmingham Autoshow. The design featured a fuel-injected, 48-valve, 530bhp V12 engine and four-wheel drive. When Jaguar was bought by Ford in 1989, it was decided that the project should be put into production by Tom Walkinshaw's Jaguar Sport division. However, the practicality of the prototype did not lend itself to a road car, so instead it was decided that the 530bhp would come from a twin-turbo 3.5 litre V6 that had been developed in the Group C XJR-10 and 11 race cars, and that it would be transferred to the road conventionally by two wheels rather than four. Production began in 1992. Built on an aluminium-honeycomb chassis, the finely sculpted bodywork was also constructed in lightweight aluminium. The powerful twin-turbo V6 engine could be seen through a glass panel, and the layout limited luggage space at the rear of the body to just enough for a briefcase, tool kit and CD player. This was not matched by the passenger area, however, as the cockpit was designed to be purposeful, yet spacious; there was ample headroom for even the tallest of pilots, and creature comforts included air conditioning and full leather upholstery.

Cadillac

Almost from its very beginnings in 1902, the name Cadillac has stood for prestige motoring, and in the luxury-car market this General Motors flagship marque has often set the standards for others to follow. In 1912, Cadillac fitted electric lighting as standard on its 5.5 litre four-cylinder model; in 1914, it introduced its first V8 engine, which has remained a feature of the marque ever since. In 1930, the extravagant V16 arrived, followed closely by the V12 models, in both cases styled by Harley Earl, who went on to create the ultimate American post-war automotive styling statements with fins, chrome and bullet-shaped bumpers.

◀ c1904 Cadillac Single-Cylinder Open Two-Seater, correct carburettor, artillery wheels, brass lamp, finished in red, black interior, running.
£6,000–7,000 / $8,700–10,200 ⚒ H&H

1929 Cadillac Series 341-B Victoria Coupé, coachwork by Fisher, 5.3 litre engine, left-hand drive, wire wheels, older restoration, recent engine and gearbox rebuild, brakes refurbished, chassis overhauled, chrome replated, correct mascot, windscreen sunvisor and V8 script, original instruments, nickel candlelight courtesy lights, light green cloth interior and grey carpets.
£15,000–18,000 / $21,750–26,000 ⚒ Bon
The first V8 Cadillac left the production line in 1915, and from the very outset this simple sidevalve unit captured a large slice of the luxury-car market, some 13,000 of the new 1915 Type 51 finding satisfied buyers. Production concentrated exclusively on V8 cars throughout the 1920s. The late 1920s saw an update in Cadillac design and styling under the guidance of Harley Earl, and no fewer than 12 production bodies by Fisher were offered for the 1929 season, with another 33 bespoke styles offered by Fleetwood. The 341-B of 1929 was particularly notable for the introduction on that model of Earl Thompson's 'Synchro-Mesh' gearbox, a feature that was soon to be standard in world-wide car production. Duplex-Mechanical brakes with all shoes internal were also adopted. Modifications to the engine included drilling the connecting rods to provide pressure lubrication to the little ends.

1926 Cadillac Series 314 Golfer Roadster, coachwork by Fisher, 314.5cu.in sidevalve V8 engine, 80bhp, 3-speed manual gearbox, leaf-spring suspension, 4-wheel drum brakes, left-hand drive, 132in (335.5cm) wheelbase, radiator with thermostatically controlled shutters and Motometer, older restoration, finished in maroon with black wings, brown interior, paintwork chipped, brightwork generally in good condition, light scratching to windscreen, interior showing signs of age, little recent use, in need of recommissioning.
£30,000–35,000 / $43,500–50,750 ⚒ C

CADILLAC (pre-war) Model	ENGINE cc/cyl	DATES	CONDITION		
			1	2	3
Type 57–61	5153/8	1915–23	£20,000+	£14,000	£6,000
Series 314	5153/8	1926–27	£22,000	£15,000	£6,000
Type V63	5153/8	1924–27	£20,000	£13,000	£5,000
Series 341	5578/8	1928–29	£22,000+	£15,000+	£6,000
Series 353–5	5289/8	1930–31	£50,000+	£30,000	£18,000
V16	7406/16	1931–32	£80,000+	£50,000+	£20,000
V12	6030/12	1932–37	£42,000+	£25,000	£15,000
V8	5790/8	1935–36	£30,000+	£15,000	£6,000
V16	7034/16	1937–40	£50,000+	£30,000	£18,000

1939 Cadillac Series 90 V16 Convertible Sedan, restored, 1 of 19 built, very good condition.
£60,000–70,000 / $87,000–101,500 ⚒ BJ

1941 Cadillac Series 62 Convertible Sedan, complete body and frame restoration 1999–2000, convertible top cover missing.
£32,000–36,000 / $46,500–52,000 ⚒ BJ

1941 Cadillac Fleetwood Limousine, 345cu.in sidevalve V8 engine, 150bhp, 3-speed manual gearbox with column change, hydraulic brakes, partition, unrestored, finished in dark grey, original mohair trim and interior wood in good condition, footrails and rear reading lights intact, retains original notepad and special user's guide with 'war-time suggestions', fewer than 83,000 miles from new.
£18,000–22,000 / $26,000–32,000 ⚒ Bon

1954 Cadillac Eldorado Convertible, 331cu.in overhead-valve V8 engine, 230bhp, 4-speed automatic transmission, power steering, power brakes, power top and windows, completely restored, finished in red, white leather interior.
£30,000–35,000 / $43,500–50,750 ⚒ Bon

1955 Cadillac Series 62 Sedan, 6-seat coachwork, finished in black, grey interior, 2 owners and c39,000 miles from new, original under-bonnet General Motors certificate of ownership.
£7,000–9,000 / $10,200–13,000 ⚒ Bon

1957 Cadillac Eldorado Seville, power brakes, refurbished at a cost of c£3,500/$5,000, bare-metal respray, new Everflex roof, new exhaust, rear bumpers rechromed, finished in red with white roof, white, grey and black interior trim, power seats, air conditioning.
£11,000–13,000 / $16,000–18,850 ⚒ COYS
In 1956, Cadillac introduced the hardtop version of the Eldorado, naming it the Seville, while the Eldorado convertible became the Biarritz. That year, the Eldorado coachwork was given a facelift with a finer textured grille and parking lights that had been moved below the bumper guards. In 1957, the engine capacity was increased to produce 325bhp, and the body restyled to include longer tapering fins and black rubber-tipped bumper guards raised to the top of the grille. The goddess mascot was replaced by the stylized V-shaped emblem synonymous with Cadillacs of this era.

◀ **1959 Cadillac Series 62 Convertible,**
complete professional restoration,
excellent condition.
£30,000–35,000 / $43,500–50,750 ⚒ BJ

Cross Reference
See Colour Review (page 68–9)

Miller's Compares

◀ **I. 1959 Cadillac Coupe De Ville,** 390cu.in overhead-valve V8 engine, 325bhp, automatic transmission, power brakes, power steering, power windows, resprayed in original pale yellow 1970s, white leather interior, unrestored, 2 owners and fewer than 56,000 miles from new.
£14,000–16,000
$20,300–23,300 ⚒ Bon

▶ **II. 1959 Cadillac Series 62 Two-Door Coupé,** 6400cc V8 engine, left-hand drive, recently resprayed in dark green, original beige interior, excellent condition.
£7,000–9,000
$10,200–13,000 ⚒ H&H

Same year, same model, but different values. Car I's higher valuation is due to several factors, including exceptional originality, complete documented history and all-round outstanding condition. But there's also another factor at play: Car I was sold in the USA, while car II was bought in the UK. With bigger roads, more space and much lower fuel prices, cars such as these are far more viable and less demanding to run in the USA than in the UK. In the UK, you'd need a deep wallet to run a big V8 gas-guzzler as an every-day car, hence the lower demand.

CADILLAC Model	ENGINE cu. in/cyl	DATES	CONDITION 1	2	3
4-door sedan	331/8	1949	£8,000	£4,500	£3,000
2-door fastback	331/8	1949	£10,000	£8,000	£5,000
Convertible Coupe	331/8	1949	£22,000	£12,000	£10,000
Series 62 4-door	331/365/8	1950–55	£7,000	£5,500	£3,000
Sedan de Ville	365/8	1956–58	£8,000	£6,000	£4,000
Coupe de Ville	331/365/8	1950–58	£12,500	£9,500	£3,500
Convertible Coupe	331/365/8	1950–58	£25,000	£20,000	£10,000
Eldorado	331/8	1953–55	£35,000	£30,000	£18,000
Eldorado Seville	365/8	1956–58	£11,500	£9,000	£5,500
Eldorado Biarritz	365/8	1956–58	£30,000	£20,000	£15,000
Sedan de Ville	390/8	1959	£12,000	£9,500	£5,000
Coupe de Ville	390/8	1959	£15,000	£9,000	£5,500
Convertible Coupe	390/8	1959	£28,000	£20,000	£10,000
Eldorado Seville	390/8	1959	£13,000	£10,000	£6,000
Eldorado Biarritz	390/8	1959	£45,000+	£25,000	£15,000
Sedan de Ville	390/8	1960	£10,000	£8,000	£4,500
Convertible Coupe	390/8	1960	£27,000+	£14,000	£7,500
Eldorado Biarritz	390/8	1960	£25,000+	£17,000	£10,000
Sedan de Ville	390/429/8	1961–64	£7,000	£5,000	£3,000
Coupe de Ville	390/429/8	1961–64	£8,000	£6,000	£4,000
Convertible Coupe	390/429/8	1961–64	£20,000	£9,000	£7,000
Eldorado Biarritz	390/429/8	1961–64	£19,500	£14,000	£9,000

◄ **1979 Cadillac Seville Gucci Limited Edition,** 5.7 litre V8 engine, automatic transmission, front-wheel drive, 1 of 25 cars produced, 71,000 miles from new, good overall condition.
£2,800–3,400 / $4,000–5,000 ✗ CGC
Introduced in 1975, the Seville was Cadillac's response to the encroachment of BMW, Mercedes-Benz, Jaguar and Volvo upon its sales territory. The company's first 'compact', it had crisp, simple lines and 'European' proportions. Thus, it was 900lb (408kg) lighter, 8in (20.3cm) narrower and 27in (68.6cm) shorter than its most popular sibling, the De Ville. This particular example is a limited edition built in conjunction with fashion emporium Gucci. Its brown leather interior is offset by the use of Gucci cloth for the headlining and head and armrest inserts. The car's white paintwork carries a red and green (Gucci colours) coachline.

Calcott

▶ **1914 Calcott 10.5hp Two-Seater,** electric starter, alternator, acetylene headlamps, bulb horn, hood, finished in dark blue, brown leather upholstery, VCC dated, good mechanical condition.
£9,000–11,000 / $13,000–16,000 ✗ Bon
Calcott was one of a profusion of small car manufacturers that sprang up in the Midlands in the pre-WWI years. It competed with the likes of Stellite, GWK and Calthorpe, and its products closely resembled the Standard light cars of the time, which were also built in Coventry. The 10.5hp model was the most successful commercially and was powered by a 1242cc four-cylinder engine.

Caterham

◄ **1985 Caterham 7,** 1600cc Ford 4-cylinder crossflow engine, twin 45DCOE Weber carburettors, full weather equipment, 1 owner and 36,000 miles from new, completely original.
£9,000–11,000 / $13,000–16,000 ⊞ VIC

1991 Caterham 7 Special Edition, 1 owner and fewer than 15,000 miles from new, original authentification document, excellent condition throughout.
£10,000–12,000 / $14,500–17,500 ✗ COYS
When ITC and Patrick McGoohan devised the revolutionary spy fantasy *The Prisoner* in 1966, there was no more suitable car for 'Number 6', McGoohan's lead character, to drive than a Lotus 7. Such is the link between the 7 and *The Prisoner* that, over the years, green with a yellow nosecone has become one of the most popular colour schemes for the car. To meet this continued demand, Caterham Cars, which took over production of the 7 from Lotus in the early 1970s, launched a special edition to commemorate the 30-year association of the 7 with *The Prisoner*. Patrick McGoohan gave his blessing and endorsement to the project. This car is only the eighth example produced (appropriately, Number 6 was given to Patrick McGoohan).

1985 Caterham 7 Supersprint, 1700cc engine, 150bhp, 4-speed Graham Sykes gearbox, Quaiffe limited-slip differential, enlarged radiator, 13in alloy wheels, immobiliser, long-cockpit version, increased-vision weather equipment, tonneau cover, electrically heated windscreen, finished in red, black cloth adjustable seats, 4-point seat belts, heater, engine recently rebuilt.
£7,500–8,500 / $11,000–12,300 ✗ H&H

Chevrolet

General Motors' mainstay brand takes its name from Swiss-born racing driver Louis Chevrolet. In the early years of the 20th century, Louis worked for, among others, De Dion Bouton in New York. But the real prime mover behind Chevrolet was the charismatic chancer William C. Durant who, in 1910, had lost control of General Motors, the firm he'd founded in 1908, and immediately had begun making his comeback. In 1911, he set up his new company,

naming it after Chevrolet, who helped design the first car. Chevrolet had left the business by 1913, but by 1916 Durant's fortunes had soared so dramatically that his company actually bought General Motors. However, by 1920, as the post-war depression took hold, Durant lost both Chevrolet and General Motors. His legacy, though, is a marque that ever since has run a steady course right through the mainstream of American motoring.

1927 Chevrolet Superior B1 Tourer, 2500cc 4-cylinder engine, 3-speed manual gearbox, right-hand drive, original Autovac, barrel speedometer, extensively restored, bare-metal respray in yellow and black, new weather equipment, new maroon interior, excellent condition.
£8,000–10,000 / $11,500–14,500 ✗ H&H

▶ **1934 Chevrolet Standard Phaeton,** right-hand drive, new kingpins, brakes overhauled, new wiper motor, finished in beige, brown interior, 1 of 234 built, believed to be South African export model, good condition.
£6,500–8,000 / $9,500–11,500 ✗ COYS

A known continuous history can add value to and enhance the enjoyment of a car.

1927 Chevrolet Capitol Four-Door Sedan, 3000cc 4-cylinder engine, left-hand drive, finished in white and black, blue interior, 41,000 miles from new, excellent condition throughout.
£5,000–6,000 / $7,250–8,750 ✗ H&H

1928 Chevrolet National Model AB Roadster, 2802cc 4-cylinder engine, disc wheels with detachable rims, right-hand drive, finished in red with black wings, good mechanical condition.
£6,000–7,000 / $8,700–10,200 ✗ BRIT
For the 1928 season, the Chevrolet range comprised eight different models, including a two-seat roadster, a coupé, a cabriolet and three different varieties of sedan. In fact, 1928 was the last year that Chevrolet was to use four-cylinder engines, as the trend towards sixes was becoming firmly established.

1948 Chevrolet Fleetline Aero Sedan, right-hand drive, interior retrimmed, otherwise unrestored, excellent condition.
£9,000–11,000 / $13,000–16,000 ✗ Bon
A sub-division of Chevrolet's range-topping Special Deluxe Series, the Fleetline was introduced early in 1941 the last full year of automobile production before the attack on Pearl Harbour ushered the USA into WWII. The late 1930s and early 1940s had seen an increasing interest on the part of car designers in streamlined models, reflecting developments in the aircraft industry, and this trend was exemplified by the new-for-1942 Fleetline Aero Sedan. Like the rest of the Chevrolet range, the fastback-styled Aero was powered by the company's famous 'stovebolt' overhead-valve six, an engine it would continue to use when production resumed after the war's end.

1951 Chevrolet Fleetline Deluxe Sedan, 6-cylinder engine, 3-speed manual gearbox, left-hand drive, restored, finished in red, black and gold interior, good condition throughout.
£8,000–10,000 / $11,500–14,500 ➤ **Bon**
In 1949, the Fleetline look was extended to Chevrolet's Special (basic) Series, and both series would feature Styleline (notchback) and Fleetline versions from then until the end of 1952, when the fastback body style was dropped.

A brass desk stand, based on a Chevrolet saloon, with enclosed fitted trays, 1940s, 10in (25.5cm) long.
£100–120 / $145–175 ➤ **G(L)**

◀ **1951 Chevrolet Station Wagon,** 216.5cu.in overhead-valve 6-cylinder engine, 92bhp, 3-speed manual gearbox with column change, 4-wheel hydraulic drum brakes, independent front suspension, heater, complete, sound running condition.
£2,500–3,000 / 3,500–4,400 ➤ **Bon**

1952 Chevrolet Styleline Deluxe Convertible, overhead-valve 6-cylinder engine, 3-speed manual gearbox, restored, finished in maroon, maroon and grey interior, noisy gearbox, otherwise good condition.
£10,000–12,000 / $14,500–17,500 ➤ **Bon**

▶ **1953 Chevrolet Two-Ten Four-Door Sedan,** 3860cc 6-cylinder engine, 115bhp, 3-speed manual gearbox, left-hand drive, restored, finished in cream and brown, beige and brown interior, fewer than 80,000 miles from new, excellent condition throughout.
£4,000–5,000 / $5,800–7,250 ➤ **H&H**

◀ **1955 Chevrolet Bel Air Hardtop,** original 265cu.in overhead-valve V8 engine, 163bhp, original 2-speed automatic transmission, finished in coral and grey.
£13,000–15,000 $18,750–21,750 ➤ **Bon**

CHEVROLET Model	ENGINE cc/cyl	DATES	CONDITION 1	2	3
H4/H490 K Series	2801/4	1914–29	£9,000	£5,000	£2,000
FA5	2699/4	1918	£8,000	£5,000	£2,000
D5	5792/8	1918–19	£10,000	£6,000	£3,000
FB50	3660/4	1919–21	£7,000	£4,000	£2,000
AA	2801/4	1928–32	£5,000	£3,000	£1,000
AB/C	3180/6	1929–36	£6,000	£4,000	£2,000
Master	3358/6	1934–37	£9,000	£5,000	£2,000
Master De Luxe	3548/6	1938–41	£9,000	£6,000	£4,000

1957 Chevrolet Bel Air Convertible, 283cu.in V8 engine, solid valve lifters, twin 4-barrel carburettors, 245bhp, automatic transmission, power brakes, power steering, power seats and top, factory continental kit, optional gold trim, spinner wheel covers, fin-mounted aerials, finished in original metallic blue, pale blue vinyl top and top cover, deluxe two-tone blue buttoned interior, 329 miles from new.
£25,000–30,000 / $36,250–43,500 ⚡ Bon

Miller's is a price GUIDE not a price LIST

1957 Chevrolet Bel Air Convertible, automatic transmission, power steering, continental kit, professionally restored, 98 miles covered since, finished in correct red, original radio, concours winner.
£30,000–35,000 / $43,500–50,750 ⚡ BJ

▶ **1962 Chevrolet Chevy II Nova Two-Door Convertible,** automatic transmission, finished in white, red interior, good to very good condition.
£4,000–5,000 / $5,800–7,250 ⚡ Bon
Introduced to compete with Ford's Falcon in the increasingly important 'compact' market, the Chevy II appeared in 1962. Of unitary construction and with no-frills styling, the Chevy II range comprised no fewer than 11 different models available with either four- or six-cylinder engines and an extensive range of options. Top of the range were the five Nova models: two sedans, a coupé, a station wagon and a convertible, all of which came with the new 194.4cu.in overhead-valve six-cylinder engine as standard. The Novas incorporated all the lower models' standard fittings plus enhanced interior trim.

◀ **1969 Chevrolet Nova SS 396 Coupé,** 396cu.in Turbo Jet V8 engine, 375bhp, 4-speed manual gearbox, power brakes, Rallye wheels, finished in red with black vinyl roof.
£14,000–16,000 / $20,500–23,200 ⚡ BJ

1966 Chevrolet Chevelle SS 396 Coupé, 396cu.in Turbo Jet V8 engine, 360bhp, complete chassis-up restoration, fewer than 1,000 miles since, alloy wheels, finished in metallic turquoise.
£13,000–15,000 / $18,750–21,750 ⚒ BJ

1969 Chevrolet Chevelle SS 396 Coupé, 396cu.in V8 engine, 4-barrel carburettor, automatic transmission with console-mounted shifter, power brakes, chrome Rallye wheels.
£11,000–13,000 / $16,000–18,850 ⚒ BJ

◀ **1970 Chevrolet Chevelle LS-6 Convertible,** 454cu.in LS-6 V8 engine, 450bhp, M22 4-speed manual gearbox, fully optioned, matching numbers, restored, complete with original build sheets, window sticker and sales contract, thought to be 1 of only 17 LS-6 convertibles built.
£115,000–130,000
$166,750–188,500 ⚒ BJ
A noted motoring journalist wrote of the LS-6, 'Driving an LS-6 Chevelle is like being the guy who's in charge of triggering atom bomb tests. You have the power, you know you have the power and you know that if you use that power, bad things may happen.'

1969 Chevrolet Camaro SS Convertible, 396cu.in. V8 engine, TH400 automatic transmission, correct chassis and engine numbers, bare-metal respray in correct dusk blue, 70,000 miles from new, concours winner.
£11,000–13,000 / $16,000–18,850 ⚒ CGC

Cross Reference
See Colour Review (page 69)

1969 Chevrolet Camaro ZL-1 Coupé, 4-speed manual gearbox, 1 of only 4 finished originally in white.
£80,000–90,000 / $116,000–130,000 ⚒ BJ
For the 1969 model year, Chevrolet agreed to build a series of ultra-high-performance Camaros for drag racing. To qualify for the Super Stock classification, 50 examples needed to be built. Eventually, production reached a total of 69. The specification called for the use of Chevrolet's 427cu.in ZL-1 aluminium engine, previously used in Can-Am racing. This was offered as the ZL-1 performance package. The Camaro cost £1,900/$2,727; the ZL-1 package added £2,900/$4,160 to the bill.

1969 Chevrolet Camaro SS 396 Coupé, 396cu.in V8 engine, 350bhp, close-ratio 4-speed manual gearbox, Positraction 3:73:1 12-bolt rear axle, front and rear spoiler package.
£12,000–14,000 / $17,500–20,500 ⚒ BJ

1954 Chevrolet Corvette Coupé, coachwork by Ghia Aigle, 235cu.in overhead-valve 6-cylinder engine, 150bhp, 2-speed automatic transmission, 4-wheel drum brakes, chrome Borrani wire wheels, aluminium body, fog lamps, Veglia instruments, unrestored, black leather interior, 2 owners and fewer than 2,500 miles from new.
£30,000–35,000 / $43,500–50,750 ➤ RM
One of the last cars created by Michellotti for Ghia Aigle, this 1954 Corvette coupé was created for a Portuguese client in 1957. It was displayed on the Ghia Aigle stand at the Geneva Show that year.

◄ **1955 Chevrolet Corvette,** 265cu.in V8 engine, 195bhp, restored 1991, museum displayed for last 5 years, oldest surviving V8-engined Corvette production model.
£80,000–90,000 / $116,000–130,500 ➤ BJ

► **1956 Chevrolet Corvette,** V8 engine, twin 4-barrel carburettors, 240bhp, automatic transmission, Positraction rear axle, spinner wheel covers, powered soft top, hardtop, unrestored apart from older respray in original metallic blue with silver side coves, original beige vinyl interior in excellent condition, Wonder Bar radio, very original.
£19,000–22,000 / $27,500–32,000 ➤ Bon
Despite the fact that all 1956 Corvettes were V8 powered and shared the same basic two-door convertible body, the colour and options lists allowed for many different configurations. Available engines included the standard 210bhp, 265cu.in unit with single four-barrel carburettor, and two twin-carburettor engines, offering 225bhp and 240bhp. Transmission choices included the standard three-speed manual gearbox, and optional four-speed manual or two-speed Power Glide automatic.

Chevrolet Corvette (1953 onwards)

The glassfibre 'plastic fantastic' was born in 1953 and started as a creeper, slowly gathering momentum and mutating with moving tastes through four decades of manufacture. In 1992, the 'Vette notched up a million sales and is still going strong. What's more, unlike Ford's Mustang and Thunderbird, the curvy Corvette has kept faith with its sports-car roots. Today, the latest Corvette is a true modern supercar, yet with its long nose and aggressive lines, it reveals its lineage as surely as any sporting Jaguar. Whether it's a 1960s Sting Ray or a definitive flame-red 1950s model, these glassfibre fantasies proudly wave the star-spangled banner as America's native sports car.
Pick of the bunch: All Corvette fanciers have their favourite eras. For some, it's the purity of the very first generation from 1953; others prefer the glamorous 1956–62 models; but for many, the

Corvette came of age in 1963 with the birth of the menacing Sting Ray. Most valuable are the early and very rare 1953–54 cars, although they're mechanically mundane with an ancient 'stovebolt' six-cylinder engine.
For: Just about any classic Corvette will have bystanders cooing at its curves. It has the advantage, too, of mass-produced stock mechanicals clothed in an exotic show-car skin.
Against: They're strictly for extroverts only and can bring on a fit of anti-American fervour. In short, they're over-sexed, over-thirsty and over here.
Famous Corvette owners: John Wayne, Dinah Shore, William Shatner, Swedish former world heavyweight boxing champion Ingemar Johansson, Shirley Bassey, all of The Beach Boys, all the original Mercury 7 astronauts, the crew of Apollo 12, Jools Holland.

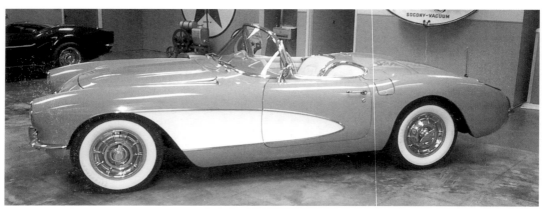

1957 Chevrolet Corvette, 283cu.in overhead-valve V8 engine, twin 4-barrel carburettors, 270bhp, 4-speed manual gearbox, coil-springs independent front suspension, rigid rear axle on semi-elliptic leaf springs, 4-wheel hydraulic drum brakes, hard and soft tops, matching numbers, completely restored early 1990s, fewer than 1,000 miles since, 31,500 miles from new.
£60,000–65,000 / $87,000–94,250 ↗ RM

1958 Chevrolet Corvette, 283 cu.in V8 engine, Ramjet fuel injection, 290bhp, 4-speed manual gearbox, 4-wheel hydraulic drum brakes, soft top, restored, finished in two-tone grey, red leather interior.
£30,000–35,000 / $43,500–50,750 ↗ Pou

1958 Chevrolet Corvette, 283cu.in V8 engine, 270bhp, hard and soft tops, restored to original specification.
£34,000–38,000 / $50,000–65,000 ↗ BJ

1960 Chevrolet Corvette, 4.7 litre V8 engine, fuel injection, 4-speed manual gearbox, hard and soft tops, finished in blue and white.
£27,000–30,000 / $39,000–43,500 ⊞ COR

1963 Chevrolet Corvette Sting Ray Roadster, 5.4 litre V8 engine, 4-speed manual gearbox, hard and soft tops, extensively restored, finished in silver.
£20,000–23,000 / $30,000–33,500 ⊞ COR

1966 Chevrolet Corvette Sting Ray Roadster, 427cu.in V8 engine, 425bhp, 4-speed manual gearbox, 4-wheel independent suspension, Positraction rear axle, 4-wheel ventilated disc brakes, centre-lock aluminium wheels, side exhaust pipes, tinted windows, black vinyl top, original interior, excellent condition.
£20,000–25,000 / $30,000–36,250 ✗ Pou

1966 Chevrolet Corvette Sting Ray Coupé, 327cu.in V8 engine, 350bhp, 4-speed manual gearbox, centre-lock alloy wheels, side exhaust pipes, finished in metallic light blue.
£15,000–17,000 / $21,750–24,750 ✗ BJ

1967 Chevrolet Corvette Sting Ray Coupé, 427cu.in V8 engine, tri-power carburation, 400bhp, 4-speed manual gearbox, 4-wheel disc brakes, 4-wheel independent suspension, power steering, power windows, air conditioning, professionally restored, fewer than 3,000 miles since, finished in Goodwood green, all parts correctly date coded to 1967, excellent condition throughout.
£33,000–37,000 / $48,000–53,750 ✗ RM

1968 Chevrolet Corvette L88 Coupé, 427cu.in V8 engine, 430bhp, 4-speed manual gearbox, 4-wheel disc brakes, 4-wheel independent suspension, resprayed in Le Mans blue, black interior, 1 of only 77 built with L88 engine, used as pace car at Donnington Motor Speedway, Minnesota, unrestored, original.
£50,000–55,000 / $72,500–80,000 ✗ RM
Originally, the new Corvette body style introduced in 1968 had been intended for 1967 production. However, delays forced the continuation of the Sting Ray for one more year. Corvette designers were instructed to carry out a minor facelift for these interim 1967 models. There were several changes to the engine line-up, including the legendary L71 435bhp tri-power 'big block' unit. Most performance buyers chose this option, assuming that it was the most powerful engine on offer. What they didn't know was that Chevrolet had hidden an even more potent option in the catalogue. The L88 engine was listed as a 430bhp option for $947.90, more than twice the price of the 435bhp L71 engine. The L88 engine featured an aluminium inlet manifold and heads, an 850cfm dual-feed Holley carburettor, transistorized ignition and 12:1 compression. In addition, the L88 package included an aluminium radiator, heavy-duty brakes and suspension, and the Muncie M22 'rock crusher' gearbox. A special cowl-induction bonnet was fitted. Although rated at 430bhp, the L88 is widely recognised as producing in excess of 500bhp – making an L88 model capable of 170mph, right off the showroom floor. Intended to homologate the engine for racing, the L88 offering was kept quiet, with the factory and dealers actively discouraging orders by the public. Although introduced in 1967, the L88 continued to be available until 1969, making it the most desirable of the next generation of Corvettes. With only 213 cars built, it is also one of the rarest.

CHEVROLET Model	ENGINE cu.in/cyl	DATES	CONDITION 1	2	3
Stylemaster	216/6	1942–48	£8,000	£4,000	£1,000
Fleetmaster	216/6	1942–48	£8,000	£4,000	£1,000
Fleetline	216/6	1942–51	£8,000	£5,000	£2,000
Styleline	216/6	1949–52	£8,000	£6,000	£2,000
Bel Air 4-door	235/6	1953–54	£6,000	£4,000	£3,000
Bel Air Sport Coupe	235/6	1953–54	£7,000	£4,500	£3,500
Bel Air convertible	235/6	1953–54	£12,500	£9,500	£6,000
Bel Air 4-door	283/8	1955–57	£8,000	£4,000	£3,000
Bel Air Sport Coupe	283/8	1955–56	£11,000	£7,000	£4,000
Bel Air convertible	283/8	1955–56	£16,000	£11,000	£7,000
Bel Air Sport Coupe	283/8	1957	£11,000	£7,500	£4,500
Bel Air convertible	283/8	1957	£22,000+	£15,000+	£8,000
Impala Sport Sedan	235/6, 348/8	1958	£12,500	£9,000	£5,500
Impala convertible	235/6, 348/8	1958	£14,500	£11,000	£7,500
Impala Sport Sedan	235/6, 348/8	1959	£8,000	£5,000	£4,000
Impala convertible	235/6, 348/8	1959	£14,000	£10,000	£5,000
Corvette	235/6	1953	£25,000+	£18,000	£10,000
Corvette	235/6, 283/8	1954–57	£20,000+	£13,000	£9,000
Corvette	283, 327/8	1958–62	£24,000+	£16,000	£9,000
Corvette Sting Ray	327, 427/8	1963–67	£19,000+	£15,000+	£10,000
Corvette Sting Ray Roadster	327, 427/8	1963–66	£22,000+	£15,000	£8,000
Corvette Sting Ray Roadster	427/8	1967	£20,000+	£13,000	£10,000

Value will also be regulated by build options, rare coachbuilding options and de luxe engine specifications etc.

1975 Chevrolet Corvette Sting Ray Coupé, 5.7 litre V8 engine, automatic transmission, T-top roof, finished in silver, blue interior.
£7,000–8,000 / $10,200–11,600 ⊞ COR

1980 Chevrolet Corvette Coupé, 5.7 litre V8 engine, 4-speed manual gearbox, full dual stainless-steel exhaust, T-top roof, finished in yellow, electric windows, black leather interior, tilt wheel.
£9,000–10,000 / $13,000–14,500 ⊞ COR

1990 Chevrolet Corvette ZR-1 Coupé, T-top roof, finished in metallic dark red, 1 of 181 ZR-1s built, 1 owner and 93 miles from new.
£24,000–27,000 / $34,800–39,000 ⚒ BJ

1989 Chevrolet Corvette Convertible, 5.7 litre V8 engine, automatic transmission, finished in white, black soft top, black leather interior, air conditioning.
£9,000–10,000 / $13,000–14,500 ⊞ COR

Chrysler

1927 Chrysler 60 Phaeton, 2953cc 6-cylinder engine, hickory spoked wheels, full weather equipment, right-hand drive, completely restored early 1990s, flashing indicators, finished in maroon and ivory, beige leatherette interior trim, excellent mechanical condition.
£16,000–18,000 / $23,000–26,000 ⚒ BRIT
Having joined Buick in 1910 in Michigan, Walter P. Chrysler rapidly proved his worth, becoming president of the company before leaving in 1919, following disagreements with William C. Durrant. During 1923, Chrysler acquired the Chalmers plant in Detroit, and in January 1924 the new Chrysler appeared, proving so successful that by the end of the year some 32,000 had been sold. For a medium-priced car, the Chrysler boasted an impressive specification, which included full-pressure lubrication, four-wheel hydraulic brakes and aluminium pistons. By 1927, Chrysler was the fourth best-selling marque in the USA, four models being available – the Series 50 powered by a four-cylinder engine, and the 60, 70 and Imperial Series 80, all utilising six-cylinder engines. The Series 60 was built on a 109in (276.9cm) wheelbase, while its 3 litre engine developed 54bhp at 3,000rpm. No fewer than eight styles of coachwork were available.

1956 Chrysler Windsor Hardtop, power steering, power brakes, finished in black and white, original white vinyl and red fabric interior, 60,000 miles from new.
£9,000–11,000 / $13,000–16,000 ⚒ Bon
The 1955 Chryslers changed the company's stodgy image almost overnight, combining crisp styling by design chief Virgil Exner with powerful engines and competent chassis. The company referred to the new style as the '100 Million Dollar Look', and it was well received. Changes to the 1956 models were modest, among them a new simplified grille and a number of trim changes, including rear lights that were integrated into subtly redesigned rear wings. The Windsor Series was offered in six body/trim styles, including two different coupés, a four-door estate, a pair of six-passenger, four-door saloons and a convertible.
All Chryslers – and therefore all Windsors – came only with V8 engines, but instead of the 'hemi-head' unit of the 300B, the Windsor was equipped with the 'wedge-head' engine. This 331cu.in overhead-valve V8 featured a cast-iron block and compression ratio of 8.5:1, resulting in 225bhp. Mated to the Powerflite automatic transmission – operated by push-button controls – the engine was more than powerful enough to propel the 3,900lb (1,769kg) Chrysler at a brisk pace.

> A known continuous history can add value to and enhance the enjoyment of a car.

Citroën

André Citroën founded his own firm in 1919 in the former Mors factory, where earlier he had worked as a chief engineer. Initially, his cars were fairly orthodox, and they quickly proliferated on French roads. The famed Traction Avant of 1934 was a rare piece of genuine and pioneering mass-market innovation, with its front-wheel drive and unitary hull. After the war, the theme of unconventional thinking continued with the wonderfully idiosyncratic 2CV, which reduced the motor car to its bare essence. The DS19 of 1955 went the other way and took technical innovation to a new level, with its pioneering hydro-pneumatic self-levelling suspension, power-assisted brakes and semi-automatic gearbox, not to mention its revolutionary shape. In 1976, Citroën was taken over by Peugeot, and since then Citroën cars have largely been more conventional.

CITROËN Model	ENGINE cc/cyl	DATES	CONDITION 1	2	3
A	1300/4	1919	£4,000	£2,000	£1,000
5CV	856/4	1922–26	£7,000	£4,000	£2,000
11	1453/4	1922–28	£4,000	£2,000	£1,000
12/24	1538/4	1927–29	£5,000	£3,000	£1,000
2½ Litre	2442/6	1929–31	£5,000	£3,000	£1,500
13/30	1628/4	1929–31	£5,000	£3,000	£1,000
Big 12	1767/4	1932–35	£7,000	£5,000	£2,000
Twenty	2650/6	1932–35	£10,000	£5,000	£3,000
Ten CV	1452/4	1933–34	£5,000	£3,000	£1,000
Ten CV	1495/4	1935–36	£6,000	£3,000	£1,000
11B/Light 15/Big 15/7CV	1911/4	1934–57	£9,000	£5,000	£2,000
Twelve	1628/4	1936–39	£5,000	£3,000	£1,000
F	1766/4	1937–38	£4,000	£2,000	£1,000
15/6 and Big Six	2866/6	1938–56	£7,000	£4,000	£2,000

CITROËN Model	ENGINE cc/cyl	DATES	CONDITION		
			1	2	3
2CV	375/2	1948–54	£1,000	£500	£250
2CV/Dyane/Bijou	425/2	1954–82	£1,000	£800	£500
DS19/ID19	1911/4	1955–69	£5,000	£3,000	£800
Sahara	900/4	1958–67	£5,000	£4,000	£3,000
2CV6	602/2	1963 on	£750	£500	£250
DS Safari	1985/4	1968–75	£6,000	£3,000	£1,000
DS21	1985/4	1969–75	£6,000	£3,000	£1,000
DS23	2347/4	1972–75	£6,000	£4,000	£1,500
SM	2670/ 2974/6	1970–75	£9,000	£6,000	£4,500

Miller's Starter Marque

- **Starter Citroën:** *Citroën 2CV, 1948–91*
- In 1935, Citroën managing director Pierre-Joules Boulanger visited the French market town where he was born, and returned to Paris with an attack of conscience and a great idea. He decreed, 'Design me a car to carry two people and 50 kilos of potatoes at 60kmh, using no more than three litres of fuel per 100km. It must be capable of running on the worst roads, of being driven by a débutante and must be totally comfortable.' The project Toute Petite Voiture also had to be like 'a settee under an umbrella', and capable of 'crossing a field carrying a basket of eggs without breaking any'.
- The rest, as they say, is history. From its Paris launch in 1948 to the end of production in 1991, over seven million 2CVs and its various derivatives have hit the road.
- It's an undeniable classic, yet a frugal utility vehicle at the same time; fun too. The fabric roof rolls right back like the lid of a sardine can and you can take the seats out for a family picnic.
- A rare wonder these days is that all the body panels simply unbolt. In fact, even the main bodyshell is only held in place by a mere 16 bolts. That means it's easy to repair rust or crash damaged panels, but it also means that fresh panels can hide serious rot on the old-style separate chassis.
- Inspect sills – especially at the base of the B-posts – front floorpan, chassis members and chassis rails running to the rear of the car. One indicator of chassis trouble is wide gaps around the triangular body section in front of the doors.
- As for that legendary twin-pot, air-cooled engine, it's a remarkably robust unit. Citroën designed it in the knowledge that is was likely to be hammered pretty much all the time and given no more routine maintenance than a farmyard pitchfork.
- In most cases, you'll be looking at a car with the 602cc engine, and the one thing these need is an oil change every 3,000 miles or so. Neglect here will be revealed by big-end knocking.
- There are two types of gearbox, one for drum-brake cars up to 1982, and the other for later disc-braked models. The 'drum' box is very robust, and only if it sounds like a lorry will there be any trouble with the bearings. The 'disc' box is a little more fragile, with a tendency to unwind the second-gear selector ring – and that may mean a new unit. Again, listen for excessive noise.
- Brakes are usually trouble free, but on disc-braked cars open up the reservoir to see if it's filled with the correct Citroën LHM clear green fluid. If not, the master cylinder rubbers will soon go, if they haven't dissolved already, and that's £300–400 to rectify.
- Naturally, for a car that's been in production until so recently, parts and spares are plentiful.

1924 Citroën 5CV Cloverleaf Three-Seater Tourer, 856cc engine, left-hand drive, restored c1993, finished in blue, black interior, very good condition throughout.
£4,500–5,500 / $6,500–8,000 ➤ H&H
The Citroën 5CV was the French equivalent of the Austin 7 and made its appearance in 1922, production continuing for almost five years. Its 856cc engine proved virtually indestructible. The car was built under licence in Germany by Opel, where it was known as the Laubfrosch (Tree Frog).

1925 Citroën B12 Tourer, 1453cc 4-cylinder engine, restored to original specification late 1990s, finished in green with black wings, tan duck hood, side screens.
£4,500–5,500 / $6,500–8,000 ➤ BRIT
The rugged Citroën B12 was also assembled in Britain, at Slough, being known as the 11.4.

1938 Citroën 11BL Cabriolet, 1911cc 4-cylinder engine, 56bhp, 3-speed manual gearbox, front-wheel drive, 4-wheel hydraulic drum brakes, torsion-bar suspension.
£28,000–34,000 / $40,000–50,000 ➤ Pou

Citroën Traction Avant (1934–57)

French production: 708,339 four-cylinder models; 50,518 six-cylinder models.
Slough production (1945–55): 14,600 four-cylinder models; 1,700 six-cylinder models.
Body styles: Saloon, cabriolet, faux-cabriolet, Commerciale tradesman's hatchback.
Engine: 1911cc, four-cylinder; 2867cc, six-cylinder.
Power output: 46–65bhp for 1911cc; 77bhp for 2867cc.
Transmission: Three-speed manual.
Brakes: Drums all-round.
Maximum speed: 70–75mph for 1911cc; 83mph for 2867cc.

Revolutionary, subversive and defiant in the movie mythology of the French resistance, a living period piece in its later production years, and today excruciatingly chic among designer types, the Traction Avant is quite simply an automotive icon. What's more, it's British – well, not quite, but it was produced in Citroën's Slough plant from 1945 to 1955. Traction Avant means 'front drive', and in 1934 that was pretty forward thinking, but it

was way out in front in many other ways too, with the gearbox mounted ahead of the engine, the wheels way out at each corner, a monocoque construction and torsion-bar suspension. With all this, and its low stance and centre of gravity, its handling was so assured that some ageing and rather more sentimental pundits still consider it modern. The two acknowledged criticisms are atrociously heavy steering at low speeds and a poor turning circle, but so sleek and touching sinister is the styling that few devotees care. The other problem is the labyrinthine nomenclature, for the Traction Avant was not so much a single model, but a whole model range, starting with the short-wheelbase Onze Légère, known in Britain as the Light 15. Then there was the Big 15 and 15/6, the six-cylinder so-called Maigret model. And that's just the start. By the end of production, the Traction looked dated, even vintage, but unlike the similarly antique MG T-series Midgets of the same period, the immortal Traction Avant was still avant garde.

1949 Citroën Big Six Saloon, left-hand drive, new radiator, new dynamo, finished in black with silver wheels, interior in good original condition, some blistering to door bottoms.
£3,000–4,000 / $4,500–5,800 ✗ CGC
The introduction of Citroën's 7C Traction Avant in 1934 broke new ground in the engineering of production cars. The model was developed continually, and eventually the 1.9 litre four-cylinder version was produced alongside a 3 litre six. This car is an example of the small-boot Big Six, which gave all the advantages of the more powerful engine with the purer body line of the earlier cars.

1988 Citroën 2CV6, 602cc twin-cylinder engine, inter-connected coil-sprung suspension, finished in maroon and black, black roll-back vinyl roof, grey fabric interior, 13,850 miles from new, excellent condition.
£2,000–2,500 / $3,000–3,500 ✗ BRIT
The Deux Chevaux originally saw the light of day in 1949, the earliest versions being powered by a diminutive 375cc engine, which eventually was enlarged to 425cc. By 1974, the engine had grown to 602cc, rendering the 2CV6 livelier than its forebears.

Cooper

◀ **1955 Cooper MG Sports,** 1250cc 4-cylinder MG TC engine, completely restored late 1990s at a cost of over £20,000/$29,000, replacement body, finished in green, brown interior.
£15,000–17,000
$21,750–24,750 ✗ H&H
Without doubt, John Cooper was one of the world's major players in racing-car design, and his name has always been linked with success and innovation. Cooper Cars also made a handful of two-seaters, but no two cars were identical.

Cord

1931 Cord L-29 Cabriolet, 298.6cu.in sidevalve 8-cylinder engine, 3-speed gearbox, front-wheel drive, restored.
£80,000–90,000 / $116,000–130,000 🔨 BJ

1937 Cord 812 Beverly Saloon, 4.7 litre V8 engine, supercharger, recent transmission overhaul.
£20,000–22,000 / $29,000–32,000 🔨 BJ

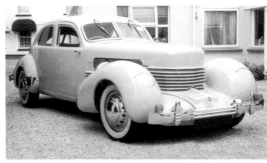

1936 Cord 812 Westchester Saloon, 4.7 litre Lycoming V8 engine, supercharger, finished in mushroom, burgundy upholstery, 1 of only 5 right-hand-drive examples known to exist.
£30,000–35,000 / $43,000–51,000 🔨 Bon
Launched in 1935 by the Auburn Automobile Company, the Cord incorporated unheard-of advances in styling and engineering, including retractable headlamps and front-wheel drive combined with independent suspension. The 812 model was introduced for 1936 and featured a 4.7 litre Lycoming V8 engine with optional supercharger, electronically controlled Bendix transmission with overdrive on fourth and distinctive exposed exhausts running from the bonnet to the front wings of supercharged models. The Schwitzer-Cummins supercharger provided nearly 200bhp, and Ab Jenkins achieved 121mph using a blown Cord. Costing more than twice as much as a Cadillac and four times that of a Ford V8, the Cord went out of production in 1937.

Cord 810 & 812 (1935–37)

Production: 2,322.
Engine: Lycoming 4729cc V8.
Power output: 125bhp, 810; 170bhp at 4,200rpm, supercharged 812.
Construction: Unitary, pressed-steel body/chassis.
Transmission: Front-wheel drive, electrically-operated four-speed pre-selector manual gearbox, synchromesh on top three gears.
Brakes: Hydraulic drums, front and rear.
Maximum speed: 90+mph, 810; 112mph, supercharged 812.
0–60mph: 13.5 seconds, supercharged 812.

Pick of the bunch: These Cords were produced as both convertibles and saloons; most-prized is the supercharged 812 two-door sports-phaeton convertible.
Cord fact: The 810 was the first production car to feature 'pop-up' headlights. In this case, they were hand cranked by a mechanism adapted from an aircraft landing-light system, rather than truly pop-up.
Striking the right Cord: In October 1999, a 1936 Cord 810 Phaeton owned by Jimmy Page, guitarist of Led Zeppelin, sold at auction in the UK for £85,000.

Crescent

◀ **1915 Crescent Cyclecar,** only 2 owners since 1920, thought to be sole surviving example.
£7,000–8,000 / $10,200–11,600 🔨 CGC
Crescent Motors existed between 1911 and 1915, being based in Walsall, Staffordshire, until 1913, when a move was made to Smethwick, Birmingham. The Crescent was more car-like in appearance than many other cyclecars, due to the radiator required to cool the c900cc Blumfield V-twin engine. The move to Birmingham saw a change of drive from belt to chain, as in this example, but in both cases a friction disc was used to provide a potentially infinite number of final-drive ratios. This car was laid up in a workshop in 1924 and remained untouched for 52 years until the building was demolished. Assuming the car to have been abandoned, the demolition company gave it to a local veteran car enthusiast. Subsequently, the original owner, then in his eighties, thought that it had been stolen, until he read about its restoration. After a visit by the police to the restorer, he and the original owner met and struck a deal, the car passing officially to the former.

Crosley

◀ **1947 Crosley Crosmobile,** fitted with later 44cu.in cast-iron overhead-camshaft engine, 26.5bhp, 3-speed manual gearbox, finished in metallic grey.
£4,000–5,000 / $5,800–7,250 ⚒ Bon

Powell Crosley had tried building a car in 1907. Unsuccessful, he made another attempt with a cyclecar, but did no better. In 1939 Crosley had another go. This time, his product was a tiny economy car powered by a 12bhp air-cooled engine. With a price of less than $300, almost 5,000 examples were built before American involvement in WWII halted production. After the war, Crosley was at it again. These post-war models used the brazed-steel COBRA engine, based on Lloyd Taylor's patents for a sheet-metal engine. Unfortunately, the 26.5bhp unit, which had proved sturdy as an industrial engine, was less reliable in a passenger vehicle. However, the venture was profitable.

Crossley

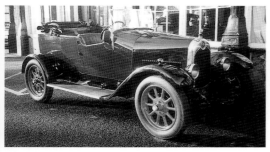

1925 Crossley 15/30 Three-Door Tourer, 2100cc engine, single updraft carburettor, foot-operated 4-wheel brakes, transmission handbrake, reversible artillery wheels, rear-mounted spare wheel, aluminium-panelled body on ash frame, folding windscreen, restored, new hood, finished in green and black, green interior, Australian import.
£7,500–8,500 / $11,000–12,500 ⚒ H&H

1928 Crossley 20.9hp Aero Saloon, side mounted spare wheel, radiator calormeter, roof ventilator, restored, finished in blue with black wings, blue interior, mechanics and electrics in good condition.
£11,000–13,000 / $16,000–19,000 ⚒ Bon

Daimler

Throughout much of Daimler's long career, its fluted radiator has moved in the highest echelons of British society. Yet it owes its name to a German inventor. The British Daimler company's origins go back to 1891, when British inventor and businessman Frederick Simms acquired British rights to Gottlieb Daimler's engines. The Daimler Motor Company Ltd was formed in 1896, and the first car – which took 60 workers to produce – emerged in March 1897. In 1910, Daimler was given welcome stability and capital following its acquisition by

Birmingham Small Arms (BSA), later a world renowned manufacturer of motorcycles. In the 1920s, Daimler's engines matched Rolls-Royce's for smoothness and silent running, and in 1926 Daimler produced Britain's first series-production V12. After WWII, Daimler struggled to retain its pre-war eminence, and certainly for a while lost direction. In 1960, Daimler was acquired by Jaguar, and the last distinct true Daimler model was the DS420 limousine (1968–92). Today, the marque lives on as a flagship brand under Jaguar's patronage.

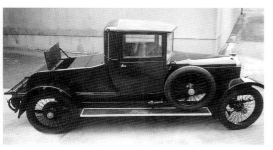

◀ **1922 Daimler TT 20hp Doctor's Coupé with Dicky,** 3306cc 4-cylinder engine, some original Watford instruments, indicators, brake lights, finished in blue, 2-seater bench seat, large dicky seat area, rear parcel shelf, brown interior trim.
£6,000–7,000 / $8,750–10,250 ⚒ H&H

DAIMLER Model	ENGINE cc/cyl	DATES	CONDITION 1	2	3
Veteran (Coventry built)	var/4	1897–1904	£75,000	£60,000	£30,000
Veteran	var/4	1905–19	£35,000	£25,000	£15,000
30hp	4962/6	1919–25	£40,000	£25,000	£18,000
45hp	7413/6	1919–25	£45,000+	£30,000	£20,000
Double Six 50	7136/12	1927–34	£40,000	£30,000	£20,000
20	2687/6	1934–35	£18,000	£14,000	£12,000
Straight 8	3421/8	1936–38	£20,000	£15,000	£12,000

Value is dependent on body style, coachbuilder and condition of the sleeve-valve engine.

1934 Daimler 20hp Six-Light Saloon, coachwork by Mulliner, 2443cc 6-cylinder engine, fluid flywheel, pre-selector gearbox, sliding sun roof, Rotax lighting to the front, Lucas Owl Eye rear light, finished in black over cream, chromework in fair condition, interior trimmed in tan Bedford cord, rear compartment with occasional seats, silk pulls, internal lighting and sun blind, wood trim, well maintained, very good condition throughout.
£7,500–9,000 / $11,000–13,000 ✗ CGC
The 1930s were particularly fruitful for Britain's oldest car manufacturer. As part of the BSA empire, Daimler benefited from the talents of an engineering pool that included George Lanchester and Laurence Pomeroy. However, royal patronage alone could not sustain the Coventry marque, and it eagerly contested the small-car market. Launched in 1934, the new 20hp was one of its first models to forsake the Knight sleeve-valve engine in favour of a more conventional overhead-valve design.

1935 Daimler 20hp Six-Light Saloon, 2443cc 6-cylinder engine, pre-selector gearbox, older restoration.
£9,000–10,000 / $13,000–14,500 ⊞ TIHO

1949 Daimler DE36 Spey Touring Limousine, coachwork by Hooper, restored, good condition, quantity of spare parts.
£14,000–17,000 / $20,500–24,500 ✗ Bon
Much favoured by royal families the world over, the DE36 was Britain's last production car with a straight-eight engine.

◀ **1950 Daimler DB18 Special Sports Drophead Coupé,** 2522cc 6-cylinder engine, pre-selector gearbox, restored 1989–90, only 6,500 miles since, finished in black and silver, new red leather interior, new carpets, woodwork repolished, concours winner, 1 of fewer than 500 built.
£23,000–27,000 / $33,000–39,000 ✗ H&H
The DB18 Special Sports Drophead had three-seater coachwork, the third passenger being provided with a side-facing seat in the back.

1955 Daimler Conquest Century Saloon, 2433cc engine, pre-selector gearbox, retains original suitcase and small tools, finished in black and gold, grey interior, 27,000 miles from new, excellent original condition.
£4,000–5,000 / $5,800–7,250 ✗ H&H

1957 Daimler Conquest Four-Door Saloon, 2400cc engine, Borg-Warner automatic transmission, restored over 10 years, black paintwork showing some signs of deterioration, original push-button radio, original grey leather upholstery and woodwork in good condition, 63,000 miles from new.
£3,500–4,000 / $5,000–5,800 ✗ H&H

Daimler Conquest Century Roadster & Drophead Coupé (1954–57)

Production: 65 roadsters; 54 drophead coupés.
Price when new: £1,673/$2,400.
Engine: 2433cc, straight-six.
Transmission: Four-speed pre-selector manual, fluid flywheel.
Power output: 100bhp at 4,400rpm.
0–60mph: 14.5 seconds.
Maximum speed: 100mph.
Brakes: Drums all round.

Announced in late 1953 for production the following year, this aluminium-bodied faux sportster is nothing if not quirky. In fact, unkinder automobile critics have suggested that it looks as if every panel came from a different car. In its day, it fitted in with few people's conventional notion of what a sports car should be and was hampered further by its high price – twice that of sporting stalwarts like the Triumph TR2, and a little more costly than Jaguar's sporting thoroughbred, the XK120. Late in 1955, Daimler discontinued the roadster and replaced it with a drophead coupé with a third sideways seat in the rear. If you fancy a rare curio, there are few rarer or curiouser, but beware the public reaction. If you are hoping for a 'What'll she do, mister?', don't be too upset when all you get is 'Did you make it yourself?'

◀ **1960 Daimler SP250 Dart,** 2548cc V8 engine, new engine and gearbox mountings, new water pump, stainless-steel exhaust, front suspension rebuilt, wire wheels, complete set of original steel wheels and aluminium embellishers, finished in grey, black soft top and tonneau cover, red interior, 1 owner for last 31 years, well maintained, would benefit from a respray.
£8,000–9,000
$11,500–13,000 ⚶ H&H

1961 Daimler SP250 Dart, restored, engine rebuilt with new valves and pistons, Rover 5-speed gearbox, new fuel tank, wire wheels, finished in metallic blue, dark blue hood, cream hardtop, cream vinyl bucket seats, in need of carpets and sundry items of trim.
£6,000–7,000 / $8,750–10,250 ⚶ CGC
Introduced in 1959, the Daimler Dart was something of a departure for a company better known for supplying royalty with limousines. Underneath the glassfibre bodyshell, with its controversial styling, was a conventional chassis with independent front suspension and all-round disc brakes. Edward Turner (of Ariel motorcycle fame) was responsible for the 2548cc V8 engine. Developing 140bhp, it could propel the Dart to a 127mph top speed and from 0 to 60mph in 8.5 seconds.

1965 Daimler 250 V8 Saloon, finished in metallic green, beige leather interior, original unused toolkit, 3 owners and c74,000 miles from new, good condition throughout.
£6,500–8,000 / $9,500–11,500 ⚶ Bon
Jaguar's acquisition of Daimler in 1960 brought with it the latter's lightweight V8 engines. First seen in the SP250 sports car, the 2.5 litre version was judged superior to Jaguar's 2.4 litre XK six, so the opportunity was taken to create an upmarket, Daimler-badged variant of the Mk II saloon using this power unit. Launched in 1962, the new Daimler came with Borg Warner automatic transmission as standard and turned out to be a fine performer, its 110mph top speed exceeding that of an overdrive-equipped 2.4 litre Mk II by a wide margin.

DAIMLER Model	ENGINE cc/cyl	DATES	CONDITION 1	2	3
DB18	2522/6	1946–49	£6,000	£3,000	£1,000
DB18 Conv S/S	2522/6	1948–53	£15,000+	£7,000	£2,000
Consort	2522/6	1949–53	£5,000	£3,000	£1,000
Conquest/Con.Century	2433/6	1953–58	£4,000	£2,000	£1,000
Conquest Roadster	2433/6	1953–56	£12,000	£7,000	£4,000
Majestic 3.8	3794/6	1958–62	£5,000	£2,000	£1,000
SP250	2547/8	1959–64	£12,000	£10,000	£4,500
Majestic Major	4561/8	1961–64	£6,000	£4,000	£1,000
2.5 V8	2547/8	1962–67	£8,000	£5,250	£2,500
V8 250	2547/8	1968–69	£8,000+	£4,000	£2,000
Sovereign 420	4235/6	1966–69	£6,500	£3,500	£1,500
Double Six Coupé	5343/12	1975–77	£8,000	£3,000	£1,500

Miller's Compares

I. 1968 Daimler 250 V8 Saloon, 2548cc V8 engine, automatic transmission, detailed engine bay, finished in white, navy blue interior, 69,000 miles from new.
£11,500–13,500 / $16,500–19,500 ➹ H&H

II. 1968 Daimler 250 V8 Saloon, 2548cc V8 engine, 140bhp, engine recently rebuilt, automatic transmission, finished in red, good overall condition.
£2,500–3,500 / $3,500–5,000 ➹ CGC

Although considerable, the difference in value between these 250 V8 Daimlers isn't as wide as sometimes can be found. These are quality cars that employed quality materials (leather, walnut and Wilton carpet), and bringing an average car up to sparkling condition could well cost more than the difference in value between the two cars. In other words, the more expensive car actually may not only be better value, but also cheaper overall.

1977 Daimler 4.2 litre XJC Coupé, 4.2 litre 6-cylinder engine, restored 1999–2000, Series III wheels, recently resprayed, black leather interior, excellent condition.
£2,500–3,000 / $3,500–4,500 ➹ COYS
The Series II XJ models were introduced in 1973 alongside another variant on the XJ theme, a two-door coupé. This model was significant in that it represented Sir William Lyons' last project before his retirement from active design in 1972. The XJC used the short-wheelbase floorpan with larger front doors and a slightly different roofline, but otherwise was substantially the same as the four-door saloon. Lyons had insisted that the front and rear windows met in a pillarless construction, which was very elegant, but posed many problems in terms of sealing and operation. Consequently, the coupé did not enter production until early 1975. When it was introduced, the option of the Daimler version was also offered, and this was made in small quantities to a higher standard of finish and trim.

1977 Daimler Double Six Coupé, V12 engine, 285bhp, 3-speed automatic transmission, finished in white, tan leather interior, 72,000 miles from new, good condition.
£3,000–4,000 / $4,400–5,800 ➹ CGC

1977 Daimler Double Six Coupé, 5343cc V12 engine, automatic transmission, alloy wheels, finished in blue, tan leather upholstery, fewer than 47,500 miles from new, 1 of 399 examples built, very good condition.
£2,500–3,000 / $3,500–4,500 ➹ H&H

1986 Daimler Double Six TWR, modified at a cost of over £20,000/$29,000, TWR engine efficiency kit with larger throttle bodies, big-bore exhaust, revalved quick-shift automatic transmission, AP Racing front brakes, ventilated rear discs, uprated suspension with Billstein shock absorbers, quick-action steering rack with semi-solid bushes, 16in alloy wheels, electric sunroof, windows, mirrors and aerial, finished in steel blue, grey leather interior, picnic tables, air conditioning, cruise control, electrically adjustable front seats.
£2,500–3,000 / $3,500–4,500 ➹ BARO
The Daimler derivative of the XJ12 offered a higher-specification interior with individual seats in the rear, in place of the bench seat found in the Jaguar.

► **1981 Daimler Sovereign Series III,** 3442cc 6-cylinder Jaguar engine, resprayed in yellow, original black leather interior trim.
£600–800 / $870–1,150 ➹ BRIT

Darracq

◄ **1903 Darracq 8hp Model G Four-Seater Rear-Entrance Tonneau,** oil sidelamps, centre-mounted Salisbury Bleriot headlamp, extensive mechanical restoration 1995, finished in green with yellow wheels, upholstered in green buttoned Connolly hide, VCC dated, own trailer.
£37,000–42,000 / $54,000–61,000 ⚒ Bon
Alexandre Darracq had experimented with electric carriages as early as 1896, but it was not until 1900 that he built his first successful car powered by an internal-combustion engine. The single-cylinder, 8hp model, introduced in 1903, was the mainstay of Darracq production. This very successful car followed conventional practice, with a vertical single-cylinder engine featuring an atmospheric inlet valve and mechanical exhaust valve. By 1904, Darracq accounted for 10 per cent of French car production.

Datsun

Datsun 240Z (1969–73)

Production: 156,076.
Engine: Single-overhead-camshaft, inline six, 2393cc.
Power output: 151bhp at 5,600rpm.
Transmission: All-synchromesh four- or five-speed manual gearbox, or automatic.
Brakes: Discs front/drums rear.
Maximum speed: 125mph.
0–60mph: 8.0 seconds.
Throughout the 1960s, Japanese car makers were teetering on the brink of a sports-car breakthrough. The revolution came with the Datsun 240Z, which at a stroke established Japan on the world sports-car stage. The breakthrough had been on the cards for a while: the E-Type Jaguar wasn't in its first flush of youth, and at the lower level the Austin-Healey was on its last legs; neither was the MGB exactly factory fresh. There was a gaping hole, particularly in America, and the Datsun 240Z filled it handsomely. In fact, where many European sports cars made unwilling

concessions for the Americans, the 240Z was aimed straight at them. It was even launched in the USA in October 1969, a month before its official Japanese release and, on a rising tide of Japanese exports to the USA, it scored a massive hit. It had looks, vigorous performance, nimble handling and high equipment levels. In its day, it was a great-value sporting package that outsold all rivals. Today, the 240Z gives plenty of show and go for not much dough, offering all the right sporting sensations for less than half the price of an E-Type Jag, which it once attempted to rival.
Pick of the bunch: The sporting Datsun gained weight and girth, and slowed down as it mutated through the 260Z and on to the 280ZX. Consequently, many Datsun Z fans favour the original incarnation, the 240Z, for its purity and performance. The ultimate 240Z was the Samurai performance package, with triple Weber carbs, special head and other mods, which gave six-second 0–60mph times.

DATSUN Model	ENGINE cc/cyl	DATES	CONDITION		
			1	2	3
240Z	2393/6	1970–71	£6,000	£4,000	£2,000
240Z	2393/6	1971–74	£5,000	£3,250	£1,500
260Z	2565/6	1974–79	£4,000	£2,800	£1,200
260Z 2+2	2565/6	1974–79	£4,000	£2,600	£1,000

De Dion Bouton

Restored values
The cost of a professional restoration will have an influence on, but no direct relation to, a car's market value. A restored car can have a market value lower than the cost of its restoration.

► **1901 De Dion Bouton 4½hp Vis-à-vis Voiturette,** rear-mounted engine, De Dion rear axle, brass accessories, older restoration, finished in green, black buttoned leather upholstery, front seat interchangeable so that passengers can sit in vis-à-vis formation or facing forwards.
£46,000–55,000 / $67,000–80,000 ⚒ Bon

Delage

1926 Delage DI All-Weather Tourer, right-hand drive, wind-up windows, central frames between front and rear doors fold away when hood and windows are retracted, twin side-mounted spare wheels, Brooks touring trunk, finished in blue over black, 2 occasional seats (enabling the car to carry 6), inlaid marquetry to wood cappings, brakes overhauled, bonnet repainted.
£18,000–22,000 / $26,000–32,000 ⚒ Bon
Louis Delage began making cars in 1905, the first being a single-cylinder De Dion-engined runabout, but within a few years he was offering multi-cylinder designs. Four-cylinder DI and six-cylinder DM models formed the mainstay of the company's touring-car production in the 1920s. Introduced in 1924, and very well specified for its day, the DI was powered by a 2.1 litre overhead-valve engine driving through a four-speed gearbox, and came with four-wheel brakes. A beautifully balanced fast touring car, it possessed exceptional performance, with comfortable suspension, light and responsive steering, and good roadholding, yet it was rugged enough to withstand the punishment meted out by cobbled roads.

1932 Delage Model DS Seven-Seater Touring Saloon, 2.5 litre engine, twin side-mounted spare wheels, Marchal headlamps, radiator calormeter, rear-mounted luggage trunk, electric trafficators, subject of major restoration, finished in maroon and cream, new West of England cloth upholstery, all interior woodwork refinished.
£11,000–13,000 / $16,000–19,000 ⚒ Bon
By the 1930s, Delage was offering a range of four-, six- and eight-cylinder cars that catered for a wide sector of the market. The Type DS, announced in the autumn of 1930, was a logical development of the earlier DR model and featured an overhead-valve, pushrod engine of 2517cc. Power was transmitted through a four-speed gearbox, and the model was offered in long- and short-wheelbase forms. In Britain, with saloon coachwork, the DS retailed at around £700/$1,000, making it significantly more expensive than comparable products from the likes of Humber and Lanchester. However, the price was reflected in the build quality.

Delahaye

1948 Delahaye Type 135M Three-Position Drophead Coupé, coachwork by Pennock, 3557cc 6-cylinder engine, triple downdraught Solex carburettors, Cotal electro-mechanical gearbox, independent transverse-leaf front suspension, rigid rear axle on semi-elliptic leaf springs, Bendix brakes, opening windscreen, finished in metallic light blue, cream leather interior, refurbished at a cost of £24,000/$35,000.
£40,000–45,000 / $58,000–65,000 ⚒ Bon
Delahaye was one of France's most exclusive marques – at £3,500/$5,000, only the very wealthy could afford a Type 135. After WWII, European car design was heavily influenced by Detroit and the move towards mass production, but the Dutch coachbuilder Pennock of The Hague resisted the temptation to remove the definition between the bonnet and wings when styling his flamboyant cars. With minimal timber framing, his coachwork was welded to the chassis, providing a rigid structure that was taut and rattle-free, unlike many other coachbuilt examples of the day. This car is understood to have been built for the noted pre- and post-war racing driver Prince Birabongse (Bira) of Siam.

1948 Delahaye 180, coachwork by Henri Chapron, 4455cc 6-cylinder engine, 125bhp, Cotal 4-speed electro-mechanical pre-selector gearbox, 4-wheel hydraulic drum brakes, independent front suspension with coil springs and hydraulic shock absorbers, De Dion rear axle with semi-elliptic leaf springs and Houdaille shock absorbers, left-hand drive, armour-plated limousine coachwork with division, restored over c10 years, c£6,500/$9,500 spent on mechanical work, finished in black, red velour interior.
£20,000–24,000 / $29,000–35,000 ⚒ C
Two Type 180s were ordered by the French Communist Party for prominent member Jacques Duclos and its president, Maurice Thorez. This car, the seventh in the series, is the latter's. It was bodied by Henri Chapron as a limousine with division and, at the request of the party, was fully armour plated. The grille design, by Philippe Charbonneaux, was developed to reinforce the marque's identity and to unify the frontal appearance of all models regardless of coachbuilder.

Dellow

◀ **1953 Dellow Mk IIB Competition Model,** engine partially overhauled, Radpanels competition model body without doors.
£4,750–5,750 / $7,000–8,500 ⚲ Bon
Dellow Motors was established in 1946 by Ken Delingpole and Ron Lowe in Alvechurch, Birmingham, as a tuning company. By 1950, series production had begun, using new Ford parts and a 3in (7.6cm) tubular A-frame chassis to Dellow's own design, the ex-War Department rocket body tubing providing exceptional strength and longevity. Dellow's products have been successful in trials, hill climbs, driving tests and other events to this day.

DeLorean

The ill-fated DeLorean DMC-12 ranks right up there with the Ford Edsel as one of the auto industry's greatest failures. A high flyer who'd risen to the height of vice-president of General Motors, John Zachary DeLorean launched his own venture in 1974. By 1982, the short flight of his gull-winged sports car was over and his reputation in tatters. With a design by Giorgetto Giugiaro's Ital Design, chassis and manufacturing development by Lotus, a unique brushed stainless-steel body and fancy gull-wing doors, the DeLorean was intended as a glimpse of the future. But with a complex series of capital-raising exercises that eventually saw the company settle in Northern Ireland, production only finally got under way early in 1981. By then, the design was outdated, and those who did buy DeLoreans found a litany of quality-control problems. Performance was also disappointing. Like the Edsel before it, the DeLorean bombed against wildly optimistic sales forecasts, and DeLorean Motor Cars foundered in a mire of court cases. Today, there is a small cult of DeLorean devotees who find the fascination of the story behind the car almost worth the frustration of owning one.

> ## DeLorean DMC–12 (1981–82)
>
> **Production:** 8,800.
> **Construction:** Y-shaped backbone chassis, glassfibre body with brushed stainless-steel outer skin.
> **Engine:** 2849cc, overhead-camshaft, V6.
> **Power output:** 130bhp at 5,500rpm.
> **Transmission:** Five-speed manual; optional three-speed automatic.
> **Maximum speed:** 130mph claimed.
> **0-60mph:** 8.5 seconds claimed.

◀ **c1981 DeLorean DMC-12,** 2849cc overhead-camshaft V6 engine, automatic transmission, right-hand drive, grey interior, 3,500 miles from new.
£9,000–11,000 / $13,000–16,000 🚗 DOCL
Of 24 right-hand-drive De Loreans built, only three were equipped with automatic transmission.

DeSoto

◀ **1929 DeSoto Series K Roadster Espanol,** 6-cylinder engine, 4-wheel hydraulic brakes, wood-spoked artillery wheels, hood and side screens, older restoration, finished in yellow and black, 1 of first Series Ks produced, earliest known surviving right-hand-drive DeSoto.
£22,000–26,000
$32,000–38,000 ⚲ Bon

1959 DeSoto Firedome Sportsman Hardtop, 383cu.in V8 engine, single 2-barrel carburettor, 305bhp, push-button automatic transmission, power steering, power brakes, push-button AM radio, restored, finished in black and white, vinyl and fabric interior in excellent condition, fewer than 77,000 miles from new.
£7,000–9,000 / $10,200–13,000 ↗ Bon

De Tomaso

1970 De Tomaso Mangusta, coachwork by Ghia, left-hand drive, restored c1989, little use since, uprated suspension with Koni adjustable shock absorbers, finished in yellow, black interior, good condition.
£14,000–16,000 / $20,500–23,500 ↗ Bon

Having dabbled unsuccessfully in racing-car construction during the early 1960s, Alejandro De Tomaso established himself as a serious automobile manufacturer with the introduction of the Mangusta coupé in 1967. His first road car had been the backbone-chassised Vallelunga, a pretty mid-engined coupé with 1.5 litre Ford four-cylinder engine. Built in small numbers, the Vallelunga was not a success, but it did provide the basis of the chassis for the Mangusta. One of the first supercars, the Mangusta was powered by a mid-mounted 4.7 litre Ford V8 engine driving through a five-speed ZF transaxle. Ghia's Giorgetto Giugiaro contributed the striking coachwork, originally intended for Giotto Bizzarrini, and with around 300bhp on tap, the aerodynamic Mangusta was good for a top speed of around 155mph.

1974 De Tomaso Pantera, 351cu.in overhead-valve V8 engine, 310bhp, 5-speed manual gearbox, 4-wheel independent suspension, 4-wheel disc brakes, power steering, electric windows, locks and sunroof, air conditioning, fewer than 42,000 miles from new, paint showing signs of age.
£10,000–12,000 / $14,500–17,500 ↗ RM

The De Tomaso Pantera, powered by Ford's 351 Cleveland V8 and sharing its mid-engine layout with the American manufacturer's successful GT40 racing cars, translated the race-bred concept of De Tomaso's Mangusta into a steel-bodied supercar with such amenities as reasonable luggage space, air conditioning and power assists that American buyers expected. Introduced at the New York Auto Show in 1970, Panteras were sold by select Lincoln-Mercury dealers from 1971 to 1974.

De Tomaso Pantera (1971–93)

Body style: Mid-engined two-seat sports coupé.
Construction: Unitary with pressed-steel chassis, aluminium and steel body panels.
Engine: 5763cc cast-iron V8 (Ford).
Transmission: ZF five-speed manual.
Power output: 350bhp at 6,000rpm.
Suspension: Independent all-round by front and rear upper and lower unequal-length wishbones, coil springs and anti-roll bar.
Brakes: All-round vacuum-assisted discs.
Maximum speed: 159mph.
0–60mph: 5.5 seconds.
Average fuel consumption: 14mpg.
Few cars descend from more mixed parentage than the De Tomaso Pantera. It's not just the Ford V8 and the Italian styling, courtesy of Ghia; the company's founder Alejandro de Tomaso was an Argentinian racing driver turned supercar builder. His first serious effort at series supercar production was the mid-engined Ford powered Mangusta of 1967, and in 1971 the Pantera developed the theme into an awesome supercar.

The project was strongly supported by Ford in the USA. Ford's Lincoln-Mercury division was pushing its performance image hard, and the Pantera gave glamour to the showrooms as a plausible Ford GT40 successor.
Somewhere between 5,000 and 6,000 were sold in the USA from 1971 to 1974 – no one knows for sure – but after that Ford withdrew showroom support and production continued at a trickle until 1993.
Nevertheless, the gloriously brawny Pantera continued to evolve into GTS and GT5 versions, sprouting wings, spoilers, flared wheel arches and other appendages like a bodybuilder on steroids. The Pantera is a flawed supercar certainly, with annoying little foibles like the tendency for the front end to lift and the steering to lighten alarmingly above 120mph, although the later spoilers and wings helped keep it down. But forget the flaws; just look at and listen to this primal expression of unleashed power. It's evil, beautifully evil.

DKW

◀ **c1958 DKW 1000 Saloon,** right-hand drive, imported into the UK from South Africa 1999, stored since, in need of recommissioning/restoration.
£1,200–1,700 / $1,750–2,450 ⚒ Bon
Originally a motorcycle manufacturer, DKW was founded in 1919 and built its first power unit, a two-stroke, in 1921, remaining faithful to this type of engine from then on for both motorcycles and cars. The first DKW car appeared in 1928, and in 1932 the firm became part of the Auto Union group of companies. After WWII, DKW production resumed in 1950. The firm had pioneered front-wheel drive on its smaller models in the early 1930s, and in the post-war era all DKW cars would have this form of transmission, beginning with the twin-cylinder Meisterklasse F89. The latter was followed by the three-cylinder 896cc Sonderklasse and 980cc 1000/1000S models, the latter being marketed as Auto Unions.

Dodge

1936 Dodge D5 Four-Dour Saloon, right-hand drive, body and chassis in good condition, seats retrimmed and in good condition, engine and paint in poor condition.
£2,500–3,000 / $3,500–4,500 ⚒ CGC

1963 Dodge Polara 500 426 Max Wedge Coupé, 1 of only 5 built with 426cu.in 'Max Wedge' engine, cast-iron headers, factory blow-off tubes, 425bhp, push-button automatic transmission, professionally restored.
£26,000–30,000 / $37,500–43,500 ⚒ BJ

Duesenberg

1930 Duesenberg Model J Derham Tourster Replica, 420cu.in double-overhead-camshaft 4-valves per-cylinder 8-cylinder engine, 265bhp, 3-speed manual gearbox, beam front axle, semi-elliptic leaf springs all-round, 4-wheel servo-assisted hydraulic drum brakes, left-hand drive, originally fitted with LeBaron limousine coachwork, replica Tourster coachwork fitted 1960s, restored mid-1980s, little use since, finished in red, tan leather interior, excellent condition.
£160,000+ / $232,000+ ⚒ C
In 1929, Gordon Buehrig was hired by Duesenberg as its chief designer. His designs were instantly successful and have become renowned as some of the finest of the era. Although Buehrig's designs were available for construction by any coachbuilder, in fact, the Tourster was only built by Derham. A distinctive aspect of the design is the steeply angled, retractable windscreen for the rear passengers, a feature that later became popular on Cadillacs and Chryslers. Fortunately, however, unlike a dual-cowl phaeton, on a Tourster there is no rear cowl or side vents to negotiate upon entry.

Edsel

The poor old Ford Edsel, consigned to the dustbin of history as the ultimate clunker. Everyone blames that unfortunate 'horse-collar' frontal treatment, but that's only part of the story. Kinder critics say that its aim was true, but the target moved. Conceived when sales of lower/medium-priced cars were booming, the Edsel was intended to be a mass-market winner. The trouble is, by the time it was officially launched on 4 September 1957, the US auto industry was in a slump, with sales particularly affected in the Edsel's market segment. It was also a victim of its own hype. Throughout its conception, the marketing men had gone into hyperdrive. They forecast 200,000 sales in the first year, and naturally would have to build extra factories to cope with the demand for a car they claimed had cost a ridiculous £172,500,000/$250,000,000 to develop. The truth is that in its first year, the Edsel set an all-time record for deliveries of a brand-new medium-priced model. Yet it fell so short of the grandiose claims that it was almost instantly dubbed a failure. Today, the Edsel is an emblem, comforting reassurance for the little man that mighty corporations can get it wrong. And, of course, its comparative failure marks it out as a prized collector's piece.

1958 Edsel Pacer Two-Door Hardtop, 361cu.in V8 engine, hardened valve seats for unleaded fuel, 303bhp, factory dual exhaust system, 3-speed automatic transmission with Teletouch push-button operation from steering-wheel centre, power steering, unrestored, original black finish, white vinyl and fabric interior, fewer than 66,500 miles from new, excellent running condition.
£6,000–7,000 / $8,700–10,200 ✍ Bon
The brief handed to Ford product planners was to develop an entirely new division of the company that would fill the perceived market void between the Ford and Mercury lines. Many components would come from the corporate parts bins, but the all-new styling was the responsibility of designer Roy Brown. He was told that the new car had to look like no other and be recognizable immediately a block away. The 1958 Edsel was certainly distinctive, with its combination of vertical and horizontal grilles, and high-mounted headlamps. Unfortunately, the distinctive styling wasn't enough to make up for production problems, which contributed to inconsistent quality and led to sales that were far below projections.

Elfin

c1961 Elfin Clubman Sports, 1500cc overhead-valve 4-cylinder Ford Cortina engine, Cosworth modifications, 4-speed close-ratio synchromesh gearbox, tubular-steel space frame, independent wishbone front suspension, rigid rear axle on coil springs, 4-wheel hydraulic drum brakes, older restoration, finished in red, black vinyl interior, 2nd example built, excellent condition.
£9,000–10,000 / $13,000–14,500 ✍ GO

Following the success of his full-width-bodied 'streamliners', which were designed along the lines of the Lotus 11, Adelaide based Elfin founder, designer and builder Garrie Cooper saw the potential to produce a Clubman model along the lines of the Lotus 7. Light weight and excellent handling, combined with a variety of proprietary mechanical components, modified and adapted to suit, provided the owners of the 14 Elfin Clubmans built with a very successful competition car at moderate cost, and one that also could be used as an exciting road car.

EMF

◀ **1910 EMF Model 30A Four-Seater Tourer,** 3000cc engine, right-hand drive, restored, finished in green and black, black interior, VCC dated, excellent condition throughout.
£13,000–15,000 / $19,000–22,000 ⬈ H&H
EMF stands for the Everitt-Metzger-Flanders Company of Detroit, Michigan, which was formed in 1908, but did not produce its first car until 1910. It soon became involved with Studebaker, which took over the company in 1912. EMF's advertising slogan was '4mph to 55mph in direct drive', but it persuaded very few to buy.

Essex

▶ **1925 Essex Six Tourer,** 2000cc 6-cylinder engine, older restoration, finished in yellow, black interior trim, excellent condition throughout.
£7,000–8,000 / $10,200–11,600 ⬈ H&H
In 1916, Hudson was a successful motor manufacturer producing 25,000 cars a year, but Roscoe B. Jackson was concerned about the threat posed by cheap mass-produced cars from the likes of Ford. Consequently, he created a separate company to compete in this market, the name Essex being chosen by studying a map of England and because it implied a large six-cylinder engine.

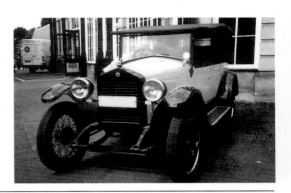

Facel Vega

Haute 'car-ture' never came much higher than Facel Vegas. These boulevard supercars were once the height of fashion, owned and driven by the rich and famous, like Tony Curtis, Joan Fontaine, Ava Gardner, Ringo Starr, Danny Kay, Stirling Moss and Pablo Picasso. But

fashion fades and so did Facel, its ten-year flirtation with car making finally crippling the company in 1964. What remains is a legacy of a little over 2,000 cars, a faddish and fanciful footnote in motoring history if you like – but a fascinating one.

1959 Facel Vega HK500, 5907cc V8 engine, 360bhp, 4-speed manual gearbox, 4-wheel disc brakes, centre-lock wheels, restored late 1990s,
£17,000–20,000 / $25,000–29,000 ⬈ Pou

1959 Facel Vega HK500, 5.9 litre Chrysler V8 engine, manual gearbox, right-hand drive, completely restored 1990–92 at a cost of over £50,000/$72,000, finished in black, red leather upholstery, very good condition throughout.
£13,000–15,000 / $19,000–22,000 ⬈ Bon
From being chiefly engaged in the supply of car bodies to Panhard, Simca and Ford of France, Facel branched out into automobile manufacture in 1954 with the launch of the Vega. A luxurious grand tourer, the Vega featured elegant coupé bodywork welded to a tubular-steel chassis. The power unit was Chrysler's 4.5 litre, 180bhp V8, and there was a choice of push-button automatic or manual transmission. An improved model, the HK500, appeared in 1957. Maximum power was around 360bhp, courtesy of the latest 5.9 litre version of Chrysler's 'hemi' V8, and top speed rose to around 140mph. Power steering became an option and Dunlop disc brakes were adopted as standard equipment in 1960.

1962 Facel Vega HKIIA, 6286cc Chrysler V8 engine, 360bhp, 5-speed ZF manual gearbox, independent front suspension by coil springs, rear suspension by semi-elliptic leaf springs, 4-wheel disc brakes, centre-lock wire wheels, 1 of 180 built.
£25,000–28,000 / $36,000–40,000 ⬈ Pou

F
E
R
R
A
R
I

Ferrari

There simply is no other marque in the world that incites passion and sets pulses racing the way Ferrari does. Although Enzo Ferrari died in 1988, there can be no doubt that his spirit inhabits every new Ferrari that leaves the factory.

Born in 1898 and already driving in his early teens, Enzo went on to race Alfa Romeos with considerable success throughout the 1920s. In 1929, he set up Scuderia Ferrari, which became, in effect, the Alfa Romeo factory team. The decisive moment in Enzo's career came in 1938, when Alfa took back control of its racing activities. In 1940, Ferrari built a Fiat-based racer of his own; even though it did not bear his name, it was surely the first Ferrari car. In late 1946, he began a series of road racers, this time bearing his name, which led to the first true Ferrari production road car, the 166 of 1948. Like the road racers on which it was based, the 166 employed a V12 engine, a configuration that would become a hallmark of the Maranello make. Throughout the 1950s and into the 1960s, Ferrari road cars were essentially hand-made and dressed with beautiful bodies by the finest Italian stylists. In 1969, Fiat took a 50 per cent interest in Ferrari and, when Enzo Ferrari died in 1988, gained complete control.

From the beginning of Fiat's interest in Ferrari, it ushered in a new era. The model range broadened throughout the 1970s, with a corresponding increase in volume; production was approaching 3,000 cars a year by 1980. While Ferrari continued to notch up a continuous string of hallmark icons from the Daytona to the 365BB, 512BBi, Testarossa, 288 GTO and F40, it was also an era during which Fiat nudged Ferrari a little closer to the automotive mainstream, some models being pitched down-market into Porsche territory, while others – a series of saloons and 2+2 coupés – made a passing pretence to every-day practicality. For the first time, with the 400 saloon, there was even an automatic option on a Ferrari, but thankfully never a production model with four doors. That would have had Ferrari fanatics seeing red. Moreover, at the same time, Ferraris were becoming less rarefied and exotic; where once some models were produced in hundreds, now many were built in their thousands. Many Ferrari purists feared that the mystique of the marque was being diluted, and it was. Throughout the 1990s, however, Ferrari regained its true course and once more is setting pulses racing with the extravagant, exotic, no-compromise creations in the spirit of Enzo Ferrari. Witness the pointless performance and sublime impracticality of the 360, 456 and 550: all good for a completely unusable 180+mph. Of course, it's pointless and that's the point.

So much for history; what about the prospect of owning one? The notion of a family man's Ferrari, or even an affordable one, may sound contradictory, but in today's market there is a whole clutch of classic 150mph Maranello hardware available at new Ford prices.

For the price of a Ford Ka 3 at £9,000/$13,000, through the middle ground of Focus and Mondeo models, to the range topping Explorer at £27,000/$40,000, you could be driving a Ferrari from the 1970s or 1980s.

Few Ferrari models are cheaper than the 308 GT4, produced from 1973 to 1979 with a 3 litre V8. The angular 2+2 styling, Bertone's first foray for Ferrari, is nobody's favourite, but 255bhp and 155mph are worth consideration. At auction, 308 GT4s regularly sell for under £10,000/$14,500, while anything much beyond £15,000/$22,000 should be a real sparkler. The 308 GT4's successor, the much prettier and softer natured Mondial, produced throughout the 1980s, was once described by Car magazine as 'the closest you'll get to supercar family transport.' Over the last year, the highest price recorded at auction was £18,000/$26,000, and I saw a 60,000km Mondial, sold at auction, for £11,000/$16,000.

More prolific at auction are the near 5 litre V12-engined 400 and 412 saloons, produced in various guises from 1976 into the early 1990s. This is a car that is the size of an XJ6 Jaguar, but actually looks a lot smaller and feels it on the inside, with accommodation that is most accurately described as an ample 2+2 rather than a true four-seater. Auction prices over the last year have ranged from £8,000/$11,500 to £17,000/$24,500. Not even the most optimistic price guides place the best above £22,000/$32,000.

For many, though, Ferrari ownership is all about two-seater hedonism, and Maranello's most affordable are the V8-engined 308 GTB and 328 GTB. Both are real purist's Ferraris with all the show, go and whoa, yet recent auction prices for 308 GTBs range from £13,000/$19,000 to £21,000/$30,000, the last for a car accompanied by £30,000/$44,000 -worth of invoices for restoration, repair and maintenance. The ceiling for 308 GTBs is around £26,000/$38,000. The younger and faster 328 GTB, produced from 1985 to 1988, generally fall within the £20,000-30,000/$80,000–$44,000 range, with excellent examples nudging £35,000/$51,000.

All of this may sound enticing, but used Ferraris are high-maintenance cars, intensive to own and often with horrendous fuel mileage. You should never buy a Ferrari without a decent, documented service and maintenance history. The last car you want is one that has spiralled down through a succession of owners, each with less means to carry out essential maintenance.

1956 Ferrari 250 GT Coupé, coachwork by Boano, chassis no. 0639GT, engine no. 0639GT, 2953cc V12 engine, 3 carburettors, 240bhp, 4-speed manual gearbox, 4-wheel drum brakes, Borrani wire wheels, 1 of 132 Boano-built examples, fewer than 43,000 miles from new, restored to original condition.
£75,000–90,000 / $109,000–140,000 ⚒ Pou

1959 Ferrari 250 GT Coupé, coachwork by Pininfarina, chassis no. 1479GT, engine no. 1479GT, 3000cc, 4-wheel drum brakes, original Borrani wire wheels, left-hand drive, finished in red, black interior, fewer than 52,500 miles from new, excellent condition throughout.
£35,000–40,000 / $51,000–58,000 ⚒ H&H

Most Ferraris' model numbers represented the approximate cubic capacity in cc of one cylinder of the engine. Thus the Ferrari 365 GTB/4 was so called because the capacity of each of its 12 cylinders was approximately 365cc. Overall capacity was 4390cc. One obvious exception is the Ferrari F40 of 1987, so named to celebrate 40 years of the famous prancing-horse marque from Maranello.

1960 Ferrari 250 GT Series II Coupé, coachwork by Pininfarina, chassis no. 2027GT, engine no. 1865GT, correct 250 GT engine, twin distributors and outside plugs, disc brakes, overdrive, Nardi steering wheel, restored 1980s, finished in metallic grey, black leather upholstery, fewer than 650 miles since 1995.
£35,000–40,000 / $51,000–58,000 ⚒ Bon
True series production of the 250 GT began with the arrival of Pininfarina's 'notchback' coupé, 350 of which were built between 1958 and 1960. However, the relatively small scale of production meant that cars could still be ordered with subtle variations according to customer choice. A number of important developments occurred during 250 GT production: the original 128C 3 litre engine was superseded by the twin-distributor 128D, which, in turn, was replaced in 1960 by the outside-plug 128F engine. The last did away with its predecessor's siamesed inlets in favour of six separate ports. On the chassis side, four-wheel disc brakes arrived late in 1959, and a four-speed-plus-overdrive gearbox the following year.

1960 Ferrari 250 GT Cabriolet Series II, coachwork by Pininfarina, chassis no. 1805, 3 litre V12 engine, 240bhp, 4-speed overdrive gearbox, coil-spring independent front suspension, multi-tubular chassis, engine and gearbox rebuilt, electrics refurbished, chassis and bodywork restored, resprayed in white, new magnolia leather interior, very good condition throughout.
£75,000–85,000 / $109,000–123,500 ⚒ Bon
The introduction of the 250 GT Series II Cabriolet brought with it increased standardization, fewer cars being built with special features to individual customer order. The overall look and proportions of the Series I were retained, with front and rear detailing identical to that of Pininfarina's contemporary 250 GT 'notchback' coupé. The Series I's covered headlights were deleted on all but one Series II, and the newcomer gained a slightly taller windscreen, providing increased headroom with the hood erected.

1960 Ferrari 250 GT Lusso, chassis no. 4635, V12 engine, left-hand drive, restored 1997–98, over £20,000 spent on the engine alone, finished in red, light tan leather upholstery, good condition throughout.
£120,000–140,000 / $174,000–203,000 ✗ COYS
When road racing came to an end in the 1960s, Ferrari made the decision to develop the 250 GT in two different ways. One was the Lusso (Luxury), which had a higher level of trim to make it suitable for road use; the other was the GTO, intended for competition use only.

1962 Ferrari 250 GTE, chassis no. 250GTE 3323, V12 engine, finished in red, black leather upholstery.
£28,000–34,000 / $41,000–49,500 ✗ COYS
In 1960, Ferrari introduced the 250 2+2 GTE, forerunner of the four-seat Ferraris. It offered more room than the other versions, yet it was a fast sports car in its own right; 240bhp translated into a top speed approachng 150mph, with acceleration to match. The model met with immediate success and soon accounted for 60 per cent of all Ferrari road-car sales. Production ceased late in 1963, by which time 950 cars had been built.

1963 Ferrari 250 GT/L Lusso, chassis no. 4425, 2953cc overhead-camshaft V12 engine, 4-speed manual gearbox, 4-wheel disc brakes, restored early 1990s at a cost of £118,000, finished in dark blue, cream leather interior, 'as new' condition.
£100,000–120,000 / $145,000–174,000 ✗ RM

▶ **1963 Ferrari 250 GTE 2+2,** coachwork by Pininfarina, chassis no. 4745, engine no. 4745, outside-plug V12 engine, 240bhp, 4-speed manual/overdrive gearbox, 4-wheel disc brakes, independent front suspension, left-hand drive, engine and gearbox overhauled, fewer than 1,200 miles since, finished in black, red leather interior.
£35,000–40,000 / $51,000–58,000 ✗ Bon

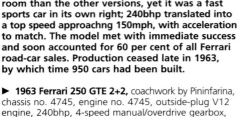

FERRARI Model	ENGINE cc/cyl	DATES	CONDITION 1	2	3
250 GTE	2953/12	1959–63	£32,000	£22,000	£20,000
250 GT SWB (steel)	2953/12	1959–62	£400,000+	£200,000+	-
250 GT Lusso	2953/12	1962–64	£85,000+	£65,000+	£50,000
250 GT 2+2	2953/12	1961–64	£32,000	£24,000	£18,000
275 GTB	3286/12	1964–66	£120,000+	£80,000	£70,000
275 GTS	3286/12	1965–67	£90,000+	£70,000	£50,000
275 GTB 4–cam	3286/12	1966–68	£190,000+	£150,000	£100,000
330 GT 2+2	3967/12	1964–67	£27,000+	£18,000	£11,000
330 GTC	3967/12	1966–68	£55,000+	£40,000+	£25,000
330 GTS	3967/12	1966–68	£80,000+	£70,000+	£60,000
365 GT 2+2	4390/12	1967–71	£30,000+	£20,000	£15,000
365 GTC	4390/12	1967–70	£40,000+	£35,000	£30,000
365 GTS	4390/12	1968–69	£190,000+	£130,000+	£80,000
365 GTB (Daytona)	4390/12	1968–74	£80,000	£60,000	£50,000
365 GTC4	4390/12	1971–74	£45,000+	£38,000	£30,000
365 GT4 2+2/400GT	4390/ 4823/12	1972–79	£25,000	£20,000	£10,000
365 BB	4390/12	1974–76	£45,000	£35,000	£25,000
512 BB/BBi	4942/12	1976–81	£50,000+	£40,000	£28,000
246 GT Dino	2418/6	1969–74	£40,000	£30,000	£20,000
246 GTS Dino	2418/6	1972–74	£50,000	£32,000	£20,000
308 GT4 2+2	2926/8	1973–80	£15,000	£10,000	£8,000
308 GTB (fibreglass)	2926/8	1975–76	£25,000	£18,000	£12,000
308 GTB	2926/8	1977–81	£22,000	£16,000	£10,000
308 GTS	2926/8	1978–81	£22,000	£18,000	£11,000
308 GTBi/GTSi	2926/8	1981–82	£24,000	£17,000	£10,000
308 GTB/GTS QV	2926/6	1983–85	£21,500	£16,500	£9,500
400i manual	4823/12	1981–85	£12,000	£10,000	£8,000
400i auto	4823/12	1981–85	£11,000	£9,000	£7,000

1965 Ferrari 275 GTB/6C Berlinetta, coachwork by Pininfarina, chassis no. 7269, engine no. 7269, 6 carburettors, largely original, uprated to 'long-nose' bodywork, original black leather upholstery and interior trim including protective plastic covering to footwell carpets, 53,500 miles from new.
£90,000–100,000 / $130,500–145,000   ⚒ Bon
Ferrari's successful 250 series was superseded in 1964 by the 275. In Ferrari nomenclature of the period, a model's designation reflected the cubic capacity of an individual cylinder, so the newcomer displaced 3.3 litres, up from its predecessor's 3 litres. The V12 engine remained the familiar Colombo type, in standard form producing 280bhp at 7,600rpm. A higher – 300bhp – state of tune employing six Weber carburettors was available and was used for the handful of 275 GTB/C (Competition) models built. Revisions to the original 275 GTB were not long coming: a longer nose, enlarged rear windows, and external boot hinges being introduced toward the end of 1965. Mechanically, the only major change was the adoption of torque-tube enclosure for the propshaft.

1965 Ferrari 275 GTS Spyder, coachwork by Pininfarina, chassis no. 07345, engine no. 07345, 3.3 litre V12 engine, 260bhp, rear-mounted 5-speed transaxle, independent double-wishbone-and-coil-spring rear suspension, multi-tubular frame, Borrani wire wheels, left-hand drive, restored, fewer than 1,000 miles since, finished in yellow, new black interior trim, 1 of only 200 275 GTS models built, concours condition.
£100,000–120,000 / $145,000–174,000   ⚒ Bon

1966 Ferrari 275 GTB/6C Aluminium Berlinetta, coachwork by Pininfarina, chassis no. 08067, 6 Weber carburettor configuration, 5-speed transaxle, independent rear suspension, Borrani wire wheels, external fuel filler, roll bar, finished in yellow, black leather upholstery, seat belts, 62,000 miles from new.
£170,000–200,000 / $246,000–290,000   ⚒ Bon
Following its launch in 1964, subtle improvements were not long in coming for the 275 GTB. Towards the end of 1965, the nose was lengthened to improve high-speed stability, while the rear window was enlarged to improve vision and the boot hinges resited to the outside to give a little more luggage space. Soon after, the open driveshaft was replaced by a solid torque tube for ease of maintenance. Options available included lighter aluminium coachwork, a six-carburettor set-up for added power, an exterior fuel filler and the choice between cast alloy wheels or Borrani wires.

1966 Ferrari 275 GTB/2 Coupé, 6 Weber carburettors, external fuel filler, competition-type outside-laced Borrani wire wheels, aluminium body, engine and running gear overhauled, bodywork refurbished, fewer than 1,000 miles since, 17,500 miles from new.
£180,000–200,000 / $260,000–290,000   ⚒ BJ

▶ **1964 Ferrari 330 GT 2+2,** coachwork by Pininfarina, 3967cc V12 engine.
£28,000–34,000 / $40,000–50,000   ⚒ BJ

1964 Ferrari 330 GT 2+2, coachwork by Pininfarina, 3967cc V12 engine, 3 carburettors, 4-speed overdrive gearbox, 4-wheel disc brakes, Borrani wire wheels, restored, finished in metallic grey, red leather upholstery.
£30,000–35,000 / $44,000–51,000 ⚒ Pou

1968 Ferrari 330 GTS Spyder, coachwork by Pininfarina, chassis no. 11011, engine no. 11011, 4 litre overhead-camshaft V12 engine, 300bhp, 5-speed all-synchromesh transaxle, torque-tube transmission, 4-wheel independent suspension by wishbones and coil springs, tubular spaceframe chassis, Borrani wire wheels, finished in red, black leather interior, electric windows, modern seat belts, engine overhauled, fewer than 40,500 miles from new.
£125,500/$140,000 / $180,000–203,000 ⚒ Bon
Only 100 330 GTS models were produced by the factory between 1966 and 1968.

1969 Ferrari 365 GTS Spyder, coachwork by Pininfarina, chassis no. 12307, engine no. 12307, radiator, steering box, rear brake calipers and rev-counter refurbished, stainless-steel exhaust manifolds, all hoses replaced, wheels rebuilt with 15in alloy rims, £18,500/$27,000 spent since 1999, finished in red, black leather upholstery, inertia-reel seatbelts, 1 of only 19 built, excellent condition.
£180,000–200,000 / $260,000–290,000 ⚒ Bon
Built only in 1969, the 365 GTS stands out as Ferrari's rarest production Spyder. It had the 4.4 litre Colombo V12, all-independent suspension and a five-speed transaxle. Top speed was 145 mph, while 0–60mph was achieved in under seven seconds.

1967 Ferrari 330 GTC, chassis no. 9537, 3967cc overhead-camshaft V12 engine, 300bhp, 5-speed transaxle, 4-wheel disc brakes, 4-wheel independent suspension, wire wheels, finished in brown, recently recommissioned at a cost of over £6,800/$10,000, fewer than 43,500 miles from new.
£45,000–55,000 / $65,000–80,000 ⚒ RM

1965 Ferrari Superfast

British comic actor Peter Sellers, star of the Pink Panther films, was also a keen motoring enthusiast. His passions ranged from Minis to Rolls-Royces, and in 1965 he bought an ultra-rare right-hand-drive Ferrari 500 Superfast.

1959 Ferrari 410 Superamerica Series III Coupé, coachwork by Pininfarina, chassis no. 1265SA, engine no. 1265SA, finished in original platinum grey, tan leather upholstery, 2nd of 12 410 Series III Superamericas built, exhibited at Geneva Salon 1959, 1 owner since 1960, fewer than 10,500 miles from new.
£425,000+ / $616,000+ ⚒ Bon
In its day, the Ferrari 410 Superamerica was one of the fastest and most potent of supercars. When tested by *Road & Track* in 1962, it recorded a maximum speed of 165mph and 0–60mph in 6.6 seconds. Ferrari had begun exploring the potential of Lampredi's very successful Grand Prix V12 engine as a road-going power unit in the early 1950s. Aimed squarely at the US market, the ultimate expression of the Lampredi-engined dynasty of Ferrari road cars – the 410 Superamerica – arrived in 1958. By then, the V12 had been enlarged to 4962cc and power increased to 340bhp. For the 410's final, Series III, incarnation, power was increased further to 400bhp.

1969 Ferrari 365 GTC, chassis no. 12245, power brakes, air conditioning, electric windows, period 8-track stereo, original, 1 of only 21 right-hand-drive 365 GTCs made, 48,000 miles from new.
£60,000–70,000 / $87,000–102,000 ↗ COYS
This car is thought to have been owned by former Beatle George Harrison under a pseudonym.

1969 Ferrari 365 GTC Coupé, coachwork by Pininfarina, chassis no. 12325, 4.4 litre overhead-camshaft V12 engine, 320bhp, 5-speed all-synchromesh transaxle, 4-wheel wishbone-and-coil-spring independent suspension, 4-wheel disc brakes, electric windows, heated rear screen, left-hand drive, cylinder heads overhauled, front suspension rebuilt, finished in metallic dark blue, black leather interior, fewer than 52,500 miles from new, original.
£60,000–70,000 / $87,000–101,500 ↗ Bon
Like so many European sports cars, the 365 GTC and convertible 365 GTS would fall victim to increasingly stringent US safety and emissions legislation, production ceasing after less than a year, during which time a mere 150 GTC and 20 GTS models left the factory.

1969 Ferrari 365 GT 2+2, coachwork by Pininfarina, left-hand drive, unrestored, finished in metallic light blue, original tan leather interior, good condition throughout.
£25,000–30,000 / $36,000–44,000 ↗ Bon
Replacement for the 330 GT 2+2, the 365 GT 2+2 was launched in October 1967. Styled in the manner of the limited-edition 500 Superfast, the 365 GT was the most refined Ferrari to date. As well as featuring all-round independent suspension (a first for a Ferrari 2+2), it boasted Koni's hydro-pneumatic self-levelling system at the rear. Further refinements included rubber-bushed mountings for the engine and drivetrain to insulate the car's occupants from noise and vibration, while power-assisted steering and air conditioning were standard. The well-proven 4.4 litre V12 engine was coupled to a five-speed gearbox, and the car's blistering performance was restrained by all-round Girling ventilated disc brakes.

1969 Ferrari 365 GT 2+2, 4.4 litre V12 engine, completely restored, magnolia interior, 77,000 miles from new.
£36,000–40,000 / $52,000–58,000 ⊞ KHP

1970 Ferrari 365 GTB/4 Daytona, coachwork by Pininfarina, chassis no. 13479, engine no. 251, Cromodora alloy wheels, finished in dark blue, reddish-brown and black Connolly leather upholstery, 8-track stereo, air conditioning, 1 owner and fewer than 61,000 miles from new, original condition, last used 1990, in need of recommissioning.
£50,000–60,000 / $72,000–87,000 ↗ Bon
The 365 GTB/4 Daytona entered production in 1969. In response to Lamborghini, Ferrari's road V12 had gained four overhead camshafts during production of the 275 GTB, to become the 275 GTB/4; the new Daytona displaced 4390cc. With a power output of 352bhp at 7,500rpm, the result was a top speed of over 170mph. This made the Daytona the world's fastest production car well into the 1970s. Dry-sump lubrication permitted the engine to be installed low in the chassis, while a five-speed transaxle transmission made it possible to achieve 50/50 front-to-rear weight distribution. In standard Ferrari practice, the chassis was built from oval-section tubing, but the all-independent wishbone-and-coil-suspension was a more recent development, having originated in the 275 GTB. The car was named in honour of Ferrari's victory in the 1967 24-hour event at Daytona, Florida, and its competition potential was soon being exploited by privateer racers. It proved a formidable opponent in international endurance events.

Miller's Compares

I. 1972 Ferrari 365 GTS/4A Daytona Spyder, coachwork by Pininfarina, chassis no. 15963, V12 engine, Borrani wire wheels, electric windows, new black mohair hood, hood cover, bare-metal respray in original metallic blue, original blue leather seats with black inserts, factory fitted air conditioning, original radio, 1 of 7 factory right-hand-drive Spyders built, fewer than 16,000 miles from new.
£275,000+ / $399,000+ ➤ Bon

II. 1973 Ferrari 365 GTB/4 Daytona Spyder Conversion, coachwork by Pininfarina, chassis no. 16761, engine no. 16761, right-hand drive, converted to spyder coachwork 1987, rebuilt 1996–98, finished in red, light tan interior with black inserts, air conditioning, over £50,000 spent since 1985, fewer than 24,500 miles from new.
£60,000–70,000 / $87,000–102,000 ➤ Bon
Ferrari made a mere 127 geniune Spyders, of which only seven were right-hand drive models. With its strong, rigid chassis – the same independently-sprung design as used on the 275 – it has been an easy option for owners of the Daytona coupé to specify subsequent conversion to spyder coachwork.

The massive difference in value between these two Ferrari Daytonas can be explained by the fact that no matter how much money and craft is expended on car II, it still can never be what car I is, namely an original Daytona Spyder. Car II was converted to a Spyder in 1987, and even though it may be completely indistinguishable from the 'real' thing, its value will never remotely approach that of an authentic Spyder. In the classic car world, authenticity holds a lot of sway, particularly in cases such as the Daytona where Ferrari produced 1,287 fixed-heads and a mere 127 Spyders.

1972 Ferrari 365 GTC/4 Spyder, 6 Weber carburettors, ZF power steering, thought to be 1 of 4 adapted by Scaglietti to Spyder configuration.
£65,000–75,000 / $94,000–109,000 ➤ BJ

1973 Ferrari 365 GT4/BB, flat-12 engine, 4 overhead camshafts, 360bhp, finished in metallic brown, beige leather interior, 1 of only 50 original right-hand-drive cars built, 19,500 miles from new, concours winner.
£30,000–35,000 / $44,000–51,000 ➤ COYS

◄ **1982 Ferrari 512 BBi,** 4942cc flat-12 engine, fuel injection, 5-speed gearbox, 4-wheel independent suspension, 4-wheel disc brakes, finished in metallic silver-grey, fewer than 6,000 miles from new.
£30,000–35,000
$44,000–51,000 ➤ Pou

1984 Ferrari 512 BBi, coachwork by Pininfarina, 4942cc flat-12 engine, fuel injection, 4-wheel independent suspension, multi-tubular frame, finished in red and black, champagne leather interior, original Blaupunkt radio/cassette, 2 owners and fewer than 3,000 miles from new, totally original.
£50,000–55,000 / $73,000–80,000 ✗ Bon

1969 Ferrari 246 GT Dino, 2400cc engine, centre-lock wheels, left-hand drive, completely restored, finished in red, black interior, concours winner, excellent condition.
£37,000–42,000 / $53,500–61,000 ✗ H&H

Cross Reference
See Colour Review (page 70)

Ferrari Dino 246 GT (1969–74)

Production: Dino 246 GT, 2,732; Dino 246 GTS (Spyder), 1,180.
Engine: Transverse mounted, four-cam, 2418cc V6.
Power output: 195bhp at 7,600rpm.
Transmission: Five-speed manual.
Brakes: Discs all-round.
Maximum speed: 142–148mph.
0–60mph: 7.1 seconds.
In its day, the pretty little Dino was the cheapest Ferrari ever marketed, in Ferrari terms at least a budget supercar that was pitched directly at the Porsche 911. It rang changes in other ways too, for in place of

Ferrari's traditional V12 lump up front, the Dino had a V6 mounted transversely amidships. In fact, it seems that the Dino was intended to emerge as a cheaper 'companion' marque in its own right, as the 246 Dino was initially completely bare of Ferrari script or any prancing-horse insignia. Even so, despite a mere 2.4 litres, its near-150mph performance was very Ferrari-like, with brilliant handling to match. As for the Pininfarina shape, many rate it as one of the prettiest and purest of all Ferraris – lithe, lean and free of the steroid strakes and brutal Rambo garnishes that infected Ferraris in the 1980s and beyond.

1971 Ferrari 246 GT Dino, coachwork by Pininfarina, completely restored 1988–90, fewer than 1,500 miles since, finished in red, tan leather upholstery, 'as new' condition.
£40,000–45,000 / $58,000–65,000 ✗ Bon

The need for a production-based engine for Formula 2 racing resulted in the introduction of a 'junior' Ferrari, the Dino 206 GT, in 1967. A compact, aluminium-bodied coupé of striking appearance, the Pininfarina-styled Dino – named after Enzo Ferrari's late son – was powered by a 2 litre four-cam V6 mounted transversely amidships and driving through a five-speed transaxle. The engine's 180bhp was good enough to propel the lightweight, aerodynamic Dino to 142mph, and while there were few complaints about its performance, the car's noisy cockpit and lack of luggage space hindered sales. A 2.4 litre version on a longer wheelbase – the 246 GT – replaced the Dino 206 in 1969. The body was steel and the cylinder block cast iron, rather than aluminium, but the bigger engine's increased power – 195bhp at 7,600rpm – was adequate compensation for the weight gain. Production of the 246 GT amounted to 2,609 units by the time the model was deleted in 1974.

▶ **1972 Ferrari 246 GTS Dino,** 2418cc engine, 4-wheel disc brakes, 4-wheel independent coil-spring suspension, multi-tubular frame, finished in red, black interior, 41,000 miles from new, very good condition throughout.
£35,000–40,000
$51,000–58,000 ✗ H&H

1972 Ferrari 246 GT Dino, subject of major renovation 1982, tuned 2.4 litre engine, Cosworth 11:1 pistons, balanced bottom-end assembly, electronic ignition, new exhaust manifolds and silencers, aluminium radiator, steering, suspension and brakes reconditioned, header tank replaced, resprayed in silver, 42,700 miles from new, very good condition throughout.
£37,000–42,000 / $53,500–61,000 ➢ **Bon**

1972 Ferrari 246 GTS Dino Spyder, 2.4 litre engine, 195bhp, Cromadora wheels, professionally rebuilt over 10 years, engine overhauled and converted to unleaded fuel, new panels fitted as necessary, interior in excellent condition, 2 owners and 38,500 miles from new.
£40,000–45,000 / $58,000–65,000 ➢ **Bon**
The final revison of the Dino came in 1972, when the GTS targa-roof version went into production.

1973 Ferrari 246 GTS Dino Spyder, coachwork by Pininfarina, 2.4 litre engine, 195bhp, 5-speed transaxle, finished in silver, black leather and cloth upholstery, 2 owners and fewer than 5,500 miles from new, unrestored, would benefit from cosmetic attention.
£32,000–37,000 / $46,500–53,500 ➢ **Bon**

1974 Ferrari 308 GT4 Dino, finished in red, seats reupholstered in black Connolly leather, good mechanical condition.
£10,000–12,000 / $14,500–17,500 ➢ **COYS**
When Ferrari replaced the 246 Dino in 1974, it broke with tradition and employed Bertone to design the coachwork. The resulting 308 GT4 was unlike anything that had come from the Maranello factory before, and all elements of the car were brand-new. Mid-mounted in a traditional tubular-steel space frame, the 3 litre aluminium quad-cam engine drove the rear wheels through a five-speed transaxle. Twin distributors were fitted to the earliest cars, leading to a small power advantage over the later cars. The 308 GT4's lines were crisp and wedge-shaped, and through clever packaging it had been possible to fit in two small rear seats – the '4' in the car's name referred to the total number of seats. The rest refers to the 3.0 litre V8 engine. This small car produced 255bhp at 7,700rpm, which meant a top speed of 155mph and an impressive acceleration time of 0–60mph in 6.5 seconds.

1978 Ferrari 308 GT4, 2926cc V8 engine, 250bhp, 5-speed manual gearbox, 4-wheel independent suspension by A-arms and coil springs, 4-wheel hydraulic disc brakes, right-hand drive, £25,000/$36,000 spent in 1989, finished in dark metallic blue, magnolia and blue interior.
£10,500–12,500 / $15,000–18,000 ➢ **C**

1977 Ferrari 308 GT4, coachwork by Bertone, 3 litre 4-camshaft V8 engine, 236bhp, 4-wheel independent suspension, left-hand drive, partially restored 1995, finished in metallic blue, beige cloth interior, fewer than 39,500 miles from new, excellent condition.
£10,000–12,000 / $14,500–17,500 ➢ **Bon**

◀ **1977 Ferrari 308 GT4,** 2926cc V8 engine, rebuilt at a cost of over £45,000 early 1990s, finished in dark blue, cream leather interior, air conditioning, very good mechanical condition.
£10,000–12,000
$14,500–17,500 ↗ BRIT

1977 Ferrari 308 GTB, engine rebuilt, 58,000 miles from new.
£25,000–35,000 / $36,000–51,000 ↗ COYS
Introduced in October 1975, the 308 GTB had all-new styling, but blended aspects of the 206/246 Dino with the later 365 GT4/BB. Examples built before the end of 1976 were fastest and handled best, thanks to a glassfibre body, which weighed substantially less than the steel coachwork that replaced it. These early cars also featured race-bred dry-sump lubrication, which also was replaced after a short period with a less-expensive wet-sump system.

1980 Ferrari 308 GTS Spyder, coachwork by Pininfarina, 3 litre carburetted engine, 255bhp, finished in bronze, beige leather interior, fewer than 18,500 miles from new.
£20,000–25,000 / $29,000–36,000 ↗ Bon

1982 Ferrari 308 GTS QV Injection Prototipo, coachwork by Pininfarina, 3 litre V8, fuel injection, 5-speed transaxle, 4-wheel independent suspension, 4-wheel disc brakes, multi-tubular chassis, Cromodora alloy wheels.
£20,000–25,000 / $29,000–36,500 ↗ Pou
This prototype QV was stolen from the factory in 1981. A year later, its 'owner', a gangster from Marseille, was killed and the car auctioned, without anyone realizing that it had been stolen. After passing through the hands of a dealer, it was purchased by a Frenchman, who subsequently left it with a Belgian Ferrari dealership for servicing. When ordering parts, the dealer quoted the engine number to the factory and the car's true identity became known. It was siezed immediately, but after an 18-month legal battle, its French owner managed to recover the car.

1985 Ferrari 308 GTS QV, 3 litre engine, 40,000 miles from new.
£27,000–30,000 / $39,000–43,500 ⊞ **KHP**

1986 Ferrari 328 GTS, 3.2 litre engine, finished in yellow, black leather interior, 21,500 miles from new.
£30,000–35,000 / $43,000–51,000 ⊞ **KHP**

1987 Ferrari 328 GTB, coachwork by Pininfarina, V8 engine, roof spoiler, finished in metallic grey, dark blue leather interior, blue leather-trimmed dashboard, air conditioning, 480 miles from new.
£35,000–40,000 / $51,000–58,000 ⚒ **Bon**
The 308 was superseded by the mechanically similar, but larger-engined, 328 GTB in 1985. By increasing the bore and stroke, the *quattrovalvole* engine's capacity was raised to 3186cc. This, together with a higher compression ratio, revised pistons and an improved Marelli engine management system, boosted maximum power to 270bhp at 7,000rpm. Top speed was raised to within a whisker of 160mph, with the sprint to 60mph covered in 5.5 seconds.

1988 Ferrari 328 GTB, 3.2 litre engine, magnolia interior, fewer than 30,000 miles from new.
£33,000–37,000 / $48,000–53,500 ⊞ **KHP**

1989 Ferrari 328 GTS, finished in red, magnolia leather interior, air conditioning, 36,000 miles from new.
£28,000–33,000 / $40,000–48,000 ⊞ **VIC**

1989 Ferrari 328 GTS Spyder, coachwork by Pininfarina, 3186cc V8 engine, 4 valves per cylinder, Bosch fuel injection, 270bhp, 4-wheel independent suspension by double wishbones and coil springs, 4-wheel servo-assisted disc brakes, multi-tubular chassis, aluminium wheels, roof aerofoil, finished in red, beige leather interior, 1 of last 328s built, 1 owner and 87 miles from new.
£40,000–45,000 / $58,000–65,000 ➶ Bon

1991 Ferrari Mondial 3.4t Cabriolet, 2 owners and fewer than 11,000 miles from new, excellent condition.
£26,000–30,000 / $38,000–43,000 ➶ COYS

1980 Ferrari 400i GT, automatic transmission, right-hand drive, £9,000 spent recently on improvements, stainless-steel exhaust system, new alloy wheels, resprayed in metallic grey, magnolia leather interior, reupholstered front seats, wood-veneer centre console, air conditioning, c50,000 miles from new.
£9,000–11,000 / $13,000–16,000 ➶ Bon

1982 Ferrari 400i, stainless-steel exhaust system, finished in metallic blue, cream leather interior, maintained virtually regardless of cost, 2 owners and fewer than 19,000 miles from new.
£9,500–11,000 / $14,000–16,000 ➶ COYS

1989 Ferrari Mondial 3.4t Cabriolet, coachwork by Pininfarina, split-rim wheels, left-hand drive, factory updates to electrical system, finished in red, cream leather interior, fewer than 12,000 miles from new.
£25,000–30,000 / $36,000–43,000 ➶ Bon
In 1984, the Ferrari Mondial Cabriolet was introduced in *quattrovalvole* form as the first true convertible Ferrari since the early 1970s. At the 1985 Frankfurt motor show, all of Ferrari's V8-engined cars had an increase in bore and stroke to give 3185cc and a further boost in power to 270bhp at 7,000rpm, the Mondial being known as the 3.2. By 1989, Ferrari announced the new Mondial 3.4t – the first appearance of the bored and stroked *quattrovalvole* in 3405cc, 296bhp form. The engine had been turned through 90 degrees in the chassis so that its crankshaft was on the car's longitudinal axis, and because it was mounted much lower, it was almost out of sight in the tall engine bay. Along with the revised engine came a new five-speed transmission, positioned as before in the chassis, but mounted transversely, hence the model designation '3.4t'. The result was a lower centre of gravity and better power-to-weight ratio. Electronically controlled, variable Bilstein gas suspension was fitted, which changed pressure with speed and cornering forces, and could be overridden by the three-position manual suspension selector. Top speed was raised to 159mph, with 0–60mph in a mere 5.6 seconds.

1984 Ferrari 400i, new stainless-steel exhaust system and manifolds at a cost of £3,500, new ECU unit, finished in metallic blue, blue leather interior, 60,000 miles from new, good condition.
£9,500–11,000 / $14,000–16,000 ➶ COYS

1986 Ferrari 412, 4943cc V12 engine, 340bhp, 3-speed automatic transmission, 4-wheel independent suspension by wishbones and coil springs, 4-wheel hydraulic disc brakes with ABS, right-hand drive, resprayed in black, 2 owners and c30,000 miles from new, previously owned by Elton John.
£15,000–25,000 / $22,000–36,500 ⚒ C

1985 Ferrari 288 GTO Berlinetta, coachwork by Pininfarina, air conditioning, black leather upholstery, 10,500 miles and 2 owners from new, 1 of only 200 built, excellent condition.
£140,000–160,000 / $203,000–232,000 ⚒ Bon
Introduced in 1984, the 288 GTO was built for Group B racing, although most of the 200 examples needed for homologation were in road-going trim. All were built from lightweight materials, including Kevlar, and came with competition brakes. The GTO bore a family resemblance to the 308 GTB, although it had a longer wheelbase, but any similarity ended there. The 3 litre V8 *quattrovalvole* engine was boosted by two IHI turbochargers and was mounted longitudinally. It was also positioned forward in the frame (the front four cylinders were beneath the rear screen) to give perfect balance and outstanding roadholding. In standard form, this engine produced 400bhp at 3,800rpm. Top speed was 190mph and 0–62mph could be achieved in under five seconds.

► **1989 Ferrari Testarossa,** coachwork by Pininfarina, left-hand drive, finished in white, magnolia leather interior, satellite tracking box, 6-CD changer, paintwork, interior and engine refurbished, 1 owner and fewer than 13,500 miles from new, excellent condition throughout.
£24,000–28,000 / $35,000–40,500 ⚒ Bon
A 'next generation' Berlinetta Boxer, the Testarossa retained its predecessor's mid-mounted, 5 litre flat-12 engine, but with maximum power output raised to 390bhp at 6,300rpm courtesy of four-valve cylinder heads. Despite the power increase, smoothness and drivability were enhanced, the car possessing excellent top-gear flexibility allied to a maximum speed of 180mph.

1992 Ferrari 512 TR, 4943cc flat-12 engine, dry-sump lubrication, 421bhp, 5-speed manual gearbox, limited-slip differential, 4-wheel independent suspension by wishbones and coil springs, 4-wheel ventilated disc brakes, right-hand drive, finished in red, magnolia interior, formerly owned by Elton John.
£40,000–50,000 / $58,000–72,000 ⚒ C

Fiat

Founded in 1899 by Giovanni Agnelli, whose family still controls the company, Fiat has grown into an Italian industrial colossus. The company's initials originally stood for Societa Anonimo Fabbrica Italiana di Automili Torini. Cars are only one area of Fiat's wide ranging interests, and in the motoring field alone Fiat controls Ferrari, Lancia, Abarth and Alfa Romeo. In its early days, Fiat devoted considerable effort to racing, and won the Targa Florio and French Grand Prix in 1907. Some of the early cars had monstrous engines, up to 11 litres. The first

model built in quantity was the 1912 Tipo Zero, of which about 200 were made. In 1919, with the 1.5 litre 501, the company became mass producers, and in 1936 the little 500 Topolino revolutionized personal transport, a feat repeated in 1957 with the 500 Nuova. From the 1960s, Fiat's model range broadened considerably. Two models that stand out and have a strong following today are the long-running 124 Spyder, which makes an interesting alternative to an MGB roadster, and the very pretty and slightly exotic Dino Spyder.

1933 Fiat 508S Balilla Ghia-Style Sports Two-Seater, left-hand drive, original steel scuttle, aluminium body panels, new ash frame.
£17,000–20,000 / $25,000–29,000 ↗ Bon
Introduced in 1932, the 508 Balilla had an excellent reputation for durability. It featured an 88in (223.5cm) wheelbase, 995cc four-cylinder sidevalve engine, a cruciform-braced chassis and hydraulic brakes. It was available in two-door saloon, and two- and four-seat tourer forms, later with a four-speed gearbox. High gearing gave the sidevalve sporting versions a top speed of around 70mph.

1967 Fiat 500 100F, rear-mounted twin-cylinder engine, 4-speed manual gearbox, disc front/drum rear brakes, fewer than 43,000 miles from new.
£2,000–3,000 / $3,000–4,500 ↗ Pou

1969 Fiat Giannini 500 TV, finished in cream, black interior, 3 owners and fewer than 38,000 miles from new, original.
£2,000–3,000 / $3,000–4,500 ↗ COYS
Following the success of the Abarth 500s, Giannini decided to renew its pre-war association with the 'baby' Fiats and provide some serious competition for Abarth on both track and road. The first example was a race prepared car that appeared in 1963, and the resulting popularity of the track cars soon led to the production of fun and accessible road-going versions. All bore the distinctive Giannini *scudetto* (little shield) in place of the Fiat emblem on the nose.

1967 Fiat 500 Giardiniera Estate, 499.6cc air-cooled engine, 3-speed manual gearbox, 4-wheel drum brakes, semi-elliptic leaf-spring suspension, full-length fabric sun roof, finished in blue, good original condition.
£5,000–7,000 / $7,250–10,250 ↗ RM

FIAT Model	ENGINE cc/cyl	DATES	CONDITION 1	2	3
501	1460/4	1920–26	£6,000	£3,500	£1,500
519	4767/6	1923–29	£9,000	£7,000	£3,000
503	1473/4	1927–29	£10,000	£4,000	£2,000
507	2297/4	1927–28	£9,000	£5,500	£3,500
522/4	2516/6	1932–34	£10,000	£8,000	£3,500
508	994/4	1934–37	£5,000	£2,500	£1,500
527 Sports	2516/6	1935–36	£14,000	£8,000	£3,500
1.5 litre Balilla	1498/6	1936–39	£10,000	£7,000	£3,000
500	570/4	1937–55	£6,000	£2,500	£1,000
1100 Balilla	1089/4	1938–40	£4,500	£2,000	£1,000

Miller's
Starter Marque

- **Starter Fiats:** *Fiat 500, 1957 onwards; Fiat 600; Fiat 850 Coupé; Fiat X1/9; Fiat 124 Coupé and Spyder.*
- **Fiat 500:** When the Fiat 500 Nuova appeared in 1957, long-time Fiat designer Dante Giacosa defended his frugal flyweight by saying, 'However small it might be, an automobile will always be more comfortable than a motor scooter.' Today though, the diminutive scootabout needs no defence, for time has justified his faith with production of more than four million 500s and derivatives up to the demise of the Giardiniera estate in 1977. In some senses, the Fiat was a mini before the British Mini, for the baby Fiat not only appeared two years ahead of its British counterpart, but it was also 3in shorter. The original 500 Nuova was rather frantic, having a 479cc tiddler of a two-pot motor. But in 1960, it grew to maturity with the launch of the 500D, which was pushed along by an enlarged 499.5cc engine. Now at last the baby Fiat could almost touch 60mph without being pushed over the edge of a cliff.
- Many Fiat 500 proponents commend the car as a usable every-day commuter classic, and fitting larger Fiat engines (up to 650cc) is a common and acceptable practice. The engines are generally robust and long-lasting, but the monocoque chassis and body are fairly rust-prone. Unless you enjoy DIY restoration, it's advisable to go for the most solid car you can find, as relatively low values mean your friends will appreciate the results of your restoration more than your bank manager.
- **Fiat 850 Coupé:** The Fiat 850 Coupé is a delectable little package combining up to 45mpg economy, peppy performance (90+mph for the 903cc versions), front disc brakes, super handling and delightfully neat styling. Again, on these Fiats, rust is the main enemy. Even though around 380,000 were built between 1965 and 1973, they have never been a common sight in Britain. If you take your time to find a good one, you'll discover a tremendously rewarding little car.
- **Fiat X1/9:** The merits of the sharp-edged Bertone design are a matter of divided opinion, but the X1/9 has a few very important things going for it. It is just about the only truly affordable and practical, volume produced, mid-engined sports car, and it also has exceptional handling. These days, it's undergoing something of a renaissance as an expression of 1970s design. The engine is a little jewel, reliable and generally long-lasting too. Unfortunately, the same can't be said of the body, so the best buy will usually be a later model that's had less time to rust.
- **Fiat 124 Spyder:** Elegant Pininfarina styling, all-round disc brakes, twin-cam power and excellent five-speed gearbox add up to a very appealing and fine handling, fresh-air sporting package. The model was produced by Fiat from 1966 to 1982; from then until 1985, Pininfarina handled production and built it as the Spyder Europe. Once again, rust can strike hard, with front suspension struts, inner sills, and the front and rear edges of the floorpan particularly susceptible. Right-hand-drive versions are very few and far between, but left-right conversion is viable. Of the 200,000 built, a large number went to the USA, so there's every chance of picking up a car that's spent most of its life in a rust-free climate. The best all-round model is the 2 litre carburettor version.

1971 Fiat Abarth 595, 30bhp, 10in wheels, sunroof, Abarth badges, finished in white with Abarth decals, Abarth (Jaeger) instruments, steering wheel and gearknob, black interior, good condition.
£3,250–4,250 / $4,700–6,200 ⚙ **Bon**
Carlo Abarth's star sign was Scorpio, and his logo incorporated a scorpion, while 'sting in the tail' neatly summed-up Abarth modified Fiats. The 595 model, introduced in 1966, was derived from the Fiat 500F and differed from its predecessors by having forward-hinged doors and a slightly longer body. Endowed with sprightly performance for its size, it dominated its class in touring car racing and proved a sales success too.

1971 Fiat 500L, brakes overhauled, blue paintwork refurbished, beige interior, 2 owners from new, original, excellent condition.
£3,500–4,500 / $5,000–6,500 ⚙ **COYS**

Miller's is a price GUIDE not a price LIST

1959 Fiat Jolly Beach Car, coachwork by Ghia, restored 1996, finished in salmon pink, wicker seats, fewer than 7,000 miles from new, good condition throughout.
£13,000–14,000 / $19,000–20,500 ⚙ **Bon**
Introduced in 1955 and produced for 15 years, Fiat's 600 and 600D were an outstanding success for the company, some 2.5 million being built. The compact, rear-engined saloon spawned numerous variants, from sport and competition versions by Abarth to the advanced Multipla people carrier. Many of Italy's finest coachbuilders offered alternatives to the original, perhaps the best known of these being Ghia's stylish Jolly beach car.

Fiat Multipla (1955–66)

Price in 1956: £811.
Production: 130,000 approx.
Engine: Water-cooled four-cylinder of 633cc; 767cc from 1960.
Power output: 22–28.5bhp, 633cc; 32bhp, 767cc.
Transmission: Four-speed manual.
Maximum speed: 55–65mph.
Average fuel consumption: 40mpg.

Fiat's new Multipla compact people carrier naturally invites comparison with a forgotten milestone, the original Multipla of 1955. This brilliantly packaged little device lays a plausible claim to being the first multi-purpose passenger vehicle (MPV). True, the original Multipla appeared some years after the Volkswagen Combi, but the Multipla was both more and less, a tiny Tardis that measured less than a 12ft (366cm) long, yet somehow accommodated six people in three rows of two. Designed by long-time Fiat chief engineer Dante Giacosa, the Multipla was based on the rear-engined Fiat 600 saloon, with the front seats brought forward over the front axle, the rear seats pushed back over the engine, and the whole encased in an egg-shaped shell. The middle and rear seats could be folded into the floor to form a flat bed and mutate the Multipla into a mini-Transit or even a camper van. In fact, you could perm any combination of two to six seats to create a brilliantly versatile vehicle that served as a family car, delivery vehicle and taxi. The one thing it wasn't was a sports car. The 633cc versions, built up to 1960, would take around 54 seconds to reach a top speed of less than 60mph. For later 767cc Multiplas, some owners claim 70mph, but 65mph seems more realistic, less if the ash-tray's full. Today, survivors anywhere are relatively rare. In Italy, most were driven into the ground, and in Britain the handful of surviving roadworthy Multiplas are highly coveted.

▶ **1967 Fiat 600D,** 767cc engine, 32bhp, 4-speed manual gearbox, completely restored, finished in red, instrument panel refurbished, red and white vinyl seats, excellent condition.
£2,500–3,500 / $3,500–5,000 ⚘ CGC

1969 Fiat Shelette Beach Car, coachwork by Michelotti, restored 1998–99, finished in white, wicker seats, 'as new' condition.
£6,000–7,000 / $8,700–10,200 ⚘ Bon

▶ **1970 Fiat 600 Jungla,** coachwork by Savio, finished in yellow, fewer than 400 miles from new, 'as new' condition throughout.
£4,000–5,000 / $5,800–7,250 ⚘ Bon

1959 Fiat 1200 Cabriolet, coachwork by Pininfarina, original Pininfarina stampings to body panels, finished in white, blue interior, swivelling driver and passenger seats, completely original, never restored or repainted, 2 owners, quantity of engine spares.
£4,000–5,000 / $5,800–7,250 ⚘ Bon

Introduced in 1957, the Fiat 1200 combined the new 1221cc overhead-valve engine with a body that had been developed from the preceding 1100 model, which was notable as Fiat's first unitary-construction small car. While Fiat produced the closed version, it was left to Pininfarina to provide an open-topped alternative in the form of the Cabriolet. First exhibited at the 1959 Geneva Salon, the two-seater had been inspired by Pininfarina's Fiat-Osca prototype, seen the previous year at Turin. Mechanically, the Cabriolet remained much the same as the saloon – although the transmission handbrake had been replaced by a conventional rear-wheel type – but came with slightly more power (58 as opposed to 55bhp) and commensurately higher (90mph) top speed. Cabriolet production continued until 1963.

1973 Fiat 124 Sports Coupé, double-overhead-camshaft 4-cylinder engine, 5-speed manual gearbox, 4-wheel disc brakes.
£2,000–2,5000 / $3,000–3,600 ⚒ H&H

1977 Fiat 124 Spyder, 2 litre double-overhead-camshaft 4-cylinder engine, 5-speed manual gearbox, 4-wheel disc brakes, left-hand drive, over £6,600 spent on renovation and maintenance since c1995, finished in black, red interior, oil leak from the gearbox, otherwise good condition.
£3,750–4,500 / $5,500–6,500 ⚒ Bon
Introduced in 1966 and based on a shortened 124 saloon floorpan and running gear, the attractive Pininfarina-styled Spyder proved an outstanding success for Fiat, over 200,000 being sold before production ended in 1982.

◄ **1978 Fiat 124 Spyder,** 1800cc double-overhead-camshaft engine, converted to unleaded fuel, finished in red, good condition.
£1,500–2,500 / $2,200–3,500 ⚒ BARO

1968 Fiat Dino Coupé, coachwork by Bertone, 1987cc 6-cylinder engine, left-hand drive, finished in white, tan interior, stored for several years, very good condition throughout.
£2,500–3,500 / $3600–5,000 ⚒ H&H

1990 Fiat X1/9, 1498cc engine, finished in dark blue, black leather interior, 28,000 miles from new, over £1,000 spent recently, very good condition throughout.
£2,750–3,500 / $4,000–5,000 ⚒ H&H

FIAT Model	ENGINE cc/cyl	DATES	CONDITION 1	2	3
500B Topolino	569/4	1945–55	£5,000	£2,000	£750
500C	569/4	1948–54	£4,000	£1,700	£1,000
500 Nuova	479,499/2	1957–75	£3,000	£1,500	£750
600/600D	633, 767/4	1955–70	£3,000	£2,000	£1,000
500F Giardiniera	479, 499/2	1957–75	£3,000	£1,500	£1,000
2300S	2280/6	1961–68	£3,000	£1,700	£1,000
850	843/4	1964–71	£1,000	£750	-
850 Coupé	843, 903/4	1965–73	£1,500	£1,000	-
850 Spyder	843, 903/4	1965–73	£3,000	£2,000	£1,000
128 Sport Coupé 3P	1116/ 1290/4	1971–78	£2,500	£1,800	£1,000
130 Coupé	3235/6	1971–77	£5,500	£4,000	£2,000
131 Mirafiori Sport	1995/4	1974–84	£1,500	£1,000	£500
124 Sport Coupé	1438/ 1608/4	1966–72	£3,000	£2,000	£1,000
124 Sport Spyder	1438/ 1608/4	1966–72	£5,500	£2,500	£1,500
Dino Coupé	1987/ 2418/6	1967–73	£8,000	£5,500	£2,500
Dino Spyder	1987/ 2418/6	1967–73	£15,000+	£10,000	£5,000
X1/9	1290/ 1498/4	1972–89	£4,000	£2,000	£1,500

Ford

In 1872, when young Henry Ford, the son of an Irish immigrant farmer, was just nine years old, he fell from a horse. As Ford folklore has it, that little mishap sparked his determination to develop a form of transport that was a little safer and more reliable than a precarious perch on top of a snorting beast.

After serving an apprenticeship to a machinist, his vision started to take shape in the winter of 1893, when he built an internal-combustion engine on the kitchen table of the Detroit home he shared with his wife Clara and new-born son Edsel. In 1896, Ford's first motorized vehicle took to the streets of Detroit. The Quadricycle, which exists to this day as an exhibit in the Henry Ford Museum, was a lightweight buggy powered by a two-cylinder four-stroke engine, producing all of 4hp. However, with no reverse gear and no brakes, motoring anywhere in the Quadricycle must have been an adventure. Other vehicles followed, and in 1903 the Ford Motor Company was established and started producing the Model A Runabout. It was the launch of its replacement, the Model T, in 1908 that really brought the company to prominence. The story of Ford in Britain also began with the Model T, when Henry Ford set up his first overseas assembly plant at Trafford Park, Manchester, in 1911; from the 1930s, Fords became as much a part of Britain's motoring landscape as our own domestic makes, like Austin and Morris once were. From the enthusiast's point of view, British built Fords offer a wide variety of affordable classic options, both from before and after WWII. American Fords from the 1950s onwards offer a touch of transatlantic glamour, and the later Mustang is firmly established as a motoring icon, coveted the world over. Ford's US-market products have been covered in a separate section, although there is some overlap with UK products (for example, the Model T, which is both a British and American Ford). In this edition, we have also placed Ford's Edsel and Lincoln products under their own headings.

1906 Ford Model N Two-Seater Runabout, original factory specification in all major respects, finished in red, black upholstery, in need of engine overhaul and recommissioning, chassis and coachwork in good condition.
£6,000–8,000 / $8,700–11,600 ➤ Bon
Henry Ford developed his first petrol driven buggy in the latter years of the 19th century, a primitive quadricycle powered by a twin-cylinder engine. It was not until 1903, however, that the Ford Motor Company was founded, building the twin-cylinder Model A in a disused wagon works in Detroit. The new car found a ready market, and Ford was on the way to realizing his dream. The Model N Runabout appeared in 1906, powered by a 15hp, four-cylinder engine. It was based on a light, but robust, chassis and carried two-seat coachwork. The deluxe Models R and S were derived directly from the Model N, and were the undoubted forerunners for the 'Universal Car', the Model T.

1914 Ford Model T Speedster, 2892cc 4-cylinder engine. finished in red and white.
£6,500–7,500 / $9,500–11,000 ⊞ TUC

1927 Ford Model T Tourer, 2892cc 4-cylinder engine, wire wheels, finished in black, white top.
£6,500–7,500 / $9,500–11,000 ⊞ TUC

FORD Model	ENGINE cc/cyl	DATES	CONDITION 1	2	3
Model T	2892/4	1908–27	£12,000	£7,000	£4,000
Model A	3285/4	1928–32	£8,500	£6,000	£3,500
Model Y and 7Y	933/4	1932–40	£5,000	£3,000	£1,500
Model C, CX & 7W	1172/4	1934–40	£4,000	£2,000	£1,000
Model AB	3285/4	1933–34	£10,000	£8,000	£4,500
Model ABF	2043/4	1933–34	£9,000	£6,000	£4,000
Model V8	3622/8	1932–40	£8,500	£6,000	£4,500
Model V8–60	2227/8	1936–40	£7,000	£5,000	£2,000
Model AF (UK only)	2033/4	1928–32	£9,000	£6,000	£3,500

A right-hand-drive vehicle will always command more interest than a left-hand-drive example in the UK. Coachbuilt vehicles, and in particular tourers, achieve a premium at auction. Veteran cars (i.e. manufactured before 1919) will often achieve a 20% premium.

1937 Ford Model Y Tudor Saloon, long-radiator model, original unrestored condition, very little rust, complete and mechanically sound.
£1,700–2,000 / $2,500–3,000 ⚡ FYC

c1950 Ford E83W Woodie Estate, recent damp and woodworm prevention treatment, very good condition throughout, spare steering column and box.
£2,500–3,500 / $3,600–5,000 ⚡ CGC

1936 Ford Model CX Fordor Saloon, restored, good condition.
£2,500–3,500 / $3,500–5,000 ⚡ FYC

1953 Ford Anglia Saloon, paintwork and interior restored, finished in black, red upholstery, original specification throughout.
£2,000–2,500 / $3,000–3,600 ⚡ Bon
Ford's Anglia, introduced in 1948, adopted the well-tried 933cc sidevalve engine, which had first appeared in the Model Y in 1933, and featured a three-speed synchromesh gearbox. Budget priced, it had a separate chassis and transverse-leaf-spring suspension, offered 60mph performance, 35–40mpg, and remained in production until 1958.

FORD (British built) Model	ENGINE cc/cyl	DATES	CONDITION 1	2	3
Anglia E494A	993/4	1948–53	£2,000	£850	£250
Prefect E93A	1172/4	1940–49	£3,500	£1,250	£900
Prefect E493A	1172/4	1948–53	£2,500	£1,000	£300
Popular 103E	1172/4	1953–59	£1,875	£825	£300
Anglia/Prefect 100E	1172/4	1953–59	£1,350	£625	£250
Prefect 107E	997/4	1959–62	£1,150	£600	£200
Escort/Squire 100E	1172/4	1955–61	£1,000	£850	£275
Popular 100E	1172/4	1959–62	£1,250	£600	£180
Anglia 105E	997/4	1959–67	£1,400	£500	£75
Anglia 123E	1198/4	1962–67	£1,550	£575	£150
V8 Pilot	3622/8	1947–51	£7,500	£5,000	£1,500
Consul Mk I	1508/4	1951–56	£2,250	£950	£400
Consul Mk I DHC	1508/4	1953–56	£6,000	£3,500	£1,250
Zephyr Mk I	2262/6	1951–56	£3,000	£1,250	£600
Zephyr Mk I DHC	2262/6	1953–56	£7,000	£4,000	£1,300
Zodiac Mk I	2262/6	1953–56	£3,300	£1,500	£700
Consul Mk II/Deluxe	1703/4	1956–62	£2,900	£1,500	£650
Consul Mk II DHC	1703/4	1956–62	£5,000	£3,300	£1,250
Zephyr Mk II	2553/6	1956–62	£3,800	£1,800	£750
Zephyr Mk II DHC	2553/6	1956–62	£8,000	£4,000	£1,500
Zodiac Mk II	2553/6	1956–62	£4,000	£2,250	£750
Zodiac Mk II DHC	2553/6	1956–62	£8,500	£4,250	£1,800
Zephyr 4 Mk III	1703/4	1962–66	£2,100	£1,200	£400
Zephyr 6 Mk III	2552/6	1962–66	£2,300	£1,300	£450
Zodiac Mk II	2553/6	1962–66	£2,500	£1,500	£500
Zephyr 4 Mk IV	1994/4	1966–72	£1,750	£600	£300
Zephyr 6 Mk IV	2553/6	1966–72	£1,800	£700	£300
Zodiac Mk IV	2994/6	1966–72	£2,000	£800	£300
Zodiac Mk IV Est.	2994/6	1966–72	£2,800	£1,200	£300
Zodiac Mk IV Exec.	2994/6	1966–72	£2,300	£950	£300
Classic 315	1340/ 1498/4	1961–63	£1,400	£800	£500
Consul Capri	1340/ 1498/4	1961–64	£2,100	£1,350	£400
Consul Capri GT	1498/4	1961–64	£2,600	£1,600	£800

Miller's
Starter Marque

- **Starter Fords:** *Anglia, Prefect, Popular models from 1948 onwards; Consul, Zephyr and Zodiac Mks I, II, III, Zephyr/Zodiac Mk IV; Consul Classic 315/Consul Capri; Cortina Mks I, II, III; Corsair, Capri, Escort.*
- Whatever your tastes, there's a Ford you can afford – in fact, more than we have space to mention above. Their list of virtues as starter classics is almost as long as the list of models there are to choose from. Importantly, many were made in their millions, which means there's generally a ready stock of cars and spares, backed by a healthy network of clubs and specialists. Better still, Fords rarely use exotic materials or obscure, hard-to-grasp, technologies, and that makes them a joy for the DIY enthusiast.
- **Consul, Zephyr and Zodiac (Mks I–III):** These are what you might term 'lifestyle' Fords – there's one to match your taste in clothes and music. The Mk I and II models are favoured as Brit-sized chunks of Americana for the retro crowd. For Mk I models, read early Elvis, rockabilly rather than rock and roll. They are also ideal for post-war swing spivs with Cesar Romero pencil moustaches, double-breasted suits and nylons to sell. The Mk II is mainstream Elvis, structurally reinforced quiffs, pedal pushers, bowling shirts and Levi 501s. As for the Mk III, that's Elvis at Vegas, Teddy-boy drape-coats, long sideboards and a tub of Swarfega in the hair. All models are eminently viable for the DIY enthusiast. While performance is hardly shattering by today's standards, they are fast enough to go with the flow of modern traffic without causing a tail-back.
- **Anglia:** In 1959, Ford's new Anglia represented the shape of fins to come, a pretty, compact little saloon that was an instant hit with buyers who might otherwise have opted for something drearily and domestically familiar, like an Austin A40, Morris Minor or Triumph Herald. Although overshadowed by the launch of the top-selling Cortina a couple of years later, the Anglia 105E was a stylish little device, with a miniature full-width version of the 'dollar-grin' grille up front and voguish US-hand-me-down rear fins. Under the skin, there was a little innovation too, with the first overhead-valve engine for a small Ford and – wonder of wonders – four gears for the first time on a British Ford. The little Anglia was a worthy and peppy little workhorse that went on to sell more than a million before making way for the Escort in 1967.
- **Pick of the bunch:** The Anglia Super 123E; this has an 1198cc engine compared with the 997cc of the 105E, so you'll get to 60mph in 22 seconds rather than 29, and eventually you'll nudge 85mph instead of running out of puff at 75mph.
- **Cortina Mk I:** The Cortina appeared late in 1962, and soon you couldn't miss it on Britain's roads as sales soared. With a mean price tag of just £639/$950, it undercut rivals and, in many cases, offered a lot more. Overall, it added up to the anatomy of a bestseller, in fact the bestselling British car of its time.
- **Pick of the bunch:** 1500 GT and Cortina Lotus; the 1500 GT gave a creditable 13-second 0–60mph and 95mph top speed; the Cortina Lotus, with 1558cc, 105bhp Lotus twin-cam and uprated suspension, scorched its way to 108mph. There were only 4,012 genuine Mk I Cortina Lotuses. They're highly prized, so watch out for fakes – there are plenty.

1961 Ford Zephyr Mk II, 2553cc 6-cylinder engine, period Lucas fog lamp, door mirror and exterior sunvisor, finished in blue and grey, original interior trim in very good condition, all major mechanical components in good condition, 51,00 miles from new, well maintained.
£2,750–3,250 / $4,000–4,700 ➶ BRIT

1967 Ford Escort 1300GT Two-Door Saloon, 1298cc engine, new alternator, gearbox reconditioned, adjustable suspension, suspension strut braces, strengthened bodyshell, Minilite-style wheels, spot lamps, full roll cage, 4-point harness, variety of spares.
£2,000–2,500 / $3,000–3,600 ➶ H&H

▶ **1962 Ford Cortina Mk I Two-Door Saloon,** mostly original apart from later 1500cc engine, finished in blue, white roof, blue vinyl upholstery, 1 owner and 49,000 miles from new, leaking fuel pipe.
£300–400 / $440–580 ↗ **CGC**

> A known continuous history can add value to and enhance the enjoyment of a car.

1968 Ford Cortina Lotus Mk II, 1558cc 4-cylinder engine, Minilite-style wheels, finished in red and gold, black interior trim in good condition, good mechanical condition.
£5,000–6,000 / $7,250–8,750 ↗ **BRIT**
Following on from the legendary Mk I Cortina Lotus, the Mk II was launched in March 1967 (five months after the standard Mk II Cortina), and was built at Dagenham rather than in the Lotus factory at Hethel, Norfolk. The 'special equipment' Lotus engine, previously a costly extra, had been standardized with modified valve timing following development work by Ford engineers. The Corsair 2000E gearbox was standard, with a Lotus ultra-close-ratio gearbox as an option for competition work; a split propshaft was utilized in place of the one-piece item found in other Mk II Cortinas. Otherwise, the new car was largely similar to the Cortina GT.

1970 Ford Cortina 1600E Four-Door Saloon, export model built for South African market, large metal sump guard, servo-assisted brakes, collapsible steering column, opening front quarterlights, no heater, right-hand drive, finished in metallic green, parchment interior, concours winner.
£7,000–9,000 / $10,000–13,000 🚗 **FCO**

FORD (British built) Model	ENGINE cc/cyl	DATES	CONDITION		
			1	2	3
Cortina Mk I	1198/4	1963–66	£1,550	£600	£150
Cortina Crayford Mk I DHC	1198/4	1963–66	£3,500	£1,800	£950
Cortina GT	1498/4	1963–66	£1,800	£1,000	£650
Cortina Lotus Mk I	1558/4	1963–66	£10,000	£7,500	£4,500
Cortina Mk II	1599/4	1966–70	£1,000	£500	£100
Cortina GT Mk II	1599/4	1966–70	£1,200	£650	£150
Cortina Crayford Mk II DHC	1599/4	1966–70	£4,000	£2,000	£1,500
Cortina Lotus Mk II	1558/4	1966–70	£6,000+	£3,500	£1,800
Cortina 1600E	1599/4	1967–70	£4,000	£2,000	£900
Consul Corsair	1500/4	1963–65	£1,100	£500	£250
Consul Corsair GT	1500/4	1963–65	£1,200	£600	£250
Corsair V4	1664/4	1965–70	£1,150	£600	£250
Corsair V4 Est.	1664/4	1965–70	£1,400	£600	£250
Corsair V4GT	1994/4	1965–67	£1,300	£700	£250
Corsair V4GT Est.	1994/4	1965–67	£1,400	£700	£350
Corsair Convertible	1664/ 1994/4	1965–70	£4,300	£2,500	£1,000
Corsair 2000	1994/4	1967–70	£1,350	£500	£250
Corsair 2000E	1994/4	1967–70	£1,500	£800	£350
Escort 1300E	1298/4	1973–74	£1,900	£1,000	£250
Escort Twin Cam	1558/4	1968–71	£8,000	£5,000	£2,000
Escort GT	1298/4	1968–73	£3,000	£1,500	£350
Escort Sport	1298/4	1971–75	£1,750	£925	£250
Escort Mexico	1601/4	1970–74	£4,000	£2,000	£750
RS1600	1601/4	1970–74	£5,000	£2,500	£1,500
RS2000	1998/4	1973–74	£4,500	£2,200	£1,000
Escort RS Mexico	1593/4	1976–78	£3,500	£2,000	£850
Escort RS2000 Mk II	1993/4	1976–80	£6,000	£3,500	£2,000
Capri Mk I 1300/ 1600	1298/ 1599/4	1969–72	£1,500	£1,000	£550
Capri 2000/ 3000GT	1996/4 2994/6	1969–72	£2,000	£1,000	£500
Capri 3000E	2994/6	1970–72	£4,000	£2,000	£1,000
Capri RS3100	3093/6	1973–74	£6,500	£3,500	£2,000
Cortina 2000E	1993/4	1973–76	£2,500	£550	£225
Granada Ghia	1993/4 2994/6	1974–77	£3,000	£900	£350

Ford Escort Mk I (1968–74)

Production: 2,228,349.
Body style: Two- and four-door saloon; estate; van.
Engine: Four-cylinder; 1098, 1298, 1558, 1599, 1840, 1993cc.
Power output: 53–120bhp.
Transmission: Four-speed manual; optional automatic on some models.
Maximum speed: 79–116+mph.
0–60mph: 8.7–19.8 seconds.

Housewives, husbands and hooligans all loved the Mk I Ford Escort, which replaced the fussy bechromed Anglia with neat lines and tasteful restraint, along with Ford's usual hard-to-beat pricing. It was, once again, a winning formula, and the unassuming Escort modestly rewrote the record books, selling a million in well under four years and easily outstripping the Cortina while no one noticed. It helped that the Escort was Ford's first true European car, built both in Germany and Britain, but the Escort was also many cars to many people – from a sensible family hack with a capacious boot to a pub car-park supercar. From the warm 1300GT with a chirpy 92mph, things became really hot with the 113mph Cortina Lotus-engined Escort Twin Cam, superseded in 1971 by the even quicker RS1600. These were cars that every white-socked adolescent hankered for, and after the Escort's domination of the 1970 World Cup London to Mexico Rally, Ford gave them a car they could afford, or at least aspire to, and even hope to insure. The Escort Mexico kept the RS1600's strengthened bodyshell, uprated running gear and suspension, but with a less fierce 86bhp, 1600cc engine. Today, it's such a 'yoof' icon that some enthusiasts dress up cooking Escorts as Mexicos, and the more unscrupulous will try to pass them off; so watch out. The final permutation of the Mk I Escort was the 1973 RS2000, which offered performance not far off the exotic RS1600, but with lots of posh bits and superior comfort; just the thing for the pushy young exec in sales.

1975 Ford Capri 2000 Ghia, 2000cc 4-cylinder engine, alloy wheels, factory fitted sun roof, finished in royal blue, blue interior, 1 owner and fewer than 9,500 miles from new, rust-proofed from new, dry-stored 7 years, recently recommissioned.
£2,500–3,000 / $3,600–4,400 ✗ H&H

1981 Ford Minster Limousine, 2.8 litre V6 engine, automatic transmission, finished in blue, excellent condition throughout.
£2,000–2,500 / $3,000–3,600 ✗ Bon
This Minster Limousine was leased from the Ford Motor Company by the Royal Household and was based at Clarence House, where it was used by HRH Queen Elizabeth The Queen Mother during 1984–87. It is based on a Ford Granada Mk II five-door estate with a 12in (30.5cm) exension to the wheelbase.

Restored values

The cost of a professional restoration will have an influence on, but no direct relation to, a car's market value. A restored car can have a market value lower than the cost of its restoration.

1986 Ford Sierra Cosworth, 2000cc engine, finished in black, grey interior, 22,000 miles from new, concours winner.
£11,500–13,500 / $16,500–19,500 ✗ H&H

1987 Sierra Cosworth, finished in black, 54,000 miles from new, original.
£9,000–10,000 / $13,000–14,500 ⊞ WbC

1984 Ford Grosvenor Limousine, coachwork by Coleman Milne, based on Granada Ghia saloon, 2.8 litre V6 engine, automatic transmission, alloy wheels, finished in metallic burgundy, tinted side and rear glass, electric windows, electric division, full grey leather interior with seating for up to 7, air conditioning, twin stereos, good condition.
£1,000–1,500 / $1,500–2,200 ✗ BARO

Ford – USA

1931 Ford Model A Two-Door Sedan, older restoration, hydraulic brakes, cowl lights, vinyl interior.
£6,000–7,000 / $8,500–10,500 ⚲ **BJ**

1930 Ford Model A Coupé, restored, 19in wire wheels, finished in black, brown cloth buttoned upholstery, rear window blind, recently recommissioned, very good condition.
£6,500–8,000 / $9,500–11,500 ⚲ **CGC**
Introduced in October 1927, the Model A was a more sophisticated and refined design than its predecessor, the Model T. Developing some 40bhp, its 3285cc four-cylinder sidevalve engine was twice as powerful as that of the 'Tin Lizzie'. The A's three-speed sliding-gear transmission was another advance, as was the adoption of four-wheel drum brakes.

1932 Ford Hi-Boy Street Rod Roadster, 1960 Chevrolet small-block V8 engine, 4-speed manual gearbox, 1949 Ford hydraulic drum brakes, left-hand drive, soft top, wind wings, original all-steel body, professionally built, featured in many magazines, *Rod & Custom* feature car October 2000, *Rod & Custom* Top Ten Rod 1999.
£50,000–55,000 / $72,000–80,000 ⚲ **BJ**

◀ **1935 Ford Roadster,** 3.6 litre sidevalve V8 engine, period speed equipment, finished in black, red interior, rumble seat.
£40,000–45,000 / $58,000–65,000 ⚲ **BJ**

▶ **1937 Ford Phantom Sportsman Woodie,** 350cu.in Chevrolet V8 engine, stainless-steel exhaust, 700-R4 automatic transmission with column change, independent front suspension with coil-spring/shock-absorber units, rigid rear axle on leaf springs with anti-roll bar and Bilstein shock absorbers, Willwood disc brakes, Chevrolet Vega steering box, 1940 Ford pick-up chassis, body based on 1937 Ford Club coupé, curved windscreen, one-piece lift-off top, finished in red.
£60,000–65,000 / $87,000–94,000 ⚲ **RM**

1950 Ford Deluxe Six Series Two-Door Business Coupé, 3700cc 6-cylinder engine, manual gearbox with column change, left-hand drive, finished in black, white interior, front bench seat, fewer than 61,000 miles from new, good condition.
£3,000–4,000 / $4,500–5,800 ⚲ **H&H**

1951 Ford Custom Deluxe Convertible, 239cu.in sidevalve V8 engine, restored, factory continental kit, finished in light green, power-operated black pinpoint vinyl top, green vinyl interior, push-button radio, fewer than 47,500 miles from new.
£12,000–14,000 / $17,500–20,500 ⚲ Bon

Like the 1949 and 1950 models that preceded them, the 1951 Fords were a combination of the old and the new. One of the very best features was the sturdy sidevalve V8, which offered good performance at a relatively low price. Ford also offered a 95bhp, 226cu.in straight-six, but most opted for the V8. For 1951, the basic Ford bodies remained the same, although trim changes were enough to give a fresh look. The large centre spinner in the grille gave way to two smaller spinners, new rear light lenses were used, and the dashboard was all new. The range included Deluxe Six, Deluxe V8, Custom Deluxe Six and Custom Deluxe V8 models. Body styles included two- and four-door sedans, three- and six-place coupés, two-door Crestliner, two-door Victoria, two-door convertible and an estate, although not all bodies were offered in all trim and engine combinations.

1951 Ford Victoria Hardtop, sidevalve V8 engine, automatic transmission, finished in pale blue and white, original push-button radio, largely unrestored, excellent condition.
£6,000–7,000 / $8,700–10,200 ⚲ Bon

1957 Ford Fairlane 500 Skyliner, 312cu.in overhead-valve V8 engine, 4-barrel carburettor, 245bhp, automatic transmission, independent front suspension, rigid rear axle, power steering, restored to correct specification.
£17,000–20,000 / $25,000–29,000 ⚲ Bon

The Fairlane 500 Skyliner was a comfortable, large, two-door coupé capable of seating six adults. It was also a convertible, as long as those six adults could travel light. Ford engineers had designed a mechanical system to lift and store the metal hardtop in the Fairlane's gaping boot. It worked smoothly, and crowds would gather whenever the Ford put on its folding-top act.

◄ **1959 Ford Fairlane 500 Skyliner,** rebuilt 5.4 litre V8 engine, new twin exhaust system, subject of cosmetic restoration, new seats, new chrome, finished in white, triple-tone bronze interior, matching numbers, excellent condition throughout.
£18,000–22,000 / $26,000–32,000 ⚲ Bon

FORD (American built) Model	ENGINE cu. in/cyl	DATES	CONDITION 1	2	3
Thunderbird	292/ 312/8	1955–57	£18,500	£13,500	£9,000
Edsel Citation	410/8	1958	£9,000	£4,500	£2,500
Edsel Ranger	223/6- 361/8	1959	£6,000	£3,500	£2,000
Edsel Citation convertible	410/8	1958	£12,000	£6,000	£4,000
Edsel Corsair convertible	332/ 361/8	1959	£10,500	£7,000	£4,500
Fairlane 2-door	223/6- 352/8	1957–59	£8,000	£4,500	£3,000
Fairlane 500 Sunliner	223/6- 352/8	1957–59	£12,000	£8,000	£6,500
Fairlane 500 Skyliner	223/6- 352/8	1957–59	£14,000	£10,000	£8,000
Mustang 4.7 V8 FHC/Conv.		1964–66	£9,000	£4,000	£2,000
Mustang GT 350		1966–67	£15,000	£10,000	£6,000
Mustang hardtop	260/6- 428/8	1967–68	£6,000	£4,000	£3,000
Mustang GT 500		1966–67	£20,000	£14,000	£6,000

1955 Ford Thunderbird, 292cu.in overhead-valve V8 engine, left-hand drive, hard and soft tops, finished in turquoise, turquoise interior, featured in many TV shows, completely original, excellent condition throughout.
£14,000–16,000 / $20,500–23,500 ⤳ H&H

1955 Ford Thunderbird, V8 engine, 3-speed manual/overdrive gearbox, finished in pale yellow, black hood, yellow and black interior, fewer than 87,500 miles from new.
£14,000–16,000 / $20,000–23,000 ⤳ Bon
Conceived to challenge Chevrolet's Corvette, the Thunderbird was one of the first Fords to be fitted with the new overhead-valve V8 engine. Introduced in two-seat 'personal car' form, the Thunderbird was aimed at image-conscious younger customers, its superior V8 engine and greater refinement enabling it to beat the Corvette handsomely in the sales war. Despite this success, the original concept soon was abandoned, a larger – and slower – four-seat version being introduced for 1958.

1956 Ford Thunderbird, overhead-valve V8 engine, 225bhp, automatic transmission, coil-spring independent front suspension, rigid rear axle on leaf springs, porthole hardtop, restored early 1980s, finished in white, black and white interior, Town and Country radio.
£19,000–23,000 / $28,000–33,000 ⤳ Bon
For 1956, changes to the Thunderbird were relatively modest. The optional removable hardtop came either with or without a porthole, and the continental kit ensured that, for the first time, boot space was ample. The biggest news could be found under the bonnet, though, where there was a choice of engines – either the 292cu.in unit or the 'Thunderbird Special' 312cu.in engine, which generated 215bhp with the manual gearbox or 225bhp with the automatic.

▶ **1959 Ford Thunderbird,** restored over 5 years, power steering, brakes, seat and windows, wire wheels, dress-up kit, leather upholstery.
£25,000–30,000 / $36,000–44,000 ⤳ BJ

1957 Ford Thunderbird, 312cu.in V8 engine, 245bhp, automatic transmission, complete body-off restoration, finished in original coral pink, concours winner.
£28,000–32,000 / $40,000–46,000 ⤳ BJ

Ford Thunderbird (1955–57)

Production: 53,166.
Engine: Cast-iron V8, 292cu.in (4785cc) and 312cu.in (5117cc).
Power output: 190–225+bhp.
Transmission: Three-speed manual with optional overdrive; three-speed Ford-0-Matic automatic transmission.
Maximum speed: 114+mph.
0–60mph: 9.5 seconds (292cu.in).
Although Chevrolet's Corvette was first out of the blocks in 1953 in the race to become America's native sports car, the late starting Ford Thunderbird cantered off into an early lead as soon as it hit the showrooms in 1955, initially outselling its rival by 24 to one. The duelling two-seaters were intended to arrest the flood of European sports cars flooding into the USA, yet both were uniquely American interpretations of the sporting idiom. The first Corvettes looked the business, but were fairly crude and powered by a

mundane six-cylinder engine. The Thunderbird, though, hit the ground with a beefy 4.7 litre V8, was lavishly equipped and well finished, with styling half-way between a Kriscraft speedboat and Riva, at least compared with the common chrome excesses of the period. The T-bird's ambience was one of well-heeled and tasteful, youthful success. It didn't last, though. In 1957, the rear deck was lengthened with the addition of flared rear wings, and in 1958 the original Thunderbird concept disappeared for good as it became a chrome-encrusted four-seater and strayed ever farther from its roots.
Doing the Continental: You can tell a 1956 Thunderbird by the continental spare-tyre kit, the encased spare being mounted vertically at the rear. It gave more space in the boot, but the extra weight set so far back severely compromised handling and steering, so the spare was put back in the boot for 1957.

1965 Ford Thunderbird Hardtop, finished in red, red vinyl interior, fewer than 68,000 miles from new.
£6,000–8,000 / $8,500–11,500 ↗ Bon
By 1964, the T-bird was into its fourth generation, although the formula was very much the same as it had been in 1958: a big lazy V8 attached to an automatic transmission, comfortable room for four adults and a choice of open or closed bodies. As before, the chassis was standard Ford, with independent front suspension and a rigid rear axle. The base Thunderbird engine was a 390cu.in overhead-valve V8 that produced 300bhp.

1965 Ford Mustang Convertible, 289cu.in V8 engine, 4-barrel carburettor, 3-speed automatic transmission, restored 1993, new exhaust, chromed steel wheels, finished in red, white power hood, white interior, good to excellent condition throughout.
£11,000–14,000 / $16,000–20,500 ↗ BRIT
During 1962, Ford saw the need for an affordable American sports car, there being a void in the market left by the demise of the two-seat Thunderbird, which was rapidly being filled by European sports cars. Ford visionaries, led by Lee A. Iacocca, understood that a large number of Americans wanted to buy into the sports-car dream. Joe Oros and David Ash set to work on producing a running prototype, the Mustang II concept car, displayed at the 1963 US Grand Prix. Many features and design cues from this prototype, such as the 108in (274.5cm) wheelbase, long bonnet and short rear deck, rear wheel scoops and tri-bar rear lights were incorporated in the production car. Clever publicity stunts, PR exercises and marketing ensured public awareness of the car prior to its launch. Oros and Ash were awarded a Gold Medal Tiffany Award for Excellence in American Design for their creation, and the affordable American sports car tradition began on 17 April 1964.

1966 Ford Mustang Coupé, 289cu.in V8 engine, 200bhp, 3-speed automatic transmission, power steering, never restored, resprayed in original pale yellow some years ago, original tan Deluxe interior, factory radio.
£7,000–8,000 / $10,200–11,600 ↗ Bon
The Mustang was built on a modified Falcon chassis, and used that car's independent front suspension and rigid rear axle. Ford's standard straight-six dropped right in, as did several V8s. The basic Mustang came with the 101bhp straight-six and a three-speed manual gearbox. Both an automatic and a four-speed manual box were available with the six, and with the 164bhp, 260cu.in V8 and 289s ranging from 210 to 271bhp. Before the year was out, a fastback version had been added, which brought the total to three body and five engine options.

1966 Shelby GT 350H (Hertz) Mustang, engine reconditioned, gearbox rebuilt, bare-metal respray in white with gold stripes, fewer than 77,000 miles from new, excellent condition.
£30,000–35,000 / $43,000–50,000 ⚲ Bon
This Mustang fastback coupé was one of a special batch commissioned by the Hertz car rental company.

> **Cross Reference**
> See Colour Review (page 71)

► **1967 Ford Mustang Convertible,** 4735cc V8 engine, automatic transmission, left-hand drive, completely overhauled and reconditioned 1994, finished in red, parchment interior trim, excellent condition throughout.
£8,000–10,000 / $11,500–14,500 ⚲ H&H

1967 Shelby GT 500, 428cu.in overhead-valve V8 engine, aluminium inlet manifold with 2x4-barrel Holley carburettors, 355bhp, 3-speed automatic transmission, competition suspension package, front disc/rear drum brakes, limited-slip differential, sport wheels, restored, finished in green, green interior, correct matching numbers on engine, transmission and rear axle, fewer than 1,000 miles in last 10 years.
£25,000–30,000 / $36,000–43,000 ⚲ RM
Carroll Shelby, who built the legendary 289 Cobra, had the idea of applying the Shelby magic to Ford's new Mustang. At the same time, Ford was looking to improve its image in the performance based youth market. Before long, the company was shipping plain-Jane Mustang fastbacks to Shelby's Los Angeles facility. The cars had few options – not even a back seat – but they did have a 271bhp, solid-lifter version of Ford's new small-block V8 engine. Shelby added competition exhausts, roll bars, suspension upgrades, tachometers and a variety of scoops and stripes, and the legendary GT 350 was born. Those initial cars were thinly disguised racers, and were highly competitive. As it turned out, however, most drivers cared more about the street than the track, and for 1966 the cars began to be friendlier and easier to drive. Although customers wanted more comfortable cars, they still had to be fast – and Shelby had the answer. The new Mustang bodyshell for 1967 had been designed to accept Ford's 390cu.in big-block engine. Shelby reasoned that if the 390 would fit, why not the Interceptor 428? And so it was that the GT 500 came into being.

1969 Shelby GT 500 Drag Pack Convertible, 428cu.in Super Cobra Jet overhead-valve V8 engine, Ram-Air induction with Holley carburettor, 335bhp, 4-speed manual gearbox, front disc/rear drum brakes, heavy-duty suspension, Traction-Lok rear axle, tinted glass, tilt steering wheel, 8-track stereo, restored, fewer than 25,000 miles from new, excellent condition.
£65,000–80,000 / $95,000–115,000 ⚲ RM
By 1969, there was little of Carroll Shelby left in the Shelby Mustangs. Powertrains were no longer unique, although by that time, Ford's standard offerings were hot enough to satisfy even the most discerning of Shelby buyers – especially the high-output big-block 428, which was standard in the GT 500. Ford stylists ensured that the cars retained their unique identities, with a longer front end, unique grille and an aggressive bonnet with no less than five NACA-type scoops. Inside, a roll bar, racing harness and special trim distinguished the Shelby Mustang from the standard pony-car fare. Only 335 GT 500 convertibles were built. This example is the most desirable variant of the final series of Shelby Mustangs, a big-block GT 500 convertible with Ford's Drag Pack high-performance option package. The standard 428 was called a Cobra Jet by Ford, but when ordered with the Drag Pack, it became a Super Cobra Jet. Included with the Drag Pack was a Traction-Lok rear axle, forged connecting rods from the legendary 427, and a specially modified crankshaft, flywheel and damper.

Frazer Nash

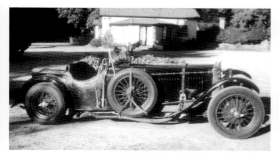

1935 Frazer Nash TT Replica, barn find, in need of renovation, unused since 1989.
£44,000–48,000 / $64,000–70,000 ⚘ COYS

Archie Frazer Nash and Ronald Godfrey joined forces in 1910 to produce the GN car; they left the company in 1922, but production continued until 1925, the GN chassis becoming the basis of innumerable 'specials' in the 1920s and 1930s. Frazer Nash set up on his own in 1924, his cars being broadly based on the GN chassis, with chain drive, dog clutches, solid rear axles, quarter-elliptic springing and very high-geared steering; these cars remained in production until 1939, despite some rather outmoded features. Over this period, around 330 were made. Various engines were used in the cars, including Plus Power, Anzani, Blackburne, Gough and Meadows, the last being the most frequently fitted. The TT Replica appeared in 1931–32, confusingly sometimes called the Boulogne 2, and later the Byfleet 2. In standard form, its top speed was around 85mph, with a 0–60mph time of 18 seconds. There was no production line in the accepted sense, and specification varied a good deal from car to car.

1988 Frazer Nash Le Mans Replica, built by Werner Oswald, 1971cc engine, converted to unleaded fuel, finished in black, new hood and weather equipment, new windscreen and aeroscreens, black interior, excellent condition.
£36,000–40,000 / $52,000–58,000 ⚘ H&H

When the Frazer Nash 'High Speed' won the 2 litre class and came third overall at Le Mans in 1949, Frazer Nash decided to rename that model as the Le Mans Replica. Only 34 Le Mans Replicas were made, but this number was swelled by a number of copies built by Crossthwaite and Gardner. There were about eight in total, which were made 'rivet for rivet' the same as the originals, being correct in every detail, including the original 120bhp, Bristol Mk IV BS1 engine; original instruments and dash; original suspension; remote-control gear change; and the centre-lock disc wheels. In addition, about 12 were made by a Werner Oswald in the late 1980s.

Ginetta

> A known continuous history can add value to and enhance the enjoyment of a car.

◀ **1991 Ginetta G32 Sports Convertible,** 1597cc 4-cylinder Ford XR3 engine, 5-speed manual gearbox, finished in British racing green, electric windows, magnolia leather upholstery, 1 of only 30 G32 convertibles built, 31,000 miles from new.
£4,000–5,000 / $5,800–7,250 ⚘ H&H

Gladiator

▶ **1900 Gladiator Type 3 Voiturette,** 3½hp Aster engine, finished in dark green, black upholstery, VCC dating certificate, excellent condition.
£32,000–36,000 / $46,000–52,000 ⚘ Bon

Gladiator's first cars came in voiturette form, with a 4hp single-cylinder horizontal engine mounted in a tubular frame, with cycle wire wheels and handlebar steering. By 1899, the company was making cars with front transversely mounted 2½ and 3½hp Aster engines, and wheel steering. With pedal controls, a two-speed gearbox and chain drive to the rear axle, the Gladiator was one of the prettiest voiturettes available. Stanley Edge's concern, the Motor Power Company, introduced the Gladiator to Britain in 1900, and by 1903 the factory was selling 80 per cent of its 1,000-a-year production to Britain. Edge continued with the Gladiator and Regent marques until he became more famously involved with Napier.

Gordon Keeble

c1965 Gordon Keeble Coupé, c£100,000 spent on restoration, finished in pale blue, good to excellent condition.
£18,000–21,000 / $26,000–30,000 ✈ Bon
Produced between 1964 and 1966, the Gordon Keeble was one of a group of 1960s GTs that combined British chassis engineering with American horsepower and Italian style. Designed by John Gordon, previously of Peerless, and produced in collaboration with garage owner Jim Keeble, the car featured a space-frame chassis with independent front suspension, De Dion rear axle and four-wheel disc brakes. Styled by Giugiaro at Bertone, its elegant glassfibre bodywork was manufactured in Britain by Williams & Pritchard. A 5.4 litre Chevrolet V8 engine provided effortless cruising and a top speed in the region of 140mph. All of which ought to have been a recipe for success, but the company failed to get its pricing right and production ceased after little more than a year. A brief revival saw a few more cars assembled, but when finally the end came, only 99 cars had been built.

c1966 Gordon Keeble Coupé, 5.4 litre Chevrolet V8 engine, space-frame chassis, 4-wheel disc brakes, independent front suspension, De Dion rear axle, restored, finished in white, black interior, not run for over 6 months, in need of recommissioning, very good condition.
£8,000–11,000 / $11,500–16,000 ✈ Bon

Auction prices

Miller's only includes cars declared sold. Our guide prices take into account the buyer's premium, VAT on the premium, and the extent of any published catalogue information relating to condition and provenance. Cars sold at auction are identified by the ✈ icon; full details of the auction house can be found on page 332.

GORDON KEEBLE Model	ENGINE cc/cyl	DATES	CONDITION 1	2	3
GKI/GKIT	5355/8	1964–67	£20,000	£15,000	£10,000

Healey

The total output of The Healey Motor Company from 1946 to 1954, when it was absorbed into BMC, amounts to little more than 1,100 cars. The engines were proprietary units from the likes of Riley, and later Nash and Alvis; the bodies were not always beautiful, but all Healey produced cars were truly sporting in character with performance to match. Most sought-after Healey is the Silverstone, a pared-to-the-bone road car that proved a favourite among club racers. These days, the name of Donald Mitchell Healey is equally or possibly better known for the true-Brit Austin-Healey breed of sports cars. At the 1952 London Motor Show, Donald Healey debuted his new Austin-engined Healey

Hundred, and such was its impact that Austin's Leonard Lord quickly decided he wanted to build the car everyone was talking about. Long before Donald Healey set up his own car company, he had already made a very significant contribution to motoring in Britain. In 1931, he had driven an Invicta to outright victory in the 1931 Monte Carlo Rally. In 1933, he joined the Riley experimental team, and in 1935 he moved across Coventry to become experimental manager and technical director at Triumph until the company collapsed in 1939. Donald Healey died in 1988, but it's no exaggeration to say that he was one of the most influential figures in the British motor industry.

▶ **1951 Healey Tickford Saloon,** finished in grey, red interior, complete and unrestored, dry stored for some years, in need of recommissioning/restoration.
£2,500–3,500 / $3,600–5,000 ✈ Bon
Healey's first offerings were the Elliott sports saloon and Westland roadster of 1946, both 2.4 litre Riley powered and built on a welded X-braced chassis featuring Healey's own trailing-arm independent front suspension. For a time, the Healey Elliott was the world's fastest closed four-seater production car, clocking 110mph at Jabbeke, Belgium, in 1947. In 1950, the Elliott and Westland were superseded by the Tickford saloon and Abbott drophead coupé, both of which enjoyed an improved chassis with Girling brakes. They were more refined and better equipped than their predecessors too, and although heavier, were still good for the 'ton'.

Hertel

◀ **1898 Hertel 3½hp Two-Seater Runabout,** 1607cc 2-cylinder horizontal water-cooled engine, 2-speed gearbox with transmission to rear wheels by friction discs, hand-operated spoon brakes on rear tyres, independent coil-spring front suspension, rear suspension by quarter-elliptic leaf springs, right-hand drive with tiller steering, tubular frame, all-steel body, 20mph top speed, restored.
£55,000–65,000 / $80,000–95,000 ⚲ C
When the first car race in the USA was announced – a 100-mile run from Chicago to Waukegan and back in 1895 – Max Hertel decided to enter with a car of his own manufacture. His entry was his first attempt at building a car, and it was much along the lines of this model. Unfortunately, his steering gear broke and he could not take part. Undeterred, he refined his vehicle further. In 1897, he met Richard Oakman, and they formed the Oakman Motor Vehicle Company. Work began in January 1898, with chassis and engines being built to the Benz patent. In 1899, however, mounting debts forced the company to close.

Hillman

William Hillman made his early fortune from bicycles, roller skates and sewing machines, before turning to car manufacture in 1907, initially producing elegant tourers and a few surprisingly large-engined cars before settling down to make quality middle-market models. Hillman died in 1926, and in 1928 the company came under the control of Humber and the Rootes Group. In the early 1930s, the Minx model name was used for the first time on a range of smart and refined small cars. By 1939, Hillman was ranked fourth in Britain, and by the 1960s Hillman was the most mainstream marque in the Rootes Group. Producing the promising, but complex, rear-engined Imp in a new Scottish factory was an ill-fated venture that led to financial troubles, and in 1964 Chrysler stepped in to take a major share of Rootes. Underfunded, neglected and misunderstood by its new parent, the Hillman marque plodded along until 1976, when the name was dropped. A curious footnote came in the form of the Peykan models assembled in Iran into the mid-1980s. These were no more than last-generation Hillman Hunters.

Miller's Starter Marque

- **Starter Hillmans:** *Californian; Minx models and variants from 1956; Imp; Avenger.*
- One of the most attractive traits of post-war Hillmans is their price. They're affordable and generally reliable, and if you're into budget top-down motoring, there's a wide choice from a company that persisted with convertibles when lots of other makers didn't bother. The 1950s Hillman Californian offers a suggestion of transatlantic glamour with straightforward Rootes underpinnings. The problem is going to be finding one because, as with later Hillmans, their low values have lured many a saveable car into the scrapyard. The Super Minx convertibles from 1962 to 1966 make an interesting four-seat, fresh-air alternative to cars like Triumph Heralds. The Super Minx is more substantially bodied and bigger engined. The Imp was a real might-have-been – if only the Mini hadn't appeared three years before, and if only it had been built better. It's redeemed, though, by a lovely engine, super gearbox and sheer entertainment value when behind the wheel. In the 1970s, the Hillman Avenger tilted against Morris Marinas, Ford Escorts and Vauxhall Vivas. The GT was surprisingly nimble and offered 100mph performance. The very rare Tiger topped 110mph and enjoyed a successful rallying career.

1931 Hillman Wizard 65 Coupé Cabriolet, considerable restoration work carried out 1991, finished in black and green, brown leather upholstery, excellent condition.
£9,500–11,000 / $13,800–16,000 ⚲ Bon
One of Coventry's oldest car manufacturers, Hillman produced a range of quality medium-sized vehicles during the 1920s and 1930s, aimed very much at the middle classes. The early 1930s saw a varied range of cars, from the four-cylinder Minx, through the six-cylinder Wizard, to the range topping Straight 8. The Wizard 65 was introduced in April 1931, a six-cylinder, sidevalve car with a capacity of 2110cc. Transmission was through a four-speed, 'silent third' gearbox, and the car had a top speed of 60mph with 21mpg fuel consumption. The Coupé Cabriolet was a factory produced two-door body that accommodated three people in the front and two in the dickey.

Miller's is a price GUIDE not a price LIST

1954 Hillman Minx Saloon Phase VII, 1265cc 4-cylinder engine, finished in black, good condition.
£2,000–2,500 / $3,000–3,600 ↗ H&H

1974 Hillman Imp Mk IV Super, 875cc rear-mounted engine, 39bhp, recent rebuild, non-standard vinyl roof.
£1,500–1,800 / $2,000–2,500 🚗 IMP

Cross Reference
See Colour Review (page 71)

HILLMAN Model	ENGINE cc/cyl	DATES	CONDITION 1	2	3
Minx Mk I–II	1184/4	1946–48	£1,750	£800	£250
Minx Mk I–II DHC	1184/4	1946–48	£3,500	£1,500	£250
Minx Mk III–VIIIA	1184/4	1948–56	£1,750	£700	£350
Minx Mk III–VIIIA DHC	1184/4	1948–56	£3,750	£1,500	£350
Californian	1390/4	1953–56	£2,000	£750	£200
Minx SI/II	1390/4	1956–58	£1,250	£450	£200
Minx SI/II DHC	1390/4	1956–58	£3,500	£1,500	£500
Minx Ser III	1494/4	1958–59	£1,000	£500	£200
Minx Ser III DHC	1494/4	1958–59	£3,750	£1,500	£400
Minx Ser IIIA/B	1494/4	1959–61	£1,250	£500	£200
Minx Ser IIIA/B DHC	1494/4	1959–61	£3,750	£1,250	£500
Minx Ser IIIC	1592/4	1961–62	£900	£500	£200
Minx Ser IIIC DHC	1592/4	1961–62	£3,000	£1,500	£500
Minx Ser V	1592/4	1962–63	£1,250	£350	£150
Minx Ser VI	1725/4	1964–67	£1,500	£375	£100
Husky Mk I	1265/4	1954–57	£1,000	£600	£200
Husky SI/II/III	1390/4	1958–65	£1,000	£550	£150
Super Minx	1592/4	1961–66	£1,500	£500	£100
Super Minx DHC	1592/4	1962–64	£3,500	£1,250	£450
Imp	875/4	1963–73	£800	£300	£70
Husky	875/4	1966–71	£800	£450	£100
Avenger	var/4	1970–76	£550	£250	£60
Avenger GT	1500/4	1971–76	£950	£500	£100
Avenger Tiger	1600/4	1972–73	£2,000	£1,000	£500

Hispano-Suiza

1930 Hispano-Suiza H6B Cabriolet, coachwork by Million-Guiet, dickey seat, hexagonal-section bumpers, centre-mounted door handles, right-hand drive, exhibited at 1930 London Motor Show, subject of ground-up restoration mid-1990s, concours winner, excellent condition throughout.
£150,000+ / $218,000 ↗ Bon

Although the marque was of Spanish origin, it was Hispano-Suiza's French-built cars that established it in the front rank of luxury automobile manufacturers after WWI. During that conflict, Hispano engines had powered some of the Allies' finest fighter aircraft. Not surprisingly, the first post-war Hispano drew heavily on this expertise, being powered by a 6597cc, overhead-camshaft six, which had been developed by halving a proposed V12 aero engine. It was built in unit with the three-speed gearbox. Maximum power was 135bhp, produced at 2,400rpm. Sensation of the 1919 Paris show, the H6B featured a light, yet rigid, four-wheel-braked chassis that matched its state-of-the-art power unit for innovation. The world's most advanced automobile at the time of its introduction and for many years thereafter, the H6B was catalogued until 1930, by which time a little over 2,000 chassis had been completed.

Honda

HONDA Model	ENGINE cc/cyl	DATES	CONDITION 1	2	3
S800 Mk I Convertible	791/4	1966–69	£7,000	£4,000	£2,500
S800 Mk I Coupé	791/4	1966–69	£5,000	£3,500	£1,000
S800 Mk II Convertible	791/4	1968–69	£7,000	£5,000	£3,000
S800 Mk II Coupé	791/4	1968–69	£6,500	£4,000	£1,200

Horstman

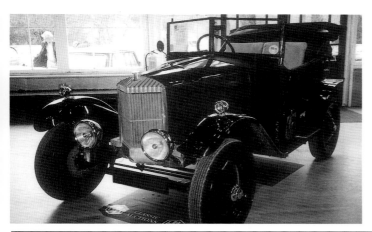

◄ **1927 Horstman Two-Seater Sports Tourer,** 1496cc Anzani engine, finished in grey and black, grey interior, good condition throughout.
£8,000–9,000
$11,500–13,000 ⚒ H&H
The Horstman Gear Company was formed in 1904 by Sidney Horstman, whose father, Gustav, was a German immigrant clock maker. The company began work on a light car in 1912, going into production two years later in Bath, initially using a bespoke 995cc four-cylinder engine. Unfortunately it ceased production in 1929, but not before it had raced at Brooklands with some success.

Hudson

1949 Hudson Super Six Two-Door Sedan, 3-speed manual gearbox, radio, heater, original wood-grained metal dashboard, rewired using correct original materials, finished in correct Hudson Rosebud pink, original two-tone grey mohair interior.
£7,000–9,000 / $10,000–13,000 ⚒ Bon
Introduced in 1948, the new post-war Hudsons were referred to as 'step-down' models because of their low construction, which allowed the driver and passengers to lower themselves into the car, instead of stepping up, as in most cars of the period. Not only were the new Hudsons low and attractive, but also they offered the then novel concept of unitary construction, with independent suspension up front and a conventional rigid axle in the rear. Under the bonnet, the sidevalve straight-six displaced 262cu.in and generated a robust 121bhp at 4,000rpm. For 1949, little was changed on the Series 481 Super Six model. Trim varied inside and out, but the car was essentially the same sturdy and attractive package of the year before.

1917 Hudson Super Six Series J Phaeton, 4736cc 6-cylinder engine, 7-seater coachwork, side curtains, black leatherette hood, older restoration, finished in blue, interior trimmed in black leather, dynamo recently overhauled, slight leak from water pump.
£18,000–20,000 / $26,000–29,000 ⚒ BRIT
The Hudson Motor Company was founded in 1908, its first car leaving the factory in the following year. So successful were Hudson products that by the conclusion of their first year's trading, over 4,000 vehicles had been sold. These auspicious beginnings spawned many finely engineered and successful models, including the redoubtable Super Six, introduced in 1916. This model was the first to be powered by an engine of Hudson's own manufacture, and established the benchmark by which the performance of production cars would be judged. Displacing 4736cc, the engine featured a four-bearing crankshaft fitted with eight counterweights, a design that Hudson was to patent. There is little doubt that at this time record-breaking dramatically assisted sales, and the Super Six set a new transcontinental record with a run from San Francisco to New York in five days, three hours and 31 minutes.

A known continuous history can add value to and enhance the enjoyment of a car.

Humber

Another once-distinguished British make that was brought low in its later days by an epidemic of badge-engineering, when the Humber name was little more than a dubious emblem of suburban rank on upmarket Hillmans and Singers. Humber, like so many early British manufacturers, had graduated to cars from bicycles in the early years of the century. In 1928, Humber took over Hillman, and the two were absorbed into the growing Rootes empire in 1931. Humber's role in those years was to furnish cars for the sober upper-middle-class market. In the 1930s, the imposing six-cylinder Humber Pullmans and Super Snipes enjoyed official patronage, and also performed stout service as staff cars in the war. The Super Snipe of the late 1940s continued the tradition as a superior bank manager's carriage. Increasingly, in the 1960s, the Humber marque lost its individual identity. Chrysler took over the Rootes Group in 1964, and in 1976 the Humber name disappeared for ever.

1904 Humber Royal Humberette 6½hp Beeston Two-Seater, 773cc engine, completely restored 1990–91, modified De Dion cylinder barrel, non-original body, VCC dated.
£16,000–18,000 / $23,000–26,000 ➢ **Bon**
Humber's reputation was established in 1903, when the first important early Humber was produced. A light two-seater with a 613cc single-cylinder 5hp De Dion engine and two-speed gearbox operated from the steering column, the new Humberette had shaft drive and a tubular chassis. An improved model with three speeds was introduced as the Royal Humberette for 1904.

1926 Humber 9/20 Four-Seater Tourer, 1056cc 4-cylinder engine, overhead inlet/side exhaust valves, 3-speed manual gearbox with right-hand gate change, older restoration, very good condition throughout.
£9,000–10,000 / $13,000–14,500 ⊞ **AVON**

Miller's Starter Marque

- **Starter Humbers:** *Hawk and Super Snipe from 1957 onwards; 1965–67 Imperial; Sceptre, 1963–76.*
- The 1959 Super Snipe and later Imperial were the last of the true Humbers. The Super Snipe was a bigger, six-cylinder, more luxurious version of the four-cylinder Hawk of 1957, with the short-lived Imperial (1965–67) topping out the range with even more luxury trimmings. The interiors were the usual British drawing-room mix of leather, wood and quietly ticking clock, and by all accounts these last big Humbers handled pretty much like a drawing-room too. Then again, Humber owners weren't really inclined to hustle a car along like those flashy types in tyre squealing Mk II Jags. And that's why, if you're lucky, you might just be able to find one that hasn't been caned into the ground by a succession of lead-footed owners.
- **Pick of the bunch:** Snipe II onwards offers better 3 litre performance and front disc brakes. Imperial is the fully loaded luxury version.
- **What to watch:** Structural rot in unitary shell; prices are low, but all the leather, wood and other luxury fittings are just as expensive to restore as in a more valuable car. Many body panels and trim items are unavailable, so you want a car that's all there.
- **Humber facts:** In 1960, the revised Super Snipe became the first British car with twin headlamps.
- **Engine:** 2655cc (Snipe I) and 2956cc, straight-six, overhead valve.
- **Power:** 105–128.5bhp.
- **Transmission:** Three-speed manual, optional overdrive; Borg Warner automatic; optional four-speed manual on Imperial.
- **Brakes:** Drums all round on 1959 Super Snipe I; front discs, rear drums from 1960.
- **Top speed:** 90–100+mph.

HUMBER Model	ENGINE cc/cyl	DATES	CONDITION 1	2	3
Veteran	var	1898			
		1918	£30,000+	£20,000+	£14,000
10	1592/4	1919	£7,000	£5,000	£3,000
14	2474/4	1919	£8,000	£6,000	£4,000
15.9–5/40	2815/4	1920–27	£9,500	£7,000	£4,000
8	985/4	1923–25	£7,000	£5,000	£2,500
9/20–9/28	1057/4	1926	£7,000	£5,000	£4,000
14/40	2050/4	1927–28	£10,000	£8,000	£5,000
Snipe	3498/6	1930–35	£8,000	£6,000	£4,000
Pullman	3498/6	1930–35	£8,000	£6,000	£4,000
16/50	2110/6	1930–32	£9,000	£7,000	£5,000
12	1669/4	1933–37	£7,000	£5,000	£3,000
Snipe/Pullman	4086/6	1936–40	£7,000	£5,000	£3,000
16	2576/6	1938–40	£7,000	£5,000	£3,000

Pre-1906 or Brighton Run eligible cars are very popular.

1963 Humber Hawk Estate, 2267cc engine, manual gearbox with floor change, finished in maroon, red interior, laid up for c14 years, interior and bodywork partially refurbished.
£2,500–3,000 / $3,500–4,500 ✈ H&H

1964 Humber Imperial Saloon, automatic transmission, bodywork restored 2000 at a cost of c£6,000/$8,700, engine converted to unleaded fuel, good to excellent condition.
£3,000–3,500 / $4,500–5,000 ✈ Bon

HUMBER Model	ENGINE cc/cyl	DATES	CONDITION 1	2	3
Hawk Mk I–IV	1944/4	1945–52	£3,700	£1,500	£600
Hawk Mk V–VII	2267/4	1952–57	£3,000	£1,500	£400
Hawk Ser I–IVA	2267/4	1957–67	£3,000	£850	£325
Snipe	2731/6	1945–48	£5,000	£2,600	£850
Super Snipe Mk I–III	4086/6	1948–52	£4,700	£2,400	£600
Super Snipe Mk IV–IVA	4138/6	1952–56	£5,500	£2,300	£550
Super Snipe Ser I–II	2651/6	1958–60	£3,800	£1,800	£475
Super Snipe SIII VA	2965/6	1961–67	£3,500	£1,800	£400
Super Snipe S.III–VA Est.	2965/6	1961–67	£3,950	£1,850	£525
Pullman	4086/6	1946–51	£4,500	£2,350	£800
Pullman Mk IV	4086/6	1952–54	£6,000	£2,850	£1,200
Imperial	2965/6	1965–67	£3,900	£1,600	£450
Sceptre Mk I–II	1592/4	1963–67	£2,200	£1,000	£300
Sceptre Mk III	1725/4	1967–76	£2,000	£900	£200

Invicta

Invicta's life was short and turbulent. The company was founded in Surrey, in 1925, by Lance Macklin and Oliver Lyle, who set out to combine in one car the American virtues of power and flexibility with British standards of road-holding and craftsmanship. The cars were known as 'assembled cars': for reasons of expediency and the quest for quality, Invicta gathered together the best proprietary components to create a car of singular quality and performance. The zenith of Invicta's short life came with the lovely and potent 4.5 litre low-chassis S-Type. Initially, the Meadows engine in the S-Type produced about 115bhp and around 95mph, so near the magic century that the car was known colloquially as

the 100mph Invicta. By the end of production, in 1935, power output was up to around 140bhp and the '100mph' appellation was no longer an exaggeration. Yet those qualities that make Invictas so prized today were also factors in the company's downfall: producing an extravagant, expensive machine – with a near-Rolls-Royce price tag – as Britain plunged into depression in the early 1930s. By 1935, Invicta production had ceased, but there were two attempted and failed revivals, first in 1937/38, then with the Black Prince, built from 1946 to 1950. What was left was a legacy of a mere 1,000 cars, most of them exquisite and none more revered than the rare 4.5 litre S-Type low-chassis tourer.

1931 Invicta Low-Chassis S-Type, fitted with Lagonda LG45 engine, dished steering wheel, period instrumentation including accelerometer, 1 of only 77 built, 1 owner for 50 years, well maintained, original Meadows engine included.
£200,000+ / $290,000+ ✈ COYS

The Invicta S-Type was not only one of the most stylish sports cars of its day, but also one of the most competitive. At the heart of the S-Type was a 4.5 litre straight-six Meadows engine that produced 115bhp, but which was more notable for its low-speed torque and flexibility. The chassis, underslung at the rear, incorporated numerous phosphor-bronze and gunmetal castings, and was built without compromise. Suspension was by semi-elliptic leaf springs and hydraulic dampers front and rear, but its exceptionally low centre of gravity endowed it with far from ordinary road-holding.

Iso

Founded in 1939 by Renzo Rivolta, the Italian Iso company's automotive products represented two extremes. In 1953, Iso began production of the Isetta bubble-car, later to be built under licence and in prodigious numbers by BMW. Then, in the 1960s, Renzo Rivolta turned his attention to producing high-performance sports and GT cars. His chief designer was Giotto Bizzarrini, whose other achievements include the Ferrari 250 GTO and Lamborghini's V12 engine. The first Iso offering was the four-seat

Rivolta, powered by a Chevrolet Corvette V8; then came the mighty Grifo two-seat coupé. Certainly its name declared its intentions, for 'grifo' is Italian for 'griffin', the mythical bird that preys on horses, an obvious allusion to Ferrari's proud emblem. It didn't quite turn out that way, though. Successive models, the Fidia and Lele, although excellent performers, didn't have quite the panache of their predecessors. Production slowed to a dribble, and by 1978 there were no more Iso cars.

1967 Iso Grifo GL 350, V8 engine, 'fuelie' heads, 350bhp, 4-speed manual gearbox, Borrani wire wheels, correct Campagnolo alloys also available, no-expense-spared restoration to original specification, finished in dark red, interior trimmed in beige Connolly leather, 1 of 30 right-hand-drive examples from a total of 412 cars, 1967 London Motor Show car.
£25,000–30,000 / $36,000–43,000 ⚲ COYS
Giotto Bizzarrini established his reputation as a skilled engineer with Alfa Romeo and Ferrari during the early 1960s, being largely responsible for developing the celebrated 250 GTO. Other cars to his credit are Lamborghini's first model, the 350GTV and his own racing car, the Bizzarrini GT. In 1963, he joined Iso. In the same year, he penned the Grifo. The Grifo was a worthy Ferrari challenger, too, with bodywork penned by Giugiaro, chassis design by Bizzarrini and power courtesy of Chevrolet's 5.3 litre V8. This combination produced a car with a top speed of over 160mph, faster than the equivalent Ferrari, an achievement that was not bettered by Ferrari until the introduction of the 275 GTB/4.

ISO Model	ENGINE cc/cyl	DATES	CONDITION 1	2	3
Rivolta V8	5359cc	1962–70	£15,000	£10,000	£3,500
Grifo V8	5359/6899		£28,000	£16,000	£12,000
Lele 2-door fastback coupé	5359	1967–74	£12,000	£8,000	£5,000
Fidia V8 4-door exec. saloon	5359	1967–74	£10,000	£7,000	£5,000

Itala

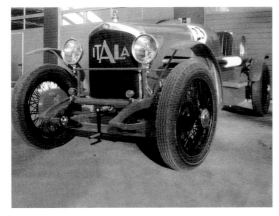

◀ **1923 Itala Tipo 51S Tourer,** 2813cc 4-cylinder sidevalve engine, 4-speed manual gearbox, rear-wheel brakes, transmission brake, right-hand drive, 65–70mph top speed, restored, little use since, engine rebuilt with aluminium pistons, forced lubrication, pumped water circulation and electric starter, SU carburettor, original bronze-bodied carburettor included, gearbox and brakes rebuilt, new aluminium coachwork on ash frame, rewired.
£30,000–35,000 / $43,000–51,000 ⚲ Bon
Founded in 1904 by Matteo Ceirano and Guido Bigio, Itala established a competition record second to none in the years leading up to WWI, winning the Targa Florio in 1906 and the Peking-Paris long-distance race the following year. The Turin based marque enjoyed similar success in the early 1920s, the highlights including class wins in the Targa Florio in 1919, 1920 and 1921; gaining first and second places in the 1921 Coppa dell Alpi; and setting a new Sydney-Melbourne record in 1924.

Jaguar

The first 'Jaguar' – although it was many years before the company would adopt the name – was not a car at all, but a motorcycle sidecar produced in 1922. Yet the aluminium-bodied sidecar already showed the traits that later would become hallmarks of Jaguar and William Lyons, the company's founder. Lyons was born in Blackpool in 1901. Before he ever dabbled with cars, he was an enthusiastic motorcyclist who, on his 21st birthday, formed the Swallow Sidecar Company with William Walmsley. In 1927, the company made the transition to four wheels, clothing a strengthened Austin 7 chassis with a stylish two-tone sports body. In 1931, the rakish SS1 appeared, and in 1935, with William Lyons now sole proprietor of the company, the Jaguar name was used for the first time. Most prized among the pre-war models is the beautifully rakish and fast SS100.

Yet Jaguar's glory years really began after the war with the 1948 launch of the XK120. Ever since, virtually every Jaguar produced – both saloon and sporting – has been an enthusiast's motor car, enjoyed by those lucky enough to own them and coveted by those who can only admire them. The best news is that in today's market, all manner of classic Jaguars are at their most affordable for years, particularly Mk II saloons and E-Types, both of which have fallen back dramatically from their over-inflated peak values of the late 1980s and early 1990s.

1935 SS1 20hp Drophead Coupé, 2.7 litre 6-cylinder sidevalve engine, largely restored, over £15,000/$22,000 spent, engine rebuilt, body with new framing and skins, all drophead fittings with car including cast aluminium cant rails, dovetail locks and chrome-plated hood frame, most chromework replated, in need of rewiring, trimming and general finishing.
£27,000–32,000 / $39,000–46,000 ⋌ CGC
Considered by many to be one of the prettiest of all the SS cars, the 20hp Drophead is also one of the rarest. Its rarity has spawned a number of convincing replicas based on the more widely available SS1 saloon, but this particular car is a genuine example.

1949 Jaguar Mk V 2½ Litre Saloon, 2664cc engine, finished in maroon, red interior.
£16,000–18,000 / $23,000–26,000 ⋌ H&H
This 2.5 litre Mk V Jaguar saloon was originally purchased in 1949 by the Duke of Bedford as an anniversary present for his wife. The Mk V was a logical progression from its predecessor, the Mk IV, but benefited from independent front suspension and a new, more substantial chassis.

1946 Jaguar Mk IV 3½ Litre Four-Door Saloon, recently out of long-term storage, engine rebuilt, Lucas P100 headlamps, original spotlamps, wire wheels, original Ace wheel discs, original wing mirrors, mascot, 6th car built after WWII, retains many SS features, original.
£6,500–8,000 / $9,000–11,500 ⋌ Bon
Jaguar Cars – as William Lyons' SS Cars had been renamed – began post-war production with a range of existing designs, the larger of which was the 2½ and 3½ Litre, retrospectively known as the Mk IV. In appearance, the cars were identical to the 1939 SS models, apart from badging, and the only significant mechanical difference was the adoption of a hypoid-bevel rear axle. Built on a 120in (305cm) wheelbase, the Mk IV's chassis featured a beam front axle and semi-elliptic leaf springs, with Girling mechanical brakes. The all-steel coachwork was available in saloon and drophead coupé versions, and featured the kind of luxurious and well-appointed interior that would become a Jaguar hallmark. The engine was Standard's rugged seven-bearing straight-six, fitted with a Weslake designed overhead-valve cylinder head and coupled to a four-speed manual gearbox. The Mk IV was marketed at a modest price to help regenerate the immediate post-war economy, and with 125bhp from the 3485cc engine, 91mph was possible.

JAGUAR Model	ENGINE cc/cyl	DATES	CONDITION 1	2	3
SSI	2054/6	1932–33	£26,000	£18,000	£12,000
SSI	2252/6	1932–33	£22,000	£17,000	£13,500
SSII	1052/4	1932–33	£18,000	£15,000	£11,000
SSI	2663/6	1934	£26,000	£22,000	£15,000
SSII	1608/4	1934	£18,000	£15,000	£12,000
SS90	2663/6	1935	£60,000+	-	-
SS100 (3.4)	3485/6	1938–39	£90,000+	-	-
SS100 (2.6)	2663/6	1936–39	£90,000+	-	-

Very dependent on body styles, completeness and originality, particularly original chassis to body.

JAGUAR Model	ENGINE cc/cyl	DATES	CONDITION 1	2	3
1½ Litre	1775/4	1945–49	£8,500	£5,500	£2,000
2½ Litre	2663/6	1946–49	£10,000	£7,500	£2,000
2½ Litre DHC	2663/6	1947–48	£17,000	£11,000	£8,000
3½ Litre	3485/6	1947–49	£12,000+	£6,000	£4,000
3½ Litre DHC	3485/6	1947–49	£19,000+	£13,500	£5,500
Mk V 2½ Litre	2663/6	1949–51	£14,000+	£8,000+	£1,500
Mk V 3½ Litre	3485/6	1949–51	£13,000	£8,000	£3,000
Mk V 3½ Litre DHC	3485/6	1949–51	£22,000+	£17,000+	£8,500
Mk VII	3442/6	1951–57	£10,000	£7,500	£2,500
Mk VIIM	3442/6	1951–57	£12,000	£8,500	£2,500
Mk VIII	3442/6	1956–59	£8,500	£5,500	£2,000
Mk IX	3781/6	1958–61	£9,000	£7,000	£2,500
Mk X 3.8/4.2	3781/6	1961–64	£7,500	£3,500	£1,500
Mk X 420G	4235/6	1964–70	£6,000	£3,000	£1,200
Mk I 2.4	2438/6	1955–59	£7,000+	£5,500	£2,000
Mk I 3.4	3442/6	1957–59	£10,000	£6,000	£2,500
Mk II 2.4	2483/6	1959–67	£9,000+	£6,000	£3,000
Mk II 3.4	3442/6	1959–67	£12,000	£8,000	£4,000
Mk II 3.8	3781/6	1959–67	£18,000+	£11,000	£5,000
S-Type 3.4	3442/6	1963–68	£9,000+	£6,500+	£2,000
S-Type 3.8	3781/6	1963–68	£10,000	£6,500	£2,000
240	2438/6	1967–68	£9,000	£6,000	£2,500
340	3442/6	1967–68	£8,000	£7,000	£3,000
420	4235/6	1966–68	£6,000	£3,000	£2,000

Manual gearboxes with overdrive are at a premium.
Some concours examples make as much as 50% over Condition 1.

1954 Jaguar Mk VII Saloon, 3422cc double-overhead-camshaft engine, 4-speed manual gearbox with overdrive, restored, cylinder head overhauled at a cost of c£900/$1,300, front suspension and steering refurbished, brakes overhauled, chromework replated, resprayed in pale blue, wood veneers restored, original front door panel mounted tool kits, original grey leather interior, 3 owners from new, excellent condition.
£9,500–11,000 / $14,000–16,000 ↗ CGC
Launched at the London Motor Show in October 1950, the Jaguar Mk VII was a full five-seat saloon that could exceed 100mph and cost less than half the price of its Bentley Mk VI rival. It proved a quantifiable success in both the home and US export markets. Despite its graceful, stately lines and generous proportions, the Mk VII had a glorious career as a rally car and circuit racer, proving itself to be one of the great sporting saloons of the 1950s, especially in 'M' specification.

▶ **1951 Jaguar XK120 Roadster,** genuine right-hand-drive car, completely rebuilt, only 1,000 miles since, fitted with larger 3800cc engine, stainless-steel exhaust, finished in white, beige and burgundy interior, excellent condition.
£20,000–25,000 / $29,000–36,000 ↗ H&H

1950 Jaguar XK120 Roadster, finished in metallic grey, dark blue leather interior, restored, near concours condition.
£40,000–45,000 / $58,000–65,000 ↗ COYS
This car was despatched from the factory to Australia where, in the hands of its original owner, it took part in many competitive events, including the 1952 Australian Grand Prix.

One of the earliest XK120 customers was car connoisseur and actor Clark Gable, who reckoned that the XK120 was 'a masterpiece of design and construction'.

◀ **1954 Jaguar XK140 MC Roadster,** left-hand drive, chrome wire wheels, original colour-coded wheels included, bodywork restored, finished in British racing green, Luke 4-point race harness, very good condition.
£40,000–45,000 / $58,000–65,000 ↗ COYS
In 1954, the XK140 replaced Jaguar's legendary XK120, offering a number of worthwhile improvements, including rack-and-pinion steering and better weight distribution due to a repositioned engine. The MC model was fitted with a C-Type head and 1¾in SU carburettors, which increased the power output to 210bhp.

◄ **1955 Jaguar XK140 SE Roadster,** restored mid-1990s, engine rebuilt, C-Type cylinder head, converted to unleaded fuel, twin exhausts, front disc brakes with Coopercraft 4-pot calipers, chrome wire wheels, chassis stove enamelled, finished in red, beige leather interior.
£45,000–50,000 / $65,000–72,000 ⊞ BC

1956 Jaguar XK140 MC Drophead Coupé, 3442cc double-overhead-camshaft 6-cylinder engine, MC-type cylinder head, 160bhp, factory sump guard, 4-speed close-ratio gearbox with overdrive, torsion-bar independent front suspension, rack-and-pinion steering, original right-hand drive, subject of complete professional restoration, retains all original mechanical components, finished in British racing green, tan interior.
£34,000–38,000 / $49,000–55,000 ⅄ RM
The most lavish of all the XKs was the XK140 drophead coupé, which was also the most expensive of the range. With its walnut woodwork and thickly padded soft top, the drophead set new standards of luxury for open-cockpit motoring. In all, fewer than 9,000 XK140s were manufactured, of which only 2,790 were drophead coupés. Of these, a mere 480 were built in right-hand-drive form.

1957 Jaguar XK140 Coupé, body-off restoration completed 1980, restored again during 1997–98, converted to unleaded fuel, driver's-side battery box adapted to house 2 paper-element carburettor air filters, finished in red, beige and black interior, fewer than 2,500 miles in last 20 years, very good condition throughout.
£17,500–20,000 / $25,000–29,000 ⅄ Bon

1958 Jaguar XK150 Roadster, matching numbers, left-hand drive, restored to original specification, retains most original panels, finished in correct pale grey with matching wire wheels, dark blue mohair hood, new red leather interior.
£28,000–32,000 / $40,000–46,000 ⅄ COYS
The XK150 was the final expression of the XK range. Announced in May 1957, it boasted a number of significant changes over the previous, similar looking XK140 model. The most noteworthy improvement was the adoption of disc brakes – Jaguar had been among the first to experiment with these in association with Dunlop in 1951. Another very welcome advance was the optional Laycock overdrive unit, which endowed the car with tremendous, long-legged cruising ability.

1958 Jaguar XK150 Drophead Coupé, 3400cc double-overhead-camshaft 6-cylinder engine, original chrome wire wheels, original right-hand drive, finished in maroon, red interior, 2 owners and 40,000 miles from new, only 700 miles in last 12 years, unrestored, very good original condition.
£30,000–34,000 / $43,000–49,000 ⅄ H&H

1960 Jaguar XK150 Roadster, 3.4 litre engine, 4-speed manual gearbox with overdrive, original right-hand drive, finished in indigo blue, grey leather interior, 2 owners and c52,000 miles from new, unrestored.
£34,000–38,000 / $49,000–55,000 ⅄ N

1957 Jaguar Mk I Saloon, manual gearbox with overdrive, finished in grey, red leather interior, 1 family owner and 60,000 miles from new.
£6,000–7,000 / $8,500–10,000 ⊞ VIC

▶ **1961 Jaguar Mk II 3.4 Saloon,** 3.4 litre double-overhead-camshaft 6-cylinder engine, 4-speed manual gearbox with overdrive, matching numbers, subject of ground-up restoration 1999–2001 at a cost of c£42,000/$61,000, fewer than 65 miles since, finished in gunmetal grey, red leather interior.
£20,000–23,000 / $29,000–33,000 ⚲ BARO

1957 Jaguar Mk I 2.4 Convertible, 2483cc 6-cylinder engine, restored and modified to 2-door convertible form in Australia, bodyshell strengthened, chrome wire wheels, double duck tonneau cover, finished in red, interior retrimmed in white leatherette, good mechanical condition throughout.
£5,000–6,000 / $7,000–9,000 ⚲ BRIT

1961 Jaguar Mk II 3.8 Saloon, refurbished and modified to Coombs specification by ex-Coombs mechanic late 1990s, close-ratio manual gearbox, power steering, finished in British racing green, dark green leather interior, Reuter leather seats, excellent condition.
£13,000–15,000 / $19,000–22,000 ⚲ COYS
It was in October 1959 that the Mk II Jaguar appeared. Similar in appearance to the Mk I, but with a much larger glass area, it boasted a wider rear track to improve road-holding, together with minor front suspension changes to reduce body roll and all-round disc brakes. Engine options comprised a 120bhp, 2.4 litre unit, a 210bhp, 3.4 litre and a 220bhp, 3.8 litre. The last provided impressive performance figures of 0–60mph in 8.5 seconds and a top speed of 125mph.

1961 Jaguar Mk II 3.8 Saloon, manual gearbox with overdrive, engine bottom-end rebuilt, new brake calipers and rear brake discs, chrome wire wheels, converted to right-hand drive, resprayed in black, new leather interior, new carpets and headlining, good to very good condition.
£8,000–10,000 / $11,500–14,500 ⚲ Bon

JAGUAR Model	ENGINE cc/cyl	DATES	CONDITION 1	2	3
XK120 roadster aluminium	3442/6	1948–49	£65,000	£30,000	£20,000
XK120 roadster	3442/6	1949–54	£30,000+	£20,000+	£15,000
XK120 DHC	3442/6	1953–54	£25,000+	£17,000+	£12,000
XK120 Coupé	3442/6	1951–55	£16,000+	£12,000+	£10,000
C-Type	3442/6	1951	£150,000+	-	-
D-Type	3442/6	1955–56	£500,000+	-	-
XKSS (original)	3442/6	1955–57	£400,000+	-	-
XK140 roadster	3442/6	1955–58	£32,000+	£23,000	£16,000
XK140 DHC	3442/6	1955–58	£28,000	£22,000	£15,000
XK140 Coupé	3442/6	1955–58	£18,000	£12,000	£7,500
XK150 roadster	3442/6	1958–60	£35,000	£22,000	£15,000
XK150 DHC	3442/6	1957–61	£28,000	£18,000	£10,000
XK150 Coupé	3442/6	1957–60	£16,000+	£10,000	£6,000
XK150S roadster	3442/ 3781/6	1958–60	£40,000+	£26,000	£20,000
XK150S DHC	3442/ 3781/6	1958–60	£36,000+	£22,000	£18,000
XK150S Coupé	3442/ 3781/6	1958–61	£22,000	£18,000	£10,000

D-Type with competition history considerably more.
Watch out for left- to right-hand-drive conversions in the XK series.

Jaguar Mk II (1960–68)

In one respect at least, 1960s cops owed a debt of gratitude to their villainous counterparts. If the Krays and kindred crooks hadn't cottoned on to the get-away capabilities of the Mk II and Mk II-based S-Type, the police probably wouldn't have been given Mk IIs to catch them. This Jag is a true sports saloon – especially the bigger-engined forms – a rare blend of grace, pace and plenty of space in the boot for loot.
Prices in 1960: 2.4, £1,534/$2,150; 3.4, £1,669/$2,400; 3.8, £1,779/$2,550.

Pick of the bunch: Post-1965 cars with much smoother, all-synchro box. Most prized is the 3.8 litre, but the extra 400cc costs a lot more than the 3.4, which runs it close in performance.
Mk II fact: Guildford dealer and saloon-car racer John Coombs created his own highly tuned Coombs Mk II, which could match an E-Type on the 0–60mph sprint. Coombs Jags are identifiable by louvred vents in the bonnet, which were taken from changing-room locker doors. Cynics say that of the 28 or so Coombs Mk IIs built, there are only 40 or 50 survivors.

Miller's Compares

I. 1961 Jaguar Mk II 3.8 Saloon, completely restored 2001 at a cost of c£40,000/$58,000, only 500 miles since, engine rebuilt and converted to unleaded fuel, electronic ignition, uprated electrics with new wiring harness, larger radiator, stainless-steel exhaust, 4-speed all-synchromesh gearbox with overdrive, Harvey Bailey handling kit, Koni shock absorbers, 4-pot front calipers, XJ6 power steering rack, body cavities rustproofed, extra sound deadening material, Coombs-type slimline rear wheel spats, wide-rim chrome wire wheels, finished in blue metallic, dark blue leather interior, XJ6 Vanden Plas-type reclining front seats, reveneered woodwork, inertia-reel seatbelts, very good mechanical and excellent cosmetic condition.
£28,000–32,000 / $40,000–46,000 ⏴ Bon

II. 1968 Jaguar 240 Saloon, 2483cc double-overhead-camshaft 6-cylinder engine, manual gearbox with overdrive, wire wheels, finished in British racing green.
£4,000–6,000 / $6,000–8,500 ⏴ Bon
The arrival of Jaguar's compact 2.4 litre saloons in 1955 heralded a new chapter in the company's history, and almost 50,000 were built between 1955 and 1969. The last of the successful line was the 240 saloon, which had refined styling – including the more elegant 'slim' bumpers – but retained essentially the same mechanical specification of the early models.

The Mk II Jaguar has many flavours and variants, and these two represent the two extremes. Car I is the ultimate standard-spec with 3.8 litre engine, manual overdrive gearbox and wire wheels. Car II, on the other hand, is not strictly a Mk II, but a 240, one of the last of the line with a budget specification that included standard Ambla (plastic) seats, slimmer bumpers and fog lamps only as an option. Its engine is the 2.4 litre unit. Additionally, car I has had over £40,000/$58,000 lavished on restoration and upgrades, but what these two comparisons demonstrate is that you can enter Mk II ownership at a level to suit you – and the price range is astonishingly wide.

Condition Guide

1. A vehicle in top class condition but not 'concours d'elegance' standard, either fully restored or in very good original condition.
2. A good, clean, roadworthy vehicle, both mechanically and bodily sound.
3. A runner, but in need of attention, probably both to bodywork and mechanics. Must have current MoT.

1968 Jaguar 340 Saloon, 3442cc double-overhead-camshaft 6-cylinder engine, wire wheels, finished in green, new red leather interior, 53,000 miles from new, good condition throughout.
£6,000–8,000 / $8,500–11,500 ⏴ H&H

◀ **1966 Jaguar 3.4 S-Type Saloon,** 3400cc 6-cylinder engine, 4-speed manual gearbox with overdrive, wire wheels, finished in red, black interior, 55,000 miles from new, excellent condition throughout.
£13,000–15,000 / $19,000–22,000 ⏴ H&H
This car was owned originally by the actor Robert Morley.

1968 Jaguar 3.8 S-Type Saloon, 4-speed manual gearbox with overdrive, right-hand drive export model, bodywork in good condition, finished in blue, vinyl interior, 2 owners and fewer than 40,000 miles from new.
£5,500–7,000 / $8,000–10,000 ⚹ Bon

1967 Jaguar 420 Saloon, manual gearbox with overdrive, power steering, finished in pale grey, red interior, 2 owners and 81,000 miles from new, bodywork in excellent condition.
£8,000–9,000 / $11,500–13,000 ⊞ BC

Market Comment

Although Jaguars of all kinds enjoy a tremendously enthusiastic following, there are several models that remain a little overlooked, which are worth considering by the Jaguar enthusiast on a budget. The S-Type saloon was, in effect, a Mk II with a stretched boot and better handling from its independent rear suspension, which made it a gangland favourite as a get-away car. The revival of the S-Type name in a new Jaguar model has done little to rejuvenate interest and increase prices, and the old S-Type remains undervalued compared to Mk II models. Another option is the 420, an S-Type with Mk X-style frontal treatment and 4.2 litre engine. Other models to consider are the 'thrift' late-model Jaguar Mk II variants, namely the 240 and 340, and the Daimler 250 V8 saloon, a Mk II with Daimler grille and a lovely compact V8 engine.

1962 Jaguar E-Type Series I 3.8 Roadster, completely restored 1990s, engine and gearbox rebuilt, rear axle overhauled, electrical ancillaries restored, bodywork refurbished, finished in white, brown mohair weather equipment, tan interior, interior fittings replaced as necessary.
£30,000–34,000 / $43,000–49,000 ⚹ COYS

1962 Jaguar E-Type Series 1 Coupé, refurbished at a cost of over £13,000/$18,850, original engine converted to unleaded fuel, hand-built racing exhaust manifold, finished in green, green interior, aluminium dashboard and centre console.
£17,000–20,000 / $24,000–29,000 ⚹ COYS
Jaguar's E-Type made immediate headlines on its launch in March 1961. Here was a sleek and beautiful 150mph car with a competition pedigree that could be bought for just over £2,000/$3,000, almost half the price of an Aston Martin or Ferrari.

1963 Jaguar E-Type 3.8 Coupé, 3800cc double-overhead-camshaft 6-cylinder engine, finished in metallic dark green, original tan interior, 73,000 miles from new, excellent condition throughout.
£17,000–20,000 / $24,000–29,000 ⚹ H&H

1965 Jaguar E-Type Series 1 4.2 Roadster, 4.2 litre double-overhead-camshaft 6-cylinder engine, restored 1991, little use since, converted to right-hand drive, excellent condition.
£38,000–42,000 / $55,000–61,000 ⊞ CMC

1965 Jaguar E-Type Series 1 4.2 Roadster, 4235cc double-overhead-camshaft 6-cylinder engine, 265bhp, 4-speed manual gearbox, 4-wheel disc brakes, independent torsion-bar front suspension, independent coil-spring rear suspension, older restoration, formerly owned by Elton John.
£25,000–30,000 / $36,000–43,000 ✗ C
Following the initial production series, Jaguar adopted an updated version of the E-Type in 1964 with the enlarged 4.2 litre six-cylinder engine. Although not improving the 145mph top speed, the engine had a noticeably increased torque range. An all-synchromesh gearbox and an improved brake servo system were standard on the 4.2 cars. There were also major technical improvements in the clutch, electrical and cooling systems. Inside, the interior had better seats, a revised dashboard, armrests and a storage compartment on the transmission tunnel.

1967 Jaguar E-Type 2+2 Coupé, 4235cc 6-cylinder engine, automatic transmission, floorpan and sills renewed 1988, finished in red, major mechanical items in good condition, in need of refurbishment.
£6,000–8,000 / $8,500–11,500 ✗ BRIT
With an extra 9in (23cm) in the wheelbase and a 2in (5cm) increase in height, the 2+2 E-Type was a viable proposition for the family man who wanted to continue driving a sports car. Although the weight had risen, the car was still an admirable performer. When an automatic version was tested by *Motor* magazine, the top speed was found to be 136.2mph, while 0–60mph took 8.9 seconds.

1968 Jaguar E-Type Series 1½ Roadster, 4235cc 6-cylinder engine, professionally refurbished 1989, converted to right-hand drive, chrome wire wheels, new bonnet, bare-metal respray in British racing green, new tan leather interior, carpets and dashboard trim, fewer than 2,000 miles since 1993, good condition.
£15,000–17,000 / $22,000–24,000 ✗ BRIT

Cross Reference
See Colour Review (page 72)

▶ **1969 Jaguar E-Type Series 1½ Coupé,** 4.2 litre engine, chrome wire wheels, finished in silver, black leather interior, good condition.
£10,000–12,000 / $14,500–17,500 ✗ COYS

Jaguar E-Type (1961–74)

Production: 72,520.
Engine: 3781 and 4235cc, straight-six; 5343cc V12.
Power output: 265–272bhp.
0–60mph: 7–7.2 seconds.
Top speed: 143–150mph.
Price new: £2,097.19s.2d/$3,000 (roadster).
A sensational showstopper at the 1961 Geneva Show. British motoring magazines had produced road tests of pre-production models to coincide with the launch – and yes, the fixed-head-coupé really could do 150.4mph (149.1mph for the roadster), although most owners found 145mph a more realistic maximum. What's more, its shattering performance came relatively cheaply. In fact, to match it you would have had to pay at least £1,000/$1,500 more, and Aston Martins and Ferraris were more than double the money. E-Types took off again in the late 1980s as grasping speculators drove prices into orbit, nudging a stratospheric £100,000/$145,000 before the gravitational pull of the market dragged them back down to earth in a big way. That's good news for today's buyers, who stand a chance of owning an E-Type for less than has been lavished on its restoration.
E-Type facts: Of every three E-Types built, two were exported. Originally, the fixed-head coupé cost £100/$145 more than the open roadster; today, roadsters are far more highly prized.

1970 Jaguar E-Type Series II Roadster, 4.2 litre 6-cylinder engine, manual gearbox, chrome wire wheels, restored 1996 at a cost of over £33,000/$48,000, finished in British racing green, green interior, no major modifications to original specification, 2 owners from new.
£22,000–25,000 / $32,000–36,000 ✗ Bon

1971 Jaguar E-Type Series III Coupé, 5.3 litre V12 engine, converted to manual gearbox, chrome wire wheels, finished in dark blue, blue leather interior, excellent condition throughout.
£20,000–23,000 / $29,000–33,000 ✗ CGC

1971 E-Type Series III Coupé, 5.3 litre V12 engine, stored since 1999.
£10,000–11,000 / $14,000–16,000 ✗ Bon
Some of the E-Type's lost performance was restored in 1971 with the arrival of the Series III V12. The new 5.3 litre overhead-camshaft engine produced 272bhp, good enough for a top speed of slightly over 140mph and a 0–100mph time of around 16 seconds. Flared wheel arches, wider tyres and a deeper radiator air intake complete with grille – plus the 'V12' boot badge – distinguished the newcomer from its six-cylinder forebears. Beneath the skin, ventilated front discs improved braking performance, while the front suspension gained anti-dive geometry.

1971 Jaguar E-Type Series III Coupé, 4.2 litre V12 engine, 3-speed automatic transmission, finished in red, black leather interior, good condition.
£8,000–10,000 / $11,500–14,500 ✗ CGC

◄ **1972 Jaguar E-Type Series III Roadster,** 5300cc V12 engine, manual gearbox, professionally restored to original specification, converted to right-hand drive, bills totalling £6,000/$8,700, finished in pale yellow, black interior, 51,000 miles from new, rust-free ex-California car.
£18,000–20,000 / $26,000–29,000 ✗ H&H

JAGUAR Model	ENGINE cc/cyl	DATES	CONDITION 1	2	3
E-Type 3.8 flat-floor roadster (RHD)		1961	£40,000+	£30,000	£22,000
E-Type SI 3.8 roadster	3781/6	1961–64	£30,000	£19,000	£15,000
E-Type 3.8 FHC	3781/6	1961–64	£20,000	£13,000	£10,000
E-Type SI 4.2 roadster	4235/6	1964–67	£28,000	£18,000	£14,000
E-Type 2+2 manual FHC	4235/6	1966–67	£16,000	£11,000	£9,000
E-Type SI 2+2 auto FHC	4235/6	1966–68	£14,000	£10,000	£9,000
E-Type SII roadster	4235/6	1968–70	£30,000	£21,000	£14,000
E-Type SII FHC	4235/6	1968–70	£18,000	£12,000	£10,000
E-Type SII 2+2 manual FHC	4235/6	1968–70	£15,000	£10,000	£8,000
E-Type SIII roadster	5343/12	1971–75	£30,000+	£26,000	£17,000
E-Type SIII 2+2 manual FHC	5343/12	1971–75	£14,000	£10,000	£9,000
E-Type SIII 2+2 auto FHC	5343/12	1971–75	£13,000	£9,000	£7,000
XJ6 2.8 Ser I	2793/6	1968–73	£3,000	£1,500	£1,000
XJ6 4.2 Ser I	4235/6	1968–73	£3,500	£2,000	£1,000
XJ6 Coupé	4235/6	1974–78	£8,000	£5,000	£3,500
XJ6 Ser II	4235/6	1973–79	£3,500	£2,000	£750
XJ12 Ser I	5343/12	1972–73	£3,500	£2,250	£1,500
XJ12 Coupé	5343/12	1973–77	£9,000	£5,000	£3,000
XJ12 Ser II	5343/12	1973–79	£3,000	£2,000	£1,000
XJS manual	5343/12	1975–78	£5,000	£4,000	£2,500
XJS auto	5343/12	1975–81	£4,000	£3,000	£2,000

Jaguar E-Type Series III Commemorative Roadsters fetch more than SIII Roadster – 50 limited editions only.

1975 Jaguar E-Type Series III Roadster, 5343cc double-overhead-camshaft V12 engine, 272bhp, ventilated front disc brakes, anti-dive front suspension, 18 gallon fuel tank, factory hardtop, finished in red, black interior, fewer than 18,000 miles from new, original.
£29,000–33,000 / $42,000–48,000 ⚒ COYS

1973 Jaguar XJ6 Series I 4.2 Saloon, gearbox replaced 1995, fuel tanks reconditioned, bare-metal respray in sable 1993, Webasto sun roof recovered, headlining replaced, light tan leather interior, 26,000 miles from new.
£2,000–2,500 / $3,000–3,500 ⚒ BARO

1974 Jaguar XJ5.3C Coupé, 5343cc V12 engine, completely restored at a cost of over £20,000/$29,000 1990s, engine rebuilt, fewer than 500 miles since, finished in white, cinnamon leather interior, good mechanical order.
£5,000–6,000 / $7,000–8,000 ⚒ BRIT
This car is a pre-production model and was used by the factory for about a year before finally being sold. It has the very rare Stromberg-carburettor engine, all production models being fuel injected. In this guise, the engine gave more power, being basically in E-Type tune.

1977 Jaguar XJ5.3C Coupé, V12 engine, finished in yellow, navy blue velour interior, 22,000 miles from new, 1 of last made, 'as new' condition.
£9,000–10,000 / $13,000–14,500 ⚒ Bon
The original XJ6 caused a sensation in 1968, when it introduced new standards of comfort and refinement. In 1973, the Series II was introduced, by this time in standard and 'L', or long-wheelbase, forms. Later in the year, the pillarless coupé was launched, being based on the original standard wheelbase. It was available with a 4.2 litre straight-six or 5.3 litre V12.

1984 Jaguar 5.3 Sovereign Avon Estate, 5343cc V12 engine, stored for many years, recommissioned, bare-metal respray in original silver 2001, light grey interior, 70,000 miles from new, 1 of only 3 examples built by Avon Coachworks.
£6,500–8,000 / $9,500–11,500 ⚒ H&H

▶ **1986 Jaguar XJS TWR Cabriolet,** V12 engine, finished in white, grey hide interior, 61,000 miles from new.
£6,000–7,000 / $8,500–10,000 ⚒ COYS
This XJS is based on the XJ-SC HE cabriolet and has been modified by renowned competition Jaguar exponent TWR. The modifications cost some £9,000/$13,000 over the list price. Included are body restyling panels, low-drag alloy wheels, upgrades to the suspension, brakes and steering, sports induction and exhaust systems, and a revalved 'quick-shift' transmission.

1988 Jaguar XJS Convertible, 5343cc V12 engine, automatic transmission, cruise control, air conditioning, 57,000 miles from new, excellent condition.
£8,500–10,000 / $12,500–14,500 ⚹ H&H

1989 Jaguar XJS Coupé, 5.3 litre V12 engine, finished in metallic grey, grey leather interior, fewer than 32,500 miles from new.
£3,500–4,000 / $5,000–6,000 ⚹ Bon
The XJS was launched in 1975, using the XJ6/XJ12 platform and running gear, but with a slightly shorter wheelbase than the saloons.

◀ **1989 Jaguar XJR-S,** alarm, car phone, finished in metallic blue, cream leather interior, 49,000 miles from new, good condition.
£7,000–8,000 / $10,000–11,500 ⚹ CGC
The limited-edition XJR-S was produced to celebrate Jaguar's return to sports car racing and its associated spate of Le Mans victories. The model was modified to give it a sportier feel compared to the base car's grand-tourer character. Stiffer spring and damper rates, together with 'meatier' steering, gave improved handling. Externally, it wore a subtle body kit, alloy wheels and a black grille.

1992 Jaguar XJ220, left-hand drive, finished in metallic British racing green, beige leather interior, 1 owner and c106 miles from new, 'as new' condition.
£85,000–95,000 / $123,000–138,000 ⚹ Bon
Planning for Jaguar's proposed 200mph supercar had begun in the mid-1980s and finally bore fruit when the prototype was shown in 1988. The XJ220 survived Ford's take-over of Jaguar in the following year, but when eventually it entered production, in 1992, it was a very different beast. Gone was the prototype's 6.2 litre V12 engine, and in its place was a Cosworth designed 3.5 litre, twin-turbo V6, as used in the XJR-11 sports-racer, while other casualties of the need to simplify the design for production included the prototype's four-wheel drive and adaptive suspension. Producing no less than 542bhp, the new engine enabled the XJ220 to meet its 200+mph design target, F1 driver Martin Brundle recording a speed of over 217mph during track testing. The 0–100mph time was a staggering 7.9 seconds. The XJ220 was constructed around a bonded and riveted monocoque chassis, formed from lightweight aluminium sheet reinforced by aluminium honeycomb sections. The race-derived double-wishbone suspension was adapted to provide acceptable comfort under road conditions, while other competition-influenced features were the AP Racing brakes, Speedline aluminium wheels and FF Developments five-speed, all-synchromesh transaxle with viscous-control, limited-slip differential.

▶ **1992 Jaguar XJ220,** 3.5 litre V6 engine, twin turbochargers, 542bhp, brakes upgraded by factory at a cost of £9,000/$13,000, 1 of 25 built, fewer than 11,500 miles from new.
£115,000–130,000 $167,000–188,500 ⚹ COYS

Colour Review

1939 Lagonda V12 Le Mans Rapide, 4.5 litre V12 engine, independent front suspension, older restoration, pale blue leather interior.
£190,000+ / $275,000 ✗ Bon
Although first seen in 1936, the Lagonda V12 did not go into production until 1938, and only 189 examples were built before the coming of WWII ended production. It was one of the outstanding British models of its day and one of an exclusive handful of 1930s road cars that could exceed 100mph in standard tune. The V12 engine produced 180bhp at 5,500rpm and sufficient torque to endow the car with a walking pace-to-105mph capability in top gear. There was a varied choice of coachwork – including a limousine – and the short-chassis Rapide roadster provided even more performance. The marque already possessed a creditable Le Mans record, and it was decided to enter a two-car team in 1939 with the aim of securing valuable data, then to mount a full-strength challenge the following year. The streamlined Le Mans two-seater used the short chassis in modified form and an improved version of the V12 engine developing 220bhp. It is thought that around 12 engines were made to the 1939 Le Mans specification, and those not used were fitted to directors' cars and those of favoured customers. Of these, only three ended up in Rapides.

▶ **1989 Lamborghini Countach Anniversary,** 5767cc 4-camshaft V12 engine, Bosch K-Jetronic fuel injection, 5-speed manual gearbox, 4-wheel disc brakes, 4-wheel independent suspension, delivery mileage only, 'as new' condition.
£60,000–70,000 / $87,000–101,000 ✗ RM
Built to celebrate Lamborghini's 25th anniversary, this special edition featured a restyled front air dam and air intakes, front and side skirts, and wide wheel arch flares.

1936 Lagonda LG45, 4.5 litre engine, Brooklands-profile camshaft, rebuilt valve gear, new pistons, new radiator core, chassis extensively rebuilt, fitted with Le Mans-type coachwork of earlier M45 model.
£50,000–55,000 / $72,000–80,000 ✗ COYS
While only in production for two years, the Lagonda M45/LG45 series gained a considerable following. Power came from Henry Meadows' 4.5 litre engine, which put Lagonda in the forefront of sports car production in 1934. In the following year, the Fox and Nicholl team of Lagondas won a notable Le Mans victory.

1910 Lanchester 20hp Torpedo Phaeton, older restoration, Lucas acetylene headlamps, oil side lamps, quadruple Testaphone-type brass horn, weather equipment, green leather upholstery, VCC dated.
£26,000–30,000 / $38,000–44,000 ✗ Bon
The Lanchester 20hp model was shown at the Olympia Motor Exhibition in February 1905. The all-new vertical inline engine was to an unconventional, 'over-square' design, with four separate cylinders and a capacity of 2.6 litres. Twin camshafts controlled the overhead valves, which were activated by leaf springs. Cantilever suspension ensured a smooth ride, and epicyclic gearing was employed. By 1910, Lanchester had adopted wheel steering, replacing the idiosyncratic tiller.

1966 Lancia Flaminia 3C 2800 Super Sport Double Bubble Coupé, coachwork by Zagato, 2775cc overhead-valve V6 engine, 150bhp, 4-speed manual transaxle gearbox, 4-wheel disc brakes, coil-and-wishbone independent front suspension, De Dion rear axle with semi-elliptic leaf springs, left-hand drive, refurbished red leather interior, correct and original, no major restoration work, former concours winner.
£37,000–44,000 / $54,000–64,000 ➢ C

The Flaminia was the first Lancia designed by Antonio Fessici and became the flagship of the range when launched in 1957. Fessici had broken with tradition and discarded the vertical-coil independent front suspension in favour of a wishbone arrangement. The engine was a 2.5 litre V6 driving through a rear-mounted gearbox and De Dion axle. In 1964, the 3C version was introduced with a 2.8 litre engine producing 152bhp. The Flaminia remained in production until 1970. The most attractive coachwork fitted was the Double Bubble coupé by Zagato, of which 187 were built.

1951 Land Rover Series I, 1595cc engine, short wheelbase, recovered from a field 1997, total chassis-up rebuild completed 1999, minimal dry-weather use since, excellent condition throughout.
£8,000–10,000 / $11,500–14,500 ➢ Bon

Rover saw the need for a tough, four-wheel-drive utility vehicle to serve the needs of the agricultural community in the immediate post-war years, but the Land Rover's runaway success took the company by surprise. The aluminium panels, necessary at a time of severe steel shortage, became a positive virtue in the Land Rover's sphere of operations, and the use of existing components – including the Rover 10 saloon's 1595cc four-cylinder sidevalve engine – kept production costs down and cut development time.

1908 Lorraine-Dietrich 20hp Type CJ Landaulette, coachwork by Pingret, Guion and Breteau, 4-cylinder T-head engine, double chain drive to rear wheels, Ducellier acetylene headlamps, high-mounted oil opera side lamps, bulb horn, chauffeur's speaking tube, landaulette compartment upholstered in cloth with brocade detailing, chauffeur's compartment with original black leather, VCC dated, thought to have been laid up for c70 years, recommissioned late 1980s.
£35,000–40,000 / $51,000–58,000 ➢ Bon

In the late 19th century, De Dietrich extended its core business as a manufacturer of railway rolling stock and began making cars. Initially, it built twin-cylinder engines under licence from Amedée Bollée, eventually developing its own engines to power a successful range of De Dietrich cars. From 1905, its well-engineered products were called Lorraine-Dietrich and sported the Cross of Lorraine on their trademark and radiator emblem. This car was found in Argentina in 1988 in very original condition, possibly even retaining its original tyres. The finely detailed coachwork was intact and original, while correct under-bonnet details included the original Bakelite Cross of Lorraine spark plug connectors.

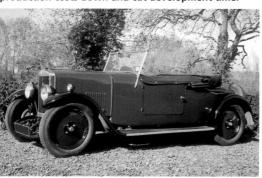

◀ **1928 Lea Francis 12/22 U-Type Two-Seater Tourer and Dickey,** 1.5 litre Meadows engine, 4-speed gearbox with right-hand gate change, new hood, well maintained.
£8,500–9,500 / $11,600–13,800 ⊞ AVON

1971 Lotus Elan Sprint Convertible, 1558cc big-valve double-overhead-camshaft engine, completely restored.
£14,000–16,000 / $20,500–23,500 HLR

1966 Maserati Mistral 4000 Spyder, coachwork by Frua, 4 litre engine, Lucas fuel injection, Borrani wire wheels, mechanics overhauled, black Connolly leather interior, fewer than 45,000 miles from new.
£33,000–38,000 / $48,000–55,000 Bon

1949 Maserati A6 1500 Coupé, coachwork by Pinin Farina, restored, chassis stripped to bare metal and zinc rustproofed, electrical system refurbished to original specification, little use since, correct in every detail.
£95,000–110,000 / $138,000–160,000 Bon
In 1947, when Maserati resumed production after WWII, the company not only returned to building Grand Prix cars, but also began small-scale production of bespoke sports-racing and road cars. Its first true road model was the A6 1500, powered by a 1488cc overhead-cam six, similar to the A6 GCS sports car's 2 litre unit, producing 65bhp at 4,700rpm. The chassis was of the ladder-frame type, with double-wishbone front suspension derived from racing practice and a rigid rear axle suspended by coil springs. Top speed, depending on coachwork, was in the region of 90–95mph.

1904 Mercedes-Simplex 28/32hp 5.3 Litre Tourer, older restoration, fitted with Brewster coachwork from a 1904 De Dietrich, Solarclipse acetylene headlamps, Dietz oil side lamps, Solar acetylene generator, hood, 2-piece cranked and folding windscreen, 10 dash oilers, Jones dashboard clock, 0–60mph speedometer, wicker picnic basket and rear luggage carrier, beige buttoned and pleated leather upholstery, recent major engine overhaul, VCC dated.
£250,000+ / $362,000+ Bon
About 100 years ago, Daimler's chief designer, William Maybach, demonstrated the potential of his new design, allowing Wilhelm Werner to show the car's paces at the Nice Speed Trials and at La Turbie Hill Climb where on both occasions he took the victor's laurels. Although designed by Maybach, the car was created at the instigation of Emil Jellinek, a pioneer motorist who had been on the Daimler board since 1900. Jellinek had combined his sporting interest in cars with the operation of an unofficial agency for Daimler products, and since the Daimler name could not be used in France because the company had sold its patents to Panhard Levassor, Jellinek called the new car after his daughter, Mercedes. This name was adopted by Daimler as its universal brand name in 1902. The 28/32hp model was one of the range of touring cars from Maybach's drawing board. The engine design followed closely that of the 18/28hp car, but displaced 5320cc. Power was transmitted through a scroll clutch, and final drive was by chain. The car was built on a tapered, pressed-steel frame, rigidity being provided by the gearbox and engine.

1933 Mercedes-Benz 380K Cabriolet A, Roots-type supercharger, independent front suspension, rear swing axles, covered fuel filler, twin rear mounted spare wheels, fitted luggage, older restoration, 1 family ownership for over 30 years, little recent use, in need of recommissioning, good condition.
£250,000+ / $362,000+ ⋏ COYS
This particular car carries what is believed to be unique factory built custom Cabriolet A coachwork. The factory coachwork on all 380K, 500K and 540K models was identical. To date, no other 380K Cabriolet A has been found with the same combination of features.

◀ **1954 Mercedes-Benz 300SL Alloy Gullwing,** 2996cc overhead-camshaft 6-cylinder engine, fuel injection, 4-speed manual gearbox, 4-wheel drum brakes, 4-wheel independent suspension, engine, chassis and body all original, extensive restoration completed 2001, red leather interior, 1 of only 29 aluminium-bodied examples built, 3 owners from new.
£500,000+ / $725,000+ ⋏ RM
The 300SL was fast, solid and handled well, and it quickly developed an enviable reputation on both road and track. To help ensure its success on the latter, Mercedes-Benz offered a special competition version of the car. A number of changes were made for these competition cars, but the most significant was the decision to build the bodies in aluminium. Production 300SLs had steel bodies with alloy doors, boot lid and bonnet; the all-alloy bodyshell trimmed more than 180lb (81kg) of the total weight. Side and rear windows were of Perspex for a further weight saving. The engines in these alloy cars were modified to improve breathing, principally by means of a special competition camshaft. Brakes were lifted directly from the 1952 works cars, with Alfin brake drums and improved cooling; suspension was updated with stiffer shock absorbers and springs. Every car was delivered with two sets of rear-axle gears – a standard ratio and a second tailored to the needs of the customer. With 3.25:1 gearing, the cars were capable of 161mph.

1970 Mercedes-Benz 280SE 3.5 Litre Convertible, V8 engine, 200bhp, 4-speed automatic transmission, self-levelling 4-wheel independent air suspension, 4-wheel disc brakes, restored late 1990s, engine and transmission overhauled, chassis and electrics refurbished, bare-metal respray, interior retrimmed in parchment hide, wood veneers polished, excellent condition.
£35,000–40,000 / $51,000–58,000 ⋏ Bon

1958 Mercedes-Benz 300SL Roadster, 2996cc overhead-camshaft 6-cylinder engine, 4-speed manual gearbox, 4-wheel disc brakes, 4-wheel independent suspension, soft top, engine completely rebuilt, resprayed, new tan interior.
£120,000–130,000 / $174,000–188,000 ⋏ RM

▶ **1946 MG TC Midget,** tuned engine, period Judson supercharger, polished aluminium bodywork, cycle front wings, full weather equipment, good condition throughout.
£25,000–28,000 / $36,000–41,000 ⋏ COYS

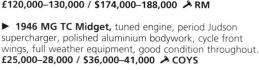

1952 MG TD Midget, 1250cc overhead-valve 4-cylinder engine, 4-speed synchromesh gearbox, rack-and-pinion steering, 4-wheel hydraulic drum brakes, independent front suspension, restored, excellent mechanical condition.
£11,000–13,000 / $16,000–19,000 ↗ RM

1939 MG VA Four-Door Saloon, 1479cc overhead-valve engine, restored at a cost of £32,000/$46,400, 86,000 miles from new.
£13,000–15,000 / $19,000–22,000 ↗ H&H
The MG VA was available in saloon, open four-seater and drop-head coupé body styles. It was produced for a two-year period, from 1937 until the start of WWII. The engine was Wolseley 12 based, it had 10in hydraulic drum brakes, and Jackall jacks were built in to the chassis. Top speed was in excess of 80mph.

1987 Mini Moke, completely rebuilt, 1300cc Cooper engine, 78bhp, oil cooler, 12in front disc brakes, 13in wheels, competition radiator, detachable top, good condition throughout.
£4,000–5,000 / $5,750–7,250 ↗ Bon

1968 MGC Roadster, 2912cc overhead-valve 6-cylinder engine, twin SU carburettors, 4-speed manual gearbox with overdrive, servo-assisted hydraulic front disc/rear drum brakes, independent front suspension by wishbones and torsion bars, rigid rear axle with semi-elliptic leaf springs, rack-and-pinion steering, hood, full-length tonneau cover, subject of £21,000/$30,450 restoration, excellent condition.
£9,000–11,0000 / $13,000–16,000 ↗ C

1954 Plymouth Plaza Convertible, 230cu.in sidevalve 6-cylinder engine, 2-speed automatic transmission, original green and white interior, radio, heater, unrestored, rust-free.
£7,000–9,000 / $10,200–13,000 ↗ Bon
According to the Plymouth catalogue, there was very little new for 1954, with only a minor facelift differentiating that year's models from 1953's offerings. The line consisted of five different body styles in the base Plaza series, four styles in the mid-market Savoy series and five styles – including a convertible – in the top-of-the-range Belvedere series. All three versions were also available in chassis form, although only a single Plaza is said to have left the factory in that condition. This car has Plaza badging and trim, but a Plaza convertible was never listed. There is no evidence that it has been modified, and the serial numbers indicate that it was built as a Plaza. It may be the single car released as a chassis, or possibly a one-off built for corporate purposes.

1930 Packard 740 Custom Eight Roadster, 384cu.in 8-cylinder sidevalve engine, 109bhp, 4-speed manual gearbox, 4-wheel drum brakes, semi-elliptic leaf-spring suspension front and rear, left-hand drive, older restoration, brown leather interior, paintwork dull, otherwise good condition.
£50,000–60,000 / $72,000–87,000 ↗ C

1958 Pontiac Star Chief Catalina Hardtop, automatic transmission, power-assisted steering, good condition.
£7,500–9,500 / $10,800–13,800 ➹ Bon
Pontiac's range-topping Star Chief line was introduced in 1953, boasting greater luxury and a longer wheelbase than the lower-priced Chieftain. The introduction of its first V8 engine in 1955 enabled Pontiac to create a new performance image, and no better examples were the Catalina convertibles and hardtops, the marque's most sporting models of the period. Pontiac styling took a giant leap forward for 1958, when a longer and lower profile was adopted across the range, together with quad headlamps and tail lamps. Advertised as 'something really special' were the all-new series 27/28 Star Chiefs – a four-door Custom Sedan, two- and four-door Catalina Hardtops and a Custom Station Wagon – all powered by the 370cu.in V8, which produced 255bhp when the three-speed manual gearbox was specified and 285bhp with automatic transmission.

1955 Porsche 356 Speedster, ground-up restoration, 7,400 miles covered since, black interior, excellent condition.
£40,000–45,000 / $58,000–65,000 ➹ Bon
The Porsche Speedster was introduced in 1954 at the request of American importer Max Hoffman. It was a stripped-out lightweight car with a cut-down windscreen.

1988 Porsche 959, 2849cc 6-cylinder double-overhead-camshaft engine, 4-valve cylinder heads, twin turbochargers, 450bhp, 4-wheel-drive, 6-speed gearbox with computer-control providing variable torque split with alternative programmes for dry, wet, icy and off-road conditions, ride height electrically controlled, ABS brakes, composite body, electric windows and mirrors, climate control, heated seats, 1 of 13 built to UK specification, c17,000 miles from new, totally original, concours condition.
£90,000–100,000 / $130,000–145,000 ➹ Bon
Conceived in the early 1980s as a four-wheel-drive Group B competitor, the Porsche 959 was first displayed in 'concept car' form in 1983 at Frankfurt and, despite the subsequent abandonment of the events for which it had been intended, entered limited production in 1987. It represented the ultimate in automobile design, successfully adapting state-of-the-art racing technology for road use. Although its *raison d'être* had ceased to exist, the Porsche 959 did achieve one major competition victory, René Metge and Dominique Lemoyne winning the gruelling Paris-Dakar Rally in 1986 in their works 959. Similar cars took second and seventh places, while the race-developed variant finished seventh at Le mans that year, winning the IMSA GT2 class.

1929 Riley 9hp Brooklands Sports, completely restored at a cost of over £55,000/$80,000, 1 of fewer than 100 examples built, excellent condition.
£50,000–55,000 / $72,000–80,000 ➹ Bon

1911 Rolls-Royce 40/50hp Silver Ghost Open-Drive Tulip Limousine, chassis no. 1582, engine no. 70B, choice of limousine or balloon car coachwork, limousine coachwork with leather aprons to the running boards, King of the Road acetylene headlamps, BRC oil sidelamps, brass klaxon horn, chauffeur's compartment upholstered in black leather and equipped with speaking tube, rear upholstered in green cloth with oatmeal carpets, fold-down rear-facing occasional seats, 3 courtesy lamps, bevelled glass to all windows, silk blinds, Swiss Omega dashboard clock, matching brass rear-view mirrors, boa constrictor horn, balloon car body in similar livery with basketweave features, deep button-back leather upholstery, hood and cranked windscreen, VCC dated.
£300,000+ / $435,000+ ➤ Bon
In production from 1907, the Rolls-Royce 40/50hp (later named Silver Ghost) was powered by a 7036cc six-cylinder engine from 1907 to 1909, later enlarged to 7428cc. This car was built originally with D-fronted limousine coachwork similar to that shown. However, it was discovered in 1950 with farm bodywork. In 1973, it was fitted with balloon car coachwork in the style of that shown. Subsequent restoration led to the replacement of the body with new D-fronted limousine coachwork. More recently, another balloon car body was acquired, giving the option of styles to match the seasons.

1927 Rolls-Royce Phantom I Derby Tourer, coachwork by Brewster, chassis no. S 144 PM, engine no. 21446, 7668cc overhead-valve 6-cylinder engine, 3-speed gearbox, rear-wheel drive, 4-wheel servo-assisted drum brakes, semi-elliptic leaf-spring front suspension, cantilever leaf springs to rear, red leather interior.
£110,000–130,000 / $160,000–189,000 ➤ C
The Phantom I was introduced in 1925 to replace the Silver Ghost model, the main changes being mechanical. The 7668cc six-cylinder engine received overhead valves and a single detachable alloy head. This provided a third more power and, with four-wheel servo-assisted brakes, the overall performance and braking were well ahead of its competitors. Since 1921, Rolls-Royce had been building cars in its Springfield, Massachusetts, plant, and by 1925 it had acquired the renowned New York coachbuilding firm of Brewster, which produced some stunning designs. Among these was the Derby Tourer, a mere 20 of which were built.

1930 Rolls-Royce Phantom II 'Woody' Estate, chassis no. 67XJ, engine no. WK55, 7.7 litre 6-cylinder engine, bodywork completely restored, interior retrimmed in black, clock missing, engine in very good condition.
£55,000–60,000 / $80,000–87,000 ➤ Bon
This car was supplied originally with Weymann fabric-covered four-door saloon coachwork, but lightweight bodies of this type rarely lasted long, and it is likely that the 'woody' bodywork was fitted within the first 20 years of the car's life. There was a tax advantage in fitting wooden utility-car bodywork under the British vehicle licensing system, and such cars were often used as 'shooting brakes' on large estates.

1934 Rolls-Royce Phantom II Cabriolet, coachwork by Henri Binder, chassis no. 162SK, engine no. ZK35, older restoration, engine overhauled.
£110,000–130,000 / $160,000–189,000 ➤ Bon
The engine and coachwork of this car were fitted originally to an earlier 1930 Phantom II chassis, the first owner of which was Octavio Guinle proprietor of the renowned Copacabana Palace Hotel in Rio de Janeiro. In 1986, they were transferred to a later restored S2 chassis.

1951 Studebaker Champion Business Coupé, manual gearbox with overdrive, grey striped mohair interior trim, original push-button radio, c77,000 miles from new, largely unrestored, very good condition.
£6,500–7,500 / $9,500–10,875 ➤ Bon
In 1951, the Champion was the base Studebaker model, being available in Custom, Deluxe and Regal lines. All three versions had a cast-iron sidevalve straight-six, which displaced 169.6cu.in and produced 85bhp. The standard transmission was a column-change, three-speed manual unit.

1932 Stutz SV-16 Convertible Coupé, coachwork by Derham, 322cu.in. overhead-valve 8-cylinder inline engine, 113bhp, 3-speed manual gearbox, vacuum-assisted 4-wheel hydraulic drum brakes, semi-elliptic leaf-spring suspension, power steering, long-wheelbase model, left-hand drive, dark red leather interior, in need of some restoration, body sound with good panel fit, chromework pitted, rear brakes seized, not run recently, thought to be 1 of 5 built with this coachwork.
£60,000–70,000 / $87,000–101,000 ⚒ C
Henry Stutz grew up on a farm in Ohio, caring for and repairing the family's agricultural machinery. In 1897, fascinated by internal-combustion engines, he built his first car, which was followed by another using an engine of his own design and manufacture. By the end of 1925, the Stutz Motor Car Company was under the stewardship of Frederick Moskovics, who had left Franklin to join the company, where he was responsible for the new Vertical Eight engine and a car that created a sensation among dealers and public alike. With overhead-cam inline engine, hydrostatic brakes and windscreen safety glass, the new model was unlike any other American car of the time. The chassis was just as radical, and the cars were inches lower than the competition, making them an immediate hit. The SV-16 (single valves, 16 of them) was eventually superseded by the DV-32 with double overhead camshafts and four valves per cylinder.

1912 Unic 10/12hp Drophead Coupé, coachwork by Alford & Alder, 4-cylinder engine, electric starter, wire wheels, acetylene headlamps, oil sidelamps, running-board mounted generator, leather hood, side windows, cloth upholstery, offset driver and passenger seats, folding side occasional seat, Watford speedometer, Smith's 8-day clock, VCC dated.
£15,000–17,000 / $22,000–25,000 ⚒ Bon
Georges Richard had established his name as a car manufacturer by building Brasier cars at Ivry-Port as early as 1897. In 1905, he moved to Puteaux, establishing his own factory and assembling a 10/12hp twin-cylinder T-head car, which he named Unic. His original one-model policy soon went by the board and four-cylinder cars joined the 10/12 on the production line. Later models of the 10/12, such as this example, were also fitted with the four-cylinder engine.

1989 Proteus Jaguar Le Mans Works-Style D-Type Replica, triple Weber carburettors, dry-sump oil system, correct torsion-bar rear suspension, correct-spec parts used where possible, hand-formed aluminium body in the style of 1956 'Longnose' factory team cars, D-Type-style instrumentation, 5th example built, excellent condition.
£42,000–48,000 / $61,000–70,000 ⚒ COYS
Developed during the early 1950s to capitalize on the success of the XK120 and C-Type models both on the track and in the showroom, the D-Type utilized much of the technology Jaguar had developed while building aircraft during the war. Proteus is recognized as creating excellent replicas of these historic cars, using many of the original construction techniques and correct parts.

1929 Vauxhall 20/60 T-Type Four-Door Saloon, 2916cc 6-cylinder engine, 4-speed manual gearbox, never restored, excellent condition throughout.
£13,000–15,000 / $19,000–22,000 ⊞ AVON

▶ 1935 Bentley 3½ Litre Sports Saloon, coachwork by Park Ward, 3669cc overhead-valve 6-cylinder engine, matching numbers, chassis and running gear restored, most chrome replated, engine running, electrics and grey leather interior to refit, last used c30 years ago.
£6,000–8,000
$8,750–11,500 ⚒ Bon

Jensen

From the 'drastic plastic' glassfibre-bodied 541 and CV8 to the growling, but refined, Interceptor with its Italian designed elegance and pioneering four-wheel drive in the FF versions, Jensens were always, at the very least, interesting. In fact, such is the charisma of the marque that although the West Bromwich company closed its doors in 1976, there have been several attempts to revive the marque, most recently with the S-V8. Brothers Richard and Allen Jensen started out as coachbuilders before producing their own cars from 1936 onwards. The original Interceptor of 1950–57 used an Austin 4 litre engine, which was also employed in the dramatic 541 of 1954. From 1962, with the launch of the CV8, Jensen adopted Chrysler V8 power. The car that really made Jensen a household name, however, was the 1967 Interceptor, which mated the massive American V8 engine with elegant Italian coachwork to create a formidable, high-performance GT. Sadly, the gas guzzling Interceptor's heyday was cut short by two oil crises and a worldwide recession.

1956 Jensen 541, mechanical work totalling £1,400 completed 2000, finished in white, black interior in need of attention, otherwise good condition.
£2,500–3,500 / $3,500–5,000 ⋋ CGC
Introduced at the 1953 Motor Show, the Jensen 541 relied on tried-and-tested Austin components, being equipped with the A135's 3993cc, 130bhp straight-six and four-speed manual gearbox. Suspension and steering parts were courtesy of the A70, although they were modified to suit the Jensen's specific chassis dynamics. Jensen designed and built its own sturdy ladder-frame chassis. The whole package was clothed in a dramatic glassfibre body penned by Eric Neale.

1962 Jensen 541S, automatic transmission, aluminium and glassfibre body, restored at a cost of over £11,000, finished in green, tan leather interior, concours condition.
£8,000–10,000 / $11,500–14,500 ⋋ Bon
Some 4½in (11.5cm) wider and offering more headroom than the original 541, together with greater luggage capacity, the 541S was generally considered to be a more practical machine. It was fitted with the proven 3993cc six-cylinder Austin engine, but featured improved road-holding, stabilility and ride.

Jensen 541 (1954–63)

Production: 531.
Price in 1956: £2,572.7s, including purchase tax.
Engine: 3993cc, overhead-valve, straight-six.
Power output: 130–140bhp at 4,000rpm.
Transmission: Four-speed manual, overdrive optional at first, then standard; four-speed automatic.
Brakes: Servo-assisted drums on early cars; discs all-round from late 1956.
Maximum speed: 115–123.5mph.
0–60mph: 9.3–11.7 seconds.
The Jensen 541 of 1954 pioneered the use of rust-free glassfibre bodywork in the UK – it was Britain's first 'plastic' four-seat saloon. The result is a seriously imposing predator of the road. It looks like it's going to gobble up anything that gets in its way. And in 1954, not much would, for under that belligerent bonnet was Austin's commercially derived 4 litre engine. It's hardly exotic, but it does the trick, powering the slowest 541 to 115mph. The 541R of 1957, with a higher-compression cylinder head was good for 125mph and 0–60mph in 9.3 seconds. It could stop too, as it was one of the very first four-seat saloons to be fitted with all-round disc brakes. Who would have bought one in the 1950s or early 1960s? Patriotic cigar chomping captains of industry, whose only other four-seat choice in this class would have been a less roomy, and more expensive, Aston Martin DB2/4. The Jensen isn't as sophisticated or as refined in its road manners as the Aston, but its in-your-face styling and up-your-khyber performance made a bold enough statement for any Toby Jug-proportioned industrialist.

JENSEN Model	ENGINE cc/cyl	DATES	CONDITION		
			1	**2**	**3**
541/541R/541S	3993/6	1954–63	£13,000	£7,000	£4,500
CV8 Mk I–III	5916/				
	6276/8	1962–66	£14,000	£7,000	£6,000
Interceptor SI–SIII	6276/8	1967–76	£9,000	£5,500	£4,000
Interceptor DHC	6276/8	1973–76	£22,000	£15,000	£10,000
Interceptor SP	7212/8	1971–76	£12,000	£8,000	£5,000
FF	6766/8	1967–71	£15,000	£10,000	£7,000

The Jensen CV8 and 541 are particularly sought after.

◀ **1975 Jensen Interceptor Series III,** 7212cc V8 engine, resprayed in dark green, magnolia interior, 50,000 miles from new, good condition throughout.
£4,000–5,000
$6,000–7,000 ✗ H&H

Jensen-Healey

▶ **1975 Jensen-Healey,** 1973cc double-overhead-camshaft 4-cylinder Lotus engine, 5-speed manual gearbox, front disc/rear drum brakes, all-round coil-spring suspension, original alloy wheels, black mohair hood, finished in white, brown vinyl interior, wooden dashboard, good condition.
£2,500–3,000 / $3,500–4,500 ✗ CGC
Launched in 1972, the Jensen-Healey was an advanced design and far removed from its Austin-Healey 3000 forebear, which had ceased production in 1968.

JENSEN-HEALEY Model	ENGINE cc/cyl	DATES	CONDITION 1	2	3
Healey	1973/4	1972–76	£4,500	£3,000	£1,500
Healey GT	1973/4	1975–76	£5,000	£3,000	£2,000

Jowett

The Bradford company founded by Benjamin and William Jowett started series car production shortly after 1910, building a string of commendable small cars powered initially by flat-twin engines, and later flat-four engines (in 1936). The company's most exciting period came after 1945 with the advanced Javelin saloon and Jupiter sports model, but it ceased car manufacture in 1954, shortly after announcing the glassfibre bodied R4 sports model, of which only three are thought to have been produced.

1950 Jowett Bradford Deluxe Estate Car, barn stored for 10 years, fewer than 61,000 miles from new, engine seized, original, many spare parts.
£2,750–3,500 / $4,000–5,000 ✗ Bon
Jowett made cars in Yorkshire from 1910 to 1953. Alongside the post-war four-cylinder Javelin and sporting Jupiter, it built the Bradford. This was a modernised version of its 1930s twin-cylinder vehicles, which were based on a horizontally-opposed-engine concept that went back to the firm's origins. The Bradford came as a no-frills light commercial vehicle, although a small number of estate cars were also built. This particular example was first used by Jowett's transport department, and lacks rear seats. It passed to Jowett's publicity and London manager and remained in his family ever since.

1950 Jowett Javelin Saloon, restored, finished in maroon, original beige interior, good condition throughout.
£3,750–4,500 / $5,500–6,500 ✗ Bon
Jowett caused a sensation when it launched the revolutionary Javelin in 1947. The design rivalled the most advanced from Continental Europe, and featured unitary construction of the all-steel, four-door saloon body, independent front suspension, torsion-bar springing and rack-and-pinion steering. The horizontally-opposed four-cylinder engine – a type Jowett had used pre-war – displaced 1.5 litres and produced 50bhp, sufficient to give the aerodynamic Javelin a top speed of around 80mph. Transmission was by four-speed manual gearbox with column change, and braking courtesy of Girling hydro-mechanical brakes – the latter replaced by a fully hydraulic system in 1952. Production ceased just before Jowett's demise in 1954.

Jowett Javelin (1947–53)

The Jowett Javelin outshone many dreary mainstream offerings in styling, engineering and performance. Its unitary construction, efficient flat-four engine, four-speed gearbox, sophisticated suspension and precise rack-and-pinion steering were combined with an up-to-the-minute, wind cheating shape and clever packaging to create a compact five-seat saloon with refined road manners, superb passenger comfort and an impressive turn of speed. Sporting successes included a class win in the 1949 Monte Carlo Rally and race-track victories over more powerful machines, certainly justification enough for Jowett to adopt the slogan, 'Take a good look when it passes you.' Unfortunately, the Javelin's reputation had been tarnished early on by weaknesses in the engine and gearbox, which later were rectified. That, combined with the model's high price – considerably more than that of an Austin A40 or Morris Oxford – helped end the brave Bradford company's car making activities in 1954.

1952 Jowett Jupiter SA, 1486cc flat-4 engine, 4-speed manual gearbox, 4-wheel hydro-mechanical drum brakes, torsion-bar suspension, rack-and-pinion steering.
£5,000–6,000 / $7,000–8,500 ⊞ JCC

Lagonda

Lagonda's distinctions are many, and some of them rather unusual. For example, how many car manufacturers do you know who were founded by opera singers? That's what Wilbur Gunn was when he came to Britain. Not only that, but the founder of one of Britain's quintessential sporting marques was also an American. In the last years of the 19th century, Gunn set up the Lagonda Engineering Company not far from London, naming the company after the local Indian name for one of the rivers in his native Ohio. Initially, Gunn's company produced motorcycles, but quickly progressed from two wheels to three, and then to four. As early as 1909, a Lagonda 16/18hp raced at Brooklands, but most early Lagondas

went for export, only becoming readily available in the Britain in 1912. Gunn died in 1920, and in the mid-1920s the company moved away from production of light cars to concentrate on the fast sporting models and tourers that have since come to characterise the marque. A Le Mans victory was gained in 1935 and, with W.O. Bentley as technical director, the company produced the magnificent V12. David Brown, owner of Aston Martin, acquired Lagonda in 1947, gaining access to Bentley's last engine design, the 2580cc twin-cam six, which was employed in the Aston Martin DB2. Since then, the Lagonda name has been used intermittently on larger, luxury-express versions of Astons.

◄ **1933 Lagonda 2 Litre Continental Drophead Coupé,** coachwork by Vanden Plas, fitted with Alvis synchromesh gearbox, finished in ivory over black, black leather interior.
£20,000–25,000 $29,000–36,000 ⋌ COYS
The Continental was a variant of Lagonda's 2 litre Speed Model, which was made in small numbers between 1930 and 1933.

LAGONDA Model	ENGINE cc/cyl	DATES	CONDITION 1	2	3
12/24	1421/4	1923–26	£14,000	£10,000	£8,000
2 Litre	1954/4	1928–32	£28,000	£25,000	£19,000
3 Litre	2931/6	1928–34	£40,000+	£30,000	£22,000
Rapier	1104/4	1934–35	£15,000	£9,000	£5,000
M45	4429/6	1934–36	£50,000+	£30,000	£20,000
LG45	4429/6	1936–37	£45,000+	£32,000	£22,000
LG6	4453/6	1937–39	£40,000+	£28,000	£20,000
V12	4480/V12	1937–39	£75,000+	£50,000	£25,000

Prices are very dependent upon body type, dhc or saloon, originality and competition history.

1937 Lagonda LG45 Four-Seater Sports, completely restored in the style of Lagonda LG45 team cars, engine, chassis and ancillaries overhauled, all chromework refurbished, new coachwork on new ash frame, finished in dark blue, blue leather interior, c9,000 miles since restoration, excellent condition.
£45,000–50,000 / $62,000–72,500 ↗ COYS
The original firm of Lagonda was replaced in 1935 by LG Motors, a new company with Alan Good as chairman and W.O. Bentley as technical director and designer. The company faced two immediate main tasks – to put the M45 model back into production and to build the best car in the world. Only two years were to be allowed for the latter exercise, and the result was the great 12-cylinder car. The M45 received some cosmetic improvements, then was replaced by the LG45 in September 1935.

1938 Lagonda LG6 Drophead Coupé, matching numbers, 4.5 litre twin-plug 6-cylinder Meadows engine, manual synchromesh gearbox, independent front suspension by unequal-length wishbones and torsion bars, centralised chassis lubrication, cylinder head and rear shock absorbers rebuilt, new fuel pumps, rewound magnetos, finished in dark green, beige leather interior and matching hood, hood bag and half tonneau, well maintained, unrestored, good condition.
£55,000–65,000 / $80,000–94,500 ↗ Bon
The LG6 was offered in two chassis lengths (standard and long) and, regardless of coachwork, the car was good for around 100mph, with lighter types capable of considerably more. Only 82 LG6s were produced between early 1938 and late 1939, of which around 50 are believed to survive.

LAGONDA (post-war) Model	ENGINE cc/cyl	DATES	CONDITION 1	2	3
3 Litre	2922/6	1953–58	£10,500	£7,000	£4,500
3 Litre DHC	2922/6	1953–56	£17,000	£12,000	£9,000
Rapide	3995/6	1961–64	£11,000+	£7,000	£4,500

Lamborghini

Having owned a number of Ferraris, wealthy industrialist Ferruccio Lamborghini was convinced that he could build a better supercar. He pursued this goal by recruiting some of the best design and engineering talent of the day for his fledgling supercar concern, names like Giotto Bizzarrini, Giampaolo Dallara, Franco Scaglione, Touring of Milan and Bertone. His first car, the 350GT of 1964, certainly looked the part and was powered by a magnificent V12,

but it was the launch of the staggering Miura, at the 1966 Geneva show, that many commentators count as the motoring sensation of the decade. When the Miura's lease of life came to an end, the brutal looking Countach debuted in 1974, and carried the company's standard as the flagship model to the end of the 1980s. By then, Ferruccio Lamborghini had long since lost interest and the company passed through several changes of ownership.

1969 Lamborghini 400GT Islero, 3929cc double-overhead-camshaft V12 engine, 325bhp, 5-speed manual synchromesh gearbox, 4-wheel independent coil-spring suspension, 4-wheel Girling disc brakes, completely restored late 1980s, engine and gearbox rebuilt, resprayed in black, black leather interior, 40,000 miles from new, well maintained.
£17,000–20,000 / $24,500–29,000 ↗ RM
Successor to the original 400GT, the Islero retained the square-tube chassis and inner structure of the 400GT 2+2, while the wheelbase remained the same. The front and rear track widths changed, and the Islero featured wider tyres on Campagnolo wheels. The first series of 125 cars was completed in December 1968, their limited production making them scarce commodities, and it wasn't until second series production began that they became readily available.

1970 Lamborghini 400GT Espada, 3929cc V12 engine, 350bhp, 5-speed manual gearbox, 4-wheel disc brakes, Campagnolo alloy wheels, 43,500 miles from new.
£6,000–8,000 / $8,500–11,500 ↗ Pou

Condition guide
1. A vehicle in top class condition but not 'concours d'elegance standard, either fully restored or in very good original condition.
2. A good, clean, roadworthy vehicle, both mechanically and bodily sound.
3. A runner, but in need of attention, probably both to bodywork and mechanics. Must have current MoT.

LAMBORGHINI Model	ENGINE cc/cyl	DATES	CONDITION 1	2	3
350 GT fhc	3500/12	1964–67	£55,000	£45,000	£25,000
400 GT	4000/12	1966–68	£45,000+	£40,000	£25,000
Miura LP400	4000/12	1966–69	£60,000	£50,000	£30,000
Miura S	4000/12	1969–71	£75,000	£60,000+	£40,000
Miura SV	4000/12	1971–72	£90,000+	£75,000	£60,000
Espada	4000/12	1969–78	£12,000	£10,000	£7,000
Jarama	4000/12	1970–78	£15,000	£13,000	£11,000
Urraco	2500/8	1972–76	£12,000	£10,000	£8,000
Countach	4000/12	1974–82	£60,000+	£40,000	£30,000

Countach limited editions are sought after as well as Miura SV.

Lamborghini Miura (1966–72)

Production: 763 (some say 764).
Engine: 3929cc, quad-overhead-cam, 24-valve, transverse mounted V12, four triple-choke Weber carburettors.
Transmission: Five-speed manual.
Power output: 350–385bhp.
0–60mph: 6–6.7 seconds.
Top speed: 165–175+mph.
Brakes: Four-wheel ventilated discs.

1969 Lamborghini Miura P400 S, coachwork by Bertone, left-hand drive, over £20,000 spent on mechanical and electrical work, converted to unleaded fuel, carburettors and distributors rebuilt, new clutch and brake master cylinders, brake calipers overhauled, new road springs and suspension bushes, wiring replaced as necessary, correct air horns, electric windows, resprayed in original orange, 2 owners and fewer than 38,500 miles from new.
£55,000–65,000 / $80,000–94,500 ✗ Bon

Having owned Ferraris as soon as he could afford them, Ferruccio Lamborghini set out to prove that he could make something better. His bold challenge began in 1964 with the 350GT, but it was the arrival of the Miura – arguably the forerunner of the modern mid-engined supercar concept – that established Lamborghini cars. Displayed as a rolling chassis at the 1965 Turin show, the finished Miura was unveiled at the 1966 Geneva Salon. It had a transverse mid-mounted engine in a box-section platform chassis, with stunning coupé coachwork by Bertone. Like the contemporary 400GT, the Miura used a 3929cc version of Lamborghini's four-cam V12 with six Weber carburettors and four valves per cylinder. With 350bhp available at 7,000rpm, the Miura was capable of shattering performance, a top speed of almost 180mph being claimed. It was equipped with a five-speed synchromesh gearbox, limited-slip differential, and all-round independent suspension by double wishbones, vertical coil springs, and front and rear anti-roll bars.

1986 Lamborghini Countach 5000S, V12 engine, 4-wheel independent double wishbone suspension, space-frame chassis, imported from USA c1998, finished in black, black leather interior, very good condition.
£32,000–36,000 / $46,500–52,000 ✗ COYS

When the first prototype for the Miura's replacement was revealed as project 112, one of the factory workers exclaimed 'Countach!', a local Piemontese expletive, roughly translated as 'Wow!' The name stuck.

1973 Lamborghini Urraco, engine rebuilt, stainless-steel exhaust front pipes, suspension and brakes overhauled, finished in red, new leather interior, very good to excellent condition.
£11,000–13,000 / $16,000–19,000 ✗ BARO

1986 Lamborghini Jalpa Targa, coachwork by Bertone, US-specification sidelights, finished in black, beige interior, fewer than 13,000 miles from new, very good condition.
£17,000–20,000 / $24,500–29,000 ✗ Bon

Intended to compete with such rivals as Ferrari's Dino and Porsche's 911, Lamborghini's Urraco 2+2 of 1970 retained the Miura's mechanical layout, but in place of the former's 4 litre V12 there was a 2.5 litre V8. A two-seater development, the Silhouette, appeared in 1976. Intended as a 308 GTB competitor, the Silhouette possessed excellent handling balance and was as quick as its Ferrari rival, but never achieved the same sales: the Silhouette was produced for little more than a year, a mere 52 being made, and had been dropped by 1978. The Urraco followed a year later, the concept of a smaller Lamborghini lapsing until the Jalpa appeared in 1982. Based on the Silhouette, the Jalpa was reworked by Giulio Alfieri, late of Maserati, who lengthened the engine's stroke for a capacity of 3485cc.. Power increased to 255bhp, and top speed to 145mph. There were a few styling changes – neater chin spoiler, altered rear quarters and different wheels – while inside the interior's ergonomics were improved. Otherwise, the Jalpa remained much as its predecessor, but would enjoy considerably greater success, remaining in production into the 1990s.

Lanchester

The name is now nearly forgotten, but Frederick Lanchester was, without doubt, one of the most important early pioneers and original thinkers of Britain's fledgling automobile industry. In fact, it was in 1895 that Fred, with his brother George, produced the very first all-British, four-wheeled petrol car, a year before the formation of the Daimler company, which is now generally credited with giving birth to the British motor industry. The cars produced under the Lanchester name were a curious blend of innovation and caution; for example, while early Lanchesters were noted for many advanced features, they persisted with tiller steering as late as 1911, when most firms had long since adopted steering wheels. By 1909, Lanchester was also a consultant to the British Daimler company, and in 1914 resigned altogether from the company that bore his name. Ironically, in 1931, Lanchester was acquired by BSA, which also owned Daimler. Thereafter, Lanchester models began to lose much of their distinction, and although the name survived WWII, the Lanchester marque faded away in 1956.

1928 Lanchester 40hp Tourer, full weather equipment including side screens, scuttle-mounted marine ventilators, radiator with water sight glass, side-mounted spare, running-board battery and tool boxes, finished in cream with black wings, brown leather interior, original.
£40,000–50,000 / $58,000–72,500 ⚘ Bon
Lanchester's six-cylinder, 38hp car had been its pre-WWI masterpiece, and the Sporting 40 had made a brief appearance shortly before the outbreak of hostilities. For the new post-war 40hp car, a more conventional appearance became the norm, the company deciding to pursue more vigorously the luxury-car market dominated by Rolls-Royce and Napier. Mounted in a pressed-steel chassis, the overhead-cam, six-cylinder, 40hp engine had a capacity of 6178cc. An epicyclic gearbox was employed, and prototype cars on test developed more power than their Rolls-Royce equivalent. The 40hp found a ready market at home, in America and from a loyal client bank in India. Some 392 40hp cars were built in a production run that lasted until 1929.

1930 Lanchester 30hp Straight Eight Weymann Limousine, fabric coachwork, twin side-mounted spare wheels, windscreen visor, side window wind deflectors, rear-mounted luggage trunk, interior upholstered in beige cloth to rear and brown leather to chauffeur's compartment, restored, engine overhauled.
£25,000–30,000 / $36,000–43,500 ⚘ Bon
The last of the real Lanchesters to be introduced before the Daimler take-over was the 30hp Straight Eight, announced in 1928. It was powered by an all-new 4437cc, overhead-camshaft eight-cylinder engine, and was clearly intended to compete with the rolls-Royce Phantom I, both in terms of performance and price. The straight-eight turbine-like engine gave the car a top speed of 80mph and the ability to hold top gear on most occasions with relatively good economy. The new model retained the distinctive Lanchester features of full cantilever rear suspension and the radiator water-level sight glass.

◀ **1932 Lanchester LA10 Six-Window Saloon,** coachwork by Mulliner, 1444cc engine, fluid flywheel, pre-selector gearbox, restored mid-to-late 1970s and displayed as a show car, finished in black over blue, blue leather interior, stored for at least 9 years, in need of some recommissioning, good condition.
£3,500–4,000 / $5,000–5,800 ⚘ BARO

LANCHESTER Model	ENGINE cc/cyl	DATES	CONDITION		
			1	2	3
LD10	1287/4	1946–49	£2,500	£1,500	£750
LD10 (Barker bodies)	1287/4	1950–51	£2,800	£1,500	£700

Lancia

The world of bookkeeping's loss was certainly the automobile enthusiast's gain, for that's how Vincenzo Lancia started out, as a humble clerk. In 1899, he got his break when he became chief inspector at Fiat after its take-over of the company for which he worked. In 1900, he began an eight-year racing career as a Fiat works driver, but while still racing Fiats, he left in 1906 to form Lancia. His first model, the Alpha, began the trend of naming Lancia cars after letters of the Greek alphabet. Early on, Lancia also gained a name for innovation and advanced engineering. The Theta, of 1913, was the first European car with full electrics, and the Lambda, of 1923, not only was a pioneer of unitary construction, but also possessed independent front suspension and a compact V4 engine. Vincenzo Lancia's final design was the Aprilia, a little gem with unitary construction, all-round independent suspension, all-round hydraulic brakes and a 1352cc V4 that gave it a commendable top speed of 80mph. The Aprilia appeared in 1937, the same year in which Vicenzo Lancia died. From the post-war era, the Aurelia fixed-head coupés have often been heralded as the first of the modern GTs. In the 1950s, Lancia made some able and beautiful machines, but could never offer a line-up that was comprehensive enough to compete with Alfa Romeo and Fiat. In 1969, mounting debts forced a sell-out to Fiat, which paid 1 million lire (around £668/$950) – plus Lancia's debts of £67 million.

LANCIA Model	ENGINE cc/cyl	DATES	CONDITION		
			1	2	3
Theta	4940/4	1913–19	£24,000	£16,500	£8,000
Kappa	4940/4	1919–22	£24,000	£16,000	£8,000
Dikappa	4940/4	1921–22	£24,000	£16,000	£8,000
Trikappa	4590/4	1922–26	£25,000	£18,000	£10,000
Lambda	2120/4	1923–28	£40,000	£20,000	£12,000
Dilambda	3960/8	1928–32	£35,000	£16,000	£10,000
Astura	2604/8	1931–39	£30,000	£20,000	£10,000
Artena	1925/4	1931–36	£9,000	£5,000	£2,000
Augusta	1196/4	1933–36	£9,000	£4,000	£2,000
Aprilia 238	1352/4	1937–39	£10,000	£5,000	£3,000

Coachbuilt bodywork is more desirable and can increase prices.

1928 Lancia Lambda 8th Series Coupé, coachwork by Airflow Streamline, aluminium cylinder head, short platform chassis, original Weymann fabric saloon coachwork replaced by aluminium-panelled, ash-framed coupé bodywork 1946, restored.
£24,000–28,000 / $35,000–40,500 ⚹ Bon

1934 Lancia Augusta Four-Door Saloon, 1196cc V4 engine, manual gearbox, right-hand drive, finished in turquoise and grey, blue leather interior, museum stored for some time, engine seized, chassis, bodywork and paintwork in fair condition, interior worn, unrestored, in need of recommissioning.
£3,750–4,500 / $5,500–6,500 ⚹ Bon

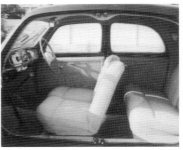

1937 Lancia Aprilia Saloon, all under-bonnet badges correct, finished in blue, grey cloth interior, period Condor radio, original rear window blind, good condition throughout.
£13,000–17,000 / $19,000–24,500 ⚡ Bon
The Aprilia had all-independent suspension – transverse leaf at the front, torsion bars at the rear – and, most unusually for a saloon, hydraulic brakes as standard. The engine was a single-overhead-camshaft, narrow-angle V4 of 1352cc, and the car featured unitary construction, a form of build that Lancia had pioneered. Not least among the Aprilia's many virtues was its generous interior space. With 46bhp, top speed was an easy 80mph.

1963 Lancia Flaminia 3C Convertible, coachwork by Touring, 2.8 litre V6 engine, triple twin-choke Weber carburettors, 150bhp, coil-spring-and-wishbone front suspension, De Dion rear suspension/transaxle, 4-wheel servo-assisted disc brakes, left-hand drive, restored at a cost of £18,000 1992–93, finished in dark silver-grey, red leather interior, 1 of only 180 convertibles built.
£18,000–20,000 / $26,000–29,000 ⚡ Bon

1972 Lancia Fulvia Saloon, 1298cc all-alloy double-overhead-camshaft V4 engine, 5-speed manual gearbox, left-hand drive, finished in burgundy, black interior, excellent condition.
£2,800–3,500 / $4,000–5,000 ⚡ H&H
The Lancia Fulvia saloon was introduced in 1969 and was produced until 1972, a total of just over 70,000 being made. It was a four-door, four-seat saloon, which was a revised version of the original 1963 design with front-wheel drive and four-wheel disc brakes.

Cross Reference
See Colour Review (page 146)

Miller's Starter Marque

- **Starter Lancias:** *Beta Coupé and Spyder, Beta HPE.*
- There are lots of lovely Lancias, and lots of models are affordable. However, in many cases they only came to the UK in penny numbers, and this relative rarity makes these models harder to keep on the road than other more populous late-era classics. In other instances, their innovative engineering, which is one of their joys, can also stretch the resources and patience of a DIY enthusiast.
- A good all-round introduction to classic Lancia ownership is the lively Lancia Beta Coupé, Spyder and HPE – the high-performance estate. For a start, they've had less time to rust than older models – and unfortunately that's an important consideration with many Lancias. The Beta saloon, introduced in 1972, was the first 'Fiat-Lancia', and one of its chief virtues was the Fiat-derived twin-overhead-cam engine, which had proved so successful in the Fiat 124. Over the model's lifetime, customers were offered a choice that ran from 1300cc to 2000cc, and all of them, even when inserted in the humblest saloon, were good for a genuine 100+mph.
- The model you'll encounter most frequently is the Beta Coupé, which was made in far greater numbers than the HPE or Spyder, and that makes the Coupé the easiest to buy and live with. The best bet is probably a clean and complete later model that's had less time to rust.

1990 Lancia Delta Integrale, 1995cc 8-valve 4-cylinder engine, turbocharger, Koni adjustable suspension, 16-valve bodyshell, electric windows, central locking, electric sunroof, finished in red, grey Alcantara Recaro interior, excellent condition throughout.
£4,000–5,000 / $5,800–7,250 ⚡ COYS
Appearing in 1978, the Delta was Lancia's first model conceived under the ownership of Fiat. From 1982, it was available with a 1585cc twin-cam engine, which later was upgraded with fuel injection, and subsequently with a turbocharger. In 1986, a turbocharged 1995cc model was introduced, known as Integrale. These cars were campaigned successfully in Group A form in international rallies.

LANCIA Model	ENGINE cc/cyl	DATES	CONDITION		
			1	2	3
Aprilia 438	1486/4	1939–50	£11,000	£6,000	£3,000
Ardea	903/4	1939–53	£10,000	£5,000	£3,000
Aurelia B10	1754/6	1950–53	£9,000	£6,000	£3,000
Aurelia B15–20–22	1991/6	1951–53	£15,000+	£10,000	£8,000
Aurelia B24–B24 Spyder	2451/6	1955–58	£40,000+	£17,000	£12,000
Aurelia GT	2451/6	1953–59	£18,000+	£11,000	£9,000
Appia C10–C105	1090/4	1953–62	£10,000	£5,000	£2,000
Aurelia Ser II/IV	2266/6	1954–59	£11,000	£6,000	£4,000
Flaminia Zagato	2458/6	1957–63	£20,000	£12,000	£7,000
Flaminia	2458/6	1957–63	£18,000	£10,000	£5,000
Flavia 1500	1500/4	1960–75	£6,000	£4,000	£2,000
Fulvia	1091/4	1963–70	£3,000	£2,000	£1,000
Fulvia S	1216/4	1964–70	£5,000	£4,000	£1,500
Fulvia 1.3	1298/4	1967–75	£6,000	£4,000	£2,000
Stratos	2418/6	1969–71	£45,000+	£20,000+	£10,000
Flavia 2000	1991/4	1969–75	£3,000	£2,000	£1,000
Fulvia HF/1.6	1584/4	1969–75	£9,000	£5,000	£2,000
Beta HPE	1585/4	1976–82	£3,000	£1,500	£500
Beta Spyder	1995/4	1977–82	£4,000	£1,500	£800
Monte Carlo	1995/4	1976–81	£6,000	£3,000	£1,000
Gamma Coupé	2484/4	1977–84	£2,500	£1,500	£500
Gamma Berlina	2484/4	1977–84	£2,500	£1,200	£300

Competition history and convertible coachwork could cause prices to vary.
Zagato coachwork striking and sometimes pricey.

Land Rover

The remarkable success story of the Land Rover began just after WWII, when Maurice Wilks, then Rover's technical chief, wanted something to replace the clapped out Willys Jeep on his Anglesey estate. Rover also needed a stop-gap model for its Solihull factory to produce while the new post-war cars were readied for production. The original Land Rover, with its galvanized chassis, permanent four-wheel drive and simple aluminium bodywork, went on sale in 1948 and has since become a powerful, world recognised brand in its own right, setting the standard for working go-anywhere vehicles. In fact, at times the unstoppable utility vehicle was more important to the company's success than its normal passenger cars. By 1977, Land Rover production topped a million and, of course, it's still going strong.

1950 Land Rover Series I, 2 litre sidevalve engine, Rover 60 head conversion, permanent 4-wheel drive, 80in (203cm) wheelbase, finished in green, full weather equipment, khaki hood, correct green vinyl interior, good condition.
£3,000–3,500 / $4,400–5,000 ↗ CGC

1950 Land Rover Series I Estate, coachwork by Tickford, 1595cc engine, restored early 1980s, new steering box, wood-framed 7-seater body, excellent condition throughout.
£8,000–10,000 / $11,500–14,500 ↗ Bon
This variant was manufactured only between 1948 and 1951, the number currently known to survive being in single figures. When new, the model was considerably more expensive than the basic 80in (203cm) Land Rover, selling at £950/$1,380. Being classed as a passenger car, it was also subject to purchase tax.

◀ **1956 Land Rover Series I,** 86in (218.5cm) wheelbase, fitted later rear chassis cross-member, new hood, 2 owners from new, excellent mechanical condition.
£1,900–2,300 / $2,750–3,350 ↗ CGC

| LAND ROVER | ENGINE | DATES | CONDITION | | |
Model	cc/cyl		1	2	3
Ser 1	1595/4	1948–51	£6,000	£3,000	£1,500
Ser 1	1995/4	1951–53	£4,500	£2,500	£1,000
Ser 1	1995/4	1953–58	£4,000	£2,000	£500
Ser 1	1995/4	1953–58	£3,000	£1,800	£800
Ser 2	1995/4	1958–59	£2,000	£950	£500
Ser 2	1995/4	1958–59	£2,800	£1,200	£500
Ser 2	2286/4	1959–71	£2,000	£950	£500
Ser 2	2286/4	1959–71	£2,500	£1,200	£500

Series 1 Land Rovers are very sought after.

Lea Francis

◄ **1927 Lea Francis 12/40 Type M Two-Seater Special,** original 1496cc Meadows 4ED twin-port engine, twin Solex carburettors, Scintilla magneto, 4-speed manual gearbox, rod operated drum brakes, engine rebuilt, coolant system upgraded following tuned Frazer Nash practice with additional feed to back of cylinder head, finished in blue, red leather interior, staggered seating, trafficators, fewer than 1,000 miles since completion.
£8,000–9,500 / $11,600–13,800 ⚒ CGC
This car was recently discovered as a 12/40 Type M rolling chassis, complete with all its running gear, that had lain disused, but carefully stored, for many years. A comprehensive professional refurbishment was begun soon afterwards. The tuned four-cylinder engine was moved further back in the chassis, giving better weight distribution and the potential to fit a supercharger at a later date. The chassis was fitted with an aluminium bob-tailed body.

| LEA-FRANCIS | ENGINE | DATES | CONDITION | | |
Model	cc/cyl		1	2	3
12HP	1944/4	1923–24	£10,000	£5,000	£3,000
14HP	2297/4	1923–24	£10,000	£5,000	£3,000
9HP	1074/4	1923–24	£7,000	£4,000	£2,000
10HP	1247/4	1947–54	£10,000	£5,500	£3,000
12HP	1496/4	1926–34	£12,000	£6,000	£4,000
Various 6-cylinder models	1696/6	1927–29	£13,500	£9,500	£5,000
Various 6-cylinder models	1991/6	1928–36	£10,500	£8,750	£5,000
14HP	1767/4	1946–54	£10,000	£6,000	£4,000
1.5 Litre	1499/4	1949–51	£11,000	£6,000	£3,000
2.5 Litre	2496/4	1950–52	£14,000	£8,000	£4,000

Lenoir

◄ **c1883 Lenoir,** 1230cc twin-cylinder 4 stroke petrol engine, tiller steering.
£20,000–30,000 / $29,000–43,500 ⚒ Pou
Étienne Lenoir (1822–1900) was a self-taught engineer. In 1900, he was awarded a medal by the Automobile Club de France for his 'invention of the petrol engine and of the first automobile ever made in the world.' In 1901, the motoring author and journalist Baudry de Saunier credited him with three discoveries: the petrol-air mixture, spark plug ignition and the intake of the mixture by the piston movement. Lenoir's first petrol engine was patented in 1860 and can be seen at the Conservatoire des Artes et Métiers. During 1862–63, he fitted one of his petrol engines into a river boat and an 'automobile', a kind of cart which covered some 11 miles (18km) in three hours. As early as 1876–79, Lenoir had patented a four-stroke petrol engine, which led in 1882–83 to the production by his associates, Rouart Frères, of a new generation of Lenoir engines in single-, two- and four-cylinder forms.

Lincoln

Henry Leland, founder of Cadillac, formed Lincoln in 1917, the company's first car appearing in 1919. Two years later, Ford stepped in to rescue the young and ailing concern. With Henry Ford's son, Edsel, at the reins, Lincoln went on to build some of the world's finest luxury cars. Perhaps it would have given Henry Leland some pleasure to have seen the marque he named after Abraham Lincoln go on to enjoy enduring presidential patronage.

1939 Lincoln Zephyr Coupé, V12 engine, overdrive gearbox, completely restored, tan leather interior, working original radio.
£22,000–26,000 / $32,000–37,700 ⚒ BJ

A known continuous history can add value to and enhance the enjoyment of a car.

1957 Lincoln Premier Two-Door Hardtop, 368cu.in V8 engine, automatic transmission, power steering, power brakes, power windows, Town and Country radio, power aerial, chrome trim in excellent condition including original hubcaps, original fabric and vinyl interior in very good condition, body sound, suitable for restoration.
£2,500–3,500 / $3,600–5,000 ⚒ Bon

1946 Lincoln Continental Club Coupé, finished in black, power windows, power seats, interior in good condition, fewer than 78,000 miles from new, complete, unrestored, very original.
£5,000–6,000 / $7,250–8,700 ⚒ Bon
The original Lincoln Continental was never intended to see production; it was only intended to see Florida. Edsel Ford wanted a unique luxury automobile to use at his Florida holiday home. Ford designer Eugene 'Bob' Gregorie began his transformation of the already spectacular Zephyr, lowering the overall car and stretching the bonnet. The one-off Continental used Lincoln Zephyr V12 running gear. When Ford took the Lincoln to Florida, it garnered so much positive attention that it was put into production as a 1940 model. The Continental employed the 292cu.in, 120bhp sidevalve V12 mated to a three-speed manual gearbox. In that first year of production, 350 cabriolets and 54 coupés were built. For 1941, there were only minor trim changes, although production did grow to 400 cabriolets and 850 coupés. The big change for 1942 came by way of a bigger V12, which displaced 306cu.in and generated 130bhp. Unfortunately, because of the United States' entry into the war, production amounted to only 113 Continentals for the year. When WWII ended, the Continental was offered again, being essentially a mildly revised 1942 model. Total production for the year amounted to only 466 cars, 265 of which were two-door Club Coupés.

LINCOLN Model	ENGINE cu. in/cyl	DATES	CONDITION 1	2	3
Première Coupé	368/8	1956–57	£6,000	£4,000	£2,000
Première Convertible	368/8	1956–57	£14,000	£8,000	£5,000
Continental Mk II	368/8	1956–57	£10,000	£6,000	£4,000
Continental 2-door	430/8	1958–60	£6,000	£4,000	£2,000
Continental Convertible	430/8	1958–60	£18,000+	£10,000+	£7,000+

Lorraine Dietrich

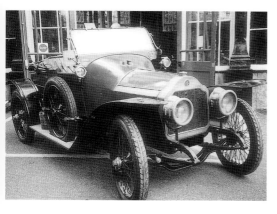

◀ **1912 Lorraine Dietrich SLF Torpedo Spyder,** subject of extensive renovation programme, 2121cc engine rebuilt, SU carburettor, new exhaust system, magneto rebuilt, new road springs, new brake drums, steering gear overhauled, radiator repaired, new beaded-edge-type spoked wheels, finished in blue, brown interior, unused since 1998.
£15,000–17,000 / $21,750–24,750 ⚒ H&H
Lorraine Dietrich began making cars as an offshoot of the long established De Dietrich company in 1905. The early years were plagued by the car division's financial troubles, but diversification kept it alive and fine touring cars abounded. Car production lasted until 1934, after which the firm concentrated on railway rolling stock. This particular car is thought to be unique in the form of its Torpedo Spyder coachwork, although a four-seater of the same vintage is in the Schlumpf Museum in eastern France.

Lotus

From selling used cars just after the end of WWII, Colin Chapman took Lotus from its birthplace in a north London lock-up to top place on the podium at the pinnacle of motor sport. The remarkable story began when Chapman was studying at London University and selling used cars in the brief post-war boom. In 1948, he took an unsold Austin 7 and created a lightweight trials car. Other competition cars followed, and in 1952 the first production Lotus emerged from the stables behind the north London pub run by Chapman's father. The Mark 6 was based around a multi-tubular frame with stressed aluminium panels, and was sold in kit form. The theme developed into the legendary Lotus 7, which remained in kit-car production as a Lotus until 1973, then was taken up by Caterham Cars. The latter still produces a much evolved version of this pulse

quickening pocket rocket. Meanwhile, back in the 1950s, the tiny Lotus company was a frenzy of activity: its first single-seater appeared in 1956; then, in 1958, Lotus produced the lovely Elite, not only the first closed Lotus, but also the world's first glassfibre monocoque and the first true Lotus road car. In 1960, the company reached another major milestone when Stirling Moss won the Monaco Grand Prix in a privately entered Lotus 18. Colin Chapman died in 1982, but the latest generation of Lotus cars – the Elise and the 340R – still bear the hallmarks of a Chapman Lotus, full of innovation with power-to-weight ratios that guarantee driving excitement and handling finesse to embarrass many a rival. Moreover, Lotus Engineering is a leading automotive consultancy, whose technical expertise is called upon by car makers the world over.

1954 Lotus 6, original-specification tuned 1172cc Ford sidevalve engine, twin SU carburettors, space-frame chassis, completely restored, most original parts retained, finished in British racing green, dark red interior, unmodified.
£18,000–20,000 / $26,000–29,000 ⋏ H&H
In 1952, Colin Chapman founded Lotus with Michael Allen. The pair's first production model was the Mark 6, which was offered in kit form based on a multi-tubular frame with stressed aluminium panels, coil-spring suspension and Ford running gear. Very few of the original 100 or so examples exist today, and the very early build date of this car is reflected in its chassis number of 23. No doubt, it would have been partly built and sold by Colin Chapman himself.

1962 Lotus Super 7 Series 2, 1600cc double-overhead-camshaft engine, twin Weber 40DCOE carburettors, dry-sump lubrication, 180bhp, 4-speed manual gearbox, 4-wheel independent suspension, 4-wheel disc brakes, completely restored, just over 2,500 miles since, engine rebuilt, new strengthened chassis, fully race-prepared but road legal, sets of road and racing tyres.
£12,000–14,000 / $17,500–20,500 ⋏ RM

Miller's is a price GUIDE not a price LIST

LOTUS Model	ENGINE cc/cyl	DATES	CONDITION 1	2	3
Six		1953–56	£13,000+	£7,000+	£5,000+
Elite 1172/4		1957–63	£22,000+	£15,000+	£10,000
7 S1 Sports	1172/4	1957–64	£12,000+	£9,000+	£5,000+
7 S2 Sports	1498/4	1961–66	£10,000+	£8,000+	£5,000+
7 S3 Sports	1558/4	1961–66	£10,000+	£8,000+	£5,000+
7 S4	1598/4	1969–72	£8,000	£5,000	£3,000
Elan S1 Convertible	1558/4	1962–64	£12,000+	£8,000	£4,500
Elan S2 Convertible	1558/4	1964–66	£12,000+	£7,000	£4,000
Elan S3 Convertible	1558/4	1966–69	£12,000+	£8,000	£5,000
Elan S3 FHC	1558/4	1966–69	£13,000	£7,000	£5,000
Elan S4 Convertible	1558/4	1968–71	£14,000+	£9,500	£7,000
Elan S4 FHC	1558/4	1968–71	£10,000+	£7,500	£5,000
Elan Sprint Convertible	1558/4	1971–73	£15,000+	£8,500+	£7,000
Elan Sprint FHC	1558/4	1971–73	£10,000+	£7,000	£6,000
Europa S1 FHC	1470/4	1966–69	£4,000+	£3,500	£2,000
Europa S2 FHC	1470/4	1969–71	£5,500+	£3,000	£2,000
Europa Twin Cam	1558/4	1971–75	£8,000	£6,000	£4,000
Elan +2S 130	1558/4	1971–74	£8,000	£5,000	£4,000
Elite S1 FHC	1261/4	1974–80	£3,500	£2,500	£1,500
Eclat S1	1973/4	1975–82	£3,500	£3,000	£1,500
Esprit 1	1973/4	1977–81	£6,500	£5,000	£3,000
Esprit 2	1973/4	1976–81	£7,000	£4,000	£2,500
Esprit S2.2	2174/4	1980–81	£7,000	£5,500	£3,000
Esprit Turbo	2174/4	1980–88	£10,000	£7,000	£4,000
Excel	2174/4	1983–85	£5,000	£3,000	£2,500

Prices vary with some limited-edition Lotus models and with competition history.

1961 Lotus Elite S2, 1216cc Coventry Climax engine, restored over last 12 years, finished in white, black and grey interior, excellent condition.
£20,000–23,000 / $29,000–33,500 ✗ H&H
Colin Chapman applied his ingenuity to a true road car looking for profit, but the Elite lost a considerable amount of money. It was, though, a technical triumph. The Elite was the world's first competition glassfibre monocoque, and it was a daring, handsome design to boot. Chapman struts were fitted at the rear, there were disc brakes all-round (inboard at the rear), and power was delivered by an aluminium Coventry Climax engine, which was light and powerful. From 1960, the car featured a close-ratio ZF gearbox.

1963 Lotus Elan S1, export specification, completely restored 1986–87 using original parts wherever possible, including chassis, suspension, cylinder block and head, carburettors and exhaust system, radiator refurbished, fitted with brake servo, halogen headlights, seat belts and battery isolation switch, new soft top and tonneau, interior retrimmed, 2 owners and fewer than 10,000 miles from new, very good condition throughout.
£16,000–20,000 / $23,000–29,000 ✗ Bon

1970 Lotus Elan S4, 1558cc 4-cylinder double-overhead-camshaft engine, twin Weber carburettors, 4-speed manual gearbox, subject of extensive restoration, new Spyder chassis, finished in red, black mohair hood, full-length mohair tonneau, new black leather seats.
£10,000–12,000 / $14,500–17,500 ⊞ BC

1971 Lotus Elan S4, 1558cc 4-cylinder big-valve engine, finished in red, excellent mechanical condition, good bodywork and chassis, 2 owners from new.
£8,750–10,000 / $13,000–14,500 ✗ BRIT

▶ **1967 Lotus Elan +2,** subject of full chassis-up rebuild, finished in white, good condition.
£5,000–6,000 / $7,250–8,750 ✗ BARO
The +2 was the first Lotus to cater for four people, having diminutive rear seats squeezed into its ultra-low body.

Lotus Elan +2 (1967–74)

Production: 3,300.
Engine: 1558cc, four-cylinder, twin-overhead-cam, cast-iron block, aluminium head.
Power output: 118–126bhp.
Transmission: Four-speed manual; five-speed manual on 130-5 model.
Brakes: Discs all-round.
Maximum speed: 115+mph for +2 and +2S; 120+mph for +2S 130.
0–60mph: 8.5 seconds for +2 and +2S; 7.5 seconds for +2S 130.
Patrick McGoohan drove a Lotus 7 in The Prisoner; Diana Rigg, as Emma Peel, drove a Lotus Elan in The Avengers; and Roger Moore was all at sea in an Esprit in the Spy Who Loved Me Bond caper. But there was one Lotus whose star never shone quite as brightly, the Elan for the family man. The +2 stood for the two extra close-coupled seats in the rear, and if the original hedonistic baby two-seater Elan shouted out that you were young, free and single, the Elan +2 meekly apologised for you – for being married and responsible, for having kids, and for not being sure that's what you wanted. With the Elan +2, Colin Chapman was aiming to spread the appeal of Lotus upmarket, on to the driveways of the posher commuter belts. It was more refined and better trimmed than the original Elan, but the +2 scarcely approached the annoying and smug self-satisfaction of the Jaguar E-Type 2+2, the car for the married man who still swung like a bachelor. The other drawback of the Elan +2 was that it was only available as a fixed-head. In truth, though, this elongated Elan possessed most of the pace, sizzling acceleration and race-bred handling of its smaller brother, but at nearly 2ft longer, it couldn't be quite as agile. In 1969, it also became the first Lotus that wasn't available for home assembly, so these later versions had none of the DIY dogma, and assembly standards were generally higher. Without doubt, the best of the bunch is the awkwardly named +2S 130-5, with the 126bhp big-valve engine from the Elan Sprint and five-speed gearbox. The Elan +2 was built in far fewer numbers than the baby Elan, but the married-with-children stigma means that, car for car, it is considerably cheaper.
Elan fact: On cars supplied to the press, the rev limiter was adjusted from 6,500 to 6,850rpm to allow the Elan to reach 120mph and sometimes a bit more.

1973 Lotus Elan +2 130-5, laid up for several years during 1990s, recommissioned 1997 at a cost of over £2,000, new steering rack and brake servo, glassfibre bodywork sound, finished in metallic blue with gold metalflake roof, faded in places, original cream vinyl interior, wooden dash in good condition.
£3,000–4,000 / $4,400–5,800 ♪ CGC
With 126bhp extracted from the 1558cc, twin-cam, four-cylinder engine and a slick five-speed manual gearbox, the 130–5 was capable of 121mph and 0–60mph in 7.4 seconds.

► **1985 Lotus Excel,** 2174cc 4-cylinder engine, stainless-steel exhaust, original alloy wheels, finished in metallic blue, cream leather interior with blue cloth inserts, good condition.
£2,250–2,750 / $3,250–4,000 ♪ BRIT
The Excel was introduced in 1982 as an update of the Eclat, and successor to the Elite, powered by a 2.2 litre, 16-valve, overhead-camshaft engine that developed 160bhp. An elegantly styled coupé with the capacity to carry four people, the Excel employed a five-speed gearbox and brakes sourced from Toyota. Performance was quoted as a respectable 6.8 seconds for the 0–60mph dash, with a maximum of 135mph.

◄ **1968 Lotus Elan +2,** 1558cc 4 cylinder engine, subject of considerable refurbishment, body stripped and resprayed in red, original black interior trim, good mechanical condition.
£5,500–6,500 / $8,000–9,500 ♪ BRIT

1969 Lotus Elan +2S, 1558cc engine, restored late 1990s, 700 miles since, gearbox replaced by 5-speed unit, galvanised chassis and sills, all brakes and suspension replaced, Spax adjustable shock absorbers, finished in yellow and green, new oatmeal interior trim, 75,500 miles from new.
£6,000–7,000 / $8,700–10,200 ♪ H&H
The Elan +2S was introduced in 1968 with the same 118bhp engine as the earlier +2, but there were no major mechanical changes apart from the addition of an alternator. It was the first Lotus not to be offered as a kit car.

1973 Lotus Elan +2S 130, 1600cc double-overhead-camshaft engine, finished in red with silver roof, black interior, good condition.
£5,000–6,000 / $7,250–8,700 ♪ BARO
The Elan +2S 130 was introduced in 1971 alongside the Elan and the Europa.

◄ **1989 Lotus Esprit Turbo SE,** finished in metallic blue-grey, grey leather interior, 30,000 miles from new.
£8,000–10,000 / £11,500–14,500 ⊞ VIC

Marcos

MARCOS Model	ENGINE cc/cyl	DATES	CONDITION 1	2	3
1500/1600/1800	1500/1600/1800/4	1964–69	£8,000	£5,000	£2,500
Mini-Marcos	848/4	1965–74	£3,500	£2,500	£1,500
Marcos 3 Litre	3000/6	1969–71	£9,000	£6,000	£4,000
Mantis	2498	1970/71	£10,000	£4,500	£1,500

Marendaz

1934 Marendaz Special, Continental engine, restored 1994, finished in red, polished aluminium bonnet, black interior, very good condition.
£16,000–20,000 / $23,000–29,000 ✗ COYS
After Marseal Motors, in which he was a partner, closed, Captain DMK Marendaz began producing cars under his own name in premises on the Brixton Road in London. He was in good company, sharing floorspace with Bugatti's London depot. His cars used Anzani engines and had a definite sporting air, with V-shaped windscreens and a Bentley-esque radiator surround. By 1932, he had moved to Maidenhead, where he built a further 60 cars, some with Marendaz assembled Continental engines and others with Coventry Climax six-cylinder inlet-over-exhaust engines. Marendaz cars featured in all manner of competition events during the 1930s, doing particularly well in rallies.

Maserati

When the five Maserati brothers formed a company to build their own cars, under their own name, in 1926, they had already gained an impressive collective track record in the automobile and engineering industries, between them manufacturing spark plugs, constructing race cars for Isotta-Fraschini and Diatto, working on aero engines, and racing motor cars and motorcycles. The impetus that turned them into a manufacturer in their own right was a supercharged grand prix car designed for Diatto. When Diatto went bankrupt, that car reverted to the Maserati brothers and led to the formation of the Maserati marque, which took as its insignia Neptune's trident, the symbol of Bologna, where the brothers were based. The Maserati competition cars were a major force from the late 1920s through to the mid-1950s, even though the brothers had sold their interest in the firm in 1937. In 1957, Juan Manuel Fangio won the world championship in a Maserati 250F, but that proved to be the company's mainstream competition swan-song. A series of accidents at the Venezuelan Grand Prix destroyed all four Maserati cars entered in that race, and with top-flight competition becoming increasingly expensive, Maserati withdrew and concentrated its limited resources on sports-racers and GTs. The first Maserati road car, the A6, had appeared a decade before at the 1947 Geneva show, but it was produced in very small numbers and was, in effect, a spin-off from the competition machines. With the withdrawal from competition, the firm could concentrate for the first time on true series-production road cars. The first of these Maseratis was the 3500GT, and a large number of memorable cars have followed, but for lots of enthusiasts, the ultimate Maserati is the gorgeous Ghibli, rated by many as the most beautiful car in the world.

◀ **1959 Maserati 3500GT Coupé,** coachwork by Touring, engine rebuilt 1999, resprayed, stored for last 18 months, good condition throughout.
£13,000–15,000
$18,850–21,750 ✗ Bon

Maserati Tipo 60/61 'Birdcage' (1959–61)

Production: 22.
Engine: 1985cc and 2890cc, four-cylinder, double-overhead-cam.
Power output: 1985cc, approx 165bhp at 6,000rpm; 2890cc, approx 250bhp at 6,500rpm.
Transmission: All-synchromesh five-speed transaxle.
Brakes: Discs all-round.

In the late 1950s, Maserati was down on its heels and on the brink of bankruptcy. In 1957, after Fangio's F1 victory in a 250F and the destruction of all four Maseratis in the Venezuelan GP, the company withdrew from racing to regroup. When Maserati returned to competition in 1959, it was with a sports-racer produced for sale to private entrants. The Tipo 60 was, in its way, a parts-bin special, with running gear based on the old F1 car and an existing 2 litre engine. Neither was it the most handsome thing, with its awkward bulges clothing a crazy mass of more than 200 steel tubes that made up its space-frame chassis and gave it the 'Birdcage' nickname, by which it has since become mythologised. Yet, against all the odds, it worked, and even more so when, in 1961, it acquired a 2.9 litre engine and became the Tipo 61. Sir Stirling Moss has a particularly fond spot for the 'Birdcage' and recalls, 'After trying the prototype at Modena I knew it was a winner. The Birdcage was light, the chassis superbly nimble with fantastic brakes and super steering... Unusually for a Maserati you could drive it hard and it still stayed together.' That's what Moss did when, with Dan Gurney, he won a heroic 1960 Nürburgring 1000km race, thrashing fully funded Ferrari and Porsche entries. Mostly, though, the 'Birdcage' was a bridesmaid. Run by enthusiastic privateers – often cash strapped and sometimes short on know-how – it led far, far more races than it ever won, but that's all part of the mythology and legend of this against-the-odds winner.

1962 Maserati 3500GTi Spyder, coachwork by Vignale, older restoration, correct Lucas fuel injection, chrome Borrani wire wheels, factory hardtop, new, mohair soft top, resprayed in red, new black leather upholstery.
£55,000–65,000 / $80,000–94,000 ⚬ **Bon**
Maserati's first series-production road car attracted the attention of Italy's finest coachbuilders: Allemano, Bertone and Frua all created bodies for the 3500GT chassis. Most coupés were built by Touring, while all but one (a Frua-bodied example) of the much less-common Spyder version were the work of Vignale. Introduced in 1959, Vignale's Maserati 3500GT Spyder was the creation of Giovanni Michelotti, at that time the company's star designer. Constructed on a slightly shorter wheelbase than the coupé, and built only to order, the Spyder lasted in production until 1964, by which time only 245 had been made.

1966 Maserati Sebring Series II Coupé, coachwork by Vignale, 5-speed manual gearbox, servo-assisted 4-wheel disc brakes, independent front suspension by wishbones and coil springs, rigid rear axle on semi-elliptic leaf springs, tubular chassis frame, Borrani wire wheels, right-hand drive, restored, original Lucas fuel injection replaced by carburettors, finished in metallic grey, red leather interior, good mechanical condition, very good bodywork and interior.
£18,000–22,000 / $26,000–32,000 ⚬ **Bon**
Introduced in 1965, the Sebring Series II came with a 3.7 litre, 245bhp engine; some cars left the factory with 4 litre units towards the end of production in 1966, by which time 96 Series IIs had been built.

1970 Maserati Mexico 4700 Coupé, coachwork by Vignale, 4.7 litre 4-camshaft V8 engine, manual gearbox, Borrani wire wheels, finished in sable, mustard Connolly hide interior, fewer than 32,500 miles from new, good original condition.
£15,000–18,000 / $21,750–26,000 ⚬ **Bon**

▶ **1967 Maserati Ghibli Coupé,** 4.7 litre 4-camshaft V8 engine, 4-wheel disc brakes.
£18,000–22,000 / $26,000–32,000 ⚬ **H&H**

1970 Maserati Ghibli Coupé, coachwork by Ghia, 4.7 litre 4-camshaft V8 engine, manual gearbox, rigid rear axle, tubular-steel chassis, alloy wheels, finished in light metallic blue, black Connolly leather interior, period Autovox radio, 2 owners and fewer than 39,500 miles from new, original condition.
£17,000–20,000 / $25,000–29,000 ⚒ Bon
Styled at Ghia by Giorgetto Giugiaro and named after a Sahara Desert wind, the Ghibli rivalled the Ferrari Daytona for straight-line performance – its top speed was close to 170mph – while beating it on price and, arguably, looks.

1970 Maserati Indy Coupé, coachwork by Vignale, manual gearbox, finished in silver, black leathercloth interior, air conditioning, fewer than 31,500 miles from new.
£13,000–15,000 / $18,750–21,750 ⚒ Bon
In 1968, Maserati followed its stunning Ghia styled Ghibli two-seater with the equally elegant Indy 2+2, although the latter was the work of Vignale and the first unitary-construction Maserati. Running gear was conventional, with independent front suspension, a live rigid rear axle and four-wheel disc brakes, while the power unit was the well-tried, 4.2 litre, four-cam V8. With 260bhp on tap, top speed was in the region of 150mph. Production ceased in 1975 after 1,104 cars had been built.

1975 Maserati Bora Coupé, coachwork by Ital Design, 4.7 litre mid-mounted 4-camshaft V8 engine, 5-speed transaxle, 4-wheel independent double-wishbone suspension, finished in silver, black leather interior, suede covered dashboard, factory radio/cassette, original spare paint canister, 330 miles from new.
£28,000–32,000 / $40,000–46,000 ⚒ Bon
One of the first models to appear after Citroën's acquisition of Maserati, the Bora employed the former's hydraulic technology to adjust seats and pedals, raise the headlamps and operate the excellent powered brakes. A slippery shape plus 310bhp made for a very fast car – top speed was around 160mph – and the Bora had acceleration and handling to match. The model was Maserati's performance flagship until production ended in 1978, by which time only 524 had been built. This particular car is one of a small number of Boras rebuilt by Maserati agent Scardovi in Bologna in the late 1980s, employing a limited number of unused bodyshells then available from the factory. These cars were built 'as new' for major collectors and commanded a substantial price. This example was purchased directly from Scardovi around 1990 and kept in storage since.

MASERATI Model	ENGINE cc/cyl	DATES	CONDITION 1	2	3
AG-1500	1488/6	1946–50	£40,000+	£30,000	£20,000
A6G	1954/6	1951–53	£50,000+	£35,000	£22,000
A6G-2000	1985/6	1954–57	£45,000+	£35,000	£20,000
3500GT fhc	3485/6	1957–64	£20,000	£14,000	£10,000
3500GT Spyder	3485/6	1957–64	£35,000+	£22,000	£15,000
5000GT	4935/8	1960–65	£60,000+	£20,000	£15,000
Sebring	3694/6	1962–66	£20,000	£15,000	£10,000
Quattroporte	4136/8	1963–74	£11,000	£9,000	£7,000
Mistral	4014/6	1964–70	£15,000	£11,000	£9,000
Mistral Spyder	4014/6	1964–70	£30,000+	£18,000	£12,000
Mexico	4719/8	1965–68	£15,000	£12,000	£9,000
Ghibli	4719/8	1967–73	£20,000	£15,000	£12,000
Ghibli-Spyder/SS	4136/8	1969–74	£50,000+	£40,000	£25,000
Indy	4136/8	1969–74	£18,000	£13,000	£10,000
Bora	4719/8	1971–80	£25,000	£18,000	£11,000
Merak/SS	2965/6	1972–81	£16,000	£14,000	£9,000
Khamsin	4930/8	1974–81	£16,000	£11,000	£9,000

Early cars with competition/Berlinetta coachwork, e.g. Zagato, command a premium; A6, A6G and A6G-2000, rare coupé and Gran Sport coachwork can see prices of £180,000–250,000.

1981 Maserati Kyalami, coachwork by Frua, 4.9 litre V8 engine, manual gearbox, Campagnolo alloy wheels, finished in silver, black Connolly hide upholstery, air conditioning, fewer than 19,500 miles from new.
£7,000–9,000 / $10,200–13,000 ✦ Bon
Parent company Citroën's financial crisis led to Maserati being acquired by Alessandro De Tomaso in 1975. One of the revitalised company's first products was the Kyalami, effectively a revised De Tomaso Longchamp fitted with a Maserati V8 engine. Restyled by Frua, it was launched at the 1976 Turin show. Production continued until 1983, by which time only 198 cars had been built.

1989 Maserati Bi-Turbo, 2491cc V6 engine, 5-speed manual gearbox, engine and turbochargers rebuilt, new door skins, resprayed in black 1999, tan interior, 59,000 miles from new, very good condition throughout.
£2,400–2,800 / $3,500–4,000 ✦ H&H

▶ **1992 Maserati Ghibli 2.0,** 1996cc 24-valve V6 engine, twin turbochargers, 306bhp, 6-speed manual gearbox, limited-slip differential, 4-wheel independent suspension, 4-wheel disc brakes, left-hand drive, c165mph top speed, 1 of only 1,133 examples built 1992–97, unused since 1998, good condition throughout.
£3,750–4,500 / $5,000–6,500 ✦ Bon
First applied to Maserati's fabulous, Ghia styled supercar of the 1960s, the Ghibli name was revived for the Bi-Turbo in the 1990s.

1984 Maserati Bi-Turbo E, 2491cc V6 engine, twin turbochargers, carburetted model, manual gearbox, finished in two-tone silver, excellent original condition.
£3,000–4,000 / $4,400–5,800 ✦ BARO

1988 Maserati Bi-Turbo Spyder, 2491cc V6 engine, blue mohair hood, finished in blue, tan hide interior, air conditioning, excellent condition.
£6,000–7,000 / $8,700–10,200 ✦ BRIT
Introduced in 1982, the Bi-Turbo was the first series-production road car to utilise a twin-turbocharger engine. Initially, it had been planned to offer an open version alongside the original coupé model, but it was not until 1984 that the Spyder appeared.

◀ **1985 Maserati Quattroporte,** finished in burgundy, magnolia hide interior, 64,000 miles from new, good condition.
£3,000–4,000
$4,400–5,800 🔨 COYS

1972 Maserati Boomerang, coachwork by Ital Design, 4719cc mid-mounted 4-camshaft V8 engine, 310bhp, 5-speed synchromesh gearbox, rear wheel drive, 4-wheel independent coil-spring suspension, servo-assisted 4-wheel ventilated disc brakes, left-hand drive, finished in two-tone metallic grey, maroon leather interior, excellent condition.
£400,000+ / $580,000+ 🔨 C
The Boomerang was first displayed as a non-functional model at the Turin motor show in 1971. By the Geneva show in March 1972, it had been transformed into a fully operational vehicle. The engine was the race-bred V8 of 4.7 litres, developing no less than 310hp, and could propel the car to an indicated top speed of 186mph.

Mathis

1920 Mathis 8/20CV Coach, 1100cc 4-cylinder sidevalve engine, 4-speed manual gearbox, single door on passenger side, set-back passenger seat, sliding side windows, side-mounted spare wheel, right-hand drive, brakes and starter motor overhauled, finished in dark green with black wings, burgundy fabric interior.
£6,500–8,000 / $9,500–11,500 🔨 Bon
Founded in Strasbourg in 1898, Mathis built only a handful of prototypes in its early years, subsequently manufacturing Ettore Bugatti's Hermès designs around 1904–05 before introducing its first own-design production car in 1910. The latter was conventional with a 2 litre, four-cylinder sidevalve engine, but Emile Mathis' reputation would be founded on a range of much smaller cars, beginning with the 1100cc Babylette and 1300cc Baby. Mathis continued to introduce larger models after WWI, but it was the success of the light cars that enabled the company to claim fourth place among French manufacturers by the mid-1920s, behind Renault, Citroën and Peugeot.

Mercedes-Benz

Mercedes-Benz motor cars have only truly existed since 1926, following the merger of the separate Daimler (Mercedes) and Benz companies, although both can claim to have fathered the motor car. Working independently, both Karl Benz and Gottlieb Daimler produced petrol-engined road vehicles in 1886. In 1894, Benz's Velo became the world's first true production automobile. The name Mercedes was first used on a Daimler in 1899. When Benz, an early pace-setter in volume production, merged with the dynamic Daimler, the combination proved formidable. In the 1930s, the range of road cars was thoroughly comprehensive, and from 1934 to the outbreak of WWII, Mercedes-Benz dominated the grand prix scene along with its compatriot, Auto Union. Following post-war reconstruction, Mercedes-Benz signalled to the

world that it was back on top with the gorgeous 300SL Gullwing, the forerunner of modern supercars. Since then, the company has concentrated on producing upmarket executive saloons, and sporting coupés and cabriolets, all formidably engineered. In most cases, Mercedes-Benz has shunned the merely voguish to produce some long-lived models whose designs have remained modern while other manufacturers have adopted and dropped the latest styling fads. A prime example is the so-called 'pagoda-roof' SL series of cars, produced from 1963 to 1971 – never the absolute zenith of high fashion, but all the better for it. While other contemporary sporting rivals aged quickly and soon looked outmoded, it's astonishing to think that the youngest of these SLs is now 30 years old, so crisp and fresh is their design.

1907 Mercedes 45hp Seven-Seat Roi des Belges Tourer, 6785cc 4-cylinder T-head engine, 4-speed manual gearbox, chain drive to rear wheels, drum brakes on rear wheels, semi-elliptic leaf-spring suspension, Ducellier self-generating acetylene headlights, scuttle mounted side lights, dashboard oiler system, older restoration, upholstery refurbished and in very good condition.
£190,000+ / $275,000+ ⚲ C

▶ **1925 Mercedes 24/100/140PS Roadster,** coachwork by Murphy, 6240cc 6-cylinder engine, supercharger, 140bhp, 4-speed manual gearbox, semi-elliptic leaf-spring suspension, 4-wheel mechanical drum brakes, wood-spoked wheels, left-hand drive, restored, finished in navy blue, red leather upholstery, in need of recommissioning.
£105,000–120,000 / $152,000–174,000 ⚲ C

◀ **1931 Mercedes-Benz 370NC Cabriolet,** 4-wheel independent suspension, artillery wheels, pillar mounted spot lamp, restored, finished in black, tan interior and hood.
£55,000–65,000 / $80,000–95,000 ⚲ COYS

▶ **1934 Mercedes-Benz 500K Cabriolet B,** 5019cc 8-cylinder engine, supercharger, 4-speed manual gearbox, 4-wheel independent suspension, 4-wheel hydraulic drum brakes, left-hand drive, museum displayed for several years.
£140,000–160,000
$203,000–232,000 ⚲ Pou

1936 Mercedes-Benz 230B Cabriolet, 2213cc 6-cylinder engine, original right-hand-drive long-chassis model, older restoration, finished in white, grey interior.
£25,000–30,000 / $36,000–43,000 ⚒ **H&H**

1952 Mercedes-Benz 170SD Diesel Saloon, 2000cc engine, original right-hand drive, ex-South Africa, subject of complete no-expense-spared restoration, engine rebuilt, new brakes and suspension, electrics overhauled, bare-metal respray in green and black, new tan leather upholstery, wood trim refurbished.
£8,000–9,000 / $11,600–13,000 ⚒ **H&H**

1952 Mercedes-Benz 220B Cabriolet, 2195cc 6-cylinder engine, left-hand drive, restored and converted from coupé late 1990s, finished in black, red interior, fewer than 54,500 miles from new, good condition throughout.
£7,500–9,000 / $10,875–13,000 ⚒ **H&H**
Only 85 220B coupés were built, and even fewer cabriolets.

1950 Mercedes-Benz 170S, 1697cc engine, 4-speed gearbox, restored by Mercedes-Benz, finished in blue, beige interior, excellent condition throughout.
£35,000–40,000 / $50,000–58,000 ⚒ **COYS**

1953 Mercedes-Benz 300S Roadster, completely restored, excellent condition.
£90,000–105,000 / $130,000–152,000 ⚒ **Bon**
Having begun post-war production in 1946 with the 170 in unchanged form, Mercedes-Benz introduced its first all-new designs of the post-war era – the 220 and 300 – in 1951. While the 220 was a big advance on the 170, the 300 re-established Mercedes-Benz in the front rank of prestige car manufacturers. The 300's oval-tube chassis followed the lines of the 170S and 220, with independent suspension all-round and four-wheel drum brakes, but incorporated the added refinements of hypoid-bevel final drive, dynamically balanced wheels and remote electrical control of the rear suspension ride height. Initially developing 155bhp, the 3 litre, overhead-camshaft six-cylinder engine was boosted in power for the succeeding 300B and 300C models, finally gaining fuel injection in the restyled 300D of 1957. The conservatively styled saloon was soon joined by the 300S (Super). Built in coupé and convertible forms on a shortened 300 saloon chassis, the 300S weighed considerably less than the former and was more powerful, its engine gaining triple (as opposed to twin) Solex carburettors and a raised compression ratio. Maximum power output was increased to 150bhp and top speed to 110mph.

MERCEDES-BENZ Model	ENGINE cc/cyl	DATES	CONDITION 1	2	3
300ABCD	2996/6	1951–62	£15,000	£10,000	£8,000
300D Cabriolet	2195/6	1951–62	£80,000	£50,000	£30,000
220A/S/SE Ponton	2195/6	1952–60	£10,000	£5,000	£3,000
220S/SEB Coupé	2915/6	1956–59	£11,000	£7,000	£5,000
220S/SEB Cabriolet	2195/6	1958–59	£28,000+	£18,000	£7,000
190SL	1897/4	1955–63	£20,000+	£15,000+	£10,000
300SL Gullwing	2996/6	1954–57	£120,000+	£100,000	£70,000
300SL Roadster	2996/6	1957–63	£110,000+	£90,000	£70,000
230/250SL	2306/ 2496/6	1963–68	£14,000+	£10,000+	£7,000
280SL	2778/6	1961–71	£16,000	£12,000	£9,000
220/250SE	2195/ 2496/6	1960–68	£10,000	£7,000	£4,000
300SE	2996/6	1961–65	£11,000	£8,000	£6,000
280SE Convertible	2778/6	1965–69	£25,000	£18,000	£12,000
280SE V8 Convertible	3499/8	1969–71	£40,000+	£20,000	£15,000
280SE Coupé	2496/6	1965–72	£12,000	£8,000	£5,000
300SEL 6.3	6330/8	1968–72	£12,000	£7,000	£3,500
600 & 600 Pullman	6332/8	1964–81	£40,000+	£15,000	£8,000

1955 Mercedes-Benz 300S Cabriolet, coachwork by Sindelfingen, cream leather interior, dashboard mounted Heuer stopwatch, fitted luggage, hood and interior restored 1990s, 2 owners from new.
£110,000–120,000 / $160,000–174,000 ✦ Bon
Mercedes-Benz introduced its first all-new designs of the post-WWII era – the 220 and 300 – in 1951. While the 220 was a big advance on the preceding 170, the 300 re-established the company in the front rank of prestige car manufacturers. Its oval-tube chassis followed the lines of the 170S and 220, with independent suspension all-round and four-wheel drum brakes, but incorporated the added refinement of hypoid-bevel final drive and remote electrical control of the rear suspension ride height. Initially developing 115bhp, the 3 litre overhead-camshaft six was boosted in power for the succeeding 300B and 300C models, gaining fuel injection in the restyled 300D of 1957. Other changes along the way included larger brakes (with servo assistance from 1954), and optional power steering and automatic transmission as standard (on the 300D). The conservatively styled saloon was soon joined by the 300S (Super). Built in coupé and convertible forms on a shortened saloon chassis, the 300S weighed considerably less and was more powerful, its engine gaining triple (as opposed to twin) Solex carburettors and a raised compression ratio. Maximum power output was increased to 150bhp and top speed to 110mph.

1957 Mercedes-Benz 300SL Roadster, fuel injection, metallic pale blue paintwork, brightwork and blue interior trim refurbished, fitted European headlamps.
£75,000–85,000 / $109,000–123,000 ✦ COYS

1955 Mercedes-Benz 300SL Gullwing, left-hand drive, restored by Daimler-Benz 1989–92 at a cost of over £140,000, everything possible replaced or refurbished, including interior, glass, bonnet and boot lids, chrome wings, undertrays and instruments, axles, engine, gearbox and other running gear rebuilt, radiator, brakes, electrics and rubbers renewed, Rudge knock-off wheels restored, resprayed in silver, red leather upholstery and matching red carpets, original speakers restored, fewer than 400 miles since rebuild, 1 of only 59 delivered new to Britain.
£170,000–190,000 / $246,000–275,000 ✦ Bon

1956 Mercedes-Benz 300SL Gullwing, restored, factory undertrays, fitted luggage, £7,000 spent recently on mechanical work, excellent condition throughout.
£130,000–145,000 / $188,000–210,000 ✦ COYS

◄ **1961 Mercedes-Benz 300SL Roadster,** 4-wheel disc brakes, finished in black, red leather interior, good original condition.
£90,000–100,000 / $130,000–145,000 ✦ Bon
Created to spearhead Mercedes-Benz' return to competition in the post-war era, the 300SL made its debut in the 1952 Mille Miglia, finishing second and fourth overall. Wins in the Carrera PanAmericana and at Le Mans followed. The first racers were open-topped, but before the season's end, the distinctive gullwing-doored coupé had appeared. Unusually high sills were a feature of the multi-tubular space-frame chassis, and while access was not a problem in the open car, the adoption of coupé bodywork required innovative thinking – hence the gullwing doors. Launched in 1954, the production 300SL retained the space-frame chassis and gullwing doors of the racer. A 2996cc, overhead-camshaft inline six, the 300SL's engine was canted at 45 degrees to achieve a lower, more aerodynamic bonnet line, and using innovative direct fuel injection, produced 215bhp at 5,800rpm. A four-speed gearbox transmitted power to the hypoid-bevel rear axle. Suspension was independent all-round. A new 300SL Roadster with conventional doors appeared in 1957.

◀ **1962 Mercedes-Benz 300SL Roadster,** 2996cc overhead-camshaft 6-cylinder engine, fuel injection, 215bhp, 4-wheel disc brakes, space-frame chassis, European lights, finished in white, black leather interior, 5th from last 'iron-block' model, fewer than 19,500 miles from new.
£120,000–135,000 $174,000–196,000 ↗ Bon

Mercedes-Benz 190SL (1955–63)

Production: 25,881.
Price in 1956: £2,776.7s, including purchase tax.
Engine: 1897cc, overhead-cam, four-cylinder.
Power output: 105bhp at 5,700rpm.
Transmission: Four-speed manual, all synchromesh.
Brakes: Hydraulic drums all-round.
Maximum speed: 108mph.
0–60mph: 13.3 seconds.
No one doubts that the gorgeous Mercedes-Benz 300SL was quite simply the world's first genuine supercar, with its tricksy multi-tubular space-frame chassis, scorching performance, sublime impracticality and drop-dead looks. Well, the Mercedes-Benz 190SL roadster shared most of the 300SL's good looks – albeit diluted for modesty – but that's where any similarity ended. The 190SL could just about match the performance of the

MGA, was no match at all for the Austin-Healey 100/Six and couldn't hold a candle anywhere near the Jaguar XK140. Yet for the price of 'the poor man's 300SL', you could have bought three MGAs or one Jaguar XK140 and an Austin-Healey as well. It doesn't seem to make any sense at all, yet for the price the 190SL sold well, particularly in the USA. And that's where it begins to make sense. As a promenade sports car with a soft boulevard ride, it was just the thing for the well-heeled folk in the Hollywood Hills, who cared more about caché than mere cash. The fact that Grace Kelly drove a 190SL in the 1956 movie *High Society* was surely a perfect piece of automotive casting.
190SL fact: Ringo Starr owned a 190SL from 1972 to 1987. Subsequently, it sold at auction in 1997 for just over £28,000.

1959 Mercedes-Benz 190SL, 1.9 litre engine, twin Dellorto carburettors, factory hardtop, left-hand drive, completely restored, finished in silver, red interior, 1 family ownership from new.
£22,000–26,000 / $32,000–38,000 ↗ Bon

1959 Mercedes-Benz 190SL, 1897cc 4-cylinder engine, right-hand drive, resprayed in black 1988, hard and soft tops, grey leather interior in good condition, fewer than 44,500 miles from new, good mechanical condition.
£14,000–16,000 / $20,500–23,000 ↗ BRIT
Smaller sister of the 300SL, the 190SL was announced during 1954, with production beginning early in the following year. Based on the 180 saloon and using a slightly modified floorpan, the 190SL was powered by a four-cylinder, overhead-valve engine equipped with twin Solex carburettors. This gave a power output of 105bhp at 5,700rpm and a top speed of around 107mph.

◀ **1962 Mercedes-Benz 190SL,** finished in red and black, hard and soft tops.
£14,000–16,000 / $20,500–23,000 ⊞ HCL

Dealer prices

Miller's guide prices for dealer cars take into account the value of any guarantees or warranties that may be included in the purchase. Dealers must also observe additional statutory consumer regulations, which do not apply to private sellers. This is factored into our dealer guide prices. Dealer cars are identified by the ⊞ icon; full details of the dealer can be found on page 332.

1964 Mercedes-Benz 220B Fintail Saloon, 2195cc engine, finished in ivory, black interior, very good condition throughout, large number of spares including engine and gearbox.
£2,000–2,500 / $3,000–3,600 ↗ H&H

1964 Mercedes-Benz 220SEB Coupé, 2195cc 6-cylinder engine, 4-speed manual gearbox, heated rear screen, older restoration, finished in white, black interior, 1 owner for 36 years.
£12,000–14,000 / $17,500–20,500 ➤ H&H

1965 Mercedes-Benz 220SEB Coupé, 2195cc 6-cylinder engine, stainless-steel exhaust, 4-speed manual gearbox, right-hand drive, full Webasto sunroof, finished in blue, grey leather interior, 2 owners from new, well maintained, good condition throughout.
£7,500–8,000 / $10,875–11,600 ➤ H&H

◄ **1967 Mercedes-Benz 250SE Coupé,** 2496cc 6-cylinder engine, power steering, electric sun roof, completely restored, braking system overhauled, all windows replaced with factory green tinted glass, bare-metal respray in original dark blue, Becker radio/cassette player, excellent condition.
£8,000–9,500
$11,600–13,800 ➤ BRIT
Sharing the same running gear as the 250S, the SEC models were launched at the Frankfurt show of 1965. Improvements included revised suspension and disc brakes all-round. The engine developed 170bhp at 5,600rpm, giving these cars a top speed of over 120mph.

1970 Mercedes-Benz 280SE 3.5 Coupé, electric sunroof, left-hand drive, finished in metallic grey, black hide interior, air conditioning, 2 owners from new, good original condition.
£8,000–9,500 / $11,600–13,800 ➤ COYS

1970 Mercedes-Benz 280SE 3.5 Cabriolet, 3499cc engine, completely restored, only genuine Mercedes parts used, some work by Mercedes factory, finished in navy blue, cream interior, complete set of fitted matching luggage.
£55,000–65,000 / $80,000–94,000 ➤ H&H

1971 Mercedes-Benz 280SE, 2778cc 6-cylinder engine, 180bhp, 4-speed automatic transmission, power steering, servo-assisted brakes, 4-wheel independent suspension, finished in white, black interior, power windows, original Becker Europa radio, air conditioning, fewer than 71,500 miles from new, excellent condition.
£4,000–5,000 / $5,800–7,250 ➤ Bon

1965 Mercedes-Benz 300SEB Coupé, 2996cc engine, finished in white, red interior, stored since 1994, recently recommissioned.
£6,000–7,500 / $8,700–10,875 ⚒ **H&H**

1975 Mercedes-Benz 280CE Coupé, 2745cc engine, left-hand drive, finished in silver, original black interior trim and upholstery, 2 owners from new, excellent condition throughout.
£2,000–2,500 / $3,000–3,600 ⚒ **H&H**

1965 Mecedes-Benz 230SL, restored 1999–2000, over £10,000/$14,500 spent, finished in white, red interior, excellent condition.
£24,000–28,000 / $35,000–40,000 ⚒ **COYS**

1966 Mercedes-Benz 230SL, 2306cc 6-cylinder engine, 4-speed manual gearbox, hard and soft tops, left-hand drive, finished in white, dark brown leather interior, excellent condition.
£13,500–15,000 / $20,000–22,000 ⚒ **CGC**
Successor to the race-bred 300SL Gullwing coupé and its roadster sister, the W113-series SL was far more of a production car in its design. Lightest of the three Super Light variants, the 230SL had sharper responses and road-holding than the later 280SL, which had softer damper and spring rates.

◄ **1967 Mercedes-Benz 250SL 2+2,** 2496cc 6-cylinder engine, right-hand drive, over £3,000/$4,400 spent since 2000, finished in white.
£10,000–12,000
$14,500–17,000 ⚒ **BARO**
The 2+2 versions of the 250SL were destined originally for the west coast of America and the south of France, but a few of these cars were produced in right-hand-drive form. The 250 was only produced for one model year, unlike the 230 and 280.

1981 Mercedes-Benz 280SL, 2752cc 6-cylinder engine, automatic transmission, finished in metallic pale blue, hard and soft tops, grey interior, air conditioning, cruise control, heated front seats, factory fitted rear seat with seat belts, 51,000 miles from new, excellent condition.
£9,500–10,500 / $14,000–15,250 ⚒ **H&H**

1972 Mercedes-Benz 350SL, 3499cc high-compression V8 engine, 230bhp, automatic transmission, original matching numbers, hardtop, all rubber door and window seals replaced, all exterior trim fittings including windscreen surround, door top trims, door mirrors and handles and bumpers renewed, new hood, bare-metal respray in silver at a cost of £5,000/$7,250, black leather interior with black carpets, fewer than 59,000 miles from new, excellent condition.
£14,000–16,000 / $20,500–23,500 ⚒ **CGC**

1979 Mercedes-Benz 450SLC, 4520cc alloy V8 engine, automatic transmission, servo-assisted brakes, finished in silver, blue velour interior, not registered until 1987, c60,000 miles from new, good condition.
£5,500–6,500 / $8,000–9,500 ⚒ **Bon**

1981 Mercedes-Benz 280SL, 2746cc 6-cylinder engine, hard top, finished in red, black interior, very good condition throughout.
£5,750–6,500 / $8,000–9,500 ⚒ **H&H**

1984 Mercedes-Benz 380SL, 3839cc V8 engine, hard and soft tops, finished in maroon, beige interior, good to very good condition.
£8,000–9,000 / $11,500–13,000 ⚒ **BRIT**

1979 Mercedes-Benz 450SEL 6.9 Saloon, 6834cc engine, original right-hand drive, lightly restored, finished in grey, black interior, 60,000 miles from new, excellent condition throughout.
£11,000–12,500 / $16,000–18,000 ⚒ **H&H**
The 450SEL with the 6.9 litre engine was produced from 1975 to 1980 and was the direct successor to the famed 300SEL 6.3, but it used the W116 S-class styling and structure. An engine delivering 286bhp pushed it to a 140mph top speed.

1987 Mercedes-Benz 560SEC, 5547cc V8 engine, fuel injection, 300bhp, automatic transmission, 4-wheel disc brakes, ABS, fewer than 24,500 miles from new.
£9,000–10,000 / $13,000–14,500 ⚒ **Pou**

MG

The origins of MG date back to 1923, when Cecil Kimber, general manager of Morris Garages in Oxford, attached a stylish two-seat sporting body to a standard Morris chassis to create the first MG. Until the outbreak of WWII, MG remained a specialist marque, rather than a real volume producer, creating a string of cars that offered the sporting driver affordable performance. In 1935, the company was incorporated into Morris, later to form BMC and British Leyland, with an ever increasing influence on MG products. Nevertheless, for many years, MG managed to keep its distinct sporting identity, producing memorable cars like the T-series Midgets, the pretty MGA, the world-beating MGB and the later Midget. The low point came in the 1980s, when the MG octagon badge was debased by being tacked on to Montegos and Maestros, and for a while it looked as though the marque would fade away. Yet in 1992, its renaissance began with the RV8, an update of the original MGB, and has since gathered real momentum with the capable little MGF.

1932 MG J2 Midget, 885cc engine, glassfibre wings, vinyl interior, engine turned aluminium dashboard, supplementary dials for water temperature, oil temperature, ammeter and clock, last used 1987, dry stored since, same family ownership for last 46 years.
£9,000–10,000 / $13,000–14,500 ⚲ CGC

The J1 and J2 Midgets were MG's first production models to truly benefit from its increasingly successful competition programme. Their 847cc version of the company's mainstay overhead-camshaft, four-cylinder engine developed some 36bhp at 5,500rpm – a prodigious output that was facilitated by using the AB crossflow cylinder head that had helped the formidable C-Type racer to victory in the Brooklands Double Twelve race and TT of 1931. A dynamic chassis complemented this advanced power unit. The under-slung rear axle kept the centre of gravity commendably low, and bronze trunnions reduced lateral loadings on the leaf springs. A four-speed manual gearbox, Rudge wire wheels and 12 volt electrics added to the specification.

> **Miller's is a price GUIDE not a price LIST**

1934 MG PA Midget, 847cc engine, optional cycle wings, full dynamo and cam drive, finished in green, red interior, rebuilt 1970s and 1980s, little use since, very good condition throughout.
£11,000–13,000 / $16,000–19,000 ⚲ H&H

1939 MG PB Midget, 939cc overhead-camshaft engine, finished in white, red wire wheels, red leathercloth interior, museum displayed for many years, original weather equipment in need of repair, chassis and bodywork in very good condition.
£13,000–15,000 / $19,000–22,000 ⚲ CGC

MG Model	ENGINE cc/cyl	DATES	CONDITION 1	2	3
14/28	1802/4	1924–27	£26,000	£18,000	£10,000
14/40	1802/4	1927–29	£25,000	£18,000	£10,000
18/80 Mk I/Mk II/Mk III	2468/6	1927–33	£40,000	£28,000	£20,000
M-Type Midget	847/4	1928–32	£11,000	£9,000	£7,000
J-Type Midget	847/4	1932–34	£15,000	£12,000	£10,000
J3 Midget	847/4	1932–33	£18,000	£14,000	£12,000
PA Midget	847/4	1934–36	£13,000+	£10,000	£8,000
PB Midget	936/4	1935–36	£15,000	£10,000	£8,000
F-Type Magna	1271/6	1931–33	£22,000	£18,000	£12,000
L-Type Magna	1087/6	1933–34	£26,000	£18,000	£12,000
K1/K2 Magnette	1087/6	1932–33	£35,000	£30,000	£20,000
N-Series Magnette	1271/6	1934–36	£30,000	£28,000	£20,000
TA Midget	1292/4	1936–39	£13,000+	£12,000	£9,000
SA 2 Litre	2288/6	1936–39	£22,000+	£18,000	£15,000
VA	1548/4	1936–39	£12,000	£8,000	£5,000
TB Midget	1250/4	1939–40	£15,000	£11,000	£9,000

Value will depend on body style, history, completeness, racing history, the addition of a supercharger and originality.

1936 MG TA Midget, 1292cc 4-cylinder engine, cycle-type front wings, full weather equipment, older restoration, finished in blue, beige leather interior trim, very good condition.
£11,000–13,000 / $16,000–19,000 ↗ BRIT
Launched early in 1936, the TA Midget succeeded the overhead-camshaft P-Type. Although the newcomer's chassis was of a similar design, in fact it was wider and had a 7ft 10in (2.64m) wheelbase, while the specification included Lockheed hydraulic brakes. The engine was derived from an overhead-valve Wolseley 10 unit and displaced 1292cc. The TA offered a standard of comfort far greater than the earlier car, with considerably more room in the cockpit, and went on to spawn a great line of sports cars.

1953 MG TD II Midget, restored, converted to right-hand drive, well-maintained, very good condition throughout.
£10,000–12,000 / $14,500–17,500 ↗ Bon
The penultimate T-series Midget, the TD, appeared in 1949. A larger car than its predecessors, it owed much to the Y-Type saloon, being based on a narrowed and modified version of the latter's chassis. While the body was roomier than before, it retained the classic looks of the traditional MG sports car and the TC's well-tried 1250cc XPAG engine. The saloon parentage was far from being a handicap, for the Y-Type employed independent front suspension and rack-and-pinion steering, the TD becoming the first MG sports car to benefit from these advances.

1938 MG TA Midget, 1292cc 4-cylinder overhead-valve engine, 4-speed gearbox, subject of nut-and-bolt rebuild, finished in two-tone blue.
£18,000–21,000 / $26,000–30,000 ⊞ AVON

1948 MG Midget TC Midget, 1250cc engine, professionally restored, only 3,000 miles since, period spot lamp and horn, finished in red, new beige leather interior and matching weather equipment.
£17,000–19,000 / $25,000–27,000 ↗ H&H

1951 MG TD Midget, independent front suspension by coil springs and double wishbones, carburettor and electrics overhauled, new distributor and coil, finished in red, black interior.
£8,500–10,000 / $12,500–14,500 ↗ Bon

MG TC/TD/TF Midget (1945–55)

Engine: 1250cc, four-cylinder; 1466cc, four-cylinder for TF 1500.
Power output: 54–57bhp for 1250cc; 63bhp for 1466cc.
Maximum speed: 75–80+mph for 1250cc; 85+mph for 1466cc.
0–60mph: 19–22 seconds for 1250cc; 18+ seconds for 1500cc.
Even at the launch of the TC in September 1945, MG's Midget theme was pretty well matured, if not pushing middle-aged. The two-seater TC was a make-over of the pre-war TB, itself an update of the 1935 TA, which carried genes dating back to the original M-Type Midget of 1929. In effect, the post-war TC Midget was a brand-new vintage sports car. Yet it took off, spearheading MG's export trail across the world, and particularly to the USA. I suppose that makes the TC the first branded product in the Britain-as-Heritage-Theme-Park souvenir shop. In any case, the TC

sold in far greater numbers than any previous MG, and two-thirds of the 10,000 built went abroad, even though they were only produced in right-hand drive. In 1950, the winning formula was warmed over slightly with the TD, which had rack-and-pinion steering, a few extra bhp from the 1250cc engine and independent front suspension. The TD, the first MG available in left-hand drive form, achieved 29,664 sales, again most going abroad. The final fling was the restyled TF, which paid passing lip service to modernity with a lower bonnet line, and a raked grille and headlamps blended into the wings. In its last year, the TF received a 1500cc engine, but with falling sales – 9,600 TFs were built – the theme was played out. Looked at differently, if they'd kept making it, the T-series Midget could have become another Morgan – but then we would never have had the pretty MGA or world beating MGB.

1953 MG TD Midget, 1250cc engine, engine block relined to standard bore, crankshaft balanced, 200 miles since, new stainless-steel exhaust, new hood, finished in Old English white, beige interior, 1 owner for 32 years, slight oil leak from engine, otherwise good condition.
£7,500–9,000 / $11,000–13,000 ➤ H&H

1953 MG TF 1250 Midget, original right-hand-drive model, bodywork and mechanics restored c1994, fewer than 3,000 miles since, finished in red, beige leather upholstery.
£9,500–11,000 / $13,800–16,000 ➤ Bon

1954 MG TF Midget, original right-hand-drive model, completely restored late 1990s, engine enlarged to 1500cc and converted to unleaded fuel, wire wheels, driver's aero screen, finished in dark blue, grey interior, ex-South Africa, excellent condition throughout.
£12,000–13,500 / $17,500–19,500 ➤ H&H

1954 MG TF Midget, 1250cc 4-cylinder engine, wire wheels, good weather equipment, original right-hand-drive model, converted to unleaded fuel, finished in red, black interior, good mechanical condition.
£10,500–13,000 / $15,000–19,000 ➤ BRIT

By 1953, the TD Midget was looking decidedly archaic when compared to the recently introduced Triumph TR2 and Austin-Healey 100. At this time, export success was crucial, and a redesign of the TD was imperative if ground was not to be lost to these newcomers. The resulting TF model was hurried into production during the autumn of 1953. Its revised front-end styling had faired-in headlamps and a slanted radiator grille. The mechanical specification, however, was largely unchanged, although the XPAG-type engine now developed 57bhp at 5,500rpm. Launched in 1953, the TF was priced at £780.5s.10d/$1,100, including purchase tax, and 9,600 were built before the model yielded to the all-new MGA in late 1955.

1954 MG TF Midget, 1250cc engine, restored 1985, fewer than 14,000 miles since, full tonneau cover, side screens, valuable registration number, well maintained.
£15,000–17,000 / $22,000–25,000 ➤ COYS

1954 MG TF 1250 Midget, older restoration, mechanics overhauled 1992, finished in black, beige leather upholstery, very good condition throughout.
£12,000–14,000 / $17,500–20,500 ➤ Bon

1954 MG TF 1250 Midget, 1250cc engine, restored and converted to right-hand drive late 1980s, full weather equipment, finished in black, red interior, little use in last 6 years, paintwork in need of attention, otherwise very good condition.
£10,500–12,000 / $15,250–17,500 ➤ H&H

1937 MG VA Tickford Drophead Coupé, coachwork by Salmons, 1549cc 4-cylinder engine, 4-speed manual gearbox, matching chassis and engine numbers, 1 of only 75 examples known to exist.
£35,000–40,000 / $50,000–58,000 ➤ BJ

1938 MG VA Drophead Coupé, coachwork by Salmons, 1500cc Wolseley-based engine, Jackall jacks, restored, engine, gearbox and back axle rebuilt, fewer than 250 miles since, finished in white, new carpets and red interior trim, woodwork repolished, correct instrumentation, excellent condition.
£18,000–21,000 / $26,000–30,000 ✈ H&H

Miller's
Starter Marque

- **Starter MG:** *MGA.*
- **Body styles:** Two-seat roadster and fixed-head coupé.
  Engine: 1489, 1588 and 1622cc, four-cylinder, overhead-valve.
  Transmission: Four-speed manual.
  Power output: 72–108bhp.
  Steering: Rack-and-pinion.
  0–60mph: 13–15.5 seconds.
  Maximum speed: 95–114mph.
- With its simple, smooth lines, the MGA seems the epitome of a 1950s traditional British sports car, just the thing to complement the cravat, corduroys and sports jacket. But back in 1955, it seemed unsportingly civilised to those die-hards who thought MGs should have separate wings, running boards and fewer creature comforts than an Outward Bound course. Apart from pert looks – a little like a scaled-down Jaguar XK120 – and lively handling, the MGA had another thing going for it: it was cheaper than both the rival Austin-Healey 100 and Triumph TR3.
- The original 1955 MGA was fitted with the rugged, 1489cc, BMC B-series engine, which eventually grew to 1622cc. The MGA 1600 of 1959 also introduced front disc brakes to the standard models, but most exotic of all was the short-lived Twin Cam, which offered 114mph and all-round disc brakes to stop it. However, only 2,111 of these fast, but temperamental, machines were built.
- Of the 101,000 MGAs built between 1956 and 1962, a staggering 81,000 were exported to America. Although that makes it rare compared with the MGB, the MGA is still eminently practical and usable. Its separate-chassis structure is a simpler proposition than the monocoque MGB, and another bonus is that so many parts – notably the unburstable BMC B-series engine – were shared with other vehicles under the Morris-BMC-Nuffield banner.
- **Pick of the bunch:** For more go and whoa, and extra refinement, look for later 1600 models; the fast and fragile Twin Cam is strictly for enthusiasts whose fingers have mutated into socket sets.

1957 MGA 1500 Roadster, 1500cc 4-cylinder engine, twin carburettors, 72bhp, new gearbox, finished in green, tan interior, only 1,000 miles since 1996, very good condition throughout.
£9,500–11,000 / $14,000–16,000 ✈ H&H

1957 MGA Roadster, 1500cc 4-cylinder engine, subject of chassis-up rebuild, converted to right-hand drive, £4,500/$6,500 of receipts for parts, Waxoyled, finished in red, black interior, in need of some tidying.
£6,500–8,000 / $9,500–11,500 ✈ H&H

1957 MGA Roadster, upgraded to disc brakes, wire wheels, new hood, side screens and chromework, finished in Old English white.
£7,000–9,000 / $10,000–13,000 ✈ COYS

1959 MGA 1600 Roadster, 1588cc 4-cylinder engine, wire wheels, finished in red, black interior, good condition.
£6,500–8,000 / $9,500–11,500 ✈ BRIT
The MGA was introduced in 1955 as a successor to the TF Midget. With its curvaceous styling, the new car was particularly appealing and sold in large numbers, both at home and overseas, a large proportion of production going to the USA. The MGA was available in both roadster and fixed-head coupé versions, and remained in production until 1962, when the MGB appeared.

1959 MGA Twin Cam Coupé, 1600cc double-overhead-camshaft engine, manual gearbox with overdrive, original right-hand-drive model, subject of considerable restoration work, many original parts, finished in black, red leather interior.
£8,750–10,000 / $12,500–14,500 ✗ **Bon**
In 1958, the more powerful twin-cam MGA model was introduced, and to cope with the added performance, disc brakes were standardized, together with centre-lock disc wheels. The new car developed 108bhp and had a top speed of 113mph.

1962 MGA 1600 Mk II Coupé, fitted reconditioned 1622cc 4-cylinder engine, c17,000 miles since, in need of cosmetic attention, otherwise good condition.
£4,000–5,500 / $5,800–8,000 ✗ **BRIT**

1959 MGA Roadster, completely restored, correct original police equipment including front 'Police' sign and public-address speaker, near-concours condition.
£15,000–17,000 / $22,000–25,000 ✗ **Bon**
This MGA was one of approximately 50 supplied to the Lancashire Constabulary for traffic patrol duties. The cars were divided into white (A-class) and black (B-class) contingents and driven exclusively by female police officers. These cars' special chassis were basically to 1600 Deluxe/Twin Cam specification, but with drum rear brakes instead of discs and extended battery carriers necessitated by the extra electrical equipment (radio, public-address amplifier, etc) carried in the boot.

Cross Reference
See Colour Review (page 148–149)

◄ **1959 MGA 1600 Roadster,** original right-hand-drive model, restored 1987, chrome wire wheels, finished in white, red leather interior.
£11,250–12,500 / $16,500–18,000 ⊞ **BC**

1961 MGA Coupé, finished in red, tan interior, fewer than 3,000 miles from new and fewer than 50 miles in last 10 years, bodywork, wheels and chromework in good condition.
£9,500–11,000 / $14,000–16,000 ✗ **COYS**

1970 MG Midget, 1275cc engine, restored, finished in British racing green, black interior with tan trim, good condition.
£4,500–5,500 / $6,500–8,000 ✗ **H&H**

Miller's Starter Marque

- **Starter MG:** *Midget (1961–79).*
- **Price in 1961:** £679.
  Production: 222,526 (plus 80,363 Austin-Healey Sprite versions).
  Engine: 948, 1098, 1275 and 1493cc, four-cylinder.
  Power output: 47–65bhp.
  Transmission: Four-speed manual.
  Maximum speed: 85–100+mph.
  0–60mph: 12–20 seconds.
- When it comes to breezy budget motoring, about the only thing that matches the MG Midget is the Austin-Healey Sprite, for apart from badging, trim and instruments, they're the same thing (the earlier Mk I 'Frog-eye' Sprite, though, was only produced as an Austin-Healey.)
- The Midget is a compelling classic cocktail for the cost conscious – in fact, about the only cheaper way of enjoying fresh-air on four wheels is probably to buy a skateboard. Midgets have a massive following, and with more than 200,000 having been built up to 1979, that means there's tremendous club support, a well established and competitive spares and remanufacturing industry, and a mature network of established marque specialists and restorers.
- Better still, the 'Spridget', as the Midget/Sprite models are often called, is a BMC parts-bin special, based on the mechanics and running gear from the likes of the million-selling Morris Minor and the Austin A35. If the body's riddled with rust, you can also get a complete new shell from Rover subsidiary British Motor Heritage.
- **What to watch:** Particular points include the inner and outer sills. Be wary of poorly fitted replacement sills and check the closing action of the doors. If they bind or snag, someone may have welded in new sills without supporting the car in the middle to ensure that the floorpan maintains its correct shape. Other trouble areas are the door pillars. Shake each door firmly in this area to reveal any flexing. The engines are generally reliable and long-lasting, but check for fluid leaks. Gearboxes can be noisy, but are similarly robust, and the rear axle – similar to the Morris Minor's – rarely gives trouble.
- **Pick of the bunch:** For classic credibility, the Sprite Mk IV and Midget Mk III (1966–70) are probably the best bet, with better performance from the 1275cc engine than earlier cars. They are still chrome-era classics, however, with all the visual appeal of the older versions. If performance matters more, the 1500cc Triumph Spitfire-engined Midgets from 1974 will touch 100mph, but they have the vast black plastic covered bumpers that some people loathe.

1967 MGB GT, 1798cc 4-cylinder engine, 4-speed manual gearbox, steel disc wheels.
£3,500–4,000 / $5,000–5,800 ⊞ PMo

1974 MG Midget, 1275cc 4-cylinder engine, 4-speed manual gearbox, hardtop, in need of renovation.
£750–1,000 / $1,000–1,500 ✗ H&H

1974 MG Midget, 1275cc 4-cylinder engine, completely restored, finished in red, black interior, 48,000 miles from new, concours winner, very good condition.
£4,000–5,000 / $5,800–7,250 ✗ H&H

1963 MGB Roadster, 1798cc engine, totally rebuilt over last 3 years including engine and bodywork, 750 miles since, new fuel tank and wiring harness, finished in red, black leather interior trim, new dash and steering wheel.
£7,000–8,000 / $10,000–11,500 ✗ H&H

1967 MGB Roadster, manual gearbox with overdrive, wire wheels, new rear springs, aluminium bonnet, new sills, castle rails, inner wheel arches, front and rear valances, door skins and carpets, resprayed in light metallic blue, leather pop-up-type hood, correct Mk I black/blue-piped leather upholstery, little recent use.
£4,000–5,000 / $5,800–7,250 ✗ Bon
Enjoying an 18-year production run and worldwide sales totalling over 500,000 cars, the MGB changed little over the years, apart from a minor facelift in 1970 and the adoption of 'rubber' bumpers from 1975. The last models rolled off the production line in October 1980. The MGB had a unitary-construction bodyshell combined with the final version of the BMC B-series power unit, with a proven gearbox, rear axle and suspension, providing a robust car that offered practical motoring.

1970 MGB GT, manual gearbox with overdrive, wire wheels, fog lamps, full-length sun roof, finished in white, black interior, good condition.
£1,800–2,200 / $2,600–3,200 ⚲ CGC
Introduced in 1965, the MGB GT was a more comfortable and versatile proposition than its roadster sibling.

1970 MGB Roadster, early Heritage bodyshell, stainless-steel exhaust, wire wheels, tonneau.
£6,000–6,500 / $8,500–9,500 ⊞ UMC

1971 MGB Roadster, 1798cc 4-cylinder engine, manual gearbox with overdrive, front fog lamps, luggage rack, finished in red, black soft top, original specification, good condition throughout.
£5,000–6,000 / $7,250–8,750 ⚲ BRIT

1972 MGB Roadster, 1800cc engine, overdrive, wire wheels, factory hardtop, finished in red, fewer than 150 miles 1990–2000, 2 owners from new, well maintained.
£3,750–4,500 / $5,500–6,500 ⚲ COYS

1973 MGB GT, 1798cc engine, overdrive gearbox, recent body overhaul, invoices totalling £2,600/$3,800, finished in red, black interior, excellent condition throughout.
£2,000–2,500 / $3,000–3,600 ⚲ H&H

Miller's Starter Marque

- **Starter MG:** *MGB.*
- Original 1962 specification:
  Engine: 1798cc, four-cylinder, twin SU carburettors.
  Transmission: Four-speed manual with optional two-speed overdrive.
  Brakes: Front discs, rear drums.
  0–60mph: 12.2 seconds.
  Top speed: 105mph.
- **Price in 1962:** £834.6s.3d/$1,200, including purchase tax.
  The MGB has to be one of the most practical, affordable and enjoyable classic sporting packages around. For a start, it's the most popular British sports car ever made, a winning formula based on rugged reliability, simple clean lines, fine road manners and adequate performance. For sheer classic credentials, models before the 1974 introduction of 'rubber-bumper' cars with higher ride height are favoured, but later cars can be even more affordable. There is also a superb parts and specialist network, even down to brand-new bodyshells made using original tooling. The fixed-head MGB GT is cheaper than the open roadster, yet offers additional practicality and comfort.
- **What to watch:** Few worries with engines and mechanics, but MGBs can rot, and because of unitary construction, particular attention must be paid to sills and other structural aspects.

MG Model	ENGINE cc/cyl	DATES	CONDITION		
			1	2	3
TC Midget	1250/4	1946–49	£13,000+	£11,000	£7,000
TD Midget	1250/4	1950–52	£13,000	£9,000	£5,000
TF Midget	1250/4	1953–55	£15,000	£13,000	£8,000
TF 1500	1466/4	1954–55	£16,000	£14,000	£9,000
YA/YB	1250/4	1947–53	£5,500+	£2,750	£1,500
Magnette ZA/ZB	1489/4	1953–58	£3,500	£2,000	£500
Magnette Mk III/IV	1489/4	1958–68	£3,500	£1,200	£350
MGA 1500 Roadster	1489/4	1955–59	£11,000+	£7,000	£4,000
MGA 1500 FHC	1489/4	1956–59	£8,000	£6,000	£3,000
MGA 1600 Roadster	1588/4	1959–61	£12,000	£9,000	£4,500
MGA 1600 FHC	1588/4	1959–61	£7,000	£5,000	£3,000
MGA Twin Cam Roadster	1588/4	1958–60	£16,000	£12,000	£9,000
MGA Twin Cam FHC	1588/4	1958–60	£13,000	£9,000	£7,000
MGA 1600 Mk II Roadster	1622/4	1961–62	£12,000	£10,000	£4,000
MGA 1600 Mk II FHC	1622/4	1961–62	£9,000	£7,000	£3,000
MGB Mk I	1798/4	1962–67	£7,000	£4,000	£1,200
MGB GT Mk I	1798/4	1965–67	£5,000	£3,500	£1,000
MGB Mk II	1798/4	1967–69	£7,500	£4,000	£1,500
MGB GT Mk II	1798/4	1969	£4,500	£2,500	£850
MGB Mk III	1798/4	1969–74	£6,500	£4,000	£1,100
MGB GT Mk III	1798/4	1969–74	£4,500	£2,500	£1,000
MGB Roadster (rubber bumper)	1798/4	1975–80	£6,000	£4,500	£1,200
MGB GT	1798/4	1975–80	£5,000	£3,000	£1,000
MGB Jubilee	1798/4	1975	£5,000	£3,000	£1,200
MGB LE	1798/4	1980	£8,500	£4,750	£2,250
MGB GT LE	1798/4	1980	£6,000	£3,750	£2,000
MGC	2912/6	1967–69	£8,000+	£6,500	£4,000
MGC GT	2912/6	1967–69	£7,000	£5,000	£2,000
MGB GT V8	3528/8	1973–76	£9,000	£6,000	£3,000
Midget Mk I	948/4	1961–62	£4,000	£2,000	£850
Midget Mk II	1098/4	1962–66	£3,000	£2,000	£850
Midget Mk III	1275/4	1966–74	£3,200	£2,000	£850
Midget 1500	1491/4	1975–79	£3,000	£2,000	£850

All prices are for British right-hand-drive cars. For left-hand-drive varieties, deduct 10–15% for UK values, even if converted to right-hand drive.

1974 MGB Roadster, completely rebuilt using mainly new parts, Heritage bodyshell, new 'unleaded' engine, new brake servo, oil cooler, Kenlowe cooling fan, finished in British racing green, leather interior.
£7,500–8,500 / $11,000–12,500 ⚮ BARO

▶ **1976 MGB GT,** 1798cc engine, completely restored at a cost of £10,000/$14,500, 1,000 miles since, converted to chrome bumpers, new wheels and body panels where necessary, finished in bronze, black and orange interior, 3 owners and 58,000 miles from new, excellent condition throughout.
£2,750–3,500 / $4,000–5,000 ⚮ H&H

1975 MGB GT, 1798cc engine, overdrive gearbox, finished in dark yellow, black cloth interior, 18,000 miles in last 16 years, good condition.
£1,600–2,000 / $2,500–3,000 ⚮ CGC

MG Milestones

1923	Cecil Kimber, general manager of Morris Garages in Oxford, introduces his first special bodies on standard Morris chassis. 1928 MG Car Company formed.
1935	Lord Nuffield sells his privately held shares in MG to Morris Motors Limited.
1955	MGA roadster launched.
1961	MGA production tops 100,000.
1962	MGB roadster launched.
1967	MGB GT fixed-head coupé launched.

1968	MG, with the rest of BMC, becomes part of British Leyland.
1980	BL discontinues MG sports cars; octagon badge applied to saloons.
1992	Return of MG sports cars with MG RV8.
1995	MGF launched at Geneva show in March; first deliveries in August.
1996	MGF voted import car of the year in Japan.
1996	10,000th MGF built in July.

◄ **1976 MGB Roadster,** converted
to unleaded fuel, bills for £7,000,
finished in burgundy, black interior.
£2,200–2,800
$3,200–4,000 ⚒ BARO

1977 MGB GT, 1798cc 4-cylinder engine, manual gearbox with overdrive, finished in blue, bodywork sound, chrome trim
untarnished, Rostyle wheels in excellent condition, black vinyl seats.
£2,200–2,800 / $3,200–4,000 ⚒ CGC

1978 MGB Roadster, 1798cc 4-cylinder engine, converted
to unleaded fuel, stainless-steel exhaust system, Waxoyled
from new, unrestored, 15in Minilite-type alloy wheels, hard
and soft tops, tonneau cover, Motolita steering wheel.
£6,000–7,000 / $8,750–10,250 ⚒ BRIT

1981 MGB Limited-Edition Roadster, 1798cc 4-cylinder
engine, overdrive gearbox, completely restored 1993, only
2,000 miles since, finished in metallic bronze, black interior,
'as new' condition.
£5,750–6,250 / $8,500–9,000 ⚒ H&H

► **1981 MGB GT Limited-Edition,**
manual gearbox with overdrive,
2 owners and 46,000 miles from new,
excellent condition.
£4,000–5,000 / $5,800–7,250 ⚒ Bon
**Introduced in 1979 to celebrate
50 years of MG production at
Abingdon, the Limited-Edition
MGB models were the last built
there before the factory's closure
in October 1980. Finished in metallic
bronze (Roadster) or metallic
pewter (GT), the duo sported chin
spoilers and Triumph Stag-type
alloy wheels, wires being an option
on the Roadster. In all, 1,000 cars
were completed, the split being
480 Roadster and 520 GT.**

1968 MGB V8 Roadster, converted 1998–2001, 3528cc modified Rover SD1 engine, Vitesse big-valve cylinder heads, 9.75:1 pistons, Lucas fuel-injection, uprated lubrication system, MG RV8 stainless-steel manifolds and competition big-bore stainless-steel exhaust system, Vitesse 5-speed close-ratio gearbox, 3.07:1-ratio V8 differential, running gear uprated using MGB V8 components, 4-pot front calipers, bodywork restored using all new panels, brightwork, light units, bumpers, hood, full/half tonneaux and interior trim, c2,500 miles covered since.
£7,000–8,000 / $10,000–11,500 ✗ Bon
Unlike BL, whose MGB V8 was built only in GT form using the Range Rover power unit and MGC four-speed manual/overdrive gearbox, concept originator Ken Costello and his imitators have been free to modify B Roadsters and use the SD1's higher-powered engine together with either the five-speed manual gearbox or Borg-Warner automatic transmission.

1968 MGC GT, finished in black, chrome wire wheels, red leather interior, good condition throughout.
£2,200–2,800 / $3,200–4,000 ✗ BARO

1968 MGC GT, 3 litre 6-cylinder engine, overdrive gearbox, finished in pale yellow, paintwork and black leather interior in good condition, original.
£3,500–4,500 / $5,000–6,500 ✗ Bon

► **1971 MG 1300 Mk II,** twin-carburettors, 70bhp, hydrolastic suspension, front disc brakes, engine top end recently rebuilt, finished in grey, black interior, fewer than 33,000 miles from new, very good to excellent condition.
£2,500–3,500 / $3,600–5,000 ✗ Bon

1973 MGB GT V8, 3.5 litre V8 engine, 137bhp, subject of extensive restoration 1992, gearbox rebuilt, suspension and brakes overhauled, correct alloy road wheels, new inner and outer sills, stainless-steel over-sills, finished in Harvest gold, black interior.
£5,000–6,000 / $7,250–8,750 ✗ BARO

1973 MGB GT V8, 3.5 litre engine, 1 owner from new.
£3,250–4,250 / $4,750–6,250 ✗ COYS

1968 MGC Roadster, overdrive gearbox, restored at a cost approaching £14,000/$20,300, chrome wire wheels, Kenlowe fan, finished in blue, tonneau, luggage rack, period Blaupunkt push-button radio, excellent condition.
£11,000–13,000 / $16,000–19,000 ✗ Bon
A six-cylinder MG sports car was proposed by Abingdon in the late 1950s, and there is little doubt that the possibility of installing a six in the MGB was in the minds of the designers all along. The 2912cc MGC was introduced in 1967. It featured 15in wheels, torsion-bar front suspension and, to accommodate the new engine, two bulges in the aluminium bonnet. Power output rose from the standard B's 95bhp to 145bhp, giving 120mph and 0–60mph in ten seconds. Only 4,544 MGC Roadsters were produced.

Mini

A commuter runabout, a racing and rallying giant killer and a living legend, the Mini is all of these things. Alec Arnold Constantine Issigonis, creator of the Morris Minor and Mini, would have made a great end-of-pier gypsy clairvoyant. For this Greek-born son of an itinerant marine engineer once showed an uncannily prophetic talent when he quipped to Italian automobile couturier Sergio Farina, 'Look at your cars, they're like women's clothes – they're out of date in two years. My cars will still be in fashion after I've gone.' Sir Alec Issigonis died in 1988, yet the Mini is still here, just. The revolutionary, front-wheel-drive Mini, with its east-west engine layout and brilliant compact packaging, was launched in 1959. Offered originally as an Austin 7 Mini or Morris Mini Minor, this pocket-sized wonder car achieved its own identity by 1970, becoming simply the Mini. The Austin Metro of 1980 was supposed to replace it, but wasn't up to the task. The Mini was so right at its launch that it's actually benefited from being left pretty much alone. Five-million-plus customers can't be wrong. It really is going to be a hard act to follow. Now, of course, the new Mini's here, but only time will tell if BMW's 'lifestyle' Mini will charm the world as much as the original.

1962 Mini, 848cc 4-cylinder engine, front-wheel drive, sliding door windows.
£2,250–2,500 / $3,300–3,600 ⊞ PMo

1965 Mini Cooper S Mk I, restored, twin tanks, finished in Almond green and Old English white, original green/brocade interior, correct and matching numbers.
£8,000–9,000 / $11,500–13,000 ⊞ WbC

1967 Morris Mini Cooper, 998cc engine, manual gearbox, finished in red with black roof, red and grey/gold vinyl seats, clear plastic seat covers, seatbelts, excellent original red carpets, fewer than 47,500 miles from new, very good original condition.
£4,000–5,000 / $5,800–7,250 ⚒ CGC

1964 Morris Mini Cooper Mk I, 998cc 4-cylinder engine, subject of full body and mechanical rebuild, finished in British racing green, white roof, Minilite-type wheels, very good mechanical condition.
£3,500–4,000 / $5,000–5,800 ⚒ BRIT

1967 Austin Mini Cooper, 998cc engine, restored, converted to unleaded fuel, carburettor overhauled, brakes rebuilt, 3 owners from new, good to very good condition.
£3,500–4,500 / $5,000–6,500 ⚒ Bon
The brainchild of racing car manufacturer John Cooper, the Mini Cooper was launched in September 1961. Enlarged to 997cc and suitably tweaked, the revised A-series engine easily met its 55bhp target, the extra power endowing the Mini Cooper with an 85+mph top speed. To cope with the increased performance, Lockheed developed special 7in-diameter disc brakes for the front wheels. The new car soon established its credentials as a rally and race winner, and the stage was set for even faster versions.

> What did John Cooper get from the original Mini Cooper? A £2/$3 royalty for each example built. But he didn't complain. He recalled, 'Harriman [then BMC chairman, George Harriman] said we had to make 1,000 – but we eventually made 150,000.' That translates into £300,000/$435,000 commission.

1968 Morris Mini, 1275cc engine, 4-speed gearbox, converted to resemble Cooper S, Minilite-type wheels, finished in white with black roof, black and blue interior, very good condition throughout.
£1,500–2,000 / $2,200–3,000 ⚒ H&H

1969 Mini Cooper S Mk II, 1275cc steel-crank engine, Hardy-Spicer driveshafts, servo-assisted brakes, twin tanks, finished in red with white roof, black interior trim, factory reclining seats, period radio, correct and matching numbers.
£7,000–8,000 / $10,200–11,500 ⊞ WbC

1969 Morris Mini Cooper S, 1275cc 4-cylinder engine completely rebuilt, only 500 miles since, Minilite-type wheels, bodywork restored, finished in dark blue with white roof, new black interior, 50,000 miles from new.
£4,500–5,500 / $6,500–8,000 ⚒ H&H

◄ **1967 Austin Mini Cooper S,** 1275cc 4-cylinder engine, close-ratio gearbox, 7in Lockheed front disc brakes, brake servo, completely restored early 1990s, little use since, finished in blue with white roof, black interior, competition-type seats.
£6,000–7,000 / $8,700–10,200 ⚒ BRIT

1968 Morris Mini Cooper Mk II, completely restored 1998, fewer than 1,000 miles since, mechanically refurbished with all worn parts renewed, bare-metal respray in white with black roof, interior retrimmed in black vinyl, matching numbers, excellent condition.
£5,500–6,500 / $8,000–9,500 ⚒ CGC

Miller's Starter Marque

- **Starter Minis:** *All models.*
- Whether yours is a 1959 car with sliding windows, cord door pulls and external hinges, or a 1995 model, all Minis are classics. Even though modern Minis are still closely related to the 1959 original, the early cars have an extra, subtle charm. Parts are rarely a problem, but the Mini's major enemy is rust, so here are a few guides to buying a sound older example.
- Before looking underneath, inspect the roof panel, guttering and pillars supporting the roof. If they are rusted or show signs of filler, it suggests that the rest of the structure may be in similar or worse shape.
- Examine floorpans from above and below, joints with the inner sill, front and rear bulkheads, cross-member and jacking points. If the subframe has welded plates, check that they've been attached properly. Look inside the parcel compartment on each side of the rear seat, beneath the rear seat, and in all corners of the boot, spare-wheel well and battery container. These are all common rust spots.
- Clicking from beneath the front of the car indicates wear in the driveshaft constant-velocity joints – not easy or cheap to rectify.
- Rear radius-arm support bearings deteriorate rapidly unless lubricated regularly; check the greasing points ahead of each rear wheel for signs of recent attention.
- The A-series engine is generally reliable and long-lived. However, expect timing-chain rattle on older units; exhaust-valve burning can be evident on high-mileage examples, as can exhaust smoke under hard acceleration, indicating cylinder/piston wear.
- Mini Coopers can be worth more than double the price of an ordinary classic Mini. Consequently, fakes abound. It's not just a question of checking the uprated specification – twin carbs, disc brakes, badges and the like – but also of unravelling engine and chassis numbers, and subtle tell-tale signs that you'll only learn about from club and professional experts. First join the club, then go shopping.

1969 Morris Mini Cooper S Mk II, 1275cc engine, completely restored 1980–82, engine overhauled, period factory replacement bodyshell, finished in red with white roof, black vinyl interior in very good condition, 10,000 miles in last 20 years, good condition.
£5,000–6,000 / $7,250–8,750 ⚲ CGC

1971 Mini Cooper S Mk III, 1275cc 4-cylinder engine, 4-speed manual gearbox, good condition.
£6,500–7,500 / $9,500–10,875 🚘 MINI

1971 Mini Cooper S, 1275cc engine, original car bodyshell, engine and twin fuel tanks, subject of some restoration, finished in blue-green with white roof, black interior, 3 owners and fewer than 66,500 miles from new.
£6,000–7,000 / $8,700–10,200 ⚲ H&H

1975 Innocenti Mini Cooper 1300, 1275cc 4-cylinder engine, older restoration, professionally converted to right-hand drive, front disc brakes, brake servo, correct pressed-steel wheels, Cooper exhaust system, finished in green with white roof, black interior trim, genuine Innocenti instrumentation, good mechanical condition.
£3,500–4,500/ $5,000–6,500 ⚲ BRIT
During 1972, Innocenti became part of the British Leyland Group, and a number of attractive Mini-based variants became available, the most popular of which were the Mini Cooper versions, especially the 1300. The specification of these models was more upmarket and comprehensive. From 1976, British Leyland ceased control, and Innocenti was taken over by De Tomaso. By the beginning of the 1980s, a Bertoni styled Mini was on offer. This, however, was powered by a Daihatsu engine, thus severing the British connection.

◄ **1976 Mini Clubman Estate,** finished in gold, 3 owners and 26,000 miles from new, good original condition.
£1,000–1,500 / $1,500–2,200 ⚲ BARO

► **1978 Mini Clubman,** 998cc 4-cylinder engine, finished in bronze, 13,000 miles from new, original specification throughout, excellent condition.
£1,400–1,800 / $2,000–2,600 ⚲ BRIT
The Clubman series was introduced in August 1969 to augment the Mini range, being available in saloon and estate forms. It was instantly recognisable by the longer nose with squared-off front panel, which had one enormous advantage from the mechanic's point of view – distributor access was far easier. The Clubman range remained available until 1980, by which time over 331,000 had been produced.

MINI Model	ENGINE cc/cyl	DATES	CONDITION 1	2	3
Mini	848/4	1959–67	£3,500	£1,200	-
Mini Countryman	848/4	1961–67	£2,500	£1,200	-
Cooper Mk I	997/4	1961–67	£8,000	£5,000	£2,500
Cooper Mk II	998/4	1967–69	£6,000	£4,000	£1,500
Cooper S Mk I	var/4	1963–67	£7,000	£5,000	£2,000
Cooper S Mk II	1275/4	1967–71	£6,000	£5,000	£2,000
Innocenti Mini Cooper	998/4	1966–75	£4,500	£2,000	£1,000

c1978 Mini, 850cc engine, finished in brown, beige vinyl interior, fewer than 12,000 miles from new, almost 'as new' condition.
£1,900–2,300 / $2,750–3,350 ✗ **Bon**

1980 Mini Clubman Estate, 998cc 4-cylinder engine, 3-speed automatic transmission, finished in orange, black interior, 3 owners and fewer than 18,500 miles from new, excellent condition throughout.
£2,500–3,000 / $3,600–4,400 ✗ **H&H**

◄ **1985 Mini Cooper S Re-creation,** 1380cc tuned engine, new alternator, close-ratio gearbox, finished in metallic dark blue with silver roof, interior trimmed in dark blue, Corbeau cloth reclining seats, good to excellent condition.
£3,750–4,250 / $5,500–6,000 ✗ **COYS**
Based on a 1985 Mini Mayfair, this car has been developed and improved to effectively re-create a 1964 Mini Cooper.

1989 Radford Mini De Ville, 1380cc engine, close-ratio gearbox, suspension lowered, 7 x 13in Minilite wheels, 2 additional driving lamps, all seams removed, Lamm Autohaus full body kit, electric tilt/slide flush-fitting 'moon' roof, resprayed in metallic dark blue, central door locking (including boot), alarm and immobiliser, tinted electric windows, rear window replaced by small tinted elliptical unit, magnolia Connolly hide upholstery, Wilton carpeting, burl-wood veneer trim, Clarion combination radio/cassette/CD player with 6-disc changer, 120watt amplifier, 6 colour-matched magnolia speakers, 16,500 miles from new, only 30th Anniversary Mini De Ville constructed.
£10,000–12,000 / $14,500–17,500 ✗ **Bon**

◄ **1990 ERA Mini Turbo,** Garrett T3 turbocharger, manual gearbox, lowered suspension, alloy wheels, twin spot lamps, flared wheel arches, chin spoiler, bonnet 'power bulge', tinted windows, finished in green, grey interior, only 900 miles from new, 'as new' condition.
£9,750–10,750 / $14,000–15,500 ✗ **Bon**
The name ERA dates back to 1934, when English Racing Automobiles produced its first single-seater racing car. The name later came to stand for Engineering Research and Application – a company involved with Zenith and Solex carburettors – but passed to Jack Knight in the mid-1980s, and shortly afterwards the ERA Mini Turbo was announced in 1989.

Colour Review

1920 Paige 6/66 Record Car, 5.4 litre engine, standard Paige 6/66 chassis, 131in (332.5cm) wheelbase, restored, German silver coachwork and wooden frame substantially original, in original racing condition without wings or headlamps, excellent condition.
£80,000–90,000 / $116,000–130,000 ⚙ BJ
On 23 January 1921, driven by Ralph Mulford, this car set the new Class B record for the mile in the USA at 102.83mph – making it the first standard-chassis vehicle of any kind to break 100mph at Daytona. Other Class B records were also broken that year. On the banked wooden track at Uniontown, Pennsylvania, records for distances from 5 to 100 miles were broken; the car covered over 89 miles in an hour and averaged 89.6mph for 100 miles. Then it was sold to P. R. A. Irons who, with J. H. Barney as co-driver, set off on the 1,600-mile run from Brisbane to Adelaide. Overcoming many obstacles, the car arrived in 54 hours and 28 minutes, breaking the record by more than 14 hours.

1923 Bugatti Type 13 Brescia, rebuilt from the remains of a car found in a scrapyard in France in the 1960s, chassis and both axles accepted as Molsheim originals by VSCC, black button-back upholstery.
£50,000–55,000 / $72,000–80,000 ⚙ COYS
Bugatti's Type 13 racing cars had won the 1920 Coupé des Voiturettes at Le Mans and filled the first four places in the Italian Voiturette GP at Brescia in 1921; from then on, the model was known as the Brescia. This name was also given to the long-wheelbase touring Types 22 and 23, the latter being also known as the Brescia Modifie. The cars were very popular, 2,000 being made before production ceased in 1926, and they were built under licence in Germany, Italy and Britain too.

1927 Bugatti Type 37A Grand Prix Car, 1496cc overhead-camshaft 12-valve 4-cylinder engine, supercharger, 90bhp, 4-speed manual gearbox, 4-wheel drum brakes, original firewall mounted chassis plate, original wire wheels replaced by replica large-drum detachable-rim aluminium wheels, cycle wings, full electrical equipment including Bosch magneto, starter motor, dynamo and Marchal headlights, red buttoned leather upholstery, retains all original major components including coachwork.
£200,000+ / $290,000+ ⚙ RM
The Type 37 Grand Prix Bugatti, introduced in 1925, was a 1.5 litre four-cylinder version of the contemporary 2 litre eight-cylinder Type 35, which the factory and a number of private owners had been utilising with considerable success in competition since its début in the French Grand Prix of 1924. Apart from its engine and wire wheels, the new model closely resembled its eight-cylinder stablemate, sharing the same chassis, axles, gearbox, radiator and coachwork. For the 1927 season, a supercharged version, designated Type 37A, was announced. When production ended in 1931, a total of 288 examples had been built, of which 78 were in supercharged form.

1934 MG K-Type Supercharged Magnette, original 6-cylinder car, restored and extensively modified to K3 specification, engine rebuilt around a brand-new block, new Phoenix crank and rods, new bearings throughout, correct Arnott 260 supercharger, Wilson pre-selector gearbox, accurate K3 coachwork.
£55,000–65,000 / $80,000–95,000 ⚙ COYS
In essence, the K3 was a supercharged 1087cc K2 with two-seater racing bodywork. Rugged and well equipped, its chassis was fitted with semi-elliptic front and rear springs. While a one-off K3 prototype was finishing the 1933 Monte Carlo Rally and gaining fastest time of the day on the Mont des Mules hill climb, another prototype was being tested on the route of the Mille Miglia. So serious was the Mille Miglia effort that the K3 was given new steering gear and a stronger front axle early in 1933 before the race. Three cars were entered, the race being a complete success for MG when they took home the Team Prize, the first time a non-Italian marque had done so.

1947 Maserati 4CLT Grand Prix Single Seater, 4-cylinder double-overhead-camshaft engine, twin-port exhausts, 4 valves per cylinder, two-stage supercharger, 260bhp, 4-speed manual gearbox, torque-tube transmission, independent front suspension by coil springs and lower wishbones, quarter-elliptic rear springs with hydraulic dampers, 4-wheel hydraulic drum brakes, completely restored, engine rebuilt with new crankcase and cylinder blocks.
£250,000+ / $362,000+ ⚒ C

c1966 Elfin Formula Vee Single Seater, 1200cc 4-cylinder air-cooled VW engine, 4-speed synchromesh VW gearbox, tubular-steel space frame, torsion-bar trailing-arm independent front suspension, Elfin modified swing-axle independent rear suspension, hydraulic drum brakes with tandem master cylinder, steel disc-type wheels, 1 of 21 Formula Vees built by Elfin, original and unmodified, excellent condition.
£4,000–5,000 / $5,800–7,250 ⚒ GO

▶ **1969 Spirit of America Rocket Dragster,** ex-Craig Breedlove, restored over 3 years to non-running show condition, complete with original rocket engine, 70-page album of published material and literature charting its provenance.
£90,000–120,000
$130,000–174,000 ⚒ RM
This car respresents a step in Craig Breedlove's 40-year quest for Land Speed Records, which saw him set the record five times between 1963 and 1965, culminating in the 600.601mph record run on 15 November 1965. The Spirit of America was built originally with support from American Motors, for the purpose of attacking the wheel-driven LSR with a single supercharged engine based on the AMC 390cu.in V8. AMC's financial troubles ended the project prematurely, but Breedlove retained the vehicle. In 1969, he acquired a NASA Lunar Module rocket engine and modified it for drag racing. With a burn rate of 4⅓ gallons of fuel per second, the engine produced 10,000lb (4,500kg) of thrust, sufficient to accelerate the 1,600lb (726kg) Spirit of America at about 146ft (44.5m) per second. Demonstrated throughout the USA during 1971–73, the Spirit of America consistently set strip records with trap speeds of over 300mph. In 1973, Breedlove took it to Bonneville. After several trial runs, he made a 4.2 second full-power burn, calculated to exceed 400mph. However, after successful completion of the run at 425mph, the braking parachute tore loose and the Spirit of America tumbled to a stop. Amazingly, Breedlove was uninjured, while the Spirit of America suffered little damage. In the run, the rocket dragster set an FIM motorcycle quarter-mile record at 377.754mph with an elapsed time of 4.65 seconds.

1948 Frazer Nash Le Mans Replica, 2 litre 6-cylinder Bristol engine, 3rd post-war chassis built, displayed at 1948 London Motor Show, engine, gearbox, suspension and brakes overhauled.
£175,000–195,000 / $254,000–283,000 ⚒ Bon
This car competed in the 1949 Mille Miglia and the 1951 Targa Florio.

◄ **1952 Siata 300BC Barchetta,** completely restored, Turismo Veloce (TV) block, Siata 7-port alloy head, cast alloy sump, twin Weber IMPE carburettors, 4-speed close-ratio TV synchromesh gearbox, Stanguellini alloy brakes, Borrani wire wheels, Stack electronic tachometer, new black interior.
£40,000–50,000 / $58,000–72,000 ✗ **Bon**
Siata was founded in 1926 by Giorgio Ambrosini, an amateur racing driver. The company tuned cars, mainly Fiats, and sold performance equipment. After WWII, Siata began making its own engines and gearboxes, and its range even included a V8. Apart from Italy, the company's largest market was the USA, where the Barchetta was sold as the Spyder. Around forty were built, ten with Siata's own version of the Fiat 1100 engine. This was fitted with twin Weber 32IMPE carburettors and a seven-port aluminium cylinder head, and was enlarged to 1221cc. It produced 60bhp and, teamed with a close-ratio four-speed gearbox, gave a top speed of about 100mph.

► **1955 Ferrari Tipo 750 Monza,** coachwork by Scaglietti, chassis no. 0518M, 3 litre 275 GTB-based V12 engine, restored, largely original.
£350,000+ / $507,000+ ✗ **Bon**

◄ **1955 Jaguar D-Type,** 3.8 litre wide-angle engine completely rebuilt 1992, triple 45DCOE3 Webers, dry-sump lubrication, original chassis, 4-spoke steering wheel, very good condition throughout.
£375,000+ / $545,000 ✗ **COYS**
The chassis of this car, the second 'long-nose' D-Type built, was driven by Mike Hawthorn in 1955 at Le Mans, where he gained victory following the withdrawal of the Mercedes team after the infamous accident in which over 80 spectators were killed. Following subsequent competition and testing use, the car is thought to have been employed as a source of parts to repair other D-Types. The chassis was fitted to another car and only came to light when that car was being restored. It was removed and the car's original chassis refitted. This car's chassis was then fitted with a reskinned original D-Type monocoque.

1956 Ferrari 410 Sport, 4962cc overhead-camshaft V12 engine, 46DCF Weber carburettors, 380bhp, 5-speed manual transaxle, independent front suspension, De Dion rear suspension, 4-wheel drum brakes, belly pans, completely original.
£2.5 million+ / $3.6 million+ ✗ **RM**
Ferrari created the 410 Sport to dominate the 1955 Carrera PanAmericana. It was among the most powerful of sports racing cars built in the 1950s, with a 4.9 litre engine of nearly 400bhp, and was virtually unbeatable. Ferrari created a total of four cars in this series. The first two were less powerful customer cars called 410 Speciales, while Ferrari retained the two more powerful 410 Sports as factory team cars. However, following the loss of life and crowd-control problems in the 1954 Carrera, not to mention the 1955 Le Mans tragedy, the 1955 Carrera PanAmericana was cancelled. Next, Ferrari entered the 410 Sports in the 1956 1000km of Buenos Aires. Driven by Peter Collins/Luigi Musso and Juan Manuel Fangio/Eugenio Castlotti, they were split on the front row by the Phil Hill/Olivier Gendebien Ferrari 857S. Ferrari's two behemoths thundered off, with Peter Collins eventually setting the fastest race lap of 102.5mph in this car before both 410 Sports retired with transaxle failures. It was the cars' first and last race for the factory, as Ferrari so them to raise capital.

1957 Porsche 550A Spyder Sports-Racing Two-Seater, rear mounted 4-overhead-camshaft flat-4 air-cooled engine, Weber carburettors, twin trailing-arm/torsion bar independent front suspension, rear swing-axle/torsion-bar suspension controlled by trailing arms, drum brakes, welded-tube space-frame, all-aluminium factory bodywork, race prepared, safety fuel cell concealed in original tank, removable headrest, new uprated oil lines.
£300,000+ / $435,000+ ⚒ **Bon**

1968 McLaren M6B Can Am Car, 355cu.in Chevrolet V8 engine, fuel injection, magneto ignition, Hewland 5-speed gearbox, front suspension by upper and lower A-arms with coil-spring/shock-absorber units, rear suspension by lower A-arms, top links, radius arms and coil-spring/shock-absorber units, riveted and bonded aluminium monocoque chassis, restored to correct historic racing configuration.
£80,000–90,000 / $116,000–130,000 ⚒ **RM**
The M6B was the customer version of McLaren's all-conquering works car of 1967, the M6A. Of standard Can Am formula design, it featured a riveted and bonded sheet-aluminium moncoque chassis with all-round independent suspension and the ubiquitous Chevrolet smallblock V8 engine. This featured Lucas/McKay fuel injection and drove the rear wheels through a Hewland transaxle. Steering was by rack-and-pinion, and the whole was clothed in open two-seat glassfibre bodywork.

1953 Jaguar XK120 Competition Road/Racer, completely rebuilt at a cost of over £70,000/$101,500, 4.2 litre engine, 300bhp, Getrag 5-speed gearbox, XK150 rear axle with limited-slip differential, uprated halfshafts and alloy differential cooling plates, XK150 rear leaf springs, panhard bar and adjustable anti-tramp bars, adjustable alloy dampers with polyurethane bushes, nickel plated and polished front suspension with polyurethane bushes and anti-roll bar, alloy 4-piston front brake calipers, XJS rear calipers, alloy XK140 radiator, D-Type alloy wheels, works-specification bonnet louvres, double-buckle leather bonnet straps, extra air ducts to engine bay, dark blue Connolly leather interior, racing seats and harnesses, break-away steering column.
£35,000–40,000 / $50,000–58,000 ⚒ **COYS**

◄ **1961 Ferrari 250 GT SWB Competition Berlinetta,** chassis no. 2443GT, engine no. 2443GT, Weber 40DCL6 carburettors, Montlhery-type exhaust system with Snap racing extractors, major body panels in steel, opening panels in aluminium, outside competition-type fuel filler cap, 130 litre racing tank.
£675,000+ / $980,000+ ⚒ **Bon**

1963 Chevrolet Corvette Sting Ray, blueprinted 327cu.in V8 engine, factory fuel injection, 375bhp, close-ratio 4-speed manual gearbox, independent coil-spring front suspension with anti-roll bar and telescopic shock absorbers, independent rear suspension with single transverse leaf spring, lateral struts, trailing arms and telescopic shock absorbers, limited-slip differential, 4-wheel disc brakes, aluminium wheels, roll cage, many spares including extra rear-end centre-sections and 2 sets of wheels.
£30,000–35,000 / $43,000–50,000 ⚒ **RM**

1964 Sunbeam Tiger Le Mans Coupé, small-block Ford overhead-valve V8 engine, Weber downdraft carburettors, c350bhp, 4-speed Borg Warner T-10 gearbox, independent front suspension by A-arms and heavy-duty springs, anti-roll bar, rigid rear Salisbury axle with limited-slip differential, leaf-spring rear suspension with trailing arms and Watts link, 4-wheel Girling disc brakes, completely restored, many spares including original Le Mans fuel tanks, Dunlop magnesium wheels and 2 carburettor intake manifolds.
£100,000–125,000 / $145,000–180,000 ⚒ RM
This car was one of two works entries for the 1964 Le Mans 24-hour race.

1966 Austin-Healey 3000 Mk III Works-Type Rally Car, fully balanced engine, triple Weber carburettors, large-capacity fuel tank with twin pumps, Aeroquip hoses throughout, all correct works modifications including aluminium bonnet with carburettor vent, hardtop with ventilation flap, aluminium big-tank boot lid, twin side mounted exhaust system, period Minilite wheels, twin Cibié spot lamps, high-back black Connolly leather rally seats, Luke harnesses, period Halda twin tripometers and Speed pilot, 2 fire extinguishers, very good condition throughout.
£32,000–35,000 / $46,000–50,000 ⚒ COYS

1982 Lancia 037 Works Group B Rally Car, rebuilt and fully prepared to Group B rally specification, 2122cc Evo II engine, supercharger, ZF transaxle, chassis, suspension and brakes rebuilt 1993, excellent condition.
£50,000–55,000 / $75,000–80,000 ⚒ Bon
During 1982–83, Lancia, in conjunction with Pininfarina and Abarth, built approximately 220 examples of the Lancia Rally (better known by its Abarth in-house code number, '037'), Group B regulations requiring a minimum of 200 cars for homologation. The factory took cars from the inventory as required for conversion to Group B specification. Subsequently, Evolution models were developed throughout 1983–85. Markku Alen drove this particular car in the 1982 Tour de Corse, in which he finished ninth overall, and again in the Acropolis Rally that same year.

1990 Chevrolet Lumina NASCAR Stock Car, 354cu.in overhead-valve V8 engine, 4-speed manual gearbox, 4-wheel disc brakes, Banjo Matthews chassis, running display condition.
£21,000–24,000 / $30,000–35,000 ⚒ RM
NASCAR stock cars are generic machines. Most teams buy standard tubular space-frame chassis from one of two vendors, and there are usually only two or three engine choices. Many important engine details are strictly regulated. Even bodies are strictly defined for conformity with rigid specifications, being subjected to frequent wind-tunnel tests to control drag coefficient, frontal area and even the aerodynamic effect upon leading and following cars.

Bob Freeman, Ferrari Dino 245 engine, an original painting depicting the famous Grand Prix racing engine, pencil and watercolour, hand-annotated and signed by the artist, commissioned illustration for *Supercar Classics* magazine, 1980s, mounted, framed and glazed, 14 x 18in (35.5 x 45.5cm).
£1,400–1,800 / $2,000–2,600 ⚹ C

◄ **Michael Wright, 1953 Carrera PanAmericana,** depicting Richie Ginther and Phil Hill at speed in the Ferrari 340 Mexico, mixed media, signed, framed and glazed, 15 x 11in (38 x 28cm).
£600–750
$870–1,100 ⚹ Bon

► **Gay Dutton, Lex Davison receiving the trophy for winning the 1961 Australian Grand Prix,** acrylic on canvas, signed by the artist, dated '91', 72 x 48½in (183 x 123cm).
£300–350
$440–500 ⚹ GO

► **Walter Gotschke, Belgian Grand Prix, Spa, 1958,** depicting Tony Brooks driving his Vanwall and leading 2nd-place Mike Hawthorn in his Ferrari, watercolour, signed by the artist, unframed, 8½ x 12in (21.5 x 30.5cm).
£3,000–4,000 / $4,400–5,800 ⚹ Bon

Gay Dutton, Stan Jones driving his Maserati 250F on the way to winning the 1959 Australian Grand Prix, acrylic on canvas, signed by the artist, dated '91', 72 x 48in (183 x 122cm).
£175–250 / $250–360 ⚹ GO

Pat Nevin, Mille Miglia 1933, depicting the MG K3 of Eyston and Lurani racing through crowded streets, oil on board, signed, titled, mounted, framed and glazed, 30 x 27in (76 x 68.5cm).
£700–800 / $1,000–1,150 ⚹ Bon

Nicholas A. Watts, Moss and Fangio in their Mercedes W196s at the 1955 British Grand Prix, mixed media, signed and dated, mounted, framed and glazed, 27 x 35in (68.5 x 89cm).
£1,400–1,600 / $2,000–2,300 ⚹ Bon

Miller's is a price GUIDE not a price LIST

Brian Hatton, a cut-away depiction of a BRM Formula 1 racing car, pen and ink with colour highlights on art paper, applied label 'BRM F1 racing car Brian Hatton FSIAD for Motor 1971', slight soiling to surface, signed, framed with Perspex shield, 14 x 24in (35.5 x 61cm).
£220–280 / $320–400 ⚹ Bon

Nick Blake, Formula 1 driver caricatures, a set of 4 limited-edition prints of watercolour caricatures of Formula 1 drivers from the 1997 season, depicting Michael Schumacher in Ferrari overalls, David Coulthard in Marlboro McLaren overalls, Jean Alesi in Benetton overalls and Damon Hill in Rothmans Williams overalls, each signed and numbered 78/500 by the artist, mounted, framed and glazed, 12 x 9in (30.5 x 23cm).
£75–100 / $110–145 ⚘ **BRIT**

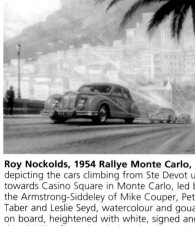

Roy Nockolds, 1954 Rallye Monte Carlo, depicting the cars climbing from Ste Devot up towards Casino Square in Monte Carlo, led by the Armstrong-Siddeley of Mike Couper, Peter Taber and Leslie Seyd, watercolour and gouache on board, heightened with white, signed and dated 1954, framed and glazed, 19¾ x 23¾in (50 x 60.5cm).
£600–700 / $870–1,000 ⚘ **Bon**
The Armstrong-Siddeley 346 Sapphire was a private entry in the 1954 Rallye Monte Carlo, and was driven by Mike Couper, with Peter Taber and Leslie Seyd as co-drivers, to 82nd place overall. It won the prize for the 'Best Equipped Car for Road Safety and Comfort'. The car was fitted with innovative revolving snow wipers on the headlights, rear wheel sand boxes and had stalk-mounted foglights, which could be extended up to 30in in front of the car. The well appointed interior featured a fold-flat passenger seat/bed, and facilities to provide hot drinks and soup en route.

Michael Wright, 1932 Alpine Trial, depicting H. J. Aldington and T. D. Ross in their Frazer Nash TT Replica, on their way to winning the Coupe des Glaciers, watercolour on paper, signed, mounted, framed and glazed, 18½ x 14½in (47 x 37cm).
£600–800
$870–1,150 ⚘ **Bon**

Brian Hatton, a cut-away depiction of a 1927 Fiat Type 406, commissioned for *The Motor*, pen and ink with coloured wash on board, board flaking with tears to margins and some loss, signed, June 1970, 22 x 25½in (56 x 65cm).
£250–300 / $360–440 ⚘ **Bon**

ADAC 1000km Rennen 1965, an advertising poster depicting a 275/330P Ferrari being followed by a Ford GT40, slight fold marks, 33 x 23¼in (84 x 59cm).
£150–200
$220–300 ⚘ **Bon**

RAC British Grand Prix, Aintree, 1955, an original advertising poster, slight fold marks and staining, 29¼ x 19¼in (74 x 49cm).
£125–150
$180–220 ⚘ **Bon**

Armin Beiber, Grosser Preis der Schweiz, 1938, an original advertising poster printed by Kummerly & Frey, Bern, good condition, framed, mounted and glazed, 36¼ x 28in (92 x 71cm).
£1,500–2,000
$2,200–3,000 ⚘ **Bon**

Hans Thoni, Grosser Preis der Schweiz, 1936, an original advertising poster printed by Polygraphische Gesellschaft Laupen, Bern, minimal wear, 39½ x 27½in (100.5 x 70cm).
£1,500–2,000
$2,200–3,000 ⚘ **Bon**

▶ **A limited-edition model of a 1989 Aston Martin AMR1 Le Mans car,** as driven by Redman, Los and Roe, made by taking a cast from the original wind-tunnel model, finished with correct sponsors' logos, mounted on a grey-painted base, believed to be 1 of 5 made, 48in (122cm) long.
£1,300–1,500
$2,000–2,200 ⚘ **Bon**

A bronze sculpture of a Mercedes-Benz Rennwagen Grand Prix car, commemorating the Mercedes-Benz factory from 1934 to 1937, made at the factory in Stuttgart as a gift from Dr Kissel to Geheimrat von Opel, c1937, 13in (33cm) long, mounted on a wooden base.
£2,500–3,000 / $3,600–4,400 ⋏ Bon

A Napier-Campbell Arrol-Aster Bluebird wind-tunnel model, carved wood of sectional construction, turned wooden wheels, front fairing attached by wooden dowels, body finished with a skim of gouache and hand-painted, underside fitted with 2 adjusting bolts, paintwork dull, minor chips and damage, offside fairing missing, 2 front wheels loose in their sockets, c1928, 26¾in (68cm) long.
£4,750–5,750 / $7,000–8,400 ⋏ Bon
The name 'Bluebird' was first adopted by Malcolm Campbell in 1912 for his six-year-old Darracq which he was racing at Brooklands. After WWI Captain Campbell applied the name – and his distinctive shade of blue racing livery – to his series of Land Speed Record contenders, and subsequently to his Water Speed Record boats. His Napier-Campbell Bluebird was built in 1926–27 with 24 litre 'broad-arrow' 12-cylinder Napier Lion aero engine developing some 500hp. In this car Campbell set a new LSR of 174.88mph at Pendine Sands in February 1927. From 1928 the car was then redeveloped with a 950bhp Napier engine and new body – developed in part through wind-tunnel testing featuring wheel fairings and a prominent tailfin.

Renzo Jarno Vandi, a 1/5-scale bronze sculpture representing 1964 F1 World Champion John Surtees at the wheel of his Ferrari 158, 29½in (75cm) long, over 20kg.
£11,000–13,000 / $16,000–19,000 ⋏ C
The Italian sculptor Vaudi spent over two years and 2,000 work hours producing this piece.

A hand-painted plaque, moulded in relief, celebrating the 1939 Le Mans 24-hour event, 42in (106.5cm) diam.
£800–900 / $1,150–1,300 ⋏ Bon

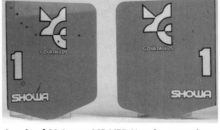

A pair of McLaren MP4/5B Honda rear-wing end plates, from Ayrton Senna's car, 1990.
£1,800–2,200 / $2,600–3,200 ⋏ Bon

▶ **A Formula 1 race helmet, suit, gloves and boots,** worn by Michael Schumacher, driver's name on suit belt.
£10,000–12,000 / $14,500–17,500 ⋏ BJ

◀ **A Stand 21 Leconte race suit,** worn by Didier Pironi during his 1978 season with the Candy Tyrrell team.
£1,300–1,600 / $2,000–2,300 ⋏ Bon

An original Jebs Formula 1 helmet, worn by Michele Alboreto during the 1986 Monaco Grand Prix, signed with dedication 'A Thomas – con amicale – M Alborato'.
£2,200–2,600 / $3,200–3,800 ⋏ C

▶ **A Bell Formula 1 helmet,** worn by Martin Brundle during the Aida and Suzuka Grands Prix while driving for McLaren, and for his last race with them at Adelaide, with radio system and clear visor with tear-off, painted by P. Vangin for Bell, 1994.
£1,700–2,000 / $2,450–3,000 ⋏ Bon

A Bell Indy helmet, worn by double World Champion Emerson Fittipaldi during the 1992 season with Penske, painted by Cleber, signed by the driver on the visor.
£1,400–1,800 / $2,000–2,600 ⋏ Bon

Moretti

1955 Moretti 750 Gran Sport, 750cc race tuned double-overhead-camshaft engine, completely restored, later 5-main-bearing engine block, new crankshaft, new Cosworth conrods, twin sidedraught Weber carburettors, later Moretti remote gear-change, finished in 2-tone blue, bucket seats retrimmed in period corduroy.
£70,000–80,000 / $101,000–116,000 ✗ COYS
Moretti made small and stylish sports cars between 1926 and 1960. Unlike many small Italian manufacturers – such as Siata, Cisitalia, Abarth and Nardi – Moretti built the entire car, relying far less on the use of Fiat components than the opposition. After WWII, the company developed a compact 350cc twin-cylinder car called La Cita. This was followed by a two-door saloon, which featured an all-new overhead-cam four-cylinder engine. Initially of 600cc capacity, it was soon enlarged to 750cc. By 1951, Moretti had developed a twin-cam version, which, with twin Webers, was estimated to produce 60bhp. This was used as the power unit for a run of Gran Sport Coupés, which were graced with bodywork by such styling houses as Vignale, Zagato and Michelotti. Based on a multi-tube frame, these machines had rigid rear axles located by a panhard rod and quarter-elliptic leaf springs, which also acted as trailing arms. At the front, quarter-elliptic leaf springs served as top and bottom wishbones. Clothed in aluminium, the cars weighed around 1,000lb (454kg) and found favour in the USA.

Morgan

If ever a car manufacturer was an anachronism, this is it, for to this day Morgan's cars are defiantly traditional, post-vintage in appearance and built with little concession to modern production-line practices – and that includes the new Aero 8, whose muscular high-tech body conceals a traditional ash frame made in time-honoured Morgan fashion. Indeed, although the Aero 8 is something of a leap forward, in the main, Morgan has stuck to what it knows best, gently refining and improving a car that displays a direct lineage back to the company's first four-wheeler of 1935. The one exception appeared during the 1960s, when Morgan made a stab at passing modernity with the glassfibre-bodied Plus Four Plus closed coupé, of which only 26 were produced. As for the classic four-wheelers, some consider later Morgans with Rover V8 powered, 125mph performance a little 'less classic' than older models, but the company still has trouble keeping abreast of demand from those who crave high-speed instant nostalgia. As for the vintage-era three-wheeled Morgans, these were produced from 1910 and soldiered on until 1952. They still enjoy a tremendously enthusiastic following, particularly in historic club racing, and their quaint charm has inspired a number of modern lookalikes.

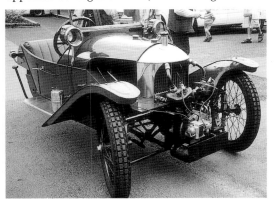

Restored values

The cost of a professional restoration will have an influence on, but no direct relation to, a car's market value. A restored car can have a market value lower than the cost of its restoration.

◀ **1925 Morgan Grand Prix,** 998cc water-cooled JAP V-twin engine, restored, engine rebuilt, finished in green, new green interior trim.
£9,500–11,000 / $14,000–16,000 ✗ H&H
Morgan's Grand Prix was given its name to commemorate W. G. McMinnies' win of the cyclecar Grand Prix at Amiens in 1913.

MORGAN Model	ENGINE cc/cyl	DATES	CONDITION		
			1	2	3
4/4 Series I	1098/4	1936–50	£10,000+	£6,000	£5,000
Plus 4	2088/4	1950–53	£15,000	£10,000	£7,000
Plus 4	1991/4	1954–68	£14,000	£11,000	£7,000
4/4 Series II/III/IV	997/4	1954–68	£10,000+	£7,000	£5,000
4/4 1600	1599/4	1960 on	£14,000+	£9,000	£6,000
Plus 8	3528/8	1969 on	£17,000+	£13,500	£10,000

c1938 Morgan 4/4 Series I Two-Seater, Coventry Climax engine, 2 rear-mounted spares, finished in red, black interior, good condition.
£12,000–14,000 / $17,500–20,500 ⊞ FHD

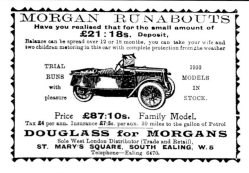

◀ **1934 Morgan Super Sports,** 1224cc JAP engine, older restoration, engine rebuilt 1995, fitted early SU carburettors, original rebuilt Amal carburettors included, factory dropped front suspension, last used 1995, stored since, in need of recommissioning.
£25,000–30,000 / $36,000–43,000 ⚒ Bon

1949 Morgan F-Super, 1172cc 4-cylinder sidevalve engine, Aquaplane twin-carburettor manifold, swinging-arm rear suspension, 2 rear-mounted spares, finished in British racing green, staggered seating to accommodate taller driver, black leather upholstery, very good overall condition.
£11,000–13,000 / $16,000–19,000 ⚒ CGC
The first production Morgan three-wheeler was shown at the Motor Cycle Show of 1911, and 40 years later the last variation on the theme left the Malvern Wells factory. Many engines were used in the three-wheelers, but all fell into one of three categories: air-cooled twins, water-cooled twins and water-cooled fours. The F-Super was the ultimate development of the three-wheeler.

1983 Morgan 4/4 Two-Seater, 4-cylinder Ford XR3 engine, finished in red, silver wire wheels, black weather equipment and tonneau, black leather seats, 2 owners and 42,500 miles from new, always garaged.
£9,500–11,000 / $14,000–16,000 ⚒ CGC

1985 Morgan 4/4 Two-Seater, 2 litre double-overhead-camshaft carburetted Fiat engine, chrome wire wheels, 1 of only 26 made, good condition.
£10,000–11,000 / $14,500–16,000 ⊞ FHD

Morris

Morris may be no more – the name disappeared from the Austin-Rover inventory in 1984 – but for 70 years, the marque founded by William Morris in 1913 stood out as a byword for stout middle-class motoring. The firm's early reputation was built on the sturdy and reliable 'bullnose' Morris Oxford and Cowley models. In fact, in 1924 Morris was Britain's number-one car manufacturer, ahead of Ford, and in 1929 Morris produced 51 per cent of all new cars built in Britain that year. Through the 1930s, Morris' market share dwindled, and in 1952 William Morris, by then Viscount Nuffield, agreed to merge with Austin to form the British Motor Corporation. Thereafter, the Morris marque struggled for prominence, but one car that was conceived before the merger, the miraculous Morris Minor, went on to become Britain's first million-selling car. In the 1960s and 1970s, other Morris offerings were little more than alternately badged Austins.

1925 Morris Cowley Two-Seater with Dickey, rebuilt 1990–99, converted to unleaded fuel, finished in grey with black wings and correct black-painted accessories, good hood and weather equipment, reupholstered in green leatherette, excellent condition.
£8,000–9,000 / $11,500–13,000 ⚒ Bon
When William Morris launched his Morris Oxford Light Car in 1913, he could have had little idea of the impact that his famous 'bullnose' cars would have on bringing motoring to the masses in the UK. Initially, Morris employed White & Poppe engines, but later he adopted the Continental engine and subsequently the Hotchkiss, a sturdy unit that powered the Cowley and Oxford models, as well as being the basis for the first MGs and Morris Commercials. The 11.9hp Cowley sold in greatest numbers and was offered in various guises, including a four-seat tourer, doctor's coupé, commercial traveller's car and the hugely popular two-seater with dickey.

◄ **1923 Morris Cowley Bullnose Two-Seater Tourer,** 1548cc engine, originally used as a tractor, rebodied as a tourer, finished in grey, grey interior, good condition.
£8,000–9,000 / $11,500–13,000 ⚒ H&H

1924 Morris Cowley Bullnose Two-Seater Tourer, 11.9hp engine, finished in maroon, original side screens, green interior, stored 17 years, good original condition.
£5,500–6,500 / $8,000–9,500 ⚒ H&H

1926 Morris Cowley Bullnose Four-Seater Tourer, 1479cc engine, front brakes, Barker dipping headlights, finished in maroon and black, new hood and upholstery, otherwise original.
£8,500–10,000 / $12,500–14,500 ⚒ H&H

MORRIS Model	ENGINE cc/cyl	DATES	CONDITION		
			1	2	3
Prices given are for saloons					
Cowley (Bullnose)	1550/4	1913–26	£12,000	£8,000	£6,000
Cowley	1550/4	1927–39	£10,000	£6,000	£4,000
Oxford (Bullnose)	1803/4	1924–27	£14,000	£10,000	£6,000
Oxford	1803/4	1927–33	£10,000	£8,000	£6,000
16/40	2513/4	1928–33	£8,000	£7,000	£6,000
18	2468/6	1928–35	£9,000	£7,000	£5,000
8 Minor	847/4	1929–34	£5,500	£4,000	£2,000
10/4	1292/4	1933–35	£5,000	£3,000	£1,500
25	3485/6	1933–39	£10,000	£8,000	£5,000
Eight	918/4	1935–39	£4,000	£3,000	£1,500
10HP	1140/4	1939–47	£4,500	£3,000	£1,500
16HP	2062/6	1936–38	£5,000	£3,500	£2,000
18HP	2288/6	1935–37	£5,000	£3,500	£2,500
21HP	2916/6	1935–36	£6,000	£4,000	£2,500

A tourer version of the above is worth approximately 30% more. Value is very dependent on body type and is greater if coachbuilt.

1927 Morris Oxford 13.9hp Two-Seater Tourer with Dickey, 1802cc sidevalve 4-cylinder engine, leaf-sprung chassis, Barker dipping headlights, restored late 1980s, mechanics overhauled, engine refurbished, dynastart and magneto recently rebuilt, finished in maroon with black wings, chocolate brown interior, recalibrated speedometer and clock, very good condition.
£8,500–10,000 / $12,500–14,500 ✗ CGC
The Morris Oxford Tourer proved to be an exceptionally reliable and endearing workhorse, so much so that even after eight years and 70,000 miles (no mean feat given the road network of the time), this car's original owner refused to replace it. Instead, he had it returned to the Morris works, where it was completely remanufactured. Invoices for all the work done, including the chrome plating of the radiator shell, have survived to this day.

1936 Morris Eight Four-Seater Tourer, 918cc 4-cylinder engine, finished in green with black wings, black leatherette interior trim, unused for several years, mechanics and weather equipment in good condition, in need of recommissioning.
£4,500–5,500 / $6,500–8,000 ✗ BRIT
The introduction of the Morris Eight in September 1934 quickly put Morris at the forefront of the competitive small-car market. Powered by a 918cc sidevalve engine, it was available in two- and four-door saloon form, and also as a two- or four-seat tourer.

1934 Morris Oxford Twenty Saloon, 1900cc 6-cylinder engine, 4-speed manual gearbox, older restoration, finished in black, original interior, very good condition.
£8,000–9,000 / $11,500–13,000 ⊞ AVON

1933 Morris 10hp Four-Door Saloon, partially restored, chassis sandblasted and repainted, new front wings, resprayed in green, red interior, upholstery worn, otherwise very good condition.
£2,000–3,000 / $3,000–4,400 ✗ CGC

1952 Morris Minor Two-Door Saloon, 918cc 4-cylinder sidevalve engine, torsion-bar independent front suspension, rack-and-pinion steering, resprayed in green, 55,000 miles from new, original in most respects, excellent condition.
£2,000–2,500 / $3,000–3,600 ✗ CGC

Morris Oxford Series II/III/IV (1954–59)

Price in 1954: £744.7s.6d.
Production: 145,458.
Body styles: Saloon and estate.
Engine: 1489cc, overhead-valve, four-cylinder.
Power output: 50–53bhp.
Transmission: Four-speed manual, column change; optional Manumatic two-pedal drive from 1956.
Brakes: Hydraulic drums all-round.
Maximum speed: 74.2–80mph.
0–60mph: 27–29 seconds.
The most remarkable thing about this Morris is that, quite incredibly, it's still being built. When UK production wound down in 1959, to make way for the new square-rigged Farina designed Oxford, the tooling for the old model was sold to India, where, to this day, it's produced as the Hindustan Ambassador. In fact, Indian production has now passed one-and-a-half million, and the sturdy plodder has even earned the affectionate nickname of the 'fatted duck'. During its production life in the UK, it inspired little affection, but earned a reputation of sorts as a generally competent, if unexciting, family hack with decent enough ride and handling. The trouble was, as Britain emerged from the strictures of rationing, cars like Ford's glamorous Consul, Zephyr and Zodiac, and Vauxhall's glitzy Wyvern and Cresta seemed to deliver the long-awaited rewards of victory. By comparison, the mediocre Morris Oxford still smacked of austerity and must hardly have seemed worth winning the war for. Today, the 1954–59 Morris Oxford has a limited period appeal among those who still consider Camp coffee, tinned peaches and Carnation exotic delicacies.

◀ **1954 Morris Minor Convertible,** restored 1989–90, split screen, immobiliser, finished in black, red leather interior, good condition throughout.
£4,000–4,500 / $5,800–6,500 🗡 COYS
Sir Alec Issogonis' Morris Minor was launched at the first post-war Motor Show in 1948. To begin with, only two body styles were available: the two-door saloon and the two-door tourer. Subsequently, a four-door saloon and estate were added, as were a van and pick-up. The total number of Morris Minors produced was 1,583,622.

1955 Morris Minor De Luxe Series II Four-Door Saloon, 803cc 4-cylinder overhead-valve engine, 4-speed synchromesh gearbox, torsion-bar independent front suspension, rack-and-pinion steering, restored early 1990s, finished in beige, original maroon interior, matching chassis/engine numbers, excellent condition.
£4,000–5,000 / $5,800–7,250 🗡 Bon

1956 Morris Minor 1000 Four-Door Saloon, 948cc 4-cylinder engine, 4-speed synchromesh gearbox, torsion-bar independent front suspension, rack-and-pinion steering, restored 1998–2000, new suspension bushes, working trafficators upgraded to flashing mode with repeaters behind front grille, all brightwork rechromed, seats in original unmarked condition, new headlining, new carpet, original toolkit and jack, good condition throughout.
£2,000–2,500 / $3,000–3,600 🗡 Bon

◀ **1959 Morris Minor 1000 Two-Door Saloon,** 948cc 4-cylinder engine, 4-speed manual gearbox.
£2,000–2,300 $3,000–3,350 ⊞ PMo

1959 Morris Minor 1000 Traveller, 4-speed synchromesh gearbox, torsion-bar independent front suspension, rack-and-pinion steering, restored 1987–88, resprayed in maroon, good running condition.
£4,000–5,000 / $5,800–7,250 🗡 Bon
Morris offered a two-door Minor saloon and convertible initially, followed by a four-door saloon in 1950 and the Traveller estate in 1953, by which time the Minor was being built in Series II form with 803cc overhead-valve engine. Restyled for 1956 with a one-piece curved windscreen, the Minor 1000 came with a 948cc engine and improved gearbox. Apart from a further capacity increase (to 1098cc) in 1962, the Minor remained virtually unchanged until the last model – a Traveller – rolled off the production line in April 1971.

Miller's Starter Marque

- **Starter Morris:** *Minor, 1948–71.*
- The Minor's a motoring milestone, Britain's first million-seller, our very own people's car and, in its day, staple transport for everyone from midwives to builders' merchants. The Jaguar XK120 was the undoubted star of the 1948 London Motor Show, the car that everybody wanted, but the Series MM Morris Minor was the car that ordinary people needed. Designed by Alec Issigonis, the genius who later went on to pen the Mini, the Minor featured the then novel unitary chassis-body construction, and its famed handling finesse and ride comfort more than made up for the lack of power. In fact, in 1950, a Minor even tempted the young Stirling Moss into high-speed cornering antics that lost him his licence for a month.
- Today, the Minor has undeniable classic credentials. Any model is eminently affordable and almost as practical to own now as when in production, due to ready availability and a blossoming cottage industry that provides everything you need to keep your Minor in fine fettle. The Minor is also generally long-lived and one of the easiest cars for DIY maintenance. The wide engine bay provides plenty of room to work; cylinder-head overhauls and even more major work, such as removing the sump and big ends, can be carried out without removing the engine. The major problem is likely to be rust. Front and rear wings are bolt-on items, and sound wings can conceal horrors underneath. On Travellers, the wood framing is structural and should be checked very carefully.
- Convertibles should be given particularly close scrutiny. They are more prized, and although there's a legitimate industry converting saloons to open tops, there are plenty of fast-buck cowboys and inept DIY bodgers. The resulting 'rogue rag-tops' are potential killers – literally – so contact the Morris Minor Owner's Club (see Directory of Car Clubs) to check out a prospective buy.

MORRIS Model	ENGINE cc/cyl	DATES	CONDITION 1	2	3
Minor Series MM	918/4	1948–52	£3,000	£1,600	£800
Minor Series MM Conv	918/4	1948–52	£4,500	£2,200	£1,200
Minor Series II	803/4	1953–56	£2,000	£1,000	£500
Minor Series II Conv	803/4	1953–56	£5,500	£3,500	£1,500
Minor Series II Est	803/4	1953–56	£3,000	£1,250	£800
Minor 1000	948/4	1956–63	£1,750	£925	£250
Minor 1000 Conv	948/4	1956–63	£4,000+	£2,000	£750
Minor 1000 Est	948/4	1956–63	£4,000	£2,200	£1,200
Minor 1000	1098/4	1963–71	£2,000	£950	£250
Minor 1000 Conv	1098/4	1963–71	£4,500	£3,000	£1,500
Minor 1000 Est	1098/4	1963–71	£4,000	£3,000	£1,500
Cowley 1200	1200/4	1954–56	£1,675	£1,000	£300
Cowley 1500	1489/4	1956–59	£1,750	£950	£350
Oxford MO	1476/4	1948–54	£2,000	£850	£250
Oxford MO Est	1476/4	1952–54	£3,000	£1,500	£350
Series II/III	1489/4	1954–59	£2,000	£1,200	£300
Series II/III/IV Est	1489/4	1954–60	£2,250	£1,350	£250
Oxford Series V Farina	1489/4	1959–61	£1,800	£800	£250
Oxford Series VI Farina	1622/4	1961–71	£1,750	£750	£200
Six Series MS	2215/6	1948–54	£2,500	£1,500	£500
Isis Series I/II	2639/6	1955–58	£2,500	£1,300	£450
Isis Series I/II Est	2639/6	1956–57	£2,600	£1,350	£500

◀ **1959 Morris Minor 1000 Tourer,** 948cc engine, boot mounted luggage rack, finished in light grey, green interior, 67,000 miles from new.
£2,000–3,000 / $3,000–4,400 ⚒ H&H

1962 Morris Minor 1000 Four-Door Saloon, professionally modified with 1275cc MG engine, alternator, stainless-steel exhaust, hydraulic clutch, higher-ratio differential, servo-assisted brakes, later-type heater, Kenlowe pre-heater, finished in blue, blue interior, 3 owners from new, very good condition throughout.
£3,500–4,400 / $5,000–6,500 ⚒ H&H

◀ **1973 Morris Marina 1.3,** 1275cc 4-cylinder engine, finished in dark blue, 21,000 miles from new, no recent use, in need of recommissioning.
£550–700 / $800–1,000 ⚒ BRIT

Muntz

▶ **1952 Muntz Jet Convertible,** original 1952 Lincoln sidevalve V8 engine, twin windscreen-pillar spot lamps, lift-off non-folding soft top, white Iguana-type interior, original 4-track tape player, 1 of 209 built, original.
£30,000–40,000
$43,000–58,000 ⚒ BJ

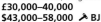

Napier

◀ **1908 Napier 45hp Type 23 Open-Drive Limousine,** 6-cylinder engine, later Zenith carburettor, non-original wings, side mounted spare wheel, coiled bulb horn, Napier oil side lamps, acetylene headlamps, finished in black with white coachlines, enclosed rear compartment with pleated and buttoned cloth upholstery, ivory pulls, silk blinds, map pockets, smoker's companions, newspaper nets to the roof, passenger sling pulls to each rear window, interior courtesy light and indicator to convey instructions to chauffeur, chauffeur's compartment with fuel and oil pressure gauges, instruction indicator and Elliott speedometer and mileage/time indicator, 1 family ownership since 1914, little use since 1925, VCC dated, museum condition.
£80,000–90,000 / $116,000–130,000 ⚘ **Bon**

Nash

1951 Nash Rambler Convertible Custom, 172.6cu.in sidevalve 6-cylinder engine, 82bhp, 3-speed manual gearbox with overdrive and column change, Hotchkiss drive, wheel discs, flashing indicators, restored, c1,500 miles since, finished in pale pink, black fabric top, black and grey interior, clock, courtesy light, excellent condition throughout.
£14,000–17,000 / $20,500–24,500 ⚘ **Bon**
This particular car was driven by Lois Lane in the 1950s *Superman* TV series and was acquired from Universal Studios, California.

Nissan

◀ **1991 Nissan Figaro,** 1100cc 4-cylinder Micra engine, turbocharger, automatic transmission, Targa top, right-hand drive, finished in green and white, cream interior, electric windows, air conditioning, CD player, little use since 1997, very good condition.
£7,500–8,500 / $11,000–12,500 ⚘ **Bon**
A field in which Nissan were pioneers was the retro-styled small car. Beginning with the BE-1 in the mid-1980s, the company progressed to the Pao, the S-Cargo and a fourth design, the Figaro, a Micra powered two-seat sports model with 1960s styling. The genre sold well in Japan, although most were limited to 10,000 production runs.

Oldsmobile

The Oldsmobile company takes its name from Ransom Eli Olds, who formed the Olds Motor Vehicle Company in Michigan in 1897 and quickly enjoyed considerable success. The Curved Dash Olds led the way in 1901 as America's first series-produced car, and also its most popular.

By 1905, however, Ransom Eli Olds had left the company to form Reo (named after his initials). Meanwhile, in 1908, Oldsmobile was bought by William Durant's fledgling General Motors and has since spent most of its life as a middle-market mainstay of the US giant.

1903 Oldsmobile Model R, single-cylinder 7hp engine, 2-speed planetary gearbox, transmission brake, steering tiller, wooden body, older restoration, finished in dark green, VCC dated.
£17,000–19,000 / $24,500–27,500 ⚒ Bon

1916 Oldsmobile Model 44 Tourer, 4100cc sidevalve V8 engine, Johnson Model D carburettor, manually operated choke and accelerator pump, 3-speed manual gearbox, 6 volt electrics, left-hand drive, mechanics refurbished, finished in red, black interior trim, exhibited at the Imperial Palace Casino Museum for many years, VCC dated.
£12,000–14,000 / $17,500–20,500 ⚒ H&H

◀ **1966 Oldsmobile Toronado,** subject of mechanical restoration early 1990s at a cost of £14,000/$20,300, engine rebuilt and converted to unleaded fuel.
£3,750–4,500 / $5,500–6,500 ⚒ COYS
The Oldsmobile Toronado created a sensation on its launch in 1966. An entirely new concept, it was America's first front-wheel-drive production car, powered by Oldsmobile's 7 litre, 385bhp Rocket V8 engine.

OLDSMOBILE Model	ENGINE cc/cyl	DATES	CONDITION		
			1	2	3
Curved Dash	1600/1	1901–04	£18,000+	£15,000	£12,000
30	2771/6	1925–26	£9,000	£7,000	£4,000
Straight Eight	4213/8	1937–38	£14,000	£9,000	£5,000

Overland

1913 Overland Model 69 Tourer, 3-speed manual gearbox, right-hand drive, VCC dated, original, unrestored.
£7,000–8,500 / $10,000–12,500 ⚒ Bon

The Overland car was developed in the early 1900s by the Standard Wheel Company, of Terre Haut, Indiana, and the fledgling firm had already changed hands once before John North Willys, a New York car dealer and major Overland customer, arrived to rescue it from oblivion in 1907. Willys had ordered 500 Overlands and paid a deposit of $10,000. When the cars were not forthcoming, he travelled to Indiana, only to find Overland on the point of closure. Willys secured credit, reorganised the company and by the summer of 1908 was in a position to build a new factory, a facility that was sorely needed, as Willys had been forced to carry out assembly in a circus tent! The revitalised company went from strength to strength, production increasing steadily until, by the beginning of WWI, only Ford could claim a higher output.

Packard

1930 Packard Standard Eight Coupé, restored 1994, finished in maroon and black, tan interior.
£12,000–14,000 / $17,500–20,500 ✗ COYS
Packard launched its first eight-cylinder model in 1923, which became known as the Packard Eight. For 1925, Bijor chassis lubrication was made standard, and from 1927 all Packards had hypoid back axles. Also new for 1927 was an increase in power from 85bhp to 109bhp, which was achieved through the use of aluminium pistons, better manifolding and an improved cylinder head. New for 1929 was the Standard Eight, which replaced the six-cylinder cars previously built alongside the earlier Eights.

1942 Packard Rollston Open Town Car, black leather top to rear, power windows, division, 2 radios, walnut fascia, silk curtains, occasional seat, cocktail cabinet, intercom, hassocks, rear compartment upholstered in beige wool broadcloth, leather and canvas tops to chauffeur's compartment, leather chauffeur's seat, excellent condition.
£50,000–60,000 / $73,000–87,000 ✗ BJ
The one-off coachwork of this Custom 180 Super 8 was built for the president of Packard.

> A known continuous history can add value to and enhance the enjoyment of a car.

PACKARD Model	ENGINE cc/cyl	DATES	CONDITION 1	2	3
Twin Six	6946/12	1916–23	£30,000	£20,000	£15,000
6	3973/6	1921–24	£20,000	£15,000	£12,000
6, 7, 8 Series	5231/8	1929–39	£35,000+	£25,000+	£14,000+
12	7300/12	1936–39	£50,000+	£30,000+	£18,000+

Peugeot

Peugeot's history dates right back to the dawn of motoring, for not long after the earliest Daimler and Benz vehicles had taken to the road, the French company was also in contention. In 1889, Peugeot turned out four vehicles and is also credited with being the first manufacturer to sell a car to a private owner. Since 1974, Peugeot has also been in control of Citroën, and in 1978 acquired Chrysler's European interests, annexing the Talbot, Sunbeam and Simca brands.

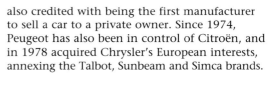

◄ **1973 Peugeot 304S Convertible,** 1.3 litre engine rebuilt 1989, finished in white, correct brown interior and hood, in need of some restoration.
£450–600 / $650–870 ✗ CGC

PEUGEOT Model	ENGINE cc/cyl	DATES	CONDITION 1	2	3
Bébé	856/4	1912–14	£25,000	£15,000	£8,000
153	2951/4	1913–26	£9,000	£5,000	£3,000
163	1490/4	1920–24	£5,000	£4,000	£2,000
Bébé	676/4	1920–25	£7,000	£6,000	£3,000
156	5700/6	1922–24	£7,000	£5,000	£3,000
174	3828/4	1922–28	£7,500	£5,000	£2,000
172	714/4	1926–28	£4,000	£3,000	£1,500
183	1990/6	1929–30	£5,000	£3,000	£1,500
201	996/4	1930–36	£6,000	£3,000	£1,500
402	2140/4	1938–40	£4,500	£3,000	£1,000
Good solid cars.					

Pick

◀ **1901 Pick 4hp Voiturette,** forward mounted vertical single-cylinder engine, water-cooled, automatic inlet valve, mechanical overhead exhaust valve, 2 forward speeds, belt and double chain drive to rear axle, restored, finished in yellow, black interior, VCC dated.
£32,000–35,000 / $46,000–50,000 ✦ Bon
Jack Pick established a reputation as a bicycle manufacturer in Stamford before beginning motor car production at the turn of the century. Early Picks were De Dion powered, and it seems that later engines were bought from Allard & Co of Coventry, before Pick began manufacturing its own engines. This 1901 car is believed to be the oldest surviving Pick, and research indicates that it may be the prototype car exhibited at The Cordingley Show at the Royal Agricultural Hall, Islington, in May 1901. It is believed that the car remained in Stamford for most of its early life, and before rescue for preservation its engine was used to drive a lathe. It was discovered in 1949 in a shed and bought for £7.10s.0d/$10.

Pierce-Arrow

1933 Pierce-Arrow 836 Club Brougham, 5998cc 8-cylinder engine, hydraulic tappets, 135bhp, rear servo-assisted brakes, thermostatically controlled bonnet shutters, Archer mascot, hinged luggage rack, triple rear lights, twin side mounted spares, restored, finished in red and maroon, fawn Bedford cord interior, c55,000 miles from new, variety of small spare parts and trim items.
£24,000–28,000 / $35,000–41,000 ✦ BRIT
Of the many prestige cars built in the USA, probably none enjoyed more favour, for a longer period, than the Pierce-Arrow. However, the 1930s proved to be a difficult time for manufacturers, with the cost of development often exceeding the revenue returned by flagging sales. Without the cushion of a large parent company, Pierce-Arrow was forced to declare bankruptcy in December 1937, following a loss of over $250,000 in the preceding 17 months, and the assets were sold at auction in May 1938. The last Pierce-Arrow was built that summer, for chief engineer Carl Wise, from parts secured from the receivers. A facility was retained for the maintenance of existing cars until the remaining parts and tooling were scrapped in 1942 for the war effort.

Plymouth

1948 Plymouth Special Deluxe Business Coupé,
217.8cu.in 6-cylinder engine, 95bhp, 3-speed manual gearbox, windscreen pillar spot lamp, fog lamps, finished in pale yellow, bench seat, radio, heater.
£5,000–6,000 / $7,250–9,000 ✦ Bon

1930 Plymouth Model 30U Coupé, older restoration, resprayed c1995, very good condition throughout.
£7,000–8,000 / $10,000–11,500 ✦ Bon

◀ **1966 Plymouth Satellite Hemi,** 426cu.in 'hemi' V8 engine, automatic transmission, servo-assisted brakes, centre-lock wheels, restored, 1 of only 364 built, 67,000 miles from new, completely original.
£20,000–24,000 / $29,000–35,000 ⚒ **BJ**

1970 Plymouth Superbird, 440cu.in 'hemi' V8 engine, 4-speed manual gearbox, power steering, servo-assisted disc brakes, Rally wheels, subject of complete ground-up restoration to original condition, AM/8-track with 3-speaker dash, 30,000 miles from new, matching numbers, 1 of 308 built, 'as new' condition.
£50,000–60,000 / $72,000–87,000 ⚒ **BJ**

1967 Plymouth Belvedere II Hardtop, 426cu.in 'hemi' V8 engine, matching numbers, only example built.
£30,000–35,000 / $43,000–50,000 ⚒ **BJ**

Pontiac

Pontiac GTO (1964–71)

Production: 497,122.
Body styles: Two-door five-seat coupé, hardtop or convertible.
Engine: 5346–7470cc, V8.
Power output: 250–360bhp.
Transmission: Three- or four-speed manual; two-speed automatic.
Brakes: Drums all-round; front discs from 1968.
Maximum speed: 135mph (7470cc).
0–60mph: 6.6 seconds (7470cc).
The car that started the whole muscle-car movement was really the result of a piece of corporate insubordination. When General Motors clamped down on performance cars, Pontiac's chief engineer, John Z. De Lorean, skirted the edict by simple 'hot-rod' methods, plonking the biggest engine available into their medium-sized Tempest Le Mans range, and with one stroke

created a new breed of home-grown performance car. The GTO immediately hit home, especially in the youth market, and Ford and Chrysler quickly picked up on the muscle-car theme with such cars as the 7 litre Galaxie and the uprated Plymouth Sport Fury. But the GTO was the first to offer near-race performance and road-holding in a full-sized car, and Americans queued to buy: 32,000 chose the GTO option in the first year it was available, more than 75,000 in the second, and almost 100,000 in the third. From the original Tempest Le Mans option package, the GTO was elevated to a separate Tempest model in 1966, and became a model in its own right in 1968. It withered back into the Le Mans range in 1972, but in the course of its joyride, the GTO had created a uniquely American expression of performance motoring.

1977 Pontiac Firebird Trans Am, 6.6 litre V8 engine, 220bhp, automatic transmission, removable glass roof, finished in black, Firebird bonnet emblem in good condition, black interior and fittings in need of attention.
£2,000–2,500 / $3,000–3,600 ⚒ **CGC**

1986 Pontiac Trans Am 5.0, 5 litre V8 engine, 4-speed automatic transmission, alloy wheels, finished in silver, cruise control, air conditioning, electric windows.
£2,750–3,500 / $4,000–5,000 ⚒ **BARO**

PONTIAC Model	ENGINE cc/cyl	DATES	CONDITION		
			1	2	3
Six–27	3048/6	1926–29	£9,000	£7,000	£4,000
Silver Streak	3654/8	1935–37	£12,000	£9,000	£5,500
6	3638/6	1937–49	£7,000	£4,000	£3,500
8	4078/8	1937–49	£7,000	£4,000	£3,500

Porsche

Volkswagen Beetle designer Ferdinand Porsche may have given the world the people's car, but it was his son, Ferry, who, with long-time associate Karl Rabe, created a car that people all over the world would prize from the day the first Porsche rolled off the production line. These days, a Porsche – virtually any Porsche – stands for precision, performance, purity and perfection, and the 356 was the first chapter in that story. Well, not quite. The 356 was so named because it was actually the 356th project from the Porsche design office since it had been set up in 1930. It was also the first car to bear the Porsche name.

Post-war expediency forced a make-do reliance on VW Beetle underpinnings, but the 356 is a true sporting machine. Some aficionados adore the first-of-breed purity of the earliest 'jelly mould' cars, but with each successive modification the Porsche detached itself farther from its humble roots. A pert, nimble, tail-happy treat, the 356 is still the prettiest production Porsche there's ever been, the foundation stone of a proud sporting tradition. Why, if you squint at more modern Porsches, like the 911 and today's models, you can still identify the genetic inheritance passed down from a true original.

1954 Porsche 356 1500 Super Coupé, 1582cc air-cooled flat-4 engine, 55bhp, 4-speed manual gearbox, independent front suspension, rear swing axles, 4-wheel hydraulic drum brakes with cooling fins, right-hand drive, finished in blue, light beige vinyl interior, 3 owners and fewer than 13,000 miles from new, all instrumentation in working order.
£65,000–75,000 / $94,000–109,000 ⚡ C
This first-series Porsche 356 was originally a special order for the wife of a major department store owner in Sydney, Australia. The intention was that it would be used at the wedding of the couple's daughter. The local Porsche distributor was asked to send the factory an order for the new car to be supplied and painted in the exact colour as the bride's pale blue wedding dress.

1955 Porsche 356 Speedster, fitted replacement 1800cc engine, original engine included, restored late 1980s, finished in black, beige hood and side screens, beige interior.
£40,000–45,000 / $58,000–65,000 ⚡ Bon
The work of Ferry Porsche, the 356 was based on the Volkswagen, designed by his father, and employed a platform-type chassis with rear mounted, air-cooled engine and torsion-bar all-independent suspension. In 1951, a works 356 finished first in the 1100cc class at the Le Mans 24-hour race, thus beginning the marque's long and illustrious association with Le Sarthe. A batch of 15 roadsters was constructed in 1952, their successful reception in the USA leading to the Speedster's introduction in 1954. Intended as a cheaper, sportier version of the 356 Cabriolet that could be raced or enjoyed as a fun road car, the Speedster featured a low windscreen, stripped interior and very basic weather equipment. Various power units were available, from the 60bhp Normal and 75bhp Super to the 100bhp, four-cam Carrera engine. The Speedster was comparatively expensive, though, and demand for a lightweight road-racer was limited. Only 4,854 Speedsters were built before Porsche dropped the model in 1958.

1957 Porsche 356 Speedster, 1488cc engine, 4-speed gearbox, independent suspension by torsion bars and trailing arms, 4-wheel drum brakes, completely restored, finished in red, red interior.
£35,000–40,000 / $51,000–58,000 ⚡ COYS

Porsche 356 (1949–65)

The Porsche 356 is the car that started it all, beginning a proud sporting tradition that continues to this day. In many ways too, the 356 is the Beetle's athletic offspring, its concept, rear-engined layout and design descending directly from the parent car. Even its flat-four, air-cooled engine – although not a Beetle engine – is Beetle derived. It hardly sounds exotic, but the 356 is much more than a Bug in butterfly's clothes. In the 356, the humble Volkswagen genes are miraculously mutated into a peppy, pert piece of precision engineering available in myriad combinations, from humble 'cooking' models for less than Mondeo money, to the exotic and very precious Speedsters and quad-cam Carreras.
Pick of the bunch: Ultimate in performance and price is the 356C Carrera II. Some connoisseur purists favour the earliest split-windscreen 'jelly mould' shape, but for all-round drivability and affordability, the last-of-the-line 1600cc 356C coupés with all-round disc brakes make most sense.

1961 Porsche 356B Coupé, 1582cc overhead-valve flat-4 engine (from a 912), 4-speed transaxle, independent front suspension, rear swing axles, resprayed in grey, new red interior, little recent use.
£12,000–14,000 / $17,500–20,500 ⚒ RM

1963 Porsche 356B 1600 Cabriolet, matching numbers, restored, engine rebuilt, transaxle and brakes overhauled, all chrome trim replated, bare-metal respray in red, black canvas top, new black leather upholstery, all new rubber seals and mats.
£28,000–32,000 / $40,000–46,000 ⚒ Bon

Cabriolets had been manufactured right from the start of 356 production, but the first open Porsche to make a significant impact was the Speedster, introduced in 1954. The Speedster was dropped in 1958 and replaced by the more civilised Convertible D, which differed principally by virtue of its larger windscreen and winding side windows. Porsche sub-contracted cabriolet body construction to a number of different coachbuilders, Convertible D production being undertaken by Drauz, of Heilbronn. By the time the 356B arrived in September 1959, the car had gained a one-piece, rounded windscreen and 15in-diameter wheels. The newcomer's introduction brought with it further styling revisions and an engine now standardised at 1600cc.

Porsche 356B (1959–63)

Production: 30,963 (all Porsche 356Bs).
Body styles: 2+2 fixed-head coupé, cabriolet and speedster.
Construction: Unitary – steel body with integral pressed-steel platform chassis.
Engine: 1582cc, air-cooled, flat-four, twin carburettors.
Power output: 90bhp at 5,500rpm (Super 90).
Transmission: Four-speed manual, all-synchromesh, rear-wheel drive.
Suspension: Front, independent by trailing arms and transverse torsion bars with anti-roll bar; rear, independent by swing axles, radius arms and transverse torsion bars; telescopic shock absorbers.
Brakes: Hydraulic drums all-round.
Maximum speed: 110mph.
0–60mph: 10 seconds.
Average fuel consumption: 30–35mpg.

▶ **1964 Porsche 356C Sunroof Coupé,** 1582cc air-cooled flat-4 engine, 75bhp, 4-speed synchromesh gearbox, 4-wheel independent suspension, 4-wheel disc brakes, finished in white.
£13,000–15,000 / $19,000–22,000 ⚒ RM

1964 Porsche 356C Coupé, restored, finished in silver, black interior.
£20,000–22,000 / $29,000–32,000 ⊞ HCL

1969 Porsche 911T 2.2 Targa Coupé, carburettors overhauled, finished in orange, original black interior, 3 owners from new, totally original, good to very good condition.
£12,000–14,000 / $17,500–20,500 ⚒ Bon

Porsche's long-running 911 arrived in 1964 as a replacement for the 356. Introduced as a new base model in 1967, the 911T (Touring) came initially with the 2 litre, six-cylinder engine, gaining the 2.2 litre unit, along with the rest of the range, in 1969. There was a convertible Targa version. First seen in 1966, the Targa represented an ingenious approach to the concept of a soft-top 911, sporting a hefty roll-over bar to protect the occupants in the event of an inversion, plus removable roof and rear hood sections that were stowable in the boot. For 1969, a quieter and less leak-prone fixed rear window replaced the rear hood, and the Targa would continue in this form into the 1990s.

1968 Porsche 911L, finished in original cream, tinted windows, correct black interior trim, front and rear seat belts, 3 owners from new, good condition throughout.
£6,000–7,000 / $8,500–10,500 ⚒ COYS

1970 Porsche 911E Coupé, 2195cc engine, 158bhp, left-hand drive, completely restored 1999, stored in a carcoon since, over £8,000 spent on parts and labour excluding respray, engine and gearbox rebuild, new exhaust system, suspension rebuilt, bare-metal respray in orange, new black leather upholstery.
£9,500–11,500 / $14,000–16,500 ⚒ H&H

1975 Porsche 911 (930) 3.0 Turbo, 2994cc 6-cylinder engine, correct Fuchs wide alloy wheels, finished in black, black leather interior, little recent use.
£11,500–13,500 / $16,500–19,500 ⚒ BRIT
Since its introduction in the mid-1960s, the Porsche 911 has undergone a programme of evolution, improvement and enlargement. One of the most radical advances came in 1975 when, with the engine size increased to 3 litres, the flagship model of the range was turbocharged to create the Type 930. It could be distinguished from its unblown siblings by wildly flared rear arches and the formidable 'whale-tail' rear wing – the first time such a device had been seen away from the race-track. Porsche later referred to this as an 'improver' rather than a spoiler. It was capable of a top speed of over 150mph and acceleration to 60mph in a little over 6 seconds.

1973 Porsche 911 Carrera 2.7 RS Coupé, 2.7 litre engine, fuel-injection, 210bhp, restored 1989, matching chassis, engine and gearbox numbers, duck's-tail spoiler, lightweight door skins, bumpers and seats, fewer than 45,500 miles from new, good condition throughout.
£35,000–40,000 / $51,000–58,000 ⚒ Bon

1977 Porsche 911 Coupé, 2700cc engine, 5-speed manual gearbox, left-hand drive, finished in red, black interior, good condition throughout.
£6,000–7,000 / $9,000–10,000 ⚒ H&H

1977 Porsche 911 Carrera 3.0, 2994cc flat-6 engine, 204bhp, 5-speed manual gearbox, rack-and-pinion steering, 4-wheel torsion-bar independent suspension, 4-wheel disc brakes, converted to right-hand drive, recent gearbox overhaul, finished in black, tan leather interior, good cosmetic condition.
£6,000–7,000 / $9,000–10,000 ⚒ CGC

PORSCHE Model	ENGINE cc/cyl	DATES	CONDITION 1	2	3
356	var/4	1949–53	£15,000+	£8,000	£5,000
356 Cabriolet	var/4	1951–53	£20,000+	£14,000	£10,000
356A	1582/4	1955–59	£13,000	£9,000	£5,000
356A Cabriolet	1582/4	1956–59	£16,000	£10,000	£7,000
356A Speedster	1582/4	1955–58	£30,000	£19,000	£14,000
356B Carrera	1582/ 1966/4	1960–65	£40,000+	£30,000+	£18,000
356C	1582/4	1963–65	£15,000+	£11,000+	£5,000
356C Cabriolet	1582/4	1963–64	£25,000+	£16,000	£10,000
911/911L/T/E	1991/6	1964–68	£12,000	£7,000	£5,000
912	1582/4	1965–68	£6,500	£5,000	£2,000
911S	1991/6	1966–69	£12,000	£8,000	£5,500
911S	2195/6	1969–71	£13,000	£9,000	£6,000
911T	2341/6	1971–73	£13,000	£8,000	£6,000
911E	2341/6	1971–73	£12,000+	£8,000	£6,000
914/4	1679/4	1969–75	£4,000	£3,000	£1,000
914/6	1991/6	1969–71	£6,000	£3,500	£1,500
911S	2341/6	1971–73	£16,000	£10,000	£8,500
Carrera RS Lightweight	2687/6	1973	£40,000	£28,000+	£16,000
Carrera RS Touring	2687/6	1973	£30,000	£26,000	£17,000
Carrera 3	2994/6	1976–77	£14,000	£9,000	£7,000
924 Turbo	1984/4	1978–83	£5,000	£4,000	£2,000
928/928S	4474/4664/V8	1977–86	£10,000	£7,000	£4,000
911SC	2993/6	1977–83	£13,000	£8,000	£6,000

Sportomatic cars are less desirable.

1979 Porsche 911SC Targa, 3 litre engine, finished in metallic bronze, biscuit upholstery, 74,000 miles from new.
£10,000–11,500 / $14,500–16,500 ⊞ WbC

1983 Porsche 911SC Targa, engine, gearbox and running gear rebuilt late 1990s, fewer than 2,000 miles since, new wheels, resprayed in white, black interior, faulty synchromesh on 1st and 2nd gears, otherwise good condition.
£7,000–8,000 / $10,500–11,500 ⚡ COYS

1985 Porsche 911 3.3 Turbo, flat-6 engine, Turbo 2 alloy wheels, finished in black, immobiliser, good condition throughout.
£13,000–15,000 / $19,000–22,000 ⚡ BARO

1987 Porsche 911 Carrera 3.2 Cabriolet, 3.2 litre engine, G50 sports gearbox, front and rear Carrera spoilers, refinished in original silver.
£12,500–14,000 / $18,000–20,500 ⚡ COYS

1991 Porsche 911 Carrera 4 Lightweight, bought direct from the factory at a cost of c£125,000/$180,000, unused and dry stored from new, finished in white, black interior, seats retain factory protective covers, rollcage still with original card covering, 1 owner and only 9 miles from new.
£40,000–45,000 / $58,000–65,000 ⚡ COYS
Over the years, Porsche has produced a number of 911 derivatives to meet the racing regulations of different countries around the world, as well as producing cars for a number of one-make series. The 964 was developed for just such a series in the USA, traditionally a very important market for Porsche. The company produced a limited number of highly developed cars using aluminium bodies to compete against each other on some of America's greatest circuits. Only 20 of these cars were built by the factory, 18 of which competed in the race series. This car is one of the remaining two.

Market comment

Despite their many virtues, Porsches need not be objects of pure fantasy. Some of the less-exotic fixed-head 356s in middling condition are, these days, enticingly affordable. The trouble is that for the price of a new modern family saloon, you could very easily end up in abject Porsche penury. The 356 may have evolved from the humble Beetle, but don't think it's just a Bug with a pretty new skin. True, the flat-four engine is VW derived, relatively easy to maintain and rewarding for the DIY enthusiast, but it's the rest of the car you've got to worry about. Those swooping wings, for example, could cost you £500 a go if you want real Porsche versions, and the rest of the bodyshell is equally pricey and complex. Beware Porsche 356s that have been tarted up on the top side and bathed in bitumen underneath to conceal shoddy repairs. As for the 911, the pre-1973 cars may not have quite the punch of the later ones, but they're affordable and – to some eyes – the purest of the breed. Buy a good one and you'll have a reliable, robust eye-catcher with performance to match. Mechanically, a well-maintained 911 should be near bulletproof. Once again, it's body bodges and underside horrors that you really have to look out for. With both the 356 and 911, a professional inspection is highly recommended, and if you end up with a good one you'll find that running costs can be surprisingly reasonable.

Cross Reference
See Colour Review (page 150)

◄ **1970 Porsche 914,** 1679cc 4-cylinder engine, stainless-steel exhaust system, Targa roof, finished in silver, slight bubbling of paintwork.
£1,500–2,000 / $2,200–3,000 ⚡ BRIT
Styled by Karmann, the 914 was a mid-engined design that utilised a VW 411 engine.

1982 Porsche 944 Coupé, 2479cc 4-cylinder engine, 4-speed automatic transmission, factory fitted sun roof, finished in white, brown interior, 80,000 miles from new.
£1,800–2,400 / $2,500–3,500 ✗ H&H

1991 Porsche 944 Cabriolet, electric hood, finished in red, black full leather interior, 45,000 miles from new.
£9,000–11,000 / $13,000–16,000 ⊞ VIC

1979 Porsche 924 Turbo, 5-speed gearbox/transaxle, 4-wheel disc brakes, rack-and-pinion steering, coil-spring front suspension, rear torsion bars, alloy wheels, 944-style body kit, finished in black, matching Porsche logo interior, electric windows, sun roof and door mirrors, good condition.
£1,500–2,000 / $2,200–3,000 ✗ CGC
Launched in 1976, the Porsche 924 received a lukewarm welcome. Few criticised its balanced handling, but many considered it underpowered. In response, Porsche turbocharged the model's 1984cc, four-cylinder engine. The result, introduced in 1979, was a car with a 144mph top speed and a 0–60mph time of 6.9 seconds – equal to the contemporary Ferrari 308. The 924 Turbo's running gear was suitably uprated to cope.

1986 Porsche 928S, 4957cc 4-camshaft V8 engine, 288bhp, automatic transmission, power steering, servo-assisted brakes, finished in metallic burgundy, tan leather interior, air conditioning, electric windows, 57,000 miles from new, excellent condition.
£9,000–10,000 / $13,000–14,500 ✗ Bon
When Porsche introduced the 928 in 1978, marque enthusiasts didn't know what to think. Like the four-cylinder 924 offered the year before, the 928 was a front-engined, rear-wheel-drive car with a water-cooled powerplant. The long nose behind the exposed, pop-up headlights concealed a 4474cc, overhead-camshaft, alloy V8. Power output reached the rear wheels through a choice of a three-speed automatic or five-speed manual transaxle. Suspension was fully independent, and the brakes were ventilated discs at all corners.

Premier

Restored values
The cost of a professional restoration will have an influence on, but no direct relation to, a car's market value. A restored car can have a market value lower than the cost of its restoration.

◄ **1914/18 Premier Raceabout,** 6-cylinder T-head engine, 100bhp, shaft-drive rear axle on cantilever rear springs, full-width touring screen, period monocle screen attached to steering column, rebuilt mid-1990s, full complement of period instruments, excellent mechanical condition.
£27,000–32,000 / $39,000–46,500 ✗ COYS

Railton

▶ **c1934 Railton Sports Tourer,** 4.2 litre 8-cylinder engine, 3-speed manual gearbox, semi-elliptic leaf-spring suspension, spoked wheels, restored in Sydney, Australia early 1990s, mechanics rebuilt, 4–5 seat touring body fitted, finished in dark green.
£20,000–24,000 / $29,000–35,000 ⚲ **GO**
Reid Railton was a notable engineer and racing-car designer. In 1930, when only 35 years old, he designed Bluebird, in which Sir Malcolm Campbell set a land speed record of 272mph on the Bonneville salt flats in the USA. Production of Railton cars began in 1933, using imported running gear in conjunction with the big eight-cylinder Hudson engine. The resultant high power-to-weight ratio resulted in a fast and accelerative car. Fitted with a variety of coachwork, the Railton bore comparison with the likes of Alvis and Lagonda.

Range Rover

◀ **1976 Range Rover,** 3500cc V8 engine, overdrive gearbox, 4-wheel disc brakes, towbar, finished in mustard yellow, brown cloth interior, 1 owner and fewer than 73,500 miles from new, unused since 2000.
£750–1,000 / $1,100–1,500 ⚲ **Bon**

Reliant

1966 Reliant Scimitar SE4, 6-cylinder engine, triple carburettors, manual gearbox with overdrive, wire wheels, electric sunroof, restored to concours condition.
£6,500–7,500 / $9,500–11,000 ⊞ **GrM**

1974 Reliant Scimitar GTE, 2994cc V6 engine, manual gearbox with overdrive, completely restored.
£3,500–4,000 / $5,000–5,800 ⊞ **TIHO**

RELIANT Model	ENGINE cc/cyl	DATES	CONDITION 1	2	3
Sabre 4 Coupé & Drophead	1703/4	1961–63	£5,500	£2,750	£1,000
Sabre 6 Coupé & Drophead	2553/6	1962–64	£6,000	£3,500	£1,500
Scimitar GT Coupé SE4	2553/6, 2994 V6	1964–70	£4,500	£2,500	£1,000
Scimitar GTE Sports Estate SE5/5A	2994/V6	1968–75	£5,000	£3,000	£750
Scimitar GTE Sports Estate SE6/6A	2994/V6	1976–80	£5,000	£3,500+	£1,250
Scimitar GTE Sports Estate SE6B	2792/V6	1980–86	£6,500	£5,000	£2,000
Scimitar GTC Convertible SE8B	2792/V6	1980–86	£8,000	£7,000	£5,500

Reliant Scimitar GTE (1968–86)

Price when new: £1,759.
Production: 16,000 approx.
Engine: Ford 2994cc V6 (1968–79); Ford 2792cc V6 (1979–86).
Power output: 128–135bhp.
Transmission: Four-speed manual, optional overdrive; automatic.
Brakes: Front discs, rear drums.
Maximum speed: 116–118mph.
0–60mph: 10.2–10.8 seconds.

Del Boy and Rodders might have suffered delusions of adequacy in their Reliant Regal van, but there was one Reliant that really was regal – the Scimitar. Princess Anne owned no less than eight Scimitar GTE estates over the years, and Prince Edward once owned a Scimitar convertible. Until the 1960s, Reliant was best known for its traders' three-wheelers, but in 1961 it turned its attention to four-wheeled sporting products, first with the rather ugly Sabre, then the more harmonious Sabre Six. The elegant Scimitar coupé of 1964 was certainly something of a breakthrough for Reliant, but it was the 1968 Scimitar GTE that marked a quiet revolution. Although there was nothing revolutionary in the production of its glassfibre body, the shape, styling, glass rear hatch and split rear seats created a new class of car, the sports estate, a sporting, four-seater carry-all with luggage space increased at a stroke from 19 to 36cu.ft (0.5 to 1cu.m). In Reliant parlance, GTE stood for 'Grand Touring Estate', and although the concept seems obvious today, it was years ahead of its time. The Scimitar GTE appeared three years before Volvo leapt on the sports-wagon bandwagon with the P1800ES. Today, it's still one of the few sports estates that actually looks right as an estate. As a work-a-day classic hack, there's also little to match its blend of sporting style and practicality at the price – with its massive and strong chassis, no-nonsense mechanics, Ford V6 engine and rust-free glassfibre body.

Renault

For the enthusiast, many of Renault's most engaging post-war cars come in small packages. The 4CV of 1947–61 was an advanced little device with a rear mounted, overhead-valve engine, rack-and-pinion steering and all-independent suspension. Eventually, it sold over one million, but the Dauphine was even more successful, claiming honours as the first French car to sell over two million. As petite sporting boulevardiers, the Floride and Caravelle made up for their lack of outright performance with plenty of charm. The long-lived Renault 4 was both innovative and versatile. Seemingly 'unstyled', it was an excellent little carry-all that could be readily adapted from family hack to utility vehicle by removing the seats and tail-gate if necessary. In production from 1962 to 1986, it sold an astonishing seven million-plus. The Renault 5 carried the theme forward and set a standard in small-car styling that's rarely been matched since.

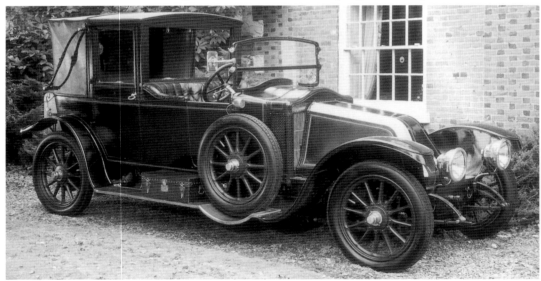

1913 Renault Type DO 22hp Landaulette de Ville, 5.1 litre 6-cylinder engine, electric starter, electric lighting, finished in original black with green coachlines, chauffeur's seat upholstered in black leather, rear passenger compartment upholstered in beige silk, 'letter box' window in glass division to allow communication with chauffeur, matching rear-view mirrors, VCC dated, fewer than 10,000 miles from new, original specification in every major respect,
£37,000–44,000 / $53,500–65,000 ➢ **Bon**
This car was supplied originally to Fred Bourne, president of the Singer Sewing Machine Company. He, in turn, presented it as a wedding gift to his daughter, May, on the occasion of her marriage to Ralph Beaver Strassburger that year. The new Mr and Mrs Strassburger engaged Russian emigré, William Obidine, as their chauffeur to look after the Renault. When the Strassburgers returned to the USA, not only did they take their wedding gift, but also Obidine went with them, and the car was to remain in his care until his death in 1980. The Renault remained in the heated coach house at the family home and was regularly washed and serviced by the faithful 'Obie', who signed his name under the scuttle each time he carried out a major service.

RENAULT Model	ENGINE cc/cyl	DATES	CONDITION		
			1	2	3
40hp	7540/6	1919–21	£30,000	£20,000	£10,000
SR	4537/4	1919–22	£10,000	£7,000	£5,000
EU-15.8HP	2815/4	1919–23	£8,000+	£5,000	£2,000
GS-IG	2121/4	1920–23	£5,000	£3,000	£2,000
JP	9123/6	1922–29	£25,000	£20,000	£15,000
KJ	951/4	1923–29	£6,000	£4,000	£2,000
Mona Six	1474/6	1928–31	£7,000	£5,000	£3,000
Reinastella	7128/8	1929–32	£25,000	£20,000	£15,000
Viva Six	3181/6	1929–34	£10,000	£7,000	£3,000
14/45	2120/4	1929–35	£7,000	£5,000	£2,000
Nervahuit	4240/8	1931	£12,000	£10,000	£7,000
UY	1300/4	1932–34	£7,000	£5,000	£2,000
ZC/ZD2	4825/8	1934–35	£12,000	£10,000	£7,000
YN2	1463/4	1934–39	£7,000	£5,000	£2,000
Airline Super and Big 6	3620/6	1935	£10,000	£8,000	£5,000
18	2383/4	1936–39	£9,000	£5,000	£3,000
26	4085/6	1936–39	£12,000	£8,000	£5,000

Veteran pre-war models like the 2-cylinder AX, AG and BB are very popular, with values ranging between £6,000 and £15,000. The larger 4-cylinder cars like the AM, AZ, XB and VB are very reliable, and coachbuilt examples command £30,000+, with 6-cylinder coachbuilt cars commanding a premium.

► **1923 Renault Type KJ 1 8.3hp Tourer,** 4-cylinder sidevalve engine, 3-speed manual gearbox, Michelin disc wheels, finished in mushroom with black wings, reupholstered in black leathercloth, museum displayed for some years, in need of recommissioning.
£6,000–7,000 / $8,500–10,500 ➢ Bon

◄ **1916 Renault Type EU 12hp Open-Drive Landaulette,** 2815cc monobloc engine, completely restored, engine, running gear and chassis rebuilt, most of bodywork re-created.
£9,000–11,000 / $13,000–16,000 ➢ Bon
The Type EU appeared at the end of 1916 and was particularly suited for use at the Front, where it served in many different guises, from staff cars to reconnaissance vehicles and ambulances. The Renault works at Billancourt had been placed on a war footing at the outbreak of hostilities in August 1914, the company also making lorries, shells, light tanks, aero engines and aircraft. In late 1918, Louis Renault was made an Officer of the Légion d'Honneur for his great contribution to the war effort. This particular Renault is understood to have been supplied to the French Army late in 1916 as a staff car, emerging with five bullet holes, which are still to be seen in the driver's door today. By about 1928, it had been sold for private use, and during WWII it was used by a lorry repair depot for carrying engines and tools, being fitted with a flat bed and heavy-duty rear axle.

Renault Floride/Caravelle (1959–68)

Engine: 845–1108cc, water-cooled, four-cylinder.
Power output: 40–55bhp.
Transmission: Three- and four-speed manual; three-speed semi-automatic.
Brakes: Drums all-round; discs all-round from 1964.
Top speed: 75–90mph.
Renault's first really sporty-looking car was a stylish little number. Launched in 1959 as the Floride in both fixed-head and convertible versions, its elegant looks saw it adopted as fashionable road wear for promenading around Cannes and Beverley Hills. But with its tiny, rear mounted, 845cc, four-cylinder engine producing a meagre 40bhp, its go came nowhere near matching its show. While the performance was more in line with an Austin-

Healey Sprite, as a full four-seater – at a pinch – it offered better accommodation than the MGB. In 1962, with a bigger 956cc engine, the Floride became the Caravelle, and from 1963 it came with an 1108cc unit, at last offering a genuine 90mph.
Pick of the bunch: Definitely a 1963-on Caravelle with the 1108cc engine that eventually will top out at 90mph.
Floride fact: After the Floride's debut at the October 1958 Paris Salon, Renault boasted that Americans were so bowled over by the car that more than 12,800 of them had placed orders before knowing the price, specifications or approximate delivery date. In the USA, the car was marketed from the start as the Caravelle.

RENAULT Model	ENGINE cc/cyl	DATES	CONDITION 1	2	3
4CV	747/ 760/4	1947–61	£3,500	£2,000	£850
Fregate	1997/4	1952–60	£3,000	£2,000	£1,000
Dauphine	845/4	1956–66	£1,500	£1,000	£350
Dauphine Gordini	845/4	1961–66	£2,000	£1,000	£450
Floride	845/4	1959–62	£3,000	£2,000	£600
Caravelle	956/ 1108/4	1962–68	£4,500	£2,800	£750
R4	747/ 845/4	1961–86	£2,000	£1,500	£350
R8/R10	1108/4	1962–71	£1,800	£750	£200
R8 Gordini	1108/4	1965–66	£8,000	£5,000	£2,000
R8 Gordini	1255/4	1966–70	£8,000	£5,500	£2,500
R8S	1108/4	1968–71	£2,000	£1,200	£400

Renault-Alpine

◀ **1969 Renault Alpine A-110,** 1300cc 4-cylinder engine, 140bhp, 4-speed manual gearbox, independent front suspension by A-arms and coil springs with anti-roll bar, rear swing axles with trailing arms and coil springs, 4-wheel hydraulic 'mountain' disc brakes, subject of no-expense-spared restoration, new chassis and body with later panel upgrades, interior fully refurbished with new leather upholstery.
£20,000–22,000 / $29,000–32,000 ⚒ RM
The A-110 was equipped with various engines throughout its 15-year life, but in that time only 7,812 examples were built, including the Group 4 rally cars that won three world championships in the late 1960s and early 1970s.

Reo

▶ **1910 Reo 30hp Tourer,** engine rebuilt at a cost of over £8,000, unused since, chassis rust-free, bodywork restored, interior retrimmed, VCC dated, in need of running in.
£20,000–23,000 / $29,000–33,500 ⚒ Bon
Founded in 1904 by Ransom Eli Olds, following his acrimonious departure from Oldsmobile, Reo took its name from the man's initials. The new company's first model was a 16hp, twin-cylinder, planetary/chain-drive tourer with a detachable tonneau. Olds' first attempt at a four-cylinder Reo was half-hearted, this 24hp model only being produced for 1906, but the introduction of the four-cylinder Ford Model T in 1908 was an event that no one could ignore. However, Olds chose not to compete head-on with Ford; instead, he placed the new 35hp Reo upmarket, where its superior specification – 3.7 litre, inlet-over-exhaust engine, multi-disc clutch, countershaft gearbox, shaft drive, worm-and-sector steering – justified a price tag of £850/$1,250, £210/$300 more than the basic Model T.

Richard

◀ **1903 Richard Brasier Model H 12hp Four-Seater Tonneau,** twin-cylinder engine with atmospheric inlet valves and mechanical exhaust valves, 4 forward gears plus reverse, Dubrille oilers, Lucas brass headlamps, professionally restored, engine and radiator rebuilt, bonnet refabricated to original pattern, finished in maroon and black, black leather upholstery, original apart from magneto and carburettor, VCC dated, very good condition.
£60,000–65,000 / $87,000–94,000 ⚒ Bon

Riley

The small firm of Riley was right at the forefront of the early British car industry, producing its first car in 1898. In the 1920s and 1930s, the Coventry firm built some very appealing and highly regarded small sporting cars, with elegant bodies and excellent power units, all of which used twin, low-set camshafts operating pushrods and overhead valves. In the later 1930s, the company spread itself too thinly, with too many models and not enough capital, and was forced to sell out to Morris in 1938. The immediate post-war products, the RM-series cars, were hallmark Riley sporting

saloons, still much appreciated by enthusiasts today for their looks, long-legged cruising ability and assured handling. For many fans, the RMs also rate as the last real Rileys. Sadly, later Rileys were rather ill-served under the BMC banner, which spawned a series of dull badge-engineered look-alikes. About the only intriguing offspring was the Elf. It's really only a Mini with a boot – or a bustle, if you like – a fancier grille and a smattering of wood veneer, but it can make a distinctive budget classic. The Riley name eventually faded away for good in 1969.

RILEY Model	ENGINE cc/cyl	DATES	CONDITION		
			1	2	3
9hp	1034/2	1906–07	£9,000	£6,000	£3,000
Speed 10	1390/2	1909–10	£10,000	£6,000	£3,000
11	1498/4	1922–27	£7,000	£4,000	£2,000
9	1075/4	1927–32	£10,000	£7,000	£4,000
9 Gamecock	1098/4	1932–33	£14,000	£10,000	£6,000
Lincock 12hp	1458/6	1933–36	£9,000	£7,000	£5,000
Imp 9hp	1089/4	1934–35	£35,000	£28,000	£20,000
Kestrel 12hp	1496/4	1936–38	£8,000	£5,000	£2,000
Sprite 12hp	1496/4	1936–38	£40,000	£35,000	£20,000

Many Riley 9hp Specials available; ideal for VSCC and club events.

1933 Riley Nine Lynx, manual gearbox, special wings without running boards, Bosch headlights, hood, side screens, tonneau cover, finished in blue-green, very good condition. **£13,000–15,000 / $18,750–21,750** ⚲ CGC

1935 Riley 12/4 Kestrel Saloon, 1.5 litre 4-cylinder engine with high camshafts and hemispherical combustion chambers, 51bhp, Wilson pre-selector gearbox, 73mph top speed, sliding sun roof, finished in grey with green wire wheels, green leather upholstery and wood veneers complete and original, dashboard with original Jaeger instruments, fuel gauge missing, 2 owners from new, very original but in need of cosmetic attention. **£4,500–5,500 / $6,500–8,000** ⚲ CGC

◀ **1952 Riley RMA 1.5 Saloon,** 1500cc 4-cylinder engine with twin high mounted camshafts, fabric-roofed bodywork finished in black and red, red interior, paintwork and bodywork in very good condition. **£2,500–3,500 / $3,500–5,000** ⚲ H&H

RILEY Model	ENGINE cc/cyl	DATES	CONDITION		
			1	2	3
1½ Litre RMA	1496/4	1945–52	£6,000	£3,500	£1,500
1½ Litre RME	1496/4	1952–55	£6,000	£3,500	£1,500
2½ Litre RMB/F	2443/4	1946–53	£9,000	£7,000	£3,000
2½ Litre Roadster	2443/4	1948–50	£18,000	£11,000	£9,000
2½ Litre Drophead	2443/4	1948–51	£18,000	£14,000	£10,000
Pathfinder	2443/4	1953–57	£3,500	£2,000	£750
2.6	2639/6	1957–59	£3,000	£1,800	£750
1.5	1489/4	1957–65	£3,000	£2,000	£850
4/68	1489/4	1959–61	£1,500	£700	£300
4/72	1622/4	1961–69	£1,600	£800	£300
Elf I/II/III	848/4	1961–66	£1,500	£850	£400
Kestrel I/II	1098/4	1965–67	£1,500	£850	£400

Rolls-Royce

Henry Royce was a Manchester electrical engineer, who built three experimental 10hp, two-cylinder cars in 1903. The Honourable Charles Rolls was an entrepreneur, who sold foreign cars in London. They teamed up in 1904 to form Rolls-Royce, a name that ever since has represented excellence with elegance and supreme luxury. From the beginning of their partnership, they established Rolls-Royce's credentials as an exclusive producer of very expensive and superb motor cars of the highest quality. The 40/50, which became known universally as the Silver Ghost, really could make a plausible claim to being the 'best car in the world', although in the 1930s, for example, such an extravagant claim was harder to justify against rival luxury contenders at home and abroad. The Silver Ghost was continually developed through the years until it was replaced, in 1925, by the New Phantom, later referred to as the Phantom I. This continued the Rolls-Royce policy of evolution rather than revolution – it was, in essence, a Ghost chassis with a new overhead-valve engine. Earlier, in

1922, Rolls-Royce had added the smaller 3127cc 20 model, which evolved in 1929 into the 3669cc 20/25, and later into the 25/30. In 1931, Rolls-Royce bought Bentley – some suggest the primary motive was to stifle competition from the magnificent 8 Litre Bentley. In 1949, Rolls-Royce entered a new era with the Silver Dawn, the first Rolls-Royce offered complete by the factory rather than as a chassis to be fitted with bespoke coachwork of the owner's choosing. Rolls-Royce continued to offer chassis to coachbuilders alongside its own factory-bodied cars until 1965 with the launch of the Silver Shadow. This new Rolls-Royce was the first to feature monocoque construction with an integral body and chassis, which, at a stroke, removed the scope for coachbuilt bodies, although the Phantom V Limousine still retained a separate chassis. In 1971, Rolls-Royce Limited became bankrupt after trouble with the RB211 aircraft engine, and the car division was separated out and floated as a public company. These days, of course, the quintessential British luxury brand is owned by BMW.

1920 Rolls-Royce Silver Ghost Salamanca, chassis no. 16LE, right-hand drive, restored to original condition at a cost of c£75,000/$109,000, coachwork original and correct, good to excellent condition.
£75,000–85,000 / $109,000–123,000 ✗ COYS
The Rolls-Royce 40/50 was introduced at the 1907 Olympia motor show, where it caused a sensation. Orders flooded in, despite a price of £895/$1,300, and by 1908 the Silver Ghost – so renamed after the silver plating and paintwork of the 13th 40/50 produced – was Rolls-Royce's only model. For 1909, capacity increased to 7428cc, and two years later a torque-tube drive was fitted, while power rose to 58bhp. Production was limited to the war effort during WWI, chassis being used for armoured cars, ambulances and staff cars, while the company diversified into aero engine production. By the time private Ghost sales resumed in 1919, power had increased to 70bhp at 2,000rpm, and a chain-driven starter motor and dynamo were standard. This car carries Salamanca cabriolet coachwork fitted at Rolls-Royce's Springfield factory in the USA. With all the weather equipment erected, the car has the appearance of a full-blown saloon, complete with glass windows and a rigid hood, but it can be transformed relatively easily into an attractive and lightweight-style tourer.

▶ **1921 Rolls-Royce 40/50hp Silver Ghost Double Cabriolet,** coachwork by Barker, chassis no. 40UG, engine no. P3, older restoration, twin side-mounted spare wheels, opening windscreen, chauffeur communication porthole in drop-down division.
£65,000–75,000 / $95,000–109,000 ✗ Bon Barker's Double Cabriolet coachwork was state of the art in 1922, offering many different configurations: open, closed or part-open according to the demands of the weather.

1922 Rolls-Royce 40/50hp Silver Ghost Open-Drive Limousine, coachwork by Wilkinsons, chassis no. 76ZG, engine no. N309AL, originally supplied with saloon body, subsequently rebodied, finished in green over black, nickel-silver coach handles and locks, engraved detailing to passenger compartment, luggage rack, leather upholstery to chauffer's compartment, cloth to rear, very good condition throughout.
£80,000–90,000 / $116,000–130,000 ✗ CGC

1928 Rolls-Royce 20hp Limousine, coachwork by Thrupp & Maberly, chassis no. GBM64, engine no. Y9E, 4-wheel servo-assisted brakes, sliding glass division, occasional seats, finished in black, fawn upholstery, used as a taxi during WWII, good original condition throughout.
£15,000–18,000 / $22,000–26,000 ✗ H&H

In 1910, the adventurous Charles Rolls was killed in a flying accident. The impact on the company was far from disastrous, as by then Rolls had largely lost interest in motor cars.

1929 Rolls-Royce 20hp Sedanca De Ville, coachwork by Windovers, chassis no. GLN62, engine no. Q8N, 2700cc engine, twin side mounted spare wheels, Grebel headlights and sidelights, finished in yellow and black, beige interior.
£24,000–28,000 / $35,000–40,000 ✗ H&H

1926 Rolls-Royce 20hp Five-Seater Tourer, coachwork by Windovers, chassis no. GCK 3, engine no. G 1480, front-wheel brakes, overdrive gearbox, Auster screen, windscreen-pillar spot lamp, front bumper, side mounted spare wheel, polished aluminium finish, original in every respect.
£45,000–50,000 / $65,000–72,000 ✗ Bon
The arrival of the 'baby' Rolls-Royce, the 20hp, in 1922 heralded a new generation of small luxury cars geared to the financial constraints of the post-WWI era. The smooth six-cylinder, 3.1 litre engine featured overhead valves and a unit-construction gearbox.

1926 Rolls-Royce Phantom I 40/50hp Coupé Cabriolet, coachwork by Barker, chassis no. 21SC, engine no. EV85, dickey seat, twin side mounted spare wheels, Ace wheel discs, luggage rack, boa constrictor horn, Stephen Grebel lighting set, Barker dipping system, windscreen-pillar spot lamp, new hood and hood bag, nickel-plated brightwork renewed or refurbished as necessary, coachwork restored, bare-metal respray in navy blue, pigskin upholstery.
£67,500–75,000 / $97,000–108,000 ✗ Bon
Long awaited successor to the Ghost, the New Phantom arrived in 1925. Retrospectively known as the Phantom I, the newcomer boasted an entirely new overhead-valve, 7688cc six-cylinder engine with detachable cylinder head, which was considerably more powerful than that of its predecessor. The New Phantom, like the 20hp model, had a disc-type clutch and adjustable radiator shutters; its chassis, though, remained essentially the same as that of the later four-wheel-braked Ghost, and would continue fundamentally unchanged until the arrival of the Phantom II in 1929 brought with it an entirely new frame. Some 2,212 Phantom I chassis had left Rolls-Royce's UK factory by the time production ceased.

ROLLS-ROYCE Model	ENGINE cc/cyl	DATES	CONDITION		
			1	2	3
Silver Ghost 40/50	7035/6	pre-WWI	£350,000+	£120,000	£80,000
Silver Ghost 40/50	7428/6	post-WWI	£110,000+	£70,000	£40,000
20hp (3-speed)	3127/6	1922–25	£29,000+	£23,000	£15,000
20hp	3127/6	1925–29	£30,000+	£24,000	£15,000
Phantom I	7668/6	1925–29	£50,000+	£28,000	£22,000
20/25	3669/6	1925–26	£30,000+	£18,000	£13,000
Phantom II	7668/6	1929–35	£40,000+	£30,000	£20,000
Phantom II Continental	7668/6	1930–35	£60,000+	£40,000	£28,000
25/30	4257/6	1936–38	£30,000+	£18,000	£12,000
Phantom III	7340/12	1936–39	£45,000+	£28,000	£14,000
Wraith	4257/6	1938–39	£38,000	£32,000	£25,000

Prices will vary considerably depending on heritage, originality, coachbuilder, completeness and body style. A poor reproduction body can often mean the value is dependent only upon a rolling chassis and engine.

1927 Rolls-Royce Phantom I 40/50hp Boat-Tail Tourer, chassis no. 95EF, engine no. ZB15, 7668cc engine, originally bodied by Barker as a 5-passenger tourer, subsequently fitted with boat-tail coachwork, finished in maroon and black, parchment hide upholstery, coachwork in very good condition, original mechanical specification in all major respects.
£30,000–35,000 / $43,000–50,000 ⚲ Bon

1930 Rolls-Royce 20/25hp Tourer, coachwork by Windovers, chassis no. GGP8, engine no. H9X, restored, professionally retrimmed early 1990s, 4 owners from new, good condition throughout.
£30,000–35,000 / $43,000–50,000 ⚲ Bon
The introduction of a small Rolls-Royce, the 20hp, in 1922 enabled the company to cater for the increasingly important owner-driver market. Its successor, the 20/25hp, introduced in 1929, updated the concept with significant improvements, featuring an enlarged (from 3127 to 3669cc) and more-powerful crossflow version of the 20hp's six-cylinder, overhead-valve engine. Apart from the revised engine, early 20/25 chassis were identical to those of the last 20hp models, both being produced during 1929. Thus the 20/25 inherited the right-hand gear-change lever and servo-assisted brakes introduced on its predecessor for 1926, as well as Phantom-style vertical radiator shutters. Built alongside the Phantom II, the 20/25 benefited from many of the features developed for the larger model, such as synchromesh gears and centralised chassis lubrication, and would become the bestselling Rolls-Royce of the inter-war period.

▶ **1930 Rolls-Royce 20/25hp All-Weather Tourer,** coachwork by Mulliner, chassis no. GNS48, engine no. W5L, 3.7 litre engine, side mounted spare wheel, twin driver's mirrors, new cylinder head and block, coachwork restored 1988–89, ash frame and panelling replaced as required, finished in burgundy and black, hood re-covered in black duck material, new beige leather upholstery.
£18,000–22,000 / $26,000–32,000 ⚲ CGC

1928 Rolls-Royce Phantom I Regent Convertible Coupé, coachwork by Brewster, engine no. 17662, 7668cc overhead-valve 6-cylinder engine, 3-speed manual gearbox, 4-wheel servo-assisted drum brakes, semi-elliptic leaf-spring suspension to front, cantilever springs to rear, rear door to dickey seat, left-hand drive, partially restored, engine rebuilt, brightwork refurbished, in need of full repaint, blue hood, beige leather upholstery, door panels missing, carpeting torn, chassis plate missing.
£43,000–48,000 / $62,000–70,000 ⚲ C

1930 Rolls-Royce 20/25hp Saloon, coachwork by Barker, chassis no. GTR9, semi-concealed rear mounted spare wheel, fitted suitcase accessed from inside car, subject of considerable renovation work, resprayed in black and burgundy, retrimmed in dark red leather, leather covered dash, correct.
£27,000–30,000 / $39,000–43,000 ⊞ RCC

▶ **1932 Rolls-Royce 20/25hp Boat-Tail Tourer,** coachwork by Ashton Keynes, chassis no. GBT54, engine no. P7T, originally fitted with sports saloon coachwork by Thrupp & Maberly, rebodied with skiff coachwork 1973, wooden decking to rear body, finished in maroon over black, cocktail cabinet in rear passenger compartment.
£25,000–30,000 / $36,000–43,000 ▸ CGC

1932 Rolls-Royce 20/25hp Sports Saloon, coachwork by Freestone & Webb, chassis no. GMU66, engine no. R9S, body restored 1997–98, engine rebuilt and fitted with oil filter, converted to unleaded fuel, gearbox fitted with overdrive unit, invoices for this work totalling over £27,000/$39,000, new honeycomb radiator core, mohair roof covering reproofed, good condition throughout.
£30,000–35,000 / $43,000–50,000 ▸ Bon

1933 Rolls-Royce 20/25hp Sedanca, coachwork by Freestone & Webb, chassis no. GBA64, 3.7 litre engine, restored 1999–2001, finished in black, burgundy upholstery, excellent condition.
£63,000–68,000 / $91,000–99,000 ▸ COYS

1933 Rolls-Royce 20/25hp Sports Saloon, coachwork by Thrupp & Maberly, chassis no. GLZ1, engine no. X4Q, twin trumpet horns, centre driving lamp, rear mounted spare wheel, glass panel with blind to roof, sun blinds to windscreen, grey leather upholstery, paintwork would benefit from refreshing, fitted replacement cylinder head, upholstery partially replaced, otherwise original in all major respects.
£14,000–16,000 / $20,000–23,000 ▸ Bon
In 1957, this car was purchased by Merchiston Motors of Edinburgh for the personal use of W. E. 'Willie' Wilkinson, as a reward for his outstanding achievements in taking the Ecurie Ecosse Jaguars to victory at Le Mans. 'Wilkie' retained the car for almost 44 years until his recent death.

1934 Rolls-Royce 20/25hp Sedanca De Ville, coachwork by Mulliner, chassis no. GRC15, engine no. YT2, twin side-mounted spare wheels, Brooks luggage trunk with fitted cases on period rack, centre mounted Lucas driving lamp, finished in burgundy over black, sedanca roof section in heavy-duty black 'elephant hide', driver's seat trimmed in heavy-duty black hide, rear compartment in cream Bedford cord with black piping, illuminated vanity mirrors in veneered cabinets, centre-mounted radio speaker, division, well maintained.
£30,000–35,000 / $43,000–50,000 ▸ CGC

1934 Rolls-Royce 20/25hp Ranalah Sedanca Drophead Coupé, coachwork by John Charles, subject of no-expense-spared restoration, concours winner.
£50,000–55,000 / $72,000–80,000 ▸ BJ

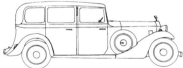

1934 Rolls-Royce 20/25hp Continental Saloon, coachwork by Mann Egerton, chassis no. GAC55, engine no. V67, subject of substantial refurbishment 1995, engine top end rebuilt, radiator recored, dynamo rebuilt, electrical system overhauled, halogen headlamp conversion, windscreen replaced, finished in black, grey leather upholstery, complete set of original tools in lock-away trays, original specification in all major respects, good condition.
£17,000–19,000 / $25,000–27,500 ↗ Bon

1929 Rolls-Royce Phantom II Four-Door Tourer, chassis no. 17WJ, P100 bull's-eye headlamps, Grebel windscreen-pillar spot lamp, twin side mounted spare wheels, new hood and side screens, finished in burgundy and black, recently reupholstered in dark red leather.
£43,000–47,000 / $62,000–68,000 ⊞ RCC

1934 Rolls-Royce 20/25hp Two-Door Faux Cabriolet, coachwork by Freestone & Webb, chassis no. GYD44, manual gearbox with synchromesh on 3rd and 4th gears, thermostatically controlled radiator grille shutters, 1-shot centralised lubrication system, electric fuel gauge, restored 1984, little use since, finished in dark green over light green, green leather interior trim, excellent condition.
£40,000–45,000 / $58,000–65,000 ↗ COYS

1930 Rolls-Royce Phantom II 40/50hp Enclosed-Drive Limousine, coachwork by Harrison & Son, chassis no. 167XJ, engine no. FC75, short-chassis model, Lucas lighting, twin chrome trumpet horns, rear-mounted luggage trunk, twin side-mounted spare wheels, 28 gallon petrol tank, finished in cream and brown, chauffeur's compartment upholstered in beige leather, rear seats trimmed in brown velour, dark brown carpeting, cocktail cabinet with decanters and glasses, walnut cappings throughout.
£23,000–27,000 / $33,000–39,000 ↗ Bon
Increasing competition from both home and overseas manufacturers saw Rolls-Royce introduce the all-new Phantom II in 1929. Unveiled at The Olympia Motor Exhibition in 1929, the 7.7 litre, 40/50hp Phantom II featured unit construction of engine and gearbox, improved handling characteristics and a significantly improved ride.

1932 Rolls-Royce Phantom II Croydon Drophead Coupé, chassis no. 302AJS, original open coachwork, finished in dark green, beige hood, beige leather interior, 1 of only 125 left-hand-drive Phantom IIs built, excellent condition throughout.
£90,000–95,000 / $130,000–138,000 ⊞ RCC

1933 Rolls-Royce Phantom II Limousine, coachwork by Hooper, chassis no. 107MW, engine no. Y865, 5646cc engine, long-chassis model, twin side mounted spare wheels with covers, finished in navy blue and ivory, beige interior.
£23,000–27,000 / $33,000–39,000 ➤ **H&H**

1933 Rolls-Royce Phantom II 40/50hp Six-Light Limousine, coachwork by Hooper, chassis no. 37MW, engine no. JD75, Lucas lighting, twin side-mounted spare wheels, luggage trunk to rear, finished in black over green, black leather interior, sliding division, 2 occasional seats, accommodation for 7 passengers.
£20,000–24,000 / $29,000–35,000 ➤ **Bon**

1933 Rolls-Royce Phantom II 40/50hp Continental Sports Touring Saloon, coachwork by Barker, chassis no. 15MW, engine no. YN45, 7.7 litre 6-cylinder engine, short-chassis model, André Telecontrol dampers, twin side mounted spare wheels, Carl Zeiss headlamps, sliding sun roof, subject of no-expense-spared mechanical overhaul and detailed cosmetic restoration, engine, suspension, brakes and electrics overhauled, chrome trim replated as necessary, polished wheel discs, finished in dark blue, original tan leather upholstery, original radio, interior woodwork repolished, set of Rolls-Royce tools, 3 owners from new, original.
£45,000–50,000 / $65,000–72,000 ➤ **Bon**
From the spring of 1933, the Continental specification engines were fitted with a high-lift camshaft; uprated leaf springing was also available on all Continentals, as was a high-compression cylinder head, while axle ratios were variable according to the owner's requirements.

1936 Rolls-Royce 25/30hp Sedanca Drophead Coupé, coachwork by Salmons & Sons, chassis no. GXM5, engine no. H25V, older restoration.
£40,000–44,000 / $58,000–64,000 ➤ **Bon**

1936 Rolls-Royce 25/30hp Sports Saloon, coachwork by Mulliner, chassis no. GXM70, Ace wheel discs, fitted suitcases, brown leather interior, 76,000 miles from new, correct, excellent condition.
£27,000–30,000 / $39,000–43,000 ⊞ **RCC**

1937 Rolls-Royce 25/30hp Owen Sedanca Coupé, coachwork by Gurney Nutting, chassis no. GUN31, engine no. M285, subject of comprehensive restoration, finished in black and grey, excellent chrome and black fabric top, newly reupholstered in grey cloth, matching leather-bound grey carpets, veneers refurbished, interior mirrors to the rear, smoker's companion, lights to each side in rear, torch fitted in passenger footwell.
£80,000–90,000 / $116,000–130,000 ➤ **Bon**
The new 'small' Rolls-Royce 25/30hp model, exhibited at Olympia in October 1936, featured an engine enlarged in capacity to 4257cc, although borrowing many of its design features from the exceptionally successful 20/25hp. The 20/30hp enjoyed a production run from 1936 to 1938, when it was replaced by the new Wraith. Some 1,201 chassis were built. This car was sold new by H.R. Owen Ltd to racing driver Prince Birabongse (Bira) of Siam and was used regularly by him while resident in London through to 1949, later passing to his cousin, Prince Chula, also a successful amateur racing driver. Eton educated Bira was just 23 years old when he placed the order for his new car. He had first taken up motor racing in 1935, campaigning Rileys, MGs and more notably his ERA, and in the year in which he ordered this car had five notable wins: the Campbell Trophy, the Light Car Race at the Isle of Man, the London Grand Prix, the 12-Hour Race at Donington and the Imperial Trophy.

1939 Rolls-Royce Phantom III 40/50hp Razor-Edge Touring Limousine, coachwork by Freestone & Webb, chassis no. 3DL154, engine no. E28A, P100 headlamps, centre driving lamp, twin chrome horns, side mounted spare wheel, sun roof, luggage boot to rear, older restoration, finished in green over sage, original brown leather upholstery to front compartment, beige West of England cloth to rear, Cartier fitted clock, lady's vanity cabinet, gentleman's cocktail cabinet, concours winner.
£42,000–47,000 / $61,000–68,000 ✠ Bon
The new 7.3 litre V12 engine of the Phantom III reflected the company's experience in building engines of this configuration for aircraft such as the Supermarine S6B seaplane, for it adopted advanced materials and design techniques, such as 'skeleton' cylinder blocks with wet liners and aluminium cylinder heads. Independent front suspension was introduced for the first time on a Rolls-Royce, considerably enhancing handling and ride, and the powerful engine ensured that little use was made of the four-speed, right-hand-change gearbox.

1949 Rolls-Royce Silver Wraith Empress Line Saloon, coachwork by Hooper, chassis no. WDC12, engine no. W12C, engine and chassis completely overhauled, finished in black over silver, black leather interior, complete with period tools.
£19,000–23,000 / $27,000–33,000 ✠ Bon
The new Silver Wraith was launched late in 1946, being Rolls-Royce's first new car since the end of WWII. It was powered by a six-cylinder, overhead-inlet/side-exhaust-valve engine, initially displacing 4257cc. The chassis was of traditional design and significantly shorter than its pre-war Wraith predecessor. The Silver Wraith production run lasted some 14 years, during which 1,144 examples were built. The coachwork of this car would appear to be the prototype for the famous Hooper Empress Line, which first appeared in production guise at the 1950 Motor Show. The car has Body No. 9505 to Design No. 8181, and a similar car appeared at the Earl's Court Motor Exhibition in 1948. It is thought that only seven cars were built to this design.

◄ **1953 Rolls-Royce Silver Wraith Empress Limousine,** coachwork by Hooper, chassis no. BLW15, manual gearbox, new stainless-steel exhaust system, full rear-wheel spats, finished in black and silver-blue, black leather upholstery to front compartment, blue leather to rear, rear facing occasional seats, division opens to form glass panel in sliding sun roof, cocktail cabinet, vanity mirrors.
£35,000–39,000
$50,000–57,000 ⊞ RCC

1955 Rolls-Royce Silver Wraith Long-Wheelbase Lightweight Touring Limousine, coachwork by Mulliner, chassis no. DLW145, engine no. L144D, traditional ash body frame replaced by tubular and cast-aluminium sub-frame, c£10,000/$14,500 spent in last 10 months, engine overhauled, braking system rebuilt, front suspension and chassis lubrication system overhauled, new headlights, resprayed in grey over dark blue, electric division, speaker cabinet flanked by twin cocktail cabinets, large reading light, extra-large rear seat, good woodwork to interior, 1 of only 21 lightweight touring limousines built, very good condition throughout.
£17,500–20,500 / $25,000–30,000 ✠ CGC

► **1956 Rolls-Royce Silver Cloud I Saloon,** transmission overhauled, little use since, finished in blue, original blue-grey leather interior, chassis and underbody in good condition.
£16,500–18,500 / $24,000–27,000 ⊞ RCC

1954 Rolls-Royce Silver Dawn Saloon, coachwork by James Young, chassis no. SOG42, engine no. S21G, 4566cc engine, automatic transmission, subject of body-off restoration, finished in silver and off-white, red hide interior, air conditioning, 1 of c63 Silver Dawns supplied to bespoke coachbuilders.
£18,000–22,000 / $26,000–32,000 ✠ Bon

1956 Rolls-Royce Silver Cloud I Saloon, coachwork by Hooper, automatic transmission, original period colour scheme of black over sand, tan leather interior, 1 of only 2 such cars bodied by Hooper in 1956, 1 family ownership and fewer than 75,000 miles from new, original condition.
£18,000–22,000 / $26,000–32,000 ⚒ COYS

◀ **1956 Rolls-Royce Silver Cloud I,** 4887cc 6-cylinder engine with overhead inlet and side exhaust valves, twin SU carburettors, 4-speed automatic transmission, 4-wheel servo-assisted drum brakes, independent front suspension by wishbones and coil springs with hydraulic dampers, rigid rear live axle with semi-elliptic leaf springs and electrically controlled dampers, left-hand drive, finished in dark grey, original grey leather interior, air conditioning, Radford Countryman fittings including folding rear seats to provide extra luggage space, speedometer in kilometres and high-frequency horns, paintwork and chrome trim in very good condition, slight tarnishing to wheel discs, little recent use.
£23,000–27,000 / $33,000–39,000 ⚒ C
The coachbuilders Harold Radford offered a Countryman conversion of the Silver Cloud saloon, which included a large number of separately available luxury fittings.

ROLLS-ROYCE Model	ENGINE cc/cyl	DATES	CONDITION 1	2	3
Silver Wraith LWB	4566/ 4887/6	1951–59	£25,000	£17,000	£10,000
Silver Wraith SWB	4257/ 4566/6	1947–59	£20,000	£13,000	£10,000
Silver Wraith Drophead	4257/ 4566/6	1947–59	£50,000	£35,000	£25,000
Silver Dawn St'd Steel	4257/ 4566/6	1949–52	£25,000	£15,000	£10,000
Silver Dawn St'd Steel	4257/ 4566/6	1952–55	£30,000	£20,000	£15,000
Silver Dawn Coachbuilt	4257/ 4566/6	1949–55	£35,000+	£25,000	£18,000
Silver Dawn Drophead	4257/ 4566/6	1949–55	£60,000	£50,000	£30,000
Silver Cloud I	4887/6	1955–59	£18,000	£10,000	£8,000
SCI Coupé Coachbuilt	4887/6	1955–59	£30,000	£20,000	£15,000
SCI Conv (HJM)	4887/6	1955–59	£80,000+	£60,000+	£40,000
Silver Cloud II	6230/8	1959–62	£19,000	£10,000	£8,000
SCII Conv (HJM)	6230/8	1959–62	£80,000	£75,000	£40,000
SCII Conv (MPW)	6230/8	1959–62	£60,000	£40,000	£32,000
Silver Cloud III	6230/8	1962–65	£25,000	£12,000	£10,000
SCIII Conv (MPW)	6230/8	1962–65	£70,000	£45,000	£35,000
Silver Shadow	6230/ 6750/8	1965–76	£14,000	£9,000	£7,000
S Shadow I Coupé (MPW)	6230/ 6750/8	1965–70	£15,000	£10,000	£8,000
SSI Drophead (MPW)	6230/ 6750/8	1965–70	£33,000	£25,000	£18,000
Corniche FHC	6750/8	1971–77	£15,000	£11,000	£8,000
Corniche Convertible	6750/8	1971–77	£28,000	£22,000	£18,000
Camargue	6750/8	1975–85	£30,000	£25,000	£18,000

◀ **1961 Rolls-Royce Silver Cloud II Saloon,** 6235cc V8 engine, power steering, finished in gold and brown, beige leather interior, woodwork in excellent condition, period HMV push-button radio, electric windows, excellent condition throughout.
£13,000–15,000
$19,000–22,000 ⚒ H&H

1965 Rolls-Royce Silver Cloud III Two-Door Convertible, good quality conversion similar in appearance to Mulliner design, finished in deep blue, matching power hood, magnolia leather interior, very good condition throughout.
£60,000–65,000 / $87,000–94,000 ⊞ RCC

1963 Rolls-Royce Phantom V Limousine, coachwork by James Young, recently restored, finished in black, black interior, air conditioning, CD player, cocktail cabinet complete with all glasses.
£28,000–32,000 / $40,000–46,000 ⚒ Bon

> Sir Henry Royce, made a baronet after Rolls-Royce engines contributed to success in the 1931 Schneider Trophy air race, died in 1933.

1975 Rolls-Royce Phantom VI Landaulette, coachwork by Mulliner Park Ward, 6.7 litre overhead-valve V8 engine, twin SU carburettors, 3-speed automatic transmission, dual-circuit 4-wheel hydraulic drum brakes, wishbone-and-coil-spring independent front suspension, rigid rear axle on semi-elliptic leaf springs, Sundym glass, vanity mirrors to drop tables in rear, electrically-operated rear seat, division cabinet incorporating television, quadrophonic tape player and cocktail compartment, stereo radios to front and rear compartments, leather Duchess straps to each D-post, period Pye telephone, rear section of hood electrically operated, good condition throughout.
£150,000+ / $218,000+ ⚒ C

From 1950 to 1956, Rolls-Royce built chassis for the Phantom IV using an eight-cylinder inline engine of 5675cc, but it was manufactured for heads of state only; a mere 18 were made. The Phantom V followed, in 1960, and was the first Phantom to have the V8 engine; it was sold without restriction. Similarly, the Phantom VI, introduced in 1968, had no restriction on sales; it was similar to the V, but the engine capacity was increased to 6.7 litres, the transmission was changed to three speeds, the brakes were operated hydraulically, and power steering was fitted. Late in Phantom V production, a coachwork style that had its origins in the earliest of the carriage designs, the Landau, was developed for the latest Rolls-Royce. The design, which featured a convertible rear section, was particularly appropriate for state limousines, as when used for parades and similar events, it enabled the public to see the passengers, while they could remain comfortably and safely seated. The design continued to be produced on Phantom VI chassis.

1972 Rolls-Royce Silver Shadow I Saloon, finished in blue, factory electric steel sun roof, original navy leather interior, original 8-track stereo, 58,000 miles from new, substantially original, excellent condition throughout.
£9,000–11,000 / $13,000–16,000 ⚲ BARO
The Silver Shadow was the first Rolls-Royce to be built using unitary construction, rather than the traditional separate chassis with a choice of standard steel or coachbuilt bodywork.

1973 Rolls-Royce Silver Shadow I Saloon, 6750cc engine, 4-wheel disc brakes, 4-wheel independent self-levelling suspension, full Webasto sun roof, finished in metallic light blue, dark blue interior, service receipts totalling over £50,000/$72,500, 2 owners from new.
£4,500–5,500 / $6,500–8,000 ⚲ H&H

> The T1 and T2 were Bentley's equivalents of the Rolls-Royce Silver Shadow I and II. Although virtually identical, apart from the distinctive radiator, Bentley versions can often be cheaper than their Rolls-Royce counterparts, despite the fact that Bentley versions are far rarer.

◀ **1976 Rolls-Royce Silver Shadow I Saloon,** last of chrome-bumper models, long wheelbase, small rear window, 2 owners and 88,000 miles from new.
£8,000–10,000 / $11,500–14,500 ⊞ VIC

1975 Rolls-Royce Corniche, 6750cc overhead-valve V8 engine, 225bhp, 3-speed automatic transmission, 4-wheel servo-assisted disc brakes, 4-wheel independent self-levelling coil-spring suspension, left-hand drive, finished in brown, magnolia leather interior, built to US specification, in need of some mechanical attention, otherwise good condition, formerly the property of Muhammad Ali.
£17,000–20,000 / $25,000–29,000 ⚲ C
The Rolls-Royce Corniche was announced in early 1971 and introduced a new practice of using names to designate specific coachwork designs, rather than just the basic chassis; with unitary construction, this no longer worked. The name and model, in fact, provided a new identity for the existing coachbuilt, two-door design based on the Silver Shadow, which had been available since 1967 from Mulliner, Park Ward. The Corniche benefited from improved performance over the standard Shadow and, for the first time, cruise control was introduced, while cosmetically the new car featured a revised dash layout.

1985 Rolls-Royce Camargue, coachwork by Pininfarina, finished in Old English white, burgundy interior, 2 owners and fewer than 5,000 miles from new, excellent condition.
£34,000–38,000 / $50,000–55,000 ✦ Bon

Styled by Pininfarina of Italy, the Camargue was launched in 1975. Based on the Silver Shadow floorpan and running gear, the rakish-looking newcomer was strikingly different from any preceding Rolls-Royce. Intended as the company's flagship model, it was priced accordingly at 50 per cent above the Corniche. Like the latter, the Camargue used an uprated version of the company's dependable 6750cc, pushrod V8. Rolls-Royce's advanced split-level air conditioning system was introduced with the Camargue, later becoming standard on the Shadow II range. The Camargue and the Corniche were the first to feature Rolls-Royce's revised rear suspension and ride-height control. The Camargue was an exclusive model even by Rolls-Royce standards, output totalling just 531 units by the time production ceased in 1986.

◀ **1978 Rolls-Royce Silver Shadow II Saloon,** finished in metallic light blue, blue leather interior, well maintained.
£8,000–10,000 / $11,500–14,500 ⊞ VIC

1980 Rolls-Royce Silver Shadow II Saloon, 6750cc V8 engine, finished in maroon, good condition.
£8,000–9,000 / $11,500–13,000 ⊞ BLE

◀ **1980 Rolls-Royce Silver Shadow II Saloon,** 6750cc V8 engine, finished in gold, barley leather interior, 2 owners from new, minor bubbling to paintwork, otherwise excellent condition throughout.
£6,000–7,000 / $8,750–10,250 ✦ H&H

1981 Rolls-Royce Silver Spirit Saloon, 6750cc V8 engine, automatic transmission, finished in dark blue, light blue leather interior, 56,000 miles from new, excellent condition.
£12,000–14,000 / $17,500–20,500 ✦ H&H

Rover

Rover's roots were in the booming bicycle industry of the last decades of the 19th century. The first Rover car appeared in 1904. In its early years, Rover had never been a high-volume car maker, and in the mid-1920s it concentrated on the solid middle-class territory that to this day is Rover's home ground. As Rover emerged from WWII, it made do with the P3, an updated pre-war design, until the now much loved and so-called 'Auntie' Rover, the P4, was ready in 1950. Thoroughly modern and at first considered even avant-garde by some more traditionally-minded motorists, it went on to establish Rover's post-war reputation for dependable and robust quality cars. The big P5 saloon, launched in 1959, became a newsreel fixture outside 10 Downing Street as a P5 fleet loyally served ministers and prime ministers from Harold Wilson to Margaret Thatcher. The stylish P6,

especially in V8 form, has also become a favourite, admired and enjoyed in enthusiastic every-day use. But while Rover models remained distinguished, Britain's motor industry was in turmoil with merger mania. Rover could no longer remain independent against this tide, and in 1967 merged into the Leyland Motor Corporation. In this environment, Rover could have slithered into oblivion, but it managed to produce one great vehicle. The Range Rover of 1970 is, without doubt, a living classic. Somehow Rover weathered the BL years and emerged on top, as the organisation was named Rover Group in 1986 and acquired by BMW in 1994. In the year 2000, BMW's troubled ownership came to an end, and today a trimmed down Rover, divested of Land Rover, is owned by a British consortium. It's going to be an interesting few years.

1924 Rover 14hp Four/Five-Seater Tourer, 2297cc 4-cylinder engine, 4-speed manual gearbox, worm-drive axle, transmission brake operated by foot pedal, rear brakes operated by hand lever, twin side mounted spare wheels, beaded-edge tyres, full weather equipment, rear Auster screen and leg protection, older restoration.
£14,000–16,000 / $20,500–23,500 ⚒ Bon
The Rover Cycle Company of Coventry was formed in 1896, and from 1899 J. Starley worked on the development of a motorcycle, the first examples going on sale from 1902, with tri-cars available during 1904–07. The Rover 8 four-wheeler from 1904 had the innovative feature of a steel backbone chassis, the 10hp and 12hp models giving Rover a strong market in the lead-up to WWI. After the Armistice, although Rover concentrated on the light car market, it also offered larger models, including a six.

1939 Rover 10hp Two-Door Sports Coupé, 1389cc overhead-valve 4-cylinder engine, manual gearbox with synchromesh on 3rd and 4th gears, automatic chassis lubrication, switchable free-wheel hubs, trafficators and modern flashing indicators, sliding sun roof, finished in black, original brown leather interior.
£5,000–6,000 / $7,250–8,750 ⚒ Bon

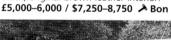

► **1939 Rover 12 Four-Door Saloon,** 1479cc engine, restored, finished in black, new blue leather upholstery, all woodwork repolished, missing 2 spot lamps.
£7,500–8,500 / $10,900–12,300 ⚒ H&H

ROVER Model	ENGINE cc/cyl	DATES	CONDITION		
			1	2	3
10hp	998/2	1920–25	£5,000	£3,000	£1,500
9/20	1074/4	1925–27	£6,000	£4,000	£2,000
10/25	1185/4	1928–33	£7,000	£4,000	£2,500
14hp	1577/6	1933–39	£6,000	£4,250	£2,000
12	1496/4	1934–37	£7,000	£4,000	£1,500
20 Sports	2512/6	1937–39	£7,000	£4,500	£2,500

1955 Rover P4 60 Saloon, finished in black, red leather interior, unused since 1995, in need of recommissioning, good condition.
£350–500 / $500–720 ⚒ CGC
The Rover P4 was launched in 1950, and its transatlantic styling disguised a competent chassis with Girling hydraulic drum brakes, independent coil-and-wishbone front suspension and a panhard rod located, leaf-sprung rear. Various engine options were available during the P4's model life, including the 60, a 2 litre, inlet-over-exhaust four-cylinder unit developing 60bhp. With the standard four-speed-plus-free-wheel manual transmission, this gave a top speed of 80mph. Marginally slower than its big brother the 75, the 60 was also close in terms of price. Only 9,261 examples of the 60 were built between 1954 and 1959.

1964 Rover 95 Saloon, export model, slightly lower compression ratio than standard, tinted sun visors, 3 owners from new.
£2,200–2,800 / $3,200–4,000 ⚒ Bon

1959 Rover P4 90 Saloon, 2.6 litre 6-cylinder engine, front suspension and shock absorbers rebuilt, finished in green, matching green vinyl and leather interior, original HMV radio and spot lamps, 85,000 miles from new, good condition throughout.
£1,300–1,700 / $2,000–2,500 ⚒ CGC

1966 Rover P5 3 Litre Coupé, 2995cc engine, 4-speed manual gearbox with overdrive, finished in grey, dark red interior, stored for many years, 1 owner since 1967.
£750–1,000 / $1,100–1,500 ⚒ H&H
The Rover 3 Litre was introduced in 1958 and remained in production for ten years, being offered in both saloon and coupé guises. The Mk III came with power steering and a 134bhp engine; externally, it was recognisable by its new radiator badge and a continuous chrome side strip.

ROVER Model	ENGINE cc/cyl	DATES	CONDITION 1	2	3
P2 10	1389/4	1946–47	£3,200	£2,500	£1,000
P2 12	1496/4	1946–47	£3,500	£2,800	£1,200
P2 12 Tour	1496/4	1947	£6,000	£3,500	£1,500
P2 14/16	1901/6	1946–47	£4,200	£3,000	£1,000
P2 14/16 Sal	1901/6	1946–47	£3,000	£2,000	£700
P3 60	1595/4	1948–49	£5,000	£2,500	£1,000
P3 75	2103/6	1948–49	£4,000	£3,000	£800
P4 75	2103/6	1950–51	£4,000	£2,000	£1,200
P4 75	2103/6	1952–64	£3,500	£1,800	£1,200
P4 60	1997/4	1954–59	£3,200	£1,200	£1,200
P4 90	2638/6	1954–59	£4,000	£1,800	£1,200
P4 75	2230/6	1955–59	£3,800	£1,200	£1,000
P4 105R	2638/6	1957–58	£4,000	£2,000	£1,000
P4 105S	2638/6	1957–59	£4,000	£2,000	£1,000
P4 80	2286/4	1960–62	£3,000	£1,200	£800
P4 95	2625/6	1963–64	£3,000	£1,600	£500
P4 100	2625/6	1960–62	£3,800	£2,000	£1,000
P4 110	2625/6	1963–64	£3,800	£2,000	£1,000
P5 3 Litre	2995/6	1959–67	£4,000	£2,500	£1,000
P5 3 Litre Coupé	2995/6	1959–67	£5,500	£3,800	£1,000
P5B (V8)	3528/8	1967–74	£6,250	£4,500	£1,500
P5B (V8) Coupé	3528/8	1967–73	£6,250	£4,500	£1,500
P6 2000 SC Series 1	1980/4	1963–65	£2,200	£800	-
P6 2000 SC Series 1	1980/4	1966–70	£2,000	£800	-
P6 2000 SC Auto Series 1	1980/4	1966–70	£1,500	£600	-
P6 2000 TC Series 1	1980/4	1966–70	£2,000	£900	-
P6 2000 SC Series 2	1980/4	1970–73	£2,000	£900	-
P6 2000 SC Auto Series 2	1980/4	1970–73	£1,500	£800	-
P6 2000 TC Series 2	1980/4	1970–73	£2,000	£900	-
P6 3500 Series 1	3500/8	1968–70	£2,500	£1,400	-
P6 2200 SC	2200/4	1974–77	£1,750	£850	-
P6 2200 SC Auto	2200/4	1974–77	£2,500	£1,000	-
P6 2200 TC	2200/4	1974–77	£2,000	£1,000	-
P6 3500 Series 2	3500/8	1971–77	£3,000	£1,700	-
P6 3500 S Series 2	3500/8	1971–77	£2,000	£1,500	-

1971 Rover P5B Saloon, 3528cc V8 engine, 3-speed automatic transmission, engine and transmission rebuilt, new electrics, bodywork rebuilt using mainly new panels, finished in magenta, cream interior refurbished, all new rubber seals, 71,000 miles from new.
£3,200–3,800 / $4,650–5,500 ✗ H&H

1968 Rover P6 2000 TC Saloon, restored, dry stored 1989–2000, recently fitted with new exhaust system, radiator core and carburettor floats, excellent condition.
£1,500–2,000 / $2,200–3,000 ✗ Bon

1971 Rover P5B Saloon, 3528cc V8 engine, converted to unleaded fuel, new radiator 1998, new front and rear screen seals, resprayed in white 1997, original burgundy leather upholstery, carpeting in poor condition, otherwise good condition throughout.
£1,000–1,500 / $1,500–2,200 ✗ BRIT

The Rover P5, beloved of captains of industry, tycoons and government ministers alike, was powered by a 3 litre straight-six from its introduction in 1958. Also available as a four-door coupé with a lowered roofline from 1962, and incorporating high levels of comfort, power steering and choice of manual/overdrive gearbox or automatic transmission, these cars were very much in the Rover tradition. For some years, Rover had experimented with alternative power units and even gas-turbine power. However, the solution was to come in the form of a light, compact V8 found in a boatyard in Wisconsin. While visiting Carl Keikhaffer, of Mercury Marine, William Martin-Hurst, then Rover's production director, spotted the Buick derived engine in the experimental shop. The all-aluminium 3.5 litre unit was adopted and modified by Rover before being installed into the P5 in 1967, giving a useful 144bhp, 108mph and 50mph in less than 9 seconds from rest. These cars, fitted with automatic transmission as standard and distinguishable by Rostyle wheels, were designated P5B – 'B' for Buick.

◄ **1972 Rover P6 3500 S,** 3.5 litre V8 engine, 4-speed manual gearbox, 4-wheel independent suspension, fitted later SD1 engine, converted to unleaded fuel, electronic ignition, electric fan, 4 new gas shock absorbers, some structural restoration carried out, 4 new wings, finished in brown, magnolia leather interior.
£750–1,000 / $1,100–1,500 ✗ CGC

Rover P6 (1963–76)

Production: 327,808.
Price in 1963: £1,265.
Engine: 1978cc, four-cylinder; 2204cc, four-cylinder; 3528cc, V8.
Power output: 90–114bhp (2000); 98–115bhp (2200); 144bhp (3500).
Transmission: Four-speed manual; Borg Warner three-speed automatic.
Brakes: Discs all-round, servo-assisted.
Maximum speed: 94mph (2000 auto); 102mph (2000 manual); 122mph (3500 manual).
0–60mph: 18 seconds (2000 auto); 15 seconds (2000 manual); 9.1 seconds (3500 manual).
In the 1950s, the warm and gentle charms of Rover's P4 had earned it the nickname of the 'Auntie' Rover, cherished affectionately by owners as one of the family. But frankly, by the early 1960s, the dumpy dowager was well past pensionable age and becoming something of a burden. That's where the P6 came in, at the October 1963 London Motor Show, young, vigorous, strikingly modern, almost avant garde and all the more surprising for being a Rover, a name then more associated with staid sobriety than with dash and daring. Rover's traditional clientele may have choked into their cravats, but the press raved about it. *The Autocar* declared it

'one of the outstanding cars of the decade', and in 1964 it was voted Car of the Year. The praise was deserved, because there was no carry-over engineering from previous models. The sleek shape, evolved from an earlier gas-turbine experimental project, doffed its hat a little to the Citroën DS, as did the construction, with a skeletal 'base unit' to which the body panels were bolted. Anchors were discs all-round, and suspension geometry was up-to-the-minute. The initial version, the 2000, contributed a large part to Rover's 24 per cent upturn in sales during 1964, and for once the company didn't sit on its laurels. A pokier 2000TC – twin-carb model – followed in 1966, along with an automatic (the only P6 that couldn't top the ton). But the most exciting development came in 1968, when Rover squeezed in the fabulous Buick derived 3.5 litre V8 to create the 3500. Initially, it was only available as an automatic, but a four-speed-manual-gearbox version, the 3500S, became available in 1971, offering serious 120+mph performance, much appreciated by the police. In the final count, the P6 sold more than one-and-half times as many as any Rover before. It should have led to greater things – but then came the SD1. You know the rest of the Rover story.

Saab

SAAB Model	ENGINE cc/cyl	DATES	CONDITION 1	2	3
92	764/2	1950–53	£3,000	£1,500	£1,000
92B	764/2	1953–55	£3,500	£1,500	£1,000
93–93B	748/3	1956–60	£3,000	£1,500	£1,000
95	841/3	1960–68	£3,000	£1,500	£1,000
96	841/3	1960–68	£4,000	£1,800	£1,000
96 Sport	841/3	1962–66	£3,500	£1,500	£1,000
Sonnett II	1698/4	1967–74	£3,500	£1,500	£1,000
95/96	1498/4	1966–80	£3,000	£1,000	£800
99	1709/4	1968–71	£2,000	£1,200	-
99	1854/4	1970–74	£2,000	£1,000	-
99	1985/4	1972–83	£2,000	£1,000	£500
99 Turbo	1985/4	1978–83	£3,000	£1,000	£500

S.C.A.T.

1913 S.C.A.T. 15hp Five-Seater Tourer, coachwork by Newton & Bennett, radiator recored, detachable wire wheels, period running-board tyre inflator, brass bulb horn, matching rear-view mirrors, electric lighting, resprayed in British racing green, full tonneau cover, full weather equipment, bills for c£10,000, VCC dated.
£23,000–26,000 / $33,500–37,500 ⚹ Bon
Societa Ceirano Automobili Torino was based, as its name implies, in Turin. Giovanni Ceirano came from an affluent Italian family and had a passion for the new-fangled motor car. Recognising the publicity value to be obtained from active participation in motor sport, Ceirano entered S.C.A.T. cars in Europe's major races, fielding a team in the 1908 Tourist Trophy Race on the Isle of Man and later achieving victory in the gruelling Italian Targa Florio of 1911, 1912 and 1914. Cyril Snipe, the nephew of a Newton & Bennett board member, drove the winning car in 1912, and Newton & Bennett contributed financially to the S.C.A.T. operation.

Sheffield Simplex

◄ **1908 Sheffield Simplex LA2 Four-Seater Tourer,** 6960cc sidevalve 6-cylinder engine built in 3 blocks of 2 cylinders, combined clutch and brake, tipping steering wheel for large drivers, older restoration, new cylinder blocks, non-original carburettor, replica 'works' Simplex trials-car coachwork.
£65,000–75,000 / $94,000–109,000 ⚹ H&H
The name Simplex is synonymous with the idea of the 'gearless car', models being manufactured between 1906 and 1922. It was developed by Peter Brotherhood and Percy Richardson. This particular car was exported originally to Australia. From 1939 to 1945, it was used as a lorry in Adelaide, delivering bricks to building sites and, at one point, the engine was detached from the chassis and used to drive a pump, while the chassis was employed as a trailer.

Shelby

1966 Shelby Cobra 427 S/C, 427cu.in overhead-valve V8 engine, 485bhp, 4-speed manual gearbox, 4-wheel coil-spring independent suspension, rack-and-pinion steering, 4-wheel disc brakes, 3 owners from new.
£300,000+ / $435,000+ ⚒ BJ
The Cobra 427 SC (Semi-Competition) was a road-going version of a pure competition model developed by Shelby. It came about when Shelby was unable to sell all of the competition models it had built to conform to FIA regulations. The only changes made were the installation of a full windscreen, rubber bushes in the suspension and a slightly muffled exhaust. In total, 31 were built.

1967 Shelby Cobra 427, original side-oiler 427cu.in V8 engine, subject of chassis-up restoration to concours condition, very low mileage.
£140,000–160,000 / $203,000–232,000 ⚒ BJ

1967 Shelby Cobra 427, 1 of 4 cars fitted originally with 428cu.in V8 engine, subsequently fitted with Holman & Moody 427cu.in overhead-camshaft V8, recently refurbished.
£130,000–150,000 / $188,000–218,000 ⚒ BJ

Singer

Having started with sewing machines and bicycles, George Singer produced his first motor car in Coventry in 1905. The Singer Nine of the 1930s had a really fine 972cc engine, and in open form was a serious rival of MG offerings. Both designs endured into the 1950s without radical changes. The other great pre-war Singer model was the 1½ Litre Le Mans. Post-war, Singer's products were too expensive to compete comprehensively with the likes of BMC, and in 1955 the company was acquired by the Rootes empire, the marque being reduced to an upmarket badge that faded away for good in 1970.

◄ **1926 Singer 10hp Tourer,** finished in red with black wings, little use since 1960s, basically sound and complete, fair condition.
£3,500–4,500 / $5,000–6,500 ⚒ CGC
Like so many Midlands car manufacturers, Singer began by producing bicycles, then graduated to motorcycles, and finally produced its first car in 1905. Pre-war production employed White and Poppe engines, and the company enjoyed great success with the 10hp model in 1912. After WWI, Singer continued production of the 10hp, gradually making improvements. The first of these was a centrally mounted gearbox; later the configuration was redesigned completely with an all-new, monobloc, four-cylinder, overhead-valve engine. From 1926, four-wheel brakes were provided.

1929 Singer Junior 8hp Porlock Sports, 848cc 4-cylinder engine, starter motor and magneto rebuilt, body professionally rebuilt 1991, finished in 2-tone green, new black canvas weather equipment, dark green leatherette interior trim to original pattern, engine and all other major mechanical components in good condition.
£7,500–8,500 / $10,900–12,300 ⚴ BRIT
Singer grew rapidly and gained an enviable reputation for quality products, becoming Britain's third largest car manufacturer, behind Austin and Morris, by the late 1920s. In 1926, the 8hp Junior range was introduced, powered by the first of a long line of excellent overhead-camshaft engines. A small car of high quality, the Junior was available with six different body styles and enjoyed a production run lasting until 1932. The Porlock sports model was so named in 1929, when such a car ascended Porlock Hill in Devon with considerable alacrity no less than 100 times.

1929 Singer Junior 8hp Porlock Sports, 848cc overhead-camshaft 4-cylinder engine, 3-speed manual gearbox, ladder-frame chassis, 4-wheel leaf-spring suspension, 4-wheel drum brakes, 6 volt electrics, wire wheels, completely restored, finished in green and white, canvas hood, black leatherette upholstery, well maintained, very good condition.
£7,000–8,000 / $10,200–11,600 ⚴ CGC

1930 Singer Junior 8hp Tourer, 848cc overhead-camshaft 4-cylinder engine, 4-speed manual gearbox, rear mounted fuel tank, hood and side screens, finished in maroon and black, red interior, good condition.
£4,500–5,500 / $6,500–8,000 ⚴ Bon

1933 Singer Nine Sports Four-Seater Tourer, subject of extensive restoration, good weather equipment, finished in red, red leather upholstery, original specification in all major respects.
£5,250–6,250 / $7,500–9,000 ⚴ Bon
Announced for the 1932 season, the Nine employed a 972cc, 26.5bhp version of the engine first used for the Junior Special in an entirely new chassis. A four-speed gearbox was standard on the Nine, sports versions of which were equipped with Rudge Whitworth wire wheels, twin Zenith carburettors initially and a radiator stone guard. A free-wheel option was available for an extra £10.10s/$17.

1930 Singer Junior 8hp Four-Door Saloon, 848cc 4-cylinder engine, restored over last 10 years, virtually unused since, engine completely rebuilt, rewired incorporating brake lights, new roof covering, finished in maroon with black wings, new red leathercloth upholstery, in need of running in.
£5,000–6,000 / $7,250–8,750 ⚴ BRIT

SINGER Model	ENGINE cc/cyl	DATES	CONDITION 1	2	3
10	1097/4	1918–24	£5,000	£2,000	£1,000
15	1991/6	1922–25	£6,000	£3,000	£1,500
14/34	1776/6	1926–27	£7,000	£4,000	£2,000
Junior	848/4	1927–32	£6,000	£3,000	£1,500
Senior	1571/4	1928–29	£7,000	£4,000	£2,000
Super 6	1776/6	1928–31	£7,000	£4,000	£2,000
9 Le Mans	972/4	1932–37	£13,000+	£8,000	£5,000
Twelve	1476/6	1932–34	£10,000	£7,000	£6,000
1.5 Litre	1493/6	1934–36	£3,000	£2,000	£1,000
2 Litre	1991/6	1934–37	£4,000	£2,750	£1,000
11	1459/4	1935–36	£3,000	£2,000	£1,000
12	1525/4	1937–39	£3,000	£2,000	£1,000

1934 Singer Nine Four-Door Saloon, 972cc overhead-camshaft 4-cylinder engine, 31bhp, 4-speed manual gearbox, 4-wheel leaf-spring suspension and drum brakes, de luxe-specification sun roof, finished in green and black, green leather interior with wood trim.
£2,750–3,500 / $4,000–5,000 ✗ CGC
The Singer Nine featured a 'clutchless gear-change' mechanism, which employed a fluid coupling and caused the *Autocar* to remark, 'The gear lever can be moved exactly as the driver wishes from one gear position to another, either up or down, without shock or jar.' With the exception of the Pedomatic starter (operated by depression of the throttle), the Nine's design was conventional.

1936 Singer Bantam Two-Door Saloon, older restoration, mechanics overhauled, wheel discs, rear mounted luggage rack, wicker picnic basket, original chrome trim, finished in grey and black, original green leather upholstery.
£3,250–3,750 / $4,750–5,500 ✗ CGC
Successor to the Nine Saloon, the Bantam was launched in 1935. Its more curvaceous form clothed a leaf-sprung, drum-braked chassis that was very similar to that of its predecessor. The staple 972cc engine was also retained, but mated to a three-speed manual gearbox. Top speed remained unchanged at 60mph.

◀ **1948 Singer Roadster,** 1497cc overhead-valve 4-cylinder engine, 58bhp, 85mph top speed, 4-speed manual gearbox, independent coil-spring front suspension, partially restored 1983–85, finished in pale blue-grey, dark blue interior, some chrome trim in need of attention, only 500 miles in last 5 years.
£5,250–6,250
$7,500–9,000 ✗ CGC

▶ **1939 Singer Twelve Four-Door Saloon,** 1525cc 4-cylinder engine, refurbished early 1990s, finished in black, original green leather upholstery in good condition.
£4,400–5,200 / $6,500–7,500 ✗ BRIT
Produced between 1937 and 1939, the Twelve's specification included a cross-braced chassis, hydraulic brakes, twin wind-tone horns and telescopic steering column. The traditional Singer overhead-camshaft engine delivered a useful 43bhp, and combined smoothness and flexibility with the normal Singer refinements.

Restored values
The cost of a professional restoration will have an influence on, but no direct relation to, a car's market value. A restored car can have a market value lower than the cost of its restoration.

◀ **1965 Singer Chamois Saloon,** 875cc engine, 39bhp, restored, finished in maroon, very good condition.
£2,000–2,500 / $3,000–3,500 🚗 IMP
The Chamois was a luxury version of the Imp saloon. It featured wood veneer, extra sound deadening and radial tyres on 4½in (11.5cm) wide rims.

◀ **1968 Singer Chamois Saloon,** 875cc engine, 39bhp, non-standard alloy wheels, finished in green, good condition.
£1,500–1,750 / $2,200–2,500 🚗 IMP
The facelifted 1968 model featured a revised interior and dashboard; it also had twin headlights, like the Stiletto.

1969 Singer Chamois Coupé, 875cc engine, standard Imp running gear, wood veneer door cappings, restored mid-1990s.
£1,800–2,200 / $2,500–3,200 🚗 IMP

◀ **1967 Singer Vogue Estate,** 1725cc overhead-valve 4-cylinder engine, 85bhp, 4-speed manual gearbox with overdrive, coil-spring independent front suspension, leaf-spring rear suspension, front disc/rear drum brakes, finished in metallic green, black upholstery, wooden dashboard, same family ownership and 68,000 miles from new.
£200–300 / $300–450 🔨 CGC

Squire

1935 Squire Short-Chassis Two-Seater Sports, coachwork by Vanden Plas, 1.5 litre engine, 1 of only 3 short-wheelbase Vanden Plas-bodied Squires built, fitted replacement engine, otherwise original condition.
£85,000–95,000 / $123,000–138,000 🔨 Bon

In 1931, aged just 21, Adrian Squire, aided by 19-year-old G.F.A. 'Jock' Manby-Colegrave and 26-year-old Reginald Slay, established Squire Motors, 'specialists in racing and sports cars with tuning and overhauls undertaken'. A small team of mechanics was recruited and worked on Manby-Colegrave's racing cars – including an MG K3 Magnette – as well as client automobiles. Once the business was established, the trio set up the Squire Car Manufacturing Company in January 1934, and the prototype Squire was on the road with a rough test body by the summer. The capacity of its supercharged, twin-cam Anzani R1 engine was 1496cc. A massive dynastarter, driving directly on the nose of the crankshaft, gave silent starting; a Wilson pre-selector gearbox provided 'practically instantaneous' gear shifting; and massive finned manganese-alloy brake drums with nickel-chrome liners gave excellent stopping power. Each Squire sold came with an official certificate confirming that it had exceeded 100mph at Brooklands. There was just one factor holding the Squire back: its price of £1,220 was immense by the standards of the day, double that of an Aston Martin Le Mans two-seater and sufficient to buy a dozen 8hp Fords! So the first car sold was bought by Jock Manby-Colegrave. In all, only seven were built. After the original Anzani engine failed during a hill climb, a subsequent owner of this car replaced it with a 1.5 litre twin-cam unit from a British Salmson sports car.

Standard

From modest beginnings, by 1906, Standard was marketing Britain's first inexpensive six-cylinder car. The company specialised in medium-range cars during the 1920s, but it was the Standard Little Nine that buoyed the company in the 1930s. In 1945, with Captain John Black at the helm, Standard acquired the defunct Triumph marque as an upmarket badge. Standard-Triumph was merged into Leyland in 1961, and ironically it was the Standard name that almost immediately was dropped, while Triumph soldiered on until 1980.

STANDARD Model	ENGINE cc/cyl	DATES	CONDITION 1	2	3
SLS	1328/4	1919–20	£5,000	£4,000	£1,000
VI	1307/4	1922	£5,000	£4,000	£1,000
SLO/V4	1944/4	1922–28	£5,000	£4,000	£1,000
6V	2230/6	1928	£10,000	£8,000	£5,000
V3	1307/4	1923–26	£4,000	£3,000	£1,000
Little 9	1006/4	1932–33	£4,000	£2,000	£1,000
9	1155/4	1928–29	£5,500	£3,000	£1,000
Big 9	1287/4	1932–33	£4,500	£3,250	£2,000
15	1930/6	1929–30	£6,000	£4,000	£2,000
12	1337/6	1933–34	£4,000	£3,000	£1,500
10hp	1343/4	1933–37	£4,000	£2,500	£1,000
9	1052/4	1934–36	£4,200	£2,500	£1,000
Flying 9	1131/4	1937–39	£3,200	£1,800	£750
Flying 10	1267/4	1937–39	£3,500	£2,200	£1,000
Flying 14	1176/4	1937–48	£4,500	£2,200	£1,000
Flying 8	1021/4	1939–48	£4,500	£2,400	£1,000

1932 Standard Big Nine Four-Door Saloon, 1287cc sidevalve 4-cylinder engine, 4-speed manual gearbox, worm-drive back axle, leaf-spring suspension, 4-wheel drum brakes, Stanlite sliding sun roof, starter and fuel pump overhauled, bulkhead restored, finished in red and black, original brown leather interior, very good condition.
£3,250–3,750 / $4,800–5,500 ⚒ CGC
This car is believed to have seen service with the RAF, there being traces of the familiar blue paint on the body and the RAF insignia on its keys.

1936 Standard Nine Two-Door Deluxe Saloon, 1052cc 4-cylinder engine, 4-speed manual gearbox, sun roof, finished in grey, new chrome trim, original blue leather interior, fewer than 77,000 miles from new, good condition.
£2,400–2,800 / $3,500–4,000 ⚒ H&H

Standard Vanguard Phase 1 (1948–52)

Body style: 5/6-seater saloon; estate car available from mid-1949.
Production: 184,799.
Engine: 2088cc, overhead-valve, four-cylinder.
Power output: 68bhp at 4,200rpm.
Transmission: Three-speed, all-synchromesh, column-change manual; optional overdrive available from mid-1950.
Maximum speed: 81mph (overdrive model).
0–60mph: 24.5 seconds.
The Standard Vanguard was aptly named because it was one of the very first all-new, post-war British designs to hit the showrooms. With full-width body, rather than separate wings, and a beetle-back shape that followed popular American practice – in particular the 1942 Plymouth – it was an object of some admiration in a cash-strapped, car-starved Britain. Unfortunately, you couldn't actually buy one, at least initially, as British industry was under orders to 'export or die' to pay off wartime debts.

Instead, the Vanguard scored considerable sales success in old outposts of commonwealth and empire, particularly Australia, before becoming available in its home market from mid-1949. What owners found was a tough, durable, well-equipped car with an easy all-synchromesh, three-speed gearbox. Handling too was adequate, although with its high ground clearance and lofty body, the pudding-shaped Vanguard teetered on corners like a loose blancmange on a runaway serving trolley. Modern drivers would also find the 9in (23cm) drum brakes more alarming than truly arresting, but what the Vanguard really has going for it is oodles of retro charm that commands a cultish following among Bakelite fetishists and ration-book romantics. Unfortunately, survivors are now a rare commodity.
Standard power: The durable 2088cc engine was also used in Ferguson tractors and, in tuned form, in the Triumph TR2 sports car.

STANDARD Model	ENGINE cc/cyl	DATES	CONDITION		
			1	2	3
12	1609/4	1945–48	£2,000	£950	£250
12 DHC	1509/4	1945–48	£3,200	£2,000	£500
14	1776/4	1945–48	£3,000	£950	£250
Vanguard I/II	2088/4	1948–55	£2,200	£1,000	£250
Vanguard III	2088/4	1955–61	£1,800	£900	£200
Vanguard III Est	2088/4	1955–61	£2,000	£1,000	£250
Vanguard III Sportsman	2088/4	1955–58	£2,500	£1,200	£400
Vanguard Six	1998/6	1961–63	£2,000	£1,000	£500
Eight	803/4	1952–59	£1,250	£500	-
Ten	948/4	1955–59	£1,400	£800	-
Ensign I/II	1670/4	1957–63	£1,000	£800	-
Ensign I/II Est	1670/4	1962–63	£2,000	£1,100	-
Pennant Companion	948/4	1955–61	£1,800	£850	£300
Pennant	948/4	1955–59	£1,650	£825	£250

1957 Standard Super Ten, 948cc 4-cylinder engine, unused for c6 years, in need of refurbishment and recommissioning.
£300–400 / $440–580 ⚒ BRIT
Produced between 1954 and 1960, the Standard Ten was seen as a cut above the majority of small cars of the period. Although sharing the same bodyshell as the Standard Eight, it benefited from a more powerful engine, together with a much improved level of trim and furnishings. The 948cc engine gave a lively performance and was retained for the Triumph Herald, which superseded the Ten.

1963 Standard Ensign Estate De Luxe Phase II, green paintwork and chrome trim in very good condition, red vinyl interior, 55,000 miles from new, original.
£3,500–4,000 / $5,000–5,800 ⚒ CGC
Originally intended as a cheaper, more austere version of the Vanguard, Standard's Ensign changed character somewhat in its Phase II incarnation, which was built during the company's last year of production. Equipped with a 2138cc, overhead-valve engine of Triumph TR4 proportions, Phase II Ensigns offered near 100mph performance, even in estate form. De Luxe versions, such as this one, benefited from overdrive in their manual four-speed gearboxes.

Studebaker

1927 Studebaker Custom Four-Door Sedan, 3.5 litre sidevalve 6-cylinder engine, 3-speed manual gearbox, opening rear quarterlights, engine rebuilt and fitted with modern oil filter, finished in black, blue cloth interior, original flower vases, very good condition.
£10,000–12,000 / $14,500–17,500 ⚒ CGC
During the 1920s, Studebakers developed an enviable reputation for strength and durability. The introduction of bodies made from welded steel pressings in 1923 was followed by the standardisation of balloon tyres in 1925 and front-wheel brakes in 1926. Performance was strong across the model range, as indicated by the various records that Studebaker set towards the end of the decade, including the impressive feat of covering 25,000 miles in 25,000 minutes!

1963 Studebaker Avanti R1, 289cu.in overhead-valve V8 engine, Carter 4-barrel carburettor, 240bhp, 3-speed automatic transmission, finished in white, turquoise leather and turquoise and beige vinyl interior trim, air conditioning, factory seat belts, 48,000 miles from new, unrestored, bodywork in excellent condition.
£10,000–12,000 / $14,500–17,500 ⚒ Bon
The striking Avanti coupé was designed by a team led by noted industrial designer Raymond Loewy. The first new body design for Studebaker in a decade, it was also the company's first venture in glassfibre. The stunning exterior shape may have been new, but the chassis was a modified version of that used under the Lark Daytona convertible. This particular car was owned originally by the actress Greer Garson.

A known continuous history can add value to and enhance the enjoyment of a car.

Stutz

c1928 Stutz Model BB Vertical Eight Speedster, 298cu.in overhead-camshaft 8-cylinder engine, 3-speed non-synchromesh gearbox with central change, rigid axles front and rear on semi-elliptic leaf springs, 4-wheel hydraulic drum brakes with dual master cylinder, channel-section chassis, centre-lock wire wheels, twin side mounted spare wheels, right-hand drive, built originally with saloon bodywork, rebuilt and fitted with Black Hawk Speedster-style coachwork 1970s, original under-slung worm-drive rear axle replaced by Salisbury unit, engine rebuilt, fewer than 2,000 miles since, subject of further restoration mid-1980s, rewired, new hood and weather equipment, chrome trim replated, body refurbished, resprayed in metallic grey, new red leather upholstery, new instruments.
£19,000–22,000 / $27,000–32,000 ⚒ GO
Introduced in 1926, the Model AA Stutz Vertical Eight was designed by Belgian engineer Paul Bastien, and was far more European in design and appearance than most of its American contemporaries. It was powered by advanced 289cu.in, single-overhead-camshaft engine. In 1928, the Model BB, named 'The Splendid Stutz', was introduced, the engine being enlarged to 298cu.in. Its specification included hydraulic brakes, centralised chassis lubrication and centre-lock wire wheels.

Sunbeam

The firm that became Sunbeam was started in 1859 by 23-year-old John Marston, initially making tin-plate and japanned goods in Wolverhampton. In 1887, he changed the name to Sunbeam Cycles, which gained a reputation for turning out fine bicycles. A Sunbeam car appeared in 1901, but it was the arrival of French designer Louis Coatalen, who had worked previously at Humber and Hillman, that propelled the company forward to its glory years in the 1920s with a string of successful GP cars, record breakers, and fine sports and touring machines. In the early 1930s, the best Sunbeams rivalled Bentley and Alvis models, although they were not quite a match in outright performance. By then, the company was in trouble as part of the unwieldy and inefficient Sunbeam-Talbot-Darracq combine, and Rootes bought the company in 1935. After WWII, Sunbeam continued its sporting tradition initially; a Sunbeam Mk III won the 1955 Monte Carlo Rally, and the Sunbeam Rapiers of the late 1950s and early 1960s proved useful in rallying and touring-car racing. Eventually though, most Sunbeams – with the exception of the 1959 Alpine and the fearsome Tiger – were nothing more than slightly peppier and posher Hillmans. Chrysler acquired Rootes in 1964, and the Sunbeam marque faded into the sunset in 1976.

◄ 1931 Sunbeam 16 (18.2)hp Four-Seater Sports Tourer, 2194cc overhead-valve 6-cylinder engine, Lockheed hydraulic drum brakes, Magna large-hub wheels, restored over 5 years, chassis and running gear overhauled, body covered in fabric from scuttle aft, mid-blue paintwork to wings and bonnet, interior retrimmed in black leathercloth, very good condition.
£10,500–13,500 / $15,250–19,600 ⚒ CGC
This Sunbeam began life as a factory-bodied two-door, four-light sliding-roof coupé. It survived in this guise for nearly 30 years until it was rebodied as a saloon. Some 13 years later, it became a 'rather crude' tourer, in which form it was run until abandoned to its fate in a scrapyard. Spotted in an *Exchange and Mart* advertisement, it was restored, using seasoned ash and 16-gauge aluminium to create a truncated version of vintage 3 litre Sunbeam sports tourer coachwork.

SUNBEAM Model	ENGINE cc/cyl	DATES	CONDITION 1	2	3
12/16	2412/4	1910–14	£`30,000	£18,000	£12,000
16/20	4070/4	1910–15	£32,000	£22,000	£15,000
24	4524/6	1919–22	£30,000	£19,000	£11,000
3 Litre	2916/6	1925–30	£48,000	£30,000	£20,000
14/40	2200/4	1925–30	£18,000	£10,000	£8,000
16	2040/6	1927–30	£16,000	£12,500	£10,000
20	2916/6	1927–30	£22,000	£15,000	£10,500
Speed 20	2916/6	1932–35	£15,000+	£10,000	£8,000
Dawn	1627/4	1934–35	£8,000	£5,000	£3,500
25	3317/6	1934	£12,000+	£8,000	£4,000

Prices can vary depending on replica bodies, provenance, coachbuilder, drophead, twin cam etc.

1931 Sunbeam 25hp Enclosed Limousine, coachwork by Weymann, sun visor, ventilated windscreen, rear mounted Scintilla direction indicators, leather upholstery, independently adjustable seats to front, drop-down division with folding occasional tables, cabinet accommodating picnic case in rear, travelling companions with reading lamps, courtesy lights to front and rear, burr-walnut interior trim, believed exhibited by Weymann at Olympia Motor Exhibition 1930, original condition, no recent use, in need of recommissioning.
£12,000–14,000 / $17,500–20,500 ⚒ Bon
Top of the range in Sunbeam's 1930 line-up was the 25hp model, a powerful luxury car with a six-cylinder, overhead-valve engine, displacing 3.6 litres. In Rolls-Royce fashion, it featured right-hand gear change and had four-wheel, servo-assisted Dewandre vacuum brakes, together with centralised chassis lubrication.

Miller's is a price GUIDE not a price LIST

1947 Sunbeam-Talbot Ten Four-Seater Drophead Coupé, 1184cc engine, completely restored 1984–86, finished in red, red interior, 64,000 miles from new.
£6,000–7,000 / $8,700–10,200 ⚒ H&H
Sunbeam-Talbot was a marque formed in 1938 by the Rootes Group, following its acquisition of the British arm of Sunbeam-Talbot-Darracq. The cars were derived from contemporary Hillmans and Humbers, but in most instances they carried individual coachwork. In 1954, the marque dropped its 'Talbot' suffix. The Sunbeam-Talbot Ten was produced for a ten-year period from 1938 and came in sports saloon, sports tourer and drophead coupé configurations. The drophead coupé coachwork was by Abbott.

1938 Sunbeam-Talbot Sports Saloon, original engine replaced by 3000cc unit, partial restoration completed 1994, finished in dark red, beige interior, 2 owners from new, concours winner, excellent condition.
£8,500–9,500 / $12,500–13,800 ⚒ H&H
The Sunbeam Talbot 4 litre sports saloon was a Humber Super Snipe in heavy disguise. It had hydraulic brakes, an X-braced chassis and four-bearing sidevalve engine, which produced enough power for 85mph performance.

1949 Sunbeam-Talbot 90 Mk I, full rear-wheel spats, sun roof, finished in metallic silver-green, reupholstered in brown Connolly leather, 56,000 miles from new, good condition.
£1,000–1,500 / $1,500–2,200 ⚒ CGC
Introduced in 1948, the Sunbeam-Talbot 90 had much in common with the marque's immediate pre-war models. However, its somewhat conservative styling belied one very important advance, namely the adoption of an overhead-valve cylinder head for its tough 2 litre, four-cylinder engine. This torquey, flexible unit developed some 65bhp and, in conjunction with the four-speed, column-change gearbox, gave a top speed of almost 80mph. The Rootes Group was quick to capitalise on the 90's sporting capabilities, and this continued development netted victory in the 1955 Monte Carlo Rally.

1955 Sunbeam-Talbot 90 Drophead Coupé, 2267cc 4-cylinder engine, fitted gas flowed cylinder head, suitable for unleaded fuel, floor-change gearbox, finished in red, black and red interior, excellent condition throughout.
£6,000–7,500 / $8,700–10,800 ➤ H&H

▶ **1967 Sunbeam Tiger,** 260cu.in Ford V8 engine, many new components, stainless-steel exhaust, Minilite-style alloy wheels, full-harness belts, finished in blue, excellent condition.
£9,500–11,000 / $14,000–16,000 ➤ BARO

1966 Sunbeam Alpine Mk V, 1725cc 4-cylinder engine, 4-speed manual gearbox, restored, period Wolfrace wheels, finished in mid-blue, black mohair hood, black leather interior, excellent condition.
£8,000–9,000 / $11,500–13,000 ⊞ BC

▶ **1972 Sunbeam Stiletto,** 875cc engine, twin carburettors, 55bhp, servo-assisted drum brakes, vinyl roof covering, rev-counter, completely restored.
£2,250–2,750 / $3,300–4,000 🚗 IMP

1960 Sunbeam Alpine, 1494cc 4-cylinder engine, 4-speed manual gearbox, wire wheels.
£4,500–5,500 / $6,500–8,000 ⊞ PMo

SUNBEAM-TALBOT/ SUNBEAM Model	ENGINE cc/cyl	DATES	CONDITION 1	2	3
Talbot 80	1185/4	1948–50	£3,500	£2,250	£1,000
Talbot 80 DHC	1185/4	1948–50	£6,000	£4,500	£2,000
Talbot 90 Mk I	1944/4	1949–50	£4,000	£2,100	£750
Talbot 90 Mk I DHC	1944/4	1949–50	£7,000	£4,750	£2,000
Talbot 90 II/IIa/III	2267/4	1950–56	£5,000	£3,000	£1,500
Talbot 90 II/IIa/III DHC	2267/4	1950–56	£7,000	£5,000	£2,250
Talbot Alpine I/III	2267/4	1953–55	£11,000	£7,500	£3,750
Talbot Ten	1197/4	1946–48	£3,500	£2,000	£750
Talbot Ten Tourer	1197/4	1946–48	£7,000	£4,000	£2,000
Talbot Ten DHC	1197/4	1946–48	£6,500	£4,000	£2,000
Talbot 2 Litre	1997/4	1946–48	£4,000	£2,500	£1,000
Talbot 2 Litre Tourer	1997/4	1946–48	£7,500	£4,000	£2,250
Rapier I	1392/4	1955–57	£1,200	£700	£300
Rapier II	1494/4	1957–59	£1,800	£900	£300
Rapier II Conv	1494/4	1957–59	£3,000	£1,500	£450
Rapier III	1494/4	1959–61	£2,000	£1,200	£400
Rapier III Conv	1494/4	1959–61	£3,500	£1,600	£600
Rapier IIIA	1592/4	1961–63	£2,000	£1,200	£400
Rapier IIIA Conv	1592/4	1961–63	£3,600	£1,700	£650
Rapier IV/V	1592/ 1725/4	1963–67	£2,000	£700	£250
Alpine I-II	1494/4	1959–62	£6,000	£3,500	£1,800
Alpine III	1592/4	1963	£6,500	£4,000	£1,250
Alpine IV	1592/4	1964	£5,500	£3,500	£1,250
Alpine V	1725/4	1965–68	£6,000	£4,000	£1,250
Harrington Alpine	1592/4	1961	£8,000	£4,750	£1,250
Harrington Le Mans	1592/4	1962–63	£10,000	£6,500	£3,000
Tiger Mk 1	4261/8	1964–67	£12,000	£10,000	£6,000
Tiger Mk 2	4700/8	1967	£13,000	£8,000	£6,000
Rapier Fastback	1725/4	1967–76	£1,100	£700	£250
Rapier H120	1725/4	1968–76	£1,500	£800	£300

Swift

◀ **1915 Swift 10hp Tourer,** 4-cylinder engine, dickey seat, completely rebuilt 1985, little use since, finished in green, double duck hood, deep buttoned burgundy leather upholstery, very good condition.
£9,000–10,000 / $13,000–14,500 ↗ Bon
Coventry bicycle maker Swift turned to car manufacture at the turn of the last century, producing a single-cylinder voiturette powered by an MMC engine, then progressing to a 10hp, twin-cylinder light car in 1904. This was replaced by an 1100cc, four-cylinder, 10hp model in 1914, which was periodically improved throughout the 1920s. Concentrating on the manufacture of small family cars while producing virtually all its own parts enabled Swift to beat its mass-producing rivals for quality, but not for price, and it closed in 1931.

Talbot

1925 Talbot (French) Model DC 12/32hp Tourer, 1600cc, original 3-door factory coachwork, running-board mounted toolbox, side mounted spare wheel, opening windscreen, Marchal lighting, original artillery wheels changed to wire wheels, recored radiator, rewired, magneto overhauled, new tonneau cover, finished in cream with black wings, black leathercloth interior, believed supplied originally to New Zealand with British instrumentation.
£9,000–11,000 / $13,000–16,000 ↗ Bon
Following the merger of Sunbeam and Talbot in 1919, that conglomerate joined with Darracq in France in 1920, and the French firm began trading as Automobiles Talbot in the old Darracq factory at Suresnes. For the 1925 season, Talbot offered the four-cylinder model DC, rated at 12/32hp, and the Model DS, rated 15/40hp. Conventional cars in every respect, their performance reflected race breeding.

1938 Talbot Ten Sports Saloon, 1185cc 4-cylinder engine, completely restored 1996–2000, all components rebuilt, finished in maroon, new grey leather upholstery.
£7,000–8,500 / $10,200–12,300 ↗ BRIT
The first new model to be introduced following the Rootes Group's acquisition of the Sunbeam-Talbot-Darracq combine in 1935, the Talbot Ten employed the mechanical components of the contemporary Hillman Minx. The engine benefited from an aluminium cylinder head, which gave the car quite respectable performance. Available as a two-door pillarless sports saloon (with the then fashionable 'aero-line' style of coachwork), drophead coupé or sports tourer, the Talbot Ten was both stylish and well appointed.

▶ **1981 Talbot-Matra Mureena,** finished in white, grey interior.
£2,300–2,700 / $3,350–4,000 ↗ BARO
Originally launched in 1973 as the Bagheera, the Mureena 1.6 and Mureena S 2.2 followed in 1980. The unique aspect of this collaboration between Talbot and Matra was the three-abreast seating, but the construction of the car was also fairly radical. The chassis came from Matra and was a fully galvanised item, while the body was built with a steel inner skin and glassfibre outer shell.

TALBOT Model	ENGINE cc/cyl	DATES	CONDITION 1	2	3
25hp and 25/50	4155/4	1907–16	£35,000	£25,000	£15,000
12hp	2409/4	1909–15	£22,000	£15,000	£9,000
8/18	960/4	1922–25	£8,000	£5,000	£2,000
14/45	1666/6	1926–35	£16,000	£10,000	£5,000
75	2276/6	1930–37	£22,000	£12,000	£7,000
105	2969/6	1935–37	£30,000+	£20,000+	£15,000

Higher value for tourers and coachbuilt cars.

Talbot-Lago

1950 Talbot-Lago T26 Record, restored 1990s, excellent condition.
£40,000–45,000 / $58,000–65,000 ⚒ COYS
The Sunbeam-Talbot-Darracq group was acquired by Rootes in 1935, at which time the Darracq name was acquired by Tony Lago, who sold cars in France under the Talbot label. His company manufactured some of the era's most notable competition cars, as that was Lago's passion. After WWII, the cars became known as Talbot-Lago or Lago-Talbot, the company continuing to produce superb Grand Prix cars. However, it also began to manufacture some beautiful road cars, primarily to support the competition programme.

Toyota

Although Toyota had been making cars in Japan since 1935, the company's products were little known in the UK until the 1960s. The first Toyota sold in Britain was the Corona 1500, which arrived in 1965 with little fanfare. If it provoked any comment at all, it was usually patronising, jingoistic ridicule. But it was a sign of things to come when James Bond forsook his traditional Aston Martin for a Toyota 2000GT in *You Only Live Twice*, even though they had to chop the roof off to accommodate the strapping Sean Connery. Although the 2000GT was only produced in very limited numbers – around 337 – it served its purpose as an attention-getter, while Toyotas came more and more into the mainstream with a comprehensive line-up of saloons, sporting coupés, 4x4s and working vehicles.

TOYOTA Model	ENGINE cc/cyl	DATES	CONDITION 1	2	3
Celica TA22 & TA23 Coupé	1588/4	1971–78	£2,500	£1,800	£500
RA28 Liftback	1968/4	1971–78	£3,500	£1,500	£400
Plus a premium of £200 to £500 for a Twin-Cam GT.					

1967 Toyota 2000GT, 1998cc double-overhead-camshaft 6-cylinder engine, 150bhp, 137mph top speed, 0–60mph in 8.4 seconds, 5-speed manual gearbox, backbone chassis, 4-wheel independent suspension by coil springs and double wishbones, aluminium body, resprayed in original dark red, complete factory tool kit including jack and emergency light, 1 owner and fewer than 15,500 miles from new, completely original.
£90,000–100,000 / $130,000–145,000 ⚒ Bon

TOYOTA Model	ENGINE cc/cyl	DATES	CONDITION 1	2	3
Crown MS65, MS63, MS75, Saloon, Estate, Coupé	2563/6	1972–75	£2,000	£1,000	£500
Plus a premium of £200 to £400 for the Coupé.					

Triumph

Triumph's long history is full or ironies. It was the most seemingly British of makes, yet it was founded by two ex-patriot Germans. In later years, when the defunct Triumph company was taken over by Standard, it went on to eclipse and outlast its parent. Starting out as a bicycle maker, founded by Siegfried Bettman and Mauritz Schulte, the company turned to motorcycles in 1902, and in 1923 the first Triumph motor car appeared. The car and motorcycle arms of the business separated in 1936, and in June 1939 the receivers were called in to close down the car manufacturer. That might have been the end of the Triumph story, but in 1944 Sir John

Black acquired the remains of Triumph for his Standard Motor Company. What he got was a name, a bit of residual goodwill – and precious little else. Yet somehow, over the next two decades, Triumph built up a sporting reputation to rival MG and Austin-Healey, and on the saloon side eclipsed Standard's own offerings. In the glory years of the 1950s and 1960s, Triumph's TR roadsters stood out as worthy best-of-breed contenders in the no-nonsense sports-car stakes. From the bluff-fronted TR2 to the chisel-chinned TR6, they were as true-Brit as sports cars could be. The Triumph name eventually passed on in 1980.

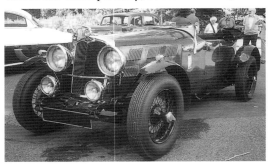

1938 Triumph Vitesse Two-Seater Sports, 1767cc engine recently rebuilt, rewired, steering and brakes overhauled, new petrol tank, originally a standard Vitesse, fitted with two-seat sports bodywork in aluminium 1950s, finished in green, unrestored hood and frame, green interior, good condition throughout.
£9,500–11,500 / $13,500–16,500 ✈ H&H
Triumph's models for 1937 saw a return to the use of its own engines, designed by Donald Healey. All came with overhead valves and there were three sizes: 1496 and 1767cc fours and a 1991cc six. In addition, the 1232cc Coventry Climax engine continued to be used in the cheapest Gloria model, so the range was a complex one. The Vitesse had the 1.8 litre four, while the Dolomite had the 2 litre six.

1950 Triumph Renown Four-Door Saloon, 2088cc 4-cylinder engine, box-section chassis, independent front suspension, hydraulic drum brakes, restored, very good condition.
£1,000–1,500 / $1,500–2,200 ✈ H&H

1954 Triumph TR2, 1991cc overhead-valve engine, overdrive gearbox, restored, finished in red, red interior, dry-stored for 25 years.
£9,500–11,000 / $14,000–16,000 ✈ H&H
Triumph introduced the TR2 in 1953, and by 1955 had produced over 8,000 examples.

◀ **1953 Triumph Mayflower Two-Door Saloon,** 1247cc sidevalve 4-cylinder engine, coil-spring independent front suspension, restored, very good condition.
£2,250–2,750 / $3,300–4,000 🚗 TMC

TRIUMPH Model	ENGINE cc/cyl	DATES	CONDITION 1	2	3
TLC	1393/4	1923–25	£6,000	£4,000	£1,500
TPC	2169/4	1926–30	£6,000	£4,000	£2,000
K	832/4	1928–34	£4,000	£2,000	£1,000
S	1203/6	1931–33	£5,000	£3,000	£1,500
G12 Gloria	1232/4	1935–37	£6,000	£4,000	£2,000
G16 Gloria 6	1991/6	1935–39	£7,000	£4,500	£2,000
Vitesse/Dolomite	1767/4	1937–39	£14,000	£10,000	£6,000
Dolomite	1496/4	1938–39	£7,000	£4,000	£2,000

Triumph TR2 (1953–55)

Production: 8,628.
Engine: 1991cc, overhead-valve, four-cylinder, twin SU carburettors.
Power output: 90bhp at 4,800rpm.
Maximum speed: 105mph.
0–60mph: 12 seconds.
If ever there was a sports car that epitomised the British bulldog spirit, it must be the Triumph TR2. Spend a minute in that cosy cockpit and your dress sense will change. You'll start smoking a pipe, wearing corduroys, cravat and flat cap, and sprouting a wing-commander's handlebar moustache. It's as true Brit as a car can be, born

in the golden age of British sports cars, but aimed at the lucrative US market, where the Jaguar XK120 had already scored a hit. The TR2 was no conventional beauty certainly, but with its bluff-fronted, honest demeanour it was a worthy best-of-breed contender in the budget sports-car arena and the cornerstone of a stout sporting tradition.
TR2 titbits: A pre-production TR2 was officially timed at a whisker under 125mph on the Jabbeke motorway in Belgium, having received careful tuning and rudimentary streamlining. The Triumph sporting tradition was firmly established when TR2s came first and second in the 1954 RAC Rally.

1956 Triumph TR3, 4-wheel hydraulic drum brakes, original right-hand drive model, restored 2001, good condition throughout.
£7,000–8,000 / $10,000–11,500 ⚲ Bon
Introduced in October 1955, the TR3 represented evolution, not revolution, and was little different from its predecessor. Changes to the Standard Vanguard derived 2 litre engine boosted power from 90 to 95bhp, but the most obvious difference was the adoption of an 'egg-box' radiator grille. By mid-1956, the engine had been given a new cylinder hear and developed 100bhp. Then, in August of that year, Girling front disc brakes and the stronger Phase III Vanguard rear axle were standardised.

1956 Triumph TR2, 1990cc overhead-valve engine, original right-hand drive model, restored, finished in red, tan interior, 60,000 miles from new, 2 owners since 1978, good condition throughout.
£7,000–8,000 / $10,000–11,500 ⚲ H&H

◄ **1956 Triumph TR3,** original right-hand drive model, restored 1985–87 at a cost of £6,000, fewer than 4,000 miles since, engine and gearbox rebuilt, many panels replaced, interior retrimmed in black, over £2,000 spent recently on mechanical work
£10,000–12,000 / $14,500–17,500 ⚲ COYS

1959 Triumph TR3A, manual gearbox with overdrive, restored 1997, used only twice since, finished in white, full weather equipment and tonneau cover, maroon interior trim and upholstery, excellent condition.
£13,000–14,000 / $19,000–20,500 ⚲ Bon
The TR3A, while retaining many features of the original, had a full-width grille, distinguishing it from its predecessors. Power was provided by a 1991cc development of the versatile 2 litre Standard Vanguard engine, also found in the Triumph Renown and the Triumph Roadster, and in sports guise was good for well over 100mph and 25mpg in regular service. Arguably, the TR3A was the most successful of the early TR variants, and whereas only 22,000 TR2s and TR3s were built in four years, no fewer than 61,567 cars TR3As left the factory in the five years of production from autumn 1957.

1959 Triumph TR3A, 1998cc 4-cylinder engine, restored, converted to right-hand drive, wire wheels, Kenlowe electric fan, finished in British racing green, black mohair hood and tonneau cover, very good condition.
£10,000–11,000 / $14,500–16,000 ⚲ BRIT

► **1964 Triumph TR4,** original right-hand drive model, professionally rebuilt, finished in red, black interior, excellent condition throughout.
£7,000–8,000 / $10,000–11,500 ⚲ CGC

1966 Triumph TR4A, 2138cc engine completely rebuilt, converted to unleaded fuel, chassis Waxoyled, converted to right-hand drive, new steering rack, rewired, new scuttle, bare-metal respray in Old English white, black interior, new dashboard, fitted rally seats, original seats included.
£7,000–8,000 / $10,000–11,500 ⏿ H&H

1970 Triumph TR6, 2.5 litre 6-cylinder engine, 150bhp, manual gearbox with overdrive, original right-hand drive model, restored 1990s, c8,000 miles since, gearbox recently overhauled at a cost of over £1,400, finished in Old English white, black vinyl trim.
£7,000–8,000 / $10,000–11,500 ⏿ CGC

TRIUMPH Model	ENGINE cc/cyl	DATES	CONDITION 1	2	3
1800/2000 Roadster	1776/ 2088/4	1946–49	£14,000	£8,000	£5,000
1800	1776/4	1946–49	£4,000	£2,000	£1,000
2000 Renown	2088/4	1949–54	£4,000	£2,000	£1,000
Mayflower	1247/4	1949–53	£2,000	£1,000	£500
TR2 long door	1247/4	1953	£10,000	£8,000	£5,000
TR2	1247/4	1953–55	£9,000	£6,000	£5,000
TR3	1991/4	1955–57	£9,000	£8,500	£3,500
TR3A	1991/4	1958–62	£11,000	£8,500	£3,500
TR4	2138/4	1961–65	£10,000	£6,000	£3,000
TR4A	2138/4	1965–67	£9,000	£6,500	£3,000
TR5	2498/6	1967–68	£11,000	£7,500	£4,000
TR6 (PI)	2498/6	1969–74	£8,000	£7,500	£3,500
Herald	948/4	1959–61	£1,000	£400	£150
Herald FHC	948/4	1959–61	£1,500	£550	£300
Herald DHC	948/4	1960–61	£2,500	£1,000	£350
Herald 'S'	948/4	1961–64	£800	£400	£150
Herald 1200	1147/4	1961–70	£1,100	£500	£200
Herald 1200 FHC	1147/4	1961–64	£1,400	£800	£300
Herald 1200 DHC	1147/4	1961–67	£2,500	£1,000	£350
Herald 1200 Est	1147/4	1961–67	£1,300	£700	£300
Herald 12/50	1147/4	1963–67	£1,800	£1,000	£250
Herald 13/60	1296/4	1967–71	£1,300	£600	£200
Herald 13/60 DHC	1296/4	1967–71	£3,500	£1,500	£500
Herald 13/60 Est	1296/4	1967–71	£1,500	£650	£300
Vitesse 1600	1596/6	1962–66	£2,000	£1,250	£550
Vitesse 1600 Conv	1596/6	1962–66	£3,500	£1,800	£600
Vitesse 2 litre Mk I	1998/6	1966–68	£1,800	£800	£300
Vitesse 2 litre Mk I Conv	1998/6	1966–68	£4,500	£2,200	£1,000
Vitesse 2 litre Mk II	1998/6	1968–71	£2,000	£1,500	£300
Vitesse 2 litre Mk II Conv	1998/6	1968–71	£5,000	£2,500	£600
Spitfire Mk I	1147/4	1962–64	£2,000	£1,750	£300
Spitfire Mk II	1147/4	1965–67	£2,500	£2,000	£350
Spitfire Mk III	1296/4	1967–70	£3,500	£2,500	£450
Spitfire Mk IV	1296/4	1970–74	£5,000	£2,500	£350
Spitfire 1500	1493/4	1975–78	£3,500	£2,500	£750
Spitfire 1500	1493/4	1979–81	£5,000	£3,500	£1,200
GT6 Mk I	1998/6	1966–68	£5,000	£4,000	£1,200
GT6 Mk II	1998/6	1968–70	£6,000	£4,500	£1,400
GT6 Mk III	1998/6	1970–73	£7,000	£5,000	£1,500
2000 Mk I	1998/6	1963–69	£2,000	£1,200	£400
2000 Mk III	1998/6	1969–77	£2,000	£1,200	£500
2.5 PI	2498/6	1968–75	£2,000	£1,500	£900
2500 TC/S	2498/6	1974–77	£1,750	£700	£150
2500S	2498/6	1975–77	£2,500	£1,000	£150
1300 (FWD)	1296/4	1965–70	£800	£400	£150
1300TC (FWD)	1296/4	1967–70	£900	£450	£150
1500 (FWD)	1493/4	1970–73	£700	£450	£125
1500TC (RWD)	1296/4	1973–76	£850	£500	£100
Toledo	1296/4	1970–76	£850	£450	£100
Dolomite 1500	1493/4	1976–80	£1,350	£750	£125
Dolomite 1850	1854/4	1972–80	£1,450	£850	£150
Dolomite Sprint	1998/6	1976–81	£5,000	£4,000	£1,000
Stag	2997/8	1970–77	£9,000	£5,000	£2,000
TR7	1998/4	1975–82	£4,000	£1,200	£500
TR7 DHC	1998/4	1980–82	£4,000	£3,000	£1,500

Triumph TR6 (1969–76)

From the original TR2 of 1953, beloved of the cravat-and-corduroy crew, Triumph's sporting road wear kept broadly abreast of the times and, in the late 1960s, combined polo-neck smartness with a touch of chest-wig brawn in the clean-cut and butch TR6. Some think the TR6 granite-jawed handsome, others find it almost thuggish. Whatever, it's just about as hairy-chested as the classic TRs got, with its 2.5 litre, six-cylinder engine, which, in fuel-injected form, heaved you along with 150 galloping horses.

The TR6 may look true-Brit, but the crisp lines came courtesy of Germany's Karmann, who squared off the friendly curves of the TR4, created in 1964 by Italian 'haute car-turier' Michelotti.

The TR6 was by far the most prolific of the TR2–6 series. More than 78,000 of the 94,619 TR6s were exported to the USA, where legislators emasculated the bulldog Brit. Many US TR6s have found their way back here, but US-spec cars had carbs instead of fuel injection and other performance wilting mods. Know what you're buying and pay less for a US-spec car.

Pick of the bunch: Beefiest and best are pre-1973, British-spec TR6s, which pumped out 152bhp. After that, revised fuel injection reduced power output to a less thrilling 125bhp.

◀ **1973 Triumph TR6,** 2498cc 6-cylinder engine, 106bhp, 4-speed manual gearbox, disc front/drum rear brakes, left-hand drive, restored.
£7,000–8,000 / $10,000–11,500 ➤ Pou

1975 Triumph TR6, 2498cc engine, 4-speed manual gearbox with overdrive, original right-hand drive model, restored 1989–90 at a cost of c£7,500, c1,000 miles since, engine rebuilt, fuel-injection system overhauled, new front wings, sills, inner rear wings and front and rear valances, resprayed in red, black interior trim.
£6,500–7,500 / $9,500–11,000 ➤ H&H

1976 Triumph TR6, 2498cc 6-cylinder engine, 106bhp, all-independent suspension, US export model, left-hand drive, new gearbox, recently resprayed, black interior, very good condition.
£5,000–6,000 / $7,250–8,750 ➤ Bon

▶ **1968 Triumph Herald 13/60 Convertible,** 1296cc overhead-valve 4-cylinder engine, twin SU carburettors, stainless-steel exhaust, manual gearbox with overdrive, new chassis outriggers and galvanised side rails and sills, wire wheels, body completely refurbished, new hood, finished in white, black interior trim, very good condition throughout.
£1,200–1,500 / $1,750–2,150 ➤ H&H

Triumph Milestones

1902 Triumph Cycle Company builds its first motorcycle.
1909 Triumph builds 3,000 motorcycles.
1923 First Triumph motor car launched in April.
1923 Motorcycle production up to 15,000 a year.
1930 Motorcycle production up to 30,000 a year. Name of Triumph Cycle Company changed to Triumph Motor Company.
1931 Triumph employing 3,000 workers on six sites in Coventry.
1936 Triumph motorcycle business sold in January to help expansion of car business.
1939 In June, Lloyd's Bank calls in receivers.

1944 Sir John Black's Standard Motor Company acquires Triumph name.
1955 Triumph TR3 is the first British volume-production car to be fitted with front disc brakes as standard.
1961 Leyland takes over Standard-Triumph.
1968 Leyland merges with British Motor Holdings to form British Leyland Motor Corporation.
1981 Triumph Acclaim is the last 'Triumph'. It's really a mildly modified Honda Ballade.
1984 Austin-Rover drops Triumph name from catalogue.

1971 Triumph Herald 13/60 Estate, 1296cc 4-cylinder engine, subject of much refurbishment, finished in maroon, fawn interior trim.
£1,000–1,300 / $1,500–2,000 ↗ BRIT

The introduction in 1959 of the Triumph Herald took the Standard Triumph Motor Company years ahead, as this striking Michelotti designed newcomer replaced the rather dated Standard Ten. The Herald enjoyed a 12-year production run, evolving in 1967 into the Herald 13/60, the 1300cc engine bringing a welcome boost in power. The most versatile variant of the range was the estate car, combining the excellent Herald virtues of economy and 24ft turning circle with a load-carrying capacity almost unrivalled in its class.

1973 Triumph GT6 Mk III, 1998cc 6-cylinder engine, 104bhp, restored over 6 years, fewer than 300 miles since, chassis fully painted, all suspension components powder coated, all mechanical items replaced, engine rebuilt, finished in red, new black interior.
£4,250–4,750 / $6,000–7,000 ↗ H&H

1966 Triumph 2000 Saloon, 1998cc engine, finished in blue and black, red interior, 3 owners from new, very good condition.
£2,750–3,250 / $4,000–4,700 ↗ H&H

1977 Triumph 2500 S Saloon, 2498cc engine, manual gearbox with overdrive, fitted Kenlowe fan, engine top-end oil feeder, alloy wheels, sun roof and towbar, Zeibart rust treatment, finished in red and black, tan interior.
£700–900 / $1,000–1,300 ↗ H&H

1978 Triumph Spitfire, 1493cc engine, finished in green, black interior trim, rust-free, excellent condition.
£2,750–3,250 / $4,000–4,700 ↗ H&H

The Triumph Spitfire was introduced in 1962 and survived until 1974.

Miller's
Starter Marque

- **Starter Triumphs:** *Herald and Vitesse saloons and convertibles; Spitfire; Dolomite, Toledo and variants.*
- A Triumph Herald's a top-down winner when it comes to budget wind-in-the-hair motoring – an Italian styled four-seater convertible with a 25ft (7.5m) turning circle that's tighter than a London taxi's, and an engine that's so accessible it's like having your own inspection pit. They are very modestly priced too. Of course, it's not all good news. The Herald's performance is hardly shattering, particularly with the early, rather asthmatic 948cc Standard Ten engine. They're also prone to rust, and the handling was legendary – for being so darned awful, in the case of the earlier models at least. In the wet and in sudden throttle-off conditions, the car's high-pivot, swing-axle rear suspension would pitch it suddenly into unpredictable oversteer.
- But who'd be daft enough to try to race a Herald on public roads? What's more relevant is the smiles per mile as you and your family potter along over hill and dale, burning fossil fuel at a miserly 35–40mpg.
- Heralds do fray quite ferociously, and you'll want to inspect the separate chassis, which provides the structural strength. The front-hinged bonnet is both a strength and a weakness. It gives unrivalled access to the front running gear and engine, but once the rot sets in, it can flap around like a soggy cardboard box.
- Finally, because of its separate chassis, the Herald saloon is one car that can be safely turned into a convertible. The roof literally unbolts, and a number of rag-top conversion kits are available.
- **Pick of the bunch:** The Herald's certainly no winged-messenger, so avoid early cars with puny 948cc engine and go for at least the 1147cc or preferably the last 1296cc cars.
- The Herald's chassis formed the basis of a number of sporting Triumphs, including the twin-headlamped Vitesse. Similar in looks to the Herald, but with a 1600 or 2000cc engine, the Vitesse will heave you along with plenty more urge – almost to 100mph in 2 litre form. The Herald chassis also formed the basis of the pretty little two-seat Triumph Spitfire, again with wonderful engine access provided by the front-hinged, one-piece bonnet. The Spitfire ran from 1961 to 1980, and that means there are plenty to choose from.

1978 Triumph Dolomite Sprint, engine rebuilt, converted to unleaded fuel, twin Weber 45DCOE carburettors, suspension lowered, ex-works limited-slip differential, competition half-shafts, regularly Waxoyled, finished in blue, black cloth interior, good condition.
£1,500–1,800 / $2,200–2,600 ⚘ CGC
Launched in June 1973, the Dolomite Sprint was a natural rival to such cars such as BMW's 2002tii and Alfa Romeo's GTV 2.0. A compact four-door sports saloon, it had a 16-valve, 1998cc, four-cylinder engine that produced some 127bhp – sufficient to propel the Sprint to 60mph in 8.7 seconds and on to a 120mph top speed. With overdrive operating on the top two ratios of its four-speed manual gearbox, such performance was always readily accessible. The all-round coil-spring suspension was upgraded with thicker anti-roll bars, and the Sprint also received uprated disc/drum brakes. A chin spoiler, vinyl roof and alloy wheels distinguished it from its less-potent brethren.

1972 Triumph Stag, 2997cc V8 engine, completely rebuilt 1990, new radiator, new cooling fans, reconditioned back axle, new fuel pump, finished in blue, black interior trim.
£2,750–3,250 / $4,000–4,700 ⚘ H&H

1976 Triumph Stag, 2997cc V8 engine, manual gearbox with overdrive, stainless-steel exhaust, Kenlowe electric fan, finished in British racing green, hard and soft tops, 67,000 miles from new, original specification throughout.
£4,500–5,500 / $6,500–8,000 ⚘ BRIT

1982 Triumph TR7 Convertible, 2 litre 4-cylinder engine, 5-speed manual gearbox, c£4,000 spent on renovation/maintenance in past 4 years, visible wear to driver's seat, worn layshaft bearing, otherwise good condition.
£1,000–1,500 / $1,500–2,200 ⚘ Bon

1982 Triumph TR7 Convertible, 1998cc 4-cylinder engine, finished in gold, black PVC hood, full-length tonneau cover, tan interior trim, 42,500 miles from new, good original condition.
£2,500–3,000 / $3,500–4,500 ⚘ BRIT
Originally introduced in 1975 as a fixed-head coupé, the TR7 appeared in convertible guise in the spring of 1979.

TVR

◄ **1969 TVR Vixen S2,** mechanics overhauled, bodyshell restored, resprayed in dark red, red and black vinyl interior, excellent condition throughout.
£5,750–6,750 / $8,500–10,000 ⚘ CGC
Launched in 1967, the Vixen featured a stiff, tubular backbone chassis clothed in a squat, purposeful glassfibre shell. Its 1599cc crossflow Ford engine and four-speed manual gearbox were set well back towards the car's centre-line, which, combined with all-round coil-spring suspension, provided notably viceless handling.

TVR Model	ENGINE cc/cyl	DATES	CONDITION 1	2	3
Grantura I	1172/4	1957–62	£4,000	£3,000	£2,000
Grantura II	1558/4	1957–62	£4,500	£3,000	£2,000
Grantura III/1800S	1798/4	1963–67	£5,000	£3,000	£2,200
Tuscan V8	4727/8	1967–70	£12,000	£7,000	£6,000
Vixen S2/3	1599/4	1968–72	£5,000	£3,000	£1,500
3000M	2994/6	1972–79	£7,000	£4,000	£3,000
Taimar	2994/6	1977–79	£7,500	£5,000	£3,500

► **1984 TVR 350i,** 3.5 litre V8 engine, finished in white, cream leather upholstery, excellent condition throughout.
£2,750–3,500 / $4,000–5,000 ✕ **COYS**
The 350i was developed from the Tasmin range, being manufactured between 1983 and 1985. The 3.5 litre V8 was similar in weight to the older V6, but the chassis had to be modified slightly to accommodate the larger engine. With these modifications and changes to the steering, the car went and handled much better than the previous models. With 190bhp on tap, performance was improved beyond recognition, a top speed of 135mph and 0–60mph in 6 seconds being quoted.

Unic

c1914 Unic Type M1 Coupé Chauffeur, coachwork by Vicard, 2.6 litre engine, acetylene headlamps, oil opera-style side lamps, loop door handles, bevelled-glass windows to rear, finished in red with black wings, unused since 1992, passenger compartment interior in need of restoration.
£11,500–13,500 / $17,000–20,000 ✕ **Bon**
Georges Richard left the firm he had founded in 1905 and began car production at Puteaux, his new products being called Unic, because of the company's intended policy of offering just one model. This was short-lived, however, when four-cylinder models were added to the range in 1906. In 1914, the M1 appeared, powered by a conventional, four-cylinder engine with a displacement of 2614cc and driving through a four-speed gearbox. It was Unic's last pre-war model.

Vanden Plas

◄ **1969 Vanden Plas Princess 1300 Saloon,** finished in white, grey leather interior, 1 owner from new, good condition.
£2,300–2,700 / $3,400–4,000 ✕ **Bon**
One of the most illustrious of Britain's coachbuilders, Vanden Plas was acquired by BMC in 1946 and reinvented as a marque some years later. In the 1960s and 1970s, the name was applied to top-of-the-range versions of Austin Morris models, most notably the 1100/1300. Vanden Plas re-equipped the car with the kind of luxurious interior long associated with the firm, using wood-veneer trim and leather upholstery, and fitted a distinctive grille and their own badging. The engine specified was the same twin-carburettor unit fitted to the MG 1100/1300, the 1.3 litre 65bhp version being good enough for a top speed of 90mph.

VANDEN PLAS Model	ENGINE cc/cyl	DATES	CONDITION 1	2	3
3 Litre I/II	2912/6	1959–64	£5,000	£3,000	£1,000
4 Litre R	3909/6	1964–67	£4,000	£2,500	£700
1100 Princess	1098/4	1964–67	£2,000	£1,000	£500
1300 Princess	1275/4	1967–74	£2,200	£1,500	£500

Vauxhall

The Griffin may be a mythical beast, but from modest beginnings the cars that sport this ancient heraldic emblem have proliferated to become an enduring fact of motoring life for millions of motorists in Great Britain and around the world. The company's first car was produced in 1903, and in the Edwardian and Vintage years the sporting Prince Henry and 30/98 models stood out as serious road-going rivals to the 3 litre Bentleys, worthy of mention alongside Invictas and Bugattis. In 1925, the firm's poor finances led to General Motors taking control and successfully moving the marque down-market into solid middle-class territory with successful models like the H-Type 10 and the J-Type 14. In the 1950s, the transatlantic influence really became prominent in the gaudy Crestas and F-Type Victors, so beloved today of ageing Teddy boys. During this period, Vauxhall's product range also expanded rapidly and aspired to compete head-to-head and model-to-model with Ford's UK offerings. For many British car buyers, the choice was a straight either/or between, say, a Vauxhall Cresta and a Ford Zephyr/Zodiac, and later between a Vauxhall Viva and a Ford Anglia or Escort. Although America's General Motors had owned Vauxhall and a majority shareholding in German car maker Opel since the 1920s, these European cousins operated independently of one another until the 1960s, when the model lines began to converge until most design input came from Germany.

◀ **1937 Vauxhall DX 14/6 Four-Door Saloon,** boot with covered exterior mounted spare wheel, period suitcase, restored, mechanics overhauled, rewired, new exhaust, resprayed in black, new leather upholstery, excellent condition throughout.
£6,000–7,000 / $8,700–10,200 ⊁ H&H
The Light Six was only made for a two-year period from 1937, and changes from the Big Six were mainly cosmetic, so it still had steel spoked wheels and a curved radiator grille. The touring saloon with its separate projecting boot was only available on the DX14, and the tiresome camshaft driven wipers had already been replaced with the electric type the previous year. This particular example is believed to have been used during WWII by the US Army Air Force in Britain and has had very little use since.

VAUXHALL Model	ENGINE cc/cyl	DATES	CONDITION 1	2	3
D/OD	3969/4	1914–26	£35,000	£24,000	£18,000
E/OE	4224/4	1919–28	£80,000	£60,000+	£35,000
Eighty	3317/6	1931–33	£10,000	£8,000	£5,000
Cadet	2048/6	1931–33	£7,000	£5,000	£3,000
Lt Six	1531/6	1934–38	£5,000	£4,000	£1,500
14	1781/6	1934–39	£4,000	£3,000	£1,500
25	3215/6	1937–39	£5,000	£4,000	£1,500
10	1203/4	1938–39	£4,000	£3,000	£1,500
Wyvern LIX	1500/4	1948–51	£2,000	£1,000	£500
Velox LIP	2200/6	1948–51	£2,000	£1,000	£500
Wyvern EIX	1500/4	1951–57	£2,000	£1,320	£400
Velox EIPV	2200/6	1951–57	£3,000	£1,650	£400
Cresta EIPC	2200/6	1954–57	£3,000	£1,650	£400
Velox/Cresta PAS/PAD	2262/6	1957–59	£2,850	£1,300	£300
Velox/Cresta PASY/PADY	2262/6	1959–60	£2,700	£1,500	£300
Velox/Cresta PASX/PADX	2651/6	1960–62	£2,700	£1,300	£300
Velox/Cresta PASX/PADX Est	2651/6	1960–62	£2,700	£1,300	£300
Velox/Cresta PB	2651/6	1962–65	£1,600	£800	£100
Velox/Cresta PB Est	2651/6	1962–65	£1,600	£800	£100
Cresta/Deluxe PC	3294/6	1964–72	£1,500	£800	£100
Cresta PC Est	3294/6	1964–72	£1,500	£800	£100
Viscount	3294/6	1964–72	£1,700	£900	£100
Victor I/II	1507/4	1957–61	£2,000	£1,000	£250
Victor I/II Est	1507/4	1957–61	£2,100	£1,100	£300
Victor FB	1507/4	1961–64	£1,500	£900	£200
Victor FB Est	1507/4	1961–64	£1,600	£1,000	£300
VX4/90	1507/4	1961–64	£2,000	£900	£150
Victor FC101	1594/4	1964–67	£1,600	£900	£150
Victor FC101 Est	1594/4	1964–67	£1,800	£1,000	£200
101 VX4/90	1594/4	1964–67	£2,000	£1,500	£250
VX4/90	1975/4	1969–71	£1,000	£600	£100
Ventora I/II	3294/6	1968–71	£1,000	£375	£100
Viva HA	1057/4	1963–66	£1,000	£350	£100
Viva SL90	1159/4	1966–70	£1,000	£350	£100
Viva Brabham	1159/4	1967–70	£2,000	£1,000	£800
Viva	1600/4	1968–70	£500	£350	£100
Viva Est	1159/4	1967–70	£500	£400	£100

Miller's
Starter Marque

- **Starter Vauxhalls:** *PA Cresta/Velox, 1957–62; F-Type Victor, 1957–61.*
- As our price table shows, all Vauxhalls of the 1950s and 1960s are affordable, but two models that really stand out for their glamorous styling are the Detroit inspired PA Cresta/Velox and F-Type Victor, both a kind of mid-Atlantic meeting between Uncle Stan and Uncle Sam, and very appealing today to anyone who enjoys nostalgia for the 1950s.
- They look for all the world like classic Yank tanks, yet their flanks clothe ordinary British mechanics and running gear, which are generally readily available and easy to maintain. The earlier E-Type Cresta, Velox and Wyvern also offer a touch of star-spangled razzamatazz, but their numbers have thinned to a level where they are not quite as practical as the later PA. Later cars, like the PB Cresta and FB Victor, are also practical buys; compared to the extravagant PA, they are almost muted.
- The glorious PA Cresta is a monster by British standards, a genuine six-seater with enough body rock and roll to please any Elvis fan. Mechanically, they offer little to worry about, with their strong 2.2 and 2.6 litre engines, and ancillaries like front discs, starter motors and dynamos straight from an MGB.
- **Pick of the PAs:** Some prefer the looks of the pre-1960 models, with their three-piece rear windows, although later models have slightly more eager 2.6 litre lumps in place of the earlier 2.2.
- But the bodies are a different matter. Legend has it that PA Crestas rusted so rapidly that by the time they reached the end of the Luton production line, they would have failed today's MoT test. Actually, their resistance to rust was pretty much in line with other cars of the era. The big difference is that there's just more metal to rust. When you go to look at one, take a metal detector, because a festering rust box will be a labour of love rather than a sound buying proposition.
- The F-Type Victor delivers a Detroit dream in a UK-sized package. Compared to contemporary saloon rivals, it was a fine car to drive, with a tough and flexible engine. The mechanics are all pretty sturdy, but the early cars really did have a deserved reputation for rusting, as their bodyshells offered more mud traps than a Florida swamp. In fact, by the end of 1959, Vauxhall was already receiving corrosion complaints, and in response added underseal and splash panels.

1962 Vauxhall Cresta PA Four-Door Saloon, 2651cc engine, 4-speed manual gearbox, finished in black and grey, grey interior trim, 26,500 miles from new, very little use since 1994, completely original, concours winner.
£5,000–6,000 / $7,250–8,750 ↗ Bon

1976 Vauxhall Viva E Saloon, 1256cc overhead-valve 4-cylinder engine, 4-speed manual gearbox, front disc brakes, 4-wheel coil-spring suspension, finished in gold, brown vinyl seats with cloth face inserts, period radio, 9,000 miles from new, last used 1990, dry stored since, some minor paint defects, otherwise very good condition.
£800–1,000 / $1,150–1,500 ↗ CGC

1984 Vauxhall Astra GTE, 1796cc 4-cylinder engine, 5-speed manual gearbox, alarm, finished in white, grey interior, 1 owner and fewer than 55,000 miles from new, completely original.
£2,500–3,000 / $3,500–4,500 ↗ H&H

Vauxhall Viva HA (1963–66)

Production: 321,332.
Price when new: £528.
Engine: 1057cc, four-cylinder.
Power output: HA, 44bhp at 5,000rpm; HA 90, 58bhp at 5,000rpm.
Transmission: Four-speed manual, all-synchromesh.
Brakes: Drums all-round, front discs optional at £12 extra; front discs standard on HA 90.
Maximum speed: 79mph (85mph for HA 90).
0–60mph: 20+ seconds.
As its first post-war entry into the growing small-car market, Vauxhall had high hopes for the Viva, and sales got off to a brisk start, notching up 100,000 in its first ten months. In place of flashy style, image and sizzling performance, Vauxhall

concentrated on value for money, pricing the Viva pretty much on a par with the Ford Anglia, and well below the Cortina, Morris 1100 and Triumph Herald. Other than that, the Viva had a big boot and light controls, which prompted the marketing hacks to target women, perhaps imagining the 'fairer sex' to be more susceptible. 'The Viva concept centres around what a woman expects to find in a car,' ran one brochure, although beyond being 'nice and slow', it's difficult to imagine what other feminine virtues the Viva possessed. The Viva was, in effect, an Anglicised version of the Opel Kadett and, although never the zenith of automotive style, sold well, swaying buyers on value for money and sheer common sense.

Volkswagen

The Volkswagen Beetle may be the best selling car in the world – a true people's car – but it had a long and painful birth. In the early 1930s, Herr Hitler's vision for mass master-race motoring began to take shape when he entrusted Dr Ferdinand Porsche with the project. Some 630 or so Beetles were made before hostilities disrupted production. Back then, they were propaganda wagons too, named KdF-Wagen, after the slogan of the Hitler Youth, 'Kraft durch Freude', which means 'strength through joy'. When production resumed in 1945, the Beetle, now a more friendly Volkswagen, gathered an irresistible momentum, notching up 10,000 sales in 1946, 100,000 in 1950 and a million by 1955. In 1972, it overtook the Model T Ford's production record of 15 million. Today, the amazing story of the world's most popular car isn't finished yet, as every car that rolls off the remaining South American production lines adds to a 21-million-plus production record that's unlikely ever to be beaten. The Volkswagen story isn't all about the Beetle though. The Beetle-based Karmann Ghia adds a bit of sporting style to the basic father-car, and remains practical and affordable, while the Golf Gti, of course, has become a latter-day icon.

◄ **1954 Volkeswagen Beetle Cabriolet,** 1192cc rear mounted air-cooled flat-4 engine, 4-speed manual gearbox, 4-wheel independent suspension, restored, Hartz cloth hood lined in beige cloth, hood cover in period pinpoint vinyl, original grey vinyl interior in excellent condition, extra glove box lock, interior light, tinted driver's visor, 82,000 miles from new.
£7,500–9,000
$11,000–13,000 ✗ Bon

1961 Volkswagen Beetle 1200, 1192cc air-cooled flat-4 engine, restored over 3 years, engine rebuilt, original 6 volt electrical system, finished in red, grey interior trim, period Blaupunkt valve radio, variety of correct-specification spare parts including fuel tank and pair of new cylinder heads, concours winner, excellent condition throughout.
£4,000–5,000 / $5,800–7,250 ✗ BRIT

1972 Volkswagen Beetle 1302S, 1600cc engine, manual gearbox, finished in red, in need of some welding for MoT.
£300–350 / $440–500 ✗ CGC

VOLKSWAGEN Model	ENGINE cc/cyl	DATES	CONDITION 1	2	3
Beetle (split rear screen)	1131/4	1945–53	£5,000	£3,500	£2,000
Beetle (oval rear screen)	1192/4	1953–57	£4,000	£2,000	£1,000
Beetle (slope headlamps)	1192/4	1957–68	£2,500	£1,000	£600
Beetle DHC	1192/4	1954–60	£6,000	£4,500	£2,000
Beetle 1500	1493/4	1966–70	£3,000	£2,000	£1,000
Beetle 1302 LS	1600/4	1970–72	£2,500	£1,850	£850
Beetle 1303 S	1600/4	1972–79	£3,000	£2,000	£1,500
1500 Variant/1600	1493/ 1584/4	1961–73	£2,000	£1,500	£650
1500/1600	1493/ 1584/4	1961–73	£3,000	£2,000	£800
Karmann Ghia/I	1192/4	1955–59	£5,000	£3,000	£1,000
Karmann Ghia/I DHC	1192/4	1957–59	£8,000	£5,000	£2,500
Karmann Ghia/I	1192/4	1960–74	£5,500	£3,000	£1,800
Karmann Ghia/I DHC	1192/4	1960–74	£7,000	£4,500	£2,000
Karmann Ghia/3	1493/4	1962–69	£4,000	£2,500	£1,250

1977 Volkswagen Beetle Cabriolet 1303S, 1584cc engine, 60bhp, front disc brakes, MacPherson-strut front suspension, original right-hand drive model, 3 owners and c20,000 miles from new, never restored, completely original condition.
£12,000–14,000 / $17,500–20,500 ✗ COYS

◀ **1973 Volkswagen Beetle Cabriolet,** original specification including steel wheels with polished aluminium trim rings and chrome hub caps, weather equipment and hood bag, original steering wheel, finished in red, black interior, very good condition throughout.
£4,250–5,250 / $6,000–7,500 ✗ CGC

Miller's Starter Marque

- **Starter Volkswagen:** *Beetle.*
- The Volkswagen Beetle is one bug they just can't find a cure for. As a starter classic, it has the benefit of still being in production, and that means readily-available, cheap spares for most models other than very early cars. That buzzing, air-cooled four-cylinder engine is well nigh unburstable too, and in mechanical terms the cars are easy to work on. One fact says it all: the world record for an engine swap – drive up to drive away – is just over three minutes.
- If you're a classic purist, choose from the first-of-breed 1131cc, 1945–53 split-screen cars or the 1953–57 oval-window 1200cc models. For drivability and less-onerous ownership costs, a good mid-way motor is the 1500cc Bug produced from 1966 to 1970. It's old enough to be classic, fast enough to keep up and still pure in design.
- The body's the Beetle's bug though. While the wings are bolted on and virtually every body panel is available, there are a lot of Beetle bodywork bodges around. Check very closely where the body attaches to the chassis, just behind the front wheels and immediately ahead of the rear wheels: severe rust here can make the vehicle unsafe.

◀ **1966 Volkswagen Karmann Ghia Coupé,** 1285cc air-cooled flat-4 engine, original right-hand-drive model, resprayed in blue, cream interior, 2 owners from new.
£4,500–5,500
$6,500–8,000 ✗ H&H
The Karmann Ghia was offered as a fixed-head coupé and a cabriolet. It had a children-only rear seat. The model was produced for 17 years, with four engine options. In all, something like half a million examples left the Volkswagen factories.

Volkswagen Karmann Ghia (1955–74)

The humble Bug turned into the belle of the boulevard when German coachbuilder Karmann clothed the Volkswagen Beetle in debutante designer wear from Italian styling house Ghia. But this Karmann's a chameleon. Its styling is loosely in the sporting idiom, although chubbier and less sharply defined, rather like a novelty bar of soap. As for performance, the cute Karmann Ghia didn't exactly sprout wings when it emerged from its Beetle chrysalis with its spluttering air-cooled engine, all buzz and fury signifying nothing much at all. Needless to say, it was the perfect Beverly Hills boulevardier, a sports car 'mule' that did it all, from the beach to the shopping mall.
Pick of the bunch: The later, the faster. From 1966 on, you get the bigger, faster 1500cc engine with front disc brakes; from 1970, the engine's uprated to 1600cc, but later cars are less pretty with heavy bumpers and large lamp clusters. Also, anything with a steering wheel on the right fetches a premium in the UK.
For: The blend of Beetle basics and sports-car looks makes for a distinctive car with cheap and readily available mechanical components.
Against: Unfortunately, it's also a classic compromise. It's got a better aerodynamic shape than the Beetle, but it's also heavier. That means a slightly higher top speed, but your Karmann will be no Beetle beater away from the lights.
What to watch: The mechanics may be of that unburstable Beetle breed, but the Karmann coachbuilt body becomes costly when it starts to rust – and rust they do.

Volvo

Although Sweden's premier car maker was founded back in 1927, it wasn't until the post-WWII era that Volvos reached a wider international audience, initially with the PV444 and PV544, which earned admiration both for the accomplished road-holding that made them rally winners and for the solid build quality that has become a Volvo hallmark. In the later 1950s, the 121 continued in the same mould and endured through various model designations (122/131/132/123GT) up to 1970. Today, they are still enjoyed in daily use as a robust and stylish classic workhorse. Perhaps the most unlikely Volvo is the P1800 sports car, a one-time flight of fancy by the sober Swedes. It's certainly stylish, robust too, and in estate form, it's an uncommonly practical sports car.

◄ **1953 Volvo PV444 Special-Edition Saloon,** 1414cc 4-cylinder engine, finished in maroon, red and beige interior trim, very good mechanical condition throughout.
£4,750–5,500 / $7,000–8,000 ➶ **BRIT**
First shown at the Stockholm exhibition in September 1944, the PV444 aroused tremendous interest, and demand was heightened by the fact that WWII had delayed its launch by a year. This new small car was unique in that it combined American design with European size. Powered by a sturdy four-cylinder engine, the car had a unitary-construction steel body and independent front suspension. Demand far outstripped supply, due to steel shortages, and it was 1947 before deliveries of the PV444 began.

Volvo PV544 (1958–65)

Production: 246,995.
Body style: Two-door saloon.
Construction: Unitary chassis/body.
Engine: 1583cc, four-cylinder; 1778cc (1961–65).
Power output: 1583cc, 60–75bhp; 1778cc, 75–90bhp.
Transmission: Three- and four-speed manual.
Maximum speed: 85–95+mph.
0–60mph: 13–20 seconds.
Even at its introduction in 1958, the Volvo PV544 wasn't so much a new model as a mild update of the earlier PV444 produced from 1947. With its quasi-American styling – often compared to the fastback Fords of the 1940s – scaled down to reasonable European proportions, the PV444 was the car that brought Volvo into the mainstream. Its modern unitary construction, high levels of comfort, fine driving dynamics and rugged dependability added up to a winning combination, both in the domestic Swedish market and abroad. The PV544 refined the theme further with a one-piece screen, more powerful engines, optional four-speed gearbox and an emphasis on sensible levels of equipment rather than mere gimmicks. The PV544 featured a padded dash, twin padded sun visors, an anti-dazzle rear-view mirror and self-parking wipers to ease the stress of driving. Seats reclined to form a double bed, and it was also the first car to offer both front and rear seat-belt anchorages. Throughout the 1950s and well into the 1960s, the PV models featured strongly in the toughest rallies all over the world. But one place where they were a rarity was on the roads of Britain; produced only in left-hand-drive form, they were never officially imported, and only a few discerning drivers were prepared to pay punitive import duty to drive a truly capable car that shamed much of our stodgy domestic fare.

► **1966 Volvo Amazon 122S Saloon,** 1780cc 4-cylinder B18 engine, 4-speed manual gearbox with overdrive, restored, concours winner.
£11,000–14,000 / $16,000–20,500 ⊞ **BC**
The subject of many thousands of hours of painstaking restoration work, this car has won every major concours event it has entered, including the Benson & Hedges Masters Trophy.

VOLVO Model	ENGINE cc/cyl	DATES	CONDITION 1	2	3
PV444	1800/4	1958–67	£4,000+	£1,750	£800
PV544	1800/4	1962–64	£4,000	£1,750	£800
120 (B16)	1583/4	1956–59	£3,000	£1,000	£300
121	1708/4	1960–67	£3,500	£1,500	£350
122S	1780/4	1960–67	£4,500	£1,500	£250
131	1780/4	1962–69	£4,000	£1,500	£350
221/222	1780/4	1962–69	£2,500	£1,500	£300
123Gt	1986/4	1967–69	£3,000	£2,500	£750
P1800	1986/4	1960–70	£4,500	£2,500	£1,000
P1800E	1986/4	1970–71	£4,200	£2,500	£1,000
P1800ES	1986/4	1971–73	£4,800	£3,000	£1,000

Volvo P1800 (1961–73)

Price when new: £1,832.12s.9d.
Engine: 1778cc, overhead-valve, four cylinder;
1985cc (1968–73).
Power output: 100–124bhp.
Maximum speed: 105–115mph.
0–60mph: 9.7–13.2 seconds.
They called it the 'second sexiest car launch of
1961' – after the E-Type Jaguar – and in its way,
this sleek Swede has always played a supporting
role. It was terminally typecast as the 'Saint'
Volvo after co-starring alongside Roger Moore in
the long-running 1960s TV series, but although

Moore went on to big-screen Bond stardom, the
P1800 remained stereotyped as a London mews
dweller's sports car, with more go than show and
a boot that you could actually put things in.
Towards the end of its life, it became more
practical still, with the introduction of the
P1800ES sports-estate. With a production run
totalling just over half the E-Type's, the P1800 is
relatively rare, always distinctive and about as
practical as a classic sports car can be. Affordable
too, as MGB money could bag you a svelte-
looking Swede.

1966 Volvo Amazon Estate, right-hand drive, restored
c1997, finished in light blue, black interior.
£1,500–2,000 / $2,200–3,000 ✦ Bon
Introduced in 1956, the Volvo 120 series remained in
production until 1970. Marketed in Sweden as the
Amazon, the original 121 four-door saloon was joined
by two-door (131) and estate (221) models in the
1960s. The overhead-valve, four-cylinder engine,
originally of 1.6 litres capacity, would grow first to 1.8
and, finally, 2 litres. This estate once featured in the
Yorkshire TV series *Heartbeat*, being used to smuggle
a stolen oil painting concealed beneath a false floor,
which the car retains.

▶ **1973 Volvo 1800ES,** 2 litre engine, fuel injection,
automatic transmission, servo-assisted brakes, independent
front suspension, original steel wheels with trim rings,
resprayed in original red, original black leather interior in
excellent condition, 15,500 miles from new.
£3,750–4,500/ $5,500–6,500 ✦ Bon

1965 Volvo P1800S, B20 engine, finished in white, very
good condition.
£3,800–4,200 / $5,500–6,000 ⊞ AMA

Restored values

The cost of a professional restoration will have
an influence on, but no direct relation to, a car's
market value. A restored car can have a market
value lower than the cost of its restoration.

Wanderer

1939 Wanderer W23 Cabriolet, coachwork by Gläser, left-hand drive, older restoration, extra headlamps, air horn, rear
fog lamp, non-period flashing indicators, finished in red and black, cream leather interior.
£18,000–22,000 / $26,000–32,000 ✦ Bon
Oldest of the four companies that merged in 1932 to form the Auto Union (the others being Audi, DKW and
Horch), Wanderer had begun life as a bicycle maker in 1885. The firm turned to motorcycle manufacture in the
early 1900s, before building its first automobile, a tandem two-seat light car popularly known as the *Püppchen*
(doll), in 1911. Wanderer entered the 1930s with a new sidevalve six-cylinder engine, designed by Ferdinand
Porsche, that would be developed steadily and enlarged as the decade progressed, ending up at 2651cc in the
W23 of 1937. The W23 which featured an advanced chassis incorporating hydraulic brakes and dampers, together
with independent suspension all-round by means of double wishbones at the front and swing axles at the rear.

Willys

◄ **1928 Willys Overland Crossley Manchester Special,** built over 6-year period, 1950s 27 litre Rolls-Royce Meteor B V12 Centurion tank engine, new ignition system, 1950s Daimler Scout armoured car fluid flywheel, Wilson pre-selector gearbox, chain drive, 1928 Manchester chassis, very good condition.
£19,000–22,000 / $27,000–32,000 ⚲ **Bon**
Willys Overland Crossley was set up in 1920 in Stockport, as a subsidiary of Crossley Motors, to assemble its cars for the UK market. The firm's biggest selling model was the Whippet, manufactured from 1926 to 1930 and available at first with a 2.4 litre, four-cylinder engine, and later with a similar-sized six. The commercial versions were known as Manchesters.

Wolseley

In some ways, Wolseley ended up where it had begun, for it was Herbert Austin who had set the wheels in motion for car manufacture at what was then the Wolseley Sheep Shearing Machine Company. Austin left in 1905, but through an ironic twist Wolseley and Austin were reunited when Austin and Morris merged in 1952 to form the British Motor Corporation. Although Wolseley was overshadowed at BMC by its big brothers, its contribution to British motoring was still important as one of the early pace setters. The first four-wheeled Wolseley motor car was produced in 1899 or 1900, and in 1901 Wolseley car manufacturing was taken over by armaments firm Vickers. Early Wolseley products usually possessed well engineered engines that didn't always get the chassis and running gear to match. Financial difficulties led to the company's acquisition in 1927 by William Morris, and after 1935 Wolseleys served as upmarket Morrises with superior interiors and overhead-valve engines. After the 1952 merger of Austin and Morris, Wolseley survived as a BMC brand until 1975. BMC-era Wolseleys offer enthusiasts a little more distinction and pampering than provided by the starker, plain-Jane Austin and Morris versions.

The Wolseley Hornet, produced from 1961 to 1969, was even more distinctive. Based on the Mini's bodyshell, it was distinguished by upmarket appointments and an extended boot, which had no Austin or Morris counterpart, although the Riley Elf had the same feature. Produced in far fewer numbers than the conventional Mini, the Hornet makes a really distinctive and rather posher alternative.

◄ **1932 Wolseley Hornet Occasional Four Coupé,** 1271cc overhead-camshaft 6-cylinder engine, 4-speed manual gearbox, finished in green and black, original interior, excellent condition.
£7,500–9,000
$11,000–13,000 ⊞ **AVON**

► **1934 Wolseley Nine Four-Door Saloon,** 1018cc 4-cylinder engine, older restoration, period accessories including Ace Avion wheels discs, matched fog and spot lamps and Wilcot trafficators, finished in green and black, green leather upholstery.
£6,000–7,000 / $8,700–10,200 ⚲ **BRIT**
Offered during the 1934 and 1935 seasons, the Wolseley Nine was a companion model to the six-cylinder Hornet. A small car of high quality with a good level of equipment, the Nine was powered by a three-bearing engine utilising the familiar bevel-driven overhead camshaft. The specification included a synchromesh gearbox and Lockheed hydraulic brakes. Only 7,201 Nines were produced before the model was replaced by the Wasp.

WOLSELEY (Veteran & Vintage) Model	ENGINE cc/cyl	DATES	CONDITION 1	2	3
10	987/2	1909–16	£16,000	£12,500	£9,000
CZ (30hp)	2887/4	1909	£18,000	£13,000	£9,000
15hp and A9	2614/4	1920–27	£12,000	£10,000	£8,000
20 and C8	3921/				
	3862/6	1920–27	£11,000	£8,000	£6,000
E4 (10.5hp)	1267/				
	1542/4	1925–30	£6,000	£4,000	£3,000
E6 and Viper and 16hp	2025/6	1927–34	£15,000	£12,000	£8,000
E8M	2700/8	1928–31	£18,000	£15,000	£12,000
Hornet	1271/4	1931–35	£10,000	£8,000	£4,500
Hornet Special	1271/				
	1604/6	1933–36	£12,000	£8,000	£5,000
Wasp	1069/4	1936	£7,000	£5,000	£3,500
Hornet	1378/6	1936	£8,000	£6,000	£4,000
21/60 and 21hp	2677/				
	2916/6	1932–39	£11,000	£6,000	£4,000
25	3485/6	1936–39	£8,500	£5,500	£4,000
12/48	1547/4	1937–39	£5,000	£3,000	£2,000
14/56	1818/6	1937–39	£6,000	£4,000	£2,000
18/80	2322/6	1938–39	£7,500	£5,500	£4,000

Early Wolseley cars are well made and very British, and those with coachbuilt bodies command a premium of at least 25 per cent.

1936 Wolseley 12/48 Series II Saloon, 1547cc engine, finished in grey and blue, blue interior, 4 owners and 97,000 miles from new, original condition.
£3,250–4,250 / $4,750–6,250 ⚒ H&H
Dating from 1936, the 12/48 Series II saloon was effectively the same as its predecessor, the 10/40, apart from the fact that it had a larger engine. Both models had SU carburettors, but the later car had hydraulic brakes and dampers, 12 volt electrics and grease-gun chassis lubrication. Moreover, it was possible to order bespoke coachwork. This particular car was used in the film *Dark Blue World*.

1938 Wolseley 14hp Series II Four-Door Saloon, finished in black, brown leather interior trim, last used 1995, very good condition.
£1,500–2,000 / $2,200–3,000 ⚒ CGC
Absorbed by William Morris' burgeoning empire in 1927, Wolseley became one of its flagship brands. While Wolseley models may have relied heavily on the communal parts bin, they were always better equipped than their Morris equivalents, and until the end of the 1930s enjoyed the benefit of overhead-valve engines. Current from 1936 to 1938, the 14/56 was powered by an 1818cc, overhead-valve, six-cylinder engine that developed 56bhp. Mated to a four-speed manual gearbox, it endowed the 14/56 with a 75mph top speed. A favourite with police forces throughout the country, these small Wolseley sixes provided rapid, reliable transport.

WOLSELEY Model	ENGINE cc/cyl	DATES	CONDITION 1	2	3
8	918/4	1939–48	£3,000	£2,000	£1,000
10	1140/4	1939–48	£3,500	£2,000	£1,000
12/48	1548/4	1939–48	£4,000	£2,000	£1,250
14/60	1818/6	1946–48	£4,500	£2,500	£1,500
18/85	2321/6	1946–48	£6,000	£3,000	£2,000
25	3485/6	1946–48	£7,000	£4,000	£2,500
4/50	1476/4	1948–53	£2,500	£1,000	£450
6/80	2215/6	1948–54	£3,000	£1,500	£750
4/44	1250/4	1952–56	£2,500	£1,250	£750
15/50	1489/4	1956–58	£1,850	£850	£500
1500	1489/4	1958–65	£2,500	£1,000	£500
15/60	1489/4	1958–61	£2,000	£700	£400
16/60	1622/4	1961–71	£1,800	£800	£400
6/90	2639/6	1954–57	£2,500	£1,000	£500
6/99	2912/6	1959–61	£3,000	£1,500	£750
6/110 MK I/II	2912/6	1961–68	£2,000	£1,000	£500
Hornet (Mini)	848/4	1961–70	£1,500	£750	£400
1300	1275/4	1967–74	£1,250	£750	£400
18/85	1798/4	1967–72	£1,000	£500	£250

Commercial Vehicles

1955 Albion Victor, last Albion supplied to Guernsey Railway Co, narrow Channel Island specification, restored late 1990s.
£2,500–4,000 / $3,600–5,800 ↗ **Bon**

1924 Austin Seven 2½cwt Commercial Van, converted from Chummy late 1920s, 6in (15cm) brakes, finished in maroon, cream interior, black leather upholstery.
£7,000–8,000 / $10,000–11,500 ↗ **Bon**

1937 Austin Ruby Van, finished in dark red with black wings, black fabric roof insert, in need of some rewiring and finishing, good condition.
£1,700–2,200 / $2,500–3,000 ↗ **CGC**

1939 Austin Heavy 12/4 Landaulette London Taxi, 4-cylinder engine, 4-speed manual gearbox, retaining all original features including illuminated 'Taxi' sign, roof rack, hand operated spot lamp, Hackney Carriage plate, wood/leather trunk, taximeter, restored, finished in black with dark blue to side swage moulding, retrimmed in correct blue Rexine fabric, fold-down rear hood in correct black leatherette.
£13,000–15,000 / $19,000–22,000 ↗ **Bon**

1957 Austin A35 Pick-up, restored, good condition.
£4,000–5,000 / $5,800–7,250 🚗 **AUS**
Fewer than 500 A35 pick-ups were built.

1960 Austin Gipsy Fire Tender, in service until late 1970s, stored for some time, suitable for restoration, sound and complete.
£1,700–2,000 / $2,500–3,000 ↗ **Bon**
Built between 1958 and 1968, the four-wheel-drive Austin Gipsy was an obvious rival to the Land Rover. More advanced than the Land Rover in some respects, most notably in its tubular-steel chassis and all-round independent suspension, the Gipsy proved somewhat less durable thanks to a steel-panelled body. The trailing-arm suspension used Flexitor rubber-in-torsion springs housed in large-diameter tubes attached to the chassis, although this arrangement was superseded by more conventional rigid axles and leaf springs on later models. A choice of engines was offered – Austin A70 2.2 litre or 2.5 litre diesel – while later Gipsies had the 2.9 litre Austin Atlantic engine.

1958 Austin A35 Van, restored, good condition.
£2,000–2,500 / $3,000–3,600 🚗 **AUS**

1960 Bedford CA Ultra-Brake Minibus, 1595cc engine, finished in green, tan interior, bodywork in need of minor cosmetic attention or restoration.
£600–1,000 / $875–1,500 ➶ H&H

1969 BMC/LD Ambulance, completely restored to original condition, Flintshire County Council Ambulance Service livery.
£2,000–3,000 / $3,000–4,500 🚌 BAm

1932 Commer 20/25 14hp 33cwt Recovery Truck, sidevalve engine, older restoration, recovery equipment including galvanised A-frame, towing ambulance, rigid towing pole and steering lock.
£5,000–6,000 / $7,250–8,750 ➶ CGC

1987 Dodge Diplomat Police Car, genuine ex-police car, restored, finished in Sheriff's Department of Middlesex County, New Jersey, livery, good condition throughout.
£2,750–3,750 / $4,000–5,500 ➶ Bon
Introduced mid-way through the 1977 model year, the all-new Diplomat slotted into the Dodge range between the compact Aspen and the full-sized Monaco and Charger models. It was built as either a two-door coupé or four-door sedan and came with a 318cu.in V8 engine as standard.

1958 Morris J2 Caravanette, 1500 B-series engine, column gear change.
£2,000–3,000 / $3,000–4,500 ⊞ BMC

1947 Chevrolet Custom Pick-up, older restoration, lowered suspension, sun visor, rolled and pleated upholstery, rust free.
£4,500–5,500 / $6,500–8,000 ➶ BJ

1930 Dennis 60/70hp Low-Load Fire Appliance, 7996cc 8-cylinder White & Poppe petrol engine, restored to original condition 1990s, full complement of accessories and tools, locker-store fittings, hoses and bell.
£15,000–17,500 / $22,000–25,500 ➶ BRIT
John and Raymond Dennis began manufacturing bicycles and motorcycles at Guildford, under the name of Speedking, during 1899. By the end of that year, they had assembled their first car, a two-seater powered by a rear mounted, De Dion 3.5hp engine. This vehicle was not intended for sale, merely being for exhibition purposes, but by 1901 production had begun, this time employing a front mounted, 8hp De Dion power unit. Over the next few years, a prolific range of motor cars was built, and by 1908 there were two factories. Also during this year, Dennis started building fire engines, which was to become a company speciality. During WWI, some 7,000 lorries were produced, while car production ceased in 1915. By 1920, Dennis was employing over 1,400 people and had acquired engine manufacturer White & Poppe.

1921 Ford Model TT 1 Ton Dropside Truck, 2-speed rear axle, finished in green with red coachlines, green upholstery, good condition.
£4,750–5,750 / $7,000–8,500 ↗ **Bon**

1928 Ford Model A Pick-up, 3.3 litre sidevalve 4-cylinder engine, right-hand drive, restored, cylinder block upgraded to Model B specification, most mechanical parts reconditioned or renewed, finished in green and black, in need of minor electrical and interior trim work.
£7,500–8,500 / $11,000–12,500 ↗ **CGC**

1971 Land Rover 110 Fire Tender, petrol engine, long-wheelbase model, large front bumper used as water carrier, equipped with hoses, ladders, rear searchlight and blue flashing lights, last used 1999, in need of recommissioning and cosmetic attention.
£700–800 / $1,000–1,150 ↗ **Bon**
Supplied new to Cheshire County Fire Brigade in 1971, this Land Rover tender was commissioned for use at Runcorn and specially lowered for use in the multi-storey car parks around the town's shopping precinct.

1926 Ford Model T Truck, restored, varnished wood artillery wheels, finished in deep red with black wings and radiator surround.
£7,500–9,000 / $11,000–13,000 ↗ **CGC**

1986 GB Cars Radnor Van, 848cc overhead-valve 4-cylinder engine, 4-speed manual gearbox, Reliant Fox running gear, Reliant galvanised box-section chassis, glassfibre body, finished in red and black, 25,000 miles from new, good condition.
£1,700–2,000 / $2,500–3,000 ↗ **BARO**
GB Cars was formed by Gavin Hooper and Brian Lewis, and was based in London. The manufacturer offered the Raglan tourer and the Radnor van. It is thought that only six vehicles were actually built and sold. GB Cars stopped production after a short time, as it was competing with both Ollerton and Asquith, which were catering for the same market.

1971 Morris Minor Van, 1098cc 4-cylinder engine, little recent use, Royal Mail livery.
£2,400–2,800 / $3,500–4,000 ↗ **BRIT**
Morris commercials introduced a new Minor 5cwt van, or more correctly, the O-series commercial van, in 1953, based on the Series II Morris Minor. The new van, powered by the 803cc, overhead-valve A-series engine, was soon adapted for use by the Post Office, early examples being fitted with separate headlights mounted on rubber wings and an opening window on the driver's side of the split screen. This specification was similar to that of the outgoing Z-series vans, then in use for Royal Mail deliveries and by GPO telephone engineers, but later the specification came more closely into line with general production. This example would appear to have been in service until 1977, and subsequently was re-acquired by the Post Office in 1987 for its Historic Fleet.

◀ **1908 Unic Type C9 12/14hp Taxi,** 4-cylinder engine, 4-passenger example, restored mid-1990s, unused since, good condition.
£19,000–23,000 / $28,000–33,000 ↗ **Bon**

Replica, Kit & Reproduction Cars

◄ **1997 Dax AC Cobra Replica,** tuned Rover V8 engine, 4-barrel Holley carburettor, Mallory competition distributor.
£13,000–14,500 / $19,000–21,000 ⊞ **WbC**

2000 Pilgrim Sumo Roadster, 2 litre Ford Zetec engine, ABS brakes, galvanised chassis, Halibrand wheels, roll bar, soft top, tonneau cover, black leather seats, woodrim steering wheel, tinted windscreen, sun visors, alarm.
£6,000–7,000 / $8,700–10,200 ↗ **Bon**
Sussex based kit-car builder Pilgrim manufactures sports cars in a variety of classic styles, the Sumo being influenced by the legendary AC Cobra. Introduced in 1987, the Sumo offered enthusiasts a less expensive route to 'Cobra' ownership, using Ford Cortina engines and running gear. In 1993, the current (Mk III) Sumo was introduced in two forms, one using Ford Sierra/Granada components, the other Jaguar parts. The steel chassis combines ladder-frame, space-frame and monocoque construction techniques, while the bodywork is in glassfibre. Like many similar vehicles, the Sumo is available for self-build or as a 'turn key' car, with a wide range of options.

1989 Teal Bugatti Type 35 Replica, 1800cc B-series engine, aluminium body, steel chassis.
£5,500–6,500 / $8,000–9,500 ↗ **BARO**

1999 Southern Roadcraft Ferrari Daytona Spyder Replica, 3900cc Rover V8 engine, modified Jaguar XJ6 suspension, steering and rear axle, built at a cost of over £33,000, all mechanical parts used either new or reconditioned apart from engine and gearbox, finished in red, cream interior.
£15,000–18,000 / $22,000–26,000 ↗ **H&H**

1994 Dax GT40 Replica, tuned 4700cc V8 engine, Holley carburettors, c350bhp, Peugeot 5-speed manual gearbox, Spax adjustable coil-spring/damper units, zinc and powder coated space-frame chassis, BRM wheels, GT40 filler caps, glassfibre body panels, finished in blue and grey, blue interior trim, air conditioning, removable steering wheel, fewer than 950 miles from new.
£20,000–23,000 / $29,000–33,000 ↗ **H&H**

1996 Jaguar SS100 Replica, correct 3.5 litre SS-type engine, 2 sidedraught SU carburettors, original beam front and rigid rear axles, period leaf springs, correct 18in wire wheels, aluminium coachwork built at a cost of over £50,000, almost £10,000 spent on paintwork and trim, correct red leather bucket seats, reproduction instruments bearing pre-war SS logo on their faces.
£45,000–55,000 / $65,000–80,000 ⚒ COYS

1983 Proteus Jaguar C-Type Replica, early Proteus prototype; 3781cc double-overhead-camshaft 6-cylinder Jaguar engine, 4-speed Moss gearbox with overdrive, 4-wheel Dunlop disc brakes, leaf-sprung rear axle with limited-slip differential, 16in wire wheels, steel box-section chassis with aluminium bulkhead, floors and bonnet reinforcement framework, alloy quick-release fuel filler cap, glassfibre body, engine and gearbox rebuilt 1993–94, resprayed, fitted electronic ignition, carburettors and hydraulics overhauled, bills for over £4,000, finished in British racing green, period tan bucket seats, woodrim steering wheel, excellent condition.
£17,500–20,000 / $25,000–29,000 ⚒ CGC

1981 JPR Wildcat Jaguar E-Type Replica, 2.3 litre engine, centre-lock wire wheels, fared-in headlamps, racing mirrors, finished in red, woodrim steering wheel.
£5,000–6,000 / $7,250–8,750 ⚒ Bon

1994 Hawk Lancia Stratos Replica, 2 litre 4-cylinder engine fitted special camshafts, lightened flywheel and twin Dell'Orto 45mm carburettors, same front suspension uprights and geometry as genuine Stratos, Ferrari 5-stud wheels, Dino hubs, right-hand drive, Bertone-style seats, professionally trimmed to replicate original Stratos road car, Sabelt harnesses, MoMo steering wheel, lined roof and panelled-in roll cage, built at a cost of over £25,000, excellent condition throughout.
£15,000–18,000 / $22,000–26,000 ⚒ Bon

Microcars

c1958 Messerschmitt KR200 Cabin Scooter, 191cc air-cooled single-cylinder 2-stroke engine, 4-speed gearbox in unit with engine, rigid steel frame, independent suspension on all 3 wheels by rubber in torsion, completely restored, little use since.
£4,000–6,000 / $5,800–8,800 ⚒ GO

1959 Nobel 200, 191cc Sachs single-cylinder 2-stroke engine, 10bhp, 4-speed gearbox, 50mph top speed, fewer than 16,000 miles from new, original unrestored condition.
£3,000–4,000 / $4,500–5,800 🚗 NR
This car is an early model, identified by its indicator lamps being roof mounted, whereas the later Model A had its indicators mounted at the front and rear. The car is reversed by starting the engine backwards.

Restoration Projects

◀ **1951 AC 2 Litre Drophead Coupé Conversion,** 4-speed Moss gearbox, converted from saloon, some genuine drophead fixtures and fittings, loosely assembled, finished in red, beige leather seats, instruments and door trims in need of fitting, hood frame but no hood.
£900–1,000 / $1,300–1,500 ⚒ CGC
Launched in 1947, the AC 2 Litre owed a lot to pre-war design trends. Its continued use of AC's overhead-camshaft six, developing some 76bhp in this guise, and a beam-axle front suspension design leant it a vintage feel.

1962 AC Ace-Zephyr Ruddspeed Sports, 2.6 litre Ford 6-cylinder engine, Raymond Mays cylinder head, mechanically dismantled, bodyshell stripped, wheel arches flared to accommodate wide wire wheels and tyres.
£18,000–22,000 / $26,000–32,000 ⚒ Bon

◀ **c1963 AC Aceca V8 Coupé,** Cobra V8 engine, left-hand drive, dry-stored.
£5,000–8,000
$7,250–11,500 ⚒ Bon
AC Cars never got around to building a closed, Aceca-style version of the Cobra, although the Frua styled AC 428, introduced in 1966, did use a lengthened Cobra Mk III chassis frame. This car represents one unknown individual's attempt to construct a 'closed Cobra'.

1934 Austin 10hp Clifton Tourer, 1125cc sidevalve
4-cylinder engine, 4-speed synchromesh gearbox, X-braced
chassis, 12 volt electrics, 2-seater-plus-dickey coachwork,
last used 1988, barn stored since.
£3,300–4,500 / $4,750–6,500 ➶ Bon

1937 Austin 20 Rolling Chassis, 3.4 litre 6-cylinder engine,
original front wings, grille, bonnet, headlamps, side lights
and chrome bumper, finished in green over black, including
drawings for van body, chassis in good drivable condition.
£1,700–2,000 / $2,500–3,000 ➶ CGC

c1955 Austin A30 Four-Door Saloon, in need of
complete restoration.
£50–100 / $75–145 🚗 Aus

1955 Austin-Healey 100/4 BN1, wire wheels, in need of
complete restoration.
£2,000–2,500 / $3,000–3,600 ➶ H&H

1926 Bentley Speed Model Tourer, coachwork by
Vanden Plas, 3 litre engine, partially restored 1989–91 at a
cost of over £30,000.
£35,000–40,000 / $51,000–58,000 ➶ Bon

1948 Bentley Mk VI Rolling Chassis, originally from a
saloon, engine and gearbox not fitted, engine dismantled,
no documentation.
£500–600 / $720–870 ➶ H&H

c1923 Citroën 5CV Boulangier (Bread Van), engine runs,
chassis in good condition, coachwork generally sound,
finished in grey, black interior, laid up since WWII,
last change of owner 1939, complete and original.
£2,500–3,000 / $3,500–4,500 ➶ Bon
**Citroën's 5CV was the Gallic equivalent of the Austin
7 and made its debut in 1922, remaining in production
for almost five years, during which approximately
88,000 examples left the factory. Powered by a four-
cylinder, 855cc sidevalve engine, it had quarter-elliptic
leaf springs all-round.**

c1909 Daimler 15hp Tourer, engine turns over, 4-seat
touring coachwork retaining many original fittings and
details, finished in maroon with black wings and upholstery,
mechanically complete, untouched for c30 years.
£16,000–19,000 / $23,000–28,000 ➶ CGC

c1958 Falcon Carribean Roadster, based on 1939 Ford Prefect components, 1172cc sidevalve 4-cylinder engine, chassis and running gear overhauled mid-1980s, hardtop, stored for past 2–3 years.
£600–700 / $870–1,000 ✗ Bon
The glassfibre-bodied Falcon Carribean was made in both open and closed forms between 1957 and 1963. Approximately 30 of the 500 or so built survive.

1918 Ford Model T Mail Carrier, in need of complete restoration.
£2,000–2,500 / $3,000–3,600 ⊞ TUC

1953 Healey Warwick Coupé, believed bodied by Mulliner, 2.4 litre double-overhead-camshaft 4-cylinder Riley engine, 104bhp, trailing-arm independent front suspension, new exhaust, aluminium coachwork finished in dark red, spare wheel, dashboard retaining original instrumentation, red leather interior incomplete, blistering to front wings, little attention since 1993, running.
£2,000–2,500 / $3,000–3,600 ✗ CGC

> **Miller's is a price GUIDE not a price LIST**

1953 Jaguar XK120 Roadster, original matching-numbers engine, some new panels, original trim.
£9,000–10,500 / $13,000–15,250 ✗ COYS

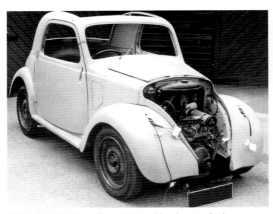

1939 Fiat 500 Topolino, 569cc sidevalve 4-cylinder engine, Lockheed hydraulic brakes, independent front suspension, 12 volt electrics, chassis and running gear rebuilt and finished to concours standard, bodyshell repaired where necessary and primed, new wiring, seats retrimmed in red leather, all components necessary to complete, 2 owners from new, running.
£1,800–2,300 / $2,500–3,500 ✗ CGC

1924 Ford Model T 1 Ton Truck, partially restored.
£2,000–2,500 / $3,000–3,600 ⊞ TUC

1948 Jaguar Mk IV Saloon, 2.5 litre 6-cylinder engine, 4-speed manual gearbox, Girling mechanical brakes, beam front axle, rigid rear axle, semi-elliptic leaf-spring suspension, sun roof, holed core plug, engine runs.
£3,000–4,000 / $4,500–5,800 ✗ Bon

1954 Jaguar XK120SE Coupé, 3.4 litre double-overhead-camshaft 6-cylinder engine, 4-wheel drum brakes, independent front suspension, left-hand drive, partially stripped, dating from final year of production, barn discovery.
£9,000–10,000 / $13,000–14,500 ✗ Bon

1930 Lagonda 2 Litre Supercharged Tourer, original engine, low-chassis model, period fold-flat windscreen, unrestored, 1 of only 5 genuine 2 litre supercharged cars, almost completely original.
£20,000–24,000 /$29,000–35,000 ⚒ COYS

◀ **c1968 Lotus Elan S3 Fixed-head Coupé,** 1558cc engine, replacement cylinder head, virtually new Weber carburettors, left-hand drive, finished in maroon, black interior.
£3,000–3,500 $4,500–5,000 ⚒ H&H

1955 Maserati A6G-2000 Coupé, coachwork by Zagato, 2 litre double-overhead-camshaft 6-cylinder engine not fitted, mechanically almost complete, aluminium bodyshell ready for final priming and painting, including original-type windscreen, 3rd A6G-2000 coupé to carry Zagato coachwork.
£250,000+ / $362,000+ ⚒ Bon

1935 MG KN Magnette Tourer, coachwork by Coachcraft, last of c20 KN chassis sold by University Motors as University Motors Speed Model, matching engine and chassis numbers, unrestored.
£12,000–15,000 / $17,500–21,500 ⚒ Bon
The KN Magnette combined the long-wheelbase chassis of the K1 with the N-Type 1271cc engine and was only offered as a saloon, thus providing University Motors with the opportunity to exploit a gap in the market with their attractive K1-style four-seat tourer using the larger and more powerful N-Type engine.

1962 Mercedes-Benz 190SL Roadster, 1900cc, left-hand drive, engine, gearbox and suspension rebuilt, bare-metal respray in silver, hard and soft tops, original tan interior, all parts to complete.
£6,500–8,000 / $9,500–11,500 ⚒ H&H

1923 Rolls-Royce 40/50hp New Phantom Experimental Car, chassis no. 46PK, engine no. 7EAC II, laid up on blocks and engine turned fortnightly since 1945, shooting-brake body, believed 15,000 miles from new.
£100,000+ / $145,000+ ✗ Bon

This car was the factory development car for the New Phantom and also Sir Henry Royce's personal car. The chassis was originally allocated engine no. G237, but was fitted with the current engine by the Experimental Department at Rolls-Royce. This engine, originally code named 'Seagull' and later designated EAC II, was the development engine for the New Phantom, which was not to be launched until 1925. Concurrently with this development, the company was working on an all-new, four-wheel braking system based on the Hispano-Suiza servo-assisted design, and it is thought that this was the first Rolls-Royce chassis to be fitted with front-wheel brakes. Moreover, this was the car that Royce used as his personal transport at his summer home in West Wittering, and clearly it was used as something of a working test-bed. In 1926, it was fitted with its second body by Hooper, remaining with the Experimental Department. It was passed to The Red Cross Society for wartime service in 1940, and in 1944 it was registered as an ambulance in Winchester.

1931 Singer Junior Saloon, 885cc engine, finished in grey, complete, in need of restoration.
£400–600 / $580–870 ✗ H&H

1955 Standard Vanguard Estate, 2088cc engine, manual gearbox with column change, original driving lamp, finished in grey, red and grey vinyl interior, fewer than 58,000 miles from new, laid up since c1973, 1 family ownership from new.
£1,000–1,200 / $1,500–1,750 ✗ CGC

1939 Rover 14 Four-Door Saloon, 1577cc engine, finished in black, tan seating and interior trim removed, no documents, complete, in need of complete restoration.
£300–500 / $450–720 ✗ H&H

1919 Scripps-Booth Model 6/39 Tourer, fewer than 8,000 miles from new, last used 1926, engine turns freely, generally sound, original.
£5,000–6,000 / $7,250–8,750 ✗ CGC

1935 Standard Flying 12 Saloon, 1608cc 4-cylinder engine, 4-speed manual gearbox, worm-drive back axle, sliding roof, safety glass, finished in pale blue, blue interior, adjustable seats, leather upholstery, thought to be oldest surviving Flying 12, chassis and interior fundamentally sound, complete.
£150–300 / $220–440 ✗ CGC

1924 Vauxhall 30/98 Tourer, special counter-balanced-crank engine, original lighting equipment, dashboard with all correct instruments, unused for 40 years, partially rebuilt.
£45,000–55,000 / $65,000–80,000 ✗ COYS

Colour Review

1919 Ford Model TT Woody, 6-seat coachwork, high-speed transmission upgrade, older restoration.
£9,000–11,000 / $13,000–16,000 ⚲ **Bon**

▶ **1951 Ford F3 Pick-up,** sidevalve V8 engine, converted to unleaded fuel, wooden stake rails, older repaint in original dark green, original cardboard headlining, two-tone vinyl interior, radio, heater, interior light.
£4,000–5,000 / $5,800–7,200 ⚲ **Bon**

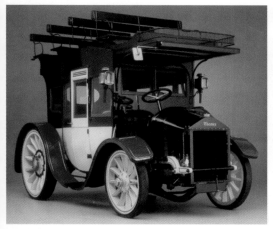

1913 Thames 25-Seater Motor Stagecoach, coachwork by Thrupp & Maberly, older restoration, maroon velour upholstery, museum displayed for some years, good to very good condition.
£40,000–50,000 / $58,000–73,000 ⚲ **Bon**
The first Thames car was a large 45hp, 6977cc, six-cylinder model, and 50hp and 60hp types followed. One of the 9648cc 60hp models took records at Brooklands in 1907, driven by Clifford Earp. Smaller models followed, including twins and fours, but in 1911 an unusual fleet of mock stagecoaches was built to the order of Motor Coaches Ltd. To make them more authentic looking, the 4960cc, six-cylinder engine was mounted in a semi-forward-control position, the driver being exposed to the elements. The coach accommodated nine passengers inside and 16 on four rows of seats on the roof. Intended for use in and around London, they proved popular with race-goers at Ascot and Epsom, providing natural grandstands for spectators. This example is the only known survivor.

1937 GMC Fire Appliance, 3548cc 6-cylinder engine, original, all correct fittings, flashing indicators, fewer than 4,500 miles from new, pump in need of attention, otherwise all major mechanical components in good condition.
£5,500–7,000 / $8,000–10,000 ⚲ **BRIT**

1971 Morris Minor Pick-up, 1098cc 4-cylinder engine, fitted new pick-up body 1982, resprayed 1992, black interior, unused since 1993, 64,000 miles from new, very good condition throughout.
£2,700–3,400 / $4,000–5,000 ⚲ **M&M**

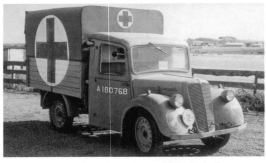

1939 Morris 11.9hp 10cwt Convertible Ambulance, older restoration, believed to be only surviving restored example, museum displayed for many years, in need of respray and attention to engine timing.
£3,000–4,000 / $4,400–5,800 ✕ Bon
The Morris Convertible Ambulance, widely used during WWII, was built to a design patented by Richard Benn of Worthing and was capable of carrying four stretchered patients at one time. The patent allowed simple conversion from lorries to ambulances when needed, the necessary apparatus being carried beneath the truck bed.

1941 Daimler Dingo Mk II Scout Car, 4-wheel drive, older restoration, 1 of oldest known surviving Dingos, finished in Engineers, 30 Corps livery, museum displayed for some time, in need of recommissioning.
£4,000–5,000 / $5,800–7,250 ✕ Bon
Daimler's armoured scout car played a significant role as a forward reconnaissance vehicle in WWII. Powered by a rear mounted, 55bhp, six-cylinder engine, it drove through a five-speed pre-selector gearbox with fluid flywheel and single-speed transfer box with differential. The Dingo was remarkably quick in action, its speed in reverse almost matching its forward speed. It was equipped with independent coil-spring suspension and hydraulic brakes, had a crew of two and weighed 5,725lb (2,597kg). Over 6,000 were built, and they saw service in Europe and North Africa.

▶ **1943 Austin Type G/YG 10hp Light Utility Truck,** 1230cc 4-cylinder sidevalve engine, Girling mechanical brakes, leaf-spring suspension, 2 occasional seats to rear, roof mounted spare wheel, full tilt cover, wartime headlamp mask, older restoration, little use since 1976, in need of recommissioning.
£5,000–6,000 / $7,250–8,750 ✕ Bon

c1944 GMC 2½ Ton 6x6 Short-Wheelbase Truck, 270cu.in 6-cylinder engine, 94bhp, hard-cab model, restored.
£2,000–3,000 / $3,000–4,400 🚚 MVT

1940 Morris Commercial CS8 Compressor Truck, released from service 1946 after complete rebuild, thought to have covered only 600 miles since, unused for several years, in need of recommissioning.
£3,750–4,500 / $5,500–6,500 ✕ Bon
Morris Commercial Cars built the first 15cwt chassis, on which the CS8 was based, in 1934. The early models had an open cab with folding windscreen, and this particular example is powered by the four-cylinder sidevalve engine introduced early in WWII. The CS8 was adopted by the military for various uses, including as a general service truck, a water carrier and, as in the case of this particular example, a compressor truck.

c1943 Willys MB Jeep, 134.2cu.in. 4-cylinder sidevalve engine, 3-speed gearbox with reverse, 2-speed transfer box, hydraulic brakes, rigid axles on leaf springs, 6 volt electrics.
£7,000–8,000 / $10,000–11,500 ⊞ RRM

1944 John Deere Model LI Petrol/Paraffin Tractor, restored, engine rebuilt, thought to be only example in UK.
£5,000–6,000 / $7,250–8,750 ✕ CGC

c1890 Single Brougham, to fit 14hh and over, interior with occasional seating to front, buttoned blue velvet upholstery, wheels rebuilt 2000, with pair of swan-neck shafts.
£4,000–5,000 / $5,800–7,250 ➢ **TSh**

c1900 Butcher's Delivery Van, to fit 14.2–15.2hh, with shafts, winner in light trade classes, finished to show standard.
£2,000–2,500 / $3,000–3,600 ➢ **TSh**

c1926 Well Bottom Milk Delivery Float, to fit 14.2–15.2hh, bow-fronted body, central driving position and canopy, pneumatic tyres, sliding doors to front storage area, slatted interior, restored, used only once since, with original crates and milk bottles from Dalton Dairy.
£10,000–12,000 / $14,500–17,500 ➢ **TSh**

c1939 London Trolley, by Vincents of Reading, to fit 14–15hh, finely carved and scalloped body, drop tailboard, stainless steel and chrome fittings, 3-stud artillery wheels, footbrake, shafts.
£2,750–3,500 / $4,000–5,000 ➢ **TSh**

1950s Austin J40 Pedal Car, restored, white interior, working lights, in need of new battery, good condition.
£900–1,200 / $1,300–1,750 ➢ **Bon**

1980s Taurus Land Rover Child's Car and Trailer, 12 volt electric motor, glassfibre and wood construction, detachable hardtop, steel chassis, 2 seats, wooden trailer with leathercloth tilt cover, finished in off-white, 72in (183cm) long.
£1,600–2,000 / $2,300–3,000 ➢ **BRIT**

1970s Child's Racing Car, 12 volt electric motor, steel chassis, glassfibre body in style of Austin Pathfinder pedal car, 84in (213.5cm) long.
£600–700 / $870–1,000 ➢ **BRIT**

▶ **1948 Austin J40 Pedal Car,** unrestored, 48in (122cm) long.
£500–700 / $720–1,000 ➢ **CGC**

Bob Murray, In The Shade, depicting a 1967 Ferrari 275 GTB/4 and a Bugatti Type 35, mixed media, signed, framed and glazed, 19 x 22in (48.5 x 56cm).
£850–950 / $1,250–1,380 ⚒ Bon

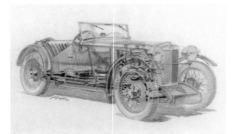

Brian Hatton, 1932 MG J2 Midget, a cut-away pen and ink drawing with watercolour wash on board, for *Motor* magazine, signed and dated 'Sept 1982', 13½ x 21in (34.5 x 53.5cm).
£200–250 / $300–360 ⚒ Bon

▶ **Dick Ellis, Austin 7,** a cut-away pen and ink line drawing with watercolour on board, for *The Autocar*, signed and dated 'Feb 1973', slight discolouration to surface, 13 x 16¼in (33 x 41.5cm).
£100–130 / $145–190 ⚒ Bon

The £100 Ford Saloon, an original poster depicting a Model Y two-door saloon and family, 29½ x 39½in (75 x 100.5cm).
£300–350 / $440–500 ⚒ CGC

▶ **An Avon Tyres advertising wall mirror,** 1930s, original, framed, 12¼ x 8¼in (31 x 21cm).
£180–220 / $260–320 ⚒ Bon

Two Dunlop advertising posters, lithographic prints, 1930s, 27 x 15in (68.5 x 38cm).
£80–100 / $115–145 ⚒ BRIT

Max Millar, Modern Trends, a labelled cut-away illustration for *The Autocar*, pen and ink with monochrome wash on board, discolouration to surface, board with flaking and loss to corners, signed, dated '20/2/31', 21 x 15in (53.5 x 38cm).
£100–150 $145–220 ⚒ Bon

▶ **R. Geri, Bugatti,** an original poster depicting the SNCF train racing a Bugatti motor car, marks for Molsheim and Alsace, very good condition.
£800–1,000 / $1,150–1,500 ⚒ Bon

Frederick Gordon-Crosby, Line Painting, pen and ink cartoon with monochrome and pink wash on paper, mounted on board, signed and dated '1937', some smudging and wear, tear to right edge of paper, 16 x 12¾in (40.5 x 32.5cm).
£800–1,100 / $1,150–1,600 ⚒ Bon

An extensive kit of maintenance tools, as used with cars dating from the 1920s, correct and period BSA spanners, box spanners, grease gun, Blower oil primer, foot pump, plug spanner, Perfect screwdrivers, painted tins and small tools, c50 tools in all, contained in heavy leather bag.
£1,200–1,400 / $1,750–2,000 ⚒ Bon

◀ **You Can Buy Your Ford Car Here,** an original poster depicting a girl at the wheel of a car, 1920s, 39½ x 29½in (100.5 x 75cm).
£300–350 / $440–500 ⚒ CGC

A set of Porsche commissioned cake plates, manufactured by Ulmer Keramik, each depicting a period scene with a Porsche 356 or RS60, glazed and unmarked, includes 1 server 11in (28cm) diam and 6 settings 8in (20.5cm) diam, excellent condition.
£1,750–2,000 / $2,500–3,000 ⚒ C

An Aston Martin DB3S six-cylinder 3 litre engine, uprated to production DB3S specification, single-plug iron head, 45DCOE152 carburettors, inlet manifold and distributor, c200bhp.
£18,000–22,000 $26,000–32,000 ⚒ Bon

A Spirit of Triumph mascot, by Françoise Victor Bazin, as used on 1920s Isotta-Fraschini cars, original German silver-on-bronze finish, display mounted, 6½in (16.5cm) high.
£1,200–1,400 / $1,750–2,000 ⚒ Bon

Porsche 356 advertising and promotional material 1950–60, factory hardbound edition, German/English/French text, colour illustrations, excellent condition.
£2,000–2,300 / $3,000–3,350 ⚒ C

A pull-cord gimmick, 'Crikey! That's Shell that was!!', in original box, 1930s, 6in (15cm) square.
£80–90 / $115–130 ⊞ MURR

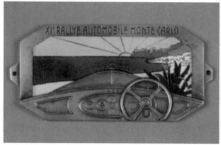

An XIe Monte Carlo Rallye plaque, by Fraisse-Demy, Paris, enamelled Riviera design, in original presentation case, 1932, plaque 3½in (9cm) wide.
£700–900 / $1,000–1,300 ⚒ Bon

A matched pair of Salsbury Flare self-contained acetylene gas headlamps, undamaged glass protective rear mirrors, bevelled-edge front glasses, burner holders, carrying bails, condenser bag aperture with hinged door to rear, hinged carbide generator covers, partially restored, slide-out square-pattern carbide generators missing, c1902, 14in (35.5cm) high.
£2,500–3,000 / $3,600–4,400 ⚒ Bon

◀ **A replica Red Ashay glass Pilot mascot,** post-war manufacture, satin glass, in metal mount, on black painted wooden base, 5½in (14cm) long.
£350–400 / $500–580 ⚒ Bon

▶ **A Mercedes-Benz three-pointed star combination mascot and thermometer,** designed for 1930s SSK cars, display mounted, original condition, 6in (15cm) high.
£1,500–1,700 / $2,150–2,450 ⚒ Bon

A set of 30 Wills Castella Classic Sports Car cards, featuring many of best-known British sports cars from 1940s to mid-1990s including Triumph Stag, Lotus Elan, Jaguar E-Type, Austin-Healey 3000 and MGB, 1996.
£25–35 / $35–50 ⊞ MUR

A nickel plated bronze Bibendum mascot, 'Combat l'obstacle', fitted with thread for radiator mounting, nickel worn and bronze patinated, c1922, 4in (10cm) high.
£950–1,100 $1,400–1,600 ⚒ CGC

A Packard Swan mascot, original chrome plating, original radiator cap cover and mounting screw, 1928–30, 9in (23cm) high.
£900–1,000 / $1,300–1,500 ➤ Bon

A Pelican mascot, by Bouraine, with carved ivory beak, the reverse with artist's signature and foundry socle, mid-1920s, 5½in (14cm) high.
£2,200–2,500 / $3,150–3,600 ➤ Bon

▶ **A satin- and frosted-glass mascot,** Boar, by René Lalique, moulded R. Lalique between legs, scripted signature under base, excellent condition, c1929.
£600–800 / $870–1,150 ➤ Bon

An Art Deco-style flying stork mascot, Cygne Sauvage, by Françoise Victor Bazin, original nickel plated finish, c1925, 5½in (14cm) high.
£700–800 / $1,000–1,150 ➤ Bon

An amber glass fish mascot, Perch, by René Lalique, unsigned.
£300–350 / $440–500 ➤ Bon

A Mickey Mouse mascot, original plated finish, excellent original condition, mid-1930s, 5¼in (13.5cm) high.
£2,750–3,250 $4,000–4,750 ➤ Bon

A cobra combination mascot and glass thermometer, by G. Rischmann, original nickel-silver plated finish, mounted on radiator cap, signed, 1924, 6in (15cm) high.
£4,500–5,500 $6,500–8,000 ➤ Bon

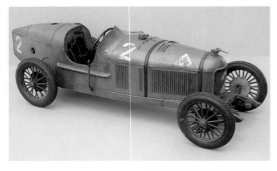

◀ **A model of a P2 Alfa Romeo racing car,** by CIJ, tinplate, clockwork motor, original Michelin tyres and fittings, French, 1920s, 20in (51cm) long.
£1,900–2,300 / $2,750–3,350 ➤ G(B)

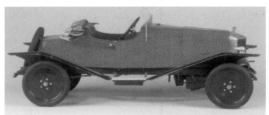

▶ **A 1/8-scale hand-built die-cast model of an 1886 Benz Patent Motorwagen,** working steering, engine with large number of moving parts, spoked wheels, solid rubber tyres, brass, steel and copper work to engine, *faux* wood-plank deck, 12in (30.5cm) long.
£100–130 $145–190 ➤ Bon

A 1/6-scale scratchbuilt metal-bodied model of a 1923 Hillman 11hp car, by C.T. Black, working canvas hood, buttoned leather bench seat, solid Dunlop Magnum rubber tyres, hinged bonnet, battery-powered headlights and side lights, nickel plated radiator, headlights and windscreen, solid wood interior body, rack-and-pinion steering, working handbrake, suspension and authentic brake shoes to rear, interior includes aluminium floor, fascia dials and switches and sprung pedals, hinged doors with working catches, 24in (61cm) long.
£750–850 / $1,100–1,250 ➤ Bon

An H.H. Hill 4-person picnic set, black leathercloth case, honey leather lined case supporting wicker covered framework, wicker covered Thermos flask, openweave wicker covered drinks bottle, bone china cups and saucers with gilt-edged Greek key pattern, 4 rectangular enamel plates, ceramic-based sandwich box, early 1920s.
£1,500–2,000 / $2,200–3,000 🔨 Bon

A Mappin & Webb combination 4-person picnic set and foot rest, dark green leather lined interior, 2 white enamel sandwich boxes with nickel plated tops, vacuum flask with brown leather covering and nickel plated top and bottom, set of drinking beakers, salt and pepper bottles and preserves jar, 4 square white enamel plates, set of 4 knives and forks, Lion armorial on lids of sandwich boxes and utensil handles.
£600–700 / $870–1,000 🔨 Bon
This picnic set was designed to be stored on the floor of a car's rear compartment, where it doubles as a foot rest for the rear-seat passengers.

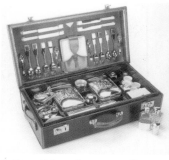

A Drew & Sons 4-person suitcase-style picnic set, black case with honey leather bindings, heavy brass catches and heavy brass rivets around lid, original ornate kettle and burner, horseshoe-shaped stand, large early-type Thermos flask, stacking nickel finished tumblers, glass bottles and food boxes, excellent condition, c1908.
£1,500–2,000 / $2,200–3,000 🔨 Bon

A Vickery 4-person picnic set, wicker case, Minton cups and saucers with matching gilt edges, matching sandwich plates, square-pattern combination kettle and teapot with correct burner, cylinder spirit flask, raffia covered drinks bottle, vesta case, tea and sugar containers, nickel plated sandwich box, excellent condition, pre-1910.
£600–700 / $870–1,020 🔨 Bon

An Albert Dunhill 4-person picnic set, figured leather covered container with stormproof corners, 4 pull-out nickel plated storage boxes, ceramic-based sandwich boxes, preserves jars, 4 raffia covered glass bottles, ceramic cups and oblong serving plates, saucers, corkscrew and cutlery, 1920s.
£12,000–13,000 / $17,000–19,500 🔨 Bon

A printed tin Shell advertising sign, mounted in wooden frame, 21¾ x 26in (55.5 x 66cm).
£75–100 / $110–145 🔨 Bon

An original polychrome Perspex Alfa Romeo garage showroom sign, 1970s, 32in (81.5cm) diam.
£600–700 / $870–1,000 🔨 C

A Servizio Assistenza Ferrari advertising sign, printed and embossed plastic, aluminium frame, 35¾in (91cm) high.
£800–1,000 / $1,150–1,500 🔨 Bon

A single-sided enamel Shell Lubricating Oil sign, 11 x 18in (28 x 45.5cm).
£375–425 / $560–620 🔨 CGC

◀ **An enamel Maserati Automobili Servizio advertising sign,** 2 small chips near base, 37¾ x 24½in (96 x 62cm).
£2,500–3,000 / $3,600–4,400 🔨 Bon

▶ **A double-sided shaped 6-colour enamel Morris Service hanging sign,** depicting a Bullnose Morris Oxford radiator, 1in diam chip to top both sides, otherwise very good condition.
£2,000–2,300 / $3,000–3,350 🔨 CGC

A double-sided enamel Vacuum Motor Car Oils sign, depicting an oil can, 24 x 36in (61 x 91.5cm).
£180–220 / $260–320 ⚒ CGC

An Angelus/Maserati stainless-steel centre seconds chronograph wristwatch, silvered dial with Arabic numerals and sweep centre seconds, blue outer scale, subsidiaries for running seconds and 45-minute recording, signed Angelus with printed Maserati emblem, nickel-finished movement jewelled to the centre in a polished case with 2 push-buttons and snap-on back, 1950.
£800–950 / $1,150–1,380 ⚒ Bon

► Christopher Hilton, *Ayrton Senna – His Full Car Racing Record*, 1994.
£14–18 / $20–28 ⊞ GPCC

Ferrari Yearbook 1959, preface by Enzo Ferrari, good clean condition, slight soiling.
£120–150 / $175–220 ⚒ Bon

► Geoffrey Williams, *McLaren – A Racing History*, 1991.
£30–35 / $45–50 ⊞ GPCC

An illuminated glass AA Hotel hanging sign, excellent condition, pre-1950, c36in (91.5cm) high.
£300–350
$440–500 ⚒ CGC

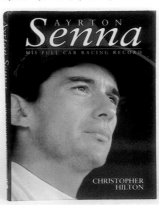

Three mechanical car clocks:
l. An S.S. Smiths & Son dash mounted veteran car watch, in angled and nickel plated case, combination rim wind and hand adjustment, Arabic numerals on white dial.
c. A car clock with Art Deco-style chapter ring on a silver dial.
r. A black 3in (7.5cm) dial, front-adjustment car clock.
£375–425 / $560–620 ⚒ Bon

A Stauffer Son & Co silver pocket watch, presented as an entrant, driver, mechanic or team award, white enamel dial, Roman numerals and subsidiary second and minute dials in very good condition, 12 o'clock wind mechanism in working order, rear inscribed 'Course d'Automobiles Gordon Bennett Cup Race – France 1905', slight chip to dial.
£1,400–1,600 / $2,000–2,300 ⚒ Bon

A Heuer Monaco stainless-steel automatic chronograph wristwatch, square grey dial with red centre seconds hand and subsidiaries for 30-minute and 12-hour recording, calendar aperture at 6 o'clock with outer calibrated track for constant minute/chronograph seconds, nickel self-winding jewelled movement in large square case with crown at 9 o'clock and 2 push-buttons to the side, Heuer strap and buckle, 1970, 1½in (4cm) wide.
£2,500–2,750 / $3,600–4,000 ⚒ Bon
The Monaco range was launched in 1969 and was sported by many celebrities of the time, the most famous being Steve McQueen, who wore the watch in the 1970 film *Le Mans*.

Racing & Rallying

1908 Napier 38.4hp Racing Car, 8650cc 6-cylinder engine, ignition by trembler coil and magneto, Rotax dynamo, 4-speed and reverse gearchange, outside handbrake, twin side mounted spare wheels, electric lighting, Rotax side lamps, spot lamp/inspection lamp, luggage grid, marine-type scuttle ventilators, fitted later 4-seat torpedo coachwork, Beatonson folding windscreen, finished in grey with dark yellow wheels, minimal dashboard instrumentation, Rotax volt and amp meters and light switch boxes, oil pressure gauge, Napier gauges for fuel and water pressure, Apollo electric klaxon, bugle horn, VCC dated, little recent use, in need of recommissioning.
£85,000–100,000 / $123,000–145,000 ⚒ Bon
For 1908, Napier challenged all comers in the 26hp, 40hp and 90hp classes, assaulted records vigorously, and produced a Grand Prix car as well as the winning four-cylinder Hutton in 'The Four Inch Race' at the Isle of Man Tourist Trophy meeting. This car is most closely related to that car's mechanical specification. The factory records list 23 special chassis allocated to the racing shop during this time, of which this and one other chassis have survived.

c1919 Ford Model T Speedster, restored 1991 as an exact re-creation of the Bee Line Special racer built by the Chevrolet brothers, fully balanced engine with 1917 overbored block, Rajo Model B overhead-valve cylinder head and Winfield camshaft, dual carburettors, wire wheels.
£6,000–8,000 / $8,500–11,500 ⚒ Bon

Miller's is a price GUIDE not a price LIST

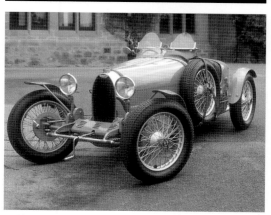

c1927 Bugatti Type 37 Grand Prix , chassis no. 37256, engine no. 227, 1496cc overhead-camshaft 4-cylinder engine, twin Solex carburettors, 4-speed gearbox with right-hand lever, 4-wheel cable operated drum brakes, centre-lock wire wheels, channel-section chassis with tubular cross-members, forged-steel front axle on semi-elliptic leaf springs, rigid rear axle on reversed quarter-elliptic leaf springs, right-hand drive, engine rebuilt with new Brineton cylinder block, quickly detachable road equipment, original body and chassis, finished in blue, black leather interior, substantially original condition.
£140,000–160,000 / $203,000–232,000 ⚒ GO
The unsupercharged Type 37 shares the same chassis, suspension, gearbox and body with its more powerful, eight-cylinder siblings, and thus has the same outstanding handling and driving characteristics. The first owner of this Type 37 was the famous racing motorist and Land Speed Record holder Sir Malcolm Campbell.

1927 Bugatti Type 37 Grand Prix, chassis no. 37292, engine no. 238, 1496cc overhead-camshaft 4-cylinder engine, 3 valves per cylinder, 60bhp, 4-speed gearbox, beam front axle on semi-elliptic leaf springs, rigid rear axle on quarter-elliptic leaf springs, cable operated drum brakes, right-hand drive, finished in blue, black leather interior.
£140–160,000 / $203,000–232,000 ⚒ C
Over the four years of production, approximately 270 Type 37s were completed.

1928 Bentley 4½ Litre Short-Chassis Racing Two-Seater, totally rebuilt 1991, finished in British racing green, green leather upholstery.
£110,000–130,000 / $160,000–188,000 ⚒ Bon
This car originally carried saloon coachwork to Weymann patents. In 1934, it was acquired by Mrs Garstin of Buckinghamshire. The Weymann coachwork was removed and the chassis shortened by well-known Bentley enthusiast and racing driver Marcus Chambers and Nobby Clark, an ex-Bentley Motors mechanic, who had joined the Bentley specialists Windrum and Garstin a year earlier. Feverish activity saw this car emerge as a serious trials/racing car for use by Terence Windrum and Mrs Garstin, who were both keen competitors. The chassis had a 9ft (274.5cm) wheelbase, 9in (23cm) shorter than the Red Label 3 Litre, and was equipped with a spartan two-seat body, large-capacity Le Mans fuel tank and outside gear lever. In its first outing on the London to Exeter Trial in 1935, it won a silver medal. Trials activity continued in 1936, when the W & G Special took a bronze medal in the London to Lands End Trial. That year, it was also entered for the Stanley Cup team race at Donington, representing the VSCC, the other two cars being driven by Harry Bowler and Tim Carson. Sadly the W & G Special, running an engine that was not yet run in, threw its conrods; nevertheless, the VSCC tied for second place. Marcus Chambers was hauled over the coals by Mrs Garstin and instructed to rebuild the engine in time for the Whitsun London to Edinburgh Trial, a task that he achieved with aplomb, and the car won a premier award in that Trial.

Auction prices

Miller's only includes cars declared sold.
Our guide prices take into account the buyer's premium, VAT on the premium, and the extent of any published catalogue information relating to condition and provenance. Cars sold at auction are identified by the ⚒ icon; full details of the auction house can be found on page 332.

1935 Riley Single-Seater Special, 1498cc engine, big valves and modified camshafts, 4 Amal carburettors, tuned inlet and exhaust manifolds, high-capacity oil pump, lightened flywheel, polished and balanced reciprocating parts, 4-speed manual gearbox, assembled on a Kestrel chassis mid-1980s, finished in red, brown interior, trophy winner.
£8,500–10,000 / $12,500–14,500 ⚒ H&H

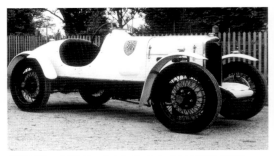

1930 Riley 9/12 Special, twin-carburettor 12/4 engine, Scintilla magneto, pre-selector gearbox, 4-wheel cable brakes, shortened 9hp chassis, aluminium body, unused for several years, in need of recommissioning.
£9,000–11,000 / $13,000–16,000 ⚒ CGC

1931 Aston Martin Sports-Racing Two-Seater Team Car, chassis no. LM5, restored 1996–2000 at a cost of c£44,000, mechanics rebuilt, converted to unleaded fuel, original 1932 factory fitted 2/4-seat bodywork, very original 1932–33 condition.
£180,000–200,000 / $260,000–290,000 ⚒ Bon
This car is the 1931–32 team car that finished second in its class in the 24-hour Brooklands Double Twelve, competed in the Le Mans 24-hour Grand Prix d'Endurance and finished sixth in the JCC Relay Race at Brooklands.

1932 Bugatti Type 51 Grand Prix, chassis no. 51150, engine no. 651, 2262cc double-overhead-camshaft 8-cylinder engine, supercharger, c185bhp, 4-speed gearbox, beam front axle on semi-elliptic leaf springs, rigid rear axle on quarter-elliptic leaf springs, cable operated 4-wheel drum brakes, right-hand drive, restored over 7-year period, used sparingly since, cylinder block replaced, replacement chassis plate issued by Bugatti Owners Club, original bonnet with widened louvres, original tail, finished in grey, black leather interior, 4 owners from new, very good condition throughout.
£600,000+ / $870,000+ ⚒ C
This particular Type 51 is almost undoubtedly Achille Varzi's official car on the works team (one of three 1933 team cars with geared-up blowers giving 185–190hp). The other two works drivers that season were René Dreyfus and W.G. Williams (William Grover). In the major races that season in the Type 51s, Varzi was first at Monaco and Tripoli, and second in Belgium. When the team's commitments in 1933 were completed, Varzi continued as an independent and had his car painted red. His Bugatti went to London in January 1934 for Lindsay Eccles, a well-known Bugatti exponent at Brooklands and Donington during 1932–36. He had many successes in a Type 35B and later in the 3.3 litre Type 59. Eccles crashed this car at the Dieppe Grand Prix in June 1934. Following the accident, it was rebuilt on an earlier frame No. 245, all the Type 51 pieces being transferred to this chassis.

1936 1½ Litre Supercharged ERA B-Type Single-Seater, 6-cylinder Riley-based engine, high proportion of original period components, race-ready condition.
£170,000–180,000 / $256,000–260,000 ⚒ Bon
English Racing Automobiles was Great Britain's very first specialist manufacturer of single-seat racing cars intended for customer sale. The company achieved enormous success within the 1.5 litre Voiturette racing class of the mid-1930s, and raced on into the early 1950s as private-owner contenders within the 1500cc supercharged Formula 1. This ERA was assembled during the late 1970s. Apart from two chassis side rails and some of the body panelling, it was assembled as new from virtually all-original period components, which had been preserved for years among a huge collection of ERA spare parts. The vast majority of those components were acquired direct from the original manufacturers/stock holders, Thomson & Taylor, the well-known Brooklands racing-car specialists, who not only co-designed and manufactured the original ERA racing chassis and suspension components, but also were responsible for such machines as the perpetual Brooklands Outer Circuit lap-record-holding Napier-Railton and the Land Speed Record breaking Railton Special.

1961 Cooper-Climax Type 53P Lowline Intercontinental/Tasman Formula Racing Single-Seater, 2.7 litre Coventry Climax Type FPF 4-cylinder engine, uprated Colotti 5-speed transaxle with re-engineered shafts, dog clutches and all gears, modern 3-plate clutch, original brake calipers, refurbished stainless-steel hoses and pipe unions, new brake lines, radiator fitted with modern core, modern 6-gallon fuel cell within original aluminium tank, stainless-steel oil lines, modern full-flow oil filter, extended roll-over bar, onboard 24 volt electric starter, original dash panel and instrumentation.
£35,000–45,000 / $51,000–65,000 ⚒ Bon

1973 Brabham BT40 Formula 2 Single-Seater, Ford BDG engine, monocoque construction, outboard suspension, side radiators, restored, engine rebuilt, new safety harness, 1 of 9 made, original.
£28,000–34,000 / $40,000–50,000 ⚒ Bon

c1937 Delahaye 135 Special Le Mans Sports-Racing Two-Seater Replica, 3.5 litre 6-cylinder engine, built from original Delahaye parts or exact replicas, apart from 4-speed manual gearbox and rear axle, correct-pattern Cotal electro-mechanical gearbox included, excellent mechanical condition, paintwork in very good condition.
£40,000–50,000 / $58,000–73,000 ⚒ Bon
Only 15 Delahaye 135 Specials were built, and 12 remain. This car was rebuilt in Argentina as an accurate replica of the most historic of the Delahaye 135 Specials, the ex-Laury Schell Ecurie Bleu racer, formerly owned by Argentinean architect Rodolfo Iriate. Iriate acted as consultant during the creation of this special in 1999.

> A known continuous history can add value to and enhance the enjoyment of a car.

1969 BRM P139 3 Litre Formula 1 Single-Seater, 3 litre P142 V12 engine, recently restored, single small-capacity fuel tank, spare set of wheels and tyres, spare steering wheel, race-ready condition.
£100,000–110,000 / $145,000–160,000 ⚒ Bon
The prototype P139 made its public debut as John Surtees' T-car in the Dutch Grand Prix at Zandvoort, but events during the race led to the team scratching its entries in the following French Grand Prix to concentrate upon development and preparation for the British race at Silverstone. In qualifying there, John Surtees set sixth-fastest time, 1.41 seconds off Jochen Rindt's pole-position time in the Lotus 49. Surtees held third before retiring early. This car, the third P139 built, made its public debut as Surtees' T-car at Watkins Glen in preparation for the US Grand Prix. Then it was driven by Surtees in his farewell appearance with the BRM team, in the Mexican Grand Prix. He qualified tenth, but went out of the race after 23 laps with transmission trouble.

1975 McLaren M25 Formula 5000 Prototype/3 Litre Formula 1 Single-Seater, engine rebuilt c1986, only 76 miles since.
£75,000–85,000 / $108,000–123,000 ⚘ Bon
Having been tested in M25 Formula 5000 form, then rendered redundant by McLaren abandoning production formulae, this machine remained at the Colnbrook factory until acquired by Spanish owner-driver Emilio de Villota, who had it converted into an M23-like, Cosworth powered Formula 1 car. De Villota was also running two other ex-works M23 chassis, and this car was acquired as a competitive spare car for his private Team Villota, later restyled Asseguredor F1. The car made its Formula 1 racing debut in 1978, in the Oulton Park Gold Cup on Good Friday. De Villota qualified third fastest and finished second in this first race for the M25/1, and at the following Easter Monday Brands Hatch meeting he finished third. Another second place followed at Snetterton and, on May Day at Mallory Park, he finished fourth and set fastest race lap.

1986 Dallara 386 Formula 3 Single-Seater, 1996cc double overhead-camshaft 4-cylinder Nova-Alfa engine, 160bhp, 5-speed transaxle, independent front and rear suspension by wishbones and coil spring/damper units, 4-wheel disc brakes, finished in yellow and blue 1986 racing livery, in need of general overhaul.
£7,000–8,000 / $10,000–11,500 ⚘ C
Gianpaolo Dallara started his career as a consultant engineer with Maserati and then Ferrari. Later, he moved to Lamborghini, where he was responsible for the marque's early road cars. His real ambition, however, was to design single-seat racing cars, which he realised in 1978 when his name was first connected with the Wolf-Dallara Formula 3 model. Over the next ten years, he moved up the ladder to F1, but it was in F3 that his designs were the most successful. This particular car was the first F3 chassis imported into France. It was campaigned independently in 1986 by future Formula 1 star Jean Alesi, who went on to finish runner-up to Yannick Dalmas in the national championship, with victories at Albi and Le Mans.

1983 Formula Fiat Abarth 2000, 1995cc double overhead camshaft 4-cylinder engine, Lancia Monte Carlo 5-speed transaxle, finished in 1983 race livery, little use since testing in 1983, original condition.
£8,000–9,000 / $11,500–13,000 ⚘ RM

1985 Alfa Romeo Formula 1 Single-Seater, experimental V6 engine, not run since 1996, good condition throughout.
£25,000–30,000 / $36,000–44,000 ⚘ Bon
The last Formula 1 car to race under the Alfa Romeo name, the 1985 185T, was the work of ex-Toleman designer John Gentry. An evolution of the previous season's 184T, the new car had an unusual suspension layout with pull rods at the front and push rods at the rear, and an aluminium honeycomb monocoque built by Monofrini, an aerospace company in Milan.

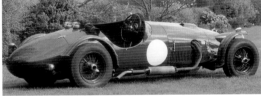

1946 HRG 1500 Le Mans Lightweight, 100bhp, leaf-sprung rigid axles, ladder frame, subject of 7-year restoration, registered for use on the road.
£32,000–36,000 / $46,000–52,000 ⚘ COYS
This car was sold to former Le Mans class winner Peter Clark. A driver of international repute, Clark proceeded to race it in international events across Europe. The pair were frequently part of the class winning team at events such as the Empire Trophy Race, Spa 24 hours and the Paris 12 hours. As one of the team cars in Ecurie Lapin Blanc, the car was continuously uprated, and for Le Mans 1949 the aerodynamic body was replaced by a lightweight body with cycle wings. Immediately after the gruelling 24-hour race, the team had to prepare for the Spa 24 hours, an event in which again they claimed the team prize, and also the Richard Seaman Cup. On return to Britain, after competing in several other races, the car was acquired by David Blakely, who continued to race it, notably in the Goodwood nine hours in 1952 and 1953. It was still in his possession at the time of his well publicised murder by Ruth Ellis, the last woman to be hanged in Britain for such a crime.

◀ **1949 Ford Sports Special,** 1172cc sidevalve 4-cylinder engine, solid billet crankshaft, competition pistons, Aquaplane competition cylinder head and matching finned side plates and manifolds, Ballamy competition front suspension, boxed Anglia frame, spare set of 17in Ballamy wheels, polished aluminium bodywork.
£6,500–7,500 / $9,500–11,000 ⚘ COYS

1949 OSCA MT4 Two-Seater Sports-Racing Siluro Spyder, 1100cc double-overhead-camshaft engine, 2 twin-choke Weber 38DCO3 carburettors, wishbone-and-coil-spring front suspension, rigid rear axle on semi-elliptic leaf springs, twin-tube chassis, subject of no-expense-spared 10-year restoration, thought to be only twin-cam OSCA to have raced internationally in both monoposto and sports-car events.
£150,000–160,000 / $217,000–232,000 ✗ Bon

The surviving Maserati brothers, Ernesto, Ettore and Bindo, sold their original specialist sports-car company to the Orsi industrial group in 1938 and accepted ten-year consultancy contracts, which expired in 1948. Then they returned to their native city of Bologna to establish a new concern of their own, entitled Officine Specializate Costruzione Automobili Fratelli, abbreviated to OSCA Maserati, and later to just OSCA. Subsequently, they manufactured a series of exceptionally good and competitive, lightweight, high-powered, predominantly small-capacity sporting cars, highlighted by the 1100 and 1300cc MT4 model. This MT4 was first seen competing in October 1950, stripped and entered as a monoposto, and finishing second overall in the hands of Francesco Nissotti in the GP de Modena. He competed with the car in this form for just under a year, notably finishing first overall in May 1951, again at the GP de Modena, and second overall at the Voiturette GP at Monza in September 1951. Then, in 1952, the car was exported to America, where it scored numerous victories in factory sports two-seater form.

1957 Elva Mark II, 1098cc FWA Coventry Climax engine, Weber carburettors, 4-speed MG manual gearbox with rare overdrive conversion, De Dion rear suspension, 4-wheel hydraulic Alfin drum brakes, recently restored to race standard, alloy body panels refurbished, resprayed in white with blue racing stripes.
£28,000–32,000 / $40,500–46,500 ✗ RM

Club racer Frank Nichols raced a CSM Special in 1954 events. Thinking he could do better with a design of his own, he founded Elva Cars in 1955 at Bexhill-on-Sea, Sussex. Legend has it that Nichols named his cars Elva for the French '*Elle va*', meaning 'she goes'. And so they did, for soon Nichols had plenty of orders for an improved version of his Mk I model, named the Elva Mk II. Early Mk IIs had handmade aluminium bodywork, but after receiving six alloy bodies contracted at £500 each, yet billed at £1,500 per, Nichols quickly switched to glassfibre panels. Elva sports-racing cars, which were built in great numbers in both front- and mid-engined configuration until the late 1960s, featured well triangulated mild-steel-tubing chassis with Ford, Coventry Climax, and even BMW and Porsche engines.

1951 Siata Grand Sport Barchetta, tuned Fiat engine, independent front suspension by coil springs and wishbones, Borrani wire wheels, tubular chassis, body styled by Farina, subject of recent extensive race preparation, engine enlarged to 1500cc, lightweight bodywork strengthened, finished in Italian racing red, black interior trim.
£40,000–45,000 / $58,000–65,000 ✗ COYS

Cross Reference
See Colour Review (page 193–197)

◀ **1958 Lister Chevrolet,** 283cu.in V8 engine, Hillborn fuel injection, original body and chassis, recently rebuilt, new gearbox and Powerloc differential, in race trim, last competitive outing 1997.
£200,000+ / $290,000+ ✗ COYS

◀ **1958 Lister-Jaguar 'Knobbly' 3.8 Litre Sports-Racing Two-Seater,** Jaguar XK 6-cylinder engine, original chassis and running gear, restored, finished in green and yellow, very original.
£250,000+ / $362,000 ↗ Bon
Under FIA Appendix J regulations, a minimum-height windscreen was required. That height was measured from the scuttle top to the upper edge of the screen, so to diminish the overall car height and thereby minimise frontal area, it was sensible to lower the scuttle height as much as possible behind the tall Jaguar engine. This was achieved by leaving the engine covered by a large hump in the bonnet, and that knobbly hump, allied to the tall wheel arches at each corner, triggered the 'Knobbly' tag that has been applied to these cars ever since.

1963 Lotus 23B Sports-Racing Two-Seater, 2 litre BMW engine, 170bhp, 5-speed Hewland gearbox, Team Lotus livery.
£30,000–35,000 / $43,000–50,000 ↗ Bon

◀ **1966 Ford GT40 Mk I,** 302cu.in V8 engine, 4 Weber 48IDA carburettors, 5-speed ZF gearbox with oil cooler, Halibrand magnesium wheels, completely restored to original specification using original components and parts, finished in Belgian racing yellow, concours winner.
£300,000+ / $435,000+ ↗ BJ

1971 Porsche-Chanabé, little recent use.
£50,000–60,000 / $72,000–87,000 ↗ COYS
With Porsche so dominant in endurance events throughout the 1960s and 1970s, when Jean Chanabé looked for components upon which he could base his creation, he turned to that marque. With its snub front, compact frame and light weight, the car caused an immediate sensation, and even Porsche was drawn to it. Apparently, the company was sufficiently impressed to allow Chanabé to use the Porsche name in the car's title when he entered it in events.

1971 Lola T292, rebuilt 2 litre BMW 4-cylinder engine, fuel injection, 300bhp, finished in silver, race-ready condition.
£55,000–65,000 / $80,000–94,500 ⌁ COYS
By the 1970s, Britain's most prolific builder of racing cars, Lola, could supply anything from Formula Ford single-seaters and sports club racers to international GT and Formula 1 machines. The T160 large-capacity Group 7 car appeared in 1968, and by 1970 the line-up included the first of a long line of successful Group 6 2 litre machines, the T210. By 1973, the latter had evolved through T212 and T290 into the T292. That year, the model won the Two Litre Championship in a vintage season that saw Lola triumph in an impressive number of different formulae on both sides of the Atlantic.

1971 Lola T222 Can Am, 465cu.in Chevrolet V8 engine, Lucas McKay fuel injection, c700bhp, Hewland LG600 5-speed gearbox with reverse, front suspension by unequal-length A-arms and coil-spring/damper units, rear suspension by lower A-arms, top links and coil-spring/damper units, 4-wheel ventilated disc brakes with 4-pot calipers, run in only 10 races, in need of restoration, very original.
£50,000–60,000 / $72,000–87,000 ⌁ RM
Only nine T222 chassis were produced for the 1971 season. This example was sold to the young and inexperienced Japanese driver Hiroshi Kazato. At Mosport for the first race, some Can Am regulars opined that he would not be able to handle the 700bhp, bewinged monster, much less qualify in it. But Kazato possessed a determination and inner fire that belied his diminutive size. The critics were silenced when he qualified and finished ninth. Proving that this result was no fluke, he scored a sixth overall at the next Can Am, also held in Canada at the Circuit Mt Tremblant in Quebec. Hiroshi's best result came in the sixth round of the series, at the ultra fast Road America circuit, where he qualified seventh and finished fifth overall. After Kazato's tragic death in 1974 at the Fuji circuit, his family installed his Lola in a shrine/museum built in honour of their son.

1985 Tiga-Mazda IMSA Camel Lights, rebuilt Mazda 13B rotary engine, Hewland 5-speed gearbox, aluminium honeycomb monocoque chassis, Kevlar reinforced carbon-weave bodywork, substantial spares package.
£20,000–25,000 / $29,000–36,000 ⌁ RM

1950 Aston Martin DB2 First Sanction Saloon, engine built to current racing and rallying standard, high-lift camshafts, high-compression pistons, DB2/4 Mk III crankshaft, steel conrods, 1¾in SU carburettors, fabricated exhaust manifold, 170bhp, DB5 clutch, 12th DB2 built and 2nd production example, body and chassis restored, c£36,000 spent on mechanical refurbishment alone.
£70,000–80,000 / $101,000–116,000 ⌁ Bon
This car is one of the 'First Sanction' DB2s, which were distinguishable by their characteristic three-piece radiator grille, side extractor grilles, all-round bumper strips, twin fuel fillers, and flush fitting front and rear screens with plated surrounds.

1951 Jaguar Mk VII Lightweight Competition Saloon, fully race prepared engine block bored to 3.8 litres, gas flowed E-Type cylinder head, 3 Weber twin-choke 45DCOE carburettors, D-Type camshafts, 'banana' exhaust manifolding, dual exhaust system with side-exit pipes, lightened flywheel, competition clutch, close-ratio gearbox with overdrive on 3rd and 4th gears, large experimental disc brakes on all 4 wheels, 4.2 litre E-Type tandem braking system, limited-slip differential, Koni dampers all-round, high-geared power steering with split steering column, 15in centre-lock Dunlop magnesium wheels with 7in rims, Kenlowe electric cooling fan, magnesium-alloy-panelled bodywork, laminated windscreen, Restall front bucket seats, 6th right-hand-drive standard production Jaguar Mk VII saloon built, 1 owner for 37 years.
£45,000–50,000 / $65,000–72,000 ⌁ Bon
This Mk VII was the personal car of Jaguar company founder and long-time chairman William Lyons. Subsequently, it was taken into Jaguar's competition department, stripped to the chassis and rebuilt with magnesium-elektron-alloy, lightweight body panels. This was carried out in preparation for the 1954 Production Touring Car Race at Silverstone. That year, the Mk VIIs proved overwhelmingly competitive, finishing 1-2-3 and being driven by winner Ian Appleyard, Tony Rolt and Stirling Moss. Not only were the three dominant Mk VIIs masters of the day, but they also shared the same time in establishing Silverstone's new saloon-car lap record, at 2 minutes, 16 seconds, at an average of 77.48mph.

1954 Aston Martin DB2/4, 2993cc 6-cylinder engine, finished in blue, tan interior, qualified competition car, FIA historic passport papers.
£15,000–17,000 / $22,000–25,000 ⚒ H&H

1957 Austin A35 Two-Door Saloon, 948cc engine, lowered suspension, wire wheels.
£2,500–3,000 / $3,500–4,500 ⊞ AUS

1958 Arnolt Bristol, prepared for endurance racing, finished in Team USA racing livery, tan leather upholstery, believed to have participated in the Carrera Mexicana.
£60,000–70,000 / $87,000–101,000 ⚒ COYS
In 1953, S.H. 'Wacky' Arnolt, Chicago businessman and vice-president of Bertone, was in London for the Motor Show. He came to an agreement with Bristol that the company would supply him with modified chassis fitted with the BS I Mk II engine; these were shipped to Bertone, who quickly produced a light two-seat body called 'Bolide', which was the cheapest of the range of three models; no hood was fitted, but one was available as an extra. The cars soon began to appear in competition, achieving notable first, second and fourth places in the 2 litre class at the Sebring 12-hour race in 1954 and 1955.

▶ **1958 Ferrari 250 GT Tour De Fance Berlinetta Competizione,** coachwork by Scaglietti, chassis no. 1139GT, engine no. 1139GT, rebuilt 3 litre 2-camshaft V12 engine, aluminium body panels, roll bar, Perspex side windows, Perspex-covered headlights, finished in red, competition-type interior, never fully restored.
£500,000+ / $725,000+ ⚒ Bon

1954 Aston Martin DB2/4, restored 1997–98 at a cost of c£50,000, returned to original right-hand-drive configuration, power-assisted steering, brake servo, roll bar, 4-point harness, Smiths racing instruments, map light, fewer than 650 miles since completion, excellent condition throughout.
£90,000–100,000 / $130,000–145,000 ⚒ Bon
The three DB2/4s campaigned by Aston Martin during the 1955 season occupy a special place in the marque's competition history, this being the only occasion that the factory entered a works team in international rallying. The cars were prepared by the works racing department for the 1955 Monte Carlo Rally, and it is interesting to note that this car was converted to left-hand drive. Team manager John Wyer hired 1953 Monte winner Maurice Gatsonides as his lead driver, alongside sports-car regulars Reg Parnell and Peter Collins. Teamed with Marcel Becquart, Gatsonides looked a certain winner as the rally entered its final stages, only to be penalised for passing a secret checkpoint many minutes ahead of schedule, a misfortune that dropped him to seventh place overall. Nevertheless, Gatsonides/Becquart had done enough to take the Over 2 Litre class to win. The other works DB2/4s of Parnell/Klemantaski and Collins/Whitehead did not fare so well, but third and fourth places in the Over Two Litre class went to privately entered DB2/4s, enabling Aston Martin to claim the team prize.

1959 Austin-Healey 3000 Works Rally Car, 3 litre 6-cylinder engine, twin SU carburettors, factory performance modifications, 4-speed manual gearbox, heavy-duty suspension, 4-wheel Girling disc brakes, subject of nut-and-bolt restoration to correct original specification, 1 of 3 works cars campaigned in 1959, class winner in 1959 Rome-Liège-Rome Rally, concours condition.
£85,000–95,000 / $123,000–138,000 ⚒ RM

1959 Fiat Abarth Double-Bubble Coupé, coachwork by Zagato, 747cc double-overhead-camshaft engine, close-ratio gearbox, transverse-leaf-spring front suspension, swing-axle/coil-spring rear suspension, restored 1996, fully modified for competition use, finished in black with red stripe.
£24,000–28,000 / $35,000–40,000 ⚒ COYS

c1959 Fiat-Abarth 750 Double-Bubble Coupé, coachwork by Zagato, battery cut-off switch, tow hook, finished in red, racing seat and harness, good condition throughout.
£15,000–20,000 / $22,000–29,000 ⚒ Bon

One of Carlo Abarth's most successful GT cars was based on the Fiat 600, the first of these little Zagato-bodied coupés – the 750 – appearing in 1956. The 600 chassis was used with scant modification, apart from changing spring rates and uprating the front brakes to twin-leading-shoe operation, yet despite this apparent handicap, it coped remarkably well with the Abarth's greatly increased performance. The latter was achieved by boring and stroking the 600's 633cc, four-cylinder engine to 747cc and modifying or replacing just about every other component, the result being an increase in maximum power from 23bhp at 4,000rpm to 44bhp at 6,000rpm.

1959 Lotus Elite Competition Coupé, restored 1990 at a cost of £33,000, further £12,000 spent recently, refurbished and resprayed glassfibre monocoque bodyshell, finished in dark blue, red interior.
£50,000–60,000 / $72,000–87,000 ⚒ Bon

This Lotus Elite began life as a 1960 Team Lotus entry in the Le Mans 24-hour endurance classic, to be driven by leading British driver Sir John Whitmore, but it was taken over prior to the race by fellow British aristocrat and sportsman Sir Gawaine Baillie. His co-driver was Michael Parkes, later to drive for Ferrari. Their Le Mans drive in this car ended in retirement at two-thirds distance, but the Elite was to compete in numerous other events that season, including the Nürburgring 1,000km.

◄ **1960 TVR Grantura Mk II,** 1600cc 4-cylinder crossflow Ford engine, special conrods, crankshaft and pistons, 4-speed close-ratio gearbox, new driveshafts, new propshaft, new suspension, shock absorbers, instruments, seats and safety harness, body refurbished and resprayed in silver, race-ready condition.
£7,000–10,000 / $10,000–14,500 ⚒ Bon

1961 Jaguar E-Type Lightweight-style Competition Roadster, 3 Weber 48DCOE carburettors, factory hardtop, lightweight aluminium opening panels in style of factory lightweight cars, uprated safety fuel tank, finished in silver, black interior.
£40,000–50,000 / $58,000–72,500 ⚒ COYS

1960 Alfa Romeo Giulietta Sprint Coupé, coachwork by Bertone, 1290cc mildly tuned engine, original single carburettor and air filter, restored and prepared for racing 1985, interior roll cage, fire extinguisher, single bucket seat, leather bonnet/boot straps, paintwork in very good condition.
£8,000–10,000 / $11,500–14,500 ⚒ Bon

1961 Jaguar E-Type Lynx Lightweight Roadster, restored and rebuilt to resemble period racers at a cost of £80,000–90,000, tuned 3.8 litre XK engine, close-ratio 5-speed Getrag gearbox, correct aluminium bonnet, doors and boot lid, Le Mans long-range fuel tank, 1 of earliest right-hand-drive roadsters built.
£50,000–60,000 / $72,000–87,000 ↗ COYS

1963 Aston Martin DB4 Vantage, 3999cc engine, c360bhp, manual gearbox, set up for racing, modified rear suspension, uprated brakes, alloy foam filled fuel tank, full roll cage, finished in red, black interior.
£33,000–37,000 / $47,000–53,500 ↗ H&H

1963 Reliant Sabre Six, original 2.6 litre engine, FIA homologated Raymond May alloy cylinder head, 3 Weber 45DCOE carburettors, tubular 6-branch exhaust manifold, side-exit exhausts, Revolution alloy wheels, finished in silver and British racing green, competition seat harness, roll cage, 1 of only 77 built.
£9,500–10,500 / $13,500–15,500 ↗ COYS

1964 Cooper S Mk I Club Racer, subject of no-expense-spared restoration, race-specification engine, full roll cage, works dash with full set of instruments, bucket seats, Willans full-harness belts, battery cut-off, armoured lines.
£11,000–13,000 / $16,000–19,000 ⊞ WbC

1964 Triumph TR4, imported from USA, rebuilt for competition and converted to right-hand drive, uprated 2289cc engine, full-race camshaft, 2 Weber carburettors, rebuilt and strengthened gearbox, full roll cage, full harness, finished in red, red and black interior, TR4 Championship winner, excellent condition.
£6,500–8,000 / $9,500–11,500 ✗ H&H

1964 Alfa Romeo Giulia Ti Saloon, extensively refurbished and modified for long-distance rallies, double-overhead-camshaft 4-cylinder engine rebuilt, new 5-speed manual gearbox, all-new independent front suspension, coil-sprung rigid rear axle, 4-wheel disc brakes, finished in original light blue, interior stripped and fitted roll cage, 2 modern seats, starter button ignition switch.
£2,500–3,000 / $3,500–4,500 ✗ Bon

1964 Ferrari 250 GT Lusso Competition Coupé, full 250 GTO 'plus'-specification engine, 6 twin-choke Weber carburettors, high-lift camshafts, high-compression pistons, modified big-valve cylinder heads, 300bhp, dry-sump lubrication system, rear-mounted oil tank, cold air box, aluminium radiator, fuel cell, twin electric pumps, 4-speed gearbox, ZF limited-slip differential, 5 Borrani 15in wire wheels, 4 Compomotive 16in aluminium race wheels, custom lightweight aluminium body in style of 330 LMB, full undertray, roll cage, Perspex side and rear windows, full instrumentation.
£120,000–130,000 / $174,000–188,000 ✗ BJ

1964 Fiat Abarth 850TC, completely rebuilt, unused since, fitted A112 engine, Weber 36DCD carburettor, full Abarth breathing system, 80bhp, aluminium tank, front-mounted radiator, Campagnolo replica alloy wheels, roll cage, competition front seats, full-harness belts, emergency cut-off switch, large amount of spares including original 850TC engine.
£8,500–10,000 / $12,500–14,500 ✗ BARO

1968 Pontiac Trans Am Supertourisme, V8 engine, 540bhp, 175+mph, not run for some time.
£6,000–7,000 / $9,000–10,000 ✗ Bon
Jean-Pierre Jarier raced this car throughout the 1986 Supertourisme series. He achieved a podium finish at Rouen and put up consistently good lap times.

1966 Lancia Fulvia, race prepared, interior stripped, single racing seat, sports steering wheel, finished in red with contrasting yellow and blue stripes, good condition throughout.
£5,000–6,000 / $7,000–9,000 ✗ Bon

► 1969 Chevrolet Camaro Trans Am, completely restored to Historic Trans Am specification, 302cu.in V8 engine, 425bhp, Borg Warner close-ratio 4-speed gearbox, independent front coil-spring suspension with anti-roll bar, 12-bolt competition rear axle on leaf springs with trailing arms, 4-wheel Corvette disc brakes, Minilite 8-spoke alloy wheels, 6-point roll cage.
£55,000–65,000
$80,000–94,500 ✗ RM

1971 Alfa Romeo Giulia 1300, double-overhead-camshaft engine, 5-speed gearbox, left-hand drive, modified for racing, chassis uprated, stripped interior, single racing seat, 3-point harness, roll cage, engine not run for 18 months.
£1,500–2,000 / $2,000–3,000 ⚒ Bon

1971 Alfa Romeo 2000 GTV, 1962cc 4-cylinder engine, 2 Weber carburettors, 150bhp, 5-speed manual gearbox, 4-wheel disc brakes.
£9,000–10,000 / $13,000–14,500 ⚒ Pou

1971 Ferrari 365 GTB/4 Daytona Group 4 Competition Berlinetta, coachwork by Pininfarina, chassis no. 13971, engine no. 001M, 4-cam V12 engine, uprated to full factory specification 1981, side exhausts, wide competition wheels, riveted Group 4 bodywork, flared arches, full-height faired-in headlamps, air splitters on front wings, chin spoiler, twin exterior fuel fillers, Perspex side windows, single pantograph wiper, trimmed in lightweight materials, harnesses for both occupants, roll cage, concours condition.
£170,000+/ $246,000+ ⚒ Bon

◀ **1971 MGB GT Sebring Replica,** extensively restored, 1950cc 4-cylinder engine built to Stage 2 standard, converted to unleaded fuel, wide alloy wheels, fitted Sebring body kit, MGC bonnet, competition wing mirrors, finished in British racing green, new interior trim panels in black and grey, original seats, Panasonic pull-out radio.
£5,500–7,000 / $8,000–10,000 ⚒ BRIT

1972 MGB GT, restored 1994, modified for sprint and hill-climb use, 1950cc Stage 3 engine, lightened and balanced crankshaft, conrods, pistons and flywheel, Kent fast road cam, Weber 45 carburettor, electronic ignition, 110bhp, 2in free-flow exhaust system, 5-speed gearbox, uprated suspension with stiffer front shock absorbers and anti-roll bar, Spax rear telescopic dampers and anti-tramp bars, new sills, wings and tailgate, Sebring rear valance, front bumper removed, bare-metal respray in original red, interior retrimmed in biscuit leather.
£2,000–2,500 / $3,000–3,500 ⚒ CGC

1973 Ferrari 365GTB/4-A Daytona Competizione Berlinetta, coachwork by Pininfarina, chassis no. 16343, 4.4 litre engine, ex-North American Racing Team Daytona 24-hour GT winning car, recently restored, finished in red with blue and white stripes, running.
£750,000+ / $1,087,000+ ⚒ Bon
This is the North American Racing Team entered car, which – driven by Woodner and Philips – actually won the GT category of the 1975 Daytona 24-hour race. It is a veteran not only of two Daytona classics, but also of the Le Mans 24-hour race.

1973 MGB Roadster, completely restored to early race specification for hill climbs, sprints and fast road use, original 1950cc engine rebuilt and balanced, Stage 3 Peter Burgess head, Weber carburettors, Venire timing gear, fast road camshaft, new braking and fuel systems, wheel bearings, steering and propshaft, Moss coil-over suspension kit, anti-roll bar, lowered springs with Spax shock absorbers, body stripped, new panels fitted, Sebring valances, headlamp covers, aluminium bonnet and strap, works hardtop, finished in red, interior completely refurbished, new bucket seats and harnesses, new dashboard, little recent use, concours condition.
£9,500–11,000 / $13,500–16,000 ⚒ H&H

► **1973 Mini Special,** fully prepared for sprints and hill climbs, 1293cc 4-cylinder engine, cross-drilled crankshaft, balanced and lightened flywheel, fast road camshaft, lightweight panels, finished in dark green with a yellow stripe, fully road legal, complete with trailer and spare set of wheels and tyres.
£2,000–2,500 / $3,000–3,500 ⚒ BRIT

1976 Chevrolet Corvette IMSA, 464cu.in V8 engine, Kinsler cross-ram fuel injection, dry-sump lubrication, Muncie T-10 4-speed gearbox, independent front suspension by upper and lower A-arms, transverse leaf springs and telescopic shock absorbers, independent rear suspension by upper wishbones, Greenwood trailing arms, transverse leaf springs and shock absorber units, 4-wheel disc brakes, mechanics refurbished, resprayed in original Greenwood-style colours.
£17,000–19,000 / $24,500–27,500 ⚒ RM
John Greenwood, a native of Florida, produced a series of wide-bodied Corvettes, all featuring big-block Chevrolet engines of not less than 427cu.in and some 600+bhp. The bodywork had to be widened to cover the enormous wheels fitted. Greenwood also worked his magic with the stock Corvette suspension, fabricating pieces to cope with the massive power and torque that the Chevrolet engine could deliver. His own cars usually sported garish paint schemes of red, white and blue to proclaim their American heritage. At the 1976 Le Mans 24-hour race, his 'Spirit of America' was timed at over 220mph along the Mulsanne Straight. This car was built in the style of Greeenwood's racers.

1979 Ferrari 308 GT/C Competizione Berlinetta, coachwork by Pininfarina, 5-speed Michelotto gearbox, AP racing brakes, glassfibre body panels, cost of initial race preparation in excess of £70,000, rebuilt late 1990s, not raced since, 'as new' condition.
£30,000–35,000 / $43,000–50,000 🔨 Bon
This car won the Pirelli backed Maranello Ferrari Challenge Series Maranello Trophy for modified cars in 1989.

◀ **1980 Audi Quattro Sport Coupé Ex-Works Team Car,** 400bhp, 4-wheel drive, restored, engine rebuilt, fewer than 70 miles since, fitted slightly larger wheels for tarmac stages, original wheels included, Bosch rally lamps, cockpit with all original fittings including Halda road computer, Recaro seats, roll cage and comprehensive array of instruments and switches, finished in original works colours, authentic race-ready condition,.
£70,000–80,000 / $102,000–116,000 🔨 Bon
This is the actual car in which Hannu Mikkola won the 1981 Swedish Rally, claimed victory on the San Remo and came a close second in Portugal.

Miller's is a price GUIDE not a price LIST

1986 Chevrolet Monte Carlo Nascar, campaigned in Winston Cup races 1986, completely restored to original condition, letter of authenticity from crew chief Kirk Shelmerdine, with Dale Earnhardt/Wrangler racing helmet complete with radio and certificate of authenticity signed by Earnhardt.
£65,000–75,000 / $94,000–108,000 🔨 BJ
This car was owned by Richard Childress and driven by Dale Earnhardt. It was instrumental in the pair's first Winston Cup Championship victory.

1989 MG Metro 6R4 Clubman, road tyres, sound insulation, self-diagnostic electronic management system, fire-extinguisher system, finished in original white, light grey cloth interior, c300 miles from new.
£14,000–17,000 / $20,500–24,500 🔨 Bon
In 1984, Austin Rover Motorsport launched a British challenge for the International Group B Rally Championship. The 6R4 featured an all-new, mid-mounted, alloy, 3 litre V6 engine with four camshafts and four valves per cylinder. Massive torque and flexibility countered the turbo opposition, and could provide around 400bhp at 9,000rpm through the five-speed, all-synchromesh gearbox to the epicyclic, torque-splitting differential and viscous coupling. Suspension is adjustable to desired settings, and massive 12in AP ventilated disc brakes ride within special Dymag magnesium-alloy wheels. A roll cage is part of what is effectively a space-frame chassis, braced by the floor and bulkheads. To homologate more than 200 production cars for World Championship status, and to help ARG's accountants balance the books, Clubman track-ready rally cars, such as this – with 250bhp at 7,000rpm – were offered for sale at £34,784.

1989 Pontiac Grand Prix Nascar, Bahari chassis no. 027, driven by Michael Waltrip 1989–91.
£24,000–27,000 / $35,000–39,000 🔨 BJ

Military Vehicles

c1940 Austin K5 Light Utility Vehicle, 1237cc sidevalve 4-cylinder engine.
£4,200–4,300 / $6,100–6,300 🚗 **MVT**

c1952 Alfa Romeo 1900 Matta, 4-wheel drive, separate chassis, finished in olive drab, period dashboard and side screens, soft top missing, never restored, substantially original, engine not run for 2 years.
£2,500–3,000 / $3,600–4,500 🔧 **Bon**
Used by the Italian Army and police, the 1900 M – also known as La Matta (mad woman) – was powered by a detuned (65bhp) version of the Alfa Romeo 1900's twin-cam, four-cylinder engine. A total of 2,000 were delivered for military police use between 1951 and 1953, a further 50 being released into the civilian market.

1943 Bedford 15cwt 4x2 Truck, restored, RAF markings.
£3,000–4,000/ $4,400–5,800 🚗 **IMPS**

c1940 Chevrolet 1½ Ton Truck, 235.5cu.in overhead-valve 6-cylinder petrol engine, 83bhp, 4-speed gearbox, 4-wheel drive, 2-speed transfer box with front axle declutch, hydraulic brakes with vacuum servo, rigid axles with semi-elliptic leaf springs, 6 volt electrics, GS body.
£2,000–3,000 / $3,000–4,500 🚗 **MVT**
In 1940. GM's Chevrolet Division became the mass producer of trucks in this class. With about 150,000 built, they constituted nearly a third of Chevrolet WWII motor vehicle ouptut.

1941 Chevrolet (Canadian) C15A Truck, 216cu.in overhead-valve 6-cylinder petrol engine, 85bhp, 2BI body, restored.
£1,500–2,700 / $2,200–3,900 PC

c1942 Chevrolet (Canadian) C30 Winch Truck, derrick equipped 3AI body.
£4,000–5,000 / $5,800–7,250 PC

Dealer prices

Miller's guide prices for dealer cars take into account the value of any guarantees or warranties that may be included in the purchase. Dealers must also observe additional statutory consumer regulations, which do not apply to private sellers. This is factored into our dealer guide prices. Dealer cars are identified by the ⊞ icon; full details of the dealer can be found on page 332.

c1942 Chevrolet (Canadian) Heavy Utility Personnel Truck, 216.5cu.in overhead-valve 6-cylinder petrol engine, 85bhp, 4-speed gearbox, 4-wheel drive, single-speed transfer box with front-axle disconnect, hydraulic brakes, rigid axles with semi-elliptic leaf springs, 6 volt electrics.
£4,000–5,000 / $ 5,750–7,250 🚗 MVT
Following interim solutions with modified estate cars, production of a purpose designed Heavy Utility was started by General Motors in Oshawa in 1942. It was the only vehicle built entirely in the GM plant.

c1942 Dodge WC54 ¾ Ton Ambulance, 230cu.in 6-cylinder engine, 92bhp, 4-speed gearbox, 4-wheel drive, single-speed transfer box, hydraulic brakes, leaf-spring suspension.
£4,000–5,000 / $6,500–7,250 ⊞ RRM
Some 26,000 WC54 ambulances were produced during 1942–44. There was accommodation in the rear for four stretcher cases or seven sitting patients. They were used by the US Army Medical Corps and allied forces.

c1942 Dodge WC51 Weapons Carrier, 230.2cu.in 6-cylinder engine, 92bhp, 4-speed gearbox, single-speed transfer box with front-axle disconnect, hydraulic brakes, semi-elliptic leaf springs.
£3,500–4,500 / $5,000–6,500 🚗 MVT

c1955 Daimler Ferret Scout Car, 4258cc 6-cylinder engine, 96bhp, 5-speed pre-selector gearbox, forward/reverse transfer box, hydraulic brakes, independent suspension by coil springs.
£4,500–5,000 / $6,500–7,250 ⊞ RRM

c1955 Daimler Ferret Mk II/III Scout Car, 4200cc 6-cylinder rear mounted engine.
£4,500–5,000 /$6,500–7,250 ⊞ RRM

Restored values

The cost of a professional restoration will have an influence on, but no direct relation to, a car's market value. A restored car can have a market value lower than the cost of its restoration.

c1942 Dodge WC53 ¾ Ton Carryall, 6-cylinder engine, 92bhp, 4-speed gearbox, 2- or 4-wheel drive, single-speed transfer box, hydraulic brakes, leaf-spring suspension.
£7,000–8,000 / $10,000–11,500 🚗 MVT

c1943 Dodge WC57 Command/Reconnaissance Car,
6-cylinder engine, 92bhp, 4-speed gearbox, 2- or 4-wheel
drive, single-speed transfer box, hydraulic brakes,
leaf-spring suspension.
£9,000–10,000 / $13,000–14,500 ⊞ RRM

▶ **c1942 Ford GPW Jeep,** 134.2cu.in sidevalve 4-cylinder
engine, 54bhp, 3-speed gearbox, 2-speed transfer box with
front axle declutch, hydraulic brakes, rigid axles with leaf
springs, 6 volt electrics.
£8,000–9,000 / $11,500–13,000 🚗 MVT

1941 Ford Heavy Utility Vehicle, 239cu.in sidevalve V8
engine, 95bhp, 3-speed gearbox, hydraulic brakes, leaf-
spring suspension, full-floating truck-type rear axle.
£5,000–6,000 / $7,250–8,750 🚗 MVT
During WWII, many basically civilian vehicles were
converted to military use. This Ford utility vehicle was
based on the company's 1941 'woody' station wagon.
The chassis and running gear were strengthened, but
the wood-framed bodywork was retained. These
vehicles saw extensive use in North Africa, often with
roof hatches or even the complete roof removed.

c1944 Ford (Canadian) 3 Ton Truck, sidevalve V8 engine,
GS body.
£2,000–2,500 / $3,000–3,500 🚗 MVT

c1943 Dodge WC56 Command Car, 6-cylinder engine,
92bhp, 4-speed gearbox, 2- or 4-wheel drive, single-speed
transfer box, hydraulic brakes, leaf-spring suspension.
£7,000–8,000 / $10,000–11,500 🚗 MVT
The WC56 was basically the same as the WC57, but
without the latter's winch.

1942 Ford GPW Jeep, sidevalve 4-cylinder engine, older
repaint, tan canvas upholstery and top, rear mounted jerry
can, shovel and axe.
£7,000–8,000 / $10,250–11,500 ↗ Bon
Just before the USA entered WWII, the US Army
invited bids for a small, light, all-wheel-drive vehicle
for use in combat. At that time, the American Bantam
Company was on its last legs, but somehow the
company managed to convince an automotive
engineer named Karl Probost to put together the
design to present to the military. Willys and Ford
were interested too, but it was the Bantam design
that was considered the best candidate. The
government considered the tiny company to have
insufficient resources to meet the army's needs, and
the bulk of the contract was split between Willys and
Ford, which began production of the Jeep Universal
Quarter-Ton. Bantam received a small portion of the
contract, but before long, the tiny company became
one of the many hundreds of American auto makers
to come and go in the first half of the 20th century.

c1944 Ford (Canadian) Light Anti-Aircraft Tractor, sidevalve V8 engine, partially restored, good condition.
£2,000–2,500 / $3,000–3,500 🚗 **MVT**

c1943 GMC 2½ Ton Shop Van, 269.5cu.in overhead-valve 6-cylinder petrol engine, 94bhp, 5-speed gearbox, 6-wheel drive, 2-speed transfer box with front-axle declutch, hydraulic brakes with vacuum servo, semi-elliptic leaf springs, 6 volt electrics.
£2,000–2,500 / $3,000–3,500 🚗 **MVT**
This house-type van was used and equipped for various roles, including artillery, automotive, electrical, instrument and small-arms repair.

▶ **c1944 GMC 2½ Ton Short-Wheelbase Truck,** 269.5cu.in 6-cylinder engine, 6-wheel drive, open cab with machine-gun ring.
£2,000–2,500 / $3,000–3,500 🚗 **MVT**

c1944 GMC 2½ Ton Air Compressor Truck, 269.5cu.in overhead-valve 6-cylinder petrol engine, 94bhp, 5-speed gearbox, 2-speed transfer box with front-axle declutch, hydraulic brakes with vacuum servo, semi-elliptic leaf springs, 6 volt electrics.
£2,000–2,500 / $3,000–3,500 🚗 **MVT**
These trucks were used by engineers to power pneumatic tools.

▶ **c1985 Hummer,** 6.2 litre diesel engine, 3-speed automatic transmission, independent suspension, limited-slip differentials.
£30,000–35,000 / $43,000–51,000 ⊞ **RRM**

c1944 Ford M8 Light Armoured Car, 320cu.in rear mounted 6-cylinder engine, 79bhp, 4-speed gearbox, 2- or 6-wheel drive, 2-speed transfer box, hydraulic brakes with vacuum servo, leaf-spring suspension, restored, deactivated gun.
£17,000–20,000 / $25,000–30,000 ⊞ **RRM**
A total of 8,523 M8 armoured cars were built between 1943 and 1945. Its turret carried a 37mm gun, and it had a crew of four. The British called it the Greyhound.

c1943 GMC 2½ Ton Truck, 259.5cu.in 6-cylinder engine, 6-wheel drive, 5 ton winch.
£2,000–3,000 / $2,900–4,400 MVT

c1948 M100 Trailer, retains original single-piece wheels.
£300–450 / £440–650 🚗 MVT
This was a post-war copy of the wartime Jeep trailer.

1941 Plymouth Four-Door Staff Car, 6-cylinder engine, 87bhp, 3-speed gearbox, hydraulic brakes, rigid axle on leaf-spring suspension at rear, independent coil-spring front suspension.
£7,000–8,000 / $10,000–11,500 🚗 MVT
At the beginning of WWII, the US military procured 2,031 1941 Plymouth saloons as well as 210 1940 models. In addition, over 10,000 new civilian saloons and coupés were requisitioned.

c1941 Willys MB Jeep, 134.2cu.in sidevalve 4-cylinder engine, 3-speed gearbox, 2-speed transfer box with front-axle declutch, hydraulic brakes, rigid axles with leaf springs, 6 volt electrics.
£5,000–6,000 / $7,250–8,750 🚗 MVT
This is an early example, indicated by its 'slatted' radiator grille. Later types had a pressed-steel grille.

c1940 Morris Commercial C8 Artillery Tractor, 3519cc 4-cylinder engine, 70bhp, 5-speed gearbox, 4-wheel drive, single-speed transfer box, hydraulic brakes, leaf-spring suspension.
£8,000–10,000 / $11,500–14,500 🚗 MVT

c1960 Reo M35 2½ Ton Truck, 331cu.in overhead-valve 6-cylinder petrol engine, 127bhp, 5-speed gearbox, 2-speed transfer box with automatic front-axle engagement, air-over-hydraulic brakes, semi-elliptic leaf springs, 24 volt electrics.
£3,000–4,000 / $4,500–6,000 ⊞ RRM
The 'Eager Beaver' M-series range was launched in 1950 by Reo and, with periodic improvements and changes, continued in production until the 1980s. Over the years, other manufacturers (Studebaker, Curtiss Wright, Kaiser Jeep, AM General and White) also built large quantities, and there was a multiplicity of body types.

1945 Willys MB Jeep, acquired early 1990s direct from NATO store in Norway where it had remained virtually unused, restored, hood, side screens, shovel and axe, 1 of lowest-mileage undamaged Jeeps in existence, very good condition throughout.
£6,500–7,500 / $9,500–11,000 ➤ Bon

◀ **c1942 Willys MB Jeep,** 134.2cu.in sidevalve 6-cylinder engine, 3-speed gearbox, 2-speed transfer box with front-axle declutch, hydraulic brakes, rigid axles with leaf springs, 6 volt electrics, fully restored, US Navy markings.
£5,000–6,000 / $7,250–8,750 🚗 MVT

Tractors

1955 Allis Chalmers Model D270 Rowcrop Tractor,
petrol/tvo engine, fitted with rear linkage and Ferguson ridger.
£800–900 / $1,150–1,300   ⚒ CGC

1955 Ferguson TEF20 Tractor, diesel engine, restored,
good condition.
£750–850/ $1,000–1,250   ⚒ CGC

1954 Field Marshall Series IIIA Tractor, diesel engine,
good ex-farm condition.
£5,000–6,000 / $7,250–8,750   ⚒ CGC

1963 Fordson Dexta Tractor, diesel engine, standard
drawbar and pick-up hitch, live drive, good ex-farm condition.
£1,400–1,800 / $2,000–2,500   ⚒ CGC

**c1942 Minneapolis Moline Model ZTU Rowcrop
Tractor,** petrol/tvo engine, older restoration.
£1,300–1,600 / $2,000–2,300   ⚒ CGC

1946 Oliver Model 80 Tractor, petrol/paraffin engine,
swinging drawbar, good condition, timing in need
of attention.
£2,000–3,000 / $3,000–4,500   ⚒ CGC

1959 Track Marshall Model 55 Crawler Tractor, Perkins
L4 diesel engine, 4 bottom track rollers, electric starter and
lighting set.
£700–800 / $1,000–1,150   ⚒ CGC

1949 Turner Yeoman of England Tractor, diesel engine,
swinging drawbar, average condition.
£2,500–3,000 /$3,500–4,500   ⚒ CGC

Caravans

1926 Eccles Caravan, completely restored 1988, many period fittings, correct leaded-light side, stable door and rear bay windows, interior repaired, new upholstery and period-style flooring, correct Rippindales cooker, non-original features include 12 volt on-board electrical installation, 240 volt mains inlet, pumped water system and stainless-steel sink, all hidden within original wooden cabinets, 1 double bed and 1 double bunk, weatherproofed.
£8,000–9,000 / $11,500–13,000 ↗ Bon

1947 Teardrop Caravan Reproduction, constructed with mahogany and hard rock maple, cocktail bar with complete set of crystal decanters, mixers and glasses, 2 TVs, video recorder, 10-disc CD player.
£11,000–13,000 / $16,000–19,000 ↗ RM
The teardrop trailer was popular from the 1930s through to the 1950s. A small door on each side allowed access to the double bed inside. The real treats, though, generally lay below the hinged panel at the rear. Most examples were equipped with a compartmentalised kitchen area that included everything from a sink to burners. The typical Teardrop was about 8ft (244cm) long, 4ft (122cm) wide and 4ft tall. Most had an aluminium skin on a plywood frame. Teardrops were sold as kits or complete units; many were homebuilt.

> **Miller's is a price GUIDE not a price LIST**

Horse-Drawn Vehicles

c1896 Stick-Back Gig, to fit 13.2–14.2hh, 47in 16-spoke Warner wheels, semi-elliptic leaf springs, sprung shafts, patent dash and splash boards, finished in blue with gold lining, navy upholstery.
£1,200–1,500 / $1,750–2,250 ↗ TSh

c1890 Continental Drosky, built in Germany, to fit 14.2–16hh, single or pair, finished in yellow and black with black lining, tan upholstery, good condition.
£650–750 / $1,000–1,100 ↗ TSh

c1900 Piano Box Buggy, built in USA, to suit 14–15hh, transverse elliptic leaf springs, finished in black with red lining, black leatherette upholstery.
£600–700 / $850–1,000 ↗ TSh

c1900 Ralli Car, to fit 14.2–15.2hh, on triple springs, fitted with louvred side panels, finished in brown with black, yellow and light brown lining.
£400–500 / $575–725 ↗ TSh

c1900 Governess Car, by Sanders & Son, to fit 11–12hh, handbrake, body spindled, finished in varnished natural wood, beige upholstery.
£650–750 / $1,000–1,100 ⚏ TSh

c1924 Wagonette, to suit 14.2–15.2hh, single or pair, handbrake, restored 1981, finished in light stained and varnished wood with green paintwork, lined in gold.
£1,500–1,800 / $2,200–2,600 ⚏ TSh

c1930 Butcher's Cart, by Harris of Chickerell, to fit 14.2–15.2hh, triple springs, 48in 14-spoke wheels with new rubbers, rear fitted with drop-down door, finished in blue with cream wheels and shafts, lined in red and blue, body decorated with pheasant pictures and sign writing, interior with small shelf.
£4,000–5,000 / $5,750–7,250 ⚏ TSh

c1980 Phaeton, to suit up to 14.2hh, single or pair, footbrake, shafts and pole, finished in maroon with cream lining, front seat and rear groom's seat upholstered in black vinyl.
£800–900/ $1,150–1,300 ⚏ TSh

c1910 Siamese Phaeton, to suit 14–15hh, single or pair, shafts, pole and swingletrees, handbrake, recently restored, finished in varnished natural wood with yellow lining, brown leather upholstery.
£2,500–3,000 / $3,500–4,500 ⚏ TSh

c1925 Ralli Car, by Brown & sons, to fit 14.2–15.2hh, re-rubbered 52in 16-spoke wheels, finished in black with yellow lining, good condition.
£700–800 / $1,000–1,200 ⚏ TSh

c1960 Ralli Car, by J. Norman, to fit 15.2–16.2hh, finished in black and grey, in need of repainting.
£550–650 / $800–1,000 ⚏ TSh

1989 Four-Wheeled Marathon Vehicle, by Fenix Carriages, to suit 14.3–16.2hh, single or pair, disc brakes, pole and shafts, driver's sprung seat, finished in dark blue with yellow lining, black vinyl upholstery.
£1,100–1,500 / $1,600–2,200 ⚏ TSh

Children's Cars

1939 Atco 98cc Junior Trainer, Villiers 98cc 2-stroke petrol engine, 1 forward gear and reverse, 10mph top speed, older restoration, finished in green, red upholstery, engine and chassis sound, cosmetics in need of attention.
£1,800–2,200 / $2,600–3,200 ⋗ Bon
Following the introduction of the driving test in 1935, greater emphasis was placed on knowledge of the Highway Code and road safety generally. Charles H. Pugh Ltd, better known for horticultural machinery, and more specifically Atco lawn mowers, designed the Junior Trainer for use in schools to demonstrate car handling and road safety.

1950s Tri-ang Ford Zephyr T-Type Pedal Car, pressed-steel construction, plastic steering wheel, chrome grille, headlamps and radiator cap, bulb horn, steel balloon wheels, chrome hubcaps, original.
£300–400 / $440–580 ⊞ CARS

Cross Reference
See Colour Review (page 275)

1950s Leeway Ford Zodiac Pedal Car, heavy-gauge pressed-steel construction, chrome windscreen surround, grille and trim, badges, restored, finished in bright orange, Perspex headlamps.
£350–450 / $500–650 ⊞ CARS

1950s Austin J40 Pedal Car, completely restored, finished in red, excellent condition.
£1,000–1,200 / $1,500–1,750 ⋗ CGC

1980s BRM Child's Electric Car, plastic and glassfibre construction, enamel badge to the nose.
£250–350 / $360–500 ⋗ CGC

1990s Grasshopper Child's Car, by Real Life Toys, 12 volt electric motor, forward and reverse gears, finished in burnished aluminium with blue wings and nose cone, good condition.
£700–900 / $1,000–1,300 ⚒ BRIT

1980s Mercedes 300SL Pedal Car, by Toys Toys, very good condition.
£150–200 / $220–300 ⚒ CGC

◀ **1918 Paige Sports Tourer Pedal Car,** by Gendron, pressed steel on wood frame, wire spoked wheels, working headlamps, bonnet mascot, bulb horn, fully restored, hand painted.
£1,500–2,000 / $2,200–3,000 ⊞ CARS

c1920 Pedal Car, rusty, barn find, in need of restoration.
£325–375 /$470–560 ⊞ JUN

c1960 Tri-ang Pedal Police Car, metal body.
£100–150 / $145–220 ⚒ BRIT

1980s Volkswagen Karmann Cabriolet Child's Car,
3½hp Briggs & Stratton engine, working lights, radio, glassfibre body, finished in white, red vinyl interior, 67in (170cm) long.
£1,000–1,250 / $1,500–1,800 ⚒ CGC

Automobile Art

Bryan de Grineau, W.O. Bentley No. 7, mixed media, signed, mounted, framed and glazed, 30 x 23¾in (76 x 60.5cm).
£1,400–1,600 / $2,000–2,300 ↗ **Bon**

Michael Wright, 1948 Dolomite Cup, depicting Bruno Sterzi in a Ferrari 166 Inter/Sport 2000, mixed media, signed, mounted framed and glazed, 18½ x 14½in (47 x 37cm).
£1,100–1,300 / $1,600–2,000 ↗ **Bon**

◀ **John Hostler, Benz 1888,** a colour cut-away for *The Autocar*, pen and ink line drawing with watercolour on board, signed and dated '8 November 1973', slight discolouration to surface, 15½ x 16½in (39.5 x 42cm).
£60–80
$90–120 ↗ **Bon**

Frederick Gordon-Crosby, Brooklands Meeting 18/4/36, depicting Driscoll's Austin spinning under the Member's Bridge, pencil highlighted with white on paper, initialled 'FGC', paper worn and discoloured, 10 x 13½in (25.5 x 34.5cm)
£500–600 / $720–870 ↗ **Bon**

Helen Taylor, Moss and Collins driving the winning Mercedes-Benz 300SLR at the Targa Florio of 1955, pen and ink with colour, framed and glazed, 14¼ x 10¼in (36 x 26cm).
£350–400 / $500–580 ↗ **Bon**

▶ **Brian Hatton, Cooper Formula II,** a cut-away depicting the racing car, pen and ink on thick card, manuscript wording on the lower right corner, verso applied with printed label 'Return to Art Department for Filing', also a *Motor* '9-Jan 57' rubber stamp and over doodles, signed, unmounted, a little soiling, 18 x 14in (45.5 x 35.5cm).
£130–150 / $190–220 ↗ **Bon**

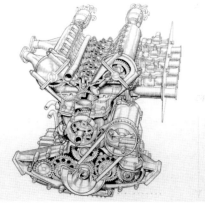

R.E. Poulton, Aston Martin DBR1 – 3 Litre, a cut-away depicting the 6-cylinder engine, pen and ink on board, pencil title and measurement on the front with four *Autocar* and IPC rubber stamps verso and encompassing the dates '15/3/57, 4/12/67 and 17 Dec 1973', signed, some soiling, unmounted, 21 x 15in (53.5 x 38cm).
£200–250 / $300–360 ↗ **Bon**

▶ Tony Upson, a large mural, depicting a DB3 driven at speed by Peter Collins at Goodwood, 1952, acrylic on board, 86 x 48in (218.5 x 122cm).
£1,500–2,000
$2,200–3,000
⚒ Bon

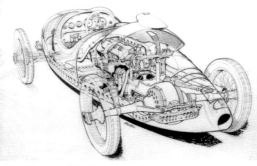

Gay Dutton, 1960 Australian Grand Prix, depicting Alec Mildren in the Cooper Maserati battling with Lex Davison in the Aston Martin DB4GP at Lowood in Queensland, acrylic on canvas, signed, dated ''91', 48 x 59¾in (122 x 152cm).
£240–280 / $350–410 ⚒ GO

Brian Hatton, 1923 Benz Tropfeawagen, a cut-away drawing, pen and ink on tracing paper laid on board with pencil notations and light corrections, applied Temple Press label to the rear with manuscript signature and dated '6-12-63', signed, some bubbling and creasing and Sellotape staining, 24 x 16in (61 x 40.5cm).
£90–110 / £130–160 ⚒ Bon

Frederick Gordon-Crosby, Paris 1925 Grand Prix de L'ACF, depicting a scene from the French Grand Prix at Montlhery in 1925 where Antonio Ascari drove his No. 8 Alfa Romeo P2 into the fencing and overturned the car, resulting in his death, mixed media, signed, framed and glazed, 14in (35.5cm) square.
£3,000–3,500 / $4,400–5,000 ⚒ Bon

A print, My Favourite Race, depicting Stirling Moss at Monaco 1961, signed by the artist and Stirling Moss, No. 447/850, in a silver frame, 31 x 25in (78.5 x 63.5cm).
£100–120 / $145–175 ⚒ CGC

▶ Max Millar, Goldie Gardner's MG, a drawing depicting the 1250cc record breaking car for The Autocar, pen and ink with monochrome wash on board, signed, dated '17/8/51', discolouration to surface, loss to bottom left corner, lower right creased, 12¼ x 29½in (31 x 75cm).
£300–350
$440–500 ⚒ Bon

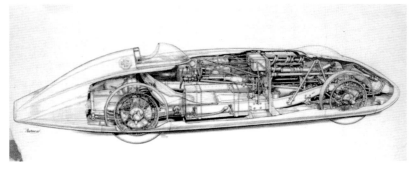

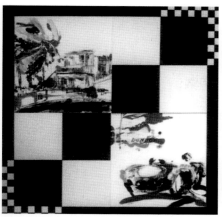

Helen Taylor, Aston Martin DBR1, a pencil and watercolour wash, signed and dated, framed and glazed, 21¾ x 29½in (55.5 x 75cm).
£850–1,000 / $1,250–1,500 ✠ Bon

Frederick Gordon-Crosby, Dundonald August 1928 – Ulster TT, depicting the battle between Hayes' Lagonda and Don's Lea-Francis, charcoal and wash heightened with white, signed and dated, mounted, framed and glazed, 17in x 23¼in (43 x 59cm).
£2,000–2,500 / $3,000–3,500 ✠ Bon

Cross Reference
See Colour Review
(page 198–199)

◄ **Max Millar, Studebaker 1935 Commander,** chassis cut-away for *The Autocar*, pen and ink on board, signed and dated '22/2/35', discolouration to surface, board with slight flaking to corners, 18¼in x 27in (46.5 x 68.5cm).
£100–150
$145–220 ✠ Bon

Helen Taylor, Wharton driving the winning BRM V16 during the Glover Trophy at Goodwood in 1954, pen and ink with colour, framed and glazed, 10¼ x 14¼in (26 x 36cm).
£450–550 / $650–800 ✠ Bon

R.W. Macbeth, A Roadside Tragedy, monochrome watercolour and mixed media, with title and dedication 'Presented by William Smith Esq., JP, Mayor of Brighouse, 1907.' on the mount, framed, the reverse of the frame applied with label 'From the Graphic Gallery, Published date Decmr 9th 1905', initialled, 18¼ x 27½in (46.5 x 70cm).
£375–450 / $560–650 ✠ Bon

▶ **Gordon Horner, Splendid Island Road Race,** charcoal and chalk with gouache highlights on paper, signed and dated 'Jersey May '49', tears to right edge, mounted on backing paper, torn with loss, 17¾ x 24in (45 x 61cm).
£3,500–4,500
$5,000–6,500 ✠ Bon

Bryan de Grineau, Thus it has been said...', pen and ink cartoon on board, signed and dated "33", the reverse applied with remains of original page from *The Motor*, some smudging and wear, missing top section of the cartoon containing two further drawings showing the four divisions in society, board broken along top margin, 13¾ x 14¾in (35 x 37.5cm).
£230–280 / $330–410 ♪ **Bon**

Frederick Gordon-Crosby, Shelsley Walsh 1936, depicting J. Stancer-Beaumont's Ford Special skidding on the S-bend, pencil highlighted in white on paper, initialled 'FGC', for *The Autocar*, published 18 September 1936, paper creased and worn with taped repair to rear, 7½ x 11in (19 x 28cm).
£350–425 /$500–620 ♪ **Bon**

Bryan de Grineau, The Motor Car has...effectively replaced the professional matchmaker, pen and ink cartoon with blue wash on board, signed and dated "33", the reverse stamped 'Motor 15 Nov 1933', some smudging and wear, 8 x 12¼in (20.5 x 31cm).
£200–250 / $300–360 ♪ **Bon**

► **Gordon Horner, Take to the Hills,** depicting a single-seat racing car ascending Prescott at speed, charcoal on paper laid on card, rubber *Autocar* stamp to the rear dated 'December 26/47', signed, sound condition with Sellotape staining at the base, 25 x 20in (63.5 x 51cm).
£300–400 / $440–580 ♪ **Bon**

► **Gordon Horner, Silverstone '49,** depicting Farina in his Maserati, leading from Viloresi in his Ferrari, charcoal and chalk on paper, published in *The Autocar* 26 August 1949, signed and dated "49", discolouration to surface, horizontal crease, paper worn with tears to lower and left edge, 24 x 21in (61 x 53.5cm).
£800–1,200
$1,150–1,750 ♪ **Bon**

Miller's is a price GUIDE not a price LIST

◄ **Algernon Rowe, Portrait of Louis Meyer,** depicting the 1928 Indianapolis 500 winner, charcoal and chalk on board, for *The Autocar* Makers of History series, published 5 October 1928, signed, framed and glazed, 22 x 16¼in (56 x 41.5cm).
£125–175 / $180–255 ♪ **Bon**

H.S.H. Gerant, an original painting depicting Charron in the Panhard-Levassor overtaking Giraud's Bollée during the Paris-Amsterdam race 1902, in the style of F. Gordon-Crosby, mixed media, 15¼ x 19in (38.5 x 48.5cm).
£200–250 / $300–360 ♪ **Bon**

Posters

Mille Miglia, 28 Aprile 1940, XVIII,
a Reale Automobile Cirolo d'Italia
original advertising poster in two
colours, slight fold marks,
39½ x 27½in (100.5 x 70cm).
£600–700 / $870–1,000 ⚲ **Bon**

**Int.Eifelrennen, Nürburgring 21
May 1939,** an original colour poster
depicting a BMW 328 and others,
good clean condition with minimal
wear, 47¼ x 33in (120 x 84cm).
£1,000–1,200 / $1,500–1,750 ⚲ **Bon**

**International Daily Express Trophy
Meeting, Silverstone 9th May
1953,** an original advertising poster,
slight marks and wear to paper,
29½ x 19in (75 x 48.5cm).
£300–350 / $440–500 ⚲ **Bon**

1960 Reims Grand Prix de L'ACF,
a printed metal poster, 12 x 6in
(30.5 x 15cm), together with a race
programme for the same event.
£130–160 / $190–230 ⚲ **CGC**

Maniacs on Wheels, a film advertising
poster featuring among others Graham
Hill and Brad Harris, multi-coloured,
1968, 27 x 40in (68.5 x 101.5cm).
£200–250 / $300–360 ⚲ **Bon**

Targa Florio, Sicily, an original poster
depicting a Ferrari 330 P3, c1968,
30 x 9in (76 x 23cm).
£50–75 / $75–110 ⚲ **Bon**

◀ **1967 British Grand Prix,** a poster
autographed by Graham Hill, common
mounted, with later Esso patch from
Hill's overalls, a contemporary
photograph of Hill and enamel helmet
badge, mounted, glazed and framed,
44 x 25¼in (112 x 64cm).
£250–300 / $360–440 ⚲ **Bon**

Cross Reference
See Colour Review (page 199)

▶ **ADAC – 1000km Rennen,** an
original poster illustrating and
outlining the Nürburgring event in
1961, good condition, slight creasing
and tear, 23 x 33in (58.5 x 84cm).
£200–250 / $300–360 ⚲ **Bon**

Congratulations Capt. Eyston,
a Castrol Land Speed Record poster, the lower left-hand corner of the poster states '(Subject to Official Confirmation), the speed was finally confirmed as 312mph for the kilometer and 311.42mph for the mile', tear to left edge, 1937, 29½ x 19¼in (75 x 49cm).
£400–500 / $580–720 ➤ Bon

The Daily Express Trophy Meeting, an original poster advertising the event held on 5th May 1951, slight fold marks, minimal wear/deterioration to paper, 29¼ x 19¼in (74.5 x 49cm).
£250–300 / $360–440 ➤ Bon

Michelin, an original monochrome poster depicting Bibendum smoking a cigar and holding aloft the Michelin building, c1920.
£175–225 / $255–325 ➤ CGC

Fiat 519, an advertising poster, linen, dated '1922', framed and glazed, 30 x 17in (76 x 43cm).
£75–100 / $110–145 ➤ BRIT

Volkswagen Beetle, an advertising poster depicting a family with their car, German text, mid-1950s, 27 x 15in (68.5 x 38cm)
£40–50 / $60–75 ➤ BRIT

Le Mans, an original film poster, featuring Steve McQueen, Italian-market version, 1972–73, 54 x 39in (137 x 99cm).
£400–600 / $580–870 ⊞ VEY

Automobilia

A 1,000 Miles Trial silver paperweight, with bevelled glass base depicting 4-seater sporting Edwardian motor car, the reverse engraved with a route map, inscribed with place names including London, Mendips, Carmarthen, Llandrindod, Ludlow, Worcester, Stratford and Oxford, hallmarked 1904, 3 x 5in (7.5 x 12.5cm).
£300–400 / $440–580 ➤ C

▶ **A silver cigarette case,** modelled as an early automobile radiator, the polished surround housing an engine turned centre grille, with enamelled Benz insignia to the top and surmounted by a clasp in the shape of the radiator cap, opening to reveal a gilt interior, German, c1910, 4 x 3¼in (10 x 8.5cm).
£1,200–1,300 / $1,750–2,000 ➤ Bon

◀ **A Gladiator sales brochure,** depicting the range of cars, motorcycles and bicycles, c1904.
£45–60 / $65–90 ➤ CGC

A leather-cased set of 37 Bartholomew's maps, with carrying handle, brass catches and road measuring device in lid, c1910, excellent condition.
£300–350 / $450–500 ⋏ Bon

A set of 37 Bartholomew's contoured road maps of England and Wales, contained in a tan-coloured leather box, with mileage recorder in lid.
£190–240 / $275–350 ⋏ Bon

A Big Tree Motor Spirit can, dented, New Zealand, 1930s, 11½in (29cm) high.
£90–1000 / $130–160 ⊞ MSMP

A Shell Motor Spirit miniature can, c1930, 6in (15cm) high.
£50–75 / $75–110 ⊞ MURR

A silver St Christopher dashboard plaque, by Jean Puifocat, with two retaining screws to the reverse, French, c1920, 2⅛in (6.5cm) square.
£600–650 / $870–950 ⋏ Bon

A Bentley brochure, for the 6-cylinder 6.5 litre, 8pp with soft cover and black print, good sound condition, slight soiling to edges, No. 22, dated October 1927.
£900–1,000 / $1,300–1,600 ⋏ Bon

A Pratts 2 gallon can, repainted green with black lettering, 1930s, 11in (28cm) high.
£5–10 / $10–15 ⊞ TPS

▶ A Shell-Mex and BP Ltd 2 gallon can, repainted red with black lettering, good condition, 1930s.
£10–12 / $15–20 ⊞ TPS

◀ A WMF nickel-plated Britannia metal inkstand, modelled as a car with driver and passenger, bonnet opens to reveal a tray for postage stamps, boot lid opens to reveal an area for envelopes, c1912, 14in (35.5cm) wide.
£2,750–3,250
$4,000–4,750 ⋏ Bon

A silver and *guilloche* enamel cigarette case 'Mein Benz', German, c1924, 3½in (9cm) high.
£3,000–3,500 / $4,500–5,000 ⋏ Bon
The young lady embracing her Benz is an enduring and popular automobile advertising image of the period. Her first appearance dates from 1913, and throughout the 15 years following, both the young lady and her automobile evolved, as did fashion and design.

A Filtrate Running-In Compound 1 pint can, 1930s, 4½in (11.5cm) high.
£40–50 / $60–75 ⊞ MSMP

A Shell Test Your Nerves game, in original envelope, 1930s, 6 x 4in (15 x 10cm).
£35–45 / $50–65 ⊞ MURR

John Player, a set of Motor Car cigarette cards, 1936.
£50–60 / $75–90 ⚒ MUR

A Pegaso brochure, 8pp, with technical details and colour illustrations outlining the 102B-series cars in their different forms, c1954.
£140–180 / $200–260 ⚒ Bon

Six plastic advertising key rings, BP, Shell, Goodyear, Gillette, Tintin, Ford, 1960s, each c1½in (4cm) long.
£5–15 / $10–20 ⚒ HUX

A Rolls-Royce Pillar Box sterling silver lighter, by Saunders & Shepherd, with hexagonal stepped base and spherical sprung cap, hinged and opening to reveal a spirit-filled cigar lighter, surmounted by a Spirit of Ecstasy, London 1934, 6½in (16.5cm) high.
£8,000–9,000
$11,500–13,000 ⚒ Bon
The series of desk pieces, of which this Pillar Box lighter formed a part, was produced between 1926 and 1936, one for each year except 1931 and 1935. Seven examples of each were made as Christmas gifts, one for the head of each major Rolls-Royce distributor.

Two plastic Esso advertising key rings, 1960s, 1½in (4cm) long.
£5–15 / $10–20 ⊞ HUX

▶ **A Porsche 356 Carrera assembly guide,** describing the complete assembly and maintenance of all Carrera engine types, July 1963 edition.
£700–800
$1,000–1,200 ⚒ C

◀ **A Ferrari 275 GTB/4 sales brochure,** 6pp, with technical specifications, 1966, 12½ x 7¾in (32 x 19.5cm).
£250–300 / $350–450 ⚒ Bon

Montague Tombs, *Third Degree,* with illustrations by F. Gordon-Crosby, 12pp, reprinted from *The Autocar* February 1939, good clean condition.
£115–130 / $165–200 ⚒ Bon

A Mobil Oil pourer, 1950, 7in (18cm) high.
£5–10 / $10–15 ⊞ BLM

A Porsche 356 Carrera tool kit, original tools in vinyl pouch, complete, 1950s, excellent condition.
£2,800–3,400 / $4,000–5,000 ⚒ C

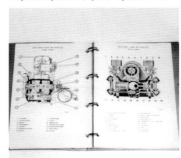

Badges

An AGEA Assurance badge, 1930s, 3in (7.5cm) diam.
£55–60 / $80–90 ⊞ GIRA

A German car club badge, 'Rund um Wilderschausen' (Trip to Wilderschausen), dated 30 May 1954.
£30–35 / $45–50 ⊞ CARS

A Belgian car club badge, 'Royal Automobile Club du Hainaut, Mons', coloured enamels on a chrome base, 1950s–60s.
£35–40 / $50–60 ⊞ CARS

A Brooklands Automobile Racing Club member's badge, by Spencer of London, with correct '120 M.P.H.' attached black enamel plaque replacing the B.A.R.C. motif, original coloured enamels in good condition, the reverse inscribed 'S.C.H. Davis 12.10.29', maker's socle to stabilising bracket, original nickel plating slightly distressed.
£4,000–4,500 / $5,800–6,500 ⚲ Bon Only 84 120mph badges were ever issued. Sammy Davis won this example during the B.R.D.C. 500 mile race held on 12 October 1929, using the outer circuit at Brooklands and driving 'Old No. 1', the 6.5 litre Bentley. Although Davis only came second in the race, turning in an average speed of 109mph, he made the fastest lap at 126.09mph.

A silver and enamel Rolls-Royce chauffeur's cap badge, numbered 4309, c1913, in original box, 2½ x 1½in (6.5 x 4cm)
£275–350 / $400–500 ⊞ MURR

▶ **A BOAC car badge,** 1960s, 5in (12.5cm) high.
£34–45 / $50–65 ⊞ COB

Cross Reference
See Colour Review (page 200)

An enamel and gilded-brass motor rally dashboard plaque, for a car trip organised by the Southern Tirol rally group, 27–28 April 1990 from Bozen to Algun in the Austrian alps.
£50–75 / $75–110 ⊞ CARS

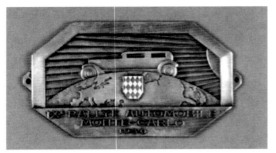

A silvered-bronze 9th Monte Carlo Rally plaque, with enamel shield, in original presentation case, 1930, 3¼in (8.5cm) wide.
£400–500 / $580–720 ⚬ Bon

▶ **An Automobile Club Nice et Côte d'Azure rally plaque,** by Drago of Nice, enamelled with club badge, for 1931 rally, in original presentation case, 3in (7.5cm) high.
£200–250
$300–360 ⚬ Bon

A silver 10th Monte Carlo Rally plaque, with enamel shield, marked 'Argent', in original Fraisse Demy of Paris presentation case, 3¾in (9.5cm) wide.
£500–600 / $720–870 ⚬ Bon

An enamelled silver Automobile Club de Cannes plaque, by A. Augis of Lyon, marked 'Argent' and signed 'A. Augis', in original presentation case, 3in (7.5cm wide).
£180–220 / $260–320 ⚬ Bon

◀ **A 25th Monte Carlo Rally car badge,** enamel and painted chrome, marked '25E Anniversaire 1911-1955', 1955, 3½in (9cm) wide.
£200–250
$300–360
⚬ **Bon**

A 27th Monte Carlo Rally car badge, enamel and painted chrome, 6in (15cm) wide.
£180–230 / $260–330 ⚬ Bon

Components

A pair of benzene lamps, as used on taxis and hire cars, correct bevel-edged glasses, small numbered tell-tale glasses, bails and socket mounting brackets, each with no. 1368 on front glasses, sound condition, in need of finishing, probably French, c1900, 12in (30.5cm) high.
£125–175 / $180–255 ⚬ Bon

An Adlake oil rear lamp, good undamaged condition, in need of re-enamelling, 10in (25.5cm) high.
£20–30 / $30–45 ⚬ BRIT

Cross Reference
See Colour Review (page 200)

A Neverout acetylene gas spot lamp, by Rose Manufacturing Company, brass body, mirror-glass reflector, 6in front glass, rear mounted positioning handle, inscribed brass nameplate, unrestored, c1905, 15½in (39.5cm) high.
£250–300 / $360–440 ⚬ Bon

A pair of Louis Blériot self-contained acetylene gas headlamps, parabolic-style, central plano condenser lens, nickel-silver reflectors, burner holders, carbide cylinders and retaining brackets, on/off gas switch, water condenser chambers beneath burners, carrying bails, Blériot name plaques fitted to heat ventilators, 2 Weldhen & Blériot retailer plates fitted on rear with Louis Blériot hand engraved signature plaque below, part restored, minor dents, c1905, 11in (28cm) wide.
£4,000–5,000 / $5,800–7,250 ➢ Bon

A pair of Besnard Brothers benzene town lamps, original nickel plating, combination rear opening doors and reflectors, burners, vestibules, double-convex front glasses, inscribed name plates, c1908, 8½in (21.5cm) high.
£375–450 / $560–650 ➢ Bon

An Eveready of New York tachometer, nickel plated case, silver-coloured dial with black numerals from 200 to 2400, angled bracket, c1908, 4½in (11.5cm) diam.
£170–200 / $250–300 ➢ Bon

A J. & R. Oldfield Dependence oil brass rear lamp, oil reservoir missing, 1910, 10in (25.5cm) high.
£275–325 / $400–470 ➢ Bon

A Grey and Davis central mounted acetylene gas projector, front glass, glass rear reflector, 12in (30.5cm) bezel and fork bracket, burner holder missing, c1908.
£250–300 / $360–440 ➢ Bon

A Lucas No. 742 oil side lamp, c1912.
£115–130
$170–190 ➢ CGC

A matched pair of Badger Solar Model 1132 oil side lamps, original nickel plating, undamaged side glasses, rear reflectors, tell-tale rear lens, spade mounting brackets, c1910, 12in (30.5cm) high.
£170–200 / $250–300 ➢ Bon

A pair of lozenge-shaped electric town lamps, c1912, 14½in (37cm) high.
£340–370 / $500–550 ➢ Bon
Fitted to the side of a limousine, these lamps were used to illuminate the dismounting steps at night.

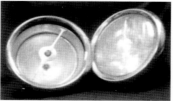

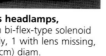

An early Rolls-Royce carburettor, on a wooden display mount.
£260–320
$380–460 ➢ COYS

A pair of Lucas headlamps,
1 complete with bi-flex-type solenoid dipping assembly, 1 with lens missing, each 10in (25.5cm) diam.
£30–40 / $45–60 ➢ BRIT

A pair of Carl Zeiss electric side lamps, correct etched and ribbed front glasses, reflectors and mounting brackets, polished brass finish.
£700–800 / $1,000–1,150 ➢ Bon

◄ **A pair of Stephen Grebel spot lamps,** completely restored, finished in original old-style nickel plating, with adjusting handles, ball-and-socket swivel mounts, armoured-cable wiring, 1920s–1930s, 10in (25.5cm) long.
£1,900–2,400
$2,750–3,500 ♪ Bon

A Stephen Grebel electric spot lamp, straw-coloured nickel plated finish, correct single-arm swivel mounting, Grebel etched front glass, oval name plate on top, late 1920s.
£950–1,150 / $1,350–1,650 ♪ Bon

► **A pair of Joseph Lucas short trumpet horns,** restored, black japanned bodies, chromium plated caps and trumpets, each retaining fly gauze.
£500–600
$720–870 ♪ Bon

Mascots

A brass combination badge and mascot, by Automobile Club Nord-France, spoked wheel device with red-enamelled ACNF entwined logo back and front, French Heraldic Cockerel at apex, original condition, c1912, 6½in (16.5cm) high, display mounted.
£900–1,000
$1,300–1,500 ♪ Bon

◄ **A bronze Dawn of Flight car mascot,** by Albert Ernest Sanchez, depicting a large baby chicken holding back a snail, representing the advance of powered flight over pioneer motoring, good dark patina, signed on the base by artist and foundry, display mounted, 1 of only 2 known to exist, c1913, 6in (15cm) high.
£2,250–2,750
$3,300–4,000 ♪ Bon

A hollow cast nickel-silver-bronze Mr Bibendum mascot, correct factory moulded markings, signed beneath the base, c1916, 4¾in (12cm) high.
£2,500–2,750
$3,600–4,000 ♪ Bon

A heavy bronze racing driver mascot, by Bocazzi, signed on the back, original mounting stud, excellent unrubbed condition, c1920, 3¼in (8.5cm) high.
£1,400–1,600
$2,000–2,300 ♪ Bon

Cross Reference
See Colour Review
(page 277–278)

◄ **A brass Old Bill car mascot,** by Bruce Bairnsfather, depicting a jovial WWI veteran wearing a scarf and helmet, original mounting stud, very good condition, c1918.
£180–220
$260–320 ♪ Bon

A nickel plated brass Joan of Arc mascot, by Real Del Sarte, signed by the foundry Susse Frères, Paris, 1916, 7¼in (18.5cm) high.
£900–1,000
$1,300–1,500 ♪ Bon

A Pegasus on Ball car mascot, Pegase, by Emile Martin, marked 'E Martin' to ball, 1921, 5¾in (14.5cm) high.
£1,200–1,400
$1,750–2,000 ♪ Bon
Created in 1921, this mascot was awarded the Gold award at the 1921 Salon de L'Auto. It was retailed originally by Hermès and appeared in the company's sales brochures and listings of the period.

A nickel-silver-on-bronze alsatian's head mascot, by Devenet, 1920s.
£350–500 /$500–720 ♣ Bon

A nickel plated leaping ram mascot, by Henri Moreau, mounted on a dog-bone-style radiator cap, 1920s, 4½in (11.5cm) high.
£300–350 / $440–500 ♣ Bon

A young girl reading a book mascot, excellent straw-coloured nickel plating, mounted on an internal-threaded radiator cap, 1920s.
£170–200 / $250–300 ♣ Bon

A La Lune qui Rit nickel-silver plated car mascot, by Elie Ottavy, depicting a nude astride a lecherous moon, signed by the artist, dépose stamp, display mounted, 1 of only 3 examples known to exist, 1920, 7½in (19cm) high.
£3,500–4,500 / $5,000–6,500 ♣ Bon

◀ **A bronze elephant with toothache mascot,** good patina, mounted on a radiator cap, 1920s.
£350–400 / $500–580 ♣ Bon

◀ **A brass St Christopher mascot,** by M. Gaumont, depicting the saint with a child traveller on his shoulder, display mounted, 1920s, 7in (18cm) high.
£1,900–2,100
$2,750–3,000 ♣ Bon

◀ **A chrome plated brass winged female mascot,** Egyptienne, circular wood base plinth inscribed 'L. Pramer, Wien IX', 1920s, 5½in (14cm) high.
£400–450 / $580–650 ♣ C

◀ **A cheeky pelican mascot,** by André-Marcel Bouraine, with nickel plated brass body and ivory beak, the base inscribed with the artist's name, foundry socle against feet, 1920s, 6¾in (17cm) high.
£3,000–3,500
$4,400–5,000 ♣ Bon

◀ **A silvered bronze Mephisto car mascot,** by Podiebrad, signature to base, mounted on a radiator cap, c1923, 6in (15cm) high.
£400–450 / $580–650 ♣ Bon

A nickel plated bronze wise owl car mascot, by Georges Lavroff, Marcel Guillemain foundry socle, 1920s, 7¼in (18.5cm) high.
£1,650–1,800
$2,400–2,600 ♣ Bon

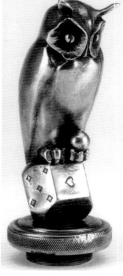

A Felix the Cat mascot, cast in bronze with cold painted black and white enamels, brass base inscribed 'Felix', mounted on a radiator cap, 1920s.
£700–800
$1,000–1,150 ⚘ **Bon**

A silver plated La Lune qui Pleure car mascot, by Elie Ottavy, depicting a nude sitting on a lecherous moon, signed by the artist, dépose stamp, display mounted, 1920, 4½in (11.5cm) high.
£2,800–3,400
$4,000–5,000 ⚘ **Bon**

A silvered bronze scarecrow mascot, Epouvantail, by 'Charles', mounted on a marble base, 1922, 5½in (14cm) high.
£600–650
$870–950 ⚘ **Bon**
This mascot was awarded a certificate of distinction at the 1922 Salon de L'Auto.

A searching Pierrot mascot, by Guiraud Rivière, nickel plated and acid etched finish, original clear glass shade, artist's signature, date and inscription to base, 1922, 6½in (16.5cm) high.
£2,250–2,750
$3,300–4,000 ⚘ **Bon**

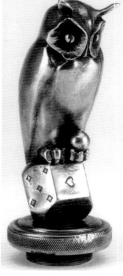

A wise owl mascot, by Bouraine, perched on a gaming dice and holding a roulette ball in his left foot, original nickel-silver plated finish, mounted on a 1920s French radiator cap, 7½in (19cm) high.
£1,300–1,500
$2,000–2,200 ⚘ **Bon**

A Mr Bibendum mascot, Combat L'Obstacle, depicting the Michelin man in a boxing post, correctly fitted to hexagonal radiator cap, finished in natural bronze, c1922, 4¼in (11cm) high.
£1,600–1,800
$2,300–2,600 ⚘ **Bon**

A nickel plated brass mountain goat mascot, by C. Laplagne, signed by the artist, Susse Frères foundry signature to base, 1920s, 4¾in (12cm) high.
£1,100–1,200
$1,600–1,750 ⚘ **Bon**

A Mr Bibendum mascot, in seated pose, 1920s, 4½in (11.5cm) high.
£1,250–1,400
$1,800–2,000 ⚘ **Bon**

A nickel plated bronze Unic Centaure mascot, by Frederick Bazin, mounted on a wooden plinth, c1925, 5¼in (13.5cm) high.
£400–450
$580–650 ⚘ **Bon**

◄ **A nickel plated bronze stork mascot,** by Charles-Joseph Artus, manufactured for Lorraine Dietrich cars, signed on the base, display mounted, mid-1920s, 6¾in (17cm) high.
£500–600 / $720–870 ⚘ **Bon**

A glass falcon mascot, Faucon, by René Lalique, slight amethyst tint, moulded 'R. Lalique France' above base, excellent condition with undamaged beak, 1925, 6in (15cm) high.
£3,000–3,500
$4,400–5,000 ⚘ **Bon**

A seated Egyptian mascot, by Weber & Ruhl, thick nickel plating on bronze, mounted on a radiator cap, thought to be only example in existence, Austrian, c1925, 6½in (16.5cm) high.
£1,700–1,900
$2,450–2,750 ⚘ **Bon**

A clear and frosted glass Coq Nain mascot, by René Lalique, 'R Lalique' and 'France' etched to sides of base, claws intact, slightly rounded beak, slight scratching to feathers, 1926, 8½in (21.5cm) high.
£850–950
$1,250–1,380 ⚖ Bon

A nickel plated brass parrot mascot, Perroquet, by Bourcart, mounted on a radiator cap, mid-1920s, 6in (15cm) high.
£1,000–1,200
$1,500–1,750 ⚖ Bon

◀ **A squirrel mascot,** holding a nut, made for Ford Model T, 1920s, 3½in (9cm) high.
£350–400
$500–580 ⊞ MSMP

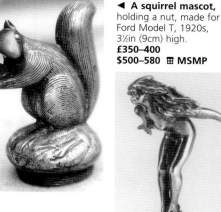

A nickel plated nude female mascot, Dans Le Vent, by Augustine and Emile Lejeune, good patina, display mounted, mid-1920s, 7in (18cm) high.
£1,700–1,900
$2,450–2,750 ⚖ Bon

▶ **A nickel plated Bentley winged 'B' mascot,** by Joseph Fray, 'Jos. Fray Birm' inscribed to the rear of the 'B', unmounted, original condition, late 1920s, 8½in (21.5cm) wide.
£850–950
$1,250–1,380
⚖ Bon

A nickel plated Rolls-Royce 20hp Spirit of Ecstasy mascot, inscribed 'C. Sykes RR Ltd' on the base, original threaded mounting stud, display mounted, c1927, 5in (12.5cm) high.
£250–300
$360–440 ⚖ Bon

A frosted glass peacock's head mascot, Tête de Paon, by René Lalique, with light grey tint, original radiator cap mounting ring, impressed mark 'R. Lalique' and moulded 'France' in the groove mounting, display mounted, original condition, 1928, 7in (18cm) high.
£1,000–1,200
$1,500–1,750 ⚖ Bon

▶ **A satin-finish glass Spirit of the Wind mascot,** by Red Ashay, with original illuminated chrome plated brass mount, 2-pin plug in the rear for connecting to vehicle's power supply, very good condition, c1930, 7½in (19cm) high.
£1,200–1,400
$1,750–2,000
⚖ Bon

◀ **A nickel plated Star Motor Company mascot,** depicting a star and dancing nymph, threaded stud missing, 1928, 4in (10cm) high.
£275–325 / $400–470 ⚖ Bon

▶ **An amethyst tinted glass frog mascot,** Grenouille, by René Lalique, etched signature to the front of the base, moulded 'R Lalique' signature to the rear leg, excellent original condition, 1929.
£11,500–13,500
$16,500–19,500
⚖ Bon

▶ **A chrome plated witch mascot,** broom replaced, dial base missing, c1930, 4in (10cm) high.
£65–85 / $95–125 ⚖ CGC
This mascot originally sat on a circular base that was inscribed with various 'fortune phrases'. When the car was on the move, the witch would rotate in the wind, her broom indicating a specific phrase when she came to rest.

► **A stained satin glass nude mascot,** Chrysis, by René Lalique, flesh tone, stencilled 'R Lalique' on base, 1931, 5in (12.5cm) high.
£3,500–4,000 / $5,000–5,800 ✈ Bon

A chrome plated Bentley winged 'B' mascot, for 3.5 and 4.25 litre cars, cornered shaped base, mounted on a radiator cap, 1930s, 3in (7.5cm) high.
£350–400 / $500–580 ✈ Bon

◄ **A chrome plated brass leaping jaguar mascot,** by Desmo, intended as an accessory for SS cars, base stamped 'Desmo Copyright', 1937, 8¼in (21cm) long.
£225–275 / $325–400 ✈ Bon

An opalescent glass female mascot, by Sabino, unmarked, mounted on a nickel radiator cap, 1930s, 9in (23cm) high.
£1,300–1,400 / $1,900–2,000 ✈ Bon

Models

A 1/4-scale scratchbuilt model of a 1994 Williams F194 Formula 1 racing car, as driven by Damon Hill, resin body, faux rubber tyres and OZ racing wheels, detailed brake disc air intakes, authentic scale decal work, fully replicated cockpit, on a plinth, sponsor's display model.
£1,500–1,800 / $2,200–2,600 ✈ Bon

► **A Ferrari Monoposto model,** by Toschi, finished in red, 22¾in (58cm) long.
£650–750
$950–1,100
✈ COYS

A wind-tunnel model of the Aston Martin Vantage Zagato, only wind-tunnel model used for the vehicle, constructed in wood, finished in grey primer, 43in (109cm) long.
£2,000–2,500 / $3,000–3,600 ✈ Bon

> **Cross Reference**
> See Colour Review (page 199–200)

A Markie 1.5in-gauge handbuilt working model of a showman's engine, spirit fired single-cylinder engine with safety valve escape, steam whistle and drip-feed oiler, copper boiler tested to 100psi, Stephenson's link steering, cast straked wheels with rubber tyres, manual spirit feed supply, hand-operated water pump system, handbrake, gears, sight glass water feed, pressure gauge, forward/reverse control, finished in maroon, removable bowed roof, 22in (56cm) long.
£1,300–1,700 / $2,000–2,450 ✈ Bon

A collection of five clockwork model cars, a Mercedes-Benz Streamliner, make unknown, a Mercedes-Benz monoposto racing car, an Austin-Healey and a BMW by Schuco, and a Porsche 356 coupé by Sixmobil.
£250–350 / $360–500 ✈ COYS

A 1/12-scale silver plated ceramic model of a Porsche 356 coupé, excellent condition.
£4,500–5,500 / $6,500–8,000 ✗ C

A 1/43-scale model of a 1992 BMW E30 racing saloon, by Minichamps.
£90–110 / $130–160 ⊞ DRAK

A 1.5in-gauge steam driven model of a traction engine, Stephenson's Link steering, single-cylinder engine with manual oilers to the pistons and drip-feed oiler to the engine, forward, neutral and reverse gearing, manual brake, straked wheels, sight-glass pressure gauge, safety valve, water tap, finished in red, in a wood and glass case, c18in (45.5cm) long.
£1,400–1,800 / $2,000–2,600 ✗ Bon

A one-off scratchbuilt 1/2-scale steel and aluminium model of a Ferrari 156 Sharknose, by Danny Davies, electrically powered, pneumatic tyres, hinged rear engine cover, faux engine hiding battery and electrics, faux sprung front and rear suspension, faux disc brakes and twin exhaust, forward/stop/reverse gear system, manual handbrake, finished in red, carpeted cockpit, padded *faux* leather seat and headrest, signed by the builder, c78in (198.1cm) long.
£1,300–1,500 / $2,000–2,200 ✗ Bon

A 1/18-scale handbuilt white-metal and alloy model of an Auto Union Type D, by CMC, Germany, as driven by Tazio Nuvolari at Donnington in 1938, rubber trimmed hand wired wheels, visible drum brakes, working steering, removable engine and forward compartment body panels, finished in silver, detailed chrome panel ties, exhaust tubes, framed aero screen, wirework radiator grille, fully replicated suspension, reproduced engine, cockpit with detailed fascia and interior, on a black velvet base, mirror-back leaded glass case, incised chromed plaque.
£500–600 / $720–870 ✗ Bon

A 1/18-scale handcast sterling silver model of a Jaguar XJ220, by Theo Fennel, blackened tyres, opening doors, detailed engine under faux glass panel, on a faux ebony plinth.
£2,500–3,000 / $3,600–4,400 ✗ Bon

A tinplate model of an Alfa Romeo P2, by CIJ, Excelsior dampers, spoked wheels, smooth tyres, spare wheel, finished in red, 1930, 20in (51cm) long.
£1,100–1,300 / $1,600–2,000 ✗ G(L)

A 1/16-scale clockwork tinplate model of a Mercedes W196 Grand Prix racing car, by Marklin, solid rubber tyres, working steering and suspension, operable handbrake, pressed upholstery, chrome-edged aero screen, chromed twin exhausts and radiator grille, finished in silver, Fangio 'signature' to the bonnet, boxed with key.
£160–200 / $230–300 ✗ Bon

Petrol Pumps & Globes

◀ **A Bowser petrol pump,** repainted in Shell livery, replica Sealed Shell globe, 1920s, 96¾in (246cm) high.
£600–700
$870–1,000 ⚲ Bon

▶ **A Regent Benzole Mixture pump lever,** 1920s, 7in (18cm) wide.
£80–100
$115–145 ⊞ MSMP

◀ **A set of 3 oil pump globes,** Duckham's NOL E.P. 140 Transmission Oil, Gargoyle Mobiloil A, Morrisol Sirrom (Regd.) Brand Engine Oil, 1933, 7½in (19cm) high.
£250–300
$360–440 each ⊞ MSMP

A White Eagle Gasoline glass pump globe, American, 21¼in (54cm) high.
£700–800
$1,000–1,200 ⚲ Bon

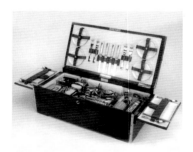

A pair of Price's Motor Oil pump globes, 1935, each 7⅛in (19cm) high.
£300–350
$440–500 each ⊞ MSMP

An Esso Extra pump globe, 1950, 20in (51cm) wide.
£125–150 / $180–220 ⊞ MSMP

A Pink Paraffin pump globe, 1960s.
£50–70 / $75–100 ⚲ CGC

Picnic Sets, Vanity Cases & Travel Goods

A Drew & Sons combination 4-person picnic set and games table, fully white lined interior, kettle with correct burner and stand, oil container, saucepan with raffia covered handle, fine-weave wicker covered glass drinks bottle, Thermos flask, 4 stacking nickel tumblers, fine china cups with gilt decoration, ceramic butter jar, spirit flask, saucers and cutlery, serving trays and spoons, top opens to reveal green baize card table, on 2 hinged legs, c1910.
£13,000–15,000
$18,750–21,750 ⚲ Bon

A Drew & Sons 6-person leather-cased picnic set, ornate kettle and burner, fine woven raffia covered drinking flasks, 6 glasses, 6 china cups, saucers, plates and side plates, Thermos Autotherm food container, sandwich boxes and food boxes, fully fitted cutlery set, original Drew vesta case, preserves and butter ceramic jars, milk bottles, condiment bottles, original leather straps, strong brass catches, brass lock, 1918.
£1,500–1,800 / $2,200–2,600 ⚲ Bon

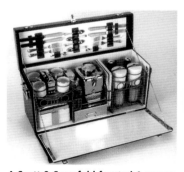

A Scott & Sons fold-fronted 4-person picnic set, rectangular kettle and burner within ornate fretwork stand, full wicker framework, 2 drinks bottles with fine openweave coverings, 4 stacking glasses, 4 white bone china cups and saucers, ceramic-based sandwich box, ceramic butter and preserves jars, milk bottle, oil container, cutlery, 2 condiment bottles, 4 gilt-edged rectangular enamel serving plates, food storage box, in a black case with brass central lock, 2 catches and brass carrying handles, c1914.
£2,500–3,000 / $3,600–4,400 ⚲ Bon

A Henckels 4-person travelling cocktail set, nickel plated cylinder, shaker lid unclips to reveal 4 stacking tumblers, lemon squeezer, 3 triangular glass spirit bottles each with nickel lid and funnel, early 1930s, 11in (28cm) high.
£500–600 / $720–870 ⚹ Bon

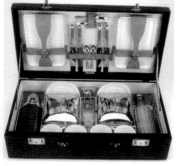

A Drew & Sons 4-person suitcase-style picnic set, raffia covered wire support holding twin ceramic Drew marked sandwich containers with nickel plated lids, raffia covered drinks bottle, leather covered Thermos flask, heavy glass milk bottle, rectangular plates, cutlery, Drew nameplate, complete, 1920s, 20in (51cm) wide.
£900–1,000 / $1,300–1,500 ⚹ Bon

Miller's is a price GUIDE not a price LIST

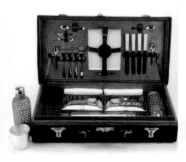

An Asprey 4-person suitcase-style picnic set, honey leather-coloured and wooden lined interior, enamel lined sandwich boxes, 2 open-weave raffia covered drinks bottles, 4 stacking metal tumblers and leather covered Thermos drinks flask, full cutlery set, enamel plates with gilt edges, corkscrew, Asprey gold tooling to the lid and body of the case, central brass lock, black leatherette covering, 1905.
£1,200–1,400 / $1,750–2,000 ⚹ Bon

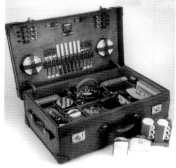

A Drew & Sons Le Grand 6-person picnic set, ceramic-based sandwich boxes, food boxes, fine china stacking cups, saucers, preserves and butter pots, twin condiment bottles, enamel plates, glasses, hidden compartment with food boxes, in a stout brown leather suitcase, 30in (76cm) wide.
£2,400–2,800 / $3,500–4,000 ⚹ Bon

A Drew & Sons 2-person wicker-cased picnic set, Thermos flask, raffia covered drinks bottle, 2 china cups and saucers, oblong plates held in lid, sandwich box, glasses, preserves jar, condiment bottles, knives and forks, wicker in excellent condition, original leather strap, 13in (33cm) wide.
£600–700 / $870–1,000 ⚹ Bon

A Drew & Sons 6-person picnic set, large cooked-meat boxes, ceramic-based sandwich box, centrally mounted ornate kettle and burner, Thermos ice flask, cups and saucers with matching china plates, vesta case, set of cutlery, twin raffia covered drinks bottles, ceramic butter jar, in a large brown leather case, brass catches, leather securing straps.
£2,300–2,700 / $3,350–4,000 ⚹ Bon

A Scott & Sons drop-front wicker-cased 6-person picnic set, nickel plated working area, 2 fine-weave wicker covered bottles, central food box, 2 pull-out sandwich boxes, ceramic butter jar, 6 rectangular plates, glasses held in raffia liners, cutlery, corkscrew and bottle opener, 1920s, 23in (58.5cm) wide.
£1,300–1,500 / $2,000–2,200 ⚹ Bon

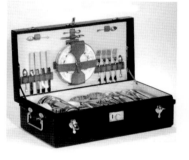

A Coracle for Saks of Fifth Avenue 4-person picnic set, twin vacuum flasks, vacuum flask consommé container, set of 4 Paragon china cups and saucers each with illustrated woodland scene, ceramic-based sandwich box, milk bottle, ceramic butter and preserves jar, set of 4 Paragon picnic-scene plates, cutlery, 1920s.
£900–1,100 / $1,300–1,600 ⚹ Bon

A Mappin & Webb gentleman's overnight case, brown watered-silk lined clothes compartment, removable opening tray, silver-topped bottles, boxes, brushes and mirror, jewellery boxes and trays, silver assayed in London 1944, finished in tan leather with chrome plated external fittings, retailer's name embossed in gold on front edge, complete with storm over-cover.
£450–600 / $650–870 ⚹ Bon

Enamel Signs

A double-sided Regent Paraffin enamelled sign, depicting a pump globe, 14 x 18in (35.5 x 45.5cm).
£60–70 / $90–100 ✎ CGC

A Ford enamelled sign, 1915.
£375–450 / $560–650 ✎ CGC

A Ferrari enamelled route direction sign, from the 50th Anniversary Rally, 12 x 36in (30.5 x 91.5cm).
£240–280
$350–410 ✎ C

▶ A double-sided AA Garage enamelled hanging sign, enamel and frame in very good condition, 36in (91.5cm) high.
£250–300
$360–440
✎ CGC

An illuminated MG Safety Fast! hanging sign, with red Perspex applied design on a white ground, 14 x 36.5in (35.5 x 92.5cm).
£375–425 / $560–620 ✎ CGC

▶ An illuminated double-sided Alfa Romeo sign, printed and embossed plastic panels within a wall mounting metal frame, 1 panel damaged with loss, 35½in (90cm) diam.
£375–450
$560–650 ✎ Bon

A double-sided Morris Trucks enamelled sign, 1920s.
£750–850
$1,100–1,250 ✎ CGC

A Dundas Garage Morris Cars dealer's enamelled sign, 1920s.
£300–350 / $440–500 ✎ CGC

An original double-sided Maserati Service garage workshop sign, printed Perspex, mounting brackets, 1970s, 39 x 31in (99 x 78.5cm).
£800–1,200 / $1,150–1,750 ✎ C

A Rolls-Royce showroom bevelled-glass sign, with chains, mid-1930s, 9 x 5in (23 x 12.5cm).
£80–100
$115–145 ✎ BRIT

◀ A Wilby AA enamelled road sign, pre-1950, 36in (91.5cm) diam.
£150–170
$220–250 ✎ CGC

▶ A Ride Grappler Tyres enamelled sign, 11 x 14in (28 x 35.5cm).
£35–45 / $50–65 ✎ CGC

An Original Sturmey Archer 3 Speed &
Tricoaster enamelled sign.
£130–150 / $200–220 ⚒ CGC

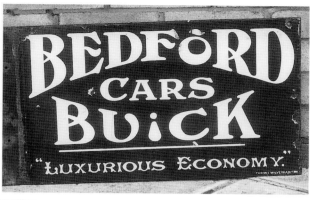

▶ A Bedford-Buick Cars enamelled sign,
1920s, 15 x 24in (38 x 61cm).
£250–300 / $360–440 ⊞ MSMP

A Dunlop Tyre Stock enamelled sign, 1920, 48 x 72in
(122 x 183cm).
£125–150 / $180–220 ⊞ MSMP

A Morris-Commercial Authorised Dealer enamelled
sign, damage to bottom edge, 1930s, 20in (51cm) wide.
£250–300 / $360–440 ⊞ MSMP

◀ A Pratt's Fill Here sign, 1920, 30in (76cm) wide.
£200–250 / $300–360 ⊞ MSMP

◀ An AA and
Royal Scottish
Automobile
Club enamelled
road sign, 1930,
30in (76cm) diam.
£120–130
$175–190
⊞ MSMP

Cross Reference
See Colour Review (page 279–280)

A double-sided Royal Laundry enamelled sign, 1930s,
18 x 30in (45.5 x 76cm).
£250–300 / $360–440 ⊞ MSMP

Watches & Clocks

An Emile Brochon 'La Reine du Jour' mantle clock, depicting the Goddess of Speed seated on and guiding an allegorical 4-wheeled car, mounted with a mechanical pendulum timepiece, the bronzed spelter construction mounted on a decorative marble base, clock dial painted with floral swags and Arabic numerals, French movement by Metris of Rouen, c1900, 19in (48.5cm) high.
£2,750–3,250 / \$4,000–4,700 ⚲ **Bon**

A Jaguar SS combination desk clock and barometer, silver plated and glazed frame, supporting rear leg, winged SS motif applied to top of frame, inscribed at base of frame 'From William Lyons'.
£350–450 / \$500–600 ⚲ **Bon**

A Craftsman stainless-steel driver's watch, silvered dial with Arabic numerals and blued-steel hands, 15-jewel nickel manual wind movement, in a crescent-shaped case with signed snap-on back, 1940s.
£1,600–1,800 / \$2,300–2,600 ⚲ **Bon**
This watch was designed to fit the side of the wrist to enable the wearer to view the time without letting go of the steering wheel.

A Stauffer & Sons gentleman's silver-cased pocket watch, as presented to finishing entrants of the 1903 Gordon Bennett race in Ireland, white dial, Roman numerals, outer seconds ring, centre seconds hand, reverse-sweep hour subsidiary dial, upper and seconds subsidiary dial lower, push-button crown performs winding, stop and return seconds hand and hand adjusting, hinged rear cover engraved 'Automobile Club Gordon Bennett Cup Race Ireland 1903', dust cover inscribed with manufacturer's name and address, small chip to right side of dial, seconds subsidiary hand loose.
£3,750–4,250 / \$5,500–6,000 ⚲ **Bon**

A Zenith chrome plated dashboard timepiece, silvered dial with Arabic numerals, subsidiary seconds and power reserve aperture, 8-day bezel wound movement, in a plated case with a back mounting bracket, Swiss, 1930, 3¾in (9.5cm) diam.
£180–220 / \$260–320 ⚲ **Bon**

A Mido wristwatch, modelled as the radiator of a Bugatti racing car, gold-cased with applied enamelled badge motif with initials 'EB', machine milled winder and time-adjust button, replacement lens to front, Continental markings, stamped to reverse, numbered 220142 to rear casing, leather strap with gold buckle, French, c1930.
£12,000–13,000
£17,500–19,000 ⚲ **C**

A chrome-cased Fiat driver's watch, silvered cross-hatched dial with raised gilt Arabic numerals, subsidiary seconds, manual wind movement, in a chrome polished case with hinged back, Swiss, 1930s.
£600–700 / \$870–1,000 ⚲ **Bon**

A Heuer twin-dial dashboard time-piece, Master Time with centre seconds, 8-day watch with revolving bezel and Arabic and baton numerals, Monte Carlo with register with digital jumping hour, large hand showing 60 minutes and small showing seconds, stop/start winding crown with return to zero by push button and revolving bezel, 1970s.
£1,300–1,400 / \$1,900–2,000 ⚲ **Bon**

◄ **A Lemania chrome plated 1/100th of a second stop watch,** white dial marked 1–3 seconds and subsidiary for 1–60 seconds recording, sweep return twin hands, frosted gilt movement signed Lemania, in a polished case with hinged back, 1960, 2½in (6.5cm) diam..
£140–160 / \$200–230 ⚲ **Bon**

Books

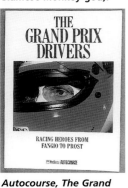

Bira, *Bits and Pieces*, 1950s, 5 x 8in (12.5 x 20.5cm).
£10–15 / $15–20 ⊞ COB
Prince Birabongse of Siam, widely known simply as 'Bira', had a successful racing career in Europe during the 1930s, late 1940s and into the 1950s. Although he drove a variety of cars, he achieved his most notable victories at the wheels of ERAs, at one time owning three of them, named 'Romulus', 'Remus' and 'Hamman' (the last after the Siamese monkey-god).

***Ferrari Yearbook 1960*,** multi-coloured covers, preface by Enzo Ferrari, good clean condition.
£150–180 / $220–260 ↗ Bon

Denis Jenkinson, *A Story of Formula 1*, 1960.
£20–25 / $30–35 ⊞ GPCC

***Ferrari Yearbook 1965*,** green covers, preface by Enzo Ferrari, very good condition.
£150–180 $220–260 ↗ Bon

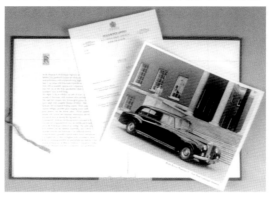

◀ ***The Rolls-Royce Phantom V*,** covering the 1961 listed car, beige and blue hardbound cover, fly leaf with text recto, with a folded flap pocket containing chassis and coachbuilding plans for the James Young and Park Ward 7 passenger limousines together with the James Young touring limousine, 2 monochrome photographs of the Park Ward car and a July 1961 price list, excellent condition, retains ribbon ties and delivery envelope.
£275–325 / $400–470 ↗ Bon

***Autocourse, The Grand Prix Drivers – Racing Heroes from Fangio to Prost*,** signed by Sir Jack Brabham and Jody Scheckter, 1987.
£75–85 / $110–125 ⊞ GPCC

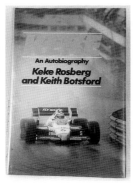

Keke Rosberg and Keith Botsford, *Keke*, an autobiography, 1985.
£55–60 / $80–90 ⊞ GPCC

David Hayhoe and David Holland, *Grand Prix Data Book*, mint condition, 1995.
£25–30 / $35–45 ⊞ GPCC

Christopher Hilton, *Mika Hakkinen Doing What Comes Naturally*, signed by Hakkinen and Hilton, 1997, 9¼ x 6½ (23.5 x 16.5cm).
£35–40 / $50–60 ⊞ GPCC

Motor Racing Memorabilia

A Chevrolet Winston cup display race engine, prepared by Bill Davis Racing.
£3,250–3,750 / $4,700–5,500 ✎ BJ

A Momo steering wheel, used by Ayrton Senna in the 1986 Spanish Grand Prix, framed and glazed, presented in a display case with a John Player Special 100th-pole-position watch, awarded to the mechanics after the qualifying session.
£4,500–5,500 / $6,500–8,000 ✎ Bon

A Fiat wall plaque, celebrating the 1922 French Grand Prix, the winning Fiat and its driver Nazzaro, enclosed by a winner's laurel, 42in (106.5cm) diam.
£180–220 / $260–320 ✎ Bon

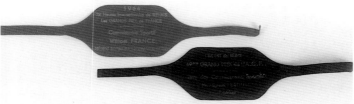

A pair of officials' arm bands, 1964 French Grand Prix, 49th Grand Prix de L'ACF, 4 x 17in (10 x 43cm).
£27–35 / $45–50 ⊞ LE

A 1965 Indianapolis 500 race programme, signed by race winner Jim Clark.
£650–750 / $950–1,100 ✎ CGC

A bronze bust of Ayrton Senna, by Sean Rice, signed, c1994, 19in (48.5cm) high.
£3,250–3,750 / $4,700–5,500 ⊞ SPA

◄ **A Fiat wall plaque,** celebrating the 1922 French Grand Prix, the winning Fiat and its driver Nazzaro, enclosed by a winner's laurel, 42in (106.5cm) diam.
£180–220 / $260–320 ✎ Bon

A set of 3 1949 race programmes, British Grand Prix at Silverstone on 14th May, Goodwood Easter Monday meeting on 18th April, Goodwood BARC meeting on 17th September.
£35–40 / $50–60 ✎ CGC

A 1973 Monaco race programme, signed by Giles Villeneuve and many other drivers, framed.
£750–850 / $1,100–1,250 ⊞ GPT

A Ferrari wall plaque, celebrating Phil Hill's win at Monza in 1961, 42in (106.5cm) diam.
£1,200–1,400 / $1,750–2,000 ✎ Bon

LOCATE THE SOURCE
The source of each illustration in Miller's can be found by checking the code letters below each caption with the Key to Illustrations, pages 332–333.

▶ **Woodcote Grandstand and Car Park Passes,** 1971, 5 x 6in (12.5 x 15cm).
£8–12 / $12–18 ⊞ LE

Race Suits & Helmets

A race suit, helmet, gloves and boots, as worn by Nigel Mansell while driving for Ferrari.
£3,500–4,000
$5,000–5,800 ⚘ BJ

A race suit, helmet, gloves and boots, as worn by Damon Hill.
£1,200–1,400
$1,750–2,000 ⚘ BJ

A 1960s Everoak white helmet, with peak and visor, signed by David Coulthard, Rubens Barrichello, Michele Alboreto, Mika Salo, René Arnoux, Johnny Servoz-Gavin, Jackie Ickx, Emerson Fittipaldi, Hans Stuck, Patrick Tambay, Marc Surer, Martin Donnelly, Roger Ward, Jochen Mass, Jack Brabham, Tony Brooks, John Watson and Jackie Oliver.
£475–575
$690–850 ⚘ Bon

A Bell helmet, worn by Jody Scheckter in 1979, won in a *Daily Express* competition in 1980, accompanied by various letters of provenance.
£5,000–6,000
$7,250–8,700 ⚘ Bon

A Simpson Bandit helmet, worn by Elio de Angelis, given by him to Lotus team manager Peter Warr during 1982–83 season.
£3,500–4,000
$5,000–5,800 ⚘ Bon

◄ **A GPA helmet,** worn by Derek Warwick during his 1983 season with Toleman, complete with radio system.
£900–1,100
$1,300–1,500 ⚘ Bon

An F1 GPA helmet, worn by Nelson Piquet during his 1983–84 season with Brabham, with full radio system and clear visor.
£2,200–2,600
$3,200–3,800 ⚘ Bon

A Simpson helmet, worn by Eddie Cheever while driving with the Target/Chip Ganassi CART team in 1990.
£750–1,000
$1,100–1,500 ⚘ Bon

▶ **A Sparco race suit,** worn by Michele Alboreto in the 1986 Monaco Grand Prix, triple-layer Nomex specification, applied sponsors' logos, embroidered name to left breast.
£1,200–1,500
$1,750–2,150 ⚘ C

◄ **A Bieffe race helmet,** worn by Eddie Irvine during the 1996 season, autographed, inscribed 'Estoril and Suzuka '96', with original soft cloth protective helmet bag.
£1,800–2,200
$2,600–3,200 ⚘ C

Photographs

A signed photograph of John Surtees, in a 1.5 litre Ferrari, framed and glazed, 16 x 14½in (40.5 x 37cm).
£160–180 / $230–260 ⚒ **Bon**

A signed photograph of Richie Ginther, showing the driver getting out of his BRM, signed 'With best wishes Richie Ginther', framed and glazed, 16 x 14½in (40.5 x 37cm).
£100–120 / $145–175 ⚒ **Bon**

An original postcard of Hans Stuck, driving the 2 litre V8 Kuchen-engined AFM, his achievements listed on the reverse, a total of 403 1st prizes and records, 1950s.
£120–140 / $175–200 ⚒ **Bon**

An original photograph of Herman Lang, in the Mercedes W125 leading the early stages of the 1937 German Grand Prix at the Nürburgring, framed and glazed, 11 x 7½in (28 x 19cm).
£600–800 / $870–1,150 ⚒ **Bon**

A signed photograph of Whitney Straight, at the wheel of his Duesenburg at Brooklands, signed 'To Jack with best wishes from Whitney Straight', together with a page from *The Illustrated Sporting and Dramatic News*, 13th May 1933, 8 x 10in (20.5 x 25.5cm).
£80–120 / $115–175 ⚒ **Bon**

▶ **A photograph of Tazio Nuvolari,** driving his Auto Union at the Swiss Grand Prix, Bremgarten circuit, Bern, 1938, signed by the photographer Louis Klemantaski, framed, mounted and glazed, 22 x 18in (56 x 46cm).
£400–500 / $580–720 ⚒ **Bon**

◀ **A set of 14 photographs featuring Graham Hill,** from Hill's own collection, 1960s–70s.
£50–80
$75–115 ⚒ **BRIT**

A signed photograph of Juan Manuel Fangio, mounted and framed.
£300–350 / $440–500 ⚒ **Bon**

Trophies

◀ **A twin-handled cup trophy,** awarded to Jochen Rindt, inscribed 'Fur die Verdiente Eines Wahlosterreichers um Osterreich, November 1966'.
£700–900
$1,000–1,300
⚒ Bon

A sterling silver trophy, by Buccelati, modelled as a stylized Shell Oils logo, with inscription 'Raduno Internazionale Madonnina Dei Centauri Castellazzo Alessandria – Italia, 20/21 Luglio 1957', mounted on a 3-step marble base, 14¼in (36cm) high.
£3,000–4,000 / $4,400–5,800 ⚒ **Bon**

A silver plated Coupe des Alpes trophy, awarded to G.A. Duff and Frazer Nash, inscribed 'XIV Rallye International des Alpes', mounted on wood, 7¼in (18.5cm) high.
£400–500 / $580–720 ⚒ Bon

◀ **A signpost trials trophy,** 1920s, 6in (15cm) high.
£100–130
$145–190
⊞ MSMP

The 24 Heures du Mans 9th Grand Prix d'Endurance 1st in Class Trophy, by Ciere Perdue, awarded to Aston Martin for gaining 1st place in the 1101–1500cc category at the 1931 event, signed cast-bronze sculpture of the figure of Victory standing on a stylised rock formation, mounted on a mahogany base, marks for Suisse Frères Paris, founders stamp, 30in (76cm) high.
£18,000–20,000
$26,000–29,000 ⚒ **Bon**
The 1496cc Aston Martin, driven by Bertelli and Harvey, covered a total of 1,420 miles at an average speed of 59mph to take the First in Class trophy.

The Rudge Cup – Coupe Biennale 1931–32, awarded to Aston Martin for consecutive achievements at Le Mans in 1931 and 1932, patinated bronze trophy with octagonal cup bearing tablet, with high-relief motor racing scenes to each face, faceted central column embossed with figures of Victory, supported by a square marble base with presentation inscription 'VII Coupe Biennale 1931–1932 Offerte par L'Automobile Club de L'Ouest, A la Société Des Automobiles Aston Martin', marks for Delannoy and Arthus Bertrand, 15¾in (40cm) high.
£20,000–23,000
$29,000–33,000 ⚒ Bon
This trophy was awarded to Bertelli in 1932, after having qualified in 1931 for arriving fifth overall, first in the 1101–1500cc class and consequently fifth in the Rudge Cup, partnered by Maurice Harvey, then in 1932 partnered by Patrick Driscoll, achieving seventh overall and second in class after covering 1,409miles at an average speed of 58.09mph, resulting in the highest index for that year. Aston Martin won the Rudge Cup three times out of a total of 15 competitions, making it the most successful team in the history of this famous series of trophies. The trophy was affectionately referred to by the Bertelli family as the 'bird bath' and was used by them as a fruit bowl.

A Lagonda Car Club tankard trophy, pewter, 5in (12.5cm) high.
£40–50 / $60–75 ⊞ DRJ

◀ **A silver trophy,** awarded to G. A. Duff, inscribed 'Ente Provinciale Per Il Turismo, Milano', mounted on wood, 1940s, 6¾in (17cm) high.
£80–100 / $115–145 ⚒ Bon

Key to Illustrations

Each illustration and descriptive caption is accompanied by a letter code. By referring to the following list of Auctioneers (denoted by *), dealers (•), Clubs, Museums and Trusts (§), the source of any item may be immediately determined. Inclusion in this edition no way constitutes or implies a contract or binding offer on the part of any of our contributors to supply or sell the goods illustrated, or similar articles, at the prices stated. Advertisers in this year's directory are denoted by †.
If you require a valuation, it is advisable to check whether the dealer or specialist will carry out this service and if there is a charge. Please mention *Miller's* when making an enquiry. A valuation by telephone is not possible. Most dealers are willing to help you with your enquiry; however, they are very busy people and consideration of the above points would be welcomed.

AMA • Amazon Cars, Top Road, Wingfield, Suffolk IP21 5QT Tel: 01379 388400 sales@amazoncars.co.uk www.amazoncars.co.uk

AUS § Austin A30–35 Owners Club, Club Secretary Alan Fox, Anna Maria Cottage, Devon Consols, Tavistock, Devon PL19 8PB Tel: 01822 833489 a3035clubsec@lineone.net www.austin-club.com

AVON • Avonvale Classics, Fleet Lane Farm, Bredon, Tewkesbury, Gloucestershire GL20 7EF Tel: 01684 772754 www.avonvale.com

B/Bon *† Bonhams, Montpelier Street, Knightsbridge, London SW7 1HH Tel: 020 7393 3900 www.bonhams.com

BAm § British Ambulance Society, Paul M. Tona, 5 Cormorant Drive, Hythe, Hampshire SO45 3GG Tel: 023 8084 1999

BARO *† Barons, Brooklands House, 33 New Road, Hythe, Southampton, Hampshire SO45 6BN Tel: 023 8084 0081 info@barons-auctions.com www.barons-auctions.com

BC • Beaulieu Garage Ltd, Beaulieu, Brockenhurst, Hampshire SO42 7YE Tel: 01590 612999

BJ *† Barrett-Jackson Auction Company, LLC, 3020 N Scottsdale Road, Scottsdale, Arizona, USA Tel: 480-421-6694 www.barrett-jackson.com

BLE • Ivor Bleaney, PO Box 60, Salisbury, Wiltshire SP5 2DH Tel: 01794 390895

BLM • Bill Little Motorcycles, Oak Farm, Braydon, Swindon, Wiltshire SN5 0AG Tel: 01666 860577 www.classicbikes.glo.cc

BRIT * British Car Auctions Ltd, Classic & Historic Automobile Division, Auction Centre, Blackbushe Airport, Blackwater, Camberley, Surrey GU17 9LG Tel: 01252 878555

C * Christie, Manson & Woods Ltd, The Jack Barclay Showroom, 2–4 Ponton Road, Nine Elms, London SW8 5BA Tel: 020 73892217

CARS •† C.A.R.S. (Classic Automobilia & Regalia Specialists), 4–4a Chapel Terrace Mews, Kemp Town, Brighton, East Sussex BN2 1HU Tel: 01273 60 1960 office 01273 622722 or 07890 836734 cars@kemptown-brighton.freeserve.co.uk www.brmmbrmm.com/barc www.carsofbrighton.com www.brmmbrmm.com/pedalcars www.brooklandsbadges.com www.brooklands-automobilia-regalia-collectors-club.co.uk

CCW •† Car Care Works (Bovingdon) Ltd, Ley Hill Road, Bovingdon, Hemel Hempstead, Hertfordshire HP3 0NW Tel: 01442 833177 www.db7centre.co.uk

CGC *† Cheffins, 8 Hill Street, Saffron Walden, Essex CB10 1JD Tel: 01799 513131 www.cheffins.co.uk

CMC • Classic Motor Cars Ltd, Building 6, Stanmore Industrial Estate, Bridgnorth, Shropshire WV15 5HR Tel: 01746 765804 mail@classic-motor-cars.co.uk

COB • Cobwebs, 78 Northam Road, Southampton, Hampshire SO14 0PB Tel: 023 8022 7458 www.cobwebs.uk.com

COR •† Claremont Corvette, Snodland, Kent ME6 5NA Tel: 01634 244444

COYS * Coys of Kensington, 2/4 Queens Gate Mews, London SW7 5QJ Tel: 020 7584 7444

DOCL § Delorean Owners Club, Hon Sec Mr Chris Parnham, 14 Quarndon Heights, Allestree, Derby DE22 2XN Tel: 01332 230823 chrisparnham@ntlworld.com www.delorean.co.uk

DRAK • John Drake, 5 Fox Field, Everton, Lymington, Hampshire SO41 0LR Tel: 01590 645623

DRJ • The Motorhouse, D. S. & R. G. Johnson, Thorton Hall, Thorton, Buckinghamshire MK17 0HB Tel: 01280 812280

FCO §† Ford Cortina 1600E Owners' Club, Dave Johnson, 16 Woodlands Close, Sarisbury Green, Southampton, Hampshire SO31 7AQ Tel: 01395 276701 davejohnson@ford-cortina-1600e-club.org.uk www.ford-cortina-1600e-club.org.uk

FCO §† Ford Cortina 1600E Owners' Club, 65 Ivydale, Exmouth EX8 4TA Tel: 01395 276701 www.ford-cortina-1600e-club.org.uk

FHD •† F. H. Douglass, 1a South Ealing Road, Ealing, London W5 4OT Tel: 020 8567 0570

FYC § Ford Y&C Model Register, Bob Wilkinson, 9 Brambleside, Thrapston, Northamptonshire NN14 4PY

G(B) * Gorringes Auction Galleries, Terminus Road, Bexhill-on-Sea, East Sussex TN39 3LR Tel: 01424 212994 bexhill@gorringes.co.uk www.gorringes.co.uk

G(L) * Gorringes inc Julian Dawson, 15 North Street, Lewes, East Sussex BN7 2PD Tel: 01273 472503 auctions@gorringes.co.uk www.gorringes co.uk

GIRA • Girauto, Porte d'Orange, 84860 Caderousse, France Tel: 04 90 51 93 72

GO * Goodmans in association with Bonhams, 7 Anderson Street, Double Bay, Sydney NSW 2028, Australia Tel: +61 (0) 9327 7311 info@goodmans.com.au

GPCC • Grand Prix World Book Service, 43 New Barn Lane, Ridgewood, Uckfield, East Sussex TN22 5EL Tel: 01825 764918 dhl@gpworld.fsnet.co.uk www.GrandPrixWorld.co.uk

GPT •† Grand Prix Top Gear, 160 Ashleigh Road, Parkstone, Poole, Dorset BH14 9BY Tel: 01202 710105

GrM • Grundy Mack Classic Cars, Corner Farm, West Napton, Malton, Yorkshire YO17 8JB Tel: 01484 450446 Nick@grundy-mack-classic-cars.co.uk

H&H *† H & H Classic Auctions Ltd, Whitegate Farm, Hatton Lane, Hatton, Warrington, Cheshire WA4 4BZ Tel: 01925 730630 www.classic-auctions.co.uk

HCL • Heritage Classics Motor Company, 8980 Santa Monica Boulevard, West Hollywood, California 90069, USA Tel: 310 657 9699 sales@heritageclassics.com www.heritageclassics.com

HLR § Historic Lotus Register, President Victor Thomas, Badgers Farm, Short Green, Winfarthing, Norfolk IP22 2EE Tel: 01953 860508

HMC • Hallmark Cars, 1 Connaught Avenue, North Chingford, London E4 7AE Tel: 020 8529 7474

HUX • David Huxtable, Sats at Portobello Road, Basement Stall 11/12, 288 Westbourne Grove, London W11 Tel: 07710 132200 david@huxtablesoldadv.demon.co.uk

IMP § Imp Club, PR/Events sec Richard Sozanski, 19 Chesford Grove, Stratford-on-Avon, Warwickshire CV37 9LS Tel: 01789 298093

IMPS § Invicta Military Vehicle Preservation Society, North Thames Branch, Tim Wood, 22 Victoria Avenue, Grays, Essex RM16 2RP www.imps.org.uk www.warandpeace.uk.com

JCC § Jowett Car Club, Mrs Pauline Winteringham, 33 Woodlands Road, Gomersal, Yorkshire BD19 4SF

JUN •† Junktion, The Old Railway Station, New Bolingbroke, Boston, Lincolnshire PE22 7LB Tel: 01205 480068

KHP • Kent High Performance Cars, Unit 1–2 Target Business Centre, Bircholt Road, Parkwood Industrial Estate, Maidstone, Kent ME15 9YY Tel: 01622 663308 www.theferraricentre.co.uk

LE • Laurence Edscer, 91 Sea Road, Carlyon Bay, St. Austell, Cornwall PL25 3SH Tel: 01726 810070 homeusers.prestel.co.uk/edscer

MINI § Mini Cooper Register, Philip Splett, Burtons Farm, Barling Road, Barling Magna, Southend, Essex SS3 0LZ

MSMP • Mike Smith Motoring Past, Chiltern House, Ashendon, Aylesbury, Buckinghamshire HP18 0HB Tel: 01296 651283

MUR • Murray Cards (International) Ltd, 51 Watford Way, Hendon Central, London NW4 3JH Tel: 020 8202 5688 murraycards@ukbusiness.com www.murraycards.com/

MURR • Murrays' Antiques & Collectables, Dorset Tel: 01202 309094

MVT § Military Vehicle Trust, PO Box 6, Fleet, Hampshire GU52 6GE www.mvt.org.uk

N * Neales, 192–194 Mansfield Road, Nottingham NG1 3HU Tel: 0115 962 4141 fineart@neales.co.uk www.neales-auctions.com

NR § Nobel Register, Mike Ayriss, 29 Oak Drive, Syston, Leicester LE7 2PX Tel: 0116 2608221(H) 0116 2601749 (W) michael.ayriss@virgin.net

PC Private Collection

PMo • Planet Motorcycles, 44–45 Tamworth Road, Croydon, Surrey CRO 1XU Tel: 020 86865650

Pou * Poulain Le Fur, Commissaires Priseurs Associes, 20 rue de Provence, 75009 Paris, France Tel: 01 42 46 81 81 mlamoure@poulainlefur.com www.poulainlefur.com

RCC •† Real Car Co Ltd, Snowdonia Business Park, Coed y Parc, Bethesda, Gwynedd LL57 4YS Tel: 01248 602649 mail@realcar.co.uk www.realcar.co.uk

RM * RM Auctions, Inc, 9300 Wilshire Boulevard, Suite 550, Beverley Hills CA 90212, USA Tel: 310 246 9880 www.rmauctions.com

RM * RM Classic Cars, One Classic Car Drive, Ontario NOP 1AO, Canada Tel: 00 519 352 4575 www.rmclassiccars.com

RRM • RR Motor Services Ltd, Bethersden, Ashford, Kent TN26 3DN Tel: 01233 820219

SPA • Sporting Antiques, 10 Union Square, The Pantiles, Tunbridge Wells, Kent TN4 8HE Tel: 01892 522661

SWO * Sworders, 14 Cambridge Road, Stansted Mountfitchet, Essex CM24 8BZ Tel: 01279 817778 www.sworder.co.uk

TEN * Tennants, The Auction Centre, Harmby Road, Leyburn, Yorkshire DL8 5SG Tel: 01969 623780 enquiry@tennants-ltd.co.uk www.tennants.co.uk

TEN * Tennants, 34 Montpellier Parade, Harrogate, Yorkshire HG1 2TG Tel: 01423 531661 enquiry@tennants-ltd.co.uk www.tennants.co.uk

TIHO •† Titty Ho, Grove Street, Raunds, Northamptonshire Tel: 01933 622206

TMC § Triumph Mayflower Club, John Oaker, 19 Broadway North, Walsall, West Midlands WS1 2QG

TPS • Trevor's Pump Shop, 2 Cement Cottages, Station Road, Rainham, Kent ME8 7UF Tel: 01634 361231

TSh * Thimbleby & Shorland, 31 Great Knollys Street, Reading, Berkshire RG1 7HU Tel: 0118 9508611

TUC •† Tuckett Bros, Marstonfields, North Marston, Buckinghamshire MK18 3PG Tel: 01296 670500

UMC •† Unicorn Motor Company, Brian R. Chant M.I.M.I., Station Road, Stalbridge, Dorset DT10 2RH Tel: 01963 363353 www.unicornmotor.com

VEY • Paul Veysey Tel: 01452 790672 www.drivepast.com

VIC •† Vicarys of Battle Ltd, 32 High Street, Battle, East Sussex TN33 0EH Tel: 01424 772425

WbC • Woodbridge Classic Cars, Blomvyle Hall Garage, Easton Road, Hacheston, Suffolk IP13 0DY Tel: 01728 746413 sales@tr6.com www.tr6.com

Glossary

We have attempted to define some of the terms that you will come across in this book. If there are any terms or technical expressions that you would like explained or you feel should be included in future, please let us know.

Aero screen A small, curved windscreen fitted to the scuttle of a sports car in place of the standard full-width screen. Used in competition to reduce wind resistance. Normally fitted in pairs, one each in front of the driver and passenger.

All-weather A term used to describe a vehicle with a more sophisticated folding hood than the normal Cape hood fitted to a touring vehicle. The sides were fitted with metal frames and transparent material, in some cases glass.

Barchetta Italian for 'little boat', an all-enveloping open sports bodywork.

Berline See **Sedanca de Ville**.

Boost The amount of pressure applied by a supercharger or turbocharger.

Boxer Engine configuration with horizontally-opposed cylinders.

Brake A term dating from the days of horse-drawn vehicles. Originally the seating was fore and aft, the passengers facing inwards.

Brake horsepower (bhp) This is the amount of power produced by an engine, measured at the flywheel (See **Horsepower**).

Cabriolet The term Cabriolet applies to a vehicle with a hood that can be closed, folded half-way or folded right back. A Cabriolet can be distinguished from a Landaulette because the front of the hood reaches the top of the windscreen, whereas on a Landaulette, it only covers the rear half of the car.

Chain drive A transmission system in which the wheels are attached to a sprocket, driven by a chain from an engine-powered sprocket, usually on the output side of a gearbox.

Chassis A framework to which the car body, engine, gearbox, and axles are attached.

Chummy An open-top, two-door body style, usually with a single door on each side, two seats in the front and one at the rear.

Cloverleaf A three-seater, open body style, usually with a single door on each side, two seats in the front and one at the rear.

Concours Concours d'Elegance is a competition in which cars are judged by their condition. Concours has become a byword for a vehicle in excellent condition.

Cone clutch A clutch in which both driving and driven faces form a cone.

Connollising Leather treatment produced by British firm Connolly to rejuvenate and restore suppleness to old and dry leather.

Convertible A general term (post-war) for any car with a folding soft top.

Continental A car specifically designed for high-speed touring, usually on the Continent. Rolls-Royce and Bentley almost exclusively used this term during the 1930s and post-WWII.

Coupé In the early Vintage and Edwardian period, Coupé was only applied to what is now termed a Half Limousine or Doctor's Coupé, which was a two-door two-seater. The term is now usually prefixed by Drophead or Fixed-Head.

Cubic capacity The volume of an engine obtained by multiplying the area of the bore by the stroke. Engine capacity is given in cubic centimetres (cc) in Europe and cubic inches (cu.in) in the USA. 1 cubic inch equals 16.38cc (1 litre = 61.02cu.in).

de Ville A style of coachwork in which the driver/chauffeur occupies an open driving position, and the passengers a closed compartment – thus, Coupé de Ville or Sedanca de Ville. In America, these vehicles are known as Town Cars.

Dickey seat A passenger seat, usually for two people, contained in the boot of the car and without a folding hood (the boot lid forms the backrest). See **Rumble seat**.

Doctor's coupé A fixed or drophead coupé without a dickey seat, the passenger seat being slightly staggered back from the driver's to accommodate the famous doctor's bag.

Dog cart A form of horse-drawn vehicle originally designed for transporting beaters and their dogs to a shoot (the dogs were contained in louvred boxes under the seats; the louvres were kept for decoration long after the practice of carrying dogs in this way had ceased).

Dos-à-dos Literally back-to-back, i.e. the passenger seating arrangement.

Double-duck Double-layered fabric used in construction of folding convertible tops.

Drophead coupé Originally a two-door two-seater with a folding roof.

Dry sump A method of lubricating engines in which the oil is contained in a separate reservoir rather than in a sump at the bottom of the cylinder block. Usually, two oil pumps are used, one to remove oil from the engine to the reservoir, the other to pump it back to the engine.

Fender American term used to describe the wing of a car.

F-head An engine design in which the inlet valve is in the cylinder head, while the exhaust valve is in the cylinder block. Also referred to as inlet-over-exhaust.

Fixed-head coupé A coupé with a solid fixed roof.

Golfer's coupé Usually an open two-seater with a square-doored locker behind the driver's seat to accommodate golf clubs.

Hansom As with the famous horse-drawn cab, an enclosed two-seater with the driver out in the elements, either behind or in front of the passenger compartment.

Homologation To qualify for entry into some race series, the rules can require that a minimum number of road-going production versions of the race car are built. These are generally known as 'homologation specials'.

Hood American term used to describe the bonnet of a car.

Horsepower (hp) The unit of measurement of engine power – one horsepower represents the energy expended in raising 33,000lb by one foot in 60 seconds.

Landau An open town carriage for four people with a folding hood at each end, which would meet in the middle when erected.

Landaulette A horse-drawn Landaulette carried two people and was built much like a coupé. The roof line of a Landaulette is always angular, in contrast to a Cabriolet, and the folding hood is very often made of patent leather. A true Landaulette only opens over the rear compartment and not over the front seat at all. (Also Landaulet.)

L-head An engine design in which the inlet and exhaust valves are contained within the cylinder block. *See* **Sidevalve.**

Limousine French in origin and used to describe a closed car equipped with occasional seats and a division between the rear and driver's compartments.

Monobloc engine An engine with all its cylinders cast in a single block.

Monocoque A method of constructing a car without a separate chassis, structural strength being provided by the arrangement of the stressed panels. Most modern, mass-produced cars are built in this way.

Monoposto Single-seater (Italian).

Nitrided Used to describe engine components, particularly crankshafts, that have been specially hardened to withstand the stresses of racing or other high-performance applications.

OHC Overhead camshaft, either single (SOHC) or double (DOHC).

OHV Overhead valves.

Phaeton A term dating back to the days of horse-drawn vehicles and used to describe an open body, sometimes with a dickey or rumble seat for the groom at the rear. It was an owner/driver carriage and designed to be pulled by four horses. A term often misused during the Veteran period, but still in common use, particularly in the USA.

Post Vintage Thoroughbred (PVT) A British term created by the Vintage Sports Car Club (VSCC) to describe selected models made in the vintage tradition between 1931 and 1942.

Roadster A two-seater, open sporting vehicle, the hood of which is removed completely rather than being folded down, as on a drophead coupé. Early versions without side windows.

Roi des Belges A luxurious open touring car with elaborately contoured seat backs, named after King Leopold II of Belgium. The term is sometimes incorrectly used to describe general touring cars.

Rotary engine A unique form of car engine in which the cylinders, pistons and crankshaft of the normal reciprocating engine are replaced by a triangular rotor that rotates about an eccentric shaft within a special waisted chamber. One or more rotor/chamber assemblies may be used. On the whole, the engine has a third of the number of parts of a comparable reciprocating engine. The engine was designed by Dr Felix Wankel and has been used in a range of sports cars by Mazda.

RPM Engine revolutions per minute.

Rumble seat An American term for a folding seat for two passengers, used to increase the carrying capacity of a standard two-passenger car. *See* **Dickey seat.**

Runabout A low-powered, lightweight, open two-seater from the 1900s.

Saloon A two- or four-door car with four or more seats and a fixed roof.

Sedan *See* **Saloon.**

Sedanca de Ville A limousine body with an open driving compartment that can be covered with a folding or sliding roof section, known in America as a Town Car.

Sidevalve Used to describe an engine in which the valves are located in the cylinder block rather than the head.

Sociable A cyclecar term used to describe the side-by-side seating of the driver and passenger.

Spider/Spyder An open two-seater sports car, sometimes a 2+2 (with two small occasional seats behind the two front seats).

Station wagon American term for an estate car.

Supercharger An engine-driven pump for forcing the fuel/air mixture into the cylinders to gain extra power.

Surrey An early 20thC open four-seater with a fringed canopy. A term from the days of horse-drawn vehicles.

Stanhope A single-seat, two-wheeled horse-drawn carriage with a hood. Later, a four-wheeled, two-seater, sometimes with an underfloor engine.

Stroke The distance an engine's piston moves up-and-down within its cylinder. The stroke is invariably measured in millimetres, although in the USA, inches may be used.

Superleggera Italian for 'super lightweight' and used to describe a method of construction devised by Touring of Milan, whereby an aluminium skin was attached to a framework of steel tubes to produce a light, yet strong, structure. One of the best-known proponents of this method was Aston Martin, which employed Superleggera construction in some of its DB series cars.

Tandem A cyclecar term used to describe the fore-and-aft seating of the driver and passenger.

Targa A coupé fitted with a removable central roof section.

Tonneau A rear-entrance tonneau is a four-seater to which access is provided through a centrally-placed rear door. A detachable tonneau meant that the rear seats could be removed to make a two-seater. Today, 'tonneau' usually refers to a waterproof cover that can be fitted over the cockpit of an open car when the roof is detached.

Torpedo An open tourer that has coachwork with an unbroken line from the bonnet to the rear of the body.

Tourer An open four- or five-seater with three or four doors, a folding hood (with or without sidescreens) and seats flush with the body sides. This body style began to appear in about 1910 and, initially, was known as a torpedo (*see above*), but by 1920, the word 'tourer' was being used instead – except in France, where 'torpedo' continued in use until the 1930s.

Turbocharger An exhaust-gas-driven pump for forcing the air/fuel mixture into the engine's cylinders to produce extra power.

Unitary construction Used to describe a vehicle without a separate chassis, structural strength being provided by the arrangement of the stressed panels. *See* **Monocoque.**

Veteran All vehicles manufactured before 31 December 1918; only cars built before 31 March 1904 are eligible for the London to Brighton Commemorative Run.

Victoria Generally an American term for a two- or four-seater with a very large folding hood. If a four-seater, the hood would only cover the rear seats. In some cases, applied to a saloon with a 'bustle' back.

Vintage Any vehicle manufactured between the end of the veteran period and 31 December 1930. *See* **Post Vintage Thoroughbred.**

Vis-à-vis Face-to-face; an open car in which the passengers sit opposite each other.

Voiturette A French term used to describe a very light car, originally coined by Léon Bollée.

Wagonette A large car for six or more passengers, in which the rear seats face each other. Entrance is at the rear, and the vehicle is usually open.

Waxoyled Used to describe a vehicle in which the underside has been treated with Waxoyl, a proprietary oil and wax spray that protects against moisture.

Weymann A system of body construction employing Rexine fabric panels over a Kapok filling to prevent noise and provide insulation.

Wheelbase The distance between the centres of the front and rear wheels of a vehicle.

Directory of Car Clubs

If you would like your Club to be included in next year's directory, or have a change of address or telephone number, please inform us by 31 May 2003.

105E Anglia Owners Club Middlesex Group, 9 Evelyn Avenue, Ruislip, Middlesex HA4 8AR Tel: 01895 672251

1958 Cadillac Owners Association, PO Box 850029, Braintree, Maine, USA Tel: 781 843 4485 coa1958@aol.com www.1958cadillac.com

2CVGB Deux Chevaux Club of GB, PO Box 602, Crick, Northampton NN6 7UW

750 Motor Club Ltd, Worth Farm, Little Horsted, West Sussex TN22 5TT

A C Owners Club, P. S. Tyler, Hopwoods House, Sewards End, Saffron Walden, Essex CB10 2LE

A40 Farina Club, Membership Secretary, 2 Ivy Cottages, Fullers Vale, Headley Down, Bordon, Hampshire GU35 8NR

ABC Owners Club, D. A. Hales, The Hedgerows, Sutton St Nicholas, Hereford HR1 3BU

Alexis Racing and Trials Car Register, Duncan Rabagliati, 4 Wool Road, Wimbledon, London SW20 0HW

Alfa Romeo 1900 Register, Peter Marshall, Mariners, Courtlands Avenue, Esher, Surrey KT10 9HZ

Alfa Romeo Owners Club, Ken Carrington Tel/Fax: 01245 473455

Alfa Romeo Section (VSCC Ltd), Allan & Angela Cherrett, Old Forge, Quarr, Nr Gillingham, Dorset SP8 5PA

Allante Owners' Association, 140 Vintage Way #456, Novato, CA, USA Tel: 415 382 1973 allantefan@aol.com www.allante.com

Allard Owners Club, Miss P. Hulse, 1 Dalmeny Avenue, Tufnell Park, London N7

Alvis Owners Club, 1 Forge Cottages, Little Bayham, Lamberhurst, Kent TN3 8BB Tel: 01892 890043 maldavey@aol.com

Alvis Register, Mr J. Willis, The Vinery, Wanborough Hill, Nr Guildford, Surrey GU3 2JR Tel: 01483 810308

American Auto Club UK, 11 Wych Elm, Colchester, Essex CO2 8PR Tel: 01206 564404

The American Motors Owners Association, Don P. Loper, 1615 Purvis Avenue, Janesville, WI 53545, USA www.amonational.com

Amilcar Salmson Register, R. A. F. King, Apple House, Wildmoor Lane, Sherfield on Lodden, Hampshire RG27 0HA

Antique Automobile Club of America, 501 W. Governor Road, PO Box 417, Hershey, PA 17033, USA www.aaca.org

Armstrong Siddeley Owners Club Ltd, Peter Sheppard, 57 Berberry Close, Bournville, Birmingham, West Midlands B30 1TB

Associated Fords of the Fifties, PO Box 33063, Portland, OR, USA Tel: 503 957 8231 tjrydzew@aol.com www.angelfire.com/or2/AssociatedFords/ind

Association of British Volkswagen Clubs, Dept PC, 76 Eastfield Road, Burnham, Buckinghamshire SL1 7PF

Association of American Car Clubs UK, PO Box 2222, Braintree, Essex CM7 9TW Tel/Fax: 01376 552478

Association of Healey Owners, John Humphreys, 2 Kingsbury's Lane, Ringwood, Hampshire BH24 1EL

Association of Old Vehicle Clubs in Northern Ireland Ltd, Trevor Mitchell (Secretary), 38 Ballymaconnell Road, Bangor, Co Down, Northern Ireland BT20 5PS Tel: 028 9146 7886 secretary@aovc.co.uk www.aovc.co.uk

Association of Singer Car Owners, Anne Page, 39 Oakfield, Rickmansworth, Hertfordshire WD3 2LR Tel: 01923 778575

Aston Martin Owners Club Ltd, Drayton St Leonard, Wallingford, Oxfordshire OX107BG Tel: 01865 400400 hqstaff@amoc.org

ATCO Car Owners Club, 106–114 Shakespeare Street, Southport, Lancashire PR8 5AJ Tel: 01704 501336 atcocar@lawnmowerworld.co.uk www.lawnmowerworld.co.uk

Atlas Register, 38 Ridgeway, Southwell, Nottinghamshire NG25 0DJ

Austin 3 Litre OC, Neil Kidby, 78 Croft Street, Ipswich, Suffolk IP2 8EF

Austin A30–35 Owners Club, Alan Fox (Club Secretary), Anna Maria Cottage, Devon Consols, Tavistock, Devon PL19 8PB Tel: 01822 833489 a3035clubsec@lineone.net www.austin-club.com

Austin Atlantic Owners Club, Lee Marshall (Membership Secretary), Wildwood, 21 Cornflower Close, Stamford, Lincolnshire PE9 2WL

Austin Big 7 Register, R. E. Taylor, 101 Derby Road, Chellaston, Derbyshire DE73 1SB

Austin Cambridge/Westminster Car Club, Arthur Swann, 21 Alexander Terrace, Corsham, Wiltshire SN13 0BW

Austin Counties Car Club, Martin Pickard, 10 George Street, Bedworth, Warwickshire CV12 8EB

Austin Eight Register, Ian Pinniger, 3 La Grange Martin, St Martin, Jersey, Channel Islands JE3 6JB

Austin Gipsy Register 1958–1968, Mike Gilbert, 24 Green Close, Rixon, Sturminster Newton, Dorset DT10 1BJ

Austin Healey Club, Colleen Holmes, REF MP, 4 Saxby Street, Leicester LE2 0ND Tel: 0116 254411 www.austin-healey-club.com

Austin Healey Club, Mike Ward, Midland Centre, 66 Glascote Lane, Tamworth, Staffordshire B77 2PH Tel/Fax: 01827 260 644 Sam.Ward@UKGateway.net

Austin J40 Pedal Car Club, Mary Rowlands, 21 Forest Close, Lickey End, Bromsgrove, Worcestershire B60 1JU

Austin Maxi Club, Mrs C. J. Jackson, 27 Queen Street, Bardney, Lincolnshire LN3 5XF

Austin Seven Mulliner Register, Mike Tebbett, Little Wyche, Walwyn Road, Upper Colwall, Nr Malvern, Worcestershire WR13 6PL

Austin Seven Van Register 1923–29, NB Baldry, 32 Wentworth Crescent, Maidenhead, Berkshire SL6 4RW

Austin Sheerline & Princess Club, Ian Coombes, 44 Vermeer Crescent, Shoeburyness, Essex S53 9TJ

Austin Swallow Register, G. L. Walker, School House, Rectory Road, Great Haseley, Oxfordshire OX44 7JP

Austin Taxi Club, A. Thomas, 52 Foss Avenue, Waddon, Croydon, Surrey CR0 4EU www.taxiclub.freeserve.co.uk

Austin Ten Drivers Club Ltd, 10–28hp Austin vehicles 1931–1939, Mike Bevan, 98 Heage Road, Ripley, Derbyshire DE5 3GH Tel/Fax: 01773 749891 mike.bevan@btinternet.com www.austintendriversclub.com

Auto Union Register, Kurt Soezen, 25 Rutland Court, London SE5 8EB Tel/Fax: 0044 207 274 6227 kurt.soezen@amserve.net

Az MG Club, PO Box 2468, Phoenix, AZ, USA Tel: 602 439 1142 azmgclub@ten4ten.com www.ten4ten.com/~azmgclub/

Battery Vehicle Society, Keith Roberts, 29 Ambergate Drive, North Pentwyn, Cardiff, Wales CF2 7AX

Bentley Drivers Club, 16 Chearsley Road, Long Crendon, Aylesbury, Buckinghamshire HP18 9AW

Berkeley Enthusiasts Club, Phil James, 55 Main Street, Sutton Bonington, Loughborough, Leicestershire LE12 5PE

Biggin Hill Car Club with XJ Register of JDC, Peter Adams, Jasmine House, Jasmine Grove, London SE20 8JY

BMC J2/152 Register, 10 Sunnyside Cottages, Woodford, Kettering, Northamptonshire NN14 4HX morris.j2@btopenworld.com www.brmmbrmm.com/bmcj21152

BMW Drivers Club, Sue Hicks, Bavaria House, PO Box 8, Dereham, Norfolk NR19 1TF

Bond Owners Club, Stan Cornock, 42 Beaufort Avenue, Hodge Hill, Birmingham, West Midlands B34 6AE

Borgward Drivers Club, Mr D. C. Farr, 19 Highfield Road, Kettering, Northamptonshire NN15 6HR

Brabham Register, Ed Walker, The Old Bull, 5 Woodmancote, Dursley, Gloucestershire GL11 4AF

Bristol Austin Seven Club, 1 Silsbury Hill Cottages, West Kennett, Marlborough, Wiltshire SN8 1QH

Bristol Microcar Club, 123 Queens Road, Bishopsworth, Bristol, Gloucestershire BS13 8QB

Bristol Owners Club, John Emery, Vesutor, Marringdean Road, Billingshurst, West Sussex RH14 9HD

British Ambulance Society, Roger Leonard (General Sec), 21 Victoria Road, Horley, Surrey RH6 9BN

British Ambulance Society, Paul M. Tona, 5 Cormorant Drive, Hythe, Hampshire SO45 3GG Tel: 023 8084 1999

British Automobile Racing Club, Thruxton Circuit, Andover, Hampshire SP11 8PN Tel: 01264 882200 info@barc.net www.barc.net

British Hotchkiss Society, Michael J. Edwards (Hon Sec), Yew Cottage, Old Boars Hill, Oxford OX1 5JJ Tel: 01865 735180 medwards@globalnet.co.uk

British Saab Enthusiasts, Mr M. Hodges, 75 Upper Road, Poole, Dorset BH12 3EN

British Salmson Owners Club, John Maddison, 8 Bartestree Close, Matchborough East, Redditch, Worcestershire B98 0AZ

British Saloon Car Club of Canada, 1404 Baldwin Street, Burlington, Ontario, L7S 1K3, Canada. tipple@procor.com www.geocities.com/MotorCity/7967/

Brough Superior Club, Justin Wand (Secretary), Flint Cottage, St Paul's Walden, Hitchin, Hertfordshire SG4 8ON

BSA Front Wheel Drive Club, Barry Baker (Membership Secretary), 164 Cottimore Lane, Walton-on-Thames, Surrey KT12 2BL

Bugatti Owners Club Ltd, Sue Ward, Prescott Hill, Gotherington, Cheltenham, Gloucestershire GL52 9RD Tel: 01242 673136 club@bugatti.co.uk www.bugatti.co.uk/club

Buick Club of America, PO Box 360775, Columbus, Ohio 43236, USA www.buickclub.org

Buick Club UK, PO Box 2222, Braintree, Essex CM7 9TW

C A Bedford Owners Club, G. W. Seller, 7 Grasmere Road, Benfleet, Essex SS7 3HF

California Sports Car Club, 9534 S. Painter Avenue, Whittier, CA 90605, USA Tel: 562 693 4110 www.calclub.com

Cambridge-Oxford Owners Club, 32 Reservoir Road, Southgate, London N14 4BG

Cape Cod Classics, PO Box 615, South Yarmouth, Massachusetts MA02664-0615, USA Tel: +1 (508) 394 1378

Capri Club International, 18 Arden Business Centre, Arden Road, Alcester B49 6HW

Capri Club International, North London Branch, 12 Chalton Road, Edmonton, London N9 8EG Tel: 020 8364 7845/020 8804 6326

Capri Drivers Association, Mrs Moira Farrelly (Secretary), 9 Lyndhurst Road, Coulsdon, Surrey CR5 3HT

Caprock Classic Car Club, PO Box 53352, Lubbock, Texas, TX 79453-5335, USA Tel: +1 (806) 794 3389 joe.martin@juno.com

Carolina C3 Corvettes, 1501 S. Blount St, Raleigh, NC, USA Tel: 919 836 7604 cwn@nc.rr.com www.c3vettes.com

Central Florida Corvette Association www.cfca.net

Citroen Car Club, PO Box 348, Bromley, Kent BR2 2QT Tel Membership: 01689 853999 General fax/answerphone: 07000 248 258 members@citroencarclub.org.uk www.citroencarclub.org.uk members@citroencarclub.org.uk www.citroencarclub.org.uk

Citroen Traction Owners Club, Peter Riggs, 2 Appleby Gardens, Dunstable, Bedfordshire LU6 3DB

Clan Owners Club, Chris Clay, 48 Valley Road, Littleover, Derbyshire DE23 6HS

The Classic Camper Club, PO Box 3, Amlwch, Anglesey LL68 9ZE Tel/Fax: 01407 832243 Mobile: 07780 618499 Classic.CamperClub@btinternet.com www.ClassicCamperClub.co.uk

The Classic Car Club of America, Inc., 1645 Des Plaines River Road, Suite 7A Des Plaines, IL 60018, USA Tel: 847 390 0443 www.classiccarclub.org

Classic Chevrolet Club, PO Box 2222, Braintree, Essex CM7 9TW

Classic Hearse Register, Paul Harris, 121 St Mary's Crescent, Basildon, Essex, SS13 2AS Tel: 01268 472313

Classic Z Register, Jon Newlyn, 11 Lawday Link, Upper Hale, Farnham, Surrey GU9 0BS

Club Alpine Renault UK Ltd, 1 Bloomfield Close, Wombourne, Wolverhampton, West Midlands WV5 8HQ

Club Lotus, Lotus Lodge, PO Box 8, Dereham, Norfolk NR19 1TF

Club Peugeot UK, Peter Vaughan, 41 Hazelwood Drive, Bourne, Lincolnshire PE10 9SZ

Club Peugeot UK, Club Regs 504 Cab/Coupe, Beacon View, Forester Road, Soberton Heath, Southampton, Hampshire SO32 3QG Tel: 01329 833029

Club Triumph, Derek Pollock, 86 Waggon Road, Hadley Wood, Hertfordshire EN4 0PP Tel: 020 8440 9000 enquiries@club.triumph.org.uk www.triumph.org.uk

Club Triumph Eastern, Mr D. A. Davies, 72 Springwater Road, Eastwood, Leigh-on-Sea, Essex SS9 5BJ

Clyno Club, Swallow Cottage, Langton Farm, Elmesthorpe, Leicestershire LE9 7SE

Commercial Vehicle and Road Transport Club, Steven Wimbush, 8 Tachbrook Road, Uxbridge, Middlesex UB8 2QS

Connaught Register, Duncan Rabagliati, 4 Wool Road, Wimbledon, London SW20 0HW

Contemporary Historical Vehicle Association, PO Box 98, Tecumesh, Kansas, KS 66542-0098, USA Tel: +1 (913) 233 6715 www.classicar.com/clubs/chva/chva.htm

Cortina Mk II Register, Mark Blows, 78 Church Avenue, Broomfield, Chelmsford, Essex CM1 7HA

The Corvair Society of America, PO Box 607, Lemont, IL 60439, USA Tel: 630 257 6530 www.corvair.org

Cougar Club of America, Barrie S. Dixon, 11 Dean Close, Partington, Greater Manchester M31 4BQ

Crayford Convertible Car Club, 58 Geriant Road, Downham, Bromley, Kent BR1 5DX Tel: 020 8461 1805

Crossley Register, Malcolm Jenner, Willow Cottage, Lexham Road, Great Dunham, Kings Lynn, Norfolk PE32 2LS Tel: 01328 701240

DAF Owners Club, S. K. Bidwell (Club Sec), 56 Ridgedale Road, Bolsover, Chesterfield, Derbyshire S44 6TX

Daimler and Lanchester Owners Club, PO Box 276, Sittingbourne, Kent ME9 7GA

Datsun Owners Club, Jon Rodwell, 26 Langton Park, Wroughton, Wiltshire SN4 0QN Tel: 01793 845271 www.datsunworld.com

De Tomaso Drivers Club, Philip Stebbings (Founder & Club Secretary), Flint Barn, Malthouse Lane, Ashington, West Sussex RH20 3BU Tel: 01903 893870 Mobile: 07711 458989

Delage Section of the VSCC Ltd, Peter Jacobs (Secretary), Clouds' Reach, The Scop, Almondsbury, Bristol BS32 4DU

Delahaye Club GB, A. F. Harrison, 34 Marine Parade, Hythe, Kent CT21 6AN

Dellow Register, Douglas Temple Design Group, 4 Roumelia Lane, Bournemouth, Dorset BH5 1EU

Delorean Owners Club, Mr Chris Parnham (Hon Sec), 14 Quarndon Heights, Allestree, Derby DE22 2XN Tel: 01332 230823 chrisparnham@ntlworld.com www.delorean.co.uk

Diva Register, Steve Pethybridge, 8 Wait End Road, Waterlooville, Hampshire PO7 7DD

DKW Owners Club GB, David Simon, Aurelia, Garlogie, Skene, Westhill, Aberdeenshire, Scotland AB32 6RX Tel: 01224 743429

Droop Snoot Group, 41 Horsham Avenue, Finchley, London N12 9BG

Dunsfold Land Rover Trust, Dunsfold, Surrey GU8 4NP Tel: 01483 200058

Dutton Owners Club, Rob Powell, 20 Burford Road, Baswich, Stafford ST17 0BT

Early Ford V8 Club, 12 Fairholme Gardens, Cranham, Upminster, Essex RM14 1HJ Tel: 01708 222729

East Anglia Fighting Group, 206 Colchester Road, Lawford, Nr Manningtree, Essex Tel: Colchester 395177

Elva Owners Club, Roger Dunbar, 8 Liverpool Terrace, Worthing, West Sussex BN11 1TA Tel/Fax: 01903 823710 email: roger.dunbar@elva.com www.elva.com roger.dunbar@elva.com www.elva.com

Enfield & District Veteran Vehicle Trust, Whitewebbs Museum, Whitewebbs Road, Enfield, Middlesex EN2 9HW Tel: 020 8367 1898

ERA Club, Guy Spollon, Arden Grange, Tanworth-in-Arden, Warwickshire B94 5AE

F and FB Victor Owners Club, Wayne Parkhouse, 5 Farnell Road, Staines, Middlesex TW18 4HT

F-Victor Owners Club, Alan Victor Pope, 34 Hawkesbury Drive, Mill Lane, Calcot, Reading, Berkshire RG3 5ZR Tel: 01635 43532

Facel Vega Car Club, Mr M. Green Secretary, 17 Stanley Road, Lymington, Hampshire SO41 3SJ

Fairthorpe Sports Car Club, Tony Hill, 9 Lynhurst Crescent, Uxbridge, Middlesex UB10 9EF

Fallbrook Vintage Car Club, PO Box 714, Fallbrook, CA, USA Tel: 760 451 0896 rover1964@Att.net

Ferrari Club of GB, Betty Mathias, 7 Swan Close, Blake Down, Kidderminster, Worcestershire DY10 3JT

Ferrari Owners Club, Peter Everingham, 35 Market Place, Snettisham, Kings Lynn PE31 7LR

Fiat 130 Owners Club, Michael Reid, 28 Warwick Mansions, Cromwell Crescent, London SW5 9QR

Fiat 500 Club, Janet Westcott Membership sec, 33 Lionel Avenue, Wendover, Aylesbury, Buckinghamshire HP22 6LP Tel: 01296 622880

Fiat Motor Club (GB), Mrs S. Robins (Hon. Membership Sec), 118 Brookland Road, Langport, Somerset TA10 9TH

Fiat Osca Register, Mr M. Elliott, 36 Maypole Drive, Chigwell, Essex IG7 6DE

Fiesta Club of GB, S. Church, 145 Chapel Lane, Farnborough, Hampshire GU14 9BN

Fifty's Automobile Club of America, Bill Schmoll, 1114 Furman Drive, Linwood, New Jersey, NJ 08221, USA Tel: +1 (609) 927 4967

Fire Service Preservation Group, Andrew Scott, 50 Old Slade Lane, Iver, Buckinghamshire SL0 9DR

Five Hundred Owners Club Association, David Docherty, 'Oakley', 68 Upton Park, Chester CH2 1DQ

Ford 105E Owners Club, Sally Harris, 30 Gower Road, Sedgley, Dudley, West Midlands DY3 3PN

Ford Avo Owners Club, D. Hensley, 11 Sycamore Drive, Patchway, Bristol, Gloucestershire BS12 5DH

Ford Capri Enthusiasts Register, Glyn Watson, 7 Louis Avenue, Bury, Lancashire BL9 5EQ www.uk-classic-cars.com/fordcapri.htm

Ford Classic and Capri Owners Club, 1 Verney Close, Covingham, Swindon, Wiltshire SN3 5EF

Ford Corsair Owners Club, Mrs E. Checkley, 4 Bexley Close, Hailsham, East Sussex BN27 1NH Tel: 01323 840655

Ford Cortina 1600E Owners' Club, Dave Johnson, 16 Woodlands Close, Sarisbury Green, Southampton, Hampshire SO31 7AQ Tel: 01395 276701 davejohnson@ford-cortina-1600e-club.org.uk www.ford-cortina-1600e-club.org.uk

Ford Cortina 1600E Owners' Club, 65 Ivydale, Exmouth EX8 4TA Tel: 01395 276701 www.ford-cortina-1600e-club.org.uk

Ford Cortina Owners Club, Mr D. Eastwood Chairman, 52 Woodfield, Bamber Bridge, Preston, Lancashire PR5 8ED Tel: 01772 627004

Ford Escort 1300E Owners Club, Robert Watt, 65 Lindley Road, Walton on Thames, Surrey KT12 3EZ

Ford Executive Owners Register, Maureen Long, 22 Warwick Green, Bulkington, Bedworth, Warwickshire CV12 9RA

Ford GT Owners, c/o Riverside School, Ferry Road, Hullbridge, Hockley, Essex SS5 6ND

Ford Mk II Independent O.C. International, B. & J. Enticknap, 173 Sparrow Farm Drive, Feltham, Middlesex TW14 0DG Tel: 020 8384 3559

Ford Mk IV Zephyr & Zodiac Owners Club, Richard Cordle, 29 Ruskin Drive, Worcester Park, Surrey KT4 8LG Tel: 020 8649 0685

Ford Model "T" Ford Register of GB, Mrs Julia Armer, 3 Strong Close, Keighley, Yorkshire BD21 4JT

Ford Sidevalve Owners Club, Membership Secretary, 30 Earls Close, Bishopstoke, Eastleigh, Hampshire SO50 8HY

Ford Y&C Model Register, Bob Wilkinson, 9 Brambleside, Thrapston, Northamptonshire NN14 4PY

Frazer-Nash Section of the VSCC, Mrs J. Blake, Daisy Head Farm, South Street, Caulcott, Bicester, Oxfordshire OX6 3NE

Friends of The British Commercial Vehicle, c/o BCVM, King Street, Leyland, Preston, Lancashire PR5 1LE

Gay Classic Car Group, Box 5901, London WC1 3XX

The Gentry Register, Barbara Reynolds General secretary, Barn Close Cottage, Cromford Road, Woodlinkin, Nottinghamshire NG16 4HD

Gilbern Owners Club, Alan Smith, Hunters Hill, Church Lane, Peppard Common, Oxon RG9 5JL Tel: 01491 628379

Gordon Keeble Owners Club, Ann Knott, Westminster Road, Helmdon, Brackley, Northamptonshire NN13 5QB Tel: 01280 702311

Great Autos of Yesteryear, PO Box 4, Yorba Linda, California, CA 93666-1314, USA

Guernsey Motorcycle & Car Club, c/o Graham Rumens, Glenesk, Sandy Hook, St Sampsons, Guernsey, Channel Islands GY2 4ER

Gwynne Register, H. K. Good, 9 Lancaster Avenue, Hadley Wood, Barnet, Hertfordshire EN4 0EP

Heinkel Trojan Owners and Enthusiasts Club, Y. Luty, Carisbrooke, Wood End Lane, Fillongley, Coventry, Warwickshire CV7 8DF

Heinz 57 Register, Barry Priestman (Secretary), 58 Geriant Road, Downham, Bromley, Kent BR1 5DX

Hermon Enthusiasts Club, 6 Westleton Way, Felixstowe, Suffolk IP11 8YG

Hillman, Commer & Karrier Club, A. Freakes, Capri House, Walton-on-Thames, Surrey KT12 2LY

Historic Caravan Club, Barbara Bissell (Secretary), 29 Linnet Close, Lodgefield Park, Halesowen, West Midlands B62 8TW www.hcclub.co.uk

Historic Commercial Vehicle Society HCVS, Michael Banfield, Iden Grange, Cranbrook Road, Staplehurst, Kent TN12 0ET Tel: 01580 892929 hcvs@btinternet.com

Historic Grand Prix Cars Association, 106 Gifford Street, London N1 0DF Tel: 020 7607 4887

Historic Lotus Register, Victor Thomas (President), Badgers Farm, Short Green, Winfarthing, Norfolk IP22 2EE Tel: 01953 860508

Historic Rally Car Register RAC, Martin Jubb, 38 Longfield Road, Bristol, Gloucestershire BS7 9AG

Historic Sports Car Club, Cold Harbour, Kington Langley, Wiltshire SN15 5LY

Historic Volkswagen Club, Rod Sleigh, 28 Longnor Road, Brooklands, Telford, Shropshire TF1 3NY

Horseless Carriage Club of America, 128 S. Cypress St, Orange, California, CA93666-1314, USA Tel: +1 (714) 538 HCCA

HRG Association, I. J. Dussek, Churcher, Church Road, Upper Farringdon, Alton, Hampshire GU34 3EG

Humber Register, R. N. Arman, Northbrook Cottage, 175 York Road, Broadstone, Dorset BH18 8ES

Imp Club, Richard Sozanski (PR/Events Sec), 19 Chesford Grove, Stratford-on-Avon, Warwickshire CV37 9LS Tel/Fax: 01789 298093

Invicta Military Vehicle Preservation Society, North Thames Branch, Tim Wood, 22 Victoria Avenue, Grays, Essex RM16 2RP www.imps.org.uk www.warandpeace.uk.com

Isetta Owners Club, 19 Towcester Road, Old Stratford, Milton Keynes, Buckinghamshire MK19 6AH Tel: 01908 569103

Jaguar Car Club, R. Pugh, 19 Eldorado Crescent, Cheltenham, Gloucestershire GL50 2PY

Jaguar Drivers Club, JDC Jaguar House, 18 Stuart Street, Luton, Bedfordshire LU1 2SL

Jaguar Enthusiasts Club, 176 Whittington Way, Pinner, Middlesex HA5 5JY

Jaguar/Daimler Owners Club, 130/132 Bordesley Green, Birmingham, West Midlands B9 4SU

Jensen Owners' Club, Keith Andrews (Membership Secretary), 2 Westgate, Fulshaw Park, Wilmslow, Cheshire SK9 1QQ Tel: 01625 525699 keithoff@virgin.net

Jowett Car Club, Mrs Pauline Winteringham, 33 Woodlands Road, Gomersal, Yorkshire BD19 4SF

JU 250 Register, Stuart Cooke, 34 Thorncliffe Drive, Darwen, Lancashire BB3 3QA

Junior Zagato Register, Kenfield Hall, Petham, Nr Canterbury, Kent CT4 5RN

Jupiter Owners Auto Club, Steve Keil, 16 Empress Avenue, Woodford Green, Essex IG8 9EA

K70 Register, SAE to: Mr Bood, 25 Cedar Grove, Penn Fields, Wolverhampton WV3 7EB Tel: 01902 566623

Karmann Ghia Owners Club, Astrid Kelly (Membership Secretary), 7 Keble Road, Maidenhead, Berkshire SL6 6BB

Kieft Racing and Sports Car Club, Duncan Rabagliati, 4 Wool Road, Wimbledon, London SW20 0HW

Lagonda Club, Colin Bugler (Hon Secretary), Wintney House, London Road, Hartley Wintney, Hook, Hampshire RG27 8RN

Lancia Motor Club, PO Box 51, Wrexham LL11 5ZE Tel: 01270 620072 www.lanciamotorclub.co.uk

Land Rover Register (1947–1951), Membership Secretary, High House, Ladbrooke, Leamington Spa, Warwickshire CV33 0BT

Land Rover Series 3 Owners Club Ltd, 23 Deidre Avenue, Wickford, Essex SS12 0AX Tel: 01268 560818

Land Rover Series One Club, David Bowyer, East Foldhay, Zeal Monachorum, Crediton, Devon EX17 6DH

Land Rover Series Two Club Ltd, Laurence Mitchell Esq, PO Box 251, Barnsley S70 5YN

Landcrab Owners Club International, 5 Rolston Avenue, Huntington, York YO31 9JD

Lea Francis Owners Club, R. Sawers, French's, High Street, Long Wittenham, Abingdon, Oxfordshire OX14 4QQ

Lincoln-Zephyr Owners Club, Colin Spong, 22 New North Road, Hainault, Ilford, Essex IG6 2XG

London Bus Preservation Trust, Cobham Bus Museum, Redhill Road, Cobham, Surrey KT11 1EF Tel: 01932 868665 nashionalbus@btclick.com www.lbpt.org

London Vintage Taxi Association, Steve Dimmock, 51 Ferndale Crescent, Cowley, Uxbridge, Berkshire UB8 2AY

Lotus Cortina Register, Andy Morrell, 64 The Queens Drive, Chorleywood, Rickmansworth, Hertfordshire WD3 2LT Tel: 01923 776219 lotuscortinareg@cs.com

Lotus Drivers Club, Lee Barton, 15 Pleasant Way, Leamington Spa, Warwickshire CV32 5XA Tel: 01926 313514

Lotus Seven Club, PO Box 777, Haywards Heath RH16 2YA Tel: 07000 L7CLUB (572582) www.lotus7club.co.uk

Manta A Series Register, Mark Kinnon, 112 Northwood Avenue, Purley, Surrey CR8 2EQ mkinnon@mantaclub.org www.mantaclub.org

Marcos Owners Club, 62 Culverley Road, Catford, London SE6 2LA

Marendaz Special Car Register, John Shaw, 107 Old Bath Road, Cheltenham, Gloucestershire GL53 7DA

Marina/Ital Drivers' Club, Mr J. G. Lawson, 12 Nithsdale Road, Liverpool, Lancashire L15 5AX

Maserati Club, Michael Miles, The Paddock, Old Salisbury Road, Abbotts Ann, Andover, Hampshire SP11 7NT

Masters Club, Barry Knight, 2 Ranmore Avenue, East Croydon, Surrey CR0 5QA

Matra Enthusiasts Club MEC, 19 Abbotsbury, Orton Goldhay, Peterborough, Cambridgeshire PE2 5PS

The Mechanical Horse Club, The Secretary, 2 The Poplars, Horsham, East Sussex RH13 5RH

Memphis Old Time Car Club, Memphis, TN, USA Tel: 901 685 3275 Email: rchance443@aol.com

Mercedes-Benz Owners Association, Upper Birchetts House, Langton Road, Langton Green, Tunbridge Wells, Kent TN3 0EG info@onpublications.com

The Mercedes-Benz Club, Paddy Long, Whitefriars, Ashton Keynes, Wiltshire SN6 6QR Tel: 07 0718 18868 join@mercedes-benzownersclub.co.uk www.mercedes-benzownersclub.co.uk

Mercedes-Benz Owners Club, Northern Ireland Area, Trevor Mitchell, 38 Ballymaconell Road, Bangor, Co Down, Northern Ireland BT20 5PS Tel: 028 91467886 tmitchell@mercedes-benzownersclub.co.uk

Messerschmitt Owners Club, Mrs Eileen Hallam, Birches, Ashmores Lane, Rusper, West Sussex RH12 4PS

Metropolitan Owners' Club, Nick Savage, The Old Pump House, Nutbourne Common, Pulborough, West Sussex RH20 2HB

MG Car Club Ltd, Kimber House, PO Box 251, Abingdon, Oxon OX14 IFF

MG Owners Club, Octagon House, Swavesey, Cambridgeshire CB4 5QZ Tel: 01954 231125 mginfo@mgownersclub.co.uk www.mgownersclub.co.uk

MG 'Y' Type Register, Mr J. G. Lawson, 12 Nithsdale Road, Liverpool, Lancashire L15 5AX

Midas Owners Club, Steve & Debbie Evans, 8 Mill Road, Kingslands, Holyhead, Anglesey LL65 2TA Tel: 01407 769544 MIDAS.MEMBERS@tinyworld.co.uk

Midget & Sprite Club, Nigel Williams, 15 Foxcote, Kingswood, Bristol, Gloucestershire BS15 2TX

Military Vehicle Trust, PO Box 6, Fleet, Hampshire GU52 6GE www.mvt.org.uk

Mini Cooper Club, Mary Fowler, 59 Giraud Street, Poplar, London E14 6EE

Mini Cooper Register, Philip Splett, Burtons Farm, Barling Road, Barling Magna, Southend, Essex SS3 0LZ

Mini Marcos Owners Club, Roger Garland, 28 Meadow Road, Claines, Worcester WR3 7PP Tel: 01905 458533

Mini Moke Club, Paul Beard, 13 Ashdene Close, Hartlebury, Herefordshire DY11 7TN

Mini Owners Club, 15 Birchwood Road, Lichfield, Staffordshire WS14 9UN

Mini Seven Racing Club, Mick Jackson, 345 Clay Lane, S. Yardley, Birmingham, West Midlands B26 1ES

MK I Consul, Zephyr and Zodiac Club, 180 Gypsy Road, Welling, Kent DA16 1JQ

Mk I Cortina Owners Club, R. J. Raisey, 51 Studley Rise, Trowbridge, Wiltshire BA14 0PD

Ford Mk II Consul, Zephyr and Zodiac Club, Del Rawlins, Bryn Gwyn Farm, Carmel, Cearnafon, Gwynedd LL54 7AP

Mk II Granada Owners Club, Paul Farrer, 58 Jevington Way, Lee, London SE12 9NQ Tel: 020 8857 4356

Model A Ford Club of Great Britain, Mr S. J. Shepherd, 32 Portland Street, Clifton, Bristol, Gloucestershire BS8 4JB

Morgan +4 Club, c/o 11423 Gradwell, Lakewood, CA, USA Tel: 714 270 MOGG elwillburn@excite.com

Morgan Sports Car Club, Carol Kennett, Old Ford Lodge, Ogston, Higham, Derbyshire DE55 6EL

Morgan Three-Wheeler Club Ltd, Dennis Plater (Membership Secretary), Holbrooks, Thoby Lane, Mountnessing, Brentwood, Essex CM15 0TA

Morris 12 Club, D. Hedge, Crossways, Potton Road, Hilton, Huntingdon, Cambridgeshire PE18 9NG

Morris Cowley and Oxford Club, Derek Andrews, 202 Chantry Gardens, Southwick, Trowbridge, Wiltshire BA14 9QX

Morris Marina Owners Club, Nigel Butler, Llys-Aled, 63 Junction Road, Stourbridge, West Midlands DY8 4YJ

Morris Minor Owners Club, Jane White, 127–129 Green Lane, Derby DE1 1RZ

Morris Minor Owners Club, N. Ireland Branch, Mrs Joanne Jeffery (Secretary), 116 Oakdale, Ballygowan, Newtownards, Co Down, Northern Ireland BT23 5TT Tel/Fax: 028 97521370 morris.minor.secretary@aovc.co.uk

Morris Register, Michael Thomas (Secretary), 14 Meadow Rise, Horam, East Sussex TN21 0LZ Tel: 01435 810133 www.morrisregister.co.uk

Moss Owners Club, David Pegler, Pinewood, Weston Lane, Bath, Somerset BA1 4AG

Motorvatin' USA American CC, T. Lynn, PO Box 2222, Braintree, Essex CM7 6TW

Mustang Club of America, 3588 Highway 138, PMB 365, Stockbridge, GA 30281, USA Tel: (770) 477 1965

Naylor Car Club, Mrs F. R. Taylor (Registrar), 21 Anglesey Place, Great Barton, Bury St Edmunds, Suffolk IP31 2TW Tel: 01284 787539 freda.naylorcarclub@btinternet.com www.naylorcarclub.org.uk

Nobel Register, Mike Ayriss, 29 Oak Drive, Syston, Leicester LE7 2PX Tel home: 0116 2608221 Work: 0116 2601749 michael.ayriss@virgin.net

Norfolk Military Vehicle Group, Fakenham Road, Stanhoe, King's Lynn, Norfolk PE31 8PX Tel: 01485 518052

North East Club for Pre War Austins, Tom Gatenby, 9 Townsend Crescent, Morpeth, Northumberland NE61 2XW

North Thames Military Vehicle Preservation Society, 22 Victoria Avenue, Grays, Essex RM16 2RP

Northern California Corvette Association, 119 Marlow Drive, Oakland, CA, USA Tel: 510 562 1025 vette74@pacbell.net www.nccacorvettes.org

Nova Owners Club, Ray Nicholls, 19 Bute Avenue, Hathershaw, Oldham, Lancashire OL8 2AQ

NSU Owners Club, Rosemarie Crowley, 58 Tadorne Road, Tadworth, Surrey KT20 5TF

Old Bean Society, P. P. Cole, 165 Denbigh Drive, Hately Heath, West Bromwich, West Midlands B71 2SP

Opel GT UK Owners Club, Dean Hayes, 11 Thrale Way, Parkwood, Rainham, Kent ME8 9LX

Opel Vauxhall Drivers Club, The Old Mill, Dereham, Norfolk NR20 5RT

Panhard et Levassor Club GB, Martin McLarence, 18 Dovedale Road, Offerton, Stockport, Cheshire SK2 5DY

Panther Enthusiasts Club UK, George Newell (Secretary), 91 Fleet Road, Farnborough, Hampshire GU14 9RE Tel: 01252 540217

Pedal Car Collectors' Club (P.C.C.C.), A. P. Gayler (Secretary), 4/4a Chapel Terrace Mews, Kemp Town, Brighton, East Sussex BN2 1HU Tel/Fax: 01273 601960 www.brmmbrmm.com/pedalcars

Piper (Sports and Racing Car) Club, Clive Davies, Pipers Oak, Lopham Rd, East Harling, Norfolk NR16 2PE

Porsche Club Great Britain, Robin Walker, c/o Cornbury House, Cotswold Business Village, London Road, Moreton-in-Marsh, Gloucestershire GL56 0JQ

Post Office Vehicle Club, John Targett, 3 Tallowood, Lower Charlton, Shepton Mallett, Somerset BA4 5QN Tel: 01749 345494

Post War Thoroughbred Car Club, 87 London Street, Chertsey, Surrey KT16 8AN

Post-Vintage Humber Car Club, Neil Gibbins, 32 Walsh Crescent, New Addington, Croydon, Surrey CR0 0BX

Potteries Vintage and Classic Car Club, B. Theobald, 78 Reeves Avenue, Cross Heath, Newcastle, Staffordshire ST5 9LA

Pre 1940 Triumph Owners Club, Jon Quiney, 2 Duncroft Close, Reigate, Surrey RH2 9DE

Pre 67 Ford Owners Club, Alastair Cuninghame, 13 Drum Brae Gardens, Edinburgh, Scotland EH12 8SY

Pre War Austin Seven Club Ltd, Steven Jones, 1 The Fold, Doncaster Road, Whitley, Nr Goole, E. Yorkshire DN14 0HZ

Pre-50 American Auto Club, Alan Murphy, 41 Eastham Rake, Wirral, Merseyside L62 9AN

Pre-War Austin Seven Club Ltd, Stephen Jones, 1 The Fold, Doncaster Road, Whitley, Nr Goole, Yorkshire DN14 0HZ

Railton Owners Club, Barrie McKenzie, Fairmiles, Barnes Hall Road, Burncross, Sheffield, Yorkshire S35 1RF

Range Rover Register, Chris Tomley, Cwm/Cochen, Bettws, Newtown, Powys, Wales SY16 3LQ

Rapier Register, D. C. H. Williams, Smithy, Tregynon, Newtown, Powys, Wales SY16 3EH

Rear Engine Renault Club, R. Woodall, 346 Crewe Road, Cresty, Crewe, Cheshire CW2 5AD

Register of Unusual Micro-Cars, Jean Hammond, School House Farm, Hawkenbury, Staplehurst, Kent TN12 0EB

Reliant Kitten Register, Brian Marshall, 16 Glendee Gardens, Renfrew PA4 0AL

Reliant Owners Club, Graham Close, 19 Smithey Close, High Green, Sheffield, Yorkshire S30 4FQ

Reliant Sabre and Scimitar Owners Club, PO Box 67, Teddington, Middlesex TW11 8QR Tel: 020 8977 6625 scimitar@scimweb.com

Renault Freres, J. G. Kemsley, Yew Tree House, Jubliee Road, Chelsfield, Kent BR6 7QZ

Renault Owners Club, J. Henderson, 24 Long Meadow, Mansfield Woodhouse, Mansfield, Nottinghamshire NG19 9QW

Riley MC Ltd, J. Hall, Treelands, 127 Penn Road, Wolverhampton WV3 0DU

Riley Register Pre 1940 cars, J. A. Clarke, 56 Cheltenham Road, Bishops Cleeve, Cheltenham, Gloucestershire GL52 8LY

Riley RM Club, Mrs J. Morris, Y Fachell, Ruthin Road, Gwernymynydd, North Wales CH7 5LQ

Ro80 Club GB, Mr Alec Coutts, 46 Molivers Lane, Bromham, Bedfordshire MK43 8LD

Rochdale Owners Club, Alaric Spendlove, 24 North Street, Ashburton, Devon TQ13 7QH www.rochdale-owners-club.com

Rolls-Royce Enthusiasts Club, Peter Baines, The Hunt House, Paulerspury, Northamptonshire NN12 7NA

Ronart Drivers Club, Simon Sutton (Membership Secretary), Orchard Cottage, Allan Lane, Fritchley, Belper, Derbyshire DE56 2FX Tel: 01773 856901

Rover P4 Drivers Guild, Colin Blowers, 32 Arundel Road, Luton, Bedfordshire LU4 8DY

Rover P5 Owners Club, Geoff Moorshead, 13 Glen Avenue, Ashford, Middlesex TW15 2JE Tel/Fax: 01784 258166

Rover P6 Owners Club, M. Jones, 48 Upper Aughton Road, Birkdale, Southport PR8 5NH

Rover Sports Register, Cliff Evans, 8 Hilary Close, Great Boughton, Chester CH3 5QP

Royal Automobile Club, PO Box 700, Bristol, Gloucestershire BS99 1RB Tel: 01454 208000

Saab Enthusiasts Club, PO Box 96, Harrow, Middlesex HA3 7DW Tel: 01249 815792

Saab Owners Club of GB Ltd, John Wood (Membership Secretary), PO Box 900, Durham DH1 2GF Tel: 01923 229945 Membership Hotline: 070 71 71 9000

Scimitar Drivers Club International, Steve Lloyd, 45 Kingshill Park, Dursley, Gloucestershire GL11 4DG

Scootacar Register, Stephen Boyd, Pamanste, 18 Holman Close, Aylsham, Norwich, Norfolk NR11 6DD

Sebring OC, D. Soundy, Hill House, Water Lane, Chelveston, Northamptonshire NN9 6AP

Simca Owners Register, David Chapman, 18 Cavendish Gardens, Redhill, Surrey RH1 4AQ

Singer Owners Club, Martyn Wray (Secretary), 11 Ermine Rise, Great Casterton, Stamford, Lincolnshire PE9 4AJ Tel: 01780 762740 www.singeroc.free-online.co.uk

Small Ford Club, 115 Woodland Gardens, Isleworth, Middlesex TW7 6LU Tel: 020 8568 3227

Solent Austin Seven Club Ltd, F. Claxton, 185 Warsash Road, Warsash, Hampshire SO31 9JE

South Devon Commercial Vehicle Club, Bob Gale, Avonwick Station, Diptford, Totnes, Devon TQ9 7LU

South Hants Model Auto Club, C. Derbyshire, 21 Aintree Road, Calmore, Southampton, Hampshire SO40 2TL

South Wales Austin Seven Club, Mr H. Morgan, 'Glynteg', 90 Ammanford Road, Llandybie, Ammanford, Wales SA18 2JY

Spartan Owners Club, Steve Andrews, 28 Ashford Drive, Ravenhead, Nottinghamshire NG15 9DE

Split Screen Van Club, Mike & Sue Mundy, The Homestead, Valebridge Road, Burgess Hill, West Sussex RH15 0RT Tel: 01444 241407

Sporting Escort Owners Club, 26 Huntingdon Crescent, Off Madresfield Drive, Halesowen, West Midlands B63 3DJ

Stag Owners Club, c/o The Old Rectory, Aslacton, Norfolk NR15 2JN stagmemsec@compuserve.com

Standard Motor Club, Tony Pingriff (Membership Secretary), 57 Main Road, Meriden, Coventry, West Midlands CV7 0LP Tel: 01676 522181 www.standardmotorclub.org.uk

Star, Starling, Stuart and Briton Register, D. E. A. Evans, New Wood Lodge, 2A Hyperion Rd, Stourton, Stourbridge, West Midlands DY7 6SB

Sunbeam Alpine Owners Club, Pauline Leese, 53 Wood Street, Mow Cop, Stoke-on-Trent, Staffordshire ST7 3PF

Sunbeam Rapier Owners Club, Ruth Kingston, Wayside, Depmore Lane, Kingsley, Nr Warrington, Cheshire WA6 6UD

Sunbeam Talbot Alpine Register, Derek Cook (Membership Secretary), 47 Crescent Wood Road, Sydenham, London SE26 6SA

Sunbeam Talbot Darracq Register, R. Lawson, West Emlett Cottage, Black Dog, Crediton, Devon EX17 4QB

Sunbeam Tiger Owners Club, Brian Postle, Beechwood, 8 Villa Real Estate, Consett, Co Durham DH8 6BJ

Swift Club and Swift Register - Coventry built cars 1901–31, John Harrison, 70 Eastwick Drive, Bookham, Leatherhead, Surrey KT23 3NX

Tame Valley Vintage and Classic Car Club, Mrs S. Ogden, 13 Valley New Road, Royton, Oldham, Lancashire OL2 6BP

Tornado Register, Dave Malins, 48 St Monica's Avenue, Luton, Bedfordshire LU3 1PN Tel: 01582 37641

Toyota Enthusiasts Club, c/o Billy Wells (Secretary/Treasurer), 28 Park Road, Feltham, Middlesex TW13 6PW Tel/Fax: 020 8898 0740

TR Drivers Club, Bryan Harber, 19 Irene Road, Orpington, Kent BR6 0HA

TR Register, 1B Hawksworth, Southmead Industrial Park, Didcot, Oxfordshire OX10 7HR Tel: 01235 818866

Trident Car Club, David Rowlinson, 23 Matlock Crescent, Cheam, Sutton, Surrey SM3 9SS Tel: 020 8644 9029

Triumph 2000/2500/2.5 Register, Alan Crussell, 10 Gables Close, Chalfont St Peter, Buckinghamshire SL9 0PR Tel: 01494 582673 t2000register@compuserve.com www.t2000register.org.uk

Triumph Dolomite Club, 39 Mill Lane, Upper Arncott, Bicester, Oxfordshire OX6 0PB Tel: 01869 242847

Triumph Mayflower Club, John Oaker, 19 Broadway North, Walsall, West Midlands WS1 2QG

Triumph Razoredge Owners Club, Stewart Langton, 62 Seaward Avenue, Barton-on-Sea, Hampshire BH25 7HP Tel: 01425 618074

Triumph Roadster Club, J. Cattaway, 59 Cowdray Park Road, Little Common, Bexhill-on-Sea, East Sussex TN39 4EZ

Triumph Spitfire Club, Mr Cor Gent, Anemoon 41, 7483 AC Haaksbergen, The Netherlands

Triumph Sporting Owners Club, G. R. King, 16 Windsor Road, Hazel Grove, Stockport, Cheshire SK7 4SW

Triumph Stag Register, M. Wattam, 18 Hazel Close, Highcliffe, Dorset BH23 4PS

Trojan Owners Club, Derrick Graham (President), Troylands, St Johns, Earlswood Common, Redhill, Surrey RH1 6QF Tel: 01737 763643

Turner Register, Dave Scott, 21 Ellsworth Road, High Wycombe, Buckinghamshire HP11 2TU

TVR Car Club, c/o David Gerald, TVR Sports Cars Tel: 01386 793239

United States Army Vehicle Club, Dave Boocock, 31 Valley View Close, Bogthorn, Oakworth Rd, Keighley, Yorkshire BD22 7LZ

United States Army Vehicle Club, Simon Johnson, 7 Carter Fold, Mellor, Lancashire BB2 7ER

Unloved Soviet Socialist Register, Julian Nowill, Earlsland House, Bradninch, Exeter, Devon EX5 4QP Tel: 01392 881748 julian.nowill@gerrard.com

Vanden Plas Owners Club, Mrs M. Hill (Hon Sec), 33 Rectory Lane, Houghton Conquest, Bedfordshire MK45 3LD

Vanguard 1&2 Owners Club, R. Jones, The Villa, The Down, Alviston, Avon BS12 2TQ Tel: 01454 419232

Vauxhall Cavalier Convertible Club, Ron Goddard, 47 Brooklands Close, Luton, Bedfordshire LU4 9EH

Vauxhall Owners Club, Roy Childers (Membership Secretary), 31 Greenbanks, Melbourn, Nr Royston, Cambridgeshire SG8 6AS

Vauxhall PA/PB/PC/E Owners Club, G. Lonsdale, 77 Pilling Lane, Preesall, Lancashire FY6 0HB Tel: 01253 810866

Vauxhall Viva OC, Adrian Miller, The Thatches, Snetterton North End, Snetterton, Norwich, Norfolk NR16 2LD Tel: 01953 498818 adrian@vivaclub.freeserve.co.uk

Vauxhall VX4/90 Drivers Club(FD/FE 1972–1978), c/o 1 Milverton Drive, Uttoxeter, Staffordshire ST14 7RE

Vectis Historic Vehicle Club, Nigel Offer, 10 Paddock Drive, Bembridge, Isle of Wight PO35 5TL

Ventura County Chevys, PO Box 309, Camarillo, CA 93011, USA Tel: 805 493 2397 www.geocities.com/MotorCity/Downs/4753/ventura.html

Veteran Car Club Of Great Britain, Jessamine Court, 15 High Street, Ashwell, Baldock, Hertfordshire SG7 5NL Tel: 01462 742818

Vintage Austin Register, Frank Smith Hon Sec, The Briars, Four Lane Ends, Oakerthorpe, Alfreton, Derbyshire DE55 7LH Tel: 0773 831646

Vintage Sports-Car Club Ltd, The Secretary, The Old Post Office, West Street, Chipping Norton, Oxon OX7 5EL Tel: 01608 644777 www.vscc.co.uk

Volkswagen '50–67' Transporter Club, Peter Nicholson, 11 Lowton Road, Lytham St Annes, Lancashire FY8 3JD Tel: 01253 720023

Volkswagen Cabriolet Owners Club (GB), Emma Palfreyman Sec, Dishley Mill, Derby Road, Loughborough, Leicestershire LE11 0SF

Volkswagen Owners Club (GB), PO Box 7, Burntwood, Walsall, West Midlands WS7 8SB

Volvo Enthusiasts Club, Kevin Price, 4 Goonbell, St Agnes, Cornwall TR5 0PH

Vulcan Register, D. Hales, The Hedgerows, Sutton St Nicholas, Herefordshire HR1 3BU Tel: 01432 880726

VW Type 3 and 4 Club, Jane Terry, Pear Tree Bungalow, Exted, Elham, Canterbury, Kent CT4 6YG

Wartburg Owners Club, Bernard Trevena, 55 Spiceall Estate, Compton, Guildford, Surrey GU3 1SE Tel: 01483 810493

West Coast Classics, 4606 N.E. 112th Ave, Vancouver, WA, USA Tel: 503 582 1213 Sunchaseme@netscape.net www.webspawner.com/user/westcoastclassics

Wolseley 6/80 and Morris Oxford MO Club, Don Gould, 2 Barleyfield Close, Heighington, Lincoln LN4 1TX Tel: 01652 635138

Wolseley Hornet Special Club, Wolseley Hornet, Sports & Specials, Chris Hyde, Lime Cottage, Orchard Lane, Winterborne Kingston, Dorset DT11 9BF whsc.sec@btinternet.com www.whsc.co.uk

Wolseley Register, M. Stanley (Chairman), 1 Flashgate, Higher Ramsgreave Road, Ramsgreave, Nr Blackburn, Lancashire BB1 9DH

XR Owners Club, PO Box 47, Loughborough, Leicestershire LE11 1XS Tel: 01509 882300 xroc.co.uk

Yankee Jeep Club, 8 Chew Brook Drive, Greenfield, Saddleworth, Lancashire OL3 7PD

Directory of Auctioneers

Auction Team Koln, Postfach 50 11 19, 50971 Koln, Germany Tel: 00 49 0221 38 70 49 auction@breker.com

Barons, Brooklands House, 33 New Road, Hythe, Southampton, Hampshire SO45 6BN Tel: 023 8084 0081 info@barons-auctions.com www.barons-auctions.com

Barrett-Jackson Auction Company, LLC, 3020 N Scottsdale Road, Scottsdale, Arizona, USA Tel: 480-421-6694 www.barrett-jackson.com

Bernaerts, Verlatstraat 18–22, 2000 Antwerpen/Anvers Tel: +32 (0)3 248 19 21 edmond.bernaerts@ping.be www.auction-bernaerts.com

Bonhams, Montpelier Street, Knightsbridge, London SW7 1HH Tel: 020 7393 3900 www.bonhams.com

Brightwells Fine Art, The Fine Art Saleroom, Ryelands Road, Leominster, Herefordshire HR6 8NZ Tel: 01568 611122 fineart@brightwells.com www.brightwells.com

British Car Auctions Ltd, Classic & Historic Automobile Division, Auction Centre, Blackbushe Airport, Blackwater, Camberley, Surrey GU17 9LG Tel: 01252 878555

Butterfields, 220 San Bruno Avenue, San Francisco, CA 94103, USA Tel: 00 1 415 861 7500

Mervyn Carey, Twysden Cottage, Benenden, Cranbrook, Kent TN17 4LD Tel: 01580 240283

Central Motor Auctions Plc, Central House, Pontefract Road, Rothwell, Leeds, Yorkshire LS26 0JE Tel: 0113 282 0707

Cheffins, 8 Hill Street, Saffron Walden, Essex CB10 1JD Tel: 01799 513131 www.cheffins.co.uk

Christie, Manson & Woods Ltd, The Jack Barclay Showroom, 2–4 Ponton Road, Nine Elms, London SW8 5BA Tel: 020 73892217 www.christies.com

Classic Automobile Auctions B. V., Goethestrasse 10, 6000 Frankfurt 1, Germany Tel: 010 49 69 28666/8

Coys of Kensington, 2/4 Queens Gate Mews, London, SW7 5QJ Tel: 020 7584 7444

DDM Auction Rooms, Old Courts Road, Brigg, Lincolnshire, DN20 8JD Tel: 01652 650172

William Doyle Galleries, 175 East 87th Street, New York, NY 10128, USA Tel: 212 427 2730

Evans & Partridge, Agriculture House, High Street, Stockbridge, Hampshire, SO20 6HF Tel: 01264 810702

Thomas Wm Gaze & Son, 10 Market Hill, Diss, Norfolk, IP22 3JZ Tel: 01379 651931 www.twgaze.com

Goodmans in association with Bonhams, 7 Anderson Street, Double Bay, Sydney, NSW 2028, Australia Tel: +61 (0) 9327 7311 info@goodmans.com.au

Greens (UK) Ltd, Worcestershire, WR14 2AY Tel: 01684 575902

H & H Classic Auctions Ltd, Whitegate Farm, Hatton Lane, Hatton, Warrington, Cheshire, WA4 4BZ Tel: 01925 730630 www.classic-auctions.co.uk

Andrew Hartley, Victoria Hall Salerooms, Little Lane, Ilkley, Yorkshire, LS29 8EA Tel: 01943 816363 info@andrewhartleyfinearts.co.uk www.andrewhartleyfinearts.co.uk

Kidson Trigg, Estate Office, Friars Farm, Sevenhampton, Highworth, Swindon, Wiltshire, SN6 7PZ Tel: 01793 861000

Kruse International, PO Box 190, 5400 County Road 11A, Auburn, Indiana 46706, USA Tel: 219 925 5600

Lambert & Foster, 77 Commercial Road, Paddock Wood, Kent, TN12 6DR Tel: 01892 832325

Lawrences Auctioneers, Norfolk House, 80 High Street, Bletchingley, Surrey, RH1 4PA Tel: 01883 743323 www.lawrencesbletchingley.co.uk

Thomas Mawer & Son, Dunston House, Portland Street, Lincoln, LN5 7NN Tel: 01522 524984 mawer.thos@lineone.net

Paul McInnis Inc. Auction Gallery, Route 88, 356 Exeter Road, Hampton Falls, New Hampshire 03844, USA Tel: 010 603 778 8989

Mealy's, Chatsworth Street, Castle Comer, Co Kilkenny, Republic of Ireland Tel: 00 353 56 41229 www.mealys.com

Morphets of Harrogate, 6 Albert Street, Harrogate, Yorkshire, HG1 1JL Tel: 01423 530030

Neales, 192–194 Mansfield Road, Nottingham, NG1 3HU Tel: 0115 962 4141 fineart@neales.co.uk www.neales-auctions.com

John Nicholson, The Auction Rooms, Longfield, Midhurst Road, Fernhurst, Surrey, GU27 3HA Tel: 01428 653727

Onslow's, The Depot, 2 Michael Road, London, SW6 2AD Tel: 020 7371 0505

Palm Springs Auctions Inc., 602 East Sunny Dunes Road, Palm Springs, California 92264, USA Tel: 760 320 3290 www.classic-carauction.com

Palmer Snell, 65 Cheap Street, Sherborne, Dorset, DT9 3BA Tel: 01935 812218

J. R. Parkinson Son & Hamer Auctions, The Auction Rooms, Rochdale Road (Kershaw Street), Bury, Lancashire, BL9 7HH Tel: 0161 761 1612/761 7372

RM Auctions, Inc., 9300 Wilshire Boulevard, Suite 550, Beverley Hills, CA 90212, USA Tel: 310 246 9880 www.rmauctions.com

RM Classic Cars, One Classic Car Drive, Ontario, NOP 1AO, Canada Tel: 00 519 352 4575 www.rmclassiccars.com

Rogers Jones & Co, The Saleroom, 33 Abergele Road, Colwyn Bay, Wales, LL29 7RU Tel: 01492 532176 www.rogersjones.ukauctioneers.com

RTS Auctions Ltd, Unit 1 Alston Road, Hellesden Park Industrial Estate, Norwich, Norfolk, NR6 5OS Tel: 01603 418200

Silver Collector Car Auctions, E204, Spokane, Washington 99207, USA Tel: 0101 509 326 4485

Sloan's Auctioneers & Appraisers, 2516 Ponce de Leon Boulevard, Coral Gables, Florida 33134, USA Tel: 305 447 0757 www.sloansauction.com

Sotheby's, 34–35 New Bond Street, London, W1A 2AA Tel: 020 7293 5000 www.sothebys.com

Sworders, 14 Cambridge Road, Stansted Mountfitchet, Essex, CM24 8BZ Tel: 01279 817778 www.sworder.co.uk

Taylors, Honiton Galleries, 205 High Street, Honiton, Devon, EX14 8LF Tel: 01404 42404

Tennants, 34 Montpellier Parade, Harrogate, Yorkshire, HG1 2TG Tel: 01423 531661 enquiry@tennants-ltd.co.uk www.tennants.co.uk

"The Auction", 3535 Las Vegas Boulevard, South Las Vegas, Nevada 89101, USA Tel: 0101 702 794 3174

Thimbleby & Shorland, 31 Great Knollys Street, Reading, Berkshire RG1 7HU Tel: 0118 9508611

Wellers Auctioneers, 70/70a Guildford Street, Chertsey, Surrey KT16 9BB Tel: 01932 568678

World Classic Auction & Exposition Co, 3600 Blackhawk Plaza Circle, Danville, California 94506, USA

Directory of Museums

Bedfordshire
Shuttleworth Collection, Old Warden Aerodrome, Nr Biggleswade SG18 9EP Tel: 01767 627288 Europe's biggest collection of flying pre-1940 aircraft, also collection of veteran and vintage vehicles including 15 motorcycles.

Stondon Museum, Station Road, Lower Stondon, Henlow SG16 6JN Tel: 01462 850339 Five museum halls with over 320 transport exhibits including Bentleys and over 30 motorcycles.

Cheshire
Mouldsworth Motor Museum, Smithy Lane, Mouldsworth, Chester CH3 8AR Tel: 01928 731781 Collection of over 60 motorcars, motorcycles and early bicycles housed in 1937 art deco building.

Cornwall
Automobilia Motor Museum, The Old Mill, St Stephen, St Austell PL26 7RX Tel: 01726 823092 www.3mc.co.uk/automobilia Over 50 vehicles and associated automobilia. Autojumble and vintage and classic vehicles purchased and for sale. Open daily April, May and October 10am–4pm, closed Saturdays early and late season, June to September 10am–6pm.

Cumbria
Cars of the Stars Motor Museum, Standish Street, Keswick CA12 5LS Tel: 017687 73757 www.members.aol.com/cotsmm World famous museum of vehicles from film and television. Phone for opening times and details of exhibits.

Lakeland Motor Museum, Holker Hall, Cark-in-Cartmel, Grange-over-Sands LA11 7PL Tel: 015395 58328 www.visitcumbria.com/sl/holkmus.htm
Over 150 cars, motorcycles, tractors, cycles and engines plus rare motoring automobilia. Also the Campbell Legend Bluebird Exhibition featuring videos, photographs and scale models of the cars and boats used by Sir Malcolm Campbell and his son Donald Campbell. Open daily 1st April to 31st October 10.30am–4.45pm except Sundays.

Western Lakes Motor Museum, The Maltings, Brewery Lane, Cockermouth Tel: 01900 824448 Located in Jennings Castle Brewery beneath the walls of Cockermouth Castle. Some 45 cars and 17 motorcycles from Vintage to Formula 3.

Derbyshire
The Donington Grand Prix Collection, Donington Park, Castle Donington DE74 2RP Tel: 01332 811027 www.donington.com/donington/museum/
World's largest collection of Grand Prix racing cars, tracing their history from the early 1900s to the present day.

Essex
Castle Point Transport Museum, Castle Point Transport Museum Society, 105 Point Road, Canvey Island SS8 7TP Tel: 01268 684272 Collection of about 35 vehicles spanning the period 1929–72. Open Sunday 10am–5pm.

Gloucestershire
Bristol Industrial Museum, Princes Wharf, City Docks, Bristol BS1 4RN Tel: 0117 925 1470 Railway exhibits, boats, workshops plus lorries and cars made at Bristol.

The Bugatti Trust, Prescott Hill, Gotherington, Cheltenham GL52 4RD Tel: 01242 677201

Cotswold Motoring Museum & Toy Collection, Sherbourne Street, Bourton-on-the-Water, Nr Cheltenham GL54 2BY Tel: 01451 821 255 Largest collection of advertising signs in the world plus toys and about a dozen motorcycles. This is the home of the Brough Superior Company and of "Brum", the small open 1920's car that has a television series.

Greater Manchester
Manchester Museum of Transport, Boyle Street, Cheetham M8 8UW Tel: 0161 205 2122 www.gmts.co.uk Collection of 80 buses and other vehicles. Open Wednesdays, Saturdays, Sundays and Bank Holidays throughout the year 10am–5pm, check for Christmas times.

Hampshire
The National Motor Museum, Brockenhurst, Beaulieu SO42 7ZN Tel: 01590 612345 www.beaulieu.co.uk Collection comprising 250 vehicles from some of the earliest examples of motoring to legendary World Record Breakers like Bluebird and Golden Arrow. Open every day except Christmas Day, May to Sept 10am–6pm, Oct to April 10am–5pm.

Humberside
Bradford Industrial Museum, Moorside Mills, Moorside Road, Bradford BD2 3HP Tel: 01274 631756 General industrial museum including many engineering items, Jowett cars, Panther and Scott motorcycles, a steam roller and Bradford's last tram.

Isle of Man
Manx Motor Museum, Crosby Tel: 01624 851236 History of the motor car illustrated mainly by unusual cars. Open May 21st to Sept 11th 10am–5pm.

Port Erin Motor Museum, High Street, Port Erin Tel: 01624 832964

Kent
Dover Transport Museum, Old Park, Honeywood Road, Whitfield, Nr Dover Tel: 01304 822409/204612 www.stayindover.co.uk/DTM General transport museum with an emphasis on East Kent. More than 30 vehicles and related displays, including a working model tramway and model railway. Open Wednesday to Saturday 1.30pm–5.30pm, Sundays & Bank Holidays 10.30am–5pm April to October.

Historic Vehicles Collection of C. M. Booth, Falstaff Antiques, 63–67 High Street, Rolvenden TN17 4LP Tel: 01580 241234
A private museum consisting mainly of Morgan three-wheelers but also some motorbikes. A most interesting collection plus memorabilia all to be found at the rear of the Antique shop.

Ramsgate Motor Museum, West Cliff Hall, Ramsgate CT11 9JX Tel: 01843 581948 Founded in 1982 and dedicated to the history of motoring, every vehicle is set out in scenes depicting the past.

Lancashire
British Commercial Vehicles Museum, King Street, Leyland, Preston PR5 1LE Tel: 01772 451011

The British Lawnmower Museum, 106–114 Shakespeare Street, Southport PR8 5AJ Tel: 01704 501336 atcocar@lawnmowerworld.co.uk www.lawnmowerworld.co.uk Engines and garden machinery. Also the head office of the ATCO Car Owners Club with one of the best 1939 ATCO cars and memorabilia on display to the general public. Open all year.

Bury Transport Museum, Castlecroft Road, off Bolton Street, Bury Tel: 0161 764 7790

London
London Transport Museum, Covent Garden Tel: 020 7565 7299/ 020 7379 6344 www.ltmuseum.co.uk Displays of vehicles telling the story of London and it's transport history since the early 1800s. Open daily 10am–6pm (11am–6pm Fridays). Not open 24–26 December.

Middlesex
Whitewebbs Museum of Transport, Whitewebbs Road, Enfield EN2 9HW Tel: 020 8367 1898 Collection of commercial vehicles, cars and 20–30 motorcycles. Ring for opening times.

Norfolk
Caister Castle Car Collection, Caister-on-Sea, Nr Great Yarmouth Tel: 01572 787251 Private collection of cars and motorcycles dating back to 1893. Open daily mid May to end September, closed Saturdays.

East Anglia Transport Museum, Chapel Road, Carlton Coleville, Lowestoft NR33 8BL Tel: 01502 518459 www.eatm.org.uk Wide range of preserved vehicles on display including cars, battery vehicles, trams and trolleybuses. Ring for opening times.

Northern Ireland
Ulster Folk and Transport Museum, Cultra, Holywood, Co. Down BT18 0EU Tel: 028 9042 8428 www.nidex.com/uftm Unique collection of wheeled vehicles, ranging from cycles and motorcycles to trams, buses and cars. Open daily (not Christmas Day or Boxing Day), opening times vary.

Nottinghamshire
Nottingham Heritage Centre, Mere Way, Ruddington NG11 6NX Tel: 0115 940 5705 Collection of around 30 vintage public road transport vehicles. Open Sundays and Bank Holidays 10.45am–5pm 1 April to 14 October.

Nottingham Industrial Museum, Courtyard Buildings, Wallaton Park Tel: 0115 915 3910

Republic of Ireland
Kilgarvan Motor Museum, Kllgarvan, Co Kerry Tel: 00 353 64 85346

Scotland
Grampian Transport Museum, Alford, Aberdeenshire AB33 8AD Tel: 019755 62292 info@gtm.org.uk www.gtm.org.uk Displays and working exhibits tracing the history of travel and transport in the locality. Open 31st March to 31st October 10am–5pm.

Moray Motor Museum, Bridge Street, Elgin IV30 2DE Tel: 01343 544933 Interesting collection of cars and motorcycles plus memorabilia and diecast models.

Museum of Transport, 1 Bunhouse Road, Glasgow G3 8DP Tel: 0141 287 2720 Museum covering road, rail and sea. Replica 1938 city street and reconstructed Glasgow Underground Station. Open daily 10am–5pm Monday to Saturday, 11am–5pm Sunday.

Myreton Motor Museum, Aberlady, East Lothian EH32 0PZ Tel: 01875 870288 Collection of over 50 cars, motorcycles, commercial vehicles and WWII military vehicles. Also collection of period advertising, posters and enamel signs.

National Museum of Scotland, The Granton Centre, 242 West Granton Road, Edinburgh EH1 1JF Tel: 0131 225 7534

Shropshire

Midland Motor Museum, Stanmore Hall, Stourbridge Road, Bridgnorth WV15 6DT Tel: 01746 762992 Collection of 60 cars and 30 motorcycles.

Somerset

Haynes Motor Museum, Sparkford, Yeovil BA22 7LH Tel: 01963 440804 www.haynesmotormuseum.co.uk Haynes Publishing Company museum with collection of vintage, veteran and classic cars and motorcycles. Open daily Mar to Oct 9.30am–5.30pm, Nov to Feb 10am–4.30pm, closed Christmas and New Years Days.

Suffolk

Ipswich Transport Museum, Old Trolleybus Depot, Cobham Road, Ipswich IP3 9JD Tel: 01473 715666 www.ipswichtransportmuseum.co.uk Collection includes 140 major road transport exhibits, also a substantial archive of documents, photographs, etc. Open some Sundays/Bank Holiday Mondays, phone for times.

Surrey

Brooklands Museum Trust Limited, The Clubhouse, Brooklands Road, Weybridge KT13 0QN Tel: 01932 857381 www.brooklandsmuseum.com Motorsport and Aviation museum including historic racing cars and aircraft, also some pre-WWII motorcycles. Open Tuesday to Sunday & Bank Holidays, Winter 10am–4pm, Summer 10am–5pm.

Dunsfold Land Rover Museum, Dunsfold GU8 4NP Tel: 01483 200567

East Sussex

Bentley Wild Fowl and Motor Museum, Halland, Nr Lewes BN8 5AF Tel: 01825 840573 www.bentley.org.uk Changing collection of veteran, Edwardian and vintage cars and motorcycles. Open daily 18th March to 31st October 10.30am–5pm.

Foulkes-Halbard of Filching, Filching Manor, Filching, Wannock, Polegate BN26 5QA Tel: 01323 487838 About 100 cars dating from 1893 to 1993, also 30 motorcycles including American pre-1940's bikes ex-Steve McQueen.

West Sussex

Amberley Museum, Amberley, Arundel BN18 9LT Tel: 01798 831370 www.showbus.co.uk Working museum including a replica bus garage with a collection of related vehicles.

Tyne & Wear

Newburn Hall Motor Museum, 35 Townfield Gardens, Newburn NE15 8PY Tel: 0191 264 2977 Private museum of about 50 cars and 10 motorcycles.

Wales

Llangollen Motor Museum, Pentrefelin, Llangollen LL20 8EE Tel: 01978 860324 Cars, motorcycles, model vehicles, signs and tools and parts.

Madog Car & Motorcycle Museum, Snowdon Street, Porthmadog Tel: 01758 713618 Cars, motorcycles plus memorabilia.

Warwickshire

Heritage Motor Centre, Banbury Road, Gaydon CV35 0BJ Tel: 01926 641188 www.heritage.org.uk The Heritage Motor Centre is home to the British Motor Industry Heritage Trust which maintains a collection of 200 vehicles on display, charting the British car industry from the turn of the century to the present day. Open daily 10am–5pm.

Museum of British Road Transport, St. Agnes Lane, Hales Street, Coventry CV1 1PN Tel: 024 7683 2425 museum@mbrt.co.uk www.mbrt.co.uk Over 230 cars and commercial vehicles, 250 cycles and 90 motorcycles. Open all year round except for Christmas Eve, Christmas Day and Boxing Day, 10am–5pm.

West Midlands

Aston Manor Road Transport Museum, 208–216 Witton Lane, Aston, Birmingham B6 6QE Tel: 0121 322 2298 This former tram depot houses a collection of buses, trucks and tramcars in an authentic setting. Open most Saturdays/Sundays & Bank Holiday Mondays 11am–5pm.

The Birmingham & Midland Museum of Transport, Chapel Lane, Wythall, Birmingham B47 6JX Tel: 01564 826471 www.bammot.org.uk Over 80 buses and coaches including the biggest collection of Midland Red vehicles, plus vehicles from the former Birmingham, West Bromwich, Walsall and Wolverhampton Corporations & West Midlands PTE. Also collection of Bristol vehicles, London Transport RT, RF, RM and RCL buses. Commercial vehicles and fire engines, also battery-electric vehicle display. Open every weekend between Easter and the last Sunday in October.

Black Country Living Museum, Tipton Road, Dudley DY1 4SQ Tel: 0121 557 9643 www.bclm.co.uk Open 1st March to 31st October daily 10am–5pm, Nov to Feb Wednesday to Sunday only 10am–4pm.

Wiltshire

Atwell-Wilson Motor Museum, Downside, Stockley, Calne SN11 0NF Tel: 01249 813119 www.atwell-wilson.org Collection of cars, lorries, motorcycles, mopeds, push-bikes and a large selection of vehicle manuals, archive material and motoring memorabilia. Open Sunday to Thursday (except Christmas Day), also open Good Friday. Summer opening hours 11am–5pm, Winter 11am–4pm.

Science Museum Transport Museum, Red Barn Gate, Wroughton, Nr Swindon SN4 9NS Tel: 01793 814466

USA

Alamo Classic Car Showcase & Museum, 6401 S Interstate 35, New Braunfels, Texas TX 78132 Tel: +1 (210) 606 4311

Alaska Historical & Transportation Museum, Box 920, Palmer, Alaska AK 99645 Tel: +1 (907) 745 4493

Alfa Heaven, Inc., 2698 Nolan Road, Aniwa, Wisconsin WI 54408-9667 Tel: +1 (715) 449 2141

Antique Auto Barn, National Parks Highway 16, Carlsbad, New York NY 88220 Tel: +1 (505) 885 2437

Auburn-Cord-Duesenberg Museum, 1600 South Wayne Street, Auburn, Indiana IN 46706 Tel: +1 (219) 925 1444

Automotive Hall of Fame, PO Box 1742, Northwood Institute, Midland, Michigan MI 48640 Tel: +1 (517) 631 5760

Bellm's Cars & Music of Yesterday, 5500 N Tamiami Trail, Sarasota, Florida FL34243 Tel: +1 (813) 355 6228

Blackhawk Collection, 1092 Eagles Nest Place, Danville, California CA 94506-5872 Tel: 925 736 3444 info@blackhawkcollection.com www.blackhawkcollection.com

Otis Chandler Museum of Transportation, 1421 Emerson Ave, Oxnard CA 93033 Tel: 805 486 5929 www.chandlerwheels.com Over 100 motorcycles, automobiles including 1930s American cars.

Chevyland USA Auto Museum, Rte 2 Box 11, Elm Creek, Nebraska NE 68836 Tel: +1 (308) 856 4208

Classic Cars International Museum, 335 W 7th Street South, Salt Lake City, Utah UT 84101 Tel: +1 (801) 322 5186

Corvette American Museum, Cooperstown, New York NY 13326 Tel: +1 (607) 547 4135

Fagan's Antique & Classic Automobile Museum, 162nd Street & Clairmont Avenue, Markham Illinois, IL 60426 Tel: +1 (312) 331 3380

Henry Ford Museum & Greenfield Village, 20900 Oakwood Blvd, Dearborn, Michigan MI 48120 Tel: +1 (313) 271 1620 www.hfmgv.org/index.html

Hall of Fame & Classic Car Museum, PO Box 240, 1 Speedway Drive, Weedsport, New York NY 12166 Tel: +1 (315) 834 6606

Imperial Palace Auto Collection, Imperial Palace Hotel & Casino, 3535 Las Vegas Blvd South, Las Vegas, Nevada NV 89109 Tel: +1 (702) 794 3174

Indianapolis Motor Speedway Hall of Fame Museum, 4790 West 16th Street, Indianapolis, Indiana IN 46222 Tel: +1 (317) 484 6747

J. E. M. Classic Car Museum, R.D.#1, Box 120C, Andreas, Pennsylvania PA 18211 Tel: +1(717) 368 3554

Justice Brothers Racing Museum, 2734 East Huntington Drive, Duarte, California CA 91010 Tel: +1 (626) 359 9174 mail@justicebrothers.com www.justicebrothers.com/jb6.html

Louisville Automobile Museum, 737 South Third Street, Louisville, Kentucky KY 40202-2150 Tel: +1 (502) 568 2277

Memoryville USA Autos of Yesteryear, Route 63 North, Rolla, Missouri MO 65401 Tel: +1 (314) 364 1810

S Ray Miller Foundation, Inc. Antique & Classic Auto Museum, 2130 Middlebury St, Elkhart, Indiana IN 46516 Tel: +1 (219) 522 0539

National Automotive & Truck Museum of the United Staes, Inc., 1000 Gordon M. Buehrig Place, Box 686, Auburn, Indiana IN 46706-686 Tel: +1 (219) 235 9714

Owls Head Transportation Museum, PO Box 277 Owls Head, Maine 04854 Tel: 207 594 4418 info@ohtm.org www.ohtm.org Antique, classic and special interest autos, motorcycles, aircraft, engines, bicycles and related vehicles. Open daily except for Thanksgiving, Christmas and New Year's Day, April to Oct 10am–5pm, Nov to March 10am–4pm.

Packard Museum (W.D. Packard Music Hall), 1703 Mahoning Ave, NW Warren, Ohio OH 44483 Tel: +1 (216) 395 8442

Shelby American Collection, 5020 Chaparral Court, PO Box 19228, Boulder, Colorado CO Tel: +1 (303) 516 9565

Silver Springs Antique Car Collection, State Road 40, Ocala, Florida FL 32670 Tel: +1 (904) 236 2121

Studebaker National Museum, 525 S Main Street, South Bend, Indiana IN 46601 Tel: +1 (219) 235 9714

David Taylor Classic Car Museum, 918 Mechanic, Galveston Island, Texas TX 77550 Tel: +1 (409) 765 6590

Toyota Museum, 1901 South Western Avenue, Torrance, California CA 90509 Tel: +1 (21 3) 618 4000

Wells Auto Museum, Rt 1, PO Box 496, Wells, Maine ME 04090 Tel: +1 (207) 646 9064.

Index to Advertisers

Bibliography

Baldwin, Nick; Georgano, G. N.; Sedgwick, Michael; and Laban, Brian; *The World Guide to Automobiles*, Guild Publishing, London, 1987

Colin Chapman Lotus Engineering, Osprey, 1993.

Flammang, James M; *Standard Catalog of Imported Cars*, Krause Publications Inc, 1992.

Georgano, G. N.; ed: *Encyclopedia of Sports Cars*, Bison Books, 1985.

Georgano, Nick; *Military Vehicles of World War II*, Osprey 1994.

Harding, Anthony; Allport, Warren; Hodges, David; Davenport, John; *The Guinness Book of the Car*, Guinness Superlatives Ltd, 1987

Hay, Michael; *Bentley Factory Cars*, Osprey, 1993.

Hough, Richard; *A History of the World's Sports Cars*, Allen & Unwin, 1961.

Isaac, Rowan; *Morgan*, Osprey, 1994.

McComb, F. Wilson; *MG by McComb*, Osprey, 1978.

Nye, Doug; *Autocourse History of the Grand Prix Car 1966–1991*, Hazleton Publishing, 1992.

Posthumus, Cyril, and Hodges, David; *Classic Sportscars*, Ivy Leaf, 1991.

Robson, Graham; *Classic and Sportscar A–Z of Cars of the 1970s*, Bay View Books, 1990.

Sedgwick, Michael; Gillies, Mark; *Classic and Sportscar A–Z of Cars of the 1930s*, Bay View Books, 1989.

Sedgwick, Michael, Gillies, Mark; *Classic and Sportscar A–Z of Cars 1945–70*, Bay View Books, 1990.

Sieff, Theo; *Mercedes-Benz*, Gallery Books, 1989.

Vanderveen, Bart; *Historic Military Vehicles Directory*, After the Battle Publications, 1989.

Willson, Quentin; Selby David, *The Ultimate Classic Car Book*, Dorling Kindersley, 1995.

347

Index

Italic Page numbers denote colour pages, **bold** numbers refer to information and pointer boxes